Assembly Language
Step-by-Step

Second Edition

Assembly Language Step-by-Step
Second Edition

Programming with DOS and Linux

Jeff Duntemann

Wiley Computer Publishing

John Wiley & Sons, Inc.

NEW YORK · CHICHESTER · WEINHEIM · BRISBANE · SINGAPORE · TORONTO

Publisher: Robert Ipsen
Editor: Cary Sullivan
Managing Editor: Micheline Frederick
Text Design & Composition: North Market Street Graphics

Library of Congress Cataloging-in-Publication Data:

Duntemann, Jeff.
    Assembly language step-by-step : programming with DOS and Linux / Jeff Duntemann.—2nd ed.
        p.   cm.
    Rev. ed. of: Assembly language, © 1992.
    ISBN 0-471-37523-3 (paper/CD-ROM : alk. paper)
    1. Assembler language (Computer program language)   I. Duntemann, Jeff. Assembly language.   II. Title.
    QA76.73.A8 D88 2000
    005.265—dc21   00-020611

Printed in the United States of America.

10 9 8 7 6 5 4

To the eternal memory of
Kathleen M. Duntemann, Godmother
1920–1999
who gave me books when all I could do
was put teeth marks on them.
There are no words for how much I owe you!

CONTENTS

ACKNOWLEDGMENTS

First of all, to the authors of the software that I am honored to provide by their permission on this book's CD-ROM:

- Robert Anderton, author of NASM-IDE: www.inglenook.co.uk/nasmide/
- Anthony Williams, author of ALINK: http://alink.home.dhs.org/
- And, of course, the NASM team: Julian "Jules" Hall, Simon Tatham, H. Peter Anvin, John Fine, Kendall Bennet, Gary Clark, and Andrew Crabtree: www.web-sites.co.uk/nasm/

Because of their generosity, there is "nothing else to buy." Everything you need to program in assembly is right here on the CD-ROM for this book.

Abundant thanks also go to Bill Schindler, for teaching me the ways of the C library, and Michael Abrash, who has always has been the rock upon whom my knowledge of assembly language itself has been anchored.

Finally, to Carol, as always, for the sacramental friendship that has challenged me, shaped me, and redeemed me every day of our 30 years together and 23 years as spouses.

Time passes. It was exactly 10 years ago this summer, back in July 1989, when I turned in the manuscript of a book called *Assembly Language from Square One*. The book was well received, but its publisher went belly-up only a few months after its introduction. That may have been a blessing, because the book was too short, had a few more errors in it than it should have had, and was printed on horrible cheap paper that ripped with almost no provocation and is now turning sickly yellow.

So, I leapt on the chance to do the book over and publish it with a real publisher, the most venerable John Wiley & Sons, who (as their T-shirts say) has been totally awesome since 1809. It was thoroughly rewritten and became a new book with a new title, and went on the shelves in September of 1992. Time passes, but in a world where the life of a computer book may well be eight months or less, Wiley kept the first edition of *Assembly Language Step-by-Step* in print for *eight years*, from 1992 to 2000.

In that time it has probably sold more copies than any other single assembly language book, and I've received hundreds of letters of advice, corrections, suggestions, and simple, "Hey, this is cool!" compliments. Thanks to you all for taking the time to write. It means a lot to me. It's unclear how long this second edition will remain in print, but as long as people keep buying it (and telling me it's been useful to them), I suspect that either this edition or one to follow will remain available.

Time passes. And before we get into the book proper, there's something else I wanted to relate. On July 8, 1999, my sister Gretchen Duntemann Roper found that Kathleen Duntemann had died peacefully in her sleep in Chicago, almost 10 years to the day since I had completed *Assembly Language from Square One*, which was also dedicated to her. She kept both books on her coffee table and would show them to anyone who came to visit, even though she never had a computer and probably never understood what assembly language was. She was my aunt and godmother, my father's sole sibling, who sang my ABCs to me and demanded that I be admitted to Adler Planetarium in Chicago when I was six, even though the rules at that time demanded that children be seven to attend the sky show. "Name the planets for the nice man," she told me, and I did, and when I had gone through all the planets I started in on the constellations. I got in, because she believed in me. And she was there through every other major milestone in my life: First Communion, Confirmation, wedding, my father's illness and death, years and years of Christmases and Thanksgivings and birthdays, always with treats for the dog and stories to tell, with a quick Irish wit and a generous heart—and truly I cannot and will not ever forget her.

I say this only because so many of you are considerably younger than I, and may forget in the fever of young life: Time passes, and so do the people who believe in us, and urge us through the walls as we hit them so that we may arrive at midlife with something to show for it. Fathers and mothers, grandparents, aunts and uncles can add immeasurably to our lives, and often do, even when we're too busy to notice. Cherish them while you have them, because cherishing them after they're gone is a lonely business indeed.

In the meantime, having been talking about assembly language in one book or another for 10 years, I've decided to make it 20. As long as there will be PCs, there will be assembly language. Stay tuned. The year 2009 will be here before you know it.

"Why Would You Want to Do *That*?"

I t was 1985, and I was in a chartered bus in New York City, heading for a press reception with a bunch of other restless media egomaniacs. I was only beginning my media career (as technical editor for *PC Tech Journal*) and my first book was still months in the future. I happened to be sitting next to an established programming writer/guru, with whom I was impressed and to whom I was babbling about one thing or another. I won't name him, as he's done a lot for the field, and will do a lot more before he's through if he doesn't kill himself smoking first.

But I happened to let slip that I was a Turbo Pascal fanatic, and what I really wanted to do was learn how to write Turbo Pascal programs that made use of the brand new Microsoft Windows user interface. He wrinkled his nose and grimaced wryly, before speaking the Infamous Question:

"Why would you want to do *that*?"

I had never heard the question before (though I would hear it many times thereafter), and it took me aback. Why? Because, well, because…I wanted to know how it *worked*.

"Heh. That's what C's for."

Further discussion got me nowhere in a Pascal direction. But some probing led me to understand that you *couldn't* write Windows apps in

Turbo Pascal. It was impossible. Or . . . the programming writer/guru didn't know how. Maybe both. I never learned the truth. But I did learn the meaning of the Infamous Question.

Note well: When somebody asks you, "Why would you want to do *that*?" what it really means is this: "You've asked me how to do something that is either impossible using tools that I favor or completely outside my experience, but I don't want to lose face by admitting it. So, . . . how 'bout those Blackhawks?"

I heard it again and again over the years:

Q: How can I set up a C string so that I can read its length without scanning it?

A: Why would you want to do *that*?

Q: How can I write an assembly language subroutine callable from Turbo Pascal?

A: Why would you want to do *that*?

Q: How can I write Windows apps in assembly language?

A: Why would you want to do *that*?

You get the idea. The answer to the Infamous Question is always the same, and if the weasels ever ask it of you, snap back as quickly as possible: *Because I want to know how it works.*

That is a completely sufficient answer. It's the answer I've used every single time, except for one occasion a considerable number of years ago, when I put forth that I wanted to write a book that taught people how to program in assembly language as their *first* experience in programming.

Q: Good grief, why would you want to do *that*?

A: Because it's the best way there is to build the skills required to understand how *all the rest* of the programming universe works.

Being a programmer is one thing above all else: It is understanding how things work. Learning to be a programmer, furthermore, is almost entirely a process of learning how things work. This can be done at various levels, depending on the tools you're working with. If you're programming in Visual Basic, you have to understand how certain things work, but those things are by and large confined to Visual Basic itself. A great deal of machinery is hidden by the layer that Visual Basic places between the programmer and the computer. (The same is true of Delphi, Java, Perl, and many other very high-level programming environments.) If you're using a C compiler, you're a lot closer to the machine, and you see a lot more of that machinery—and must, therefore, understand how it works to be able to use it. However, quite a bit remains hidden, even from the hardened C programmer. (Many C programmers fool themselves into thinking they know way more than they actually do—and have the bad karma to be pretty damned arrogant about it.)

If, on the other hand, you're working in assembly language, you're as close to the machine as you can get. Assembly language hides nothing, and withholds no power. The flip side, of course, is that no magical layer between you and the machine will absolve any ignorance and take care of things for you. If you don't understand how something works, you're dead in the water—unless you know enough to be able to figure it out on your own.

That's a key point: My goal in creating this book is not entirely to teach you assembly language *per se*. If this book has a prime directive at all, it is to impart a certain disciplined curiosity about the machine, along with some basic context from which you can begin to explore the machine at its lowest levels. That, and the confidence to give it your best shot. This is difficult stuff, but it's nothing you can't master given some concentration, patience, and the time it requires—which, I caution, may be considerable.

In truth, what I'm really teaching you is how to learn.

The Master Plan

You need an Intel-based computer. For a lot of what I'll be explaining, literally any Intel-based machine will do—right back to the primordial 8088-based IBM PC from 1981. However, to be able to try all the examples, you'll need at least a 386. Most of the book relates to 16-bit DOS, which comes with Windows 95 and 98, and (in a slightly limited form) is emulated by Windows NT. Toward the end of the book, I explain how to work with assembly under Linux, and for that you will definitely need a 386 or more-advanced Intel machine.

Although most people think of mastering assembly language as the process of learning a collection of machine instructions, that's actually the easy part. The real challenge in assembly is learning the machine's memory models—so that's actually what I'll be emphasizing.

There are three general memory models for the Intel processor family: 16-bit flat model (sometimes called the Tiny model, or just the "COM file model"), 16-bit segmented model, and 32-bit flat model. I'm spending a fair amount of time on 16-bit flat model, because it's very much like the 32-bit flat model in miniature. The segmented model ruled for a good many years (including the time when I wrote the first edition of this book), but it's actually a compromise that lived far longer than it deserved to. Whatever future Intel computing may have, it will happen in a flat memory model. You need to know about segments—but I hope you'll never actually have to *use* them.

The CD-ROM for this book contains an assembler: NASM, the Net-Wide Assembler. It's free, it's easy to learn, and full source code is available, free of charge, from the Internet. That's the assembler I'll be teaching. If you can understand NASM, you can pick up Microsoft's MASM without trouble. NASM can generate programs for both 16-bit DOS and 32-bit Linux, so it's the ideal assembler for me to teach in this book. Although NASM is included on the CD-ROM, you might check the NASM Web site to see if a newer version is available. (The first edition of this book remained in print for *eight years*. You could be reading these words in the year 2005 or later—by which time most of the software I speak of will be in a much more highly evolved state.) The Web locations of all the software mentioned or used in this book are given in Appendix C.

In the first edition of this book I presented a simple editor/environment called JED. JED is history, gone with some Borland code libraries that were pulled from the market. In its place I present NASM-IDE, a conceptually similar utility created for NASM by Robert Anderton of the United Kingdom. NASM-IDE operates only under DOS. It won't help you with Linux. But in Linux there are a multitude of editors available, and in the process of learning Linux you certainly learned one of them. Whatever it is, use it. (I use, and will recommend, EMACS.) If I've learned nothing else about Linux, it's that people get very attached to their text editors. I won't ask you to learn another one.

The way to get the most from this book is to start at the beginning and read it through, one chapter at a time, in order. Even if you roll your eyes and say you already know what hexadecimal is, read it anyway.

It's a good review—and you won't miss any of my jokes and funny stories. Load and run all the example programs. Try your best to understand what every single line in every program does.

That is, ultimately, what I'm after: to show you the way to understand what every however-distant corner of your machine is doing, and how all its many pieces work together. This doesn't mean I'll explain every corner of it myself—no one will live long enough to do that; computing isn't simple anymore—but if you develop the discipline of patient research and experimentation, you can probably work it out for yourself. Ultimately, that's the only way to learn it: by yourself. The guidance you find—in friends, on the Net, in books like this—is only guidance, and grease on the axles. You have to decide who's to be the master, you or the machine, and make it so. Assembly programmers are the only programmers who can truly claim to be the masters, and that's a truth worth meditating on.

If it means anything at all (optimist and thoroughgoing Pelagian that I am), I believe in you. Go for it.

—*Jeff Duntemann*
Scottsdale, Arizona
May 2000

CHAPTER 1

Another Pleasant Valley Saturday

Understanding What Computers Really Do

It's All in the Plan

"Quick, get the kids up, it's past 7. Nicky's got Little League at 9 and Dione's got ballet at 10. Mike, give Max his heartworm pill! (We're out of them, Ma, remember?) Your father picked a great weekend to go fishing . . . Here, let me give you 10 bucks and go get more pills at the vet's . . . My God, that's right, Hank needed gas money and left me broke. There's a teller machine over by Kmart, and if I go there I can take that stupid toilet seat back and get the right one.

"I guess I'd better make a list . . . "

It's another Pleasant Valley Saturday, and thirty-odd million suburban homemakers sit down with a pencil and pad at the kitchen table to try and make sense of a morning that would kill and pickle any lesser being. In her mind she thinks of the dependencies and traces the route:

Drop Nicky at Rand Park, go back to Dempster and it's about 10 minutes to Golf Mill Mall. Do I have gas? I'd better check first—if not, stop at Del's Shell or I won't make it to Milwaukee Avenue. Milk the teller machine at Golf Mill, then cross the parking lot to Kmart to return the toilet seat that Hank bought last weekend without checking what shape it was. Gotta remember to throw the toilet seat in back of the van—write that at the top of the list.

By then it'll be half past, maybe later. Ballet is all the way down Greenwood in Park Ridge. No left turn from Milwaukee—but there's the sneak path around behind the Mall. I have to remember not to turn right onto Milwaukee like I always do—jot that down. While I'm in Park Ridge I can check and see if Hank's new glasses are in—should call but they won't even be open until 9:30. Oh, and groceries—can do that while Dione dances. On the way back I can cut over to Oakton and get the dog's pills.

In about 90 seconds flat the list is complete:

- Throw toilet seat in van.
- Check gas—if empty, stop at Del's Shell.
- Drop Nicky at Rand Park.
- Stop at Golf Mill teller machine.
- Return toilet seat at Kmart.
- Drop Dione at ballet (remember back path to Greenwood).
- See if Hank's glasses are at Pearle Vision—if they are, make double sure they remembered the extra scratch coating.
- Get groceries at Jewel.
- Pick up Dione.
- Stop at vet's for heartworm pills.
- Drop off groceries at home.
- If it's time, pick up Nicky. If not, collapse for a few minutes, then pick up Nicky.
- Collapse!

In what we often call a "laundry list" (whether it involves laundry or not) is the perfect metaphor for a computer program. Without realizing it, our intrepid homemaker has written herself a computer program and then set out (acting as the computer) to execute it and be done before noon.

Computer programming is nothing more than this: You the programmer write a list of steps and tests. The computer then performs each step and test in sequence. When the list of steps has been executed, the computer stops.

A computer program is a list of steps and tests, nothing more.

Steps and Tests

Think for a moment about what I call a "test" in the preceding laundry list. A *test* is the sort of either/or decision we make dozens or hundreds of times on even the most placid of days, sometimes nearly without thinking about it.

Our homemaker performed a test when she jumped into the van to get started on her adventure. She looked at the gas gauge. The gas gauge would tell her one of two things: (1) She has enough gas, or (2) no, she doesn't. If she has enough gas, she takes a right and heads for Rand Park. If she doesn't have enough gas, she takes a left down to the corner and fills the tank at Del's Shell. (Del takes credit cards.) Then, with a full tank, she continues the program by taking a U-turn and heading for Rand Park.

In the abstract, a test consists of those two parts:

- First, you take a look at something that can go one of two ways.
- Then you do one of two things, depending on what you saw when you took a look.

Toward the end of the program, our homemaker got home, took the groceries out of the van, and took a look at the clock. If it isn't time to get Nicky back from Little League, she has a moment to collapse on the couch in a nearly empty house. If it *is* time to get Nicky, there's no rest for the ragged: She sprints for the van and heads back to Rand Park.

(Any guesses as to whether she really gets to collapse when the program is complete?)

More than Two Ways?

You might object, saying that many or most tests involve more than two alternatives. Ha-hah, sorry, you're dead wrong—in every case. Furthermore, you're wrong whether you think you are or not.

Except for totally impulsive or psychotic behavior, every human decision comes down to the choice between two alternatives.

What you have to do is look a little more closely at what goes through your mind when you make decisions. The next time you buzz down to Moo Foo Goo for fast Chinese, observe yourself while you're poring over the menu. The choice might seem, at first, to be of one item out of 26 Cantonese main courses. Not so—the choice, in fact, is between choosing one item and *not* choosing that one item. Your eyes rest on Chicken with Cashews. Naw, too bland. *That was a test.* You slide down to the next item. Chicken with Black Mushrooms. Hmmm, no, had that last week. *That was another test.* Next item: Kung Pao Chicken. Yeah, that's it! *That was a third test.*

The choice was not among chicken with cashews, chicken with black mushrooms, or chicken with kung pao. Each dish had its moment, poised before the critical eye of your mind, and you turned thumbs up or thumbs down on it, individually. Eventually, one dish won, but it won in that same game of "to eat or not to eat."

Let me give you another example. Many of life's most complicated decisions come about due to the fact that 99.99867 percent of us are not nudists. You've been there: You're standing in the clothes closet in your underwear, flipping through your rack of pants. The tests come thick and fast. This one? No. This one? No. This one? No. This one? Yeah. You pick a pair of blue pants, say. (It's a Monday, after all, and blue would seem an appropriate color.) Then you stumble over to your sock drawer and take a look. Whoops, no blue socks. *That was a test.* So you stumble back to the clothes closet, hang your blue pants back on the pants rack, and start over. This one? No. This one? No. This one? Yeah. This time it's brown pants, and you toss them over your arm and head back to the sock drawer to take another look. Nertz, out of brown socks, too. So it's back to the clothes closet . . .

What you might consider a single decision, or perhaps two decisions inextricably tangled (like picking pants and socks of the same color, given stock on hand), is actually a series of small decisions, always binary in nature: Pick 'em or don't pick 'em. Find 'em or don't find 'em. The Monday morning episode in the clothes closet is a good analogy of a programming structure called a *loop:* You keep doing a series of things until you get it right, and then you stop. (Assuming you're not the kind of nerd who wears blue socks with brown pants.) But whether you get everything right always comes down to a sequence of simple either/or decisions.

Computers Think Like Us

I can almost hear what you're thinking: "Sure, it's a computer book, and he's trying to get me to think like a computer." Not at all. Computers think like *us*. We designed them; how else could they think? No, what I'm trying to do is get you to take a long, hard look at how *you* think. We run on automatic for so much of our lives that we literally do most of our thinking without really thinking about it.

The very best model for the logic of a computer program is the very same logic we use to plan and manage our daily affairs. No matter what we do, it comes down to a matter of confronting two alternatives and picking one. What we might think of as a single large and complicated decision is nothing more than a messy tangle of many smaller decisions. The skill of looking at a complex decision and seeing all the little decisions in its tummy will serve you well in learning how to program. Observe yourself the next time you have to decide something. Count up the little decisions that make up the big one. You'll be surprised.

And, surprise! You'll be a programmer.

Had This Been the Real Thing . . .

Do not be alarmed. What you have just experienced was a metaphor. It was not the real thing. (The real thing comes later.)

I use metaphors a lot in this book. A metaphor is a loose comparison drawn between something familiar (such as a Saturday morning laundry list) and something unfamiliar (such as a computer program). The idea is to anchor the unfamiliar in the terms of the familiar, so that when I begin tossing facts at you, you'll have someplace comfortable to lay them down.

The most important thing for you to do right now is keep an open mind. If you know a little bit about computers or programming, don't pick nits. Yes, there are important differences between a homemaker following a scribbled laundry list and a computer executing a program. I'll mention those differences all in good time.

For now, it's still Chapter 1. Take these initial metaphors on their own terms. Later on, they'll help a lot.

Do Not Pass GO

"There's a reason *bored* and *board* are homonyms," said my best friend Art one evening, as we sat (two super-sophisticated twelve-year-olds) playing some game in his basement. (He may have been unhappy because he was losing.) Was it Mille Bornes? Or Stratego? Or Monopoly? Or something else entirely? I confess, I don't remember. I simply recall hopping some little piece of plastic shaped like a pregnant bowling pin up and down a series of colored squares that told me to do dumb things like go back two spaces or put $100 in the pot or nuke Outer Mongolia.

Outer Mongolia notwithstanding, there are strong parallels to be drawn between that peculiar American obsession, the board game, and assembly-language programming. First of all, everything we said before still holds: Board games, by and large, consist of a progression of steps and tests. In some games, such as Trivial Pursuit, *every* step on the board is a test: to see if you can answer, or not answer, a question on a card. In other board games, each little square on the board contains some sort of instruction: Lose One Turn; Go Back Two Squares; Take a Card from Community Chest; and, of course, Go to Jail.

Certain board games made for some lively arguments between Art and myself (it was that or be bored, as it were) concerning what it meant to Go Forward or Backward Five Steps. It seemed to me that you should count the square you were already on, and Art, traditionalist always, thought you should start counting with the first step in the direction you had to go. This made a difference in the game, of course. (I conveniently forgot to press my point when doing so would land me on something like Park Place with 15 of Art's hotels on it . . .)

The Game of Big Bux

To avoid getting in serious trouble, I have invented my own board game to continue down the road with this particular metaphor. In the sense that art mirrors life, the Game of Big Bux mirrors life in Silicon Valley, where money seems to be spontaneously created (generally in somebody else's pocket) and the three big Money Black Holes are fast cars, California real estate, and messy divorces.

A portion of the Big Bux Game Board is shown in Figure 1.1. The line of rectangles on the left side of the page continues all the way around the board. In the middle of the board are cubbyholes to store your play money and game pieces; stacks of cards to be read occasionally; and short detours with such names as Messy Divorce and Start a Business, which are brief sequences of the same sort of action rectangles as those forming the path around the edge of the board.

Unlike many board games, you don't throw dice to determine how many steps around the board you take. Big Bux requires that you move *one* step forward on each turn, *unless* the square you land on instructs you to move forward or backward or go somewhere else, such as through a detour. This makes for a considerably less random game. In fact, Big Bux is a pretty deterministic game, meaning that whether you win or lose is far less important than just going through the ringer and coming out the other side. (Again, this mirrors Silicon Valley, where you come out either bankrupt or ready to flee to Peoria and open a hardware store. That *other* kind of hardware.)

There is some math involved. You start out with one house, a cheap car, and $50,000 in cash. You can buy CDs at a given interest rate, payable each time you make it once around the board. You can invest in stocks and other securities whose value is determined by a changeable index in economic indicators, which fluctuates based on cards chosen from the stack called the Fickle Finger of Fate. You can sell cars on a secondary market, buy and sell houses, and wheel and deal with the other players. Each time you make it once around the board you have to recalculate your net worth. All of this involves some addition, subtraction, multiplication, and division, but there's no math more complex than compound interest. Most of Big Bux involves nothing more than taking a step and following the instructions at each step.

Is this starting to sound familiar?

Playing Big Bux

At one corner of the Big Bux board is the legend **Move In,** since that's how people start life in California—no one is actually *born* there. Once moved in, you begin working your way around the board, square by square, following the instructions in the squares.

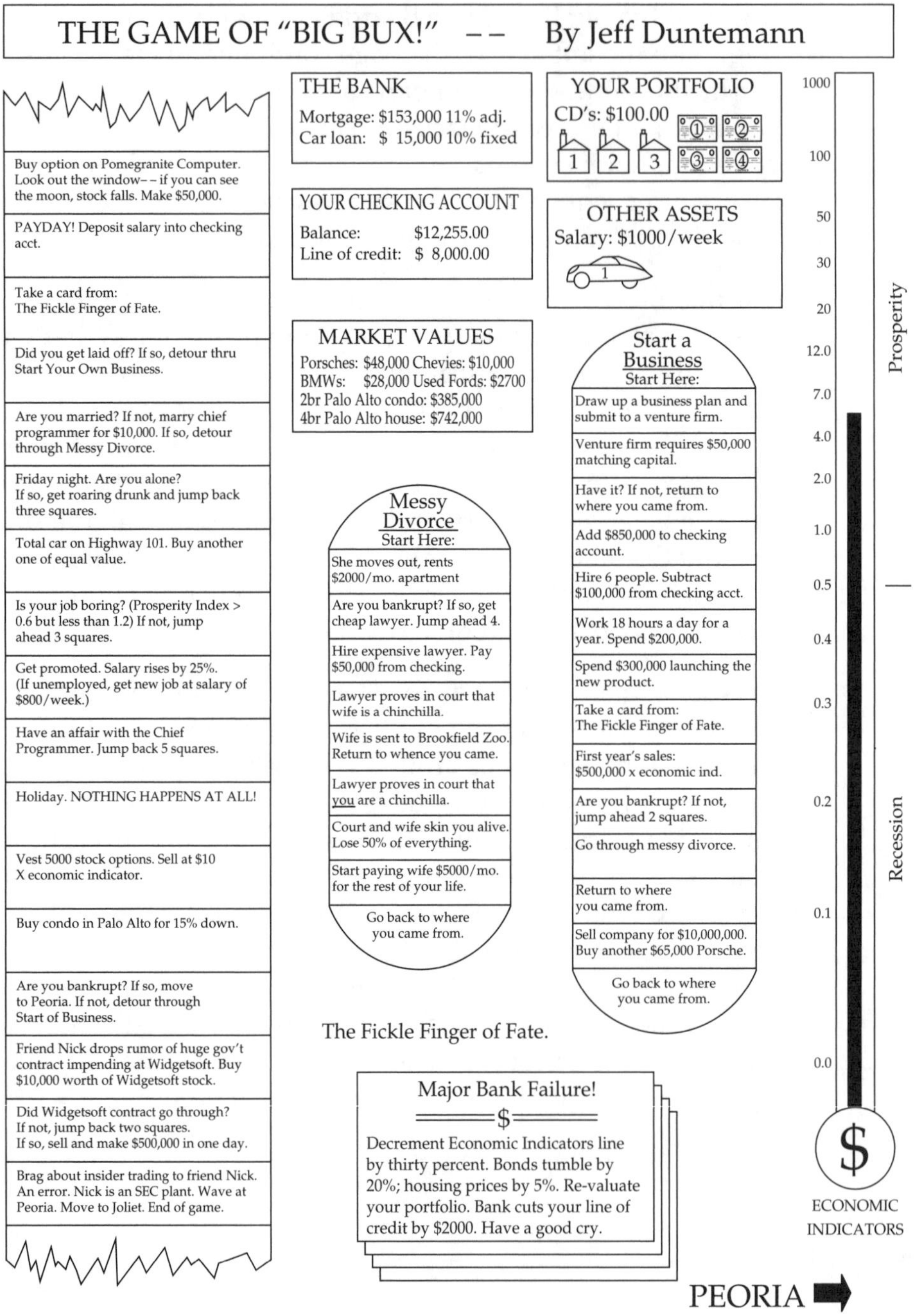

THE GAME OF "BIG BUX!" – – By Jeff Duntemann

THE BANK
Mortgage: $153,000 11% adj.
Car loan: $ 15,000 10% fixed

YOUR PORTFOLIO
CD's: $100.00

YOUR CHECKING ACCOUNT
Balance: $12,255.00
Line of credit: $ 8,000.00

OTHER ASSETS
Salary: $1000/week

MARKET VALUES
Porsches: $48,000 Chevies: $10,000
BMWs: $28,000 Used Fords: $2700
2br Palo Alto condo: $385,000
4br Palo Alto house: $742,000

Buy option on Pomegranite Computer.
Look out the window– – if you can see
the moon, stock falls. Make $50,000.

PAYDAY! Deposit salary into checking
acct.

Take a card from:
The Fickle Finger of Fate.

Did you get laid off? If so, detour thru
Start Your Own Business.

Are you married? If not, marry chief
programmer for $10,000. If so, detour
through Messy Divorce.

Friday night. Are you alone?
If so, get roaring drunk and jump back
three squares.

Total car on Highway 101. Buy another
one of equal value.

Is your job boring? (Prosperity Index >
0.6 but less than 1.2) If not, jump
ahead 3 squares.

Get promoted. Salary rises by 25%.
(If unemployed, get new job at salary of
$800/week.)

Have an affair with the Chief
Programmer. Jump back 5 squares.

Holiday. NOTHING HAPPENS AT ALL!

Vest 5000 stock options. Sell at $10
X economic indicator.

Buy condo in Palo Alto for 15% down.

Are you bankrupt? If so, move
to Peoria. If not, detour through
Start of Business.

Friend Nick drops rumor of huge gov't
contract impending at Widgetsoft. Buy
$10,000 worth of Widgetsoft stock.

Did Widgetsoft contract go through?
If not, jump back two squares.
If so, sell and make $500,000 in one day.

Brag about insider trading to friend Nick.
An error. Nick is an SEC plant. Wave at
Peoria. Move to Joliet. End of game.

Messy Divorce
Start Here:

She moves out, rents
$2000/mo. apartment

Are you bankrupt? If so, get
cheap lawyer. Jump ahead 4.

Hire expensive lawyer. Pay
$50,000 from checking.

Lawyer proves in court that
wife is a chinchilla.

Wife is sent to Brookfield Zoo.
Return to whence you came.

Lawyer proves in court that
you are a chinchilla.

Court and wife skin you alive.
Lose 50% of everything.

Start paying wife $5000/mo.
for the rest of your life.

Go back to where
you came from.

The Fickle Finger of Fate.

Start a Business
Start Here:

Draw up a business plan and
submit to a venture firm.

Venture firm requires $50,000
matching capital.

Have it? If not, return to
where you came from.

Add $850,000 to checking
account.

Hire 6 people. Subtract
$100,000 from checking acct.

Work 18 hours a day for a
year. Spend $200,000.

Spend $300,000 launching the
new product.

Take a card from:
The Fickle Finger of Fate.

First year's sales:
$500,000 x economic ind.

Are you bankrupt? If not,
jump ahead 2 squares.

Go through messy divorce.

Return to where
you came from.

Sell company for $10,000,000.
Buy another $65,000 Porsche.

Go back to where
you came from.

Major Bank Failure!
— $ —
Decrement Economic Indicators line
by thirty percent. Bonds tumble by
20%; housing prices by 5%. Re-valuate
your portfolio. Bank cuts your line of
credit by $2000. Have a good cry.

1000
100
50
30
20
12.0
7.0
4.0
2.0
1.0
0.5
0.4
0.3
0.2
0.1
0.0

Prosperity

Recession

$

ECONOMIC
INDICATORS

PEORIA ➡

Figure 1.1 The Game of Big Bux.

Some of the squares simply tell you to do something, such as **Buy condo in Palo Alto for 15% down**. Many of the squares involve a test of some kind. For example, one square reads: **Is your job boring? (Prosperity Index 0.3 but less than 4.0) If not, jump ahead 3 squares.** The test is actually to see if the Prosperity Index has a value between 0.3 and 4.0. Any value outside those bounds (that is, runaway prosperity or Four Horsemen–class recession) is defined as Interesting Times, and causes a jump ahead by three squares.

You always move one step forward at each turn, unless the square you land on directs you to do something else, such as jump forward three squares or jump back five squares.

The notion of taking a detour is an interesting one. Two detours are shown in the portion of the board I've provided. Taking a detour means leaving the main run around the edge of the game board and stepping through a series of squares elsewhere on the board. The detours involve some specific process, that is, starting a business or getting divorced.

You can work through a detour, step by step, until you hit the bottom. At that point you simply pick up your journey around the board right where you left it. You may also find that one of the squares in the detour instructs you to go back to where you came from. Depending on the logic of the game (and your luck and finances), you may completely run through a detour or get thrown out somewhere in the middle.

Also note that you can take a detour from within a detour. If you detour through Start a Business and your business goes bankrupt, you leave Start a Business temporarily and detour through Messy Divorce. Once you leave Messy Divorce, you return to where you left Start a Business. Ultimately, you also leave Start a Business and return to wherever it was you were when you took the detour.

The same detour (for example, Start a Business) can be taken from any of several different places along the game board.

Assembly Language Programming as a Board Game

Now that you're thinking in terms of board games, take a look at Figure 1.2. What I've drawn is actually a fair approximation of assembly language as it was used on some of our simpler microprocessors about 15

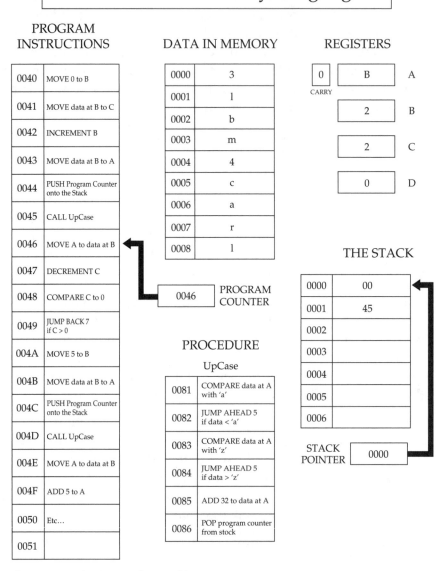

Figure 1.2   The Game of Assembly Language.

or 20 years ago. The column marked "PROGRAM INSTRUCTIONS" is the main path around the edge of the board, of which only a portion can be shown here. This is the assembly language computer program, the actual series of steps and tests that, when executed, causes the computer to do something useful. Setting up this series of program instructions is what programming in assembly language actually is.

Everything else is odds and ends in the middle of the board that serve the game in progress. You're probably noticing (perhaps with sagging spirits) that there are a *lot* of numbers involved. (They're weird numbers, too—what, for example, does "004B" mean? I deal with that issue in Chapter 2, Alien Bases.) I'm sorry, but that's simply the way the game is played. Assembly language, at the innermost level, is nothing *but* numbers, and if you hate numbers the way most people hate anchovies, you're going to have a rough time of it. (I like anchovies, which is part of my legend. Learn to like numbers. They're not as salty.)

I should caution you that the Game of Assembly Language represents no real computer processor like the Pentium. Also, I've made the names of instructions more clearly understandable than the names of the instructions in Intel assembly language. In the real world, instruction names are typically things like **STOSB**, **DAA**, **INC**, **SBB**, and other crypticisms that cannot be understood without considerable explanation. We're easing into this stuff sidewise, and in this chapter I have to sugarcoat certain things a little to draw the metaphors clearly.

Code and Data

Like most board games (including the Game of Big Bux), the assembly language board game consists of two broad categories of elements: game steps and places to store things. The "game steps" are the steps and tests I've been speaking of all along. The places to store things are just that: cubbyholes into which you can place numbers, with the confidence that those numbers will remain where you put them until you take them out or change them somehow.

In programming terms, the game steps are called *code*, and the numbers in their cubbyholes (as distinct from the cubbyholes themselves) are called *data*. The cubbyholes themselves are usually called *storage*. (The difference between the places you store information and the information you store in them is crucial. Don't confuse them.)

The Game of Big Bux works the same way. Look back to Figure 1.1 and note that in the Start a Business detour, there is an instruction reading **Add $850,000 to checking account**. The checking account is one of several different kinds of storage in the Game of Big Bux, and money values are a type of data. It's no different conceptually from an instruction in the Game of Assembly Language reading **ADD 5 to Register A**. An **ADD** instruction in the code alters a data value stored in a cubbyhole named Register A.

Code and data are two very different kinds of critters, but they interact in ways that make the game interesting. The code includes steps that place data into storage (**MOVE** instructions) and steps that alter data that is already in storage (**INCREMENT** and **DECREMENT** instructions). Most of the time you'll think of code as being the master of data, in that the code writes data values into storage. Data does influence code as well, however. Among the tests that the code makes are tests that examine data in storage, the **COMPARE** instructions. If a given data value exists in storage, the code may do one thing; if that value does not exist in storage, the code will do something else, as in the **JUMP BACK** and **JUMP AHEAD** instructions.

The short block of instructions marked **PROCEDURE** is a detour off the main stream of instructions. At any point in the program you can duck out into the procedure, perform its steps and tests, and then return to the very place from which you left. This allows a sequence of steps and tests that is generally useful and used frequently to exist in only one place rather than exist as a separate copy everywhere it is needed.

Addresses

Another critical concept lies in the funny numbers at the left side of the program step locations and data locations. Each number is unique, in that a location tagged with that number appears only *once* inside the computer. This location is called an *address*. Data is stored and retrieved by specifying the data's address in the machine. Procedures are called by specifying the address at which they begin.

The little box (which is also a storage location) marked **PROGRAM COUNTER** keeps the address of the next instruction to be performed. The number inside the program counter is increased by one (we say, "incremented") each time an instruction is performed *unless the instructions tells the program counter to do something else*. For example: Notice the **JUMP BACK 7** instruction at address 0049. When this instruction is performed, the program counter will "back up" by seven counts. This is analogous to the "go back three spaces" concept in most board games.

Metaphor Check!

That's about as much explanation of the Game of Assembly Language as I'm going to offer for now. This is still Chapter 1, and we're still in metaphor territory. People who have had some exposure to computers will recognize and understand more of what Figure 1.2 is doing. (There's a real, traceable program going on in there—I dare you to figure out what it does—and how!) People with no exposure to computer innards at all shouldn't feel left behind for being utterly lost. I created the Game of Assembly Language solely to put across the following points:

- *The individual steps are very simple.* One single instruction rarely does more than move a single byte from one storage cubbyhole to another, or compare the value contained in one storage cubbyhole to a value contained in another. This is good news, because it allows you to concentrate on the simple task accomplished by a single instruction without being overwhelmed by complexity. The bad news, however, is the following.

- *It takes a lot of steps to do anything useful.* You can often write a useful program in such languages as Pascal or BASIC in five or six lines. You can actually create useful programs in Visual Basic and Delphi without writing any code at all. (The code is still there . . . but the code is "canned" and all you're really doing is choosing which chunks of canned code in a collection of many such chunks will run.) A useful assembly language program cannot be implemented in fewer than about 50 lines, and anything challenging takes hundreds or thousands of lines. The skill of assembly language programming lies in structuring these hundreds or thousands of instructions so that the program can be read and understood.

- *The key to assembly language is understanding memory addresses.* In such languages as Pascal and BASIC, the compiler takes care of where something is located—you simply have to give that something a name, and call it by that name whenever you want to look at it or change it. In assembly language, you must always be cognizant of where things are in your computer's memory. So, in working through this book, pay special attention to the concept of addressing, which is nothing more than the art of specifying where something is. The Game of Assembly Language is peppered with addresses and instructions that work with addresses (such as **MOVE data at B to C**, which means move the data stored at the address specified by register B to the address specified by register C). Addressing is by far the trickiest part of assembly language, but master it and you've got the whole thing in your hip pocket.

Everything I've said so far has been orientation. I've tried to give you a taste of the big picture of assembly language and how its fundamental principles relate to the life you've been living all along. Life is a sequence of steps and tests, and so are board games—and so is assembly language. Keep those metaphors in mind as we proceed to get real by confronting the nature of computer numbers.

CHAPTER 2

Alien Bases

Getting Your Arms around Binary and Hexadecimal

The Return of the New Math Monster

The year 1966. Perhaps you were there. New Math burst upon the grade school curricula of the nation, and homework became a turmoil of number lines, sets, and alternate bases. Middle-class parents scratched their heads with their children over questions like, "What is 17 in Base Five?" and "Which sets does the Null Set belong to?" In very short order (I recall a period of about two months), the whole thing was tossed in the trash as quickly as it had been concocted by addle-brained educrats with too little to do.

This was a pity, actually. What nobody seemed to realize at the time was that, granted, we were learning New Math—except that *Old* Math had never been taught at the grade school level either. We kept wondering of what possible use it was to know what the intersection of the set of squirrels and the set of mammals was. The truth, of course, was that it was no use at all. Mathematics in America has always been taught as *applied* mathematics—arithmetic—heavy on the word problems. If it won't help you balance your checkbook or proportion a recipe, it ain't real math, man. Little or nothing of the logic of mathematics has *ever* made it into the elementary classroom, in part because elementary school in America has historically been a sort of trade school for everyday life. Getting the little beasts fundamentally literate is difficult enough. Trying to get them to appreciate the beauty of alternate number systems simply went over the line for practical middle-class America.

I was one of the few who enjoyed fussing with math in the New-Age style back in 1966, but I gladly laid it aside when the whole thing blew over. I didn't have to pick it up again until 1976, when, after working like a maniac with a wire-wrap gun for several weeks, I fed power to my COSMAC ELF computer and was greeted by an LED display of a pair of numbers in *base 16!*

Mon dieu, New Math *redux . . .*

This chapter exists because at the assembly language level, your computer does not understand numbers in our familiar base 10. Computers, in a slightly schizoid fashion, work in base 2 *and* base 16—all at the same time. If you're willing to confine yourself to higher-level languages such as Basic or Pascal, you can ignore these alien bases altogether, or perhaps treat them as an advanced topic once you get the rest of the language down pat. Not here. *Everything* in assembly language depends on your thorough understanding of these two number bases. So before we do anything else, we're going to learn how to count all over again—in Martian.

Counting in Martian

There is intelligent life on Mars.

That is, the Martians are intelligent enough to know from watching our TV programs these past 50 years that a thriving tourist industry would not be to their advantage. So they've remained in hiding, emerging only briefly to carve big rocks into the shape of Elvis's face to help the *National Enquirer* ensure that no one will ever take Mars seriously again. The Martians do occasionally communicate with science fiction writers like me, knowing full well that nobody has *ever* taken *us* seriously. Hence the information in this section, which involves the way Martians count.

Martians have three fingers on one hand, and only one finger on the other. Male Martians have their three fingers on the left hand, while females have their three fingers on the right hand. This makes waltzing and certain other things easier.

Like human beings and any other intelligent race, Martians started counting by using their fingers. Just as we used our 10 fingers to set things off in groups and powers of 10, the Martians used their four fingers to set things off in groups and powers of four. Over time, our civilization standardized on a set of 10 digits to serve our number system. The Martians, similarly, standardized on a set of four digits for their number system. The four digits follow, along with the names of the digits as the Martians pronounce them: Θ (xip), ſ (foo), ∩ (bar), ≡ (bas).

Like our zero, xip is a placeholder representing no items, and while Martians sometimes count from xip, they usually start with foo, representing a single item. So they start counting: *Foo, bar, bas . . .*

Now what? What comes after bas? Table 2.1 demonstrates how the Martians count to what we would call 25.

With only four digits (including the one representing zero) the Martians can only count to bas without running out of digits. The number after bas has a new name, *fooby*. Fooby is the base of the Martian number system, and probably the most important number on Mars. Fooby is the number of fingers a Martian has. We would call it *four*.

The most significant thing about fooby is the way the Martians write it out in numerals: ſΘ. Instead of a single column, fooby is expressed in two columns. Just as with our decimal system, each column has a value that is a power of fooby. This means only that as you move from the rightmost column toward the left, each column represents a value fooby times the column to its right.

The rightmost column represents units, in counts of foo. The next column over represents fooby times foo, or (given that arithmetic works the same way on Mars as here, New Math notwithstanding) simply fooby. The next column to the left of fooby represents fooby times fooby, or foobity, and so on. This relationship should become clearer through Table 2.2.

Dissecting a Martian Number

Any given column may contain a digit from xip to bas, indicating how many instances of that column's value are contained in the number as a whole. Let's work through an example. Look at Figure 2.1, which is a dissection of the Martian number ∩≡ ſΘ≡, pronounced "Barbididity-basbidity-foobity-bas." (A visiting and heavily disguised Martian precipitated the doo-wop craze while standing at a Philadelphia bus stop in 1954, counting his change.)

Table 2.1 Counting in Martian, Base Fooby

MARTIAN NUMERALS	MARTIAN PRONUNCIATION	EARTH EQUIVALENT
Θ	Xip	0
ſ	Foo	1
∩	Bar	2
≡	Bas	3
ſΘ	Fooby	4
ſſ	Fooby-foo	5
ſ∩	Fooby-bar	6
ſ≡	Fooby-bas	7
∩Θ	Barby	8
∩ſ	Barby-foo	9
∩∩	Barby-bar	10
∩≡	Barby-bas	11
≡Θ	Basby	12
≡ſ	Basby-foo	13
≡∩	Basby-bar	14
≡≡	Basby-bas	15
ſΘΘ	Foobity	16
ſΘſ	Foobity-foo	17
ſΘ∩	Foobity-bar	18
ſΘ≡	Foobity-bas	19
ſſΘ	Foobity-fooby	20
ſſſ	Foobity-fooby-foo	21
ſſ∩	Foobity-fooby-bar	22
ſſ≡	Foobity-fooby-bas	23
ſ∩Θ	Foobity-barby	24
ſ∩ſ	Foobity-barby-foo	25

The rightmost column tells how many units are contained in the number. The digit there is bas, indicating that the number contains bas units. The second column from the right carries a value of fooby times foo (fooby times one) or fooby. A xip in the fooby column indicates that there are no foobies in the number. The xip digit in ſΘ is a placeholder,

Table 2.2 Powers of Fooby

ſ	Foo	x Fooby = ſ⊖	(Fooby)
ſ⊖	Fooby	x Fooby = ſ⊖⊖	(Foobity)
ſ⊖⊖	Foobity	x Fooby = ſ⊖⊖⊖	(Foobidity)
ſ⊖⊖⊖	Foobidity	x Fooby = ſ⊖⊖⊖⊖	(Foobididity)
ſ⊖⊖⊖⊖	Foobididity	x Fooby = ſ⊖⊖⊖⊖⊖	(Foobidididity)
ſ⊖⊖⊖⊖⊖	Foobidididity	x Fooby = ſ⊖⊖⊖⊖⊖⊖	and so on ...

just as zero is in our numbering system. Notice also that in the columnar sum shown to the right of the digit matrix, the foobies line is represented by a double xip. Not only is there a xip to tell us that there are no foobies, but also a xip holding the foos place as well. This pattern continues in the columnar sum as we move toward the more significant columns to the left.

Fooby times fooby is foobity, and the ſ digit tells us that there is foo foobity (a single foobity) in the number. The next column, in keeping

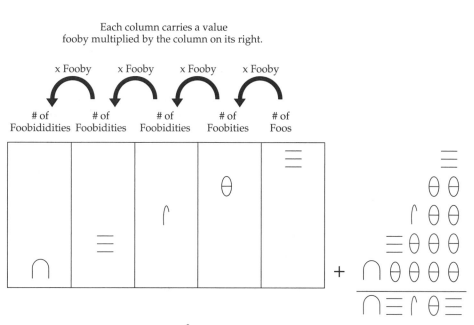

Figure 2.1 The anatomy of ∩≡ ſ⊖≡.

with the pattern, is foobity times fooby, or foobidity. In the columnar notation, foobidity is written as ⌈ΘΘΘ. The ≡ digit tells us that there are bas foobidities in the number. Bas foobidities is a number with its own name, basbidity, which may be written as ≡ΘΘΘ. Note the presence of basbidity in the columnar sum.

The next column to the left has a value of fooby times foobidity, or foobididity. The ∩ digit tells us that there are bar foobididities in the number. Bar foobididities (written ∩ΘΘΘΘ) is also a number with its own name, barbididity. Note also the presence of barbididity in the columnar sum, and the four xip digits that hold places for the empty columns.

The columnar sum expresses the sense of the way a number is assembled: The number contains barbididity, basbidity, foobity, and bas. Roll all that together by simple addition and you get ∩≡ ⌈Θ≡. The name is pronounced simply by hyphenating the component values: barbididity-basbidity-foobity-bas. Note that there is no part in the name representing the empty fooby column. In our own familiar base 10 we don't, for example, pronounce the number 401 as "four hundred, zero tens, one." We simply say, "four hundred one." In the same manner, rather than say "xip foobies," the Martians just leave it out.

As an exercise, given what I've told you so far about Martian numbers, figure out the Earthly value equivalent to ∩ ≡ ⌈Θ ≡.

The Essence of a Number Base

Since tourist trips to Mars are unlikely to begin any time soon, of what Earthly use is knowing the Martian numbering system? Just this: It's an excellent way to see the sense in a number base without getting distracted by familiar digits and our universal base 10.

In a columnar system of numeric notation like both ours and the Martians', the *base* of the number system is the magnitude by which each column of a number exceeds the magnitude of the column to its right. In our base 10 system, each column represents a value *10* times the column to its right. In a base fooby system like the one used on Mars, each column represents a value fooby times that of the column to its right. (In case you haven't already caught on, the Martians are actually using base 4—but I wanted you to see it from the Martians' own perspective.) Each has a set of digit symbols, the number of which is equal to the base. In our base 10, we have 10 symbols, from 0 to 9. In base 4, there are four digits from 0 to 3. *In any given number base, the base itself can never be expressed in a single digit!*

Octal: How the Grinch Stole Eight and Nine

Farewell to Mars. Aside from lots of iron oxide and some terrific *a capella* groups, they haven't much to offer us 10-fingered folk. There are some similarly odd number bases in use here, and I'd like to take a quick detour through one that occupies a separate world right here on Earth: the world of Digital Equipment Corporation, better known as DEC.

Back in the sixties, DEC invented the minicomputer as a challenger to the massive and expensive mainframes pioneered by IBM. (The age of minicomputers is long past, and what's left of DEC is now owned by Compaq, a microcomputer company.) To ensure that no software could possibly be moved from an IBM mainframe to a DEC minicomputer, DEC designed its machines to understand only numbers expressed in base *8*.

Let's think about that for a moment, given our experience with the Martians. In base 8, there must be eight digits. DEC was considerate enough not to invent its own digits, so what it used were the traditional digits from 0 to 7. *There is no digit 8 in base 8!* That always takes a little getting used to, but it's part of the definition of a number base. DEC gave a name to its base 8 system: *octal.*

A columnar number in octal follows the rule we encountered in thinking about the Martian system: Each column has a value eight times that of the column to its right.

Who Stole Eight and Nine?

Counting in octal starts out in a very familiar fashion: one, two, three, four, five, six, seven . . . *10.*

This is where the trouble starts. In octal, 10 comes after seven. What happened to eight and nine? Did the Grinch steal them? (Or the Martians?) Hardly. They're still there—but they have different names. In octal, when you say "10" you mean "eight." Worse, when you say "11" you mean "nine."

Unfortunately, what DEC did *not* do was invent clever names for the column values. The first column is, of course, the units column. The next column to the left of the units column is the tens column, just as it is in our own decimal system. But there's the rub, and the reason I dragged Mars into this: *Octal's "tens" column actually has a value of 8.*

A counting table will help. Table 2.3 counts up to 30 octal, which has a value of 24 decimal. I dislike the use of the terms *eleven*, *twelve*, and so on in bases other than 10, but the convention in octal has always been to

Table 2.3 Counting in Octal, Base 8

OCTAL NUMERALS	OCTAL PRONUNCIATION	DECIMAL EQUIVALENT
0	Zero	0
1	One	1
2	Two	2
3	Three	3
4	Four	4
5	Five	5
6	Six	6
7	Seven	7
10	Ten	8
11	Eleven	9
12	Twelve	10
13	Thirteen	11
14	Fourteen	12
15	Fifteen	13
16	Sixteen	14
17	Seventeen	15
20	Twenty	16
21	Twenty-one	17
22	Twenty-two	18
23	Twenty-three	19
24	Twenty-four	20
25	Twenty-five	21
26	Twenty-six	22
27	Twenty-seven	23
30	Thirty	24

pronounce the numbers as we would in decimal, only with the word *octal* after them. Don't forget to say *octal*—otherwise, people get *really* confused!

Remember, each column in a given number base has a value base times the column to its right, so the tens column in octal is actually the eights column. (They call it the tens column because it is written 10, and pronounced "ten.") Similarly, the column to the left of the tens column is the hundreds column (because it is written 100 and pronounced "hundreds"), but the hundreds column actually has a value of 8 times 8, or 64. The next column to the left has a value of 64 times 8, or 512, and the column left of that has a value of 512 times 8, or 4,096.

This is why if someone talks about a value of "ten octal," they mean 8; "one hundred octal," they mean 64; and so on. Table 2.4 summarizes the octal column values and their decimal equivalents.

A digit in the first column (the units, or ones column) tells how many units are contained in the octal number. A digit in the next column to the left, the tens column, tells how many eights are contained in the octal number. A digit in the third column, the hundreds column, tells how many 64s are in the number, and so on. For example, 400 octal means that the number contains four 64s; that is 256 in decimal.

Yes, it's confusing, in spades. The best way to make it all gel is to dissect a middling octal number, just as we did with a middling Martian number. This is what's happening in Figure 2.2: The octal number 76225 is pulled apart into columns and added up again.

It works here the same way it does in Martian, or in decimal, or in any other number base you could devise. In general: Each column has a

Table 2.4 Octal Columns as Powers of Eight

OCTAL	POWER OF 8		DECIMAL	OCTAL
1	$= 8^0$	=	$1 \times 8 =$	10
10	$= 8^1$	=	$8 \times 8 =$	100
100	$= 8^2$	=	$64 \times 8 =$	1000
1000	$= 8^3$	=	$512 \times 8 =$	10000
10000	$= 8^4$	=	$4096 \times 8 =$	100000
100000	$= 8^5$	=	$32768 \times 8 =$	1000000
1000000	$= 8^6$	=	$262144 \times 8 =$	10000000

Consider the Octal Number 76225

Each column carries a value
eight multiplied by the column on its right.

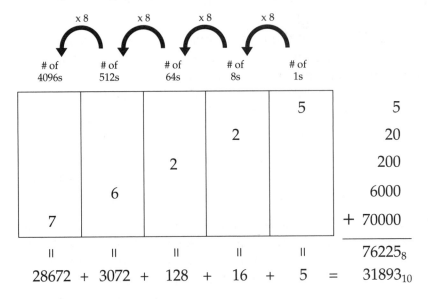

$$28672 + 3072 + 128 + 16 + 5 = 31893_{10}$$

The sum of each column's decimal equivalent
is the value of the octal number in decimal.

Figure 2.2   The anatomy of 76225 octal.

value consisting of the number base raised to the power represented by the ordinal position of the column minus one. For example, the value of the first column is the number base raised to the 1 minus 1, or zero, power. Since any number raised to the zero power is one, the first column in *any* number base always has the value of one and is called the *units column*. The second column has the value of the number base raised to the 2 minus 1, or first power, which is the value of the number base itself. In octal this is 8; in decimal, 10; in Martian base fooby, fooby. The third column has a value consisting of the number base raised to the 3 minus 1, or second power, and so on.

Within each column, the digit holding that column tells how many instances of that column's value is contained in the number as a whole. Here, the 6 in 76225 octal tells us that there are six instances of its column's value in the total value 76225 octal. The six occupies the fourth column, which has a value of 8^{4-1}, which is 8^3, or 512. This tells us that there are six 512s in the number as a whole.

You can convert the value of a number in any base to decimal (our base 10) by determining the value of each column in the alien base, then multiplying the value of each column by the digit contained in that column (to create the decimal equivalent of each digit), and then finally taking the sum of the decimal equivalent of each column. This is done in Figure 2.2, and the octal number and its decimal equivalent are shown side by side. Something to notice in Figure 2.2 is the small subscript numerals on the right-hand side of the columnar sums. These subscripts are used in many technical publications to indicate a number base. The subscript in the value 76225_8, for example, indicates that the value 76225 is here denoting a quantity in octal, which is base 8. Unlike the obvious difference between Martian and decimal, there's really nothing about an octal number itself that sets it off as octal. (We encounter something of this same problem a little later on when we confront hexadecimal.) The value 31893_{10}, by contrast, is shown by its subscript to be a base 10, or decimal, quantity. This is mostly done in scientific and research writing. In most computer publications (including this one) other indications are used, on which more later.

Now that we've looked at columnar notation from both a Martian and an octal perspective, make sure you understand how columnar notation works in any arbitrary base before we go on.

Living Fossils

Octal as a number base is very nearly extinct. The DEC PDP8 machines that were octal's home turf are now dishwasher-sized museum pieces with about the same computing power as a Furby toy. There is, however, one small domain where octal numbers still (literally) roam the Earth. People who have used the CompuServe online system for some time may be known by their numeric IDs. (Newer CompuServe accounts use alphabetic IDs, just as all Internet systems use.) Back when I had a CompuServe account, it was 76711,470. Note that nowhere in that numeric ID is any digit larger than 7. In fact, *nowhere* in *any* old-style CompuServe ID number will you find either the digit 8 or the digit 9. CompuServe was created a good many years ago on a (large) bank of old DEC computers, and their login IDs are all in octal. But as with most living fossils, look quick. CompuServe's old octal IDs are getting rarer and rarer all the time.

Hexadecimal: Solving the Digit Shortage

Octal is unlikely to be of use to you unless you do what a friend of mine did and restore an ancient DEC PDP8 computer that he had purchased as surplus from his university, by the pound. (He said it was considerably cheaper than potatoes, if not quite as easy to fry. Not quite.) As I mentioned earlier, the *real* numbering system to reckon with in the microcomputer world is base 16, which we call *hexadecimal*, or (more affectionately) simply "hex."

Hexadecimal shares the essential characteristics of any number base, including both Martian and octal: It is a columnar notation, in which each column has a value *16* times the value of the column to its right. It has 16 digits, running from 0 to . . . what?

We have a shortage of digits here. From zero through nine we're in fine shape. However, 10, 11, 12, 13, 14, and 15 need to be expressed in single digits. Without any additional numeric digits, the people who developed hexadecimal notation in the early 1950s borrowed the first six letters of the alphabet to act as the needed digits.

Counting in hexadecimal, then, goes like this: 1, 2, 3, 4, 5, 6, 7, 8, 9, A, B, C, D, E, F, 10, 11, 12, 13, 14, 15, 16, 17, 18, 19, 1A, 1B, 1C, and so on. Table 2.5 restates this in a more organized fashion, with the decimal equivalents up to 32.

One of the conventions in hexadecimal which I favor is the dropping of words such as *eleven* and *twelve* that are a little too tightly bound to our decimal system and only promote gross confusion. Confronted by the number 11 in hexadecimal (usually written 11H to let us know what base we're speaking), we would say, "one-one hex." Don't forget to say "hex" after a hexadecimal number, again to avoid gross confusion. This is unnecessary with the digits 0 through 9, which represent the exact same values in both decimal and hexadecimal.

Some people still say things like "twelve hex," which is valid, and means 18 decimal. But I don't care for it, and advise against it. This business of alien bases is confusing enough without giving the aliens Charlie Chaplin masks.

Table 2.5 Counting in Hexadecimal, Base 16

HEXADECIMAL NUMERALS	PRONUNCIATION (FOLLOW WITH "HEX")	DECIMAL EQUIVALENT
0	Zero	0
1	One	1
2	Two	2
3	Three	3
4	Four	4
5	Five	5
6	Six	6
7	Seven	7
8	Eight	8
9	Nine	9
A	A	10
B	B	11
C	C	12
D	D	13
E	E	14
F	F	15
10	Ten (or, One-oh)	16
11	One-one	17
12	One-two	18
13	One-three	19
14	One-four	20
15	One-five	21
16	One-six	22
17	One-seven	23
18	One-eight	24
19	One-nine	25
1A	One-A	26
1B	One-B	27
1C	One-C	28
1D	One-D	29
1E	One-E	30
1F	One-F	31
20	Twenty (or, Two-oh)	32

Table 2.6 Hexadecimal Columns as Powers of 16

HEXADECIMAL	POWER OF 16	DECIMAL
1H	$= 16^0 =$	1 x 16 = 10H
10H	$= 16^1 =$	16 x 16 = 100H
100H	$= 16^2 =$	256 x 16 = 1000H
1000H	$= 16^3 =$	4096 x 16 = 10000H
10000H	$= 16^4 =$	65536 x 16 = 100000H
100000H	$= 16^5 =$	1048576 x 16 = 1000000H
1000000H	$= 16^6 =$	16777216 etc...

Each column in the hexadecimal system has a value 16 times that of the column to its right. (The rightmost column, as in *any* number base, is the units column and has a value of 1.) As you might imagine, the values of the individual columns go up frighteningly fast as you move from right to left. Table 2.6 shows the values of the first seven columns in hexadecimal. For comparison's sake, note that the seventh column in decimal notation has a value of 1 million, while the seventh column in hexadecimal has a value of 16,777,216.

To help you understand how hexadecimal numbers are constructed, I've dissected a middling hex number in Figure 2.3, in the same fashion that I dissected numbers earlier in both Martian base fooby, and in octal, base 8. Just as in octal, zero holds a place in a column without adding any value to the number as a whole. Note in Figure 2.3 that there are 0, that is, no, 256s present in the number 3C0A9H.

As in Figure 2.2, the decimal values of each column are shown beneath the column, and the sum of all columns is shown in both decimal and hex. (Note the subscripts!)

From Hex to Decimal and from Decimal to Hex

Most of the manipulation of hex numbers you'll be performing will be simple conversions between hex and decimal, in both directions. The easiest way to perform such conversions is by way of a hex calculator, either a "real" calculator like the venerable TI Programmer (which I still have, wretched battery-eater that it is) or a software calculator with hexadecimal capabilities. (The old Sidekick TSR calculator for DOS was my con-

Consider the Hexadecimal Number 3C0A9

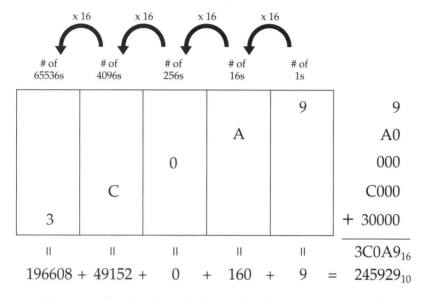

Each column carries a value sixteen times
that of the column on its right.

The sum of each column's decimal equivalent
is the value of the hex number in decimal.

Figure 2.3 The anatomy of 3C0A9H.

stant companion in years past, because it did hexadecimal arithmetic so well.) Using a calculator demands nothing of your gray matter, of course, and won't help you understand the hexadecimal number system any better. So while you're a relatively green student, lay off anything that understands hex, be it hardware, software, or human associates.

In fact, the best tool is a simple four-function memory calculator. The conversion methods I describe here all make use of such a calculator since what I'm trying to teach you is number base conversion, not decimal addition or long division.

From Hex to Decimal

As you'll come to understand, converting hex numbers to decimal is a good deal easier than going the other way. The general method is to do what we've been doing all along in the number-dissection Figures 2.1,

2.2, and 2.3: Derive the value represented by each individual column in the hex number, and then add up the total of all the column values in decimal.

Let's try an easy one. The hex number is 7A2. Start at the right column. This is the units column in any number system. You have 2 units, so enter 2 into your calculator. Now store that 2 into memory. (Or press the SUM button, if you have a SUM button.)

So much for units. Keep in mind that what you're really doing is keeping a running tally of the values of the columns in the hex number. Move to the next column to the left. Remember that each column represents a value 16 times the value of the column to its right. So, the second column from the right is the 16s column. (Refer to Table 2.6 if you lose track of the column values.) The 16s column has an A in it. A in hex is decimal 10. The total value of that column, therefore, is 16 x 10, or 160. Perform that multiplication on your calculator, and add the product to the 2 that you stored in memory. (Again, the SUM button is a handy way to do this if your calculator has one.)

Remember what you're doing: evaluating each column in decimal and keeping a running total. Now, move to the third column from the right. This one contains a 7. The value of the third column is 16 x 16, or 256. Multiply 256 x 7 on your calculator, and add the product to your running total.

You're done. Retrieve the running total from your calculator memory. The total should be 1954, which is the decimal equivalent of 7A2H.

Okay—let's try it again, more quickly, with a little less natter and a much larger number: C6F0DBH.

1. First, evaluate the units column. B x 1 = 11 x 1 = 11. Start your running total with 11.

2. Evaluate the 16s column. D x 16 = 13 x 16 = 208. Add 208 to your running total.

3. Evaluate the 256s column. 0 x 256 = 0. Move on.

4. Evaluate the 4,096s column. F x 4,096 = 15 x 4,096 = 61,440. Add it to your running total.

5. Evaluate the 65,536s column. 6 x 65,536 = 393,216. Add it to the running total.

6. Evaluate the 1,048,576s column. C x 1,048,576 = 12 x 1,048,576 = 12,582,912. Add it to your total.

The running total should be 13,037,787.

Finally, do it yourself without any help for the following number: 1A55BEH.

From Decimal to Hex

The lights should be coming on about now. This is good, because going in the other direction, from our familiar decimal base 10 to hex, is *much* harder and involves more math. What we have to do is find the hex column values within a decimal number—and that involves some considerable use of that fifth-grade bogeyman, long division.

But let's get to it, again, starting with a fairly easy number: 449. The calculator will be handy with a vengeance. Tap in the number 449 and store it in the calculator's memory.

What we need to do first is find the *largest* hex column value that is contained in 449 at least *once*. Remember grade-school "gazintas"? (12 *gazinta* 855 how many times?) Division is often introduced to students as a way of finding out how many times some number is present in—"goes into"—another. It's something like that. Looking back at Table 2.6, we can see that 256 is the largest power of 16, and hence the largest hex column value, that is present in 449 at least once. (The next largest power of 16—512—is obviously too large to be present in 449.)

So, we start with 256, and determine how many times 256 "gazinta" 449: 449 / 256 = 1.7539. At least once, but not quite twice. So, 449 contains only one 256. Write down a 1 on paper. *Don't enter it into your calculator.* We're not keeping a running total here; if anything, we could say we're keeping a running remainder. The "1" is the leftmost hex digit of the hex value that is equivalent to decimal 449.

We know that there is only one 256 contained in 449. What we must do now is *remove* that 256 from the original number, now that we've "counted" it by writing a 1 down on paper. Subtract 256 from 449. Store the difference, 193, into memory.

The 256 column has been removed from the number we're converting. Now we move to the next column to the right, the 16s. How many 16s are contained in 193? 193 / 16 = 12.0625. This means the 16s column in the hex equivalent of 449 contains a . . . 12? Hmmmm . . . remember the digit shortage, and the fact that in hex, the value we call 12 is represented by the letter C. From a hex perspective, we have found that the original number contains C in the 16s column. Write a C down to the right of your 1: 1C. So far, so good.

We've got the 16s column, so just as with the 256s, we have to remove the 16s from what's left of the original number. The total value of the 16s column is C x 16 = 12 x 16 = 192. Bring the 193 value out of your calculator's memory, and subtract 192 from it. A lonely little 1 is all that's left.

So we're down to the units column. There is one unit in one, obviously. Write that 1 down to the right of the C in our hexadecimal number: 1C1. Decimal 449 is equivalent to hex 1C1.

Now perhaps you'll begin to understand why programmers like hexadecimal calculators so much.

Let's glance back at the big picture of the decimal-to-hex conversion. We're looking for the hexadecimal columns hidden in the decimal value. We find the largest column contained in the decimal number, find that column's value, and subtract that value from the decimal number. Then we look for the next smallest hex column, and the next smallest, and so on, removing the value of each column from the decimal number as we go. In a sense, we're dividing the number by consecutively smaller powers of 16 and keeping a running remainder by removing each column as we tally it.

Let's try it again. The secret number is 988,664.

1. Find the largest column contained in 988,664 from Table 2.6: 65,536. 988,664 / 65,536 = 15 and change. Ignore the change. 15 = F in hex. Write down the F.

2. Remove F x 65,536 from 988,664. Store the remainder: 5,624

3. Move to the next smallest column. 5,624 / 4,096 = 1 and change. Write down the 1.

4. Remove 1 x 4,096 from the remainder: 5,624 - 4096 = 1528. Store the new remainder: 1,528.

5. Move to the next smallest column. 1,528 / 256 = 5 and change. Write down the 5.

6. Remove 5 x 256 from the stored remainder, 1,528. Store 248 as the new remainder.

7. Move to the next smallest column. 248 / 16 = 15 and change. 15 = F in hex. Write down the F.

8. Remove F x 16 from stored remainder, 248. The remainder, 8, is the number of units in the final column. Write down the 8.

There you have it: 988,664 decimal = F15F8H.

Note the presence of the *H* at the end of the hex number. From now on, every hex number in the text of this book will have that H affixed to its hindparts. It's important, because not *every* hex number contains letter digits. There is a 157H as surely as a 157 decimal, and the two are *not* the same number. (Quick, now: By how much are they different?) Don't forget that H in writing your assembler programs, as I'll be reminding you later on.

Practice. Practice! PRACTICE!

The best (actually, the only) way to get a gut feel for hex notation is to use it lots. Convert *each* of the following hex numbers to decimal. Lay each number out on the dissection table and identify how many 1s, how many 16s, how many 256s, how many 4,096s, and so on, are present in the number, and then add them up in decimal.

```
CCH
157H
D8H
BB29H
7AH
8177H
A011H
99H
2B36H
FACEH
8DB3H
9H
```

That done, now turn it inside out, and convert each of the following decimal numbers to hex. Remember the general method: From Table 2.6, choose the largest power of 16 that is *less* than the decimal number to be converted. Find out how many times that power of 16 is present in the decimal number, and write it down as the leftmost hex digit of the converted number. Then subtract the total value represented by that hex digit from the decimal number. Then repeat the process, using the next smallest power of 16 until you've subtracted the decimal number down to nothing.

```
39
413
22
67,349
6,992
41
```

```
1,117
44,919
12,331
124,217
91,198
307
112,374,777
```

(Extra credit for that last one . . .) If you need more practice, choose some decimal numbers and convert them to hex, and then convert them back.

Arithmetic in Hex

As you become more and more skilled in assembly language, you'll be doing more and more arithmetic in base 16. You may even (good grief) come to do it in your head. Still, it takes some practice.

Addition and subtraction are nothing more than what we know in decimal, with a few extra digits tossed in for flavor. The trick is nothing more than knowing your addition tables to 0FH. This is best done not by thinking to yourself, "Now, if C is 12 and F is 15, then C + F is 12 + 15, which is 27 decimal but 1BH." Instead, you should simply say inside your head, "C + F is 1BH."

Yes, that's asking a lot. But I ask you now, as I will ask you again on this journey, *Do you wanna hack assembly . . . or do you just wanna fool around?* It takes practice to learn the piano, and it takes practice to get really greased up on the foundation concepts of assembly language programming.

So let me sound like an old schoolmarm and tell you to memorize the following. Make flash cards if you must:

9	8	7	6	5	
+1	+2	+3	+4	+5	
0AH	0AH	0AH	0AH	0AH	

A	9	8	7	6	
+1	+2	+3	+4	+5	
0BH	0BH	0BH	0BH	0BH	

B	A	9	8	7	6
+1	+2	+3	+4	+5	+6
0CH	0CH	0CH	0CH	0CH	0CH

C	B	A	9	8	7		
+ 1	+ 2	+ 3	+ 4	+ 5	+ 6		
0DH	0DH	0DH	0DH	0DH	0DH		
D	C	B	A	9	8	7	
+ 1	+ 2	+ 3	+ 4	+ 5	+ 6	+ 7	
0EH	0EH	0EH	0EH	0EH	0EH	0EH	
E	D	C	B	A	9	8	
+ 1	+ 2	+ 3	+ 4	+ 5	+ 6	+ 7	
0FH	0FH	0FH	0FH	0FH	0FH	0FH	
F	E	D	C	B	A	9	8
+ 1	+ 2	+ 3	+ 4	+ 5	+ 6	+ 7	+ 8
10H	10H	10H	10H	10H	10H	10H	10H
F	E	D	C	B	A	9	
+ 2	+ 3	+ 4	+ 5	+ 6	+ 7	+ 8	
11H	11H	11H	11H	11H	11H	11H	
F	E	D	C	B	A	9	
+ 3	+ 4	+ 5	+ 6	+ 7	+ 8	+ 9	
12H	12H	12H	12H	12H	12H	12H	
F	E	D	C	B	A		
+ 4	+ 5	+ 6	+ 7	+ 8	+ 9		
13H	13H	13H	13H	13H	13H		
F	E	D	C	B	A		
+ 5	+ 6	+ 7	+ 8	+ 9	+ A		
14H	14H	14H	14H	14H	14H		
F	E	D	C	B			
+ 6	+ 7	+ 8	+ 9	+ A			
15H	15H	15H	15H	15H			
F	E	D	C	B			
+ 7	+ 8	+ 9	+ A	+ B			
16H	16H	16H	16H	16H			
F	E	D	C				
+ 8	+ 9	+ A	+ B				
17H	17H	17H	17H				
F	E	D	C				
+ 9	+ A	+ B	+ C				
18H	18H	18H	18H				

```
  F          E          D
+ A        + B        + C
 19H        19H        19H

  F          E          D
+ B        + C        + D
 1AH        1AH        1AH

  F          E
+ C        + D
 1BH        1BH

  F          E
+ D        + E
 1CH        1CH

  F
+ E
 1DH

  F
+ F
 1EH
```

If nothing else, this exercise should make you glad computers don't work in base 64.

Columns and Carries

With all of the single-column additions committed (more or less) to memory, you can tackle multicolumn addition. It works pretty much the same way it does with decimal. Add each column starting from the right, and carry into the next column anytime a single column's sum exceeds 0FH.

For example:

```
  1       1
  2 F 3 1 A DH
+ 9 6 B A 0 7H
  C 5 E B B 4H
```

Carefully work this one through, column by column. The sum of the first column (that is, the rightmost) is 14H, which cannot fit in a single column, so we must carry the one into the next column to the left. Even with the additional 1, however, the sum of the second column is 0BH, which fits in a single column and no carry is required.

Keep on adding toward the left. The second-to-last column will again overflow, and you will need to carry the one into the last column. As long as you have your single-digit sums memorized, it's a snap.

Well, more or less.

Now, here's something you should take note of:

The most you can ever carry out of a single-column addition of two numbers is 1.

It doesn't matter what base: 16, 10, fooby, or 2. You will either carry a 1 (in Martian, foo) out of a column, or carry nothing at all. This fact surprises people for some reason, so ask yourself: What two single digits in old familiar base 10 can you add that will force you to carry a 2? The largest digit is 9, and 9 + 9 = 18. Put down the 8 and carry the 1. Even if you have to add in a carry from a previous column, that will bring you up (at most) to 19. Again, you carry a 1 and no more. This is important when you add numbers on paper, or within the silicon of your CPU, as we'll learn a few chapters on.

Subtraction and Borrows

If you have your single-column sums memorized, you can usually grind your way through subtraction with a shift into a sort of mental reverse: "If E + 6 equals 14H, then 14H - E must equal 6." The alternative is memorizing an even larger number of tables, and since I haven't memorized them, I won't ask you to.

But over time, that's what tends to happen. In hex subtraction, you should be able to dope out any given single-column subtraction by turning a familiar hexadecimal sum inside-out. And just as with base 10, multicolumn subtractions are done column by column, one column at a time:

```
 F76CH
-A05BH
 5711H
```

During your inspection of each column, you should be asking yourself: "What number added to the bottom number yields the top number?" Here, you should know from your tables that B + 1 = C, so the difference between B and C is 1. The leftmost column is actually more challenging: What number added to A gives you F? Chin up; even I have to think about it on an off-day.

The problems show up, of course, when the top number in a column is smaller than its corresponding bottom number. Then (like the federal government on a bomber binge) you have no recourse but to borrow.

Borrowing is one of those grade-school rote-learned processes that very few people really understand. (To understand it is tacit admittance that something of New Math actually stuck, horrors.) From a height, what happens in a borrow is that one count is taken from a column and applied to the column on its right. I say *applied* rather than *added to* because in moving from one column to the column on its right, that single count is multiplied by 10, where 10 represents the number base. (Remember that 10 in octal has a value of 8, while 10 in hexadecimal has a value of 16.)

It sounds worse than it is. Let's look at a borrow in action, and you'll get the idea.

```
 9 2H
-4 FH
```

Here, the subtraction in the rightmost column can't happen as-is, because F is larger than 2. So, we borrow from the next column to the left.

Nearly 30 years out of the past, I can still hear old Sister Marie Bernard toughing it out on the blackboard, albeit in base 10: "Cross out the 9; make it an 8. Make the 2 a 12. And 12 minus F is what, class?" It's 3, Sister. And that's how a borrow works. (I hope the poor dear will forgive me for putting hex bytes in her mouth . . .)

Think about what happened there, functionally. *We subtracted 1 from the 9 and added 10H to the 2.* One obvious mistake is to subtract 1 from the 9 and add 1 to the 2, which (need I say it?) won't work. Think of it this way: We're moving part of one column's surplus value over to its right, where some extra value is needed. The *overall* value of the upper number doesn't change (which is why we call it a *borrow* and not a *steal*), but the recipient of the loan is increased by *10*, not *1*.

After the borrow, what we have looks something like this:

```
 8¹2H
- 4 FH
```

(On Sister Marie Bernard's blackboard, we crossed out the 9 and made it an 8. I just made it an 8. Silicon has advantages over chalk—except that the 8's earlier life as a 9 is not so obvious.)

And of course, once we're here, the columnar subtractions all work out, and we discover that the difference is 43H.

People sometimes ask if you ever have to borrow more than 1. The answer, plainly, is *no*. If you borrow 2, for example, you would add 20 to the recipient column, and *20 minus any single digit remains a two-digit number*. That is, the difference won't fit into a single column. Subtraction contains an important symmetry with addition:

The most you ever need to borrow in any single-column subtraction of two numbers is 1.

Borrows across Multiple Columns

Understanding that much about borrows gets you most of the way there. But, as life is wont, you will *frequently* come across a subtraction similar to this:

```
  F 0 0 0H
- 3 B 6 CH
```

Column 1 needs to borrow, but neither column 2 nor column 3 have anything at all to lend. Back in grade school, Sister Marie Bernard would have rattled out with machine-gun efficiency: "Cross out the F, make it an E. Make the 0 a 10. Then cross it out, make it an F. Make the next 0 a 10; cross it out, make it an F. Then make the last 0 a 10." Got that? (I got it. In Catholic school, the consequences of *not* getting it are too terrible to consider.)

What happens is that the middle two 0s act as loan brokers between the F and the rightmost 0, keeping their commission in the form of enough value to allow their own columns' subtractions to take place. Each column to the right of the last column borrows 10 from its neighbor to the left, and loans 1 to the neighbor on its right. After all the borrows trickle through the upper number, what we have looks like this (minus all of Sister's cross-outs):

```
  E F F¹0H
- 3 B 6 CH
```

At this point, each columnar subtraction can take place, and the difference is B494H.

In remembering your grade-school machinations, don't fall into the old decimal rut of thinking, "cross out the 10, make it a 9." In the world of hexadecimal, 10H - 1 = F. Cross out the 10, make it an *F*.

What's the Point?

. . . if you have a hex calculator, or a hex-capable screen calculator? The point is *practice*. Hexadecimal is the lingua franca of assemblers, to multiply-mangle a metaphor. The more you burn a gut-level understanding of hex into your reflexes, the easier assembly language will be. Furthermore, understanding the internal structure of the machine itself will be much easier if you have that intuitive grasp of hex values. We're laying important groundwork here. Take it seriously now and you'll lose less hair later on.

Binary

Hexadecimal is excellent practice for taking on the strangest number base of all: *binary*. Binary is base 2. Given what we've learned about number bases so far, what can we surmise about base 2?

- Each column has a value two times the column to its right.
- There are only two digits (0 and 1) in the base.

Counting is a little strange in binary, as you might imagine. It goes like this: 0, 1, 10, 11, 100, 101, 110, 111, 1,000 . . . Because it sounds absurd to say, "Zero, one, 10, 11, 100, . . . " it makes more sense to simply enunciate the individual digits, followed by the word *binary*. For example, most people say "one zero one one one zero one binary" instead of "one million, eleven thousand, one hundred one binary" when pronouncing the number 1011101—which sounds enormous until you consider that its value in decimal is only 93.

Odd as it may seem, binary follows all of the same rules we've discussed in this chapter regarding number bases. Converting between binary and decimal is done using the same methods described for hexadecimal in an earlier section of this chapter.

Because counting in binary is as much a matter of counting columns as counting digits (since there are only two digits) it makes sense to take a long, close look at Table 2.7, which shows the values of the binary number columns out to 32 places.

Table 2.7 Binary Columns as Powers of 2

BINARY	POWER OF 2	DECIMAL
1	$=2^0=$	1
10	$=2^1=$	2
100	$=2^2=$	4
1000	$=2^3=$	8
10000	$=2^4=$	16
100000	$=2^5=$	32
1000000	$=2^6=$	64
10000000	$=2^7=$	128
100000000	$=2^8=$	256
1000000000	$=2^9=$	512
10000000000	$=2^{10}=$	1024
100000000000	$=2^{11}=$	2048
1000000000000	$=2^{12}=$	4096
10000000000000	$=2^{13}=$	8192
100000000000000	$=2^{14}=$	16384
1000000000000000	$=2^{15}=$	32768
10000000000000000	$=2^{16}=$	65536
100000000000000000	$=2^{17}=$	131072
1000000000000000000	$=2^{18}=$	262144
10000000000000000000	$=2^{19}=$	524288
100000000000000000000	$=2^{20}=$	1048576
1000000000000000000000	$=2^{21}=$	2097152
10000000000000000000000	$=2^{22}=$	4194304
100000000000000000000000	$=2^{23}=$	8388608
1000000000000000000000000	$=2^{24}=$	16777216
10000000000000000000000000	$=2^{25}=$	33554432
100000000000000000000000000	$=2^{26}=$	67108864
1000000000000000000000000000	$=2^{27}=$	134217728
10000000000000000000000000000	$=2^{28}=$	268435456
100000000000000000000000000000	$=2^{29}=$	536870912
1000000000000000000000000000000	$=2^{30}=$	1073741824
10000000000000000000000000000000	$=2^{31}=$	2147483648
100000000000000000000000000000000	$=2^{32}=$	4294967296

One look at that imposing pyramid of zeroes implies that it's hopeless to think of pronouncing the larger columns as strings of digits: "One zero zero zero zero zero zero zero . . . " and so on. There's a crying need for a shorthand notation here, so I'll provide you with one in a little while—and its identity will surprise you.

You might object that such large numbers as the bottommost in the table aren't likely to be encountered in ordinary programming. Sorry, but a 32-bit microprocessor such as the Pentium (and even its antiquated forbears like the 386 and 496) can swallow numbers like that in one electrical gulp, and eat billions of them for lunch. You *must* become accustomed to thinking in terms of such numbers as 2^{32}, which, after all, is only a trifling 4 billion in decimal. Think for a moment of the capacity of the hard drive on your own desktop computer. New PCs in the spring of 2000 are routinely shipped with 10 gigabytes or more of hard disk storage. A gigabyte is a billion bytes . . . so that monster 32-bit number can't even count all the bytes on your hard drive! This little problem has actually bitten some vendors of old (no, sorry, the word is *legacy*) software. Ten or 12 years ago, a 6-gigabyte hard drive seemed like a distant fantasy for most of us. Now CompUSA sells that fantasy for $129.95. And I have a file utility that throws up its hands in despair any time it has to confront a disk drive with more than 2 gigabytes of free space . . .

Now, just as with octal and hexadecimal, there can be identity problems when using binary. The number 101 in binary is *not* the same as 101 in hex, or 101 in decimal. For this reason, always append the suffix "B" to your binary values to make sure people reading your programs (including you, six weeks after the fact) know what base you're working from.

Values in Binary

Converting a value in binary to one in decimal is done the same way it's done in hex—more simply, in fact, for the simple reason that you no longer have to count how many times a column's value is present in any given column. In hex, you have to see how many 16s are present in the 16s column, and so on. In binary, a column's value is either present (1 time) or not present (0 times).

Running through a simple example should make this clear. The binary number 11011010B is a relatively typical binary value in small-time computer work. (On the small side, actually—many common binary numbers are twice its size or more.) Converting 11011010B to decimal comes down to scanning it from right to left with the help of Table 2.7, and tallying any column's value where that column contains a 1, while ignoring any column containing a 0.

Clear your calculator and let's get started:

1. Column 0 contains a 0; skip it.
2. Column 1 contains a 1. That means its value, 2, is present in the value of the number. So we punch 2 into the calculator.
3. Column 2 is 0. Skip it.
4. Column 3 contains a 1. The column's value is 2^3, or 8; add 8 to our tally.
5. Column 4 also contains a 1; 2^4 is 16, which we add to our tally.
6. Column 5 is 0. Skip it.
7. Column 6 contains a 1; 2^6 is 64, so add 64 to the tally.
8. Column 7 also contains a 1. Column 7's value is 2^7, or 128. Add 128 to the tally, and what do we have? 218. That's the decimal value of 11011010B. It's as easy as that.

Converting from decimal to binary, while more difficult, is done *exactly* the same way as converting from decimal to hex. Go back and read that section again, searching for the *general method* used. In other words, see what was done and separate the essential principles from any references to a specific base like hex.

I'll bet by now you can figure it out without much trouble.

As a brief aside, perhaps you noticed that I started counting columns from 0 rather than 1. A peculiarity of the computer field is that we always begin counting things from 0. Actually, to call it a peculiarity is unfair; the computer's method is the reasonable one, because 0 is a perfectly good number and should not be discriminated against. The rift occurred because in our real, physical world, counting things tells us *how many* things are there, while in the computer world counting things is more generally done to *name* them. That is, we need to deal with bit number 0, and then bit number 1, and so on, far more than we need to know how many bits there are.

This is not a quibble, by the way. The issue will come up again and again in connection with memory addresses, which as I have said and will say again are the key to understanding assembly language.

In programming circles, always begin counting from 0!

A practical example of the conflicts this principle can cause grows out of the following question: What year begins the new millennium? Most people would intuitively say the year 2000, but technically, the twentieth century will continue until January 1, 2001. Why? *Because there was no year 0.* When historians count the years moving from B.C. to A.D., they go 1B.C. to 1A.D. Therefore, the first century began with year 1 and ended with year 100. The second century began with year 101 and ended with year 200. By extending the sequence you can see that the twentieth century began in 1901 and will end in 2000. On the other hand, if we had had the sense to begin counting years in the current era computer style, from year 0, the twentieth century would end at the end of 1999. My suggestion? Call this the *Short Century* (which it certainly seems to those of us who have been around for any considerable chunk of it) and begin the *Computer Millennium* on January 1, 2000.

This is a good point to get some practice in converting numbers from binary to decimal and back. Sharpen your teeth on these:

```
110
10001
11111
11
101
1100010111010010
11000
1011
```

When that's done, convert these decimal values to binary:

```
77
42
106
255
18
6309
121
58
18,446
```

Why Binary?

If it takes eight whole digits (11011010) to represent an ordinary three-digit number such as 218, binary as a number base would seem to be a bad intellectual investment. Certainly for us it would be a waste of mental bandwidth, and even aliens with only two fingers would probably have come up with a better system.

The problem is, lights are either on or they're off.

This is just another way of saying (as I discuss in detail in Chapter 3) that at the bottom of it, *computers are electrical devices*. In an electrical device, voltage is either present or it isn't; current either flows or it doesn't. Very early in the game, computer scientists decided that the presence of a voltage in a computer circuit would indicate a 1 digit, while lack of a voltage at that same point in the circuit would indicate a 0 digit. This isn't many digits, but it's enough for the binary number system. This is the only reason we use binary, but it's a pretty compelling one, and we're stuck with it. However, you will not necessarily drown in ones and zeroes, because I've already taught you a form of shorthand.

Hexadecimal as Shorthand for Binary

The number 218 expressed in binary is 11011010B. Expressed in hex, however, the same value is quite compact: DAH. The two hex digits comprising DAH merit a closer look. AH (or 0AH as your assembler will require it for reasons I explain later) represents 10 decimal. Converting any number to binary simply involves detecting the powers of two within it. The largest power of 2 within 10 decimal is 8. Jot down a 1 digit and subtract 8 from 10. What's left is 2. Now, 4 is a power of 2, but there is no 4 hiding within 2, so we put a 0 to the right of the 1. The next smallest power of 2 is 2, and there is a 2 in 2. Jot down another 1 to the right of the 0. Two from 2 is 0, so there are no 1s left in the number. Jot down a final 0 to the right of the rest to represent the 1s column. What you have is this:

```
1 0 1 0
```

Look back at the binary equivalent of 218: 11011010. The last four digits are 1010—the binary equivalent of 0AH.

The same will work for the upper half of DAH. If you work out the binary equivalence for 0DH as we just did (and it would be good mental exercise), it is 1101. Look at the binary equivalent of 218 this way:

```
    218      decimal
1101 1010    binary
  D    A     hex
```

It should be dawning on you that you can convert long strings of binary 1s and 0s into more compact hex format by converting every four binary digits (starting from the right, *not* from the left!) into a single hex digit.

As an example, here is a 32-bit binary number that is not the least bit remarkable:

```
11110000000000001111101001101110
```

This is a pretty obnoxious collection of bits to remember or manipulate, so let's split it up into groups of four from the right:

```
1111 0000 0000 0000 1111 1010 0110 1110
```

Each of these groups of four binary digits can be represented by a single hexadecimal digit. Do the conversion now. What you should get is the following:

```
1111 0000 0000 0000 1111 1010 0110 1110
  F    0    0    0    F    A    6    E
```

In other words, the hex equivalent of that mouthful is

```
F000FA6E
```

In use, of course, you would append the *H* on the end, and also put a 0 at the beginning, so in any kind of assembly language work the number would actually be written 0F000FA6EH.

This is still a good-sized number, but unless you're doing things like counting hard drive space or other high-value things, such 32-bit numbers are the largest quantities you would typically encounter in journeyman-level assembly language programming.

Suddenly, this business starts looking a little more graspable.

Hexadecimal is the programmer's shorthand for the computer's binary numbers.

This is why I said earlier that computers use base 2 (binary) and base 16 (hexadecimal) both at the same time in a rather schizoid fashion. What I didn't say is that the computer isn't really the schizoid one; *you* are. At their very hearts (as I explain in Chapter 3) computers use *only* binary. Hex is a means by which you and I make dealing with the computer easier. Fortunately, every four binary digits may be represented by a hex digit, so the correspondence is clean and comprehensible.

Prepare to Compute

Everything up to this point has been necessary groundwork. I've explained conceptually what computers *do* and have given you the tools to understand the slightly alien numbers they use. But I've said nothing so far about what computers actually *are*, and it's well past time. We return to hexadecimal numbers again and again in this book; I've said nothing thus far about hex multiplication or bit-banging. The reason is plain: Before you can bang a bit, you must know where the bits live. So, let's lift the hood and see if we can catch a few in action.

CHAPTER 3

Lifting the Hood

Discovering What Computers Actually *Are*

RAXie, We Hardly Knew Ye . . .

In January 1970 I was on the downwind leg of my senior year in high school, and the Chicago Public Schools had installed a computer somewhere. A truckful of these fancy typewriter gimcracks was delivered to Lane Tech, and a bewildered math teacher was drafted into teaching computer science (they had the nerve to call it) to a high school full of rowdy males.

I figured it out fairly quickly. You pounded out a deck of these goofy computer cards on the card punch machine, dropped them into the hopper of one of the typewriter gimcracks, and watched in awe as the typewriter danced its little golfball over the greenbar paper, printing out your inevitable list of error messages. It was fun. I got straight A's. I even kept the first program I ever wrote that did something useful: a little deck of cards that generated a table of parabolic correction factors for hand-figuring telescope mirrors, astronomy being my passion at the time. (The card deck is still in its place of honor on the narrow shelf here in my second-floor office, next to my 8-inch reel-to-reel tape deck and my father's venerable slide rule.)

The question that kept gnawing at me was exactly what sort of beast RAX (the computer's wonderfully appropriate name) actually was. What we had were ram-charged typewriters that RAX controlled over phone lines—that much I understood. But what was RAX itself?

I asked the instructor. In brief, the conversation went something like this:

ME: "Umm, sir, what exactly *is* RAX?"

HE: "Eh? Um, a computer. An electronic computer."

ME: "That's what it says on the course notes. But I want to know what RAX is made of and how it works."

HE: "Well, I'm sure RAX is all solid-state."

ME: "You mean, there's no levers and gears inside."

HE: "Oh, there may be a few. But no vacuum tubes."

ME: "I wasn't worried about tubes. I suppose it has a calculator in it somewhere. But what makes it remember that A comes before B? How does it know what FORMAT means? How does it tell time? What does it have to do to answer the phone?"

HE: "Now, come on, that's why computers are so great! They put it all together so that we don't have to worry about that sort of thing! Who cares what RAX is? RAX knows FORTRAN and will execute any correct FORTRAN program. That's what matters, isn't it?"

He was starting to sweat. So was I. End of conversation.

That June I graduated with three inches of debugged and working FORTRAN punch cards in my bookbag, and still had absolutely no clue as to what RAX was.

It has bothered me to this day.

Gus to the Rescue

I was thinking about RAX six years later, while on the Devon Avenue bus heading for work, with the latest copy of *Popular Electronics* in my lap. The lead story involved a little thing called the COSMAC ELF, which consisted of a piece of perfboard full of integrated circuit chips, all wired together, plus some toggle switches and a pair of LED numeric displays.

It was a computer. (Said so right on the label, heh.) The article told us how to put it together, and that was about all. What did those chips do? What did the whole thing do? It was driving me nuts.

As usual, my friend Gus Flassig got on the bus at Ashland Avenue and sat down beside me. I asked him what the damned thing did. He was the first human being to make the concept hang together for me:

"These are memory chips. You load numbers into the memory chips by flipping these switches in different code patterns. Each number means something to the CPU chip. One number makes it add; another number makes it subtract; another makes it write different numbers into memory, and lots of other things. A program consists of a bunch of these instruction-numbers in a row in memory. The computer reads the first number, does what the number tells it to do, and then reads the second one, does what *that* number says to do, and so on until it runs out of numbers."

If *you* don't find that utterly clear; don't worry. I had had the advantage of being an electronics hobbyist (so I knew what some of the chips did) and had already written some programs in RAX's FORTRAN. But for me, my God, everything suddenly hit critical mass and exploded in my head until the steam started pouring out of my ears.

No matter what RAX was, I knew that it had to be something like the COSMAC ELF on a larger scale. I built an ELF. It was quite an education, and allowed me to understand the nature of computers at a very deep level. I don't recommend that anybody but total crazies wirewrap their own machines out of loose chips anymore, although it was a common enough thing to do in the mid-late seventies.

As a sidenote, someone has written a Windows-based simulation of the COSMAC ELF that looks just like the one I built, and will actually accept and execute COSMAC programs. It's a lot of fun and might give you some perspective on what passed for computing in early 1976. The URL is as follows:

```
www.incolor.inetnebr.com/bill_r/computer_simulators.htm
```

The site's author, Bill Richman, has also reprinted the *Popular Electronics* article that I built the device from. All fascinating reading—and a very good education in the deepest silicon concepts underlying computing as it was then and remains to this day.

In this chapter I try and provide you with some of the insights that I obtained while assembling my own machine the hard way. (You wonder where the "hard" in "hardware" comes from? Not from the sound it makes when you bang it on the table, promise . . .)

Switches, Transistors, and Memory

Switches remember.

Think about it. You flip the switch by the door, and the light in the middle of the ceiling comes on. It stays on. When you leave the room, you flip the switch down again, and the light goes out. It stays out. Poltergeists notwithstanding, the switch will remain in the position you last left it until you or someone else comes back and flips it to its other position.

In a sense, it remembers what its last command was until you change it, and "overwrite" that command with a new one. In this sense, a light switch represents a sort of rudimentary memory element.

Light switches are more mechanical than electrical. This does not prevent them from acting as memory; in fact, the very first computer (Babbage's nineteenth-century Difference Engine) was entirely mechanical. In fact, the far larger version he designed but never finished was to have been *steam-powered*. Babbage's machine had lots of little cams that could be flipped by other cams from one position to another. Numbers were encoded and remembered as patterns of cam positions.

One if by Land . . .

Whether a switch is mechanical, or electrical, or hydraulic, or something else is irrelevant. What counts is that a switch contains a pattern: on or off; up or down; flow or no flow. To that pattern can be assigned a meaning. Paul Revere told his buddy to set up a code in the Old North Church: "One if by land, two if by sea." Once lit, the lamps in the steeple remained lit (and thus remembered that very important code) long enough for Paul to call out the militia and whup the British.

In general then, what we call *memory* is an aggregate of switches that will retain a pattern long enough for that pattern to be read and understood by a person or a mechanism. For our purposes, those switches will be electrical, but keep in mind that both mechanical and hydraulic computers have been proposed and built with varying degrees of success.

Memory consists of containers for alterable patterns that retain an entered pattern until someone or something alters the pattern.

Transistor Switches

One problem with building a computer memory system of light switches is that light switches are pretty specialized: They require fingers to set them, and their output is a current path for electricity. Ideally, a computer memory switch should be operated by the same force it controls. This allows the patterns in memory locations to be passed on to other memory locations. In the gross electromechanical world, such a switch is called a relay.

A *relay* is a mechanical switch that is operated by electricity, for the purpose of controlling electricity. You "flip" a relay by feeding it a pulse of electricity, which powers a little hammer that whaps a lever to one side or another. This lever then opens or closes a set of electrical contacts, just as your garden-variety light switch does. Computers have been made out of relays, although as you might imagine (with a typical relay being about the size of an ice cube), they weren't especially powerful computers.

Fully electronic computers are made out of transistor switches. *Transistors* are tiny crystals of silicon that use the peculiar electrical properties of silicon to act as switches. I won't try to explain what those peculiar properties are, since that would take an entire book unto itself. Let's consider a transistor switch a sort of electrical black box and describe it in terms of inputs and outputs.

Figure 3.1 shows a transistor switch. (It is a *field-effect* transistor, which in truth is only one type of transistor, but the type that our current computers are made of.) When an electrical voltage is applied to pin 1, current flows between pins 2 and 3. When the voltage is removed from pin 1, current ceases to flow between pins 2 and 3.

In real life, a tiny handful of other components (typically diodes and capacitors) are necessary to make things work smoothly in a computer memory context. These are not necessarily little gizmos connected by wires to the outside of the transistor (although in early transistorized computers they were) but are now cut from the same silicon crystal the

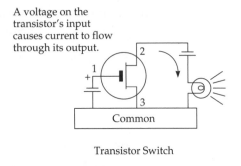

A voltage on the transistor's input causes current to flow through its output.

Transistor Switch

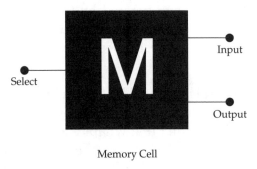

Memory Cell

Figure 3.1   Transistor switches and memory cells.

transistor itself is cut from, and occupy almost no space at all. Taken together, the transistor switch and its support components are called a *memory cell*. I've hidden the electrical complexity of the memory cell within an appropriate black-box symbol in Figure 3.1.

A memory cell keeps current flow through it to a minimum, because electrical current flow produces heat, and heat is the enemy of electrical components. The memory cell's circuit is arranged so that if you put a tiny voltage on its input pin and a similar voltage on its *select* pin, a voltage will appear *and remain* on its output pin. That output voltage will remain in its set state until you take away the voltage from the cell as a whole, or else remove the voltage from the input pin while putting a voltage on the select pin.

The "on" voltage being applied to all of these pins is kept at a consistent level. (Except, of course, when it is removed entirely.) In other words, you don't put 12 volts on the input pin and then change that to 6 volts or 17 volts. The computer designers pick a voltage and stick with it. The pattern is binary in nature: You either put a voltage on the input pin, or you take the voltage away entirely. The output pin echoes that: It either holds a fixed voltage or no voltage at all.

We apply a code to that state of affairs: *The presence of voltage indicates a binary 1, and the lack of voltage indicates a binary 0.* This code is arbitrary. We could as well have said that the *lack* of voltage indicates a binary 1 and vice versa (and computers have been built this way for obscure reasons) but the choice is up to us. Having the *presence* of something indicate a binary 1 is more natural, and that is the way things have evolved in the computing mainstream.

A single computer memory cell, such as the transistor-based one we're speaking of here, holds one binary digit, either a 1 or a 0. This is called a bit. A *bit* is the indivisible atom of information. There is no half-a-bit, and no bit-and-a-half. (This has been tried. It works badly. But that didn't stop it from being tried.)

A bit is a single binary digit, either 1 or 0.

The Incredible Shrinking Bit

One bit doesn't tell us much. To be useful, we need to bring a lot of memory cells together. Transistors started out small (the originals from the 1950s looked a lot like stovepipe hats for tin soldiers) and went down from there. The first transistors were created from little chips of germanium or silicon crystal about an eighth of an inch square. The size of the crystal chip hasn't changed outrageously since then, but the transistors themselves have shrunk almost incredibly.

Where, in the beginning, one chip held one transistor, in time semiconductor designers crisscrossed the chip into four equal areas and made each area an independent transistor. From there it was an easy jump to adding the other minuscule components needed to turn a transistor into a computer memory cell.

The chip of silicon was a tiny and fragile thing, and was encased in an oblong molded-plastic housing, like a stick of Dentyne gum with metal legs for the electrical connections.

What we had now was a sort of electrical egg carton: four little cubbyholes, each of which could contain a single binary bit. Then the shrinking process began. First 8 bits, then 16, then multiples of 8 and 16, all on the same tiny silicon chip. By the late 1960s, 256 memory cells could be made on one chip of silicon, usually in an array of 8 cells by 32. In 1976, my COSMAC ELF computer contained two memory chips. On each chip was an array of memory cells 4 wide and 256 long. (Picture a *real* long egg carton.) Each chip could thus hold 1,024 bits.

This was a pretty typical memory chip capacity at that time. We called them "1K RAM chips," because they held roughly 1,000 bits of *random-access memory* (RAM). The *K* comes from *kilobit*, that is, one thousand bits. We'll get back to the notion of what *random access* means shortly.

Toward the mid-1970s, the great memory-shrinking act was kicking into high gear. One kilobyte chips were crisscross divided into 4K chips containing 4,096 bits of memory. The 4K chips were almost immediately divided into 16K chips (16,384 bits of memory). These 16K chips were the standard when the IBM PC appeared in 1981. By 1982, the chips had been divided once again, and 16K became 64K, with 65,536 bits inside that same little gumstick. Keep in mind that we're talking more than 65,000 transistors (plus other odd components) formed on a square of silicon about a quarter-inch on a side.

Come 1985 and the 64K chip had been pushed aside by its drawn-and-quartered child, the 256K chip (262,144 bits). Chips always increase in capacity by a factor of 4 simply because the current-generation chip is divided into 4 equal areas, onto each of which is then placed the same number of transistors that the previous generation of chip had held over the whole silicon chip.

By 1990, the 256K chip was history, and the 1 megabit chip was state of the art. (*Mega* is Greek for million.) By 1992, the 4 megabit chip had taken over. The critter had a grand total of 4,194,304 bits in its tummy, still no larger than that stick of cinnamon gum. About that time, the chips themselves grew small and fragile enough so that eight of them were soldered to tiny printed circuit boards so that they would survive handling by clumsy human beings.

The game has continued, and today, in the early months of 2000, you can purchase these little circuit board memory sticks (called SIMMs, for Single Inline Memory Module) with as much as 128 mega*bytes* in them—which is just a hair over a *billion* bits.

Will it stop here? Unlikely. More is better, and we're bringing some staggeringly powerful technology to bear on the creation of ever-denser memory systems. Some physicists warn that the laws of physics may soon call a time-out in the game, since the transistors are now so small that it gets hard pushing more than one electron at a time through them. At that point some truly ugly limitations of life called quantum mechanics begin to get in the way. We'll find a way around these limitations (we always do), but in the process the whole nature of computer memory may change.

For now, what we have are billion-bit memory sticks. My computer here has two of them, for a total of 256 megabytes of electronic memory.

That should hold me until next week, heh-heh.

Random Access

These chips are called RAM chips, since what they contain is random-access memory. Newcomers sometimes find this a perplexing and disturbing word, since *random* often connotes chaos or unpredictability. What the word really means is "at random," indicating that you can reach into a random-access memory chip and pick out any of the bits it contains without disturbing any of the others, just as you might select one book at random from your public library's many shelves of thousands of books without sifting through them in order.

Memory didn't always work this way. Before memory was placed on silicon chips, it was stored on magnetic gadgets of some kind, usually rotating drums or disks distantly related to the hard drives we use today. Rotating memory sends a circular collection of bits beneath a magnetic sensor. The bits pass beneath the sensor one at a time, and if you miss the one you want, like a Chicago bus in January, you simply have to wait for it to come by again. These are *serial-access devices*. They present their bits to you, in a fixed order, one at a time, and you have to wait for the one you want to come up in its order.

No need to remember that; we've long since abandoned serial-access devices for main computer memory. We still use such systems for *mass storage*, as I describe a few pages down the road. (Your hard drive is a serial-access device.)

Random access works like this: Inside the chip, each bit is stored in its own memory cell, identical to the memory cell diagrammed in Figure 3.1. Each of the however-many memory cells has a unique number. This number is a cell's (and hence a bit's) *address*. It's like the addresses on a street: The bit on the corner is number 0 Silicon Alley, and the bit next door is number 1, and so on. You don't have to knock on the door of bit 0 and ask which bit it is, then go to the next door and ask there too, until you find the bit you want. If you have the address, you can zip right down the street and park square in front of the bit you intend to visit.

Each chip has a number of pins coming out of it. (This is the computer room's equivalent of the Killer Rake: Don't step on one in the dark!) The bulk of these pins are called *address pins*. One pin is called a *data pin*. (See Figure 3.2.) The address pins are electrical leads that carry a binary address code. Your address is a binary number, expressed in 1s and 0s only. You apply this address to the address pins by encoding a binary 1 as (say) 5 volts, and a binary 0 as 0 volts. Special circuits inside the RAM chip decode this address to one of the select inputs of the numerous memory cells inside the chip. For any given address applied to the address pins, only *one* select input will be raised to five volts, thereby selecting that cell.

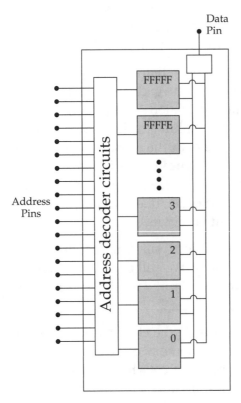

Figure 3.2   A RAM chip.

Depending on whether you intend to read a bit or write a bit, the data pin is switched between the memory cells' inputs or outputs, as shown in Figure 3.2.

But that's all done internally to the chip. As far as you on the outside are concerned, once you've applied the address to the address pins, *voila!* The data pin will contain a voltage representing the value of the bit you requested. If that bit contained a binary 1, the data pin will contain a 5-volt signal; otherwise, the binary 0 bit will be represented by 0 volts.

Memory Access Time

Chips are graded by how long it takes for the data to appear on the data pin after you've applied the address to the address pins. Obviously, the faster the better, but some chips (for electrical reasons that again are difficult to explain) are faster than others.

The times seem so small as to seem almost insignificant: 70 nanoseconds is a typical memory chip access time. A nanosecond is a *billionth* of a second, so 70 nanoseconds is significantly less than one 10-millionth of a second. Great stuff—but to accomplish anything useful, a computer needs to access memory hundreds of thousands or millions of times. Those nanoseconds add up. If you become an expert assembly language programmer, you will jump through hoops to shave the number of memory accesses your program needs to perform, because memory access is the ultimate limiting factor in a computer's performance. Michael Abrash, in fact, has published a whole book on doing exactly that, in the realm of high-speed graphics programming, which can be (badly) summarized in just these few words: *Stay out of memory whenever you can!* (You'll discover just how difficult this is soon enough . . .) The book is *Michael Abrash's Graphics Programming Black Book* (Coriolis Group Books, 1997). It's one of the few genuinely useful advanced assembly language texts available, and I strongly recommend it.

Bytes, Words, Double Words, and Quad Words

The days are long gone when a serious computer can exist on only one memory chip. My poor 1976 COSMAC ELF needed at least two. Today's computers need many, regardless of the fact that today's memory chips can hold as much as 100 megabits or more rather than the

ELF's paltry 2,048 bits. Understanding how a computer gathers its memory chips together into a coherent memory *system* is critical when you wish to write efficient assembly language programs. Whereas there is an infinity of ways to hook memory chips together, the system I describe here is that of the Intel-based PC type of computer, which has ruled the world of desktop computing since 1982.

Our memory system must store our information. How we organize a memory system out of a hatful of memory chips will be dictated largely by how we organize our information.

The answer begins with this thing called a *byte*. The fact that the granddaddy of all computer magazines took this word for its title indicates its importance in the computer scheme of things. (Alas, *Byte Magazine* ceased publishing late in 1998.) From a *functional* perspective, memory is measured in bytes. A byte is eight bits. Two bytes side by side are called a *word*, and two words side by side are called a *double word*. A *quad word*, as you might imagine, consists of two double words, for four words or eight bytes in all. Going in the other direction, some people refer to a group of four bits as a nybble—a *nybble* being somewhat smaller than a byte.

Here's the quick tour:

- A bit is a single binary digit, 0 or 1.
- A byte is 8 bits side by side.
- A word is 2 bytes side by side.
- A double word is 2 words side by side.
- A quad word is 2 double words side by side.

Computers were designed to store and manipulate human information. The basic elements of human discourse are built from a set of symbols consisting of letters of the alphabet (two of each for upper and lower case), numbers, and symbols including commas, colons, periods, exclamation marks. Add to these the various international variations on letters such as ä and ò plus the more arcane mathematical symbols, and you'll find that human information requires a symbol set of well over 200 symbols. (The symbol set used in all PC-style computers is given in Appendix D.)

Bytes are central to the scheme because one symbol out of that symbol set can be neatly expressed in one byte. A byte is 8 bits, and 2^8 is 256. This means that a binary number 8 bits in size can be one of 256 different values, numbered from 0 to 255. Because we use these symbols so much, most of what we do in computer programs is done in byte-sized chunks. In fact, except for the very odd and specialized kind of computers we are now building into intelligent food processors, *no* computer processes information in chunks smaller than 1 byte. Most computers today, in fact, process information either a word or (more and more commonly) a double word at a time.

Pretty Chips All in a Row

One of the more perplexing things for beginners to understand is that a standard 64-megabit RAM chip does not even contain 1 byte . . . just 64 million bits. Remember that the RAM chips we use today have only *one* data pin. To store a byte you would have to store eight bits in sequence at eight consecutive addresses, and to retrieve that byte you would have to retrieve eight bits in sequence. Since it takes 70 nanoseconds at the very least to store a bit in one of those chips, storing a byte would take at least 560 nanoseconds, and in practical terms, close to a microsecond, which (believe it!) is far, far too slow to be useful.

What is actually done is to distribute a single stored byte across eight separate RAM chips, with one bit from the stored byte in each chip, at the same address across all chips. This way, when a single address is applied to the address pins of all eight chips, all eight bits appear simultaneously on the eight output pins, and we can retrieve a full byte in 70 nanoseconds instead of 560 nanoseconds. See Figure 3.3.

We call this row of eight chips a *bank* of memory, and how much memory is contained in a bank depends on the type of chips incorporated in the bank. A row of eight 1-megabit chips like that shown in Figure 3.3 contains one mega*byte*. (That megabyte taken as a whole contains 8 x 1 or 8 million *bits*, however. Remember, computers deal with information a minimum of 8 bits at a time.) A row of eight 256K bit chips contains 256K bytes, and so on. The memory SIMMs in current use today typically contain a row of eight chips, each of which contains 32 or 64 megabits. Some high-end SIMMs are formed of eight 128-megabit chips and contain 128 megabytes.

Actual computers combine various combinations of memory banks in various ways to produce different amounts of memory. I'll take up the subject again when we begin talking specifically about the PC in Chapter 6.

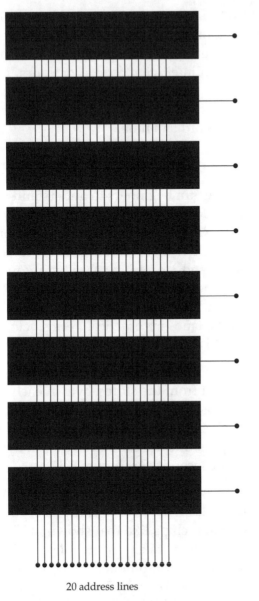

Each black box is a chip like that shown in Figure 3.2.

Each of eight chips contains 1,048,576 bits. The eight chips taken together contain 1,048,576 bytes, with each chip contributing one bit to every byte. Bytes of data may be written to and read from the eight data lines shown here.

20 address lines

Figure 3.3   A 1-megabyte memory bank.

The Shop Foreman and the Assembly Line

The gist of the previous section was only this: Electrically, your computer's memory consists of one or more rows of memory chips, each chip containing a *large* number of memory cells consisting of transistors and other minuscule electrical components. Most of the time, it's just as useful to forget about the transistors and even the rows of chips to avoid confusion. (My high school computer science teacher was not *entirely* wrong . . . but he was right for the wrong reasons.)

Over the years, memory systems have been accessed in different ways. Eight-bit computers (now ancient and mostly extinct) accessed memory eight bits (one byte) at a time. Sixteen-bit computers access memory 16 bits (one word) at a time. And today's 32-bit computers (everything in the PC realm since the 386) access memory 32 bits (one double word) at a time. This can be confusing, so it's better in most cases to envision a very long row of byte-sized containers, each with its own address. Don't assume that in computers which process information a word at a time that only *words* have addresses; it is a convention with the PC architecture that *every* byte has its own address regardless of how many bytes are pulled from memory at one time.

Every byte of memory in the computer has its own unique address, even in computers that process two bytes or even four bytes of information at a time.

If this seems counterintuitive, yet another metaphor will help: When you go to the library to take out the three volumes of Tolkien's massive fantasy *The Lord of the Rings*, you'll find that each of the three volumes has its own card catalog number (essentially that volume's address in the library) but that you take all three down at once and process them as a single entity. If you really *want* to, you can take only one of the books out at a time, but to do so will require yet another trip to the library to get the next volume, which is wasteful of your time and effort.

So it is with 16-bit or 32-bit computers. Every byte has its own address, but when a 16-bit computer accesses a byte, it actually reads *two* bytes starting at the address of the requested byte. You can use the second byte or ignore it if you don't need it—but if you later decide you do need the second byte, you'll have to access memory again to get it. Best to save time and get it all at one swoop.

The Honcho Chip

All of this talk about reading things from memory and writing things to memory has thus far carefully skirted the question of *who* is doing the read and writing. The who is almost always a single chip, and a remarkable chip it is, too: the *central processing unit*, or CPU. If you are the president and CEO of your personal computer, the CPU is your shop foreman, who sees that your orders are carried out down in the chips where the work gets done.

Some would say that the CPU is what actually does the work, but that's an oversimplification. Plenty of real work is done in the memory system, and especially in what are called *peripherals*, such as video display boards, serial and parallel ports, and modems. So, while the CPU does do a good deal of the work, it parcels out quite a bit to other components within the computer. I think its role of foreman outweighs its role as assembly-line grunt.

Most of the CPU chips used in the machines we lump together as a group and call PCs come from a company called Intel, which pretty much invented the single-chip CPU back in the early 1970s. Intel's first bang-up success was the 8080, which helped trigger the personal computer revolution by being chosen for the seminal MITS Altair 8800 computer introduced in *Popular Electronics* in December 1974. The 8080 was an 8-bit computer because it accessed memory 8 bits (1 byte) at a time. The 8080 is long extinct, but it gave birth to a pair of next-generation CPU chips called the 8086 and the 8088. These two chips are nearly identical except that the 8088 is an 8-bit CPU, while the 8086 is a 16-bit CPU, and accesses memory a word (2 bytes) at a time. IBM chose the 8088 for its original 1981 IBM PC and later the PC XT, but the 8086 never made it into a true IBM computer until the forgettable (and now largely forgotten) PS/2 models 25 and 30 appeared in 1987.

Intel produced yet another generation of CPU chip in 1983, and by 1984 the 80286 became the beating heart of the enormously successful PC/AT. The 80286 is a more powerful 16-bit CPU, capable of everything the 8086 can do, plus numerous additional things that were mostly never used in real computers. Early 1986 brought Intel's 80386 CPU chip to market. The 80386 upped the ante by being a 32-bit machine. It reads and writes memory a double word (32 bits—4 bytes) at a time. The 80386 was enormously more powerful than the 80286, and a great deal faster. From there to the 80486, to the Pentium, the Pentium II, the Pentium Pro, the Pentium MMX, and most recently the Pentium III, was a straight-line march along the 32-bit pathway toward more speed, power, and capacity. Irrespective of its 500-MHz speed, the Pentium III remains a 32-bit machine because it fetches information from memory 4 bytes at a time.

We thought for a long time that 32 bits is an ideal "fetch size" for CPU memory access, and that increasing memory access beyond 32 bits at a time would begin to slow things down. Well, that was then . . . and some time in the next few months as I write this, Intel will begin shipping samples of its first 64-bit CPU, code-named Merced. Merced fetches memory 8 bytes (a quad word) at a time and will run at speeds of 1 GHz (*gigahertz:* a billion clock cycles per second) or more. It has plenty of new internal machinery to make sure that expanding its silicon jaws to swallow 64 bits at a time will not slow anything down.

Is 64 bits an optimal size? No bets taken here. I've been in this business long enough to see the foolishness of making sweeping statements like that.

Talking to Memory

All the assorted Intel CPUs operate at varying speeds with various features, but at the bottom of things they are conceptually identical, and this discussion will apply to all of them.

The CPU chip's most important job is to communicate with the computer's memory system. Like a memory chip, a CPU chip is a small square of silicon onto which a great many transistors have been placed. The fragile silicon chip is encased in a plastic or ceramic housing with a large number of pins protruding from it. Like the pins of memory chips, the CPU's pins transfer information encoded as voltage levels, typically 3 to 5 volts. Five volts indicate a binary 1, and zero volts indicate a binary 0.

Like the memory chips, the CPU chip has a number of pins devoted to memory addresses, and these pins are connected directly to the computer's banks of memory chips. When the CPU desires to read a byte (or a word, or double word) from memory, it places the memory address of the byte to be read on its address pins, encoded as a binary number. Seventy nanoseconds or so later, the byte appears (also as a binary number) on the data pins of the memory chips. The CPU chip also has data pins, and it slurps up the byte presented by the memory chips through its own data pins. See Figure 3.4.

The process, of course, also works in reverse: To write a byte into memory, the CPU first places the memory address where it wants to write onto its address pins. Some number of nanoseconds later (which varies from system to system depending on how memory is arranged) the CPU places the byte it wishes to write into memory on its data pins. The memory chips obediently store the byte inside themselves at the requested address.

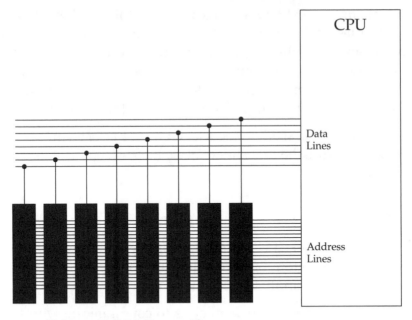

Eight megabit RAM chips, providing
1,048,576 bytes of memory total.

Figure 3.4 The CPU and memory.

Riding the Bus

This give-and-take between the CPU and the memory system represents the bulk of what happens inside your computer. Information flows from memory into the CPU and back again. Information flows in other paths as well. Your computer contains additional devices called *peripherals* that are either sources or destinations (or both) for information.

Video display boards, disk drives, printer ports, and modems are the most common peripherals in PC-type computers. Like the CPU and memory, they are all ultimately electrical devices. Most modern peripherals consist of one or two large chips and several smaller chips that support the larger chips. Like both the CPU and memory chips, these peripheral devices have both address pins and data pins. Some peripherals, video boards in particular, have their own memory chips.

Peripherals "talk" to the CPU (that is, they pass the CPU data or take data from the CPU) and sometimes to one another. These conversations take place across the electrical connections linking the address pins and data pins that all devices in the computer have in common. These electrical lines are called a *data bus* and form a sort of party line linking the

CPU with all other parts of the computer. There is an elaborate system of electrical arbitration that determines when and in what order the different devices can use this party line to talk with one another. But it happens the same way: An address is placed on the bus, followed by a byte (or word or double word) of data. Special signals go out on the bus with the address to indicate whether the address is of a location in memory, or of one of the peripherals attached to the data bus. The address of a peripheral is called an *I/O address* to differentiate between it and a *memory address* such as those we've been discussing all along.

The data bus is the major element in the *expansion slots* present in most PC-type computers, and most peripherals are boards that plug into these slots. The peripherals talk to the CPU and to memory through the data bus connections brought out as electrical pins in the expansion slots.

The Foreman's Pockets

Every CPU contains a very few data storage cubbyholes called *registers*. These registers are at once the foreman's pockets and the foreman's workbench. When the CPU needs a place to tuck something away for a while, an empty register is just the place. The CPU could always store the data out in memory, but that takes considerably more time than tucking it in a register. Because the registers are actually inside the CPU, placing data in a register or reading it back again from a register is *fast*.

But more important, registers are the foreman's workbench. When the CPU needs to add two numbers, the easiest and fastest way is to place the numbers in two registers and add the two registers together. The sum (in usual CPU practice) replaces one of the two original numbers that were added, but after that the sum could then be placed in yet another register, or added to still another number in another register, or stored out in memory, or any of a multitude of other operations.

The CPU's immediate work-in-progress is held in temporary storage containers called registers.

Work involving registers is always fast, because the registers are within the CPU and very little movement of data is necessary—and what data does move doesn't have to move very far.

Like memory cells and, indeed, like the entire CPU, registers are made out of transistors. But rather than having numeric addresses, registers have names such as AX or DI. To make matters even more complicated, while all CPU registers have certain common properties, some registers have unique special powers not shared by other registers. Understanding the ways and the limitations of CPU registers is something like following the Kosovo peace process: There are partnerships, alliances, and always a bewildering array of secret agendas that each register follows. I devote most of a chapter to registers later in this book.

Most peripherals also have registers, and peripheral registers are even more limited in scope than CPU registers. Their agendas are quite explicit and in no wise secret. This does not prevent them from being confusing, as anyone who has tried programming the VGA video board at the register level will attest.

The Assembly Line

If the CPU is the shopforeman, then the peripherals are the assembly-line workers, and the data bus is the assembly line itself. (Unlike most assembly lines, however, the foreman works the line as hard or harder than the rest of his crew!)

As an example: Information enters the computer through a modem peripheral, which assembles bits received from the telephone line into bytes of data representing characters and numbers. The modem then places the assembled byte onto the bus, from which the CPU picks it up, tallies it, and then places it back on the data bus. The video board then retrieves the byte from the bus and writes it into video memory so that you can see it on your screen.

Obviously, lots is going on inside the box. Continuous furious communication along the data bus between CPU, memory, and peripherals is what accomplishes the work that the computer does. The question then arises: Who tells the foreman and crew what to do? *You* do. How do you do that? You write a program. Where is the program? It's in memory, along with all the rest of the data stored in memory. In fact, the program *is* data, and that is the heart of the whole idea of programming as we know it.

The Box That Follows a Plan

Finally, we come to the essence of computing: the nature of programs and how they direct the CPU to control the computer.

We've seen how memory can be used to store bytes of information. These bytes are all binary codes, patterns of 1s and 0s stored as minute electrical voltage levels and making up binary numbers. We've also spoken of symbols, and how certain binary codes may be interpreted as meaning something to us human beings, things like letters, digits, punctuation, and so on.

Just as the table in Appendix D contains a set of codes and symbols that mean something to us, there is a set of codes that mean something to the CPU. These codes are called *machine instructions*, and their name is evocative of what they actually are: instructions to the CPU.

Let's take an example or two that is common to all modern CPU chips from Intel. The 8-bit binary code 01000000 (40H) means something to the CPU. It is an order: *Add 1 to register AX*. That's about as simple as they get. Most machine instructions occupy more than a single byte. The binary codes 11010110 01110011 (0B6H 73H) comprise another order: *Load the value 73H into register DH*. On the other end of the spectrum, the binary codes 11110011 10100100 (0F3H 0A4H) direct the CPU to do the following (take a deep breath): *Begin moving the number of bytes specified in register CX from the 32-bit address stored in registers DS and SI to the 32-bit address stored in registers ES and DI, updating the address in both SI and DI after moving each byte, and also decreasing CX by one each time, and finally stopping when CX becomes zero.*

The rest of the several hundred instructions understood by the Intel CPUs falls somewhere in between these extremes in terms of complication and power. There are instructions that perform arithmetic operations (addition, subtraction, multiplication, and division) and logical operations (AND, OR, etc; see Chapter 4), and instructions that move information around memory or exchange information with peripherals.

Fetch and Execute

A computer program is nothing more than a table of these machine instructions stored in memory. There's nothing special about the table nor where it is positioned in memory; it could be anywhere, and the bytes in the table are nothing more than binary numbers.

The binary numbers comprising a computer program are special only in the way that the CPU treats them. When the CPU is started running, it *fetches* a double word (for modern CPUs) from an agreed-upon address in memory. This double word, consisting of four bytes in a row, is read from memory and loaded into the CPU. The CPU examines the pattern of binary bits contained in the double word, and then begins performing the task that the fetched machine instruction directs it to do.

Ancient 8088-based machines such as the original IBM PC only fetched one byte at a time, rather than the four bytes that modern Pentium-class machines fetch. Because most machine instructions are more than a single byte in size, the 8088 CPU had to return to memory to fetch a second (or a third or a fourth) byte to complete the machine instruction before it could actually begin to obey the instruction and begin performing the task that the instruction specified.

As soon as it finishes executing an instruction, the CPU goes out to memory and fetches the next machine instruction in sequence. Inside the CPU is a register called the *instruction pointer* that quite literally contains the address of the next instruction to be fetched and executed. Each time an instruction is completed, the instruction pointer is updated to point to the next instruction in memory. (There is some silicon magic afoot inside modern CPUs that guesses what's to be fetched next and keeps it on a side shelf so it'll be there when fetched only much more quickly—but the process as I've described it is true in terms of the outcome.)

So the process goes: Fetch and execute; fetch and execute. The CPU works its way through memory, with the instruction pointer register leading the way. As it goes, it works: Moving data around in memory, moving values around in registers, passing data to peripherals, crunching data in arithmetic or logical operations.

Computer programs are lists of binary machine instructions stored in memory. They are no different from any other list of data bytes stored in memory except in how they are treated when fetched by the CPU.

The Foreman's Innards

I made the point earlier that machine instructions are *binary* codes. This is something we often gloss over, yet to understand the true nature of the CPU, we have to step away from the persistent image of machine instructions as *numbers*. They are *not* numbers. They are binary patterns designed to throw electrical switches.

Inside the CPU is a *very* large number of transistors. Some small number of those transistors go into making up the fireman's pockets: machine registers for holding information. The vast bulk of those transistors (which now number in the several millions in such CPUs as the Pentium III) are switches connected to other switches, which are connected to still more switches in a mind-numbingly complex network.

The very simple machine instruction 01000000 (40H) directs the CPU to add one to the value stored in register AX. It's very instructive of the true nature of computers to think about the execution of machine instruction 01000000 in this way:

The CPU fetches a byte from memory. This byte contains the code 01000000. Once the byte is fully within the CPU, the CPU in essence lets the machine instruction byte push eight transistor switches. The lone 1 digit pushes its switch "up" electrically; the rest of the digits, all 0s, push their switches "down."

In a chain reaction, those eight switches flip the states of first dozens, then hundreds, then thousands, and finally tens of thousands of tiny transistor switches within the CPU. It isn't random—this furious moment of electrical activity within the CPU operates utterly according to patterns etched into the silicon of the CPU by Intel's teams of engineers. Ultimately—perhaps after hundreds of thousands of individual switch throws—the value contained in register AX is suddenly one greater than it was before.

How this happens is difficult to explain, but you must remember that *any* number within the CPU can also be looked upon as a binary code, including numbers stored in registers. Also, most switches within the CPU contain more than one handle. These switches are called *gates* and work according to the rules of logic. Perhaps two, or three, or even more up switch throws have to arrive at a particular gate at the same time in order for one down switch throw to pass through that gate.

These gates are used to build complex internal machinery within the CPU. Collections of gates can add two numbers in a device called an *adder*, which again is nothing more than a crew of dozens of little switches working together first as gates and then as gates working together to form an adder.

As part of the cavalcade of switch throws kicked off by the binary code 01000000, the value in register AX was dumped trapdoor style into an adder, while at the same time the number 1 was fed into the other end of the adder. Finally, rising on a wave of switch throws, the new sum emerges from the adder and ascends back into register AX—and the job is done.

The foreman of your computer, then, is made of switches—just like all the other parts of the computer. It contains a mind-boggling number of such switches, interconnected in even more mind-boggling ways. But the important thing is that whether you are boggled or (like me on off-days) merely jaded by it all, the CPU, and ultimately the computer, *does exactly what we tell it to.* We set up a list of machine instructions as a table in memory, and then, by God, that mute iron brick comes alive and starts earning its keep.

Changing Course

The first piece of genuine magic in the nature of computers is that a string of binary codes in memory tells the computer what to do, step by step. The second piece of that magic is really the jewel in the crown: *There are machine instructions that change the order in which machine instructions are fetched and executed.*

In other words, once the CPU has executed a machine instruction that does something useful, the next machine instruction may tell the CPU to go back and play it again—and again, and again, as many times as necessary. The CPU can keep count of the number of times that it has executed that particular instruction or list of instructions and keep repeating them until a prearranged count has been met.

Or it can arrange to skip certain sequences of machine instructions entirely if they don't need to be executed at all.

What this means is that the list of machine instructions in memory does not necessarily begin at the top and run without deviation to the bottom. The CPU can execute the first 50 or a hundred or a thousand instructions, then jump to the end of the program—or jump back to the start and begin again. It can skip and bounce up and down the list like a stone tossed over a calm pond. It can execute a few instructions up here, then zip down somewhere else and execute a few more instructions, then zip back and pick up where it left off, all without missing a beat or even wasting too much time.

How is this done? Recall that the CPU contains a register that always contains the address of the next instruction to be executed. This register, the instruction pointer, is not essentially different from any of the other registers in the CPU. Just as a machine instruction can add one to register AX, another machine instruction can add—or subtract—some number to or from the address stored in the instruction pointer. Add 100 to the instruction pointer, and the CPU will *instantly* skip 100 bytes down the list of machine instructions before it continues. Subtract 100 from the address stored in the instruction pointer, and the CPU will *instantly* jump *back* 100 bytes up the machine instruction list.

And finally, the Third Whammy: *The CPU can change its course of execution based on the work it has been doing.* The CPU can decide whether to execute a given instruction or group of instructions, based on values stored in memory, or based on the state of special one-bit CPU registers called *flags*. The CPU can count up how many times it needs to do something, and then do that something that number of times.

So, not only can you tell the CPU what to do, you can tell it where to go. Better, you can sometimes let the CPU, like a faithful bloodhound, sniff out the best course forward in the interest of getting the work done the quickest possible way.

In Chapter 1, I spoke of a computer program being a sequence of steps and tests. Most of the machine instructions understood by the CPU are steps, but others are tests. The tests are always two-way tests, and in fact the choice of what to do is always the same: Jump or don't jump. *That's all*. You can test for any of numerous different conditions, but the choice is always one of jumping to another place in the program, or just keep truckin' along.

The Plan

I can sum it all up by borrowing one of the most potent metaphors for computing ever uttered: *The computer is a box that follows a plan.* These are the words of Ted Nelson, author of the uncanny book *Computer Lib/Dream Machines*, and one of those very rare people who have the infuriating habit of being right most of the time.

You write the plan. The computer follows it by passing the instructions, byte by byte, to the CPU. At the bottom of it, the process is a hellishly involved electrical chain reaction involving hundreds of thousands of switches composed of many hundreds of thousands or even millions of transistors. That part of it, however, is hidden from you so that you don't have to worry about it. Once you tell all those heaps of transistors what to do, they'll know how to do it.

This plan, this list of machine instructions in memory, is your assembly language program. The whole point of this book is to teach you to correctly arrange machine instructions in memory for the use of the CPU.

With any luck at all, by now you'll have a reasonable conceptual understanding of both what computers do and what they are. It's time to start looking more closely at the nature of the operations that machine instructions force the CPU to perform.

CHAPTER 4

The Right to Assemble

The Process of Making Assembly Language Programs

Nude with Bruises and Other Perplexities

Years ago (back in the 1960s—had to be!) I recall reading about a comely female artist who produced her oil paintings by the intriguing process of rolling naked on a tarp splattered with multicolored oil paint, and then throwing herself against a canvas taped to the studio wall. (I can see the headline now: "NUDE WITH BRUISES" FETCHES RECORD PRICE AT NY AUCTION . . .)

I've seen people write programs this way. The old GWBASIC language that was included free with every copy of DOS worked like that. So does Perl, its counterpart in the Linux universe: You roll in an intoxicating collection of wild and powerful program statements, and then smear them around on the screen until something works. And something invariably *does* work, no matter how little thought goes into the program's design. GWBASIC and Perl are like that. They pay a cost in program performance to make it easy to create safe code that doesn't require a lot of forethought or design work. The programs that result, while workable in that they don't crash the machine, can take seven seconds to paint a screen, or 20 minutes to sort a database with 150 check records in it.

You can't paint "Nude with Bruises" in assembly language. Trust me.

Sweet Blindness: The Software Components Conundrum

But there are other perfectly proper programming paradigms that won't work with assembly language, either. One is commonly used with my own beloved Delphi: Decide what you want to do, sketch out a design based on a reasonable amount of forethought, and then go hunting through a veritable Sears Catalog of software component products looking for canned code that will do more or less what you need. In fact, you design your program to cater to the quirks and limitations of the software components that you have, can find, or can afford to buy.

The goal here is, in some respects, to do as little programming as possible. You attempt to wire together a collection of black boxes that will get the job done, while spending as little time as possible at it. Delphi works this way, as does its evil twin, Visual Basic, along with most of the high-level Java products including JBuilder and Visual Café. The software components have various names (VCL, ActiveX, Java Beans) but they are conceptually alike in one important way: They hide what they do internally so that you don't have to spend a lot of time understanding them.

This sounds like something I frown on, but people who know me will understand that it's been a major portion of my professional life: I founded and edited *Visual Developer Magazine*, which focused on only these products and this way of developing software. When I write code these days, that's how I do it. (In Delphi.)

I do it because I've made the conscious decision *not* to understand all of what's going on in my software. For me it's a time thing: Sure, I'm interested in what's going on inside, but if I spent all the time it took to understand it at a very deep level, I'd never finish writing the software. I do have a life, and not all of it is bashing code.

Remember what I said in the introduction to this book: You learn assembly language to understand how things work. Like all forms of education, you trade time and disciplined energy for knowledge. I've made the conscious decision (and you probably will too) that the time and energy required to learn Windows (or Linux X11) programming at the assembly level costs more than the knowledge is worth.

This wasn't true with DOS, which in truth most people don't use anymore. Nor is it true for Linux, where a deep knowledge of the operating system and how it works is *extremely* valuable. In this book I'm largely treating DOS as training wheels for Linux, where I'm convinced that most of the serious assembly work in the near future is going to happen. Learn DOS and 16-bit flat model (which is the old "Tiny" or "COM file" model) and you will slide into Linux like a hot knife into butter.

I started this chapter this way as a warning: You can't write assembly language programs by trial and error, nor can you do it by letting other people do your thinking for you. It is a complicated and tricky process compared to GWBASIC or Perl or such we-do-it-all-for-you environments as Delphi and Visual Basic. You have to pay attention. You have to read the sheet music. And most of all, you have to practice.

DOS and DOS files

In the previous chapter, I defined what a computer program is, *from the computer's perspective*. It is, metaphorically, a long journey in very small steps. A *long* list of binary codes directs the CPU to do what it must to accomplish the job at hand. These codes are, even in their hexadecimal shorthand form, gobbledygook to us here in meatspace:

```
FE FF A2 37 4C 0A 29 00 91 CB 60 61 E8 E3 20 00 A8 00 B8 29 1F FF 69 55
7B F4 F8 5B 31
```

Is this a real program or isn't it? You'd probably have to ask the CPU, unless you were a machine-code maniac of the kind that hasn't been seen since 1977. (It isn't.)

But the CPU has no trouble with programs presented in this form. In fact, the CPU can't handle programs any other way. The CPU simply isn't equipped to understand a string of characters such as

```
LET X = 42
```

or even something that we out here would call assembly language:

```
MOV AX,42
```

To the CPU, it's binary only and hold the text, please.

So, while it is possible to write computer programs in pure binary (I have done it, but not since 1977), it's unpleasant work and will take you until the next Ice Age to accomplish anything useful.

The process of developing assembly language programs is a path that runs from what we call *source code* that you can read, to something called *machine code* that the CPU can execute. In the middle is a resting point called *object code* that we'll take up a little later.

The process of creating true machine-code programs is one of translation. You must start with something that you and the rest of us can read and understand, and then somehow convert that to something the CPU can understand and execute. Before examining either end of that road, however, we need to understand a little more about the land on which the road is built.

The God Above, the Troll Below

Most of all, we need to understand DOS, both for its own sake and as a sort of idiot younger brother of Linux. Some people look upon DOS as a god; others as a kind of troll. In fact, DOS is a little of both. Mostly what you must put behind you is the common notion that DOS is a part of the machine itself and somehow resides in the same sort of silicon as the CPU. Not so! DOS is a computer program of an only slightly special nature, called an operating system.

In part, an *operating system* is a collection of routines that do nothing but serve the hardware components of the computer itself. By hardware components I mean such things as disk drives, printers, scanners, and so on. DOS acts something like a troll living under the bridge to your disk drive. You tell the troll what you want to do with the disk drive, and the troll does it, his way, and at some cost (in machine cycles) to you.

You could write a program that handled every little aspect of disk operation itself (many game programmers have done exactly that) but it would be more trouble than it was worth, since *every* program that runs on a computer needs to access the disk drives. And regardless of how grumpy the troll is, he *does* get the job done, and (assuming your disk drives aren't falling-down damaged) does it right every time. Can *you* guarantee that you know all there is to know about running a disk drive? Forgive me if I have my doubts. That is, in my opinion, what trolls are for.

The other (and more interesting) thing that operating systems do is run programs. It is here that DOS seems more godlike than troll-like. When you want to run a program on your computer, you type its name at the DOS command line. DOS goes out and searches one or more disk drives for the named program, loads it into memory at a convenient spot, sets the instruction pointer to the start of the program, and boots the CPU in the rear to get it going.

DOS then patiently waits for the program to run its course and stop. When the program stops, it hands the CPU obediently back to DOS, which again tilts a hand to its ear and listens for your next command from the command line.

So, as programmers, we use DOS two ways: One is as a sort of toolkit, an army of trolls if you will, each of which can perform some service for your program, thereby saving your program that effort. The other is as a means of loading a program into memory and getting it going, and then catching the machine gracefully on the rebound when your program is through.

I mention DOS again and again in this book. Everywhere you look in 16-bit assembly language, you're going to see the old troll's face. Get used to it.

DOS Files: Magnetic Memory

Very simply, DOS files are memory banks stored on a magnetic coating rather than inside silicon chips. A DOS file contains some number of bytes, stored in a specific order. One major difference from RAM memory is that DOS files stored on disk are sequential-access memory banks.

A disk (be it floppy or hard) is a circular platform coated with magnetic plastic of some sort. (Here, *magnetic plastic* is simply a polymer in which iron oxide particles or something similar is embedded.) In a floppy disk drive, the platform is a flexible disk of tough plastic; in a hard disk, the platform is a rigid platter of aluminum metal. Data is stored as little magnetic disturbances on the plastic coating in a fashion similar to that used in audio cassettes and VCRs. A sensor called a *read/write head* sits very close beside the rotating platform and waits for the data to pass by.

A simplified illustration of a rotating disk device is shown in Figure 4.1. The area of the disk is divided into concentric circles called *tracks*. The tracks are further divided radially into sectors. A *sector* (typically con-

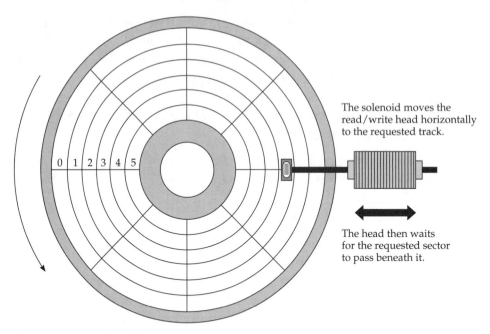

The solenoid moves the read/write head horizontally to the requested track.

The head then waits for the requested sector to pass beneath it.

Figure 4.1 Rotating disk storage.

taining 512 bytes) is the smallest unit of storage that can be read or written at one time. A DOS disk file consists of one or more sectors containing the file's data.

The read/write head is mounted on a sliding shaft that is controlled by a solenoid mechanism. The solenoid can move the head horizontally to position the head over a specific track. (In Figure 4.1, the head is positioned over track 2—counting from 0, remember!) However, once the head is over a particular track, it has to count sectors until the sector it needs passes beneath it. The tracks can be accessed at random, just like bytes in the computer's memory banks, but the sectors within a track must be accessed sequentially.

Perhaps the single most valuable service DOS provides is handling the headaches of distributing data onto empty sectors on a disk. Programs can hand sectors of data to DOS, one at a time, and let DOS worry about where on the disk they can be placed. Each sector has a number, and DOS keeps track of what sectors belong together as a file. The first sector in a file might be stored on track 3, sector 9; the second sector might be stored on track 0, sector 4, and so on. You don't have to worry about that. When you ask for sector 0 of your file, DOS looks up its location in its private tables and goes directly to track 3, sector 9 and brings the sector's data back to you.

Binary Files

The data stored in a file are just binary bytes and can be anything at all. Files like this, where there are *no* restrictions on the contents of a file, are called binary files, since they can legally contain any binary code. Like all files, a *binary file* consists of some whole number of sectors, with each sector (typically) containing 512 bytes. The least space any file on your disk occupies is 512 bytes; when you see the DOS DIR command tell you a file has 17 bytes it in, that's the count of how many bytes were *stored* in that file. But like a walk-in closet with only one pair of shoes in it, the rest of the sector is still there, empty but occupying space on the disk.

A binary file has no structure, but is simply a long series of binary codes divided into numbered groups of 512 and stored out on disk in a scheme that for now is best left to DOS to understand. Later on, you can study up on it, especially once you learn more about Linux, in which entire file systems can be loaded as though they were just more programs—which, of course, they are.

Text Files

If you've ever tried to use the DOS TYPE command to display a binary file (like an .EXE or .COM file) to the screen, you've seen some odd things indeed. There's no reason for such files to be intelligible on the screen; they're intended for other "eyes," typically the CPU's.

There is a separate class of files that is specifically restricted to containing human-readable information. These are *text files*, because they contain the letters, digits, and symbols of which printed human information (text) is composed.

Unlike binary files, text files have a certain structure to them. The characters in text files are divided into lines. A *line* in a text file is defined not so much by what it contains as by how it ends. A special series of invisible characters called an *end-of-line* (EOL) marker tags the end of a line. The first line in a text file runs from the first byte in the file to the first EOL marker; the second line starts immediately after the first EOL marker and runs to the second EOL marker, and so on. The text characters falling between two sequential EOL markers are considered a single line.

This scheme is the same for both DOS and Linux. What differs is the exact nature of the EOL marker. The EOL marker for DOS is not one character but two: the carriage return character (called CR by those who know and love it) followed by the linefeed character (similarly called LF). You don't see these characters on the screen as separate symbols, but you see what they do: They end the line. Anywhere a line ends in an ordinary DOS text file, you'll find a mostly invisible partnership of one CR character and one LF character hanging out. With Linux things are different: a single LF, without a partner CR.

Why two characters to end a line in a DOS text file? Long ago, there was (and still is, at hamfests) an incredible mechanical nightmare called a Teletype machine. These were invented during World War II as robot typewriters that could send written messages over long distances through electrical signals that could pass over wires. It was a separate mechanical operation to return the typing carriage to the left margin of the paper (carriage return) and another to feed the paper up one line to expose the next clean line of paper to the typing carriage (line feed). A separate electrical signal was required to do each of these operations, and while I don't know why that was necessary, it has carried over into the dawn of the twenty-first century in the form of those two characters, CR and LF. Not only is this a case of the tail wagging the dog, it's a case of the tail walking around 30 years after the poor dog rolled over and died.

Figure 4.2 shows how CR and LF divide what might otherwise be a single meaningless string of characters into a structured sequence of lines. It's important to understand the structure of a text file because that structure dictates how some important software tools operate, as I explain a little later.

The CR character is actually character 13 in the ASCII character set summarized in Appendix D. The LF character is character 10. They are two of a set of several invisible characters called *whitespace*, indicating their role in positioning visible text characters ('a', '*', etc.) within the white space of a text page. The other whitespace characters include the space character itself (character 32), the tab character (character 9), and the form feed character (character 12), which can optionally divide a text file further into *pages*.

Living Fossils

Another character, the *bell character* (BEL), falls in between binary and text characters. When displayed or printed, it signals that a tone should

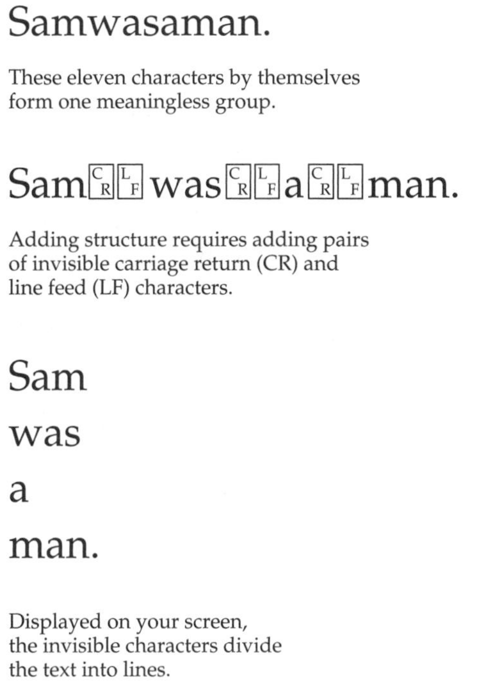

Samwasaman.

These eleven characters by themselves
form one meaningless group.

Sam⟨CR⟩⟨LF⟩was⟨CR⟩⟨LF⟩a⟨CR⟩⟨LF⟩man.

Adding structure requires adding pairs
of invisible carriage return (CR) and
line feed (LF) characters.

Sam

was

a

man.

Displayed on your screen,
the invisible characters divide
the text into lines.

Figure 4.2 The structure of a DOS text file.

be sounded. Back in the old Teletype days, the BEL character caused the teletype machine to ring its bell—which was literally a mechanical bell struck by a little hammer. BEL characters are allowed in text files, but are little used these days and considered sloppy practice. Many modern printers and most displays don't handle them correctly anyway; like the CR/LF pair, they are a barely surviving remnant of an increasingly fossilized past.

Another one of these fossilized characters will eventually cause you some trouble: the end-of-file (EOF) marker character. Unlike EOL, EOF is a single character, ASCII character 26, sometimes written as Ctrl+Z because you will generate the EOF character by holding the control key down and pressing the Z key.

The EOF character, properly, is not a DOS convention at all. DOS inherited EOF from the even older days of CP/M-80, which reigned between 1976 and 1982. In CP/M's archaic file system, there was no precise count of how many bytes were present in a text file. The operating system counted how many disk *sectors* were allocated to a text file, but within the last sector CP/M could not simply count its way to the final byte. Instead, CP/M insisted on there being an end-of-file marker at the very end of the significant data and would ignore anything after that marker.

DOS and Windows, by contrast, keep a precise count of how many characters are present in a text file, and therefore do not require any sort of EOF marker at all. However, some older DOS utilities recognize EOF, as a nod to older CP/M text files that were sometimes carried forward into the DOS world. As character 26 (Ctrl+Z) is not a displayable character and not true white space, this ordinarily did no harm. However, some editors and other utilities will not display or manipulate text past an embedded Ctrl+Z.

Some DOS utilities recognize EOF, and some do not. If you find a text file that seems to end prematurely, use a binary viewer such as DEBUG (more on which shortly) to see if a Ctrl+Z character has found its way into the interior of the file. Ctrl+Z is not otherwise useful in any text files I'm aware of, so removing it will not damage the file.

Keep in mind that *this only applies to text files*. Binary files may contain *any* character values at all, and thus may be shot full of Ctrl+Z characters, any or all of which may be vital to the file's usefulness. We return to the issue of inspecting and changing the contents of binary files in a little while.

Text Editors

Manipulating a text file is done with a program called a text editor. A *text editor* is a word processor for program source code files. In its simplest form, a text editor works like this: You type characters at the keyboard, and they appear on the screen. When you press the Enter key, an EOL marker (for DOS, the two characters CR and LF) is placed at the end of a line, and the cursor moves down to the next line.

The editor also allows you to move the cursor back up into text you've already entered, in order to change it. You can delete words and whole lines and replace them with newly entered text.

Ultimately, when you decide that you're finished, you press some key like F2, or some combination of keys like Ctrl+K+D, and the text editor saves the text you entered from the keyboard as a text file. This text file is the source code file you'll eventually present to the assembler for processing. Later on, you can load that same text file back into the editor to make repairs on faulty lines that cause errors during assembly or bugs during execution.

It's possible to use a word processor as a program text editor. In older times, many programmers used WordStar, WordPerfect, Microsoft Word, and other available word processors to edit their program text. This works—as long as you remember to write your text file to disk in "non-document mode" or "ASCII text mode." Most true word processors embed countless strange little codes in their text files, to control such things as margin settings, font selections, headers and footers, and soft page and line breaks. These codes are not recognized ASCII characters but binary values and actually turn the document file from a text file to a binary file. The codes will give the assembler fits. *If you write a program source code file to disk as a document file, it will not assemble.* See the word processor documentation for details on how to export a document file as a pure ASCII text file.

Software was expensive in years past, and programmers (who tend to be cheap, yours truly not excluded) understandably wanted to get the most bang for their software budget and used word processors for everything they could. These days, software has become cheap or (increasingly) even free, and there are a multitude of plain ASCII text editors available freely for download from the Internet.

I'll even go you better than that. On the CD-ROM associated with this book I've arranged to distribute a programming text editor specifically designed for assembly language programmers—in fact, specifically designed to work seamlessly with the assembly that I teach in this book (which is also on the CD-ROM—what a deal!). NASM-IDE was written in Turbo Pascal, and its editor works a great deal like the editors you may have used in Borland's DOS-based programming products. I explain how to use NASM-IDE in great detail in the next chapter.

In earlier editions of this book I spoke of something called JED, which was a simple assembly-programming editor that I had written for my own use—also in Turbo Pascal. JED is history, and while you can still use it if you have it, it doesn't interface well with NASM, the assembler I teach throughout this book. NASM-IDE is a great deal like JED but much more sophisticated—and obviously, it was created to work with NASM.

If for some reason the CD-ROM didn't come to you with the book, both NASM-IDE and NASM itself can be downloaded from the Internet without charge, along with the listing files. See Appendix C, "Web URLS for Assembly Programmers."

If you have a text editor that you've used for some time and prefer, there's no reason not to use it. It just won't make following along with the text quite as easy.

Compilers and Assemblers

With that understanding of DOS files under your belt, you can come to understand the nature of two important kinds of programs: *compilers* and *assemblers*. Both fall into a larger category of programs we call translators.

A *translator* is a program that accepts human-readable source code files and generates some kind of binary file. The binary file could be an executable program file that the CPU can understand, or it could be a font file, or a compressed binary data file, or any of a hundred other types of binary file.

Program translators are translators that generate machine instructions that the CPU can understand. A program translator reads a source code file line by line, and writes a binary file of machine instructions that accomplishes the computer actions that the source code file describes. This binary file is called an *object code file*.

A compiler is a program translator that reads in source code files written in higher-level languages such as C++ and Pascal and writes out object code files.

An assembler is a special type of compiler. It, too, is a program translator that reads source code files and outputs object code files for execution by the CPU. However, an assembler is a translator designed specifically to translate what we call *assembly language* into object code. In the same sense that a language compiler for Pascal or C++ compiles a source code file to an object code file, we say that an assembler *assembles* an assembly language source code file to an object code file. The process, one of translation, is similar in both cases. Assembly language, however, has an overwhelmingly important characteristic that sets it apart from compilers: *total control over the object code*.

Assembly Language

Some people define assembly language as a language in which one line of source code generates one machine instruction. This has never been literally true, since some lines in an assembly language source code file are instructions to the translator program (rather than to the CPU) and do not generate machine instructions at all.

Here's a better definition:

Assembly language is a translator language that allows total control over every individual machine instruction generated by the translator program. Such a translator program is called an assembler.

Pascal or C++ compilers, on the other hand, make a multitude of invisible and inalterable decisions about how a given language statement will be translated into machine instructions. For example, the following single Pascal instruction assigns a value of 42 to a numeric variable called **I**:

```
I := 42;
```

When a Pascal compiler reads this line, it outputs a series of four or five machine instructions that take the value 42 and store it in memory at a location encoded by the name **I**. Normally, you the Pascal programmer have *no idea* what these four or five instructions actually are, and you have utterly no way of changing them, even if you know a sequence of machine instructions that is faster and more efficient than the sequence that the compiler uses. The Pascal compiler has its own way of generating machine instructions, and you have no choice but to accept what it writes to disk to accomplish the work of the Pascal statements in the source code file.

An assembler, however, has at least one line in the source code file for every machine instruction it generates. It has more lines than that to handle numerous other things, but *every* machine instruction in the final object code file is controlled by a corresponding line in the source code file.

Each of the CPU's many machine instructions has a corresponding *mnemonic* in assembly language. As the word suggests, these mnemonics began as devices to help programmers remember a particular binary machine instruction. For example, the mnemonic for binary machine instruction 9CH, which pushes the flags register onto the stack, is **PUSHF**—which is a country mile easier to remember than 9CH.

When you write your source code file in assembly language, you will arrange series of mnemonics, typically one mnemonic per line in the source code text file. A portion of a source code file might look like this:

```
MOV  AH,12H      ; 12H is Motor Information Service
MOV  AL,03H      ; 03H is Return Current Speed function
XOR  BH,BH       ; Zero BH for safety's sake
INT  71H         ; Call Motor Services Interrupt
```

Here, the words **MOV**, **XOR**, and **INT** are the mnemonics. The numbers and other items to the immediate right of each mnemonic are that mnemonic's *operands*. There are various kinds of operands for various machine instructions, and some instructions (such as **PUSHF** mentioned previously) have no operands at all. I thoroughly describe each instruction's operands when we cover that instruction.

Taken together, a mnemonic and its operands are called an *instruction*. This is the word I'll be using most of the time in this book to indicate the human-readable proxy of one of the CPU's pure binary machine code instructions. To talk about the binary code specifically, we'll always refer to a *machine instruction*.

The assembler's most important job is to read lines from the source code file and write machine instructions to an object code file. See Figure 4.3.

Comments

To the right of each instruction is some information starting with a semicolon. This information is called a *comment*, and its purpose should be plain: to cast some light on what the associated assembly language

Mnemonic	Operands		Comment
MOV AX,BX			; Put byte count into AX

The assembler reads a line like this one from the source code file
and writes the equivalent machine instruction to the object code file:

8BH 0C3H

Figure 4.3   What the assembler does.

instruction is *for*. The instruction **MOV AH,12H** places the value 12H in register AH—but *why*? What is the instruction accomplishing in the context of the assembly language program that you're writing? The comment provides the why.

Far more than in any other programming language, comments are critical to the success of your assembly language programs. My own recommendation is that *every* instruction in your source code files should have a comment to its right.

Structurally, a comment begins with the first semicolon on a line, and continues to the EOL marker at the end of that line. This is one instance where understanding how a text file is structured is very important—because in assembly language, comments end at the ends of lines. In most other languages such as Pascal and C++, comments are placed *between* pairs of comment delimiters like **(*** and ***)**, and EOL markers at line ends are ignored.

Comments begin at semicolons and end at EOL.

Beware "Write-Only" Source Code!

This is as good a time as any to point out a serious problem with assembly language. The instructions themselves are almost vanishingly terse, and while each instruction states what it does, there is *nothing* to indicate a context within which that instruction operates. You can build that context into your Pascal or Basic code with some skill and discipline (along with identifiers that point to their purpose), but in assembly language you can *only* add context through comments.

Without context, assembly language starts to turn into what we call "write-only" code. It can happen like this: On November 1, in the heat of creation, you crank out about 300 instructions in a short utility program that does something important. You go back on January 1 to add a feature to the program—and discover that *you no longer remember how it works*. The individual instructions are all correct, and the program assembles and runs as it should, but knowledge of how it all came together and how it works from a height have vanished under Christmas memories and eight weeks of doing other things. In other words, you *wrote* it, but you can no longer *read* it, or change it. Voila! Write-only code.

Comment like crazy. Each individual line should have a comment, and every so often in a sizeable source code file, take a few lines out and make entire lines into comments, explaining what the code is up to at this point in its execution.

While comments do take room in your source code disk files, they are *not* copied into your object code files, and a program with loads of comments runs *exactly* as fast as the same program with no comments at all.

You will be making a considerable investment in time and energy when you write assembly language programs—far more than in "halfway to heaven" languages like C and C++, and unthinkably more than in "we do it all for you" IDEs like Delphi and Visual Basic. It's more difficult than just about any other way of writing programs, and if you don't comment, you may end up having to simply toss out hundreds of lines of inexplicable code and write it again, *from scratch*.

Work smart. Comment till you drop.

Object Code and Linkers

There's no reason at all why an assembler cannot read a source code file and write out a finished, executable program file as its object code file. The assembler I'm teaching in this book, NASM, can do precisely that, and for much of the book we'll use it that way. Most of the older assemblers, including Microsoft's MASM and Borland's TASM, don't have this ability, however. Object code files produced by such assemblers are a sort of intermediate step between source code and executable program. This intermediate step is a type of binary file called a *relocatable object module*, or (more simply) an .OBJ file, after the file extension used by the assembler when it creates the file. For example, a source code file called FOO.ASM would be assembled into an object file called FOO.OBJ. (The "relocatable" portion of the concept is crucial, but a little advanced for this chapter. More on it later.)

.OBJ files cannot themselves be run as programs. An additional step, called *linking*, is necessary to turn .OBJ files into executable program files.

The reason for .OBJ files as intermediate steps is that a single large source code file may be cut up into numerous smaller source code files to keep them manageable in size and complexity. The assembler assembles the various component fragments separately, and the several resulting .OBJ files are woven together into a single, executable program file. This process is shown in Figure 4.4.

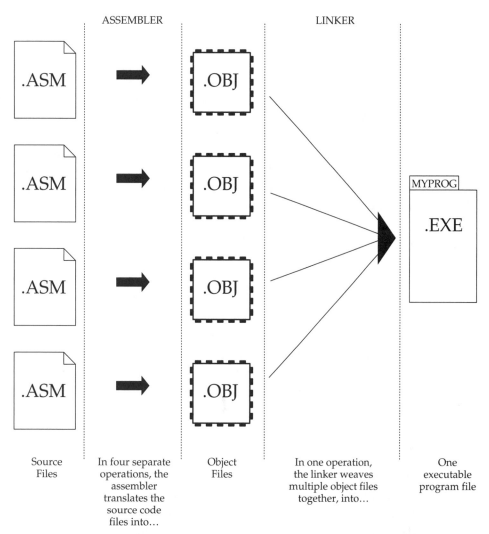

Figure 4.4   The assembler and linker.

When you're first starting out, it's unlikely that you will be writing programs spread out across several source code files. That's why we won't be using a linker initially. However, once you get into certain more advanced assembly ideas, you'll want to use the linker to change even a single .OBJ file into an executable program file. The larger your programs become, however, the more time can be saved by cutting them up into components. There are two reasons for this:

1. You can move tested, proven routines into separate libraries and link them into any program you write that might need them. This way, you

can reuse code over and over again and not build the same old wheels every time you begin a new programming project in assembly language.

2. Once portions of a program are tested and found to be correct, there's no need to waste time assembling them over and over again along with newer, untested portions of a program. Once a major program gets into the tens of thousands of lines of code (and you'll get there sooner than you might think), you can save an enormous amount of time by assembling only the portion of a program that you are currently working on, and linking the finished portions into the final program without reassembling the whole thing every time.

Executable Program Files

Programs are written to be executed, and the file that you ultimately create in assembly language programming (or most any programming, actually) is called an *executable program file*. Under Linux (as I describe toward the end of this book), there is only a single kind of executable program file. In DOS work, however, there are two types of executable program files: .COM files and .EXE files. I deal with both in this book, and the specific technical differences will have to wait until I've covered a little more ground. But in purely practical terms, .COM files are produced directly by the NASM assembler, whereas .EXE files are generated by a linker.

The linker program may be seen as a kind of translator program, but its major role lies in combining multiple object code files into a single executable program file. The linker would accept, for example, three object code files: FOO.OBJ, BAR.OBJ, and BAS.OBJ, and knit them together into a single executable program file. This file would by default be called FOO.EXE, but you can specify any name you like to the linker.

An executable file can be run by typing its name (without the .COM or .EXE extension) at the DOS prompt and pressing Enter:

```
C:\>FOO
```

A Real Assembler: NASM

For quite a few years there was only one assembler product in general use for the PC: Microsoft's Macro Assembler, better known as MASM. MASM was and remains an enormously popular program and has established a standard for assembler operation on the PC. In 1988, Borland International released its answer to MASM in the form of Turbo Assembler, which was quickly christened TASM by syllable-conserving programmers. TASM was a great deal faster than MASM and started an arms race with MASM that went on for some years. Borland's products (and eventually Borland itself) began losing the race with Microsoft in the later 1990s, and today TASM is no longer available. MASM can be purchased from Microsoft, and is included in several of Microsoft's developer product bundles. It's an excellent product, and if you go on to do professional (that is, paying) work in assembly language, you're more than likely to be called upon to use it.

I'm not, however, going to be covering MASM in any detail in this book.

Something wonderful happened in the mid-1990s that changed the world of software forever. The idea of *open source software* caught fire and caught the imagination of programmers everywhere. In open source software, programmers collaborate (generally over the Internet) with dozens or even hundreds of other programmers and create software products that no single programmer (or even two or three) could have produced alone. To facilitate the collaborative process (and to eliminate fights over who owns the software), open source software is turned loose with all of its source code and documentation, and made available for free to whoever wants it.

When the idea first got the attention of the mainstream, it seemed simply nuts. Why would programmers do all this work for nothing? While some of the founders of the open source movement, such as the estimable Richard Stallman, insist that software should ideally be free for ethical reasons, the practical reality is that the open source concept of free software makes projects possible that would never happen otherwise. Many hands are required to create complex software, and the arguments that arise over ownership, marketing, and distribution have killed many good software products that the world could well have used. By making software "no secrets" by design and letting anyone who wants it have it, these arguments go away and collaborative effort becomes possible.

The largest and most visible open source project, of course, is the Linux operating system, begun by Linus Torvalds, a Finnish college student, in 1991. I have a couple of chapters on writing assembly language under Linux toward the end of this book. But the big win for us assembly language geeks is that in 1997, an open source assembler appeared. Its name is NASM, the Net-Wide Assembler, and it has improved relentlessly since its first release. Now, in 2000, it is brutally effective, easy to learn, and best of all, it's still free. I explain lots more about NASM through the course of this book, but you should fire up your Web browser and go look at the NASM Web site at www.web-sites.co.uk/nasm/tools.html.

In case the copy of the book you own no longer has the CD-ROM in it, or if the CD-ROM is damaged or otherwise unreadable, you can download NASM from this Web site and many other places. The version of NASM I'm using throughout this book (the one that is on the CD-ROM) is 0.98. If you have an older version from somewhere, please obtain the 0.98 release so you don't get confused when I talk about features that don't exist in your copy!

Most commercial assemblers (such as MASM and TASM) come with their own special debugging tools, called *debuggers*. MASM's debugger is called CodeView, and TASM's debugger is called Turbo Debugger. Both are enormously sophisticated programs, and I won't be discussing either in this book, in part due to their intimate connection with their associated assemblers, but mostly because there is a debugger shipped with every copy of DOS and Windows—even Windows NT. This debugger, simply named DEBUG, is more than enough debugger to cut your teeth on and will get you familiar enough with debugger concepts to move up to a commercial debugger later on.

I describe DEBUG much more fully in a following section.

Setting Up a Working Directory

The process of creating and perfecting assembly language programs involves a lot of different kinds of DOS files and numerous separate software tools. Unlike the tidy, fully integrated environments of Turbo Pascal, Delphi, or Visual Basic, assembly language development comes in a great many pieces with (as it were) some assembly required.

I recommend setting up a development subdirectory on your hard disk and putting all of the various pieces in that subdirectory. For ease of understanding, let's call this directory ASM. I've actually created an ASM directory for you on the CD-ROM that comes with this book. It's completely set up and ready to go, software and all, and all you need to do is copy the contents of the CD-ROM directory FORDOS\ASM to one of your hard disk drive units. *You can't run any of the software correctly from the CD-ROM!* (CD-ROMs are by nature read-only devices, and you'll need to be writing files right and left.) If you're doing your assembly work in a DOS box under Windows, it's easy: Go back "up" into Windows and drag the contents of the FORDOS directory from the CD-ROM to an appropriate hard drive location, most likely on C: or D: but wherever you have room for it. ASM and all its subdirectories will come right along.

If you're using DOS, you'll need to use the XCOPY command, like this:

```
C:\>XCOPY F:\FORDOS C: /s
```

Note that by convention here, the CD-ROM drive is F: and the destination hard disk drive unit is C:. Use whatever your particular drive units might be. Don't forget the /s parameter. It tells XCOPY to bring the directory structure along as it copies, so the subdirectories on the CD-ROM will be reproduced on your hard drive.

Once you've copied the ASM directory from the CD-ROM, that's all the copying you'll need to do.

If you don't have a usable CD-ROM for this book (and if you bought it used, the CD-ROM is often missing or damaged), you'll have to create the ASM directory and load it yourself. Create and move into ASM by using these DOS commands:

```
C:\>MD ASM
C:\>CD ASM
```

(Obviously, you don't have to put the ASM directory on the C: drive. Put it where it goes best on your system.) Then, install the following:

1. *Your text editor or development environment.* If you're using NASM-IDE (see Chapter 5), you'll need to obtain the archive file NASMIDE.ZIP and unzip it into the ASM directory. Make sure you've enabled your ZIP utility to create directories, because the NASM-IDE archive contains example code residing in a subdirectory called EXAMPLES. You can download NASM-IDE from its home page www.inglenook.co.uk/ nasmide/. (This URL was current late winter 2000.) For other text editors such as Brief or Epsilon, you'll need to consult the product's documentation.

2. *The assembler NASM itself.* Like NASM-IDE, NASM comes in a ZIP archive, and you must unzip it into the ASM directory. Make sure the

copy you obtain is version 0.98! (Version 0.97 is still widely present on download sites like SimTel. Don't use it!) The archive file name is NASM098.ZIP. You can download the latest version of NASM from the NASM home page www.web-sites.co.uk/nasm/.

3. *The subdirectories.* As with NASM-IDE, there are subdirectories encoded in the NASM ZIP archive file, and you must enable your unzip utility to create those subdirectories during the process of extracting the files from the archive.

4. *Your linker.* Commercial assemblers such as MASM and TASM include their own linkers. Many people who use NASM under DOS use the ALINK linker, created by Anthony Williams. With Anthony's permission I've included ALINK on the CD-ROM. It's the only linker I discuss in this book. ALINK has a home page from which you can download the latest version in case you're reading this book long after its publication date: http://alink.home.dhs.org/.

5. *DEBUG.* A copy of DEBUG.EXE is installed with all current copies of DOS and Windows, even Windows NT. In ancient times, DEBUG.EXE was actually DEBUG.COM. If your version of DOS is that old, you probably ought to upgrade. Find DEBUG.EXE on your system and copy it to the ASM directory or to some directory on your DOS path.

6. *Odds and ends.* A source code listing program, while not essential, can be very helpful—such programs print out neatly formatted listings on your printer. I have written a useful one called JLIST10 that I have placed on the CD-ROM for this book—but you need to understand that it only operates with LaserJet or compatible laser printers. Add anything else that may be helpful, keeping in mind that a lot of files are generated during assembly language development, and you should strive to keep unnecessary clutter to a minimum.

The Assembly Language Development Process

As you can see, there are a lot of different file types and a fair number of programs involved in the cycle of writing, assembling, and testing an assembly language program. The cycle itself sounds more complex than it is. I've drawn you a map to help you keep your bearings during the discussions in this chapter. Figure 4.5 shows the most complex form of the assembly language development process in a "view from a height." At first glance it may look like a map of the LA freeway sys-

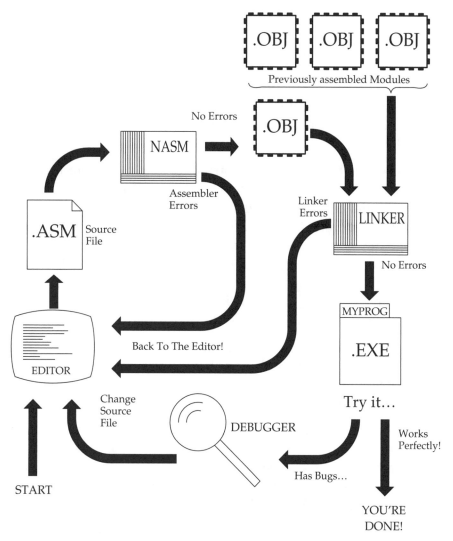

Figure 4.5 The assembly language development process.

tem, but in reality the flow is fairly straightforward. And NASM allows you to remove a certain amount of the complexity—the separate linker operation—for simple, single-source-file programs like those you'll write while learning your way around the instruction set. Finally, NASM-IDE helps even further by invoking some of the utilities automatically, so you're not constantly hammering on the keyboard.

Nonetheless, if you pursue professional-level assembly language programming, this is the map you'll need to follow. Let's take a quick tour.

Assembling the Source Code File

The text editor first creates a new text file, and later changes that same text file, as you extend, modify, and perfect your assembly language program. As a convention, most assembly language source code files are given a file extension of .ASM. In other words, for the program named FOO, the assembly language source code file would be named FOO.ASM.

It is possible to use file extensions other than .ASM, but I feel that using the .ASM extension can eliminate some confusion by allowing you to tell at a glance what a file is for—just by looking at its name. All told, about nine different kinds of files can be involved during assembly language development—more if you take the horrendous leap into Windows software development. (We're only going to speak of four or five in this book.) Each type of file will have its own standard file extension. Anything that will help you keep all that complexity in line will be worth the (admittedly) rigid confines of a standard naming convention.

As you can see from the flow in Figure 4.5, the editor produces a source code text file, which we show as having the .ASM extension. This file is then passed to the assembler program itself, for translation to a relocatable object module file with an extension of .OBJ.

When you invoke the assembler, DOS will load the assembler from disk and run it. The assembler will open the source code file you named after the name of the assembler and begin processing the file. Almost immediately afterward, it will create an object file with the same name as the source file, but with an .OBJ extension.

As the assembler reads lines from the source code file, it will examine them, construct the binary machine instructions the source code lines represent, and then write those machine instructions to the object code file.

When the assembler comes to the end of the source code file, it will close both source code file and object code file and return control to DOS.

Assembler Errors

Note well: The previous paragraphs describe what happens if the .ASM file is *correct*. By correct, I mean that the file is completely comprehensible to the assembler and can be translated into machine instructions without the assembler getting confused. If the assembler encounters something it doesn't understand when it reads a line from the source code file, we call the misunderstood text an *error*, and the assembler displays an *error message*.

For example, the following line of assembly language will confuse the assembler and summon an error message:

```
MOV AX,VX
```

The reason is simple: There's no such thing as a "VX." What came out as "VX" was actually intended to be "BX," which is the name of a register. (The *V* key is right next to the *B* key and can be struck by mistake without your fingers necessarily knowing that they done wrong.)

Typos like this are by far the easiest kind of error to spot. Others that take some study to find involve transgressions of the assembler's many rules. For example:

```
MOV ES,0FF00H
```

This looks like it should be correct, since ES is a real register and 0FF00H is a real 16-bit quantity that will fit into ES. However, among the multitude of rules in the fine print of the 86-family of assemblers is one that states you cannot directly move an immediate value (any number like 0FF00H) directly into a segment register like ES, DS, SS, or CS. It simply isn't part of the CPU's machinery to do that. Instead, you must first move the immediate value into a register like AX, and *then* move AX into ES.

You don't have to remember the details here; we'll go into the rules later on when we discuss the individual instructions. For now, simply understand that some things that look reasonable are simply against the rules for technical reasons and are considered an error.

There are much, *much* more difficult errors that involve inconsistencies between two otherwise legitimate lines of source code. I won't offer any examples here, but I wanted to point out that errors can be truly ugly, hidden things that can take a lot of study and torn hair to find. Toto, we are definitely *not* in Basic anymore . . .

The error messages vary from assembler to assembler, and they may not always be as helpful as you might hope. The error NASM displays upon encountering the "VX" typo follows:

```
testerr.asm:20: symbol 'vx' undefined
```

This is pretty plain, assuming you know what a "symbol" is. The error message NASM will present when you try to load an immediate value into ES is far less helpful:

```
Testerr.asm:20: invalid combination of opcode and operands
```

It'll let you know you're guilty of performing illegal acts with an opcode and its operands, but that's it. *You* have to know what's legal and what's illegal to really understand what you did wrong. As in running a stop sign, ignorance of the law is no excuse.

Assembler error messages do not absolve you from understanding the CPU's or the assembler's rules.

I hope I don't frighten you too terribly by warning you that for more abstruse errors, the error messages may be almost no help at *all*.

You may make (or *will* make—let's get real) more than one error in writing your source code files. The assembler will display more than one error message in such cases, but it may not necessarily display an error for *every* error present in the source code file. At some point, multiple errors confuse the assembler so thoroughly that it cannot necessarily tell right from wrong anymore. While it's true that the assembler reads and translates source code files line by line, there is a cumulative picture of the final assembly language program that is built up over the course of the whole assembly process. If this picture is shot too full of errors, in time the whole picture collapses.

The assembler will stop and return to DOS, having printed numerous error messages. *Start at the first one* and keep going. If the following ones don't make sense, fix the first one or two and assemble again.

Back to the Editor

The way to fix errors is to load the .ASM file back into your text editor and start hunting up the error. This loopback is shown in Figure 4.5.

The error message will almost always contain a line number. Move the cursor to that line number and start looking for the false and the fanciful. If you find the error immediately, fix it and start looking for the next.

Here's a little logistical snag: How do you make a list of the error messages on paper so that you don't have to memorize them or scribble them down on paper with a pencil? You may or may not be aware that you can *redirect* the assembler's error message displays to a DOS text file on disk.

It works like this: You invoke the assembler just as you normally would, but add the *redirection operator* ">" and the name of the text file to which you want the error messages sent. If you were assembling FOO.ASM with NASM and wanted your error messages written out to a disk file named ERRORS.TXT, you would invoke NASM this way:

```
C:\ASM>NASM FOO > ERRORS.TXT
```

(I've omitted certain command-line parameters for simplicity's sake.) Here, error messages will be sent to ERRORS.TXT in the current DOS directory C:\ASM. When you use redirection, the output does *not* display on the screen. The stream of text from NASM that you would ordinarily see is quite literally steered in its entirety to another place, the file ERRORS.TXT.

Once the assembly process is done, the DOS prompt will appear again. You can then print the ERRORS.TXT file on your printer and have a handy summary of all that the assembler discovered was wrong with your source code file.

Note well that if you're using an interactive development environment like NASM-IDE (which is provided on this book's CD-ROM and described in detail in the next chapter), you won't have to bother with redirection to a file or to the printer. NASM-IDE and other development environments accumulate error messages in a separate window that you can keep on display while you go back and edit your .ASM file. This is a much more convenient way to work, and I powerfully recommend it.

Assembler Warnings

As taciturn a creature as an assembler may appear to be, it genuinely tries to help you any way it can. One way it tries to help is by displaying *warning messages* during the assembly process. These warning messages are a monumental puzzle to beginning assembly language programmers: Are they errors or aren't they? Can I ignore them or should I fool with the source code until they go away?

Alas, there's no clean answer. Sorry about that.

Warnings are the assembler acting as experienced consultant, and hinting that something in your source code is a little dicey. Now, in the nature of assembly language, you may fully *intend* that the source code be dicey. In an 86-family CPU, dicey code may be the only way to do something fast enough, or just to do it at all. The critical factor is that you had *better* know what you're doing. (And if you're reading this book, my guess is that you probably don't.)

The most common generator of warning messages is doing something that goes against the assembler's default conditions and assumptions. If you're a beginner doing ordinary, 100-percent-by-the-book sorts of things, you should crack your assembler reference manual and figure out why the assembler is tut-tutting you. Ignoring a warning *may* cause peculiar bugs to occur later on during program testing. Or, ignoring a warning message may have no undesirable consequences at all. I feel, however, that it's always better to know what's going on. Follow this rule:

Ignore an assembler warning message only if you know exactly *what it means.*

In other words, until you understand why you're getting a warning message, treat it as though it were an error message. Only once you fully understand why it's there and what it means should you try to make the decision whether to ignore it or not.

In summary: The first part of the assembly language development process (as shown in Figure 4.5) is a loop. You must edit your source code file, assemble it, and return to the editor to fix errors until the assembler spots no further errors. *You cannot continue until the assembler gives your source code file a clean bill of health.*

When no further errors are found, the assembler will write an .OBJ file to disk, and you will be ready to go on to the next step.

Linking

As I explain shortly, there's nothing to prevent an assembler from generating an executable program file (that is, an .EXE or .COM file) direct from your source code file. NASM can do this, and we'll take advantage of that shortcut while we're getting started. However, in traditional assembly language work, what actually happens is that the assembler writes an intermediate object code file with an .OBJ extension to disk. You can't run this .OBJ file, even though it generally contains all the machine instructions that your assembly language source code file specified. The .OBJ file needs to be processed by another translator program, the linker.

The linker performs a number of operations on the .OBJ file, most of which would be meaningless to you at this point. The most obvious task the linker does is to weave several .OBJ files into a single .EXE executable program file. Creating an assembly language program from multiple .ASM files is called *modular assembly*, and I explain how to do it (with an example) in Chapter 9.

Why create multiple .OBJ files when writing a single executable program? One of two major reasons is size. A middling assembly language application might be 50,000 lines long. Cutting that single monolithic .ASM file up into multiple 8,000-line .ASM files would make the individual .ASM files smaller and much easier to understand.

The other reason is to avoid assembling completed portions of the program every time *any* part of the program is assembled. One thing you'll be doing is writing assembly language *procedures*, which are small detours from the main run of steps and tests that can be taken from anywhere within the assembly language program. Once you write and perfect a procedure, you can tuck it away in an .ASM file with other completed procedures, assemble it, and then simply link the resulting .OBJ file into the working .ASM file. The alternative is to waste time by reassembling perfected source code over and over again every time you assemble the main portion of the program.

This is shown in Figure 4.5. In the upper-right corner is a row of .OBJ files. These .OBJ files were assembled earlier from correct .ASM files, yielding binary disk files containing ready-to-go machine instructions. When the linker links the .OBJ file produced from your in-progress .ASM file, it adds in the previously assembled .OBJ files, which are called *modules*. The single .EXE file that the linker writes to disk contains the machine instructions from all of the .OBJ files handed to the linker when then linker is invoked.

Once the in-progress .ASM file is completed and made correct, its .OBJ module can be put up on the rack with the others and added to the *next* in-progress .ASM source code file. Little by little you construct your application program out of the modules you build one at a time.

A very important bonus is that some of the procedures in an .OBJ module may be used in a future assembly language program that hasn't even been begun yet. Creating such libraries of "toolkit" procedures can be an extraordinarily effective way to save time by reusing code over and over again, without even passing it through the assembler again!

Many traditional assemblers, such as MASM and TASM, *require* that you use a linker to process even a single small .OBJ file into an executable .COM or .EXE file. Connecting multiple modules is only one of several things the linker is capable of doing. More recent assemblers such as NASM can often take up some of the work that a linker normally does and allow you to create simple executable programs from single .ASM files. But keep in mind that to produce an executable .EXE file from multiple assembly language source code files, you *must* invoke the linker.

The linker I discuss in this book is called ALINK, and like NASM and NASM-IDE, it's a free utility created by a dedicated assembly programmer. Anthony Williams is its creator, and he was kind enough to allow me to redistribute ALINK on the CD-ROM for this book.

Invoking the linker is again done from the DOS command line. Linking multiple files involves naming each file on the command line. With ALINK, you simply name each .OBJ file on the command line after the word ALINK, with a space between each file name. You do *not* have to include the .OBJ extension—ALINK assumes that all modules to be linked end in .OBJ:

```
C:\ASM>ALINK FOO BAR BAS
```

There are many different options and commands that may be entered along with the file names, to do things slightly (or considerably) fancier. We use ALINK a lot more later on in this book, and at that point I'll explain its command syntax in greater detail.

Linker Errors

As with the assembler, the linker may discover problems as it weaves multiple .OBJ files together into a single .EXE file. Linker errors are subtler than assembler errors and are usually harder to find. Fortunately, they are rarer and not as easy to make.

As with assembler errors, when you are presented with a linker error you have to return to the editor and figure out what the problem is. Once you've identified the problem (or *think* you have) and changed something in the source code file to fix the problem, you must reassemble and relink the program to see if the linker error went away. Until it does, you have to loop back to the editor, try something else, and assemble/link once more.

If possible, avoid doing this by trial and error. Read your assembler and linker documentation. Understand what you're doing. The more you understand about what's going on within the assembler and the linker, the easier it will be to determine who or what is giving the linker fits.

Testing the .EXE File

If you receive no linker errors, the linker will create and fill a single .EXE file with the machine instructions present in all of the .OBJ files named on the linker command line. The .EXE file is your executable program. You can run it by simply naming it on the DOS command line and pressing Enter:

```
C:\ASM>FOO
```

When you invoke your program in this way, one of two things will happen: The program will work as you intended it to, or you'll be confronted with the effects of one or more program bugs. A *bug* is anything in a program that doesn't work the way you want it to. This makes a bug somewhat more subjective than an error. One person might think red characters displayed on a blue background is a bug, while another might consider it a clever New Age feature and be quite pleased. Settling bug versus feature conflicts like this is up to you. Consensus is called for here, with fistfights only as a last resort.

There are bugs and there are bugs. When working in assembly language, it's *quite* common for a bug to completely "blow the machine away," which is less violent than some think. A *system crash* is what you call it when the machine sits there mutely and will not respond to the keyboard. You may have to press Ctrl+Alt+Delete to reboot the system, or (worse) have to press the Reset button, or even power down and then power up again (that is, flip the power switch off, wait 10 seconds, and switch it on again). Be ready for this—it *will* happen to you, sooner and oftener than you will care for.

Figure 4.5 announces the exit of the assembly language development process as happening when your program works perfectly. A very serious question is this: How do you know when it works perfectly? Simple programs assembled while learning the language may be easy enough to test in a minute or two. But any program that accomplishes anything useful at all will take *hours* of testing at *minimum*. A serious and ambitious application could take weeks—or months—to test thoroughly. A program that takes various kinds of input values and produces various kinds of output should be tested with as many different combinations of input values as possible, and you should examine every possible output every time.

Even so, finding every last bug is considered by some to be an impossible ideal. Perhaps—but you should strive to come as close as possible, in as efficient a fashion as you can manage. I have a lot more to say about bugs and debugging throughout the rest of this book.

Errors versus Bugs

In the interest of keeping the Babel effect at bay, I think it's important to carefully draw the distinction between errors and bugs. An *error* is something wrong with your source code file that either the assembler or the linker kicks out as unacceptable. An error prevents the assembly or link process from going to completion and will thus prevent a final .EXE file from being produced.

A *bug*, by contrast, is a problem discovered during *execution* of a program under DOS. Bugs are not detected by either the assembler or the linker. Bugs can be benign, such as a misspelled word in a screen message or a line positioned on the wrong screen row; or a bug can make your DOS session run off into the bushes and not come back.

Both errors and bugs require that you go back to the text editor and change something in your source code file. The difference here is that most errors are reported with a line number telling you where to go in your source code file to fix the problem. Bugs, on the other hand, are left as an exercise for the student. You have to hunt them down, and neither the assembler nor the linker will give you much in the line of clues.

Debuggers and Debugging

The final, and almost certainly the most painful, part of the assembly language development process is debugging. *Debugging* is simply the systematic process by which bugs are located and corrected. A *debugger* is a utility program designed specifically to help you locate and identify bugs.

Debugger programs are among the most mysterious and difficult to understand of all programs. Debuggers are part X-ray machine and part magnifying glass. A debugger loads into memory *with* your program and remains in memory, side by side with your program. The debugger then puts tendrils down into both the operating system (for our purposes, DOS, and later Linux) and into your program and enables some truly peculiar things to be done.

One of the problems with debugging computer programs is that they operate so quickly. Thousands of machine instructions can be executed in a single second, and if one of those instructions isn't quite right, it's past and gone long before you can identify which one it is by staring at the screen. A debugger allows you to execute the machine instructions in a program *one at a time*, allowing you to pause indefinitely between each one to examine the effects of the last instruction on the screen. The debugger also lets you look at the contents of any location in memory, and the values stored in any register, during that pause between instructions.

Commercial assemblers such as MASM are generally packaged with their own advanced debuggers. MASM's CodeView is a brutally powerful (and hellishly complicated) creature that I don't recommend to beginners. For this reason, I won't try to explain how to use CodeView in this book.

Besides, CodeView is bundled with expensive Microsoft development tools and thus costs a fair amount of money. Very fortunately, every copy of DOS and Windows, irrespective of version, is shipped with a more limited but perfectly good debugger called DEBUG. DEBUG can do nearly anything that a beginner would want from a debugger, and in this book we'll do all our DOS debugging with DEBUG.

Because DEBUG is included with your operating system, it's not one of the provided tools on the CD-ROM included with this book. And because its location has changed from version to version of DOS and Windows, I recommend looking around in your system directories until you locate it. In older versions of DOS it's called DEBUG.COM. In newer versions of DOS and all versions of Windows, it's DEBUG.EXE.

I've found that on most systems, DEBUG is already on your path, and you can invoke it from any directory you happen to be in. Try invoking DEBUG before you suffer too much looking for it. If a dash character

("-") prompt appears, DEBUG is on your path and you don't need to know precisely where it is. (Type a *Q* to quit DEBUG.)

DEBUG and How to Use It

The assembler and the linker are rather single-minded programs. As translators, they do only one thing: Translate. This involves reading data from one file and writing a translation of that data into another file.

That's all a translator needs to do. The job isn't necessarily an easy thing for the translator to do, but it's easy to describe and understand. Debuggers, by contrast, are like the electrician's little bag of tools: They do lots of different things in a great many different ways and take plenty of explanation and considerable practice to master.

In this section, I introduce you to DEBUG, a program that will allow you to *single-step* your assembly language programs and examine their innards (and the machine's innards) between each and every machine instruction. This section is only an introduction—DEBUG is learned best by doing, and you'll be both using and learning DEBUG's diverse powers all through the rest of this book. By providing you with an overview of what DEBUG does here, you'll be more capable of integrating its features into your general understanding of assembly language development process as we examine it through the rest of the book.

DEBUG's Bag of Tricks

It's well worth taking a page or so simply to describe what sorts of things DEBUG can do before actually showing you how they're done. It's actually quite a list:

Display or change memory and files. Your programs will both exist in and affect memory, and DEBUG can show you *any* part of memory—which implies that it can show you any part of any program or binary file as well. It displays memory as a series of hexadecimal values, with a corresponding display of any printable ASCII characters to its right. We'll show you some examples a little later on. In addition to seeing the contents of memory, you can change those contents as well, and if the contents of memory represent a file, you can write the changed file back out to disk.

Display or change the contents of all CPU registers. CPU registers allow you to work *very* quickly, and you should use them as much as you can. This means that you need to see what's going on in the registers while you use them, and with one command, DEBUG can display the contents of all machine registers and flags at one time. If you want to change the contents of a register while stepping through a program's machine instructions, you can do that as well.

Fill a region of memory with a single value. If you have an area of memory that you want blanked out, DEBUG will allow you to fill that area of memory with any character or binary value.

Search memory for sequences of binary values. You can search any area of memory for a specific sequence of characters or binary values. This could include names stored in memory or sequences of machine instructions. This allows you to examine or change something that you know exists somewhere in memory but not *where*.

Assemble new machine instructions into memory. DEBUG contains a simple assembler that does much of what NASM can do—one machine instruction at a time. If you want to replace a machine instruction somewhere within your program, you can type **MOV AX,BX** rather than have to look up and type the raw binary machine code values 8BH 0C3H.

Unassemble binary machine instructions into their mnemonics and operands. The flip side of the last feature is also possible: DEBUG can take the two hexadecimal values 8BH and 0C3H and tell you that they represent the assembly language mnemonic **MOV AX,BX**. This feature is utterly essential when you need to trace a program in operation and understand what is happening when the next two bytes in memory are read into the CPU and executed. If you don't know what machine instruction those two bytes represent, you'll be totally lost.

Single-step a program under test. Finally, DEBUG's single most valuable skill is to run a program one machine instruction at a time, pausing after each instruction for as long as you like. During this pause you can look at or change memory, look at or change registers, search for things in memory, patch the program by replacing existing machine instructions with new ones, and so on. This is what you'll do most of the time with DEBUG.

Taking DEBUG for a Spin

DEBUG can be a pretty forbidding character, terse to the point of being almost mute. You'll be spending a lot of time standing on DEBUG's shoulders and looking around, however, so you'd best get used to it now.

The easiest way to start is to use DEBUG to load a file into memory and examine it. On the CD-ROM associated with this book is a file called SAM.TXT. It's an ordinary DOS text file, whose contents were used to demonstrate the line structuring of text files with CR and LF. (See Figure 4.2.) If you don't have the CD-ROM for some reason, you can simply load your text editor and enter the following lines:

```
Sam
was
a
man.
```

Make sure you press Enter after the period at the end of "man." Then save the file to disk as SAM.TXT.

Let's lay SAM out on DEBUG's dissection table so that we can take a look at his innards. DEBUG will load itself and the file of your choice into memory at the same time, with only one command. Type DEBUG followed by the name of the file you want to load:

```
C:\ASM>DEBUG SAM.TXT
```

Make sure you use the full file name. Some assembler programs such as MASM and TASM will allow you to use only the first part of the file name and assume a file extension like .ASM, but DEBUG requires the full file name.

Like dour old Cal Coolidge, DEBUG doesn't say much, and never more than it has to. Unless DEBUG can't find SAM.TXT, all it will respond with is a single dash character (-) as its prompt, indicating that all is well and that DEBUG is awaiting a command.

Looking at a Hex Dump

Looking at SAM.TXT's interior is easy. Just type a D at the dash prompt. (Think, *D*ump.) DEBUG will obediently display a hex dump of the first 128 bytes of memory containing the contents of SAM.TXT read from disk. The hexadecimal numbers will probably look bewilderingly mysterious, but to their right you'll see the comforting words "Sam was a man" in a separate area of the screen. To help a little, I've taken the hex dump of SAM.TXT as you'll see it on your screen and annotated it in Figure 4.6.

This is a *hex dump*. It has three parts:

1. The leftmost part on the screen is the address of the start of each line of the dump. Each line contains 16 bytes. An address has two parts, and you'll notice that the left part of the address does not change while the right part is 16 greater at the start of each succeeding line. The 86-family CPU's two-part addresses are a source of considerable confusion and aggravation, and I'll take them up in detail in Chapter 5. For now, ignore the unchanging part of the address and consider the part that changes to be a count of the bytes on display, starting with 100H.

2. The part of the hex dump in the middle is the hexadecimal representation of the 128 bytes of memory being displayed. Sixteen bytes are shown in each row.

3. The part to the right of the hexadecimal values (and thus on the right-hand side of the hex dump) are those same 128 bytes of memory displayed as ASCII characters. Now, not all binary values have corresponding printable ASCII characters. Any invisible or unprintable characters are shown as period (.) characters.

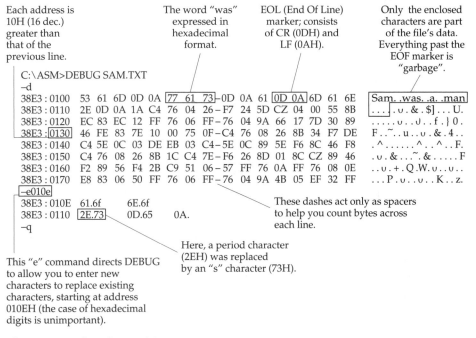

Figure 4.6 A hex dump of SAM.TXT.

This can be confusing. The last displayable character in SAM.TXT *is* a period and is actually the very first character on the second line of the hex dump. The ASCII display portion of the dump shows four identical periods in a row. To find out what's a period and what's simply a nondisplayable character, you must look back to the hexadecimal side and recognize the ASCII code for a period, which is 2EH.

Here is a good place to point out that an ASCII table of characters and their codes is an utterly essential thing to have. In ancient days, Borland's seminal Sidekick product included a very good ASCII table, and it had the advantage of always waiting in memory only a keystroke away. Sidekick and Windows didn't get along, however, and once Windows became ubiquitous, Sidekick went away. Assuming you don't have Sidekick (or some other memory-resident utility with an ASCII table), I'd advise you to take a photocopy of the ASCII table provided in Appendix D and keep it close at hand.

Memory Garbage

Take a long, close look at the hexadecimal equivalents of the characters in SAM.TXT. Notice that SAM.TXT is a very short file (20 bytes), but that 128 bytes are displayed. Any time you enter the D command, DEBUG will display 128 bytes of the area of memory you're looking at. (That area may contain a file—as it does here—or it may not. You're perfectly free to examine memory whether you've loaded a file into it or not.)

How, then, do you know where your file ends? This is an interesting problem that presents us with some interesting challenges. DEBUG doesn't tell you where a file ends—one of its few serious shortcomings, in my view. You have to know going in—and the best way to do that, for short files especially, is to use the DOS DIR command and write down its length value for the file. DOS knows how large a file is, down to the byte, and DIR will tell you for any file you list.

DIR will tell you that the SAM.TXT file is 19 bytes long. (Try it!) You can then count bytes in the hex dump until you find the last character, which in SAM's case is the final 0AH value of the last line feed character. Anything after that final 0AH value is garbage in memory and *not* part of the file! So, it matters where the end of the file is.

Some very old DOS text editors appended a single invisible byte at the end of every text file they wrote to disk. This byte, 1AH, was intended as a marker to show you very clearly where the end of the file was. Some of these text editors are still kicking around, and it's possible that you have one. (To see if you do, type in a simple sentence like "Where will it all end?" and save to disk. Go in with debug and see if there is a 1AH byte immediately after the end of the sentence.) The 1AH marker is a holdover from even more ancient times, from the CP/M operating system, which was simpler than DOS and remembered only the number of disk storage blocks a file occupied. The precise byte where the file's data ended within the final block was unknown to CP/M, so the text editors of the time used a 1AH byte to mark the tail end of the file.

There's a file on your CD-ROM, OLDSAM.TXT, which was created with such a text editor and has the final 1AH marker. (Note the time stamp on OLDSAM.TXT!) OLDSAM is otherwise identical to SAM.TXT. Note that when you do a DOS DIR command on the directory containing the two files, that OLDSAM.TXT is 20 bytes long—the 1AH marker byte is considered part of the file and counted with all the rest of the data.

Most of the time, memory garbage is not entirely random, but instead may be part of the code or data left over from the last program to be loaded and executed in that area of memory. You can safely ignore memory garbage, but should know what it is and why it appears in your hex dumps.

You might occasionally see recognizable data strings from other programs in memory garbage and wonder how they got into your current program. Note well: *They didn't get into your current program*. They were just there, and now show through beyond the end of the file you last loaded under DEBUG. Knowing where legitimate information ends and where garbage begins is always important and not generally as clear-cut as it is here.

Changing Memory with DEBUG

DEBUG can easily change bytes in memory, whether they are part of a file loaded from disk or not. The DEBUG command to change bytes is the E command. (Think, *E*nter new data.) You can use the E command to change some of the data in SAM.TXT. Part of this process is shown toward the bottom of Figure 4.6.

Notice the command line:

```
-e 010e
```

To taciturn Mr. Debug, this means, "Begin accepting entered bytes at address 010EH." I show the lowercase *E*s used in the command to put across the point that DEBUG is not sensitive to case, *even for letters used as hexadecimal digits*. In other words, there is nothing sacred about using uppercase A through E for hex digits. They can be lowercase or uppercase as you choose, and you don't even have to be consistent about it.

What DEBUG does in response to the E command shown in Figure 4.6 is display the following prompt:

```
38E3:010E 61.
```

The cursor waits after the period for your input. What DEBUG has done is shown you what value is *already* at address 010EH, so that you can decide whether you want to change it. If not, just press Enter, and the dash prompt will return. Here, it's asking you whether you want to replace the value 61. There's no *H* after it, but you must never forget that *DEBUG always works in hex*. That "61" is intended to be 61H.

Otherwise, enter a hexadecimal value to take the place of value 61H. In Figure 4.6, I wanted to use 6FH, and typed it as "6f." *Don't type the* H! Once you type a replacement value, but *before* you press Enter, you have two choices:

1. That is all, in fact, that you wish to change. Press Enter and return to the dash prompt.
2. You wish to change the byte at the next address as well. In this case, press the space bar instead. DEBUG will display the byte at the next highest address and wait for your replacement value, just as it did the first time.

This is shown in Figure 4.6. In fact, Figure 4.6 shows *four* successive replacements of bytes starting at address 010EH. Notice the lonely hex byte 0A followed by a period. What happened there is that I pressed Enter *without* typing a replacement byte, ending the E command and returning to the dash prompt.

You'll also note that the next command typed at the dash prompt was "q," for Quit. Typing Q at the dash prompt will return you immediately to DOS.

The Dangers of Modifying Files

Keep in mind that what I've just demonstrated was not changing a *file*, but simply changing the contents of a file loaded into memory. A file loaded into memory through DEBUG as we did with SAM.TXT is called a *memory image* of that file. *Only the memory image of the file was changed*. SAM.TXT remains on disk, unchanged and unaware of what was happening to its doppelganger in memory.

You can save the altered memory image of SAM.TXT back to disk with a simple command: Type W and then Enter. (Think, *Write*.) DEBUG remembers how many bytes it read in from disk, and it writes those bytes back out again. It provides a tally as it writes:

```
Writing 0013 bytes
```

The length figure here is given in hex, even though DEBUG does not do us the courtesy of displaying an *H* after the figure. 13H is 19 decimal, and there are exactly 19 bytes in SAM.TXT. DEBUG writes out *only* the significant information in the file. It does not write out anything that it didn't load in, *unless* you explicitly command DEBUG to write out additional bytes beyond the end of what was originally read.

If you haven't already figured out what was done to poor SAM.TXT, you can dump it again and take a look. If you simply press D for another dump, however, you're in for a surprise: The new dump does not contain any trace of SAM.TXT at all. (Try it!) If you're sharp you'll notice that the address of the first line is not what it was originally, but instead is this:

```
38E3:0180
```

(The first four digits will be different on your system, but that's all right—look at the second four digits instead during this discussion.) If you know your hex, you'll see that this is the address of the *next* eight lines of dumped memory, starting immediately after where the first dump left off.

The D command works that way. Each time you press D, you get the *next* 128 bytes of memory, starting with 0100H. To see SAM.TXT again, you need to specify the starting address of the dump, which was 0100H:

```
-d 0100
```

Enter that command, and you'll see a dump of the altered memory image of SAM.TXT:

```
38E3:0100 53 61 6D 0D 0A 77 61 73-0D 0A 61 0D 0A 6D 6F 6F   Sam..was..a..moo
38E3:0110 73 65 0A B2 C4 76 04 26-F7 24 5D C2 04 00 55 8B   se...v.&.$]...U.
38E3:0120 EC 83 EC 12 FF 76 06 FF-76 04 9A 66 17 7D 30 89   .....v..v..f.}0.
38E3:0130 46 FE 83 7E 10 00 75 0F-C4 76 08 26 8B 34 F7 DE   F..~..u..v.&.4..
38E3:0140 C4 5E 0C 03 DE EB 03 C4-5E 0C 89 5E F6 8C 46 F8   .^......^..^..F.
```

```
38E3:0150 C4 76 08 26 8B 1C C4 7E-F6 26 8D 01 8C C2 89 46   .v.&...~.&.....F
38E3:0160 F2 89 56 F4 2B C9 51 06-57 FF 76 0A FF 76 08 0E   ..V.+.Q.W.v..v..
38E3:0170 E8 83 06 50 FF 76 06 FF-76 04 9A 4B 05 EF 32 FF   ...P.v..v..K..2.
```

Sam, as you can see, is now something else again entirely.

Now, something went a little bit wrong when you changed Sam from a man to a moose. Look closely at memory starting at address 0111H. After the "e" (65H) is *half* of an EOL marker. The carriage return character (0DH) is gone, because you wrote an "e" over it. Only the line feed character (0AH) remains.

This isn't fatal, but it isn't right. A lonely line feed in a text file can cause trouble or not, depending on what you try to do with it. If you load the altered SAM.TXT into the NASM-IDE text editor (I explain NASM-IDE in Chapter 5), you'll see a peculiar symbol (a rectangle with a circle in the middle of it) after the word "moose." This is how the NASM-IDE editor indicates certain invisible characters that are not EOL or EOF markers, by using the graphical symbol set from the PC character ROM. The rectangle tells you that a nonprintable character is present at that point in the file. (Load the CD-ROM file MOOSE.TXT into NASM-IDE and you'll see what I mean.)

The lesson here is that DEBUG is a loaded gun without a safety catch. There are no safeguards. You can change *anything* inside a file with it, whether it makes sense or not, or whether it's dangerous or not. All safety considerations are up to you. You must be aware of whether or not you're overwriting important parts of the file.

This is a theme that will occur again and again in assembly language: *Safety is up to you.* Unlike Basic, which wraps a protective cocoon around you and keeps you from banging yourself up too badly, assembly language lets you hang yourself without a whimper of protest.

Keep this in mind as we continue.

Examining and Changing Registers

If you saved SAM.TXT back out to disk in its altered state, you created a damaged file. (I did this for you, by creating the file MOOSE.TXT.) Fixing SAM.TXT requires reconstructing the last EOL marker by inserting the CR character that you overwrote using the E command. Unfortunately, this means you'll be making SAM.TXT larger than it was when DEBUG read it into memory. To save the corrected file back out to disk, we need to somehow tell DEBUG that it needs to save more than 13H bytes out to disk. To do this we need to look at and change a value in one of the CPU registers.

Registers, if you recall, are special-purpose memory cubbyholes that exist inside the CPU chip itself, rather than in memory chips outside the CPU. DEBUG has a command that allows us to examine and change register values as easily as we examine and change memory.

At the dash prompt, type R. (Think, *R*egisters.) You'll see a display like this:

```
- r
AX=0000 BX=0000 CX=0014 DX=0000 SP=FFEE BP=0000 SI=0000 DI=0000
DS=1980 ES=1980 SS=1980 CS=1980 IP=0100  NV UP EI PL NZ NA PO NC
1980:0100 53            PUSH  BX
```

The bulk of the display consists of register names followed by equal signs, followed by the current values of the registers. The cryptic characters **NV UP EI PL NZ NA PO NC** are the names of *flags*; we discuss them later in the book.

The line beneath the register and flag summaries is a *disassembly* of the byte at the address contained by the instruction pointer. (The *instruction pointer* is a register which is displayed by the DEBUG R command, under the shorter name **IP**. Find **IP**'s value in the preceding register display—it should be 0100H, which is also the address of the "S" in "Sam.") This line will be useful when you're actually examining an executable program file in memory. In the case of SAM.TXT, the disassembly line is misleading, because SAM is *not* an executable program and contains nothing we intend to be used as machine instructions.

The hexadecimal value 53H, however, *is* a legal machine instruction—just as it is the ASCII code for uppercase *S*. DEBUG doesn't know what kind of file SAM.TXT is. SAM could as well be a program file as a text file; DEBUG makes no assumptions based on the file's contents or its file extension. DEBUG examines memory at the current address and displays it as though it were a machine instruction. If memory contains data instead of machine instructions, the disassembly line should be ignored, even though it will always be there.

This is once again an example of the problems you can have in assembly language if you don't know exactly what you're doing. Code and data look the same in memory. They are only different in how you interpret them. In SAM.TXT, the hex value 53H is the letter *S*; in an executable program file, 53H would be the machine instruction **PUSH BX**. We make good use of the disassembly line later on in the book, when we get down to examining real assembly language programs. For now, just ignore it.

When DEBUG loads a file from disk, it places the number of bytes in the file in the CX register. CX is a general-purpose register, but it is often used to contain such count values and is therefore sometimes called the *count register*.

Notice that the value of CX is 13H—just the number DEBUG reported when it wrote the altered SAM.TXT out to disk in response to the W command. If we change the value in CX, we change the number of bytes DEBUG will write to disk.

So let's fix SAM.TXT. In changing the word "man" to "moose" we wrote over two characters: the period at the end of the sentence and the CR character portion of the last line's EOL marker. We could start at address 0112H and enter a period character (2EH—use your ASCII table!) followed by a CR character (0DH). In doing so, however, we would overwrite the LF character, which is just as bad or worse.

Unlike a text editor, DEBUG will not just shove over the values to the right of the point where you wish to insert new values. DEBUG has no insert mode. You have to enter all three characters: The period, the CR, and the LF.

Use the E command to enter them, and then display a dump of the file again:

```
- e 0112
1980:0112 0D.2e  0A.0d  1A.0a

- d 0100
38E3:0100 53 61 6D 0D 0A 77 61 73-0D 0A 61 0D 0A 6D 6F 6F   Sam..was..a..moo
38E3:0110 73 65 2E 0D 0A 76 04 26-F7 24 5D C2 04 00 55 8B   se.....&.$]...U.
38E3:0120 EC 83 EC 12 FF 76 06 FF-76 04 9A 66 17 7D 30 89   .....v..v..f.}0.
38E3:0130 46 FE 83 7E 10 00 75 0F-C4 76 08 26 8B 34 F7 DE   F..~..u..v.&.4..
38E3:0140 C4 5E 0C 03 DE EB 03 C4-5E 0C 89 5E F6 8C 46 F8   .^......^..^..F.
38E3:0150 C4 76 08 26 8B 1C C4 7E-F6 26 8D 01 8C C2 89 46   .v.&...~.&.....F
38E3:0160 F2 89 56 F4 2B C9 51 06-57 FF 76 0A FF 76 08 0E   ..V.+.Q.W.v..v..
38E3:0170 E8 83 06 50 FF 76 06 FF-76 04 9A 4B 05 EF 32 FF   ...P.v..v..K..2.
```

Now the file is repaired, and we can write it back to disk. Except—SAM.TXT in memory is now two bytes longer than SAM.TXT on disk.

We need to tell DEBUG that it needs to write two additional bytes to disk when it writes SAM.TXT back out.

DEBUG keeps its count of SAM.TXT's length in the BX and CX registers. The count is actually a 32-bit number split between the two 16-bit registers BX and CX, with BX containing the high half of the 32-bit number. This allows us to load very large files into DEBUG, with byte counts that cannot fit into a single 16-bit register like CX. Sixteen-bit registers can only contain values up to 65,535. If we wanted to use DEBUG on an 80,000-byte file (which is not big at all these days, as files go), we'd be out of luck if DEBUG only kept a 16-bit count of the file size in a single register.

But for small changes to files, or for working with small files, we only have to be aware of and work with the count in CX. Adding 2 to the byte count only changes the low half of the number, contained in CX. Changing the value of CX is done with the R command, by specifying CX after R:

```
-r cx
```

DEBUG responds by displaying the name "CX," its current value, and a colon prompt on the next line:

```
CX 0013
:
```

Add 2 to the value of CX and enter 0015 at the colon prompt. Press Enter. DEBUG simply returns the dash prompt without congratulating you on your success—remember, it's a utility of few words.

Now, however, when you enter a W command to write SAM.TXT back to disk, DEBUG displays this message:

```
Writing 0015 bytes
```

The new, longer SAM.TXT has been written to disk in its entirety. Problem solved.

One final note on saving files back out to disk from DEBUG: If you change the values in either BX or CX to reflect something other than the true length of the file, and then execute a W command to write the file to disk, DEBUG will write as many bytes to disk as are specified in BX and CX. This could be 20,000 bytes more than the file contains, or it could be zero bytes, leaving you with an empty file. You can destroy a file this way. Either leave BX and CX alone while you're examining and patching a file with DEBUG, or write the initial values in BX and CX down, and enter them back into BX and CX just before issuing the W command.

The Hacker's Best Friend

There is a *great* deal more to be said about DEBUG, but most of it involves concepts we haven't yet covered. DEBUG is the single most useful tool you have as an assembly language programmer, and I'll be teaching you more of its features as we get deeper and deeper into the programming process itself.

The next chapter describes NASM-IDE, a simple program editor and development environment created specifically for people who are using the NASM assembler. If you do not intend to use NASM-IDE, you can skip right over Chapter 5 and meet us on the other side in Chapter 6, where we begin our long trek through the 86-family instruction set.

NASM-IDE: A Place to Stand

Give me a lever long enough, and a place to stand, and I will move the Earth.

—ARCHIMEDES

Access to Tools

The old guy was speaking literally about the mechanical advantage of the lever here, but behind his words there is a larger truth about work in general: To get something done, you need a place to work, with access to tools. My radio bench in the garage is set up that way: a large, flat space to lay ailing transmitters down, and a shelf above where my oscilloscope, VTVM, frequency counter, signal generator, and dip meter are within easy reach.

Much of the astonishing early success of Turbo Pascal was grounded in that truth. For the first time, a compiler vendor gathered up the most important tools of software development and put them together in an intuitive fashion so that the various tasks involved in creating software flowed easily from one step to the next. From a menu that was your place to stand, you pressed one key, and your Pascal program was compiled. You pressed another one, and the program was run. It was simple, fast, and easy to learn. Turbo Pascal literally took Pascal from a backwater language favored by academics to the most popular compiled language in history at that time.

What Borland so boldly introduced in 1983 was adopted (reluctantly at times) by its major competitor, Microsoft. Today, Microsoft's Visual Studio (including Visual C++ and Visual Basic) and Borland's Delphi are the best examples of what we call *integrated development environments* (IDEs). They provide well-designed menus to give you that place to stand and a multitude of tools that are only one or two keystrokes away.

A little remarkably, there is no true equivalent to Turbo Pascal in the assembly language field. Neither MASM nor Borland's Turbo Assembler (TASM) has that same comfortable place to stand. The reasons for this may seem peculiar to you, the beginner: Seasoned assembly language programmers either create their own development environments (they are, after all, the programming elite) or they simply work from the naked operating system command prompt. The appeal of a Turbo Pascal–type environment is not so strong to them as it is to you.

NASM-IDE

Robert Anderton of the United Kingdom had a slightly radical idea some time back that challenges that notion: He wanted to create an IDE for assembly language work, one that would be simple enough for beginners to use. Out of this radical idea came NASM-IDE, which was written—most appropriately—in Borland Pascal, the mature successor to Turbo Pascal, which made the idea of a built-in programming IDE mainstream. NASM-IDE is a DOS-based utility, and there is no version for Linux. (When we get to Linux we're going to do it the way the big boys do: from the command line.) Robert is working on a more advanced IDE, in Java, that will function for both DOS and Linux, but that's for another time, and perhaps the next edition of this book. For now, we're learning under DOS and starting from square one. NASM-IDE is just the thing.

I've arranged with Robert to distribute NASM-IDE on the CD-ROM in this book. If for some reason your copy of the book lacks a CD-ROM (as used computer books often do) or has a damaged and unreadable CD-ROM, you can download NASM-IDE free of charge from Robert's home page at www.inglenook.co.uk/nasmide/index.html.

NASM-IDE has the advantage for us that it was created specifically for use with the NASM assembler, which we'll begin using shortly. NASM has the power to assemble directly to a DOS .COM executable file, making the separate link step (as I describe in Chapter 4) unnecessary for simple programs that you write in only one source code file. NASM-IDE takes advantage of this power and allows you to edit, assemble, and test simple assembly language programs very quickly. (We explore modular assembly and linking in a later chapter, as it remains a very important topic for intermediate and advanced assembly work.)

NASM-IDE's Place to Stand

Like Turbo Pascal and the other integrated development environments from both Borland and Microsoft, NASM-IDE's most visible part is a text editor. If you look back once again to Figure 4.5, you'll see that all roads seem to lead back to the text editor in good time. In general, you do most of your *thinking* while staring at the text editor screen, so it seems a logical location to put your place to stand.

So, one way to think of NASM-IDE is as a text editor from which you can do additional, assembly-language-related things. You invoke NASM-IDE like a text editor, in fact. If you're working from DOS, the first time you want to work on a particular source code file, you type the name NAS-MIDE followed by the name of the source code file:

```
C:\ASM>NASMIDE EAT2.ASM
```

(Here, "EAT2.ASM" is the name of an assembly language source code file that we'll be working on later in this book.)

I recommend that you place the directory containing NASM-IDE on your DOS path. That way, no matter where you are on your hard drive, you can type "NASMIDE" and NASM-IDE will come up, ready for work.

When you bring up NASM-IDE using the preceding command line, what you'll see should look a lot like Figure 5.1.

NASM-IDE consists of an empty space (with a texture to fill it, indicating that it's empty) in which you can open windows containing information. At the top of the screen is a menu bar. At the bottom of the screen is a prompt bar. The menu bar provides several menus of options that you can pull down (either from the keyboard or with the mouse) to accomplish the various things that NASM-IDE can do. The prompt bar gives you terse reminders of the most important commands that you can issue via the function keys and various hot keys. Square in the middle of the screen is an edit window containing the file you opened when you invoked NASM-IDE.

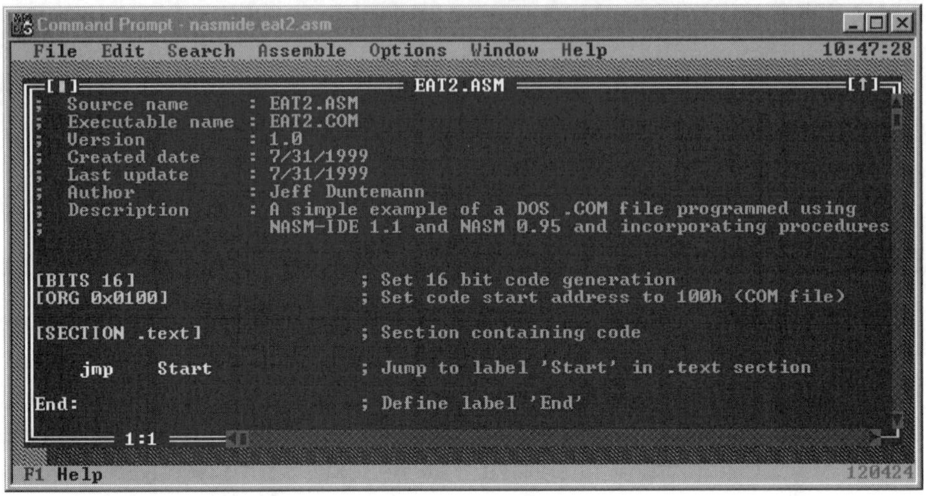

Figure 5.1 The NASM-IDE environment.

Telling NASM-IDE Where NASM Is

There isn't a lot of installing or configuring to be done with either NAS-MIDE or NASM itself. I've arranged a directory on this book's CD-ROM called ASM with all the various tools in it in the right places. However, you need to copy that directory to a place on your hard drive, because you cannot write files to the CD-ROM. You can drag the ASM directory from the CD-ROM to one of your hard drive units using Windows Explorer, and all of the subdirectories under ASM will come along. However, if you're working purely from DOS, you need to use XCOPY to do the copying.

Once you get NASM-IDE running, you need to do one essential piece of configuration before you can use it: You must tell it the exact path where the NASM executable file resides. This cannot be the path of the CD-ROM! I recommend making ASM a subdirectory on the root of one of your hard drives; for example, C:\ASM rather than C:\programming\ASM. The drive unit doesn't have to be C:, especially in these days of multigigabyte hard drives where a typical Windows 95 PC has units C:, D:, E:, and possibly even F:, all with 2 gigabytes of storage or more. (A Windows 95 hard drive unit cannot contain more than 2 gigabytes.)

Choose one and copy the ASM directory from your CD-ROM to your hard drive. Then bring up NASM-IDE and pull down the Options menu.

Select the Options | Assembler item by either highlighting it and pressing Enter, or double-clicking on it with your mouse. A dialog box will appear. You shouldn't change anything in this box except for one item: the edit line labeled NASM Location. When the dialog box appears, this line will be blank. You need to enter the full path of the NASM executable file where it was copied to your hard drive.

If you copied the ASM directory to the root of your D: drive (probably better than putting it on C: since everybody wants to be on C: and C: is often a little crowded), the path to NASM will be this:

```
D:\ASM\nasm16.exe
```

Obviously, if you copied the ASM directory to C: or E:, the initial letter will not be D:. Think it through. But this is the line you should type into the field marked NASM Location. Then click on the button labeled OK. NASM-IDE now knows where the assembler lives and will be able to invoke it for you behind the scenes.

With that accomplished, you're ready to rock. So let's see what NASM-IDE and NASM can do.

The Edit Window

The *edit window* is the part of NASM-IDE that you'll be seeing most often. It contains the assembly language source code file you're working on at any given time. Within the edit window you can type text, delete text, change text, and search for sequences of characters (*strings*) in your text. This is where you'll write new code and change code that doesn't work correctly. The cursor moves in response to the mouse, and you can move it from the keyboard as well.

The edit window works a great deal like the edit window present in the last generation of DOS-based Borland language products, Borland Pascal and Borland C++. If you have any experience in those DOS-based products, you'll feel right at home. The various hot keys and function keys all do pretty much the same things as they did in those products.

When you first bring up a file in the edit window (as you did with EAT2.ASM just now), the file will be in an edit window centered in the middle of the screen. There will be a line of empty space on all four sides. If all you're doing is editing that one file, there's no need to waste the empty space all around the edit window. At the top edge of the edit window are two controls: a small square on the left, and an upward-pointing arrow on the right. The upward-pointing arrow expands (or zooms) your edit window to occupy the full screen. The small square closes the edit window, which then vanishes.

Text screens are small enough as it is. I always zoom my edit windows so that they become as large as possible. One click on the arrow control on the top edge of the edit window is all it takes.

At the top edge of the edit window is the full path of the file currently loaded and being edited in that window.

The Menu Bar

All along the top edge of the NASM-IDE screen is the *menu bar*. Each word in the menu bar is the name of a separate menu. If you click on one of these menu names with the mouse, the menu proper (containing a number of menu *items*) will drop down beneath the name, and the top item on the menu will be highlighted with a green bar. Each item in a menu represents a command of some sort. You can move the highlight bar up and down by pressing the up/down arrow keys on the keyboard. To execute the menu command represented by the highlighted item, you press Enter. You can click on a menu option with the mouse, and the command it represents will be executed right then.

Sometimes a menu item's name is followed by three dots or periods. This indicates that this menu item, when selected, brings up a *dialog box* that you must fill out with some additional information in order to execute the command. I describe these dialog boxes a little later in this chapter.

At the right edge of the menu bar is a time display. The time is taken from your machine's system clock.

Although nearly all PC systems these days are equipped with a mouse, it's possible to use NASM-IDE without a mouse. (The mouse makes many things quicker and easier, however.) Note that the menu names in the menu bar have the first letters of their names highlighted in a separate color. (This will be red unless you change it.) The distinctive color on the first characters of the menu names reminds you of the hot keys associated with the menus. You can pull down any of the menus by pressing Alt followed by the highlighted letter.

For example, the *E* in "Edit" in the menu bar is in red. If you press Alt-E, you'll pull down the Edit menu. Then you can use the up/down arrow keys on the keyboard to move the item highlight bar up and down. When the highlight bar is over the option that you want, you simply press Enter to select that item and issue the command that it represents.

Note that the items in some of the menus are divided into groups by single horizontal lines. These lines are there only to help you recall that certain menu items are related to one another. The dividing lines cannot be selected and have no command-related function themselves.

I go through most of NASM-IDE's menu items in detail later in this chapter.

The Prompt Bar

At the bottom of the screen is another horizontal bar. This one, called the *prompt bar*, contains little reminders of certain hot keys that are functional at various times in NASM-IDE, depending on what you have open on the screen and what you're doing with it.

However, the most useful function of the prompt bar is to enlarge upon NASM-IDE's menu items a little. When you have a menu pulled down, the prompt bar will show you a short description of what the highlighted menu item is for. This will help you a *lot* while you're learning NASM-IDE and will make it a lot less necessary to be constantly flipping through this book looking for an explanation of a particular menu item that you haven't quite committed to memory.

Keep in mind that the prompt bar is not interactive; that is, there's nothing you can select in it, and nothing you can click on. It's there to give you little mental noodges, especially while you're learning the NASM-IDE system.

Other Windows

Files under edit aren't the only things that appear in windows in NASM-IDE. In fact, anything that isn't on the menu bar or the prompt bar *must* be in a window. Most of the time, it'll be assembly source code text files in the window. But you will see other information in windows as well.

The most significant of these is probably the help window. If you press F1 from almost anywhere in NASM-IDE, the help window will appear, and you can navigate around in it to read up on many of NASM-IDE's features. I have more to say about the help window later in this chapter.

When NASM-IDE invokes NASM to assemble a source code file for you, it will create a window for any error or warning messages that NASM generates while translating your source code file. This window will appear even when it's empty, to indicate that the assembly process went through completely and correctly.

There are error message boxes that will appear if certain things (such as loading a file from disk) don't go quite right. These are windows, too. Finally, several of the menu items bring up small windows called dialog boxes that must be filled in (by you) with additional information to complete the job the menu item was intended to accomplish. I discuss these dialog box windows in connection with the menu items that bring them up.

NASM-IDE windows have a few things in common. All windows have some sort of title at the center of their top edges, to indicate what they're for. Windows containing source code files will have the full path of the file shown in the window. All windows in NASM-IDE have the close control on their top edge. This is the small square toward the left side of the top edge of the window. Dialog box windows, however, lack the zoom control on the right edge. You can close any window, but it only makes sense to zoom certain types of windows, primarily the help window and the edit windows containing your source code files.

Using NASM-IDE's Tools

The very best way to explain NASM-IDE's various features and how they are used is to run through a simple programming session with a real assembly language program and explain what happens as we go. The program we'll use is EAT2.ASM, which is shown later in this book. It's not much of a program, really, and exists only to get you started in understanding the internal mechanisms of a real, working assembly language program.

The goal of EAT2.ASM is to be assembled into the executable program file EAT2.COM. When run (either from inside NASM-IDE or from the DOS prompt), EAT2.COM displays this simple message on your screen:

```
Eat at Joe's . . .
 . . . ten million flies can't ALL be wrong!
```

That's all it does. After it displays those two lines, it ceases executing and returns control to DOS.

The file EAT2.ASM is present on the CD-ROM, along with NASM-IDE and the other tools provided for you. If you don't have or can't read the CD-ROM for this book, you can download all the example code files from my Web site at www.duntemann.com/downloads.htm.

If, as I have suggested earlier, you have created a subdirectory on your hard disk called ASM (or if you've copied the CD-ROM directory ASM over to your hard drive), all the .ASM example files need to be in the ASM directory. In order for NASM-IDE to operate correctly, the assembler executable NASM.EXE must be available on your hard drive where NASM-IDE can find it. Your best bet is to copy the ASM directory over from the CD-ROM either using Windows Explorer (if you're working from within Windows) or using DOS XCOPY.

Invoking NASM-IDE

Make the current directory your working assembly language subdirectory, which I have suggested you (nay, have pestered you mercilessly) to call ASM. From the DOS prompt, invoke NASM-IDE with the file name EAT2 after it:

```
C:\ASM>NASMIDE EAT2.ASM
```

Two things: Notice first that you *must* type the ".ASM" at the end of the file name EAT2! Unlike many similar utilities, NASM-IDE has no *default file extension* and will not automatically append ".ASM" at the end of a file name entered without an extension. In other words, if you don't enter the ".ASM" file extension, NASM-IDE will not be able to find the file and will put up an error message window like the one shown in Figure 5.2.

Also, keep in mind that while NASM-IDE's official name (when we're talking about it in this book) has a hyphen between "NASM" and "IDE," *the name of the file that you type on the command line* is "NASMIDE" *without* a hyphen. If you type "NASM-IDE" at the DOS command line, DOS will not know what you're talking about.

What happens if you simply run NASM-IDE *without* specifying a file name? If you have been working on a .ASM file of some sort and last

Figure 5.2 A NASM-IDE error message box.

exited NASM-IDE with that file still in a window, NASM-IDE will load that file from disk and put it in a window, just as it was when you last shut down NASM-IDE. If, on the other hand, you're bringing up NASM-IDE for the very first time, or if there was no file in a window when you last shut NASM-IDE down, there will be no file in a window when the NASM-IDE environment appears. NASM-IDE remembers what it was doing when you last shut it down, and absent other instructions, it will pick up precisely where it left off.

NASM-IDE's ability to remember the name of the last file you worked on makes it unnecessary for *you* to remember what project you were in the middle of when you pulled the plug and went to bed. Furthermore, NASM-IDE also remembers the exact cursor position where the cursor was when you saved your file and exited, as well as whether the edit window was zoomed. So, most of the time, if you're in the middle of a project and want to get back down to it, you only need to type "NAS-MIDE" followed by Enter on the DOS command line. If you were working on EAT2.ASM before and had it open when you shut NASM-IDE down, you don't have to type EAT2.ASM again on the command line when you invoke NASM-IDE.

When you create a new file or load a file into the editor for the first time, it becomes, by default, the *current file*. This means it is the file that will be assembled when you tell NASM-IDE to invoke NASM to translate your source code file to an executable or an object code file. I explain more about the concept of the current file later in this book. Typically, unless you begin doing fancier things, the current file will simply be the source code file you have open in an edit window.

Moving Around the Edit Window

When you're in NASM-IDE and an assembly language source code file is displayed in an edit window, any characters you type on the keyboard will be inserted into the file and displayed on your screen. You can move the cursor around within the current file by using any of a number of cursor movement keys.

The easiest to remember are the PC's cursor keypad keys. The four arrow keys will move the cursor one character position in the direction the arrow points. The PgUp key will move the cursor up one page (that is, the size of your text screen; typically 25, 43, or 50 lines depending on how you set it up—more on that shortly) whereas PgDn will move the cursor one page down. The Home key will move the cursor immediately to the left screen margin, and the End key will move the cursor immediately to the end of the current line. (The *end of the line* is defined as the character *after* the rightmost *nonblank* character in the line.)

There are numerous other cursor movement keys that you can use within JED. I describe them all in detail later in this chapter. You can also zero in on a particular location in the file by clicking on a character with the mouse. The cursor will move immediately to the point at which you clicked. You can use the mouse to slide up and down within the file by clicking on the "thumb" of the scroll bar on the right-hand edge of the edit window, and then dragging the thumb up or down. (The thumb is a small rectangle set into the scroll bar.)

Take a few moments scooting around inside EAT2.ASM until you feel comfortable with it.

Making Changes to the File

The simplest way to change the file is simply to type something at the keyboard. All such characters will appear at the cursor, and the cursor will move one position to the right for each character.

You can insert a new line beneath the current line by pressing Enter.

Getting rid of unwanted text is as important as adding new text. Deleting one character at a time can be done by moving the cursor to the immediate right of the offending character, and simply using the backspace key to back the cursor over it. The character will disappear. You can also place the cursor to the *left* of the text you want to delete, and then press the Del key once for each character to be deleted. Text to the right of the cursor will be pulled in toward the left as characters disappear.

You can delete an entire line by placing the cursor on the line and pressing Ctrl-Y. This can be done all too easily by accident, and you lose a line that you may or may not have in your head or written down on paper. Be careful!

NASM-IDE contains several other ways to delete text, all of which will be described later in this chapter. For the sake of the current guided tour through NASM-IDE, move the cursor to the blank line immediately beneath EAT2.ASM's comment header (line 9 in the file) and type the phrase "MVO ax,bx." That done, press Enter and add a new line beneath it.

Saving Changes to a File

As they say in Chicago, that grand old (and cold) town where I grew up, "Vote early and often." The same philosophy applies to saving the changes you make to your current file within NASM-IDE. Every so often, perhaps when you kick back in your chair to think for a bit, save your work. It's easy: one keystroke, the function key F2. There's no visible indicator that anything's actually happening, but pressing F2 will save your file in its entirety back to the place from which you loaded it, wherever that might be on your system.

Get in the habit of pressing F2 once in a while. Keep in mind that if you save your work every five minutes, you will never lose more than five minutes of work!

NASM-IDE keeps an eye on things and does its level best to keep you from losing any of your work. If you try to exit NASM-IDE without saving your file to disk, it will remind you with the dialog box shown in Figure 5.3.

Before it will exit back to DOS, NASM-IDE will require some response from you. If you click on the green button reading "Yes," NASM-IDE

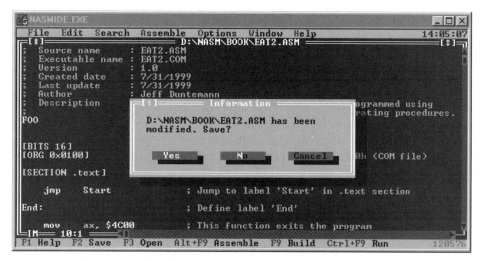

Figure 5.3 When you exit without saving.

will save your work to disk, just as though you had pressed F2. Clicking on the button reading "No" will allow you to exit NASM-IDE without saving your work—and any changes you made that you have not saved will be lost. Finally, if you click on the button reading "Cancel," the command will be cancelled, and nothing else will happen. Your work will not be saved, nor will NASM-IDE exit back to DOS.

If you don't have a mouse, you can press Enter to select "Yes," which is the default option for this dialog box. (NASM-IDE gives you every opportunity *not* to lose your changes!) If you want to move to one of the other buttons but don't have a mouse, you must use the Tab key to bounce from one button to another. The buttons will change when they are selected: The text after the initial character of the button labels will be in white rather than yellow. The three buttons cycle, so if you tab right past the button you want, press it a few more times and you'll get back to your chosen button. Then when you press Enter, that button will be clicked and the appropriate action taken.

Assembling the Current File

If you're satisfied that you've understood all the various NASM-IDE features I've described so far on this tour, it's time to assemble EAT2.ASM and make an actual runnable program file out of it. Press function key F9. NASM-IDE will invoke the assembler NASM behind the scenes. You won't see anything to indicate it on your screen; NASM-IDE will remain there as always.

However, assuming you did what I told you earlier and typed some new text at line 9 of EAT2.ASM, the screen will split horizontally and a new window will be displayed beneath the text window containing EAT2.ASM. This window has the title "Error Information" and will look a lot like Figure 5.4.

If you recall, you made a change to EAT2.ASM a little earlier by typing the phrase "MVO ax,bx" on line 9. This phrase is something like an assembly language mnemonic—but only something, and in the form I gave it to you the assembler NASM will have no idea what to do with it. So, NASM dutifully complained in the form of an error message. You can see this error message in Figure 5.4. When NASM tells you "Parser: Instruction Expected" that means that what it got in the line it paused at was *not* an instruction. You've inserted an error into EAT2.ASM here because no instruction in the 86-family instruction set is named MVO. This may not prevent your fevered fingers from transforming MOV (which *is* a legal instruction) to MVO in the furious passion of creation—or under the influence of the caffeine shakes.

The error information window will remain on the screen until you close it, which you can do by clicking on the close control at the upper-left corner of the window. And until you fix the error you inserted into EAT2.ASM, that's as far as we can go here.

Fixing it, however, is easy. NASM-IDE is reasonably smart and has placed the cursor right where it thinks the error is in the edit window.

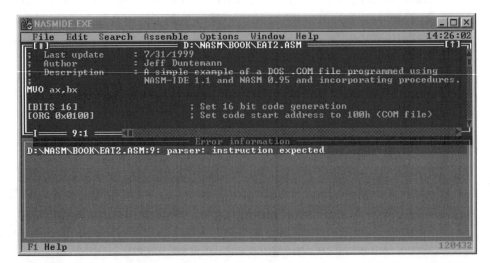

Figure 5.4 The error information window appears.

In this case, the error was pretty blatant, and NASM-IDE has no trouble spotting it. *That may not always be the case.* There is no ironclad guarantee that after spotting an error, the cursor will be placed at the location of the error. Assembly language is nothing if not tricky. You have to be able to identify errors based on what you've written, *not* simply on where NASM-IDE suggests they may be hiding.

In this case NASM-IDE has the error dead to rights, and you can fix the error by nuking the whole line with a quick Ctrl-Y. After that, press F2 to save the file to disk again. Then press F9 again to try the assembly process once more.

Note that the error information window will still appear. However, it carries a brighter message this time: "No errors occurred." Every time you assemble, the error information message will appear, either with this message—or with an error message or a warning. (More on warnings later on.)

Running the Executable File

If you don't see any error messages in the error information window, that means NASM got through it all right and created the executable .COM file that is the point of the whole exercise. You can run the EAT2.COM file from the DOS prompt, just like you can run any .COM or .EXE file from the DOS prompt. However, it's easier than even that. NASM-IDE can run your executable program file for you, right from inside NASM-IDE.

The shortcut is Ctrl-F9. If you prefer, you can pull down the Assemble menu and select Run. NASM-IDE will go away for a moment, and instead you'll see a blank DOS screen with the output of your program on it—in this case, the backhanded advertising slogan for Joe's Restaurant. See Figure 5.5.

Getting back to NASM-IDE is no big deal: Just do as the screen instructs you, and press any key.

NASM-IDE's Editor in Detail

As NASM-IDE's beating heart, the text editor deserves a little space all to itself. People who have read earlier editions of this book (there were two, in fact, though the first one didn't live very long and really doesn't count) may notice a remarkable resemblance between NASM-IDE's text

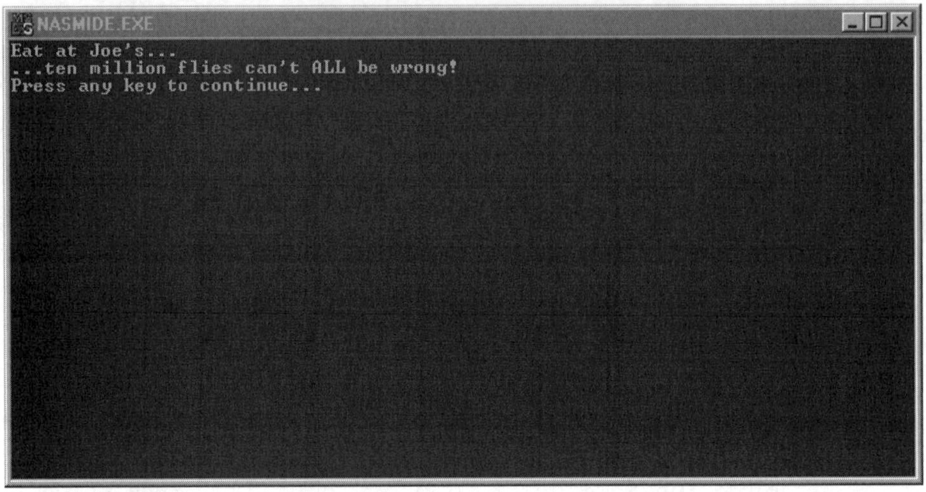

Figure 5.5 Running the executable program file.

window and my own JED editor, which is what I described for the two earlier editions of this book. The reason is pretty simple: Both JED and NASM-IDE were based on the Borland Binary Editor, a text editor module that could be linked into Turbo Pascal and Borland Pascal programs.

NASM-IDE uses a newer version of the editor than the one I incorporated into JED (which I originally wrote in 1989 with Turbo Pascal 5.0), and has the further advantage of using the Turbo Vision application framework, which provides all the window controls, the buttons, the scrollbars, and so on. But the two are remarkably alike in many ways, especially from the standpoint of the keystrokes that control their text editors.

Loading Files into the Editor

When you invoke NASM-IDE and it begins running, it loads either the file you named on the command line when you invoked it (as I described and showed you earlier) or else the last file it worked on, as recorded in a configuration file called NASMIDE.INI. (You can inspect this file, which is maintained by NASM-IDE, but *don't* alter it yourself!)

Individual lines within an edit file are limited to 254 characters. Loading a file with longer lines will cause the editor to insert hyphens at the 254-character point. You'll get an error box if you try to type past the 254-character point on any line.

Although it's not something you'll do a lot, it's useful to know that you can load more than one text file into NASM-IDE's environment at once. This can be handy when you want to cut or copy text out of one file and paste it into another. Each file remains in a separate edit window.

Opening a file in an edit window from inside NASM-IDE is done using either the menus or hotkeys. Selecting the File | Open menu item with the mouse will bring up a dialog box that will allow you to specify the file you want to open. The same dialog box can be invoked with the F3 hot key.

File | Open or F3 brings up the Open File dialog box.

The dialog is one of the more complex ones you'll encounter in using NASM-IDE, and I've shown it in Figure 5.6. Like all parts of NASM-IDE, the dialog box allows you to work either with the mouse or purely from the keyboard. Most people have a mouse, so I'll emphasize mouse-enabled techniques in my explanations.

From a height, what the dialog presents you with is a list of files (marked Files) from which you can choose (these are shown in the rectangular area in the center) as well as an edit line where the currently selected file's name is displayed. (That's the line at the top, marked Name.) If you click once on a file listed in the Files box, its name will appear in the Name box. You can move the highlight bar around the list of files with the arrow keys if you prefer to work from the keyboard.

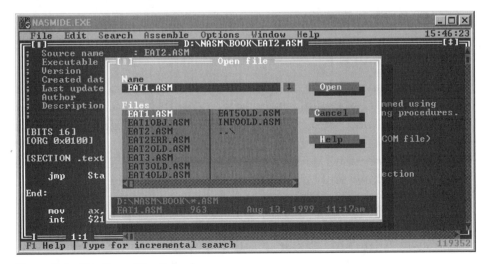

Figure 5.6 The Open File dialog box.

By default, the only files that will appear in the dialog box are those with a .ASM file extension. Directories will appear as well, indicated by a backslash character after the directory name. You can display files with file extensions other than .ASM, but you will have to place the cursor after the .ASM extension in the Name edit box, and backspace over ".ASM." Then type whatever extension you wish to display and press Enter.

Choosing a file to open is simple: You double-click on a file name in the Files list box, or else press Enter when the file you want to open is highlighted. The file will be opened and placed in an edit window.

You also have the option of typing the name of a file in the Name line at the top of the dialog. If another file name is already there, you will have to backspace over it before you type the new name in.

You can navigate through a DOS directory structure using the dialog box. Directories are shown with a backslash character after them to let you know that they are directories. Double-clicking on a directory name will take you into that directory and display any files present there.

A special symbol, "..\" indicates the parent directory. If you double-click on ..\, you will move up one level in the directory hierarchy. This is the same way you move to the parent directory using the DOS CD command, so it should come as no surprise.

A two-line blue bar at the bottom of the dialog box displays detailed information about the highlighted file, including its size, its timestamp (that is, the last time and date that it was modified), and the directory path where it resides.

Moving the Cursor

If you have a mouse, use it. Putting the cursor where you want it is easy: You click on a point on the screen and the cursor is simply *there*. Moving up and down through the file is done by grabbing the edit window's scroll bar thumb and dragging it. Most people who have any experience at all with graphical user interface (GUI) environments such as Windows will take to this without any trouble.

Many people who do a lot of text editing prefer to do their in-file cursor navigation strictly from the keyboard, to avoid having to take their hands away to grab the mouse. It's up to you. The mouse is there if you want it, but mouse or no mouse, there is a whole elaborate system for moving the cursor around without ever taking your hands away from the keyboard.

Apart from the obvious keypad keys, all editor commands are hot keys based on the Ctrl key. That is, you must hold the Ctrl key down while pressing another key or two keys. All of the hot keys that control cursor movement are grouped together for you in a cluster toward the left side of the keyboard:

```
W   E   R
 A   S   D   F
 Z   X   C
```

This arrangement of cursor command keys will be familiar to anyone who has worked with the WordStar word processor, which in ancient times was almost everybody—and today is almost nobody except those of us who were around in ancient times.

One Character at a Time

Moving the cursor one character at a time can be done in all four directions:

Ctrl-E or **Up Arrow** moves the cursor **up** one character.

Ctrl-X or **Down Arrow** moves the cursor **down** one character.

Ctrl-S or **Left Arrow** moves the cursor **left** one character.

Ctrl-D or **Right Arrow** moves the cursor **right** one character.

The position of these four keys (E, X, S, and D) provides a hint as to which way they move the cursor. Look at how they are arranged on the keyboard:

```
    E
 S   D
    X
```

Until the directions become automatic to your fingers (as they will, if you do enough editing!), thinking of the "magic diamond" will remind you which way the cursor will move for which keypress.

When you move the cursor to the bottom of the screen and press Ctrl-X one more time, the screen will scroll. All the lines on the screen will jump up by one, and the top line will disappear. As long as the cursor is on the bottom line of the screen and you continue to press Ctrl-X, the screen will scroll upward. If you use Ctrl-E to move the cursor back in the opposite direction (upward) until it hits the top of the screen, further Ctrl-Es will scroll the screen downward one line per Ctrl-E.

One Word at a Time

NASM-IDE will also move the cursor one word at a time to the left or right:

Ctrl-A or **Ctrl-Left Arrow** moves the cursor **left** one word.

Ctrl-F or **Ctrl-Right Arrow** moves the cursor **right** one word.

More hints are given here, since the A key is on the left side of the magic diamond, and the F key is on the right side of the magic diamond.

One Screen at a Time

It is also possible to move the cursor upward or downward through the file one whole screen at a time. *Upward* in this sense means toward the beginning of the file; *downward* means toward the end of the file. A screen is the height of your CRT display (25, 43, or 50 lines, depending on how you've configured the NASM-IDE environment) minus four lines for the menu and prompt bars and the edit window borders.

Ctrl-R or **PgUp** moves the cursor **up** one screen.

Ctrl-C or **PgDn** moves the cursor **down** one screen.

Moving the Cursor by Scrolling the Screen

I have described how the screen will scroll when you use the one-character-at-a-time commands to move upward (Ctrl-E) from the top line of the screen or downward (Ctrl-X) from the bottom line of the screen. You can scroll the screen upward or downward no matter where the cursor happens to be by using the scrolling commands:

Ctrl-W scrolls the screen **down** one line.

Ctrl-Z scrolls the screen **up** one line.

When you scroll the screen with these commands, the cursor rides with the screen as it scrolls upward or downward, *until* the cursor hits the top or bottom of the screen. Then further scrolling will make the screen slip past the cursor. The cursor will never vanish and will always be visible.

These are all of the cursor movement commands that may be invoked by one Ctrl keystroke. There are a few more that are accomplished by holding the Ctrl key down and pressing *two* keys in succession. *You must hold the Ctrl key down through both keypresses!*

Moving to the Ends of the Line

No matter where your cursor is on the screen, it is always within a line, even if that line happens to be empty of characters. There are two commands that will move the cursor either to the beginning (left end) of the line (screen column 1) or to the end of the line, which is the position following the last visible character on the line:

Ctrl-Q/S or **Home** sends the cursor to the **beginning** of the line.

Ctrl-Q/D or **End** sends the cursor to the **end** of the line.

Moving to the Ends of the File

The last set of cursor movement commands I describe takes the cursor to the beginning of the file or to the end of the file. If the file you are editing is more than a few screens long, it can save you a great deal of pounding on the keyboard to move one screen at a time.

Ctrl-Q/R or **Ctrl-PgUp** sends the cursor to the **beginning** of the file.

Ctrl-Q/C or **Ctrl-PgDn** sends the cursor to the **end** of the file.

Because all of the current file is in memory all of the time, moving between the ends of the file can be done *very* quickly.

Insert Mode and Cursor Coordinates

At the bottom edge of every edit window, toward the left side, are a pair of numbers indicating where the cursor is within the file. While you were moving the cursor around, the line and column numbers were continually changing to reflect the cursor's coordinates.

The number on the left is the line number, counting from the beginning of the file. The number on the right is the column number, reflecting the position of the cursor within its line. The line number always indicates the line in the file that contains the cursor—again, counting from the beginning of the file, *not* from the top of the screen.

There's another matter that you may or may not have noticed, and that is the state of the Insert toggle. A *toggle* is a condition that may exist in one of two different states. A toggle is like a switch controlling the lights in a room; the switch may be either on or off. The way you control the Insert toggle is with the Ins key: Tap Ins and you flip the state of the Insert toggle. Tap it again and you flip the state again.

The way you can monitor its state is by the shape of the text cursor in the edit window. The default is for Insert to be *on*. When Insert is on, the text cursor is a small flashing line. When Insert is off, the text cursor is a flashing block instead.

But what does it *do?* The Insert toggle determines how newly typed characters are added to your work file. When Insert is on (that is, if the cursor is a flashing line), characters that you type are *inserted* into the file. The characters appear over the cursor and immediately push the cursor and the rest of the line to the right to make room for themselves. The line becomes one character longer for each character that you type. If you press Enter, the cursor moves down one line, carrying with it the part of the line lying to its right.

When Insert is off (that is, if the cursor is a flashing block), characters that you type will *overwrite* characters that already exist in the file. Assuming you're typing in the middle of the file, somewhere within a line, you will overwrite one character for every character that you type. Only if you overwrite existing characters all the way to the end of the line or the end of the file and keep typing will the total number of characters in the file actually increase. If you press Enter, the cursor will move down to the first character of the next line down, but nothing else will change. A line will only be added to the file if you press Enter with the cursor on the *last* line of the file.

Turning Insert on and off is done with a single control keypress:

Ctrl-V or **Ins** toggles **Insert** on and off.

The Indent Toggle

Indent is another toggle. It indicates whether NASM-IDE's auto-indent feature is on or off. When Indent is on, the cursor will automatically move beneath the first visible character on a new line when you press Enter. In other words (assuming that Indent is on), given this little bit of text on your screen:

```
Adjust:
    MOV AX, [BP] + 6
    SUB AX, Increment_  <--Before pressing Enter

    _

  ^
  | After pressing Enter
```

Before pressing Enter, the cursor is at the end of the last line of text, immediately after the word "Increment." When you press Enter, the cursor will move down one line, but it will also space over to the right automatically until it is beneath the *S* in "SUB." This allows you to begin typing the next line of code without having to space the cursor over so that it is beneath the start of the previous line.

Like Insert, Indent can be toggled on and off. It takes a double control keystroke to do it:

Ctrl-Q/I toggles **Indent** on and off.

Indent is considered on when the letter *I* appears in the bottom line of the edit window frame, to the left of the cursor coordinates, almost in the corner. If the *I* is there, you will get an automatic indent to the start of the previous line when you press Enter to insert a new line.

Deleting Text

There are also a number of different ways to *delete* text in NASM-IDE. The simplest is to use the Del (Delete) key. Pressing Ctrl-G performs exactly the same delete function:

Ctrl-G or **Del** deletes one **character** to the **right** of the cursor.

The cursor does not move. It swallows the character to its right, and the rest of the line to its right moves over to fill in the position left by the deleted character. The Backspace key can be used to delete characters to the *left* of the cursor; another way it differs from Del is that the cursor rides to the left on each deletion:

Backspace deletes one **character** to the **left** of the cursor.

You can think of backspace as eating one character to the left as it moves the cursor leftward. You can also (to save a few keystrokes) delete one *word* to the right of the cursor:

Ctrl-T deletes one **word** to the **right** of the cursor.

When you press Ctrl-T, all characters from the cursor position rightward to the end of the current word will be deleted. If the cursor happens to be on a space or group of spaces between words, that space or spaces will be deleted up to the beginning of the next word. It's possible to delete from the cursor position to the end of the cursor line:

Ctrl-Q/Y deletes from the cursor to the **end of the line**.

And finally, it's possible to delete the entire cursor line with a single control keystroke:

Ctrl-Y deletes the entire **line** containing the cursor.

The line beneath the cursor moves up to take the place of the deleted line, pulling up the rest of the file behind it.

A warning here for those of you with thick fingers: The T and Y characters are right next to one another on the keyboard. In a late-night frenzy at the keyboard you may find yourself reaching for Ctrl-T to delete a word and hit Ctrl-Y instead, losing the entire line irretrievably. I've done this often enough that I simply broke myself of the habit of using Ctrl-T at all.

Undoing Changes to a Line

NASM-IDE's editor keeps a backup copy of each line while you're working on it, and retains that copy as long as the cursor remains within the line. Therefore, if you delete a word or some other portion of the line, or add something to a line by mistake, you can undo those changes to the line *as long as you haven't yet left the line*. Once you leave the line even momentarily, the editor throws away the backup copy, and Undo is no longer possible.

Ctrl-Q/L restores a line to its condition before you entered it.

One drawback is that the undo feature will *not* restore a line deleted partially with Ctrl-Q/Y or entirely with the Ctrl-Y command. Once a line is deleted, the cursor (by necessity) leaves the line, and so the editor does not retain the backup copy of the line. Be careful how you use Ctrl-Y!

Marking Text Blocks

For several kinds of operations, it's useful to be able to mark a text block. You might want to copy the text to the clipboard, cut the text to the clipboard, or delete the block of text entirely. A logical pointer embedded invisibly in your text called a *marker* is used to specify the beginning and end of a text block. There are only two of these markers, and in consequence only one block may be marked within a given file at any given time. These block markers are named B and K, after the commands that position them in your file. (You can try and remember them this way: B and K are on opposite ends of the word *block* and the markers mark opposite ends of a block of text.)

The block markers are invisible and do not appear on your screen in any way. If both are present in a file, however, all the text between them (that is, the currently marked block) is shown as highlighted text.

As with most things in NASM-IDE, there are two ways to mark a block of text with the block markers. The easy way is with the mouse. Simply click the mouse at the point in the file where you want the marked block of text to begin, and hold the left button down. With the left button held down, drag the cursor to the other end of the block. The text between the two ends of the block will become highlighted as you drag the mouse. When the end of the block is where you want it to be, just let go of the left mouse button. The block will remain highlighted until you move the cursor again.

Placing the block markers can be done from the keyboard with a pair of two-character control keystrokes:

Ctrl-K/B places the **B** marker.

Ctrl-K/K places the **K** marker.

Again, when you mark a block from the keyboard, the block will remain marked only until you move the cursor somehow. So, once you mark a block, do whatever you intend to do with the block immediately. As soon as you move the cursor by even one character, the block vanishes and is no longer marked.

The Clipboard and Block Commands

The simplest block command to understand is *Delete Block*. Getting rid of big chunks of text that are no longer needed is easy: Mark the text as a block, and then issue the Delete Block command:

Ctrl-K/Y or Ctrl-Del will **delete** a **block** of text.

For some reason, this command is called Clear in NASM-IDE's Edit menu. Delete or clear, it does the same thing: It wipes away the highlighted block of text.

The rest of the block commands mostly concern the clipboard. The *clipboard* is a special text buffer built into NASM-IDE, into which you can copy blocks of text, and from which you can insert text into different places in the same text file, or into entirely different text files. People who use Windows a lot will be familiar with the clipboard, though there was no direct equivalent under DOS.

Copy is useful when you have some standard text construction (a standard boilerplate comment header for procedures, perhaps) that you need to use several times within the same text file. Rather than type it from the keyboard each time, you type it once, mark it as a block, and then copy it to the clipboard by pressing Ctrl-Ins.

Ctrl-Ins will **copy** the highlighted block of text to the **clipboard**.

Once it's in the clipboard, you move the cursor position to where you need it. Simply put the cursor where the first character of the copied text must go, and then issue the *Paste* command:

Shift-Ins will **paste** the clipboard contents to the cursor position.

Moving a block of text is similar to copying a block of text. The difference, of course, is that the marked block of text vanishes from its original position and reappears at the cursor position. It must pass through the clipboard on its way from one place to another. As with copying a block, the process of moving text requires two operations: First you *cut* the block from its original position into the clipboard, and then you paste the block from the clipboard to the cursor position. Cutting the block is done by highlighting a block of text and then pressing Shift-Del:

Shift-Del will **cut** the highlighted **block** of text to the **clipboard**.

Once the block of text is in the clipboard, you can use the Shift-Ins hot key to paste the text from the clipboard to the cursor position, just as you did to copy a block to multiple places in the file or in different files.

All of the clipboard-related commands may also be given from the Edit menu. Once you mark a block by highlighting it, you can pull down the Edit menu and select the Cut, Copy, or Clear items to act on the marked block. Once you have some text in the clipboard, you can pull down the Edit menu and select Paste to paste the clipboard text into the current file at the cursor position.

One final clipboard command allows you to actually look at what text is currently in the clipboard. This command is available only from the Edit menu. When you select Edit | Show clipboard, a text window will open that shows exactly what text is in the clipboard. You can edit the text if you like, and your changes will be reflected in the text that you paste into your other file or files.

When you're finished looking at the clipboard text in its window, click on the close control (the small square on the left end of the top edge of the window) and it will close. The clipboard text, however, remains on the clipboard.

Searching for Text

Much of the power of electronic text editing lies in its ability to search for a particular character pattern in a text file. Furthermore, once found, it's a logical extension of the search concept to replace the found text string with a different text string. For example, if you decide to change the name of a variable to avoid conflict with another identifier in a program, you might wish to have the text editor locate *every* instance of the old variable name in a program and replace each one with the new variable name.

NASM-IDE's editor can do both search and search/replace operations with great ease—and such easy searching makes page numbering unnecessary. If you wish to work on the part of a program that contains a particular procedure, all you need do is search for that procedure's name and you will move the cursor right to the spot you want:

Ctrl-Q/F will **find** a given text string.

The Find command can also be issued from the menu bar by selecting the Search | Find menu item. When you issue the Find command (either from the keyboard or from the menu; it doesn't matter), NASM-IDE brings up a dialog box to find out what you want to find and how you want to configure the search. This dialog is shown in Figure 5.7.

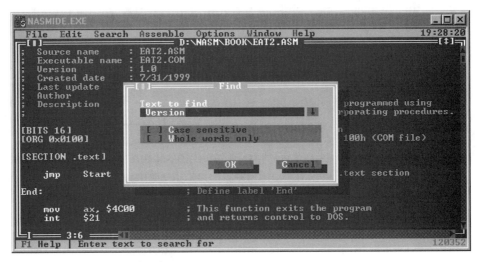

Figure 5.7 The Find dialog box.

The text that you're searching for goes in the Text to find edit field in the dialog box. You then tab down to the two options fields. These are check boxes, and they both default to blank. The first specifies a case-sensitive search. If you check it, the text found must match the text you enter in Text to find both in characters and in case.

The second check box specifies that the search must be for Whole words only. This allows you to avoid finding strings inside of larger strings. For example: Suppose you're looking for the register name "AX." In the middle of your assembly file, you have a comment that reads like this:

```
; Axe the dead space at the end of the string
```

If you don't check Whole words only, your search for "AX" will also find "Axe" because "ax" is inside "axe." You could also discriminate between the two by case, but that's less reliable, especially when you're searching source code files written by other people who may have entirely different habits in using character case. (Or who aren't consistent in how they use it—that's even worse.)

If Whole words only is checked, a search for "AX" will not find "Axe," or "Tax," or "maximum," or anything else that isn't simply . . . "AX."

Once you have the Find dialog box filled in the way you want it, press the OK button. The search will commence, and if the search is successful the cursor will move to the first character of the first instance of the found text string. If the editor cannot find any instance of the requested text string in the work file, it displays an error message box containing the message "Search string not found." You must then click on the OK button to continue editing.

Searching for Additional Instances

Most assembly language source code files will have multiple instances of common identifiers like "AX." If you want to find not the first one but the third or fourth (or one further down that you know you can identify from its context), you need to search for additional instances of the text. NASM-IDE has a command for this as well: Search again. This command may be issued from the menu bar, by selecting menu item Search | Search again. The shortcut for Search again is Ctrl-L, which is *very* handy. (Sometimes using the mouse is more hand motion than it needs to be.)

Ctrl-L will **find** (or **replace**) the **next instance** of a given text string.

Replacing Found Text

Many times, the whole reason for finding a text string is to replace it with something else—sometimes not simply once but for every instance of the text string in the file. NASM-IDE has special machinery to do exactly this: the Replace command. Once the search text is found, NASM-IDE will replace the search text with replacement text that you provide.

As with Find, you can issue the Replace command either from the menu bar by selecting the Search | Replace menu item, or from the keyboard, by pressing Ctrl-QA.

Ctrl-QA will **find** and **replace** a given text string with your text.

As with Find, the Replace command brings up a dialog box, (shown in Figure 5.8) into which you must enter:

1. The text you're searching for.
2. The text you want to replace the found text with.
3. The kind of search you want to conduct (that is, whole words only or case-sensitive or both).
4. Whether to prompt for each replacement.
5. Whether to swoop through the file and replace all instances of the original text with your replacement text.

The search options are the same as those I described for the Find command. If you leave the Replace dialog box in its default state and click OK, the editor will locate the first instance of the search string, highlight it, and display another dialog box that asks the question: "Replace this instance?" You can click on the Yes button to replace the instance, the No button to leave it alone, or the Cancel button to end the Replace operation entirely. (Cancel is most useful when you're doing a Replace all operation and running through the whole file replacing every instance of some text string.)

Note that just as with the Find command, you can use the Ctrl-L hot key to perform a subsequent Replace command on the next instance of the text string you just replaced. Each Ctrl-L will locate and replace the next instance of the search text until no more instances of the search text are found in the file.

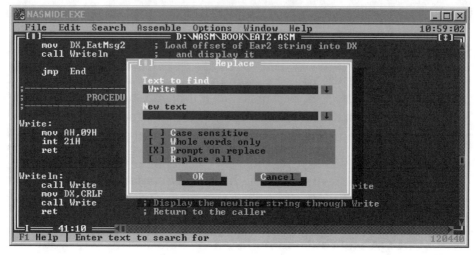

Figure 5.8 The Replace dialog box.

Saving Your Work

It's *very* important to keep in mind what is happening while you edit text files with the editor. *You are editing entirely within memory.* Nothing goes out to disk while you are actually doing the edit. You can work on a file for hours, and one power failure or dog tripping over your PC's power cord will throw it all away. You must develop the discipline of saving your work every so often.

You can save your work by going to the menu bar, pulling down the File menu, and selecting the Save item. But the easiest way to execute a Save command from within the editor is with the Save shortcut, F2.

F2 saves your work file.

Press F2 early and often. Everything depends on it.

Other NASM-IDE Features

Most of what you do with NASM-IDE involves editing assembly language source code files, but by no means all. In this final section of the chapter I discuss some of the other things that NASM-IDE can do.

Exiting NASM-IDE

There is more than one way to get out of NASM-IDE once you're finished with the job at hand. The File menu has an Exit item, and that's the easiest to remember, and it will do the job. The shortcut for the File | Exit menu item is Alt-X:

Alt-X **exits** to DOS.

NASM-IDE keeps track of whether a file has been changed by you since the last time it was saved to disk. If you attempt to exit NASM-IDE with unsaved changes on deck, NASM-IDE will bring up a dialog box asking if you want to save your changes. Most of the time you do—and in most cases you'll click the Yes button. But other occasions might arise when the best thing to do is abandon a changed file and start again. The most common example of this is a careless Replace all command that went through your entire file and did a lot of unintended and difficult-to-reverse things. The best thing to do in such a case is leave NASM-IDE without saving the damaged file, and then coming back in with the most recent copy. This is another good reason to save often: You don't want to abandon a bad "Replace all" change (what some programmers have with grim remembrance come to call a "search and destroy") along with two hours' worth of useful work.

Save often. And know when not to save. It's all part of the game.

Changing the Display Size

By default, NASM-IDE brings up a traditional 25-line by 80-character DOS text screen. This isn't a lot of room to move, especially when virtually every modern display adapter is capable of showing you either 43 lines (on some ancient hardware) or 50 lines on a text screen. When I use NASM-IDE in my own work, I use 50 lines, every time.

Setting it up is easy. Pull down the Options | Environment menu item. The dialog box shown in Figure 5.9 will appear. The top pane governs your screen size. The default is 25 lines, but you can check 43/50 instead by clicking on the 43/50 lines button. Then when you click on OK, the screen size will change immediately.

What it changes to depends on your hardware. If you have an EGA (Enhanced Graphics Adapter) (which is most unlikely in the year 2000),

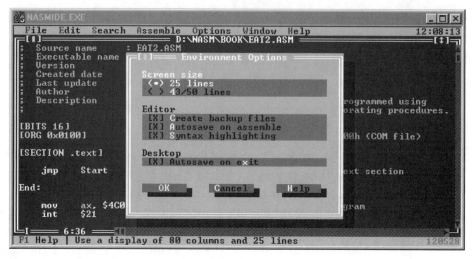

Figure 5.9 The Environment Options dialog box.

you'll get a 43-line screen. If you have a VGA (Video Graphics Array) or anything more recent than the VGA, you'll get a 50-line screen. Note that these are mutually exclusive; a single system cannot (as far as I know) let you choose from 43 lines or 50 lines. You get the big screen, however many lines that works out to on your particular hardware.

DOS Shell

People who have grown up using nothing but Microsoft Windows have a little trouble sometimes understanding what a DOS shell is or why it's useful. The answer, of course, is that there was a time when we didn't have Windows and couldn't just click on a window and open up another program without closing the first one.

But a DOS shell was a very handy thing to have in the DOS era, and NASM-IDE provides one. If you select the File I DOS shell menu item, NASM-IDE will tuck itself away and open up a DOS shell. It's like exiting NASM-IDE without really exiting it. You can run DOS programs, look at and copy files, and so on. When you're done, you simply type "exit" and press Enter and in a pop you're back inside NASM-IDE as though you'd never left.

This is still useful for doing things like invoking your linker, since NASM-IDE doesn't do that for you. I return to the DOS shell when we discuss linking modular files later in this book.

CHAPTER 6

An Uneasy Alliance

The x86 CPU and Its Segmented Memory System

As comedian Bill Cosby once said: I told you that story so I could tell you *this* one . . . We're pretty close to a third finished with this book, and I haven't even begun describing the principal element in PC assembly language: the x86 CPU. Most books on assembly language, even those targeted at beginners, assume that the CPU is as good a place as any to start their story, without considering the mass of groundwork without which most beginning programmers get totally lost and give up.

That's why I began at the *real* beginning, and took 150 pages to get to where the other guys start.

Keep in mind that this book was created to supply that essential groundwork. It is *not* a complete course in PC assembly language. Once you run off the end of this book, you'll have one leg up on any of the multitude of beginner books on assembly language from other publishers.

And it's high time we got right to the heart of things, and met the foreman of the PC itself.

The Joy of Memory Models

I wrote this book in large part because I could not find a beginning text in assembly language that I respected in the least. Nearly all books on assembly start by introducing the concept of an instruction set, and then begin describing machine instructions, one by one. This is moronic, and the authors of such books should be hung. *Even if you've learned every single instruction in an instruction set, you haven't learned assembly language.*

You haven't even come close.

The naïve objection that a CPU exists to execute machine instructions can be disposed of pretty easily: It executes machine instructions once it has them in its electronic hands. The *real* job of a CPU, and the real challenge of assembly language, lies in locating the required instructions and data in memory. Any idiot can learn machine instructions. (Many do.) *The skill of assembly language consists of a deep comprehension of memory addressing.* Everything else is details—and easy details, at that.

This is a difficult business, made much more difficult by the fact that there are a fair number of different ways to address memory in the x86 CPU family. (The "x86" indicates any member of Intel's microprocessor family that includes the 8086, 8088, 80286, 80386, 80486, Pentium, and the Pentium descendents.) Each of these ways is called a *memory model*. There are three major memory models that you can use with the more recent members of the x86 CPU family, and a number of minor variations on those three, especially the one in the middle.

The oldest memory model is called *real mode flat model*. It's relatively straightforward. The middle-aged memory model is called the *real mode segmented model*. It may be the most hateful thing you ever have to learn in *any* kind of programming, assembly or otherwise. DOS programming at its peak used the real mode segmented model. The newest memory model is called *protected mode flat model*, and it's the memory model behind modern operating systems such as Windows NT and Linux. (Note that the protected mode flat model is available only on the 386 and newer CPUs. The 8086, 8088, and 286 do not support it.) Windows 9*x* falls somewhere between models, and I doubt anybody except the people at Microsoft really understands all the kinks in the ways it addresses memory—maybe not even them. Windows 9*x* crashes all the time, and one main reason in my view is that it has a completely insane memory model. (Dynamic link libraries, or DLLs—a pox on *homo computationis*—are the other major reason.) Its gonzo memory model isn't the only reason you shouldn't consider writing Win 9*x* programs in assembly, but it's certainly the best one.

I have a strategy in this book, and before we dive in, I'll lay it out: I will begin by teaching you programming under the real mode flat model, under DOS. It's amazingly easy to learn. I will discuss real mode segmented model because you will keep stubbing your toe on it here and there and need to know it, even if you never do any serious programming in it. However, the future lies in protected mode flat model, especially under Linux. It's also amazingly easy to learn—the hard part is fooling with all the Linux system calls that don't exist under DOS. And the key is this: *Real mode flat model is very much like protected mode flat model in miniature.*

There is a big flat model, and a little flat model. If you grasp real mode flat model, you will have no trouble with protected mode flat model. That monkey in the middle is just the dues you have to pay to consider yourself a real master of memory addressing.

So let's go see how this crazy stuff works.

16 Bits'll Buy You 64K

The year I graduated from college, Intel introduced the 8080 CPU and basically invented microcomputing. (Yes, I'm an old guy, but I've been blessed with a sense of history—by virtue of having lived through quite a bit of it.) That was 1974, and the 8080 was a white-hot little item at the time. I had one that ran at 1 MHz, and it was a pretty effective word processor, which is mostly what I did with it.

The 8080 was an 8-bit CPU, meaning that it processed 8 bits of information at a time. However, it had 16 address lines coming out of it. The "bitness" of a CPU—how many bits wide its accumulator and general-purpose registers are—is important, but to my view the far more important measure of a CPU's effectiveness is how many address lines it can muster in one operation. In 1974, 16 address lines was aggressive, because memory was *extremely* expensive, and most machines had 4K or 8K bytes at very most—and some had a lot less.

Sixteen address lines will address 64K bytes. If you count in binary (which computers always do) and limit yourself to 16 binary columns, you can count from 0 to 65,535. (The colloquial "64K" is shorthand for the number 66,536.) This means that every one of 65,536 separate memory locations can have its own unique number, from 0 up to 65,535. This number is an *address*, a concept I introduced functionally back in Chapter 3. If you want to find out what's recorded in memory location number 24,263, you place the number 24,263 on a memory system's address lines, and the memory system will read the contents at that location and send them back to you.

The 8080 memory-addressing scheme was very simple: You put a 16-bit address out on the address lines, and you got back the 8-bit value that was stored at that address. Note well: There is *no* necessary relation between the number of address lines in a memory system and the size of the data stored at each location. The 8080 stored 8 bits at each location, but it could have stored 16 or even 32 bits at each location, and still had 16 memory address lines.

By far and away, the operating system most used with the 8080 was CP/M-80. CP/M-80 was a little unusual in that it existed at the *top* of installed memory—sometimes so that it could be contained in ROM, but mostly just to get it out of the way and allow a consistent memory starting point for *transient programs*—those that (unlike the operating system) were loaded into memory and run only when needed. When CP/M-80 read a program in from disk to run it, it would load the program into low memory, at address 0100H—that is, 256 bytes from the bottom of memory. The first 256 bytes of memory were called the *program segment prefix* (PSP) and contained various odd bits of information as well as a general-purpose memory buffer for the program's disk input/output (I/O). But the executable code itself did not begin until address 0100H.

I've drawn the 8080 and CP/M-80 memory model in Figure 6.1.

The 8080's memory model as used with CP/M-80 was simple, and people used it a lot. So, when Intel created its first 16-bit CPU, the 8086, it wanted to make it easy for people to translate CP/M-80 software from the 8080 to the 8086—what we call *porting*. One way to do this was to make sure that a 16-bit addressing system such as that of the 8080 still worked. So, even though the 8086 could address 16 times as much memory as the 8080 (16 x 64K = 1 MB), Intel set up the 8086 so that a program could take some 64K byte segment within that megabyte of memory and run entirely inside it, just as though it were the smaller 8080 memory system.

This was done by the use of *segment registers*—which are basically memory pointers located in CPU registers that point to a place in memory where things begin, whether this be data storage, code execution, what-

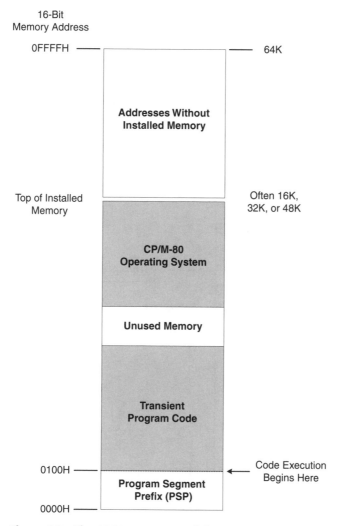

16-Bit
Memory Address

0FFFFH ———— 64K

**Addresses Without
Installed Memory**

Top of Installed
Memory

Often 16K,
32K, or 48K

**CP/M-80
Operating System**

Unused Memory

**Transient
Program Code**

0100H ———— Code Execution
Begins Here

**Program Segment
Prefix (PSP)**

0000H ————

Figure 6.1 The 8080 memory model.

ever. We'll have a lot more to say about the use of segment registers very shortly. For now, it suffices to think of them as pointers indicating where, within the 8086's megabyte of memory, a program ported from the 8080 world would begin. See Figure 6.2.

When speaking of the 8086 and 8088, there are four segment registers to consider—and again, we'll be dealing with them in detail very soon. But for the purposes of Figure 6.2, consider the register called CS— which stands for *code segment*. Again, it's a pointer pointing to a location within the 8086's megabyte of memory. This location acts as the starting

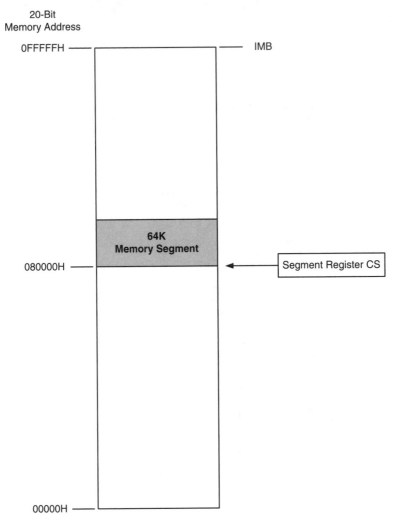

Figure 6.2 The 8080 memory model inside an 8086 memory system.

point for a 64K region of memory, within which a quickly converted CP/M-80 program can run very happily.

This was very wise short-term thinking—and catastrophically bad long-term thinking. Any number of CP/M-80 programs were converted to the 8086 within a couple of years. The problems began big time when programmers attempted to create new programs from scratch that had never seen the 8080 and had no need for the segmented memory model. Too bad—the segmented model dominated the architecture of the 8086. Programs that needed more than 64K of memory at a time had to use memory in 64K chunks, switching between chunks by switching values into and out of segment registers.

This was, and is, a nightmare. There is one good reason to learn it, however: Understanding the way segments work will help you understand how the two x86 flat models work, and in the process you will come to understand the nature of the CPU a lot better.

So, having worked my way up to the good stuff, I find myself faced with a tricky conundrum. Programming involves two major components of the PC: the CPU and memory. Most books begin by choosing one or the other and describing it. My own opinion is that you can't really describe memory and memory addressing without describing the CPU, and you can't really describe the CPU without going into memory and memory addressing.

So let's do both at once.

The Nature of a Megabyte

When running in segmented real mode, the x86 CPUs can use up to a megabyte of directly addressable memory. This memory is also called *real mode memory*. Most modern x86 machines have a lot more memory than that—typically 32 MB or more. (My own machines have 256 MB of memory.) However, most modern x86 machines run in protected mode, which can address up to 4 gigabytes of memory. We return to protected mode in a big way toward the end of this book, in discussing Linux.

As I discussed briefly in Chapter 3, a megabyte of memory is actually not 1 million bytes of memory, but 1,048,576 bytes. It doesn't come out even in our base 10 because computers insist on base 2. Those 1,048,576 bytes expressed in base 2 are 100000000000000000000B bytes. (We don't use commas in base 2—that's yet another way to differentiate binary notation from decimal apart from the suffixed *B*.) That's 2^{20}, a fact that we'll return to shortly. The number 100000000000000000000B is so bulky that it's better to express it in the compatible (and much more compact) base 16, which we call hexadecimal. The quantity 2^{20} is equivalent to 16^5, and may be written in hexadecimal as 100000H. (If the notion of number bases still confounds you, I'd recommend another trip through Chapter 2, if you haven't been through it already. Or, perhaps, even if you have.)

Now, here's a tricky and absolutely critical question: In a bank of memory containing 100000H bytes, what's the address of the very last byte in the memory bank? The answer is *not* 100000H. The clue is the flip side to that question: What's the address of the *first* byte in memory? That answer, you might recall, is 0. *Computers always begin counting from 0.* It's a dichotomy that will occur again and again in computer programming. The last in a row of four items is item number 3, because the first item in a row of four is item number 0. Count: 0, 1, 2, 3.

The address of a byte in a memory bank is just the number of that byte *starting from zero.* This means that the last, or highest, address in a memory bank containing 1 megabyte is 100000H minus one, or 0FFFFFH. (The initial zero, while not mathematically necessary, is there for the convenience of your assembler. Get in the habit of using an initial zero on any hex number beginning with the hex digits A through F.)

The addresses in a megabyte of memory, then, run from 00000H to 0FFFFFH. In binary notation, that is equivalent to the range of 00000000000000000000B to 11111111111111111111B. That's a lot of bits— 20, to be exact. If you look back to Figure 3.3 in Chapter 3, you'll see that a megabyte memory bank has 20 address lines. One of those 20 bits is routed to each of those 20 address lines, so that any address expressed as 20 bits will identify one and only one of the 1,048,576 bytes contained in the memory bank.

That's what a megabyte of memory is: some arrangement of memory chips within the computer, connected by an address bus of 20 lines. A 20-bit address is fed to those 20 address lines to identify 1 byte out of the megabyte.

Backward Compatibility

Modern x86 CPUs such as the Pentium can address much more memory than this and have a lot of machinery that I won't be discussing in this book. With the 8086 and 8088 CPUs, the 20 address lines and 1 megabyte of memory was literally all they had. They didn't speak of the real mode segmented model back in the 8088 era because that one model was all there was.

More powerful memory models didn't really come about until the appearance of the 80386 in 1986. The 386 was Intel's first true 32-bit CPU, and the first to fully implement a 32-bit protected mode. The 80286 was a transitional CPU that tried—but did not completely succeed—in implementing a protected mode. People simply used it as a faster 8088. (Later on, I talk more about what the "protected" in "protected mode" means.) The 386 and later Intel CPUs could address 4 gigabytes of memory without carving it up into smaller segments. In the 32-bit CPUs, a segment *is* 4 gigabytes—so one segment is, for the most part, plenty.

However, a huge pile of DOS software written to make use of segments was everywhere around and had to be dealt with. So, to maintain *backward compatibility* with the ancient 8086 and 8088, newer CPUs were given the power to limit themselves to what the older chips could address and execute. When a Pentium CPU places itself into real mode segmented model, it very nearly *becomes* an 8086. This may seem a waste, but it allows the Pentium to run old DOS software originally written for the 8086. Think of it as training wheels to get you up to speed in assembly language.

Whenever a newer CPU such as the 386 or Pentium is set up to look like an 8086, we say that it is in *real mode*. The term *real mode* was coined as a contrast to *protected mode*, which is the much more powerful mode used in newer operating systems (such as Windows 9*x* and NT, as well as Linux) that allows the operating system much more control over what programs running on the machine can do.

When you launch an MS-DOS window or "DOS box" under Windows 9*x* or NT, you're creating what amounts to a little real mode island inside the Windows protected mode memory system. If you have a Windows machine, you should do all your assembly language for this book in an MS-DOS window, so that real mode conventions apply. (For Linux, obviously, this limitation does not apply!)

16-Bit Blinders

In real mode segmented model, an x86 CPU can "see" a full megabyte of memory. That is, the CPU chips set themselves up so that they can use 20 of their 32 address pins and can pass a 20-bit address to the memory system. From that perspective, it seems pretty simple and straightforward. However, . . . the bulk of all the trouble you're ever likely to have in understanding real mode segmented model stems from this fact: that whereas those CPUs can see a full megabyte of memory, they are constrained to look at that megabyte through 16-bit blinders.

You may call this peculiar. (If you do any significant amount of programming in this mode, you'll probably call it much worse.) But you *must* understand it, and understand it thoroughly.

The blinders metaphor is closer to literal than you might think. Look at Figure 6.3. The long rectangle represents the megabyte of memory that the CPU can address in real mode segmented model. The CPU is off to the right. In the middle is a piece of metaphorical cardboard with a slot cut in it. The slot is 1 byte wide and 65,536 bytes long. The CPU can slide that piece of cardboard up and down the full length of its memory system. However, *at any one time*, it can only access 65,536 bytes.

The CPU's view of memory in real mode segmented model is peculiar. It is constrained to look at memory in chunks, where no chunk is larger than 65,536 bytes in length—what we call "64K." Making use of those chunks—that is, knowing which one is currently in use and how to move from one to another—is the real skill of real mode segmented model programming. The chunks are called *segments*, and it's time to take a closer look at what they are and how they're used.

The Nature of Segments

We've spoken informally of segments so far as chunks of memory within the larger megabyte memory space that the CPU can see and use in real mode segmented model. More formally, a *segment* is a region of memory that begins on a paragraph boundary and extends for some number of bytes. In real mode segmented model this number is less than or equal to 64K (65,536). We've spoken of the number 64K before. But paragraphs?

Time out for a lesson in 86-family trivia. A *paragraph* is a measure of memory equal to 16 bytes. It is one of numerous technical terms used to describe various quantities of memory. We've spoken of some of them before, and all of them are even multiples of 1 byte. Bytes are data atoms, remember; loose memory bits never exist in the absence of a byte of memory to contain them. These terms are of uneven usefulness, but you should be aware of all of them, which are given in Table 6.1.

Table 6.1 lists two names for each term. Some of these terms, such as ten byte, occur very rarely, and others, such as page, occur almost never. The term *paragraph* is almost never used, *except* in connection with the places where segments may begin.

Any memory address evenly divisible by 16 is called a *paragraph boundary*. The first paragraph boundary is address 0. The second is address

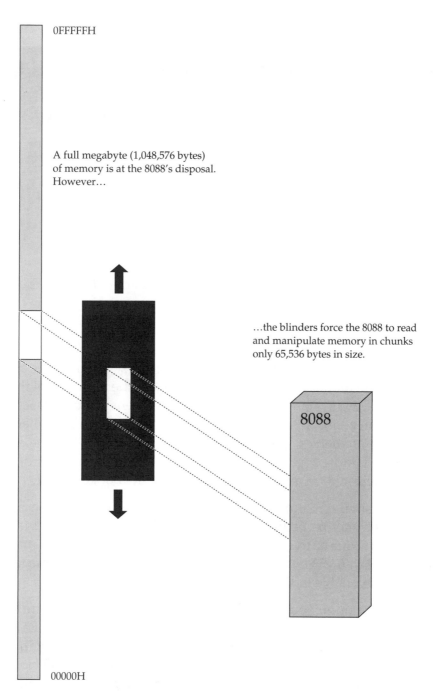

0FFFFFH

A full megabyte (1,048,576 bytes)
of memory is at the 8088's disposal.
However…

…the blinders force the 8088 to read
and manipulate memory in chunks
only 65,536 bytes in size.

8088

00000H

Figure 6.3 Seeing a megabyte through 64K blinders.

Table 6.1 Collective Terms for Memory

NAME	VALUE DECIMAL	HEX
Byte	1	01H
Word	2	02H
Double word	4	04H
Quad word	8	08H
Ten byte	10	0AH
Paragraph	16	10H
Page	256	100H
Segment	65,536	10000H

10H; the third address 20H, and so on. (Remember that 10H is equal to decimal 16.) Any paragraph boundary may be considered the start of a segment.

This *doesn't* mean that a segment actually starts every 16 bytes up and down throughout that megabyte of memory. A segment is like a shelf in one of those modern adjustable bookcases. On the back face of the bookcase are a great many little slots spaced one-half inch apart. A shelf bracket can be inserted into any of the little slots. However, there aren't hundreds of shelves, but only four or five. Nearly all of the slots are empty and unused. They exist so that a much smaller number of shelves may be adjusted up and down the height of the bookcase as needed.

In a very similar manner, paragraph boundaries are little slots at which a segment may be begun. An assembly language program may make use of only four or five segments, but each of those segments may begin at any of the 65,536 paragraph boundaries existing in the megabyte of memory available in the real mode segmented model.

There's that number again: 65,536—our beloved 64K. There are 64K different paragraph boundaries where a segment may begin. Each paragraph boundary has a number. As always, the numbers begin from 0, and go to 64K minus one; in decimal 65,535, or in hex 0FFFFH. Because a segment may begin at any paragraph boundary, the number of the paragraph boundary at which a segment begins is called the *segment address* of that particular segment. We rarely, in fact, speak of paragraphs or paragraph boundaries at all. When you see the term *segment address*, keep in mind that each segment address is 16 bytes (one paragraph) farther along in memory than the segment address before it. See Figure 6.4.

In short, segments may begin at any segment address. There are 65,536 segment addresses evenly distributed across real mode's full megabyte of memory, 16 bytes apart. A segment address is more a permission than a compulsion; for all the 64K possible segment addresses, only five or six are ever actually used to begin segments at any one time. Think of segment addresses as slots where segments may be placed.

So much for segment addresses; now, what of segments themselves? The most important thing to understand is that a segment may be up to

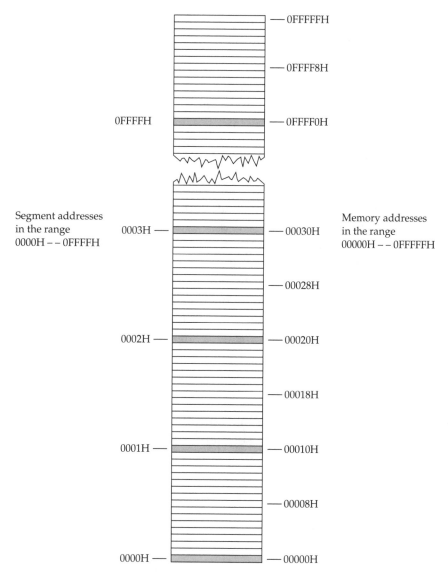

Figure 6.4 Memory addresses versus segment addresses.

64K bytes in size, but it doesn't *have* to be. A segment may be only 1 byte long, or 256 bytes long, or 21,378 bytes long, or any length at all short of 64K bytes.

A Horizon, Not a Place

You define a segment primarily by stating where it begins. What, then, defines how *long* a segment is? Nothing, really—and we get into some really tricky semantics here. A segment is more a *horizon* than a *place*. Once you define where a segment begins, that segment can encompass any location in memory between that starting place and the horizon— which is 65,536 bytes down the line.

Nothing says, of course, that a segment must use all of that memory. In most cases, when you define a segment to exist at some segment address, you only end up considering the next few hundred bytes as part of that segment, until you get into some truly world-class programs. Most beginners read about segments and think of them as some kind of memory allocation, a protected region of memory with walls on both sides, reserved for some specific use.

This is about as far from true as you can get. In real mode nothing is protected within a segment, and segments are not reserved for any specific register or access method. Segments can overlap. (People often don't think about or realize this.) In a very real sense, segments don't really exist, *except* as horizons beyond which a certain type of memory reference cannot go. It comes back to that set of 64K blinders that the CPU wears, as I drew in Figure 6.3. I think of it this way: *A segment is the location in memory at which the CPU's 64K blinders are positioned.* In looking at memory through the blinders, you can see bytes starting at the segment address and going on until the blinders cut you off, 64K bytes down the way.

The key to understanding this admittedly metaphysical definition of a segment is knowing how segments are used. And coming to understand that finally brings us to the subject of registers.

Making 20-Bit Addresses
out of 16-Bit Registers

A *register*, as I've hinted before, is a memory location *inside* the CPU chip rather than outside the CPU in a memory bank somewhere. The

8088, 8086, and 80286 are often called 16-bit CPUs because their internal registers are almost all 16 bits in size. The 80386 and its successors are called 32-bit CPUs because most of their internal registers are 32 bits in size. The x86 CPUs have a fair number of registers, and they are an interesting crew indeed.

Registers do many jobs, but one of their more important jobs is holding addresses of important locations in memory. If you'll recall, the 8086 and 8088 have 20 address pins, and their megabyte of memory (which is the real mode segmented memory we're talking about) requires addresses 20 bits in size.

How do you put a 20-bit memory address in a 16-bit register?

Easy. You don't.

You put a 20-bit address in *two* 16-bit registers.

What happens is this: All memory locations in real mode's megabyte of memory have not one address but *two*. Every byte in memory is assumed to reside in a segment. A byte's complete address, then, consists of the address of its segment, along with the distance of the byte from the start of that segment. The address of the segment is (as we said before) the byte's *segment address*. The byte's distance from the start of the segment is the byte's *offset address*. Both addresses must be specified to completely describe any single byte's location within the full megabyte of real mode memory. When written out, the segment address comes first, followed by the offset address. The two are separated with a colon. Segment:offset addresses are always written in hexadecimal. Make sure that the colon is there so that people know you're specifying an address and not just a couple of numbers!

I've drawn Figure 6.5 to help make this a little clearer. A byte of data we'll call **MyByte** exists in memory at the location marked. Its address is given as 0001:001D. This means that **MyByte** falls within segment 0001H and is located 001DH bytes from the start of that segment. Note that when two numbers are used to specify an address with a colon between them, you do *not* end each of the two numbers with an *H* for hexadecimal.

You can omit leading zeros if you like; that is, instead of saying 00B2:0004 you could write 0B2:4. (The leading zero is retained in front of the *B* in keeping with assembly language policy of never allowing a hex number to begin with the hex digits A through F.) As a good rule of

MyByte could have any of three
possible addresses:

0000H : 002DH
0001H : 001DH
0002H : 000DH

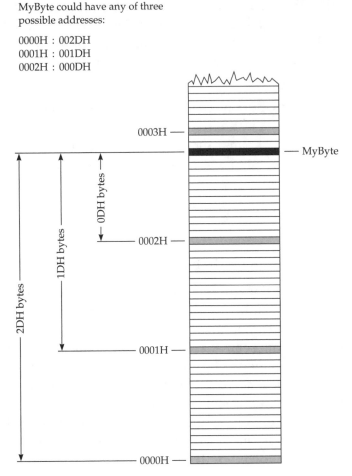

Figure 6.5 Segments and offsets.

thumb, however, I recommend using all four hex digits in both components of the address *except* when all four digits are zeros. In other
words, you can abbreviate 0000:0061 to 0:0061 or 0B00:0000 to 0B00:0.

The universe is perverse, however, and clever eyes will perceive that
MyByte can have two other perfectly legal addresses: 0:002D and
0002:000D. How so? Keep in mind that a segment may start every 16
bytes throughout the full megabyte of real memory. A segment, once
begun, embraces all bytes from its origin to 65,535 bytes further up in
memory. There's nothing wrong with segments overlapping, and in
Figure 6.3 we have three overlapping segments. **MyByte** is 2DH bytes
into the first segment, which begins at segment address 0000H. **MyByte**
is 1DH bytes into the second segment, which begins at segment address

0001H. It's not that **MyByte** is in two or three places at once. It's in only one place, but that one place may be described in any of three ways.

It's a little like Chicago's street-numbering system. Howard Street is 76 blocks north of Chicago's "origin," Madison Street. Howard Street is, however, only 4 blocks north of Touhy Avenue. You can describe Howard Street's location relative to either Madison Street or Touhy Avenue, depending on what you want to do.

An arbitrary byte somewhere in the middle of real mode's megabyte of memory may fall within literally tens of thousands of different segments. Which segment the byte is *actually* in is strictly a matter of convention.

This problem appears in real life to confront programmers of the IBM PC. The PC keeps its time and date information in a series of memory bytes that starts at address 0040:006C. There is also a series of memory bytes containing PC timer information located at 0000:046C. You guessed it—we're talking about exactly the same starting byte. Different writers speaking of that same byte may give its address in either of those two ways, and they'll all be completely correct.

The way, then, to express a 20-bit address in two 16-bit registers is to put the segment address into one 16-bit register, and the offset address into another 16-bit register. The two registers taken together identify 1 byte among all 1,048,576 bytes in real mode's megabyte of memory.

Is this awkward? You bet. But it was the best we could do for a good many years.

16-Bit and 32-Bit Registers

Think of the segment address as the starting position of real mode's 64K blinders. Typically, you'll move the blinders to encompass the location where you wish to work, and then leave the blinders in one place while moving around within their 64K limits.

This is exactly how registers tend to be used in real mode segmented model assembly language. The 8088, 8086, and 80286 have exactly four segment registers specifically designated as holders of segment addresses. The 386 and later CPUs have two more that can be used in real mode. (You need to be aware of the kind of machine you're running on if you intend to use the two additional segment registers.) Each segment register is a 16-bit memory location existing within the CPU chip itself. No matter what the CPU is doing, if it's addressing some location in memory, the segment address of that location is present in one of the six segment registers.

The segment registers have names that reflect their general functions: CS, DS, SS, ES, FS, and GS. FS and GS exist only in the 386 and later Intel x86 CPUs—but are still 16 bits in size. *All segment registers are 16 bits in size, irrespective of the CPU.*

- *CS stands for code segment.* Machine instructions exist at some offset into a code segment. The segment address of the code segment of the currently executing instruction is contained in CS.

- *DS stands for data segment.* Variables and other data exist at some offset into a data segment. There may be many data segments, but the CPU may only use one at a time, by placing the segment address of that segment in register DS.

- *SS stands for stack segment.* The *stack* is a very important component of the CPU used for temporary storage of data and addresses. I explain how the stack works a little later; for now simply understand that, like everything else within the 8086/8088's megabyte of memory, the stack has a segment address, which is contained in SS.

- *ES stands for extra segment.* The extra segment is exactly that: a spare segment that may be used for specifying a location in memory.

- *FS and GS are clones of ES.* They are both additional segments with no specific job or specialty. Their names come from the fact that they were created after ES. (Think, E, F, G.) Don't forget that they exist *only* in the 386 and later x86 CPUs!

General-Purpose Registers

The segment registers exist only to hold segment addresses. They can be forced to do a very few other things, but by and large, segment registers should be considered specialists in segment address containing. The x86 CPUs have a crew of generalist registers to do the rest of the work of assembly language computing. Among many other things, these *general-purpose registers* are used to hold the offset addresses that must be paired with segment addresses to pin down a single location in memory. They also hold values for arithmetic manipulation, for bit-shifting (more on this later), and many other things. They are truly the craftsman's pockets inside the CPU.

But we come here to one of the biggest and most obvious differences between the older 16-bit x86 CPUs (the 8086, 8088, and 80286) and the newer 32-bit x86 CPUs starting with the 386: the *size* of the general-purpose registers. When I wrote the very first edition of this book in 1989, the 8088 still ruled the PC computing world, and I limited myself to discussing what the 8088 had within it.

Those days are long gone. Even the fully 32-bit 386 is considered an antique, and the 486 is considered ever more quaint as the years go by. It's a 32-bit world, and I'd be cheating you out of some useful CPU power if I neglected to explain the 32-bit general-purpose registers. Chances are overwhelming that your machine is fully 32-bit in nature, so all of these registers (with one or two minor exceptions) can be used in assembly language programs written for DOS or a DOS window under Microsoft Windows.

Like the segment registers, the general-purpose registers are memory locations existing inside the CPU chip itself. Also, like the segment registers, they all have names rather than numeric addresses. The general-purpose registers really are generalists in that all of them share a large suite of capabilities. However, some of the general-purpose registers also have what I call a hidden agenda: a task or set of tasks that only it can perform. I explain all these hidden agendas as I go—keeping in mind that some of the hidden agendas are actually limitations of the older 16-bit machines. The newer general-purpose registers are much more . . . , er, . . . general.

The general-purpose registers fall into three general classes: the 16-bit general-purpose registers, the 32-bit extended general-purpose registers, and the 8-bit register halves. These three classes do not represent three entirely distinct sets of registers at all. The 16-bit and 8-bit registers are actually names of regions *inside* the 32-bit registers. Register growth in the x86 CPU family has come about by *extending* registers existing in older CPUs. Adding a room to your house doesn't make it two houses—just one bigger house. And so it has been with the x86 registers.

There are eight 16-bit general-purpose registers: AX, BX, CX, DX, BP, SI, DI, and SP. (SP is a little less general than the others, but we'll get to that.) These all existed in the 8086, 8088, and 80286 CPUs. They are all 16 bits in size, and you can place any value in them that may be expressed in 16 bits or fewer. When Intel expanded the x86 architecture to 32 bits in 1986, it doubled the size of all eight registers and gave them new names by prefixing an *E* in front of each register name, resulting in EAX, EBX, ECX, EDX, EBP, ESI, EDI, and ESP.

So . . . were these just bigger registers, or new registers?

Both.

As with a lot of things in assembly language, this becomes a lot clearer by drawing a diagram. See Figure 6.6, which shows how SI, DI, BP, and SP doubled in size and got new names—without entirely losing their old ones.

Each of the four registers shown in Figure 6.6 is fully 32 bits in size. However, in each register, the lower 16 bits have a name of their own. The lower 16 bits of ESI, for example, may be referenced as SI. The lower 16 bits of EDI may be referenced as DI. If you're writing programs

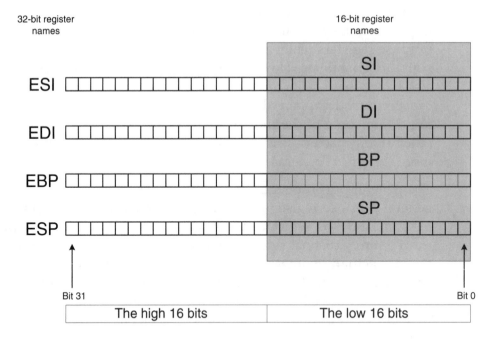

Figure 6.6 Extending the 16-bit general-purpose registers.

for an 8088 machine such as the ancient IBM PC, you can *only* reference the DI part—the high 16 bits don't exist on that CPU!

Unfortunately, the high 16 bits of the 32-bit general-purpose registers do not have their own names. You can access the low 16 bits of ESI as SI, but to get at the high 16 bits, you must refer to ESI and get the whole 32-bit shebang.

Register Halves

The same is true for the other four general-purpose registers EAX, EBX, ECX, and EDX, but there's an additional twist: The low 16 bits are themselves divided into two 8-bit halves. So, what we have are register names on not two but *three* levels. The 16-bit registers AX, BX, CX, and DX are present as the lower 16-bit portions of EAX, EBX, ECX, and EDX. But AX, BX, CX, and DX are themselves divided into 8-bit halves, and assemblers recognize special names for the two halves. The A, B, C, and D are retained, but instead of the *X*, a half is specified with an *H* (for high half) or an *L* (for low half). Each register half is 1 byte (8 bits) in size. Thus, making up 16-bit register AX, you have byte-sized register halves AH and AL; within BX there is BH and BL, and so on.

Again, this can best be shown in a diagram. See Figure 6.7. As I mentioned earlier, one quirk of this otherwise very useful system is that there is no name for the *high* 16-bit portion of the 32-bit registers. In other words, you can read the low 16 bits of EAX by specifying AX in an assembly language instruction, but there's no way to specify the high 16 bits by themselves. This keeps the naming conventions for the registers a little simpler (would you like to have to remember EAXH, EBXH, ECXH, and EDXH on top of everything else?), and the lack is not felt as often as you might think.

One nice thing about the 8-bit register halves is that you can read and change one half of a 16-bit number without disturbing the other half. This means that if you place the word-sized hexadecimal value 76E9H into register AX, you can read the byte-sized value 76H from register AH, and 0E9H from register AL. Better still, if you then store the value 0AH into register AL and then read back register AX, you'll find that the original value of 76E9H has been changed to 760AH.

Being able to treat the AX, BX, CX, and DX registers as 8-bit halves can be extremely handy in situations where you're manipulating a lot of 8-bit

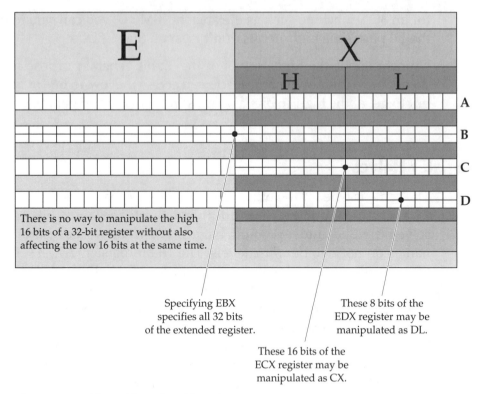

There is no way to manipulate the high 16 bits of a 32-bit register without also affecting the low 16 bits at the same time.

Specifying EBX specifies all 32 bits of the extended register.

These 8 bits of the EDX register may be manipulated as DL.

These 16 bits of the ECX register may be manipulated as CX.

Figure 6.7   8-bit, 16-bit, and 32-bit registers.

quantities. Each register half can be considered a separate register, leaving you twice the number of places to put things while your program works. As you'll see later on, finding a place to stick a value in a pinch is one of the great challenges facing assembly language programmers.

Keep in mind that this dual nature involves *only* the 16-bit general-purpose registers AX, BX, CX, and DX. The other 16-bit general-purpose registers SP, BP, SI, and DI, are not similarly equipped. There are no SIH and SIL 8-bit registers, for example, as convenient as that would sometimes be.

The Instruction Pointer

Yet another type of register lives inside the x86 CPUs. The *instruction pointer* (usually called IP) is in a class by itself. In radical contrast to the gang of eight general-purpose registers, IP is a specialist *par excellence*— more of a specialist than even the segment registers. It can do only one thing: It contains the offset address of the next machine instruction to be executed in the current code segment.

A *code segment* is an area of memory where machine instructions are stored. The steps and tests of which a program is made are contained in code segments. Depending on the programming model you're using, there may be many code segments in a program, or only one. The *current code segment* is that code segment whose segment address is currently stored in code segment register CS. At any given time, the machine instruction currently being executed exists within the current code segment.

While executing a program, the CPU uses IP to keep track of where it is in the current code segment. Each time an instruction is executed, IP is *incremented* by some number of bytes. The number of bytes is the size of the instruction just executed. The net result is to bump IP further into memory, so that it points to the start of the next instruction to be executed. Instructions come in different sizes, ranging typically from 1 to 6 bytes. (Some of the more arcane forms of the more arcane instructions may be even larger.) The CPU is careful to increment IP by just the right number of bytes, so that it does in fact end up pointing to the start of the next instruction, and not merely into the middle of the last instruction or some other instruction.

If IP contains the offset address of the next machine instruction, where is the segment address? The segment address is kept in the code segment register CS. Together, CS and IP contain the full address of the next machine instruction to be executed.

The nature of this address depends on what CPU you're using, and what programming model you're using it for. In the 8088, 8086, and 80286, IP is 16 bits in size. In the 386 and later CPUs, IP (like all the other registers except the segment registers) graduates to 32 bits in size.

In real mode segmented model, CS and IP working together give you a 20-bit address pointing to one of the 1,048,576 bytes in real mode memory. In both of the two flat models (more on which shortly), CS is set by the operating system and held constant. IP does all the instruction pointing that you the programmer have to deal with. In the 16-bit flat model (real mode flat model), this means IP can follow instruction execution all across a full 64K segment of memory. The 32-bit flat model does far more than double that; 32 bits can represent 4,294,967,290 different memory addresses. So, in 32-bit flat model (that is, protected mode flat model), IP can follow instruction execution across over 4 gigabytes of memory—considerably more than most people are likely to have in their machines.

This week, at least.

IP is notable in being the *only* register that can neither be read nor written to directly. It's possible to obtain the current value of IP, but the method involves some trickery that will have to wait until we discuss branching instructions in Chapter 10.

The Flags Register

There is one additional type of register inside the CPU: what we generically call the *flags register*. It is 16 bits in size in the 8086, 8088, and 80286, and its formal name is FLAGS. It is 32 bits in size in the 386 and later CPUs, and its formal name in the 32-bit CPUs is EFLAGS. Most of the bits in the flags register are single-bit registers called *flags*. Each of these individual flags has a name, such as CF, DF, OF, and so on, and each has a very specific meaning within the CPU.

When your program performs a test, what it tests are one or another of the single-bit flags in the flags register. Since a single bit may contain one of only two values, 1 or 0, a test in assembly language is truly a two-way affair: Either a flag is set to 1 or it isn't. If the flag is set to 1, the program takes one action; if the flag is set to 0, the program takes a different action.

The flags register is almost never dealt with as a unit. What happens is that many different machine instructions test the various flags to decide which way to go on some one-way-or-the-other decision. We're concentrating on memory addressing at the moment, so for now I'll simply promise to go into flag lore in more detail at more appropriate moments later in the book, when we discuss machine instructions that test the various flags in the flags register.

The Three Major Assembly Programming Models

I mentioned earlier that there are three major programming models that you might encounter in assembly language work. The differences between them lie (mostly) in the use of registers to address memory. (And the other differences, especially on the high end, are for the most part hidden from you by the operating system.) In this section I'm going to lay out the three models, all of which we'll touch on throughout the course of the rest of this book.

Real Mode Flat Model

In real mode, if you recall, the CPU can see only 1 megabyte (1,048,576) of memory. You can access every last one of those million-odd bytes by using the segment:offset trick shown earlier to form a 20-bit address out of two 16-bit addresses. Or . . . you can be content with 64K of memory, and not fool with segments at all.

In the real mode flat model, your program and all the data it works on must exist within a single 64K block of memory. Sixty-four kilobytes! Pfeh! What could you possibly accomplish in only 64K bytes? Well, the first version of WordStar for the IBM PC fit in 64K. So did the first three major releases of Turbo Pascal—in fact, the Turbo Pascal program itself occupied a lot less than 64K because it compiled its programs into memory. The whole Turbo Pascal package—compiler, text editor, and some odd tools—came to just over 39K. Thirty-nine kilobytes! You can't even write a letter to your mother (using Microsoft Word) in that little space these days!

True, true. But that's mostly because we don't have to. Memory's gotten cheap, and our machines now contain what by historical standards is an enormous amount of it. So we've gotten lazy and hoggish and wasteful, simply because we can get away with it.

But if you take pains to make effective use of memory, you can do spectacular things in 64K. Certainly, for your first simple steps in assembly language programming, you won't need anything near 64K—and the simplicity of the model will make it much easier to become familiar with the machine instructions you'll use to write your programs. Finally, real mode flat model is the "little brother" of protected mode flat model, which is the code model you use when programming under Linux. If you learn the ways of real mode flat model, protected mode flat model will be a snap. (All the trouble you'll have won't be with assembly code or memory models, but with the byzantine requirements of Linux itself.)

The real mode flat model is shown diagrammatically in Figure 6.8. There's not much to it. The segment registers are all set to point to the beginning of the 64K block of memory you can work with. (The operating system sets them when it loads and runs your program.) They all point to that same place and never change as long as your program is running. That being the case, you can simply forget about them. Poof! No segment registers, no fooling with segments, and none of the ugly complication that comes with them.

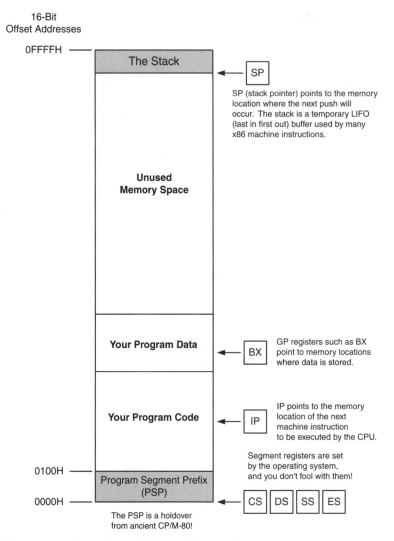

16-Bit
Offset Addresses

0FFFFH — The Stack ← SP

SP (stack pointer) points to the memory
location where the next push will
occur. The stack is a temporary LIFO
(last in first out) buffer used by many
x86 machine instructions.

**Unused
Memory Space**

Your Program Data ← BX

GP registers such as BX
point to memory locations
where data is stored.

Your Program Code ← IP

IP points to the memory
location of the next
machine instruction
to be executed by the CPU.

Segment registers are set
by the operating system,
and you don't fool with them!

0100H — Program Segment Prefix (PSP)
0000H — ← CS DS SS ES

The PSP is a holdover
from ancient CP/M-80!

Figure 6.8 The real mode flat model.

Because a 16-bit register such as BX can hold any value from 0 to 65,535, it can pinpoint any single byte within the full 64K your program has to work with. Addressing memory can thus be done without the explicit use of the segment registers. The segment registers are still functioning, of course, from the CPU's point of view. They don't disappear and are still there, but the operating system sets them to values of its own choosing when it launches your program, and those values will be good as long as the program runs. You don't have to access the segment registers in any way to write your program.

Most of the general-purpose registers may contain addresses of locations in memory. You use them in conjunction with machine instructions to bring data in from memory and write it back out again.

At the top of the single segment that your program exists within, you'll see a small region called the *stack*. The stack is a LIFO (last in, first out) storage location with some very special uses. I explain what the stack is and how it works in considerable detail in Chapter 8.

Real mode flat model is the programming model we'll use for our first several example programs.

Real Mode Segmented Model

The first two editions of this book focused entirely on real mode segmented model, which was the mainstream programming model throughout the MS-DOS era, and still holds true when you boot your Windows 9x machine into MS-DOS mode, or launch an MS-DOS window. It's a complicated, ugly system that requires you to remember a lot of little rules and gotchas. I'm still going to teach it here, because some people may still wish to write code to run under MS-DOS, and also because it illustrates the use of segments very clearly. (Under real mode flat model you can squint a little and pretend that segments don't really exist.)

In real mode segmented model, your program can see the full 1MB of memory available to the CPU in real mode. It does this by combining a 16-bit segment address with a 16-bit offset address. It doesn't just glom them together into a 32-bit address, however. You need to think back to my discussion of segments earlier in this chapter. A segment address is not really a memory address. A segment address specifies one of the 65,535 slots at which a segment may begin. One of these slots exists every 16 bytes from the bottom of memory to the top. Segment address 0000H specifies the first such slot, at the very first location in memory. Segment address 0001H specifies the next slot, which lies 16 bytes higher in memory. Jumping up-memory another 16 bytes gets you to segment address 0002H, and so on. You can translate a segment address to an actual 20-bit memory address by multiplying it by 16. Segment address 0002H is thus equivalent to memory address 0020H, which is the 32nd byte in memory.

But such multiplication isn't something you have to do. The CPU handles the combination of segments and offsets into a full 20-bit address.

Your job is to tell the CPU where the two different components of that 20-bit address are. The customary notation is to separate the segment register and the offset register by a colon. For example:

```
SS : SP
SS : BP
ES : DI
DS : SI
CS : BX
```

Each of these five register combinations specifies a full 20-bit address. ES:DI, for example, specifies the address as the distance in DI from the start of the segment called out in ES.

I've drawn a diagram outlining real mode segmented model in Figure 6.9. In contrast to real mode flat model (shown in Figure 6.8), the diagram here shows *all* of memory, not just the one little 64K chunk that your real mode flat model program is allocated when it runs. A program written for real mode segmented model can see all of real mode memory.

The diagram shows two code segments and two data segments. In practice you can have any reasonable number of code and data segments, not just two of each. You can access two data segments at the same time, because you have two segment registers available to do the job: DS and ES. Each can specify a data segment, and you can move data from one segment to another using any of several machine instructions. (We speak more of this in later chapters.) However, you only have one code segment register, CS. CS always points to the current code segment, and the next instruction to be executed is pointed to by the IP register. You don't load values directly into CS to change from one code segment to another. Machine instructions called *jumps* change to another code segment as necessary. Your program can span several code segments, and when a jump instruction (there are several kinds) needs to take execution into a different code segment, it changes the value in CS for you.

There is only one stack segment for any single program, specified by the stack segment register SS. The stack pointer register SP points to the memory address (relative to SS, albeit in an upside-down direction) where the next stack operation will take place. The stack will require some considerable explaining, which I take up in Chapter 8.

You need to keep in mind that in real mode, there will be pieces of the operating system (and if you're using an 8086 or 8088, that will be the

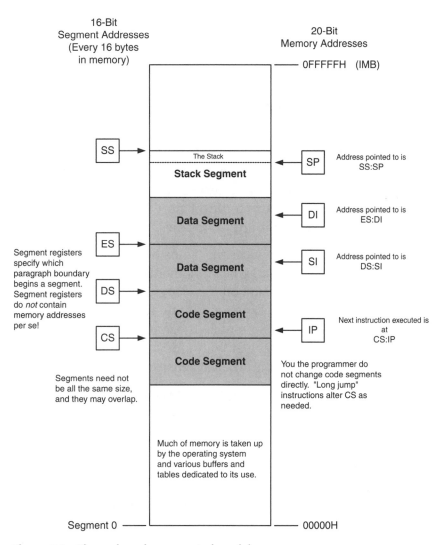

16-Bit
Segment Addresses
(Every 16 bytes
in memory)

20-Bit
Memory Addresses

0FFFFFH (IMB)

SS

The Stack

Stack Segment

SP

Address pointed to is
SS:SP

Data Segment

DI

Address pointed to is
ES:DI

ES

Data Segment

SI

Address pointed to is
DS:SI

Segment registers
specify which
paragraph boundary
begins a segment.
Segment registers
do *not* contain
memory addresses
per se!

DS

Code Segment

IP

Next instruction executed is
at
CS:IP

CS

Code Segment

You the programmer do
not change code segments
directly. "Long jump"
instructions alter CS as
needed.

Segments need not
be all the same size,
and they may overlap.

Much of memory is taken up
by the operating system
and various buffers and
tables dedicated to its use.

Segment 0

00000H

Figure 6.9 The real mode segmented model.

whole operating system) in memory with your program, along with important system data tables. You can destroy portions of the operating system by careless use of segment registers, which will cause the operating system to crash and take your program with it. This is the danger that prompted Intel to build new features into its 80386 and later CPUs to support a protected mode. In protected mode, application programs (that is, the programs that you write, as opposed to the operating system or device drivers) cannot destroy the operating system nor other applications programs that happen to be running elsewhere in memory in a multitasking system. That's what the *protected* means.

(Yes, it's true that there is a sort of rudimentary protected mode present in the 80286, but no one ever really used it and it's not much worth discussing today.)

Protected Mode Flat Model

Intel's CPUs have implemented a very good protected mode architecture since the 386 appeared in 1986. However, application programs cannot make use of protected mode by themselves. The operating system must set up and manage a protected mode before application programs can use it. MS-DOS couldn't do this, and Microsoft Windows couldn't really do it either until Windows NT first appeared in 1994.

Other protected mode operating systems have since appeared. The best known is probably Linux, the implementation of Unix written from scratch by a young Finnish college student during the first half of the 1990s. Windows NT and Linux are vying for the same general market, and while NT will probably remain the market leader for years to come, Linux is showing surprising strength for something that no one organization actually owns in the strictest sense of the word.

Protected mode assembly language programs may be written for both Windows NT and Linux. The easiest way to do it under NT is to create *console applications*, which are text-mode programs that run in a text-mode window called a *console*. The console is controlled through a command line almost identical to the one in MS-DOS. Console applications use protected mode flat model and are fairly straightforward compared to writing Windows applications. The default mode for Linux is a text console, so it's even easier to create assembly programs for Linux, and a lot more people appear to be doing it. The memory model is very much the same.

I've drawn the protected mode flat model in Figure 6.10. Your program sees a single block of memory addresses running from zero to a little over 4 gigabytes. Each address is a 32-bit quantity. All of the general-purpose registers are 32 bits in size, and so one GP register can point to any location in the full 4-GB address space. The instruction pointer is 32 bits in size as well, so EIP can indicate any machine instruction anywhere in the 4 GB of memory.

The segment registers still exist, but they work in a radically different way. Not only don't you have to fool with them; you *can't*. The segment

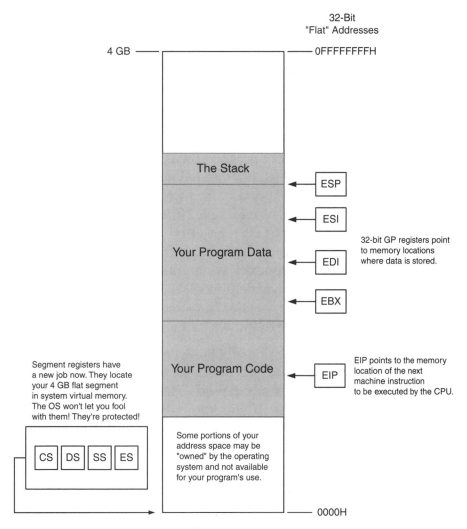

Figure 6.10   The protected mode flat model.

registers are now to be considered part of the operating system, and in most cases you can neither read nor change them directly. Their new job is to define where your 4GB memory space exists in physical or virtual memory. If these terms mean nothing to you, don't fret—you'll pick them up over time, and I don't have the space to explain them in detail here.

It's enough to understand that when your program runs, it receives a 4-GB address space in which to play, and any register can potentially address any of those 4 billion memory locations, all by itself. Not all of the 4 GB is at your program's disposal, and there are certain parts of the memory space that you can't use or even look at. Unfortunately, the rules are specific to the operating system you're running under, and I can't generalize too far without specifying Linux or Windows NT or some other protected mode OS.

But it's worth taking a look back at Figure 6.8 and comparing real mode flat model to protected mode flat model. The main difference is that in real mode flat model, your program owns the full 64K of memory that the operating system hands it. In protected mode flat model, you are given a portion of 4 GB of memory as your own, while other portions will still belong to the operating system. Apart from that, the similarities are striking: A general-purpose (GP) register by itself can specify any memory location in the full memory address space, and the segment registers are really the tools of the operating system and not you the programmer. (Again, in protected mode flat model, a GP register can *hold* the address of any location in its 4-GB space, but attempting to actually read or write certain locations will be forbidden by the OS and will trigger an error.)

Note well that we haven't really talked about machine instructions yet, and we've been able to pretty crisply define the universe in which machine instructions exist and work. Memory addressing and registers are key in this business. If you know them, the instructions will be a snap. If you don't know them, the instructions won't do you any good!

What difficulty exists in programming for protected mode flat model lies in understanding the operating system, its requirements, and its restrictions. This can be a substantial amount of learning: Windows NT and Linux are major operating systems that can take years of study. I'm going to introduce you to protected mode assembly programming in flat model later in this book, but you're going to have to learn the operating system on your own. This book is only the beginning—there's a long road out there to be walked, and you're barely off the curb.

Reading and Changing Registers with DEBUG

Much or most of what defines your assembly language programs lies in your use of registers. Machine instructions act on registers, and registers define how memory is addressed and what is read from or placed there. While you're developing and debugging your programs, a lot of what you'll be looking at is the contents of your registers.

The DOS DEBUG utility provides a handy window into the CPU's hidden world of registers. How DEBUG does this is the blackest of all black arts and I can't begin to explain it in an introductory text. For now, just consider DEBUG a magic box. One thing to keep in mind is that DEBUG is a real mode creature. It doesn't work in protected mode. You can only use it while debugging real mode programs, whether segmented or flat model. Protected mode debuggers do exist, but DEBUG isn't one of them.

Looking at the registers from DEBUG doesn't even require that you load a program into DEBUG. Simply run DEBUG, and at the dash prompt type the single-letter command R. The display will look something very close to this:

```
- R
AX=0000 BX=0000 CX=0000 DX=0000 SP=FFEE BP=0000 SI=0000 DI=0000
DS=1980 ES=1980 SS=1980 CS=1980 IP=0100   NV UP EI PL NZ NA PO NC
1980:0100 389A5409    CMP    [BP+SI+0954],BL        SS:0954=8A
```

I say "something very close" because details of the display will vary depending on what resident programs you have loaded in memory, which version of DOS you're using, and so on. What will vary will be the values listed as present in the various registers, and the machine instruction shown in the third line of the display (here, **CMP [BP+SI+0954],BL**).

What will *not* vary is the fact that every CPU register has its place in the display, along with its current value shown to the right of an equals sign. The characters "NV UP EI PL NZ NA PO NC" are a summary of the current values of the flags in the flags register.

The preceding display is that of the registers when *no* program has been loaded. All of the general-purpose registers except for SP have been set to 0, and all of the segment registers have been set to the value 1980H. These are the default conditions set up by DEBUG in the CPU when no program has been loaded. (The 1980H value will probably be different for you—it represents the first available segment in memory above DOS, and where that segment falls depends on what else exists in memory both above and below DOS.)

Changing a register is done very simply, again using DEBUG's R command. To change the value of AX, type R AX and press Enter:

```
-R AX
AX:0000
:0A7B
-
```

DEBUG will respond by displaying the current value of AX (here, "0000") and then, on the following line, a colon prompt. It will wait for you to either enter a new numeric value for AX, or else for you to press Enter. If you press Enter, the current value of the register will not be changed. In the preceding example, I typed "0A7B" (you needn't type the *H* indicating hex) followed by Enter.

Once you do enter a new value and then press Enter, DEBUG does nothing to verify that the change has been made. To see the change to register AX, you must display all the registers again using the R command:

```
- R
AX=0A7B BX=0000 CX=0000 DX=0000 SP=FFEE BP=0000 SI=0000 DI=0000
DS=1980 ES=1980 SS=1980 CS=1980 IP=0100   NV UP EI PL NZ NA PO NC
1980:0100 389A5409    CMP   [BP+SI+0954],BL        SS:0954=8A
```

Take a few minutes to practice entering new values for the general-purpose registers, then display the registers as a group to verify that the changes were made. While exploring, you might find that the IP register can be changed, even though I said earlier that it can't be changed directly. The key word is *directly*; DEBUG knows all the dirty tricks.

Inspecting the Video Refresh Buffer with DEBUG

One good way to help your knowledge of memory addressing sink in is to use DEBUG to take a look at some interesting places in the PC's memory space.

One easy thing to do is look at the PC's video display adapter's text screen video refresh buffer. A *video refresh buffer* is a region of memory with a difference: Any characters written to buffer memory are instantly displayed on the computer's screen. This is accomplished electrically through special use of the information that comes out of the memory data pins. Precisely how it is done is outside the scope of this book. For now, simply understand that writing a character to your text mode display screen (which is *not* the Windows graphical UI screen!) can be done by writing the ASCII code for that character into the correct address in the video refresh buffer portion of memory.

The text mode display buffer is the screen that appears when you're running DOS or else working in a DOS window (or "DOS box") from within MS Windows. It consists not of icons or graphical images or figures but simple textual characters, arranged in a matrix typically 25 high and 80 wide. This used to be the mainstay of all computing; now, text screens seem downright quaint to most people.

As with any memory location anywhere within the PC, the video refresh buffer has a segment address. What that segment address is depends on the kind of display installed in the PC. There are two separate possibilities, and which is present is easy enough to determine: If your PC has a *color* screen, the segment address of the video refresh buffer is 0B800H. If you have a *monochrome* screen (a situation now becoming vanishingly rare), the segment address is 0B000H instead.

It takes 2 bytes in the buffer to display a character. The first of the two (that is, first in memory) is the ASCII code of the character itself. For example, an *A* would require the ASCII code 41H; a *B* would require the ASCII code 42H, and so on. (The full ASCII code set is shown in Appendix D.) The second of the two bytes is the character's *attribute*. Think of it this way: In the display of a character on the screen, the ASCII code says *what* and the attribute says *how*. The attribute dictates the color of a character and its background cell on a color screen. On a monochrome screen, the attribute specifies whether a character is underlined or displayed in reverse video. (*Reverse video* is a character display mode in which a dark character is shown on a light background, rather than the traditional light character on a dark or black background.) Every character byte has an attribute byte and every attribute byte has its character byte; neither can ever exist alone.

The very first character/attribute pair in the video refresh buffer corresponds to the character you see in the upper-left-hand corner of the text screen. The next character/attribute pair in the buffer is the character on the second position on the top line of the screen, and so on. I've drawn a diagram of the relationship between characters on the screen and byte values in the video refresh buffer in Figure 6.11.

In Figure 6.11, the three letters "ABC" are displayed in the upper-left corner of the screen. Notice that the "C" is underlined. The screen shown in Figure 6.11 is a monochrome screen. The video refresh buffer therefore begins at 0B000:0. The byte located at address 0B000:0 is ASCII code 41H, corresponding to the letter "A." The byte at address 0B00:0001 is the corresponding attribute value of 07H. The 07H value as an attribute dictates normal text in both color and monochrome displays, in which *normal* means white characters on a black background.

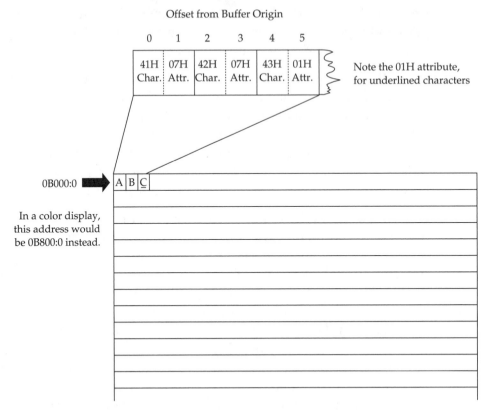

Offset from Buffer Origin

Figure 6.11 The PC's video refresh buffer.

The byte at 0B000:0005 is also an attribute byte, but its value is 01H. On a monochrome screen, 01H makes the corresponding character underlined. On a color display, 01H makes the character blue on a black background.

There is nothing about the video refresh buffer to divide it into the lines you see on the display. The first 160 characters (80 ASCII codes plus their 80 attribute bytes) are shown as the first line, and the subsequent 160 characters are shown on the next line down the screen.

You might rightfully ask what ASCII code is in the video refresh buffer for locations on the screen that show no character at all. The answer, of course, is that there *is* a character there in every empty space: the space character, whose ASCII code is 20H.

You can inspect the memory within the video refresh buffer directly, through DEBUG. Take the following steps:

1. Clear the screen by entering CLS at the DOS prompt and pressing Enter.

2. Invoke DEBUG.

3. Decide where your video refresh buffer is located, and enter the proper segment address into the ES register through the R command. Remember: Color screens use the 0B800H segment address, while monochrome screens use the 0B000H segment address. (In the year 2000, it's a 98 percent chance that your screen is color and not monochrome.) Note from the following session dump that 0B800H must be entered into DEBUG as "B800," *without* the leading zero. NASM (your assembler) *must* have that leading zero, and DEBUG *cannot* have it. Sadly, no one ever said that all parts of this business had to make perfect sense.

4. Dump the first 128 bytes of the video refresh buffer by entering D ES:0 and pressing Enter.

5. Dump the next 128 bytes of the video refresh buffer simply by entering the D command by itself a second time. (I won't say "press Enter" every time. It's assumed: You must follow a command by pressing Enter.)

What you'll see should look a lot like the following session dump:

```
C:\ASM>debug
- r es
ES 1980
:b800
- d es:0
B800:0000 20 07 20 07 20 07 20 07-20 07 20 07 20 07 20 07   . . . . . . . .
B800:0010 20 07 20 07 20 07 20 07-20 07 20 07 20 07 20 07   . . . . . . . .
B800:0020 20 07 20 07 20 07 20 07-20 07 20 07 20 07 20 07   . . . . . . . .
B800:0030 20 07 20 07 20 07 20 07-20 07 20 07 20 07 20 07   . . . . . . . .
B800:0040 20 07 20 07 20 07 20 07-20 07 20 07 20 07 20 07   . . . . . . . .
B800:0050 20 07 20 07 20 07 20 07-20 07 20 07 20 07 20 07   . . . . . . . .
B800:0060 20 07 20 07 20 07 20 07-20 07 20 07 20 07 20 07   . . . . . . . .
B800:0070 20 07 20 07 20 07 20 07-20 07 20 07 20 07 20 07   . . . . . . . .
- d
B800:0080 20 07 20 07 20 07 20 07-20 07 20 07 20 07 20 07   . . . . . . . .
B800:0090 20 07 20 07 20 07 20 07-20 07 20 07 20 07 20 07   . . . . . . . .
B800:00A0 43 07 3A 07 5C 07 41 07-53 07 4D 07 3E 07 64 07   C.:.\.A.S.M.>.d.
B800:00B0 65 07 62 07 75 07 67 07-20 07 20 07 20 07 20 07   e.b.u.g. . . . .
B800:00C0 20 07 20 07 20 07 20 07-20 07 20 07 20 07 20 07   . . . . . . . .
B800:00D0 20 07 20 07 20 07 20 07-20 07 20 07 20 07 20 07   . . . . . . . .
B800:00E0 20 07 20 07 20 07 20 07-20 07 20 07 20 07 20 07   . . . . . . . .
B800:00F0 20 07 20 07 20 07 20 07-20 07 20 07 20 07 20 07   . . . . . . . .
```

The first 80 character/attribute pairs are the same: 20H/07H, which display as plain, ordinary blank space. When you execute the CLS command on most machines, the screen is cleared, and the DOS prompt reappears on the *second* line from the top of the screen, *not* the top line. The top line is typically left blank, as is the case here.

You'll see in the second block of 128 dumped bytes the DOS prompt and the invocation of DEBUG in lowercase. Keep in mind when reading DEBUG hex dumps that any character not readily displayed as one of the standard ASCII letters, numbers, or punctuation marks is represented as a period character. This is why the 07H attribute character is shown on the right portion of DEBUG's display as a period character, since the ASCII code 07H has no displayable equivalent.

You can keep dumping further into the video refresh buffer by pressing DEBUG's D command repeatedly.

Reading the Basic Input/Output System Revision Date

Another interesting item that's easy to locate in your PC is the revision date in the ROM BIOS. *ROM* (read-only memory) chips are special memory chips that retain their contents when power to the PC is turned off. The *BIOS* (Basic Input/Output System) is a collection of assembly language routines that perform basic services for the PC: disk handling, video handling, printer handling, and so forth. The BIOS is kept in ROM at the very top of the PC's megabyte of address space.

The BIOS contains a date, indicating when it was declared finished by its authors. This date is always at the same address and can be easily displayed using DEBUG's D command. The address of the date is 0FFFF:0005. The DEBUG session is shown in the following listing. Note again that the hex number 0FFFFH must be entered without its leading zero:

```
- d ffff:0005
FFFF:0000                   30 34 2F-33 30 2F 39 37 00 FC B8    04/30/97...
FFFF:0010 00 00 00 00 00 00 00 00-00 00 00 00 00 00 00 00    ................
FFFF:0020 00 00 00 00 00 00 00 00-00 00 00 00 00 00 00 00    ................
FFFF:0030 00 00 00 00 00 00 00 00-00 00 00 00 00 00 00 00    ................
FFFF:0040 00 00 00 00 00 00 00 00-00 00 00 00 00 00 00 00    ................
FFFF:0050 00 00 00 00 00 00 00 00-00 00 00 00 00 00 00 00    ................
FFFF:0060 00 00 00 00 00 00 00 00-00 00 00 00 00 00 00 00    ................
FFFF:0070 00 00 00 00 00 00 00 00-00 00 00 00 00 00 00 00    ................
FFFF:0080 00 00 00 00 00                                     .....
```

One useful peculiarity of DEBUG illustrated here is that when you begin a hex dump of memory at an address that is *not* evenly divisible by 16, DEBUG spaces the first byte of the dump over to the right so that paragraph boundaries still fall at the left margin.

Another rather peculiar thing to keep in mind while looking at the particular dump shown in the preceding is that *only the first line of memory shown in the dump really exists*. The segment 0FFFFH begins only 16 bytes before the end of real mode's megabyte of memory space. (See Figure 6.4 for a good illustration of this.) The byte at 0FFFF:000F is the *last* byte in real mode memory—and DEBUG is a real mode creature. Addresses from 0FFFF:0010 to 0FFFF:0FFFF would require more than 20 address bits to express, so in real mode they might as well not exist. (They do exist—but DEBUG can't see them!)

DEBUG won't tell you that—it'll just give you endless pages of zeroes for memory beyond the real mode megabyte pale. (Several readers have told me that certain versions of DEBUG take a different approach, and wrap their display around to the *bottom* of memory instead, and begin displaying bytes at 0000:0000 once they run out of high memory. It's something to watch out for, and if memory beyond the FFFF:000F point is *not* zeros, you're in fact seeing such a wrap to low memory.)

Transferring Control to Machine Instructions in Read-Only Memory

So far we've looked at locations in memory as containers for data. All well and good—but memory contains machine instructions as well. A very effective illustration of a machine instruction at a particular address is also provided by the ROM BIOS—and right next door to the BIOS revision date, at that.

The machine instruction in question is located at address 0FFFF:0. Recall that, by convention, the *next* machine instruction to be executed is the one whose address is stored in CS:IP. Run DEBUG. Load the value 0FFFFH into code segment register CS, and 0 into instruction pointer IP. Then dump memory at 0FFFF:0.

```
- r cs
CS 1980
:ffff
- r ip
IP 0100
:0
```

```
- r
AX=0000 BX=0000 CX=0000 DX=0000 SP=FFEE BP=0000 SI=0000 DI=0000
DS=1980 ES=1980 SS=1980 CS=FFFF IP=0000   NV UP EI PL NZ NA PO NC
FFFF:0000 EA5BE000F0   JMP     F000:E05B
- d cs:0
FFFF:0000 EA 5B E0 00 F0 30 34 2F-33 30 2F 38 37 00 FC B8  .[...04/30/87...
FFFF:0010 00 00 00 00 00 00 00 00-00 00 00 00 00 00 00 00  ................
FFFF:0020 00 00 00 00 00 00 00 00-00 00 00 00 00 00 00 00  ................
FFFF:0030 00 00 00 00 00 00 00 00-00 00 00 00 00 00 00 00  ................
FFFF:0040 00 00 00 00 00 00 00 00-00 00 00 00 00 00 00 00  ................
FFFF:0050 00 00 00 00 00 00 00 00-00 00 00 00 00 00 00 00  ................
FFFF:0060 00 00 00 00 00 00 00 00-00 00 00 00 00 00 00 00  ................
FFFF:0070 00 00 00 00 00 00 00 00-00 00 00 00 00 00 00 00  ................
```

Look at the third line of the register display, which we've been ignoring up until now. To the right of the address display FFFF:0000 is this series of five bytes: EA5BE000F0.

These five bytes make up the machine instruction we want. Notice that the first line of the memory dump begins with the same address, and, sure enough, shows us the same five bytes.

Trying to remember what machine instruction EA5BE000F0 is would try anyone's intellect, so DEBUG is a good sport and translates the five bytes into a more readable representation of the machine instruction. This translation is placed to the right of the binary machine code EA5BE000F0. We call this process of translating binary machine codes back into human-readable assembly language mnemonics *unassembly* or, more commonly, *disassembly*:

```
JMP F000:E05B.
```

What this instruction does, quite simply, is tell the CPU to jump to the address 0F000:0E05B and begin executing the machine instructions located there. If we execute the machine instruction at CS:IP, that's what will happen: The CPU will jump to the address 0F000:0E05B and begin executing whatever machine instructions it finds there.

All IBM-compatible PCs have a JMP instruction at address 0FFFF:0. The address to which that JMP instruction jumps will be different for different makes and models of PC. This is why on your machine you won't necessarily see the exact five bytes EA5BE000F0, but whatever five bytes you find at 0FFFF:0, they will *always* begin with 0EAH. The 0EAH byte specifies that this instruction will be a JMP instruction. The remainder of the machine instruction is the address to which the CPU must jump. If that address as given in the machine instruction looks a little scrambled, well, it is . . . but that's the way the x86 CPUs do things. We return to the issue of funny-looking addresses a little later.

DEBUG has a command, G (for Go), that begins execution at the address stored in CS:IP. If you enter the G command and press Enter, the CPU will jump to the address built into the JMP instruction and begin executing machine instructions. What happens then?

If you're running under DOS, your machine will go into a *cold boot*, just as it would if you powered down and powered up again. (So make sure you're ready for a reboot before you try it!)

This may seem odd. But consider: The CPU chip has to begin execution somewhere. When the CPU "wakes up" after being off all night with the power removed, it must get its first machine instruction from somewhere and start executing. Built into the silicon of the x86 CPU chips is the assumption that a legal machine instruction will exist at address 0FFFF:0. When power is applied to the CPU chip, the first thing it does is place 0FFFH in CS, and 0 in IP. Then it starts fetching instructions from the address in CS:IP and executing them, one at a time, in the manner that CPUs must.

This is why *all* PCs have a JMP instruction at 0FFFF:0, and why this JMP instruction always jumps to the routines that bring the PC up from stone cold dead to fully operational.

Unfortunately, if you're running in a DOS window under Windows 9*x* or NT, jumping to 0FFFF:0 won't initiate a cold boot. Under Windows 9*x*, the JMP will close your DOS window. Under NT, it won't even do that . . . It'll just exit DEBUG. You see, Windows lives in protected mode, and it's . . . um . . . *protected* from little tricks like idle jumps to 0FFFF:0.

But if you're running DOS—what the heck, go ahead: Load 0FFFFH into CS and 0 into IP, and press G. Feel good?

It's what we call the feeling of *power.*

CHAPTER 7

Following Your Instructions

Meeting Machine Instructions up Close and Personal

The most visible part of any assembly language program is its machine instructions, those atoms of action that are the steps a program must take to get its work done. The collection of instructions supported by a given CPU is that CPU's *instruction set*. For example, the 8086 and 8088 CPUs share the same instruction set, which is why most people consider them the same CPU.

This cannot be said for the later CPUs in the family, all of which offer additional instructions not found in the original 8086/8088. I can't cover *all* the x86 machine instructions in this book, even the original set introduced with the 8086. Those that I will describe are the most common and the most useful, and the easiest for newcomers to understand. It's not just a space issue, either. Some of the instructions (and for the most recent CPUs, such as the Pentium, a good many of them) are dedicated to way-down-deep functions that support the workings of protected mode operating systems and virtual memory. I could spend a whole book the size of this one just explaining the concepts that go into such operating systems and would *have* to before I could explain the instructions from which one builds them.

Nor will I abandon the discussion of memory addressing begun in the last chapter. As I've said before, understanding how the CPU and its instructions address memory is more difficult but probably more important than understanding the instructions themselves. In and around the descriptions of the machine instructions I'll present from this point on there will be discussions and elaboration on memory addressing. Pay attention! If you don't learn that, memorizing the entire instruction set will do you no good at all.

Assembling and Executing Machine Instructions with DEBUG

The most obvious way to experiment with machine instructions is to build a short program out of them and watch it go. This can easily be done (and we'll be doing it a lot in later chapters), but it's far from the fastest way to do things. Editing source code and assembling it (and linking, when you must link) all take time, and when you only want to look at *one* machine instruction in action (rather than a crew of them working together), the full development cycle is overkill.

Once more, we turn to DEBUG.

At the close of the last chapter we got a taste of a DEBUG feature called *unassembly*, which is a peculiar way of saying what most of us call *disassembly*. This is the reverse of the assembly process we looked at in detail in Chapter 3. Disassembly is the process of taking a binary machine instruction such as 42H and converting it into its more readable assembly language equivalent, **INC DX**.

In addition to all its other tools, DEBUG also contains a simple assembler, suitable for taking assembly language mnemonics such as **INC DX** and converting them to their binary machine code form. (That is, taking "INC DX" from you, and translating it to 42H.) Later on we'll use a stand-alone assembler program called NASM to assemble complete assembly language programs. For the time being, we can use DEBUG to do things one or two instructions at a time and get a feel for the process.

Assembling a MOV Instruction

The single most common activity in assembly language work is getting data from here to there. There are several specialized ways to do this, but only one truly general way: The **MOV** instruction. **MOV** can move a byte, word (16 bits), or double word (32 bits) of data from one register to another, from a register into memory, or from memory into a register. What **MOV** *cannot* do is move data directly from one address in memory to a different address in memory. (To do that, you need two separate **MOV** instructions—one from memory to a register, and second from the register back out to memory.)

The name **MOV** is a bit of a misnomer, since what is actually happening is that data is *copied* from a source to a destination. Once copied to the destination, however, the data does not vanish from the source, but continues to exist in both places. This conflicts a little with our intuitive notion of moving something, which usually means that something disappears from a source and reappears at a destination.

Because **MOV** is so general and obvious in its action, it's a good place to start in working with DEBUG's assembler.

Bring up DEBUG and use the R command to display the current state of the registers. You should see something like this:

```
- r
AX=0000 BX=0000 CX=0000 DX=0000 SP=FFEE BP=0000 SI=0000 DI=0000
DS=1980 ES=1980 SS=1980 CS=1980 IP=0100  NV UP EI PL NZ NA PO NC
1980:0100 701D    JO    011F
```

We more or less ignored the third line of the register display in the previous chapter. Now let's think a little bit more about what it means.

When DEBUG is loaded *without* a specific file to debug, it simply takes the empty region of memory where a file would have been loaded (had a file been loaded when DEBUG was invoked) and treats it as though a program file were really there. The registers all get default values, most of which are zero. IP, however, starts out with a value of 0100H, and the code segment register CS gets the segment address of DEBUG's workspace, which is theoretically empty.

But . . . memory is never really empty. A byte of memory always contains some value, whether true garbage that happened to reside in memory at power-up time, or else a leftover value remaining from the last time that byte of memory was used in some computing operation. In the preceding register dump, memory at CS:IP contains a **JO** instruction. This rather obscure instruction (**J**ump on **O**verflow) was not placed there deliberately, but is simply DEBUG's interpretation of the two bytes 701DH that happen to reside at CS:IP. Most likely, the 701D value was part of some data table belonging to the last program to use that area of memory. It could have been part of a word processor file, or a spreadsheet, or anything else. Just don't think that some program *necessarily* put a **JO** instruction in memory. Machine instructions are just numbers, after all, and what numbers in memory do depends completely on how you interpret them—and what utility program you feed them to.

DEBUG's internal assembler assembles directly into memory, and places instructions one at a time—as you enter them at the keyboard—into memory at CS:IP. Each time you enter an instruction, IP is incremented to the next free location in memory. So, by continuing to enter instructions, you can actually type an assembly language program directly into memory.

Try it. Type the A command (for **A**ssemble) and press Enter. DEBUG responds by displaying the current value of CS:IP and then waits for you to enter an assembly language instruction. Type **MOV AX,1**. Press Enter. DEBUG again displays CS:IP and waits for a second instruction. It will continue waiting for instructions until you press Enter without typing anything. Then you'll see DEBUG's dash prompt again.

Now, use the R command again to display the registers. You should see something like this:

```
- r
AX=0000 BX=0000 CX=0000 DX=0000 SP=FFEE BP=0000 SI=0000 DI=0000
DS=1980 ES=1980 SS=1980 CS=1980 IP=0100   NV UP EI PL NZ NA PO NC
1980:0100 B80100     MOV    AX,0001
```

The registers haven't changed—but now the third line shows that the **JO** instruction is gone, and that the **MOV** instruction you entered has taken its place. Notice once again that CS contains 1980H, and IP contains 0100H. The address of the **MOV** instruction is shown as 1980:0100; in other words, at CS:IP.

Executing a MOV Instruction with the Trace Command

Note that you haven't *executed* anything. You've simply used DEBUG's Assemble command to write a machine instruction into a particular location in memory.

There are two ways to execute machine instructions from within DEBUG. One way is to execute a program in memory, starting at CS:IP. This means that DEBUG will simply start the CPU executing whatever sequence of instructions begins at CS:IP. We looked at the G command very briefly at the end of the last chapter, when we found the **JMP** instruction that reboots your PC on power-up, and used G to execute that instruction. The command is quite evocative: **Go**. But don't type G just yet . . .

Here's the reason: You haven't entered a program. You've entered *one* instruction, and one instruction does not a program make. The instruction *after* your **MOV** instruction could be anything at all, recalling that DEBUG is simply interpreting garbage values in memory as random machine instructions. A series of random machine instructions could easily go berserk, locking your system into an endless loop or writing zeroes over an entire segment of memory that may contain part of DOS or Windows, or of DEBUG itself. We'll use DEBUG's G command a little later, once we've constructed a complete program in memory.

Go executes programs in memory starting at CS:IP; Trace executes the single instruction at CS:IP.

For now, let's consider the mechanism DEBUG has for executing one machine instruction at a time. It's called **T**race, and you invoke it by typing T. The Trace command will execute the machine instruction at CS:IP, then give control of the machine back to DEBUG. Trace is generally used to single-step a machine-code program one instruction at a time, in order to watch what it's up to every step of the way. For now, it's a fine way to execute a single instruction and examine that instruction's effects.

So type T. DEBUG will execute the **MOV** instruction you entered at CS:IP, and then immediately display the registers before returning to the dash prompt. You'll see this:

```
AX=0001 BX=0000 CX=0000 DX=0000 SP=FFEE BP=0000 SI=0000 DI=0000
DS=1980 ES=1980 SS=1980 CS=1980 IP=0103  NV UP EI PL NZ NA PO NC
1980:0103 6E    DB    6E
```

Look at the first line. DEBUG says AX is now equal to 0001. It held the default value 0000 before; obviously, your **MOV** instruction worked.

And there's something else to look at here: The third line shows an instruction called **DB** at CS:IP. Not quite true—**DB** is not a machine instruction, but an assembly language *directive* that means **D**efine **B**yte. **DB** has other uses, but in this case it's simply DEBUG's way of saying that the number 6EH does not correspond to *any* machine instruction. It is truly a garbage byte sitting in memory, doing nothing. Executing a 6EH byte as though it were an instruction, however, could cause your machine to do unpredictably peculiar things, up to and including locking up hard.

Remember, of course, that the 6EH was what happened to lie in memory one address up from the **MOV AX,1** instruction on my machine at that particular time. You almost certainly encountered something else when you tried the experiment just now. In fact, I just rebooted my machine and tried it again and found an **XCHG BP,[8001]** instruction there instead. There's nothing meaningful about the instructions you find in memory with DEBUG this way. DEBUG is interpreting random values in memory as instructions, so almost any instruction may turn up—and if the random values do not represent a legal machine instruction, you'll see a **DB** directive instead.

Machine Instructions and Their Operands

As we said earlier, **MOV** copies data from a source to a destination. **MOV** is an extremely versatile instruction, and understanding its versatility demands a little study of this notion of source and a destination.

Source and Destination Operands

Most machine instructions, **MOV** included, have one or more *operands*. (Some instructions have no operands.) In the machine instruction **MOV AX,1**, there are two operands. The first is **AX**, and the second is the digit 1.

By convention in assembly language, the first operand belonging to a machine instruction is the *destination operand*. The second operand is the *source operand*.

With the **MOV** instruction, the sense of the two operands is pretty literal: The source operand is copied to the destination operand. In **MOV AX,1**, the source operand 1 is copied into the destination operand **AX**. The sense of source and destination is not nearly so literal in other instructions, but a rule of thumb is this: Whenever a machine instruction causes a new value to be generated, that new value is placed in the destination operand.

There are three different flavors of data that may be used as operands. These are *memory data*, *register data*, and *immediate data*. I've laid some example **MOV** instructions out on the dissection pad in Table 7.1 to give you a flavor for how the different types of data are specified as operands to the **MOV** instruction.

Table 7.1 MOV and Its Operands

MACHINE INSTRUCTION	DESTINATION OPERAND	SOURCE OPERAND
MOV AX,	1	Source is immediate data.
MOV BX,	CX	Both are 16-bit register data.
MOV DL,	BH	Both are 8-bit register data.
MOV [BP],	DI	Destination is memory data at SS:BP.
MOV DX,	[SI]	Source is memory data at DS:SI.
MOV BX,	[ES:BX]	Source is memory data at ES:BX.

Immediate data is by far the easiest to understand. We look at it first.

Immediate Data

The **MOV AX,1** machine instruction that I had you enter into DEBUG was a good example of what we call immediate data accessed through an addressing mode called immediate addressing. *Immediate addressing* gets its name from the fact that the item being addressed is immediate data built right into the machine instruction. The CPU does not have to go anywhere to find immediate data. It's not in a register, nor is it stored in a data segment somewhere out in memory. Immediate data is always right inside the instruction being fetched and executed.

Immediate data must be of an appropriate size for the operand. In other words, you can't move a 16-bit immediate value into an 8-bit register half such as AH or DL. Neither DEBUG nor the stand-alone assemblers will allow you to assemble an instruction like this:

```
MOV CL,67EF
```

CL is an 8-bit register, and 67EFH is a 16-bit quantity. Won't go!

Because it's built right into a machine instruction, you might think immediate data would be quick to access. This is true only to a point: Fetching *anything* from memory takes more time than fetching anything from a register, and instructions are, after all, stored in memory. So, while addressing immediate data is somewhat quicker than addressing ordinary data stored in memory, neither is anywhere near as quick as simply pulling a value from a CPU register.

Also keep in mind that *only* the source operand may be immediate data. The destination operand is the place where data *goes*, not where it comes from. Since immediate data consists of literal constants (numbers such as 1, 0, or 7F2BH), trying to copy something *into* immediate data rather than *from* immediate data simply has no meaning and is always an error.

Register Data

Data stored inside a CPU register is known as *register data*, and accessing register data directly is an addressing mode called *register addressing*. Register addressing is done by simply naming the register we want to work with. Here are some entirely legal examples of register data and register addressing:

```
MOV AX,BX
MOV BP,SP
MOV BL,CH
MOV ES,DX
ADD DI,AX
AND DX,SI
```

The last two examples point up the fact that we're not speaking *only* of the **MOV** instruction here. Register addressing happens any time data in a register is acted on directly, irrespective of what machine instruction is doing the acting.

The assembler keeps track of certain things that don't make sense, and one such situation is having a 16-bit register and an 8-bit register half within the same instruction. Such operations are not legal—after all, what would it mean to move a 2-byte source into a 1-byte destination? And while moving a 1-byte source into a 2-byte destination might seem more reasonable, the CPU does not support it and it cannot be done.

Playing with register addressing is easy using DEBUG. Bring up DEBUG and assemble the following series of instructions:

```
MOV AX,67FE
MOV BX,AX
MOV CL,BH
MOV CH,BL
```

Now, reset the value of IP to 0100 using the R command. Then execute the four machine instructions by issuing the T command four times in a row. The session under DEBUG would look like this:

```
- A
333F:0100 MOV AX,67FE
333F:0103 MOV BX,AX
```

```
333F:0105 MOV CL,BH
333F:0107 MOV CH,BL
333F:0109
- R IP
IP 0100
:0100
- R
AX=0000 BX=0000 CX=0000 DX=0000 SP=FFEE BP=0000 SI=0000 DI=0000
DS=333F ES=333F SS=333F CS=333F IP=0100  NV UP EI PL NZ NA PO NC
333F:0100 B8FE67    MOV   AX,67FE
- T

AX=67FE BX=0000 CX=0000 DX=0000 SP=FFEE BP=0000 SI=0000 DI=0000
DS=333F ES=333F SS=333F CS=333F IP=0103  NV UP EI PL NZ NA PO NC
333F:0103 89C3      MOV   BX,AX
- T

AX=67FE BX=67FE CX=0000 DX=0000 SP=FFEE BP=0000 SI=0000 DI=0000
DS=333F ES=333F SS=333F CS=333F IP=0105  NV UP EI PL NZ NA PO NC
333F:0105 88F9      MOV   CL,BH
- T

AX=67FE BX=67FE CX=0067 DX=0000 SP=FFEE BP=0000 SI=0000 DI=0000
DS=333F ES=333F SS=333F CS=333F IP=0107  NV UP EI PL NZ NA PO NC
333F:0107 88DD      MOV   CH,BL
- T

AX=67FE BX=67FE CX=FE67 DX=0000 SP=FFEE BP=0000 SI=0000 DI=0000
DS=333F ES=333F SS=333F CS=333F IP=0109  NV UP EI PL NZ NA PO NC
333F:0109 1401      ADC   AL,01
```

Keep in mind that the T command executes the instruction displayed in the third line of the most recent R command display. The **ADC** instruction in the last register display is yet another garbage instruction, and although executing this particular instruction would not cause any harm (it's just an **ADC**: Add with Carry), I recommend against executing random instructions just to see what happens. Executing certain jump or interrupt instructions could wipe out sectors on your hard disk or, worse, cause internal damage to DOS that would not show up until later on.

Let's recap what these four instructions accomplished. The first instruction is an example of immediate addressing: The hexadecimal value 067FEH was moved into the AX register. The second instruction used register addressing to move register data from AX into BX. Keep in mind that the way the operands are written is slightly contrary to the common-sense view of things. The destination operand comes *first*. Moving something from AX to BX is done by executing **MOV BX,AX**. Assembly language is just like that sometimes—if that were the most peculiar thing about it, I for one would be mighty grateful . . .

The third instruction and fourth instruction both move data between register halves rather than full, 16-bit registers. These two instructions accomplish something interesting. Look at the last register display, and compare the value of BX and CX. By moving the value from BX into CX a byte at a time, it was possible to reverse the order of the two bytes making up BX. The high half of BX (what we sometimes call the *most significant byte*, or MSB, of BX) was moved into the low half of CX. Then the low half of BX (what we sometimes call the *least significant byte*, or LSB, of BX) was moved into the high half of CX. This is just a sample of the sorts of tricks you can play with the general-purpose registers.

Just to disabuse you of the notion that the **MOV** instruction should be used to exchange the two halves of a 16-bit register, let me suggest that you do the following: Before you exit DEBUG from your previous session, assemble this instruction and execute it using the T command:

```
XCHG CL,CH
```

The **XCHG** instruction exchanges the values contained in its two operands. What was interchanged before is interchanged again, and the value in CX will match the values already in AX and BX. A good idea while writing your first assembly language programs is to double-check the instruction set periodically to see that what you have cobbled together with four or five instructions is not possible using a single instruction. The x86 instruction set is very good at fooling you in that regard! (One caution: Later on, you might find that cobbling something together from simple instructions might run more quickly than the same thing accomplished by a single specialized instruction, especially on the newest Pentium-class CPUs. Pentium optimization is a truly peculiar business—but we're way ahead of ourselves now in speaking of what's fast and what's not. Learn how it works *first*—and then we can explore how fast it is!)

Memory Data

Immediate data is built right into its own machine instruction. Register data is stored in one of the CPU's limited collection of internal registers. In contrast, *memory data* is stored somewhere in the megabyte vastness of real mode memory. Specifying that address is much more complicated than simply reaching into a machine instruction or naming a register.

You should recall that a memory location must be specified in two parts: a *segment address*, which is one of 65,536 segment slots spaced every 16 bytes in memory, and an *offset address*, which is the number of bytes by which the specified byte is offset from the start of the segment. Within the CPU, the segment address is kept in one of the four segment registers, while the offset address (generally just called the *offset*) may be in one of a select group of general-purpose registers that includes *only* BP, BX, SI, and DI. (Register SP is a special case and addresses data located on the stack, as I explain in Chapter 8. To pin down a single byte anywhere within real mode's megabyte of memory, you need both the segment and offset components. We generally write them together, specified with a colon to separate them, as either literal constants or register names: 0B00:0167, DS:SI or CS:IP.

BX's Hidden Agenda

One of the easiest mistakes to make early on is to assume that you can use *any* of the general-purpose registers to specify an offset for memory data. Not so! If you try to specify an offset in AX, CX, or DX, the assembler will flag an error.

In real mode, only BP, BX, SI, and DI may hold an offset for memory data.

(This isn't true for more advanced CPUs working in protected mode, as we'll see toward the end of this book.) So, in fact, general-purpose registers AX, CX, and DX aren't quite so general after all. Why was general-purpose register BX singled out for special treatment? Think of it as the difference between dreams and reality for Intel. In the best of all worlds, every register could be used for all purposes. Unfortunately, when CPU designers get together and argue about what their nascent CPU is supposed to do, they are forced to face the fact that there are only so many transistors on the chip to do the job.

Each chip function is given a budget of transistors (sometimes numbering in the tens or even hundreds of thousands). If the desired logic cannot be implemented using that number of transistors, the expectations of the designers have to be brought down a notch and some CPU features shaved from the specification.

The early x86 CPUs including the 8086 and 8088 are full of such compromises. There were not enough transistors available at design time to allow all general-purpose registers to do everything, so in addition to the truly general-purpose ability to hold data, each 8086/8088 register has what I call a "hidden agenda." Each register has some ability that none of the others share. I describe each register's hidden agenda at some appropriate time in this book, and I call it out as such.

In the 20-odd years since the 8086 was created, Intel has hugely expanded the power of its x86 family of CPUs. And sure enough, when you get into 32-bit protected mode, most of the limitations imposed by early transistor budgets go away, and general-purpose registers become almost completely general. However, when acting in real mode (as we're speaking of here), the Pentium, 486, and 386 CPUs take on just about all the characteristics of the 8086 and 8088, including this sort of limitation, which is built into the logic that decodes the instruction set for real mode.

Should you, then, be learning this sort of bad-old-days limitation? I think so. What it teaches you is that *limitations exist and need to be remembered*. Even the mighty Pentium II has limitations and restrictions. You need to develop a grasp of them, or you'll be floundering around wondering why things don't work.

Using Memory Data

With one or two important exceptions (the string instructions, which I cover to a degree—but not exhaustively—later on), only *one* of an instruction's two operands may specify a memory location. In other words, you can move an immediate value to memory, or a memory value to a register, or some other similar combination, but you *can't* move a memory value directly to another memory value. This is just an inherent limitation of the CPU, and we have to live with it, inconvenient as it gets at times.

Specifying a memory address as one of an instruction's operands is a little complicated. The offset address must be resident in one of the general-purpose registers that can legally hold an offset address. (Remember, that's only BP, BX, SI, and DI—not any of the others such as AX, CX, or

DX.) To specify that we want the data at the memory location contained in the register rather than the data in the register itself, we use square brackets around the name of the register. In other words, to move the word at address DS:BX into register AX, we would use the following instruction:

```
MOV AX,[BX]
```

Similarly, to move a value residing in register DX into the word at address DS:DI, you would use this instruction:

```
MOV [DI],DX
```

Segment Register Assumptions

The only problem with these examples is this: "DS" isn't anywhere in either instruction. Where does it say to use DS as the segment register?

It doesn't. To keep addressing notation simple, the x86 CPUs in real mode make certain assumptions about certain instructions in combinations with certain registers. There is no comprehensible system to these assumptions, and like dates in history or Spanish irregular verbs, you'll just have to memorize them, or at least know where to look them up. (The where is in Appendix B in this book.)

One of these assumptions is that in working with memory data, the **MOV** instruction uses the segment address stored in segment register DS unless you explicitly tell it otherwise. In the case of the two preceding examples, we did *not* tell the **MOV** instruction to use some segment register other than DS, so it fell back on its assumptions and used DS. However, had you specified the offset as residing in register SP instead of BX or DI, the **MOV** instruction would have assumed the use of segment register SS instead. This assumption involves a memory mechanism known as the stack, which we won't really address until the next chapter.

Overriding Segment Assumptions for Memory Data

But what if you *want* to use ES as a segment register for memory data addressed in the **MOV** instruction? It's not difficult. The instruction set includes what are called *segment override prefixes*. These are not precisely instructions, but are more like the filters that may be snapped in front of a camera lens. The filter is not itself a lens, but it alters the way the lens operates.

There is one segment override prefix for each of the four segment registers: CS, DS, SS, and ES. In assembly language they are written as the name of the segment register followed by a colon, as shown in Table 7.2.

In use, the segment override prefix is placed immediately in front of the memory data reference whose segment register assumption is to be overridden. For example, to force a **MOV** instruction to copy a value from the AX register into a location at some offset (contained in SI) into the code segment, you would use this instruction:

```
MOV [CS:SI],AX
```

Without the CS: override prefix, this instruction would move the value of AX into the data segment, at an address specified as DS:SI.

Prefixes in use are very reminiscent of how an address is written; in fact, understanding how prefixes work will help you keep in mind that in *every* reference to memory data within an instruction, there is a ghostly segment register assumption floating in the air. You may not see the ghostly DS: assumption in your **MOV** instruction, but if you forget that it's there, the whole concept of memory data will begin to seem arbitrary and magical.

Every *reference to memory data includes either an assumed segment register or else a segment override prefix to specify a segment register other than the assumed segment register.*

At the machine-code level, a segment override prefix is a single binary byte. The prefix byte is placed *in front of* rather than within a machine instruction. In other words, if the binary bytes comprising a **MOV AX,[BX]** instruction are 8BH 07H, adding the ES segment override prefix to the instruction (**MOV AX,[ES:BX]**) places a single 26H in front of the opcode bytes, giving us 26H 8BH 07H as the full binary equivalent.

Table 7.2 Segment Override Prefixes

SEGMENT OVERRIDE PREFIX	FUNCTION
CS:	Forces use of code segment register CS
DS:	Forces use of the data segment register DS
SS:	Forces use of the stack segment register SS
ES:	Forces use of the extra segment register ES

If you're sharp, the question will already have occurred to you: What about the flat models? Recall that in both real mode flat model and protected mode flat model, the segment registers all point to the same place and are not changed during the run of the program. *In the flat models you do not use segment overrides.* What I have explained previously about segment overrides applies *only* to the real mode segmented model!

Real Mode Memory Data Summary

Real mode memory data consists of a single byte or word in memory, addressed by way of a segment value and an offset value. The register containing the offset address is enclosed in square brackets to indicate that the contents of *memory*, rather than the contents of the register, are being addressed. The segment register used to address memory data is usually assumed according to a complex set of rules. Optionally, a segment override prefix may be placed in the instruction to specify some segment register other than the default segment register.

Figure 7.1 shows diagrammatically what happens during a **MOV AX,[ES:BX]** instruction. The segment address component of the full 20-bit memory address is contained inside the CPU in segment register ES. Ordinarily, the segment address would be in register DS, but the **MOV** instruction contains the ES: segment override prefix. The offset address component is specified to reside in the BX register.

The CPU sends out the values in ES and BX to the memory system side by side. Together, the two values pin down one memory location where **MyWord** begins. **MyWord** is actually two bytes, but that's fine—all the x86 CPUs working in real mode (except for the 8088) can bring both bytes into the CPU at once, while the 8088 brings both bytes in separately, one after the other. The CPU handles details like that and you needn't worry about it. Because AX is a 16-bit register, of course, two 8-bit bytes can fit into it quite nicely.

The segment address may reside in any of the four segment registers: CS, DS, SS, or ES. However, the offset address may reside only in registers BX, BP, SP, SI, or DI. AX, CX, and DX may *not* be used to contain an offset address during real mode memory addressing.

Limitations of the MOV Instruction

The **MOV** instruction can move nearly any register to any other register. For reasons having to do with the limited budget of transistors on

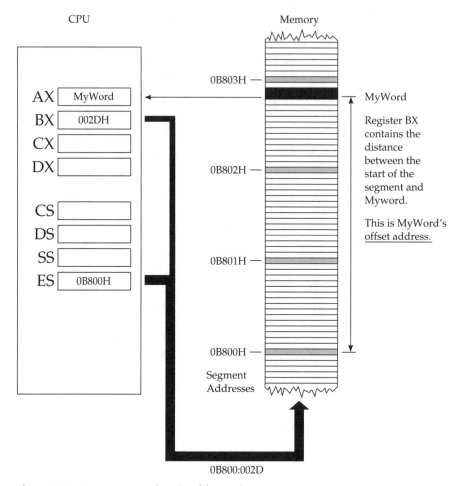

Figure 7.1 How memory data is addressed.

the 8086 and 8088 chips, **MOV** can't quite do any move you can think of—in real mode, at least. Here's a list of **MOV**'s real mode limitations:

1. *MOV cannot move memory data to memory data.* In other words, an instruction like **MOV [SI],[BX]** is illegal. Either of **MOV**'s two operands may be memory data, but *both* cannot be at once.

2. *MOV cannot move one segment register into another.* Instructions like **MOV CS,SS** are illegal. This could have been handy, but it simply can't be done.

3. *MOV cannot move immediate data into a segment register.* You can't code up **MOV CS,0B800H**. Again, it would be handy but you just can't do it.

4. *MOV cannot move one of the 8-bit register halves into a 16-bit register, nor vice versa.* There are easy ways around any possible difficulties here, and preventing moves between operands of different sizes can keep you out of numerous kinds of trouble.

These limitations, of course, are over and above those situations that simply don't make sense: moving a register or memory into immediate data, moving immediate data into immediate data, specifying a general-purpose register as a segment register to contain a segment, or specifying a segment register to contain an offset address. Table 7.3 shows numerous illegal **MOV** instructions that illustrate these various limitations and nonsense situations.

Some Notes on Assembler Syntax

Although we haven't talked about it a whole lot just yet, this book focuses on a particular assembler called NASM. And if this book is your first exposure to assembly language, nothing I've said so far should cause you any cognitive dissonance with your earlier experience, since you have no earlier experience. However, if you've played with assembly language using other assemblers, you will soon begin to see small differences between what you once learned in writing assembly language mnemonics and what I'm teaching in this book. These differences are matters of *syntax,* and they may become important, especially

Table 7.3 Rogue **MOV** Instructions

ILLEGAL MOV INSTRUCTION	WHY IT'S ILLEGAL
MOV 17,1	Only one operand may be immediate data.
MOV 17,BX	Only the source operand may be immediate data.
MOV CX,DH	The operands must be the same size.
MOV [DI],[SI]	Only one operand may be memory data.
MOV DI,[DX:BX]	DX is not a segment register.
MOV ES,0B800	Segment registers may not be loaded from immediate data.
MOV DS,CS	Only one operand may be a segment register.
MOV [AX],BP	AX may not address memory data (nor may CX or DX).
MOV SI,[CS]	Segment registers may not address memory data.

if you ever try to convert source code to NASM from another assembler such as MASM, TASM, or A86.

In the best of all worlds, every assembler would respond in precisely the same way to all the same mnemonics and directives set up all the same ways. In reality, syntax differs. Here's a common example: In Microsoft's MASM, memory data that includes a segment override must be coded like this:

```
MOV AX,ES:[BX]
```

Note here that the segment override "ES:" is *outside* the brackets enclosing BX. NASM places the overrides inside the brackets:

```
MOV AX,[ES:BX]
```

These two lines perform precisely the same job. The people who wrote NASM feel (and I concur) that it makes far more sense to place the override inside the brackets than outside. The difference is purely one of syntax. The two instructions mean precisely the same thing, right down to generating the very same binary machine code: 3E 8B 07.

Worse, when you enter the same thing in DEBUG, it must be done *this* way:

```
ES: MOV AX,[BX]
```

Differences in syntax will drive you crazy on occasion, especially when flipping between NASM and DEBUG. It's best to get a firm grip on what the instructions are doing, and understand what's required to make a particular instruction assemble correctly. I point out some common differences between NASM and MASM throughout this book, since MASM is by far the most popular assembler in the x86 world, and more people have been exposed to it than any other.

Reading and Using an Assembly Language Reference

The **MOV** instruction is a good start. Like a medium-sized screwdriver, you'll end up using it for normal tasks and maybe some abnormal ones, just as I use screwdrivers to pry nails out of boards, club black widow spiders in the garage bathroom, discharge large electrolytic capacitors, and other intriguing things over and above workaday screw turning. (Not all of these are a good idea . . . but then again, many have said that assembly language programming isn't a good idea . . .) The x86 instruction set contains dozens of instructions, however, and over the course of the rest of this book, I mix in descriptions of various other instructions with further discussions of memory addressing and program logic and design.

Remembering a host of tiny, tangled details involving dozens of different instructions is brutal and unnecessary. Even the Big Guys don't try to keep it all between their ears at all times. Most keep a blue card or some other sort of reference document handy to jog their memories about machine instruction details.

Blue Cards

A *blue card* is a reference summary printed on a piece of colored card stock. It folds up like a road map and fits in your pocket. The original blue card may actually have been blue, but knowing the perversity of programmers in general, it was probably bright orange.

Blue cards aren't always cards anymore. One of the best is a full sheet of very stiff shiny plastic, sold by Micro Logic Corporation of Hackensack, New Jersey. The one sold with Microsoft's MASM is actually published by Intel and has grown to a pocket-sized booklet stapled on the spine.

Blue cards contain very terse summaries of what an instruction does, which operands are legal, which flags it affects, and how many machine cycles it takes to execute. This information, while helpful in the extreme, is often so tersely put that newcomers might not quite fathom which edge of the card is up.

An Assembly Language Reference for Beginners

In deference to people just starting out in assembly language, I have put together a beginner's reference to the most common x86 instructions and called it Appendix A. It contains at least a page on every instruction I cover in this book, plus a few additional instructions that everyone ought to know. It does *not* include descriptions on *every* instruction, but only the most common and most useful. Once you've gotten skillful enough to use the more arcane instructions, you should be able to read the NASM documentation (or that of some other assembler) and run with it.

On page 213 is a sample entry from Appendix A. Refer to it during the following discussion.

The instruction's mnemonic is at the top of the page, highlighted in a box to make it easy to spot while flipping quickly through the appendix. To the mnemonic's right is the name of the instruction, which is a little more descriptive than the naked mnemonic.

Flags

Immediately beneath the mnemonic is a minichart of machine flags in the Flags register. I haven't spoken in detail of flags yet, but the Flags register is a collection of 1-bit values that retain certain essential information about the state of the machine for short periods of time. Many (but by no means all) x86 instructions change the values of one or more flags. The flags may then be individually tested by one of the **JMP** instructions, which then change the course of the program depending on the state of the flags.

We'll get into this business of tests and jumps in Chapter 10. For now, simply understand that each of the flags has a name, and that for each flag is a symbol in the flags minichart. You'll come to know the flags by their two-character symbols in time, but until then, the full names of the flags are shown to the right of the minichart. The majority of the flags are not used frequently in beginning assembly language work. Most of what you'll be paying attention to, flags-wise, is the Carry flag (CF). It's used, as you might imagine, for keeping track of binary arithmetic when an arithmetic operation carries out of a single byte or word.

There will be an asterisk (*) beneath the symbol of any flag affected by the instruction. *How* the flag is affected depends on what the instruction does. You'll have to divine that from the Notes section. When an instruction affects no flags at all, the word <none> will appear in the minichart.

In the example page, the minichart indicates that the **NEG** instruction affects the Overflow flag, the Sign flag, the Zero flag, the Auxiliary carry flag, the Parity flag, and the Carry flag. The ways that the flags are affected depend on the results of the negation operation on the operand specified. These ways are summarized in the second paragraph of the Notes section.

NEG Negate (Two's Complement; That Is, Multiply by -1)

Flags affected:

```
O D I T S Z A P C   OF: Overflow flag  TF: Trap flag AF: Aux carry
F F F F F F F F F   DF: Direction flag SF: Sign flag PF: Parity flag
*       * * * * *   IF: Interrupt flag ZF: Zero flag CF: Carry flag
```

Legal forms: 8086/8 286 386 486 Pentium

	8086/8	286	386	486	Pentium
NEG r8	X	X	X	X	X
NEG m8	X	X	X	X	X
NEG r16	X	X	X	X	X
NEG m16	X	X	X	X	X
NEG r32			X	X	X
NEG m32			X	X	X

Examples:

```
NEG AL
NEG ECX
NEG BYTE [BX] ; Negates byte quantity at DS:BX
NEG WORD [DI] ; Negates word quantity at DS:BX
```

Notes:

This is the assembly language equivalent of multiplying a value by –1. Keep in mind that negation is *not* the same as simply inverting each bit in the operand. (Another instruction, NOT, does that.) The process is also known as generating the *two's complement* of a value. The two's complement of a value added to that value yields zero. –1 = $FF; –2 = $FE; –3 = $FD; and so forth.

If the operand is 0, CF is cleared and ZF is set; otherwise, CF is set and ZF is cleared. If the operand contains the maximum negative value (–128 for 8-bit or –32768 for 16-bit), the operand does not change, but OF and CF are set. SF is set if the result is negative, else SF is cleared. PF is set if the low-order 8 bits of the result contain an even number of set (1) bits; otherwise, PF is cleared.

NOTE: You *must* use a type override specifier (BYTE or WORD) with memory data.

```
r8 = AL AH BL BH CL CH DL DH      r16 = AX BX CX DX BP SP SI DI
sr = CS DS SS ES
m8 = 8-bit memory data            m16 = 16-bit memory data
i8 = 8-bit immediate data         i16 = 16-bit immediate data
d8 = 8 bit signed displacement    d16 = 16-bit signed displacement
```

Legal Forms

A given mnemonic represents a single x86 instruction, but each instruction may include more than one legal form. The form of an instruction varies by the type and order of the operands passed to it.

What the individual forms actually represent are different binary number opcodes. For example, beneath the surface, the **POP AX** instruction is the number 58H, whereas the **POP SI** instruction is the number 5EH.

Sometimes there will be special cases of an instruction and its operands that are shorter than the more general cases. For example, the **XCHG** instruction, which exchanges the contents of the two operands, has a special case when one of the operands is register AX. Any **XCHG** instruction with AX as one of the operands is represented by a single-byte opcode. The general forms of **XCHG** (for example, **XCHG r16,r16**) are always 2 bytes long instead. This implies that there are actually two different opcodes that will do the job for a given combination of operands; for example, **XCHG AX,DX**. True enough—and some assembler programs are smart enough to choose the shortest form possible in any given situation. If you are hand-assembling a sequence of raw opcode bytes, say, for use in a higher-level language **INLINE** statement, you need to be aware of the special cases, and all special cases will be marked as such in the Legal forms section.

When you want to use an instruction with a certain set of operands, make sure you check the Legal forms section of the reference guide for that instruction to make sure that the combination is legal. The **MOV** instruction, for example, cannot move one segment register directly into another, nor can it move immediate data directly into a segment register. Neither combination of operands is a legal form of the **MOV** instruction, though they make sense and would be nice to have.

In the example reference page on the **NEG** instruction, you see that a segment register cannot be an operand to **NEG**. (If it could, there would be a **NEG sr** item in the Legal forms list.) If you want to negate the value in a segment register, you'll first have to use **MOV** to move the value from the segment register into one of the general-purpose registers before using **NEG** on the general-purpose register, and finally moving the negated value back into the segment register. (Note well that using **NEG** on a segment register is an almighty peculiar thing to do, and for that reason, that form of **NEG** was not given any transistor budget in the real mode portion of the x86 CPUs.)

Operand Symbols

The symbols used to indicate the nature of the operands in the Legal forms section are summarized at the bottom of every page in the reference appendix. They're close to self-explanatory, but I'll take a moment to expand upon them slightly here:

- **r8**—An 8-bit register half, one of AH, AL, BH, BL, CH, CL, DH, or DL.

- **r16**—A 16-bit general-purpose register, one of AX, BX, CX, DX, BP, SP, SI, or DI.

- **sr**—One of the four segment registers, CS, DS, SS, or ES.

- **m8**—An 8-bit byte of memory data.

- **m16**—A 16-bit word of memory data.

- **m32**—A 32-bit word of memory data.

- **i8**—An 8-bit byte of immediate data.

- **i16**—A 16-bit word of immediate data.

- **i32**—A 32-bit word of immediate data.

- **d8**—An 8-bit signed displacement. We haven't covered these yet, but a *displacement* is a distance between the current location in the code and another place in the code to which we want to jump. It's *signed* (that is, either negative or positive) because a positive displacement jumps you higher (forward) in memory, whereas a negative displacement jumps you lower (back) in memory. We examine this notion in detail in Chapter 10.

- **d16**—A 16-bit signed displacement. Again, for use with jump and call instructions. See Chapter 10.

- **d32**—A 32-bit signed displacement.

Examples

Whereas the Legal forms section shows what combinations of operands is legal for a given instruction, the Examples section shows examples of the instruction in actual use, just as it would be coded in an assembly language program. I've tried to put a good sampling of examples for each instruction, demonstrating the range of different possibilities with the instruction. This includes situations that require type override specifiers, which I cover in the next section.

Notes

The Notes section of the reference page describes the instruction's action briefly and provides information on how it affects the flags, how it may be limited in use, and any other detail that needs to be remembered, especially things that beginners would overlook or misconstrue.

What's Not Here . . .

Appendix A differs from most detailed assembly language references in that it does not have the binary opcode encoding information, nor indications of how many machine cycles are used by each form of the instruction.

The binary encoding of an instruction is the actual sequence of binary bytes that the CPU digests and recognizes as the machine instruction. What we would call **POP AX**, the machine sees as the binary number 58H. What we call **ADD SI,07733H**, the machine sees as the 4-byte sequence 81H 0C6H 33H 77H. Machine instructions are encoded into anywhere from one to four (rarely more) binary bytes depending on what instruction they are and what their operands are. Laying out the system for determining what the encoding will be for any given instruction is extremely complicated, in that its component bytes must be set up bit by bit from several large tables. I've decided that this book is not the place for that particular discussion and have left encoding information out of the reference appendix.

Finally, I've included nothing anywhere in this book that indicates how many machine cycles are expended by any given machine instruction. A *machine cycle* is one pulse of the master clock that makes the PC perform its magic. Each instruction uses some number of those cycles to do its work, and the number varies all over the map depending on criteria that I won't be explaining in this book.

Furthermore, as Michael Abrash explains in his immense book *Michael Abrash's Graphics Programming Black Book* (Coriolis Group Books, 1997), knowing the cycle requirements for individual instructions is rarely sufficient to allow even an expert assembly language programmer to calculate how much time a given series of instructions will take. He and I both agree that it is no fit subject for beginners, and I will let him take it up in his far more advanced volume.

Rally Round the Flags, Boys!

We haven't studied the Flags register as a whole. Flags is a veritable junk drawer of disjointed little bits of information, and it's tough (and perhaps misleading) to just sit down and describe all of them in detail at once. What I do is describe the flags as we encounter them in discussing the various instructions in this and future chapters.

Flags as a whole is a single 16-bit register buried inside the CPU. Of those 16 bits, 9 are actually used as flags in real mode on the x86. The remaining 7 bits are undefined in real mode and ignored. You can neither set them nor read them. Some of those 7 bits become defined and useful in protected mode on the 386 CPU and its successors, but their uses are fairly arcane and I won't be covering them in this book.

A *flag* is a single bit of information whose meaning is independent from any other bit. A bit can be set to 1 or cleared to 0 by the CPU as its needs require. The idea is to tell you, the programmer, the state of certain conditions inside the CPU, so that your program can test for and act on the states of those conditions.

I often imagine a row of country mailboxes, each with its own little red flag on the side. Each flag can be up or down, and if the Smiths' flag is up, it tells the mailman that the Smiths have placed mail in their box to be picked up. The mailman looks to see if the Smiths' flag is raised (a test) and, if so, opens the Smiths' mailbox and picks up the waiting mail.

Each of the Flags register's nine flags has a two-letter symbol by which most programmers know them. I use those symbols most of the time, and you should become familiar with them. The flags, their symbols, and brief descriptions of what they stand for follows:

- **OF**—The **Overflow flag** is set when the result of an operation becomes too large to fit in the operand it originally occupied.

- **DF**—The **Direction flag** is an oddball among the flags in that it tells the *CPU* something that you want it to know, rather than the other way around. It dictates the direction that activity moves (up-memory or down-memory) during the execution of string instructions. When DF is set, string instructions proceed from high memory toward low memory. When DF is cleared, string instructions proceed from low memory toward high memory. I take this up again when I discuss the string instructions.

- **IF**—The **Interrupt enable flag** is a two-way flag. The CPU sets it under certain conditions, and you can set it yourself using the **STI** and **CLI** instructions. When IF is set, interrupts are enabled and may occur when requested. When IF is cleared, interrupts are ignored by the CPU.

- **TF**—When set, the **Trap flag** allows DEBUG's Trace command to do what it does, by forcing the CPU to execute only a single instruction before calling an interrupt routine. This is not an especially useful flag for ordinary programming and I won't have anything more to say about it.

- **SF**—The **Sign flag** becomes set when the result of an operation forces the operand to become negative. By *negative*, we only mean that the highest-order bit in the operand (the *sign bit*) becomes 1 during a signed arithmetic operation. Any operation that leaves the sign positive will clear SF.

- **ZF**—The **Zero flag** becomes set when the results of an operation become zero. If the operand becomes some nonzero value, ZF is cleared.

- **AF**—The **Auxiliary carry flag** is used only for BCD arithmetic. BCD arithmetic treats each operand byte as a pair of 4-bit "nybbles" and allows something approximating decimal (base 10) arithmetic to be done directly in the CPU hardware by using one of the BCD arithmetic instructions. These instructions are not much used anymore; I discuss BCD arithmetic only briefly later on.

- **PF**—The **Parity flag** will seem instantly familiar to anyone who understands serial data communications, and utterly bizarre to anyone who doesn't. PF indicates whether the number of set (1) bits in the low-order byte of a result is even or odd. For example, if the result is 0F2H, PF will be cleared because 0F2H (11110010) contains an odd number of 1 bits. Similarly, if the result is 3AH (00111100),

PF will be set because there is an even number (four) of 1 bits in the result. This flag is a carryover from the days when all computer communications were done through a serial port, for which a system of error detection called *parity checking* depends on knowing whether a count of set bits in a character byte is even or odd. PF has no other use and I won't be describing it further.

- CF—The **Carry flag** is by far the most useful flag in the Flags register, and the one you will have to pay attention to most. If the result of an arithmetic or shift operation "carries out" a bit from the operand, CF becomes set. Otherwise, if nothing is carried out, CF is cleared.

Check That Reference Page!

What I call "flag etiquette" is the way a given instruction affects the flags in the Flags register. You *must* remember that the descriptions of the flags on the previous pages are generalizations *only* and are subject to specific restrictions and special cases imposed by individual instructions. Flag etiquette for individual flags varies widely from instruction to instruction, even though the *sense* of the flag's use may be the same in every case.

For example, some instructions that cause a zero to appear in an operand set ZF, while others do not. Sadly, there's no system to it and no easy way to keep it straight in your head. When you intend to use the flags in testing by way of conditional jump instructions (see Chapter 10), you have to check each individual instruction to see how the various flags are affected.

Flag etiquette is a highly individual matter. Check the reference for each instruction to see if it affects the flags. Assume nothing!

A simple lesson in flag etiquette involves two new instructions, **INC** and **DEC**, and yet another interesting ability of DEBUG.

Adding and Subtracting One with INC and DEC

Several x86 machine instructions come in pairs. Simplest among those are **INC** and **DEC**, which increment and decrement an operand by one, respectively.

Adding one to something or subtracting one from something are actions that happen a *lot* in computer programming. If you're counting the number of times a program is executing a loop, or counting bytes in a table, or doing something that advances or retreats one count at a time, **INC** or **DEC** can be very quick ways to make the actual addition or subtraction happen.

Both **INC** and **DEC** take only one operand. An error will be flagged by DEBUG or by your assembler if you try to use either **INC** or **DEC** with two operands, or without any operands.

Try both by using the Assemble command and the Trace command under DEBUG. Assemble this short program, display the registers after entering it, and then trace through it:

```
MOV AX,FFFF
MOV BX,002F
DEC BX
INC AX
```

The session should look very much like this:

```
- A
1980:0100 MOV AX,FFFF
1980:0103 MOV BX,002D
1980:0106 INC AX
1980:0107 DEC BX
1980:0108
- R
AX=0000 BX=0000 CX=0000 DX=0000 SP=FFEE BP=0000 SI=0000 DI=0000
DS=1980 ES=1980 SS=1980 CS=1980 IP=0100   NV UP EI PL NZ NA PO NC
1980:0100 B8FFFF     MOV    AX,FFFF
- T

AX=FFFF BX=0000 CX=0000 DX=0000 SP=FFEE BP=0000 SI=0000 DI=0000
DS=1980 ES=1980 SS=1980 CS=1980 IP=0103   NV UP EI PL NZ NA PO NC
1980:0103 BB2D00     MOV    BX,002D
- T

AX=FFFF BX=002D CX=0000 DX=0000 SP=FFEE BP=0000 SI=0000 DI=0000
DS=1980 ES=1980 SS=1980 CS=1980 IP=0106   NV UP EI PL NZ NA PO NC
1980:0106 40         INC    AX
- T

AX=0000 BX=002D CX=0000 DX=0000 SP=FFEE BP=0000 SI=0000 DI=0000
DS=1980 ES=1980 SS=1980 CS=1980 IP=0107   NV UP EI PL ZR AC PE NC
1980:0107 4B         DEC    BX
- T
```

```
AX=0000 BX=002C CX=0000 DX=0000 SP=FFEE BP=0000 SI=0000 DI=0000
DS=1980 ES=1980 SS=1980 CS=1980 IP=0108  NV UP EI PL NZ NA PO NC
1980:0108 0F        POP      CS
```

Watch what happens to the registers. Decrementing BX predictably turns the value 2DH into value 2CH. Incrementing 0FFFFH, on the other hand, rolls over the register to 0 since 0FFFFH is the largest unsigned value that can be expressed in a 16-bit register. Adding 1 to it rolls it over to zero, just as adding 1 to 99 rolls the rightmost two digits of the sum to zero in creating the number 100. The difference with **INC** is that *there is no carry*. The Carry flag is not affected by **INC**, so don't try to use it to perform multidigit arithmetic.

Using DEBUG to Watch the Flags

When **INC** rolled AX over to zero, the Carry flag was not affected, but the Zero flag (ZF) became set (that is, equal to 1). The Zero flag works that way: When the result of an operation becomes zero, ZF is almost always set.

DEC sets the flags in the same way. If you were to execute a **DEC DX** instruction when DX contained 1, DX would become zero and ZF would be set.

Apart from looking at a reference guide, how can you tell what flags are affected by a given instruction? DEBUG allows you to see the flags as they change, just as it lets you dump memory and examine the values in the general-purpose and segment registers. The second line of DEBUG's three-line register display contains eight cryptic symbols at its right margin. You've been seeing them, I'm sure, without having a clue as to their meaning.

Eight of the nine 8086/8088 flags are represented by two-character symbols. (The odd flag out is Trap flag TF, which is reserved for exclusive use by DEBUG itself and cannot be examined while DEBUG has control of the machine.) Unfortunately, the symbols DEBUG uses are not the same as the standard flag symbols that programmers call the flags by. The difference is that DEBUG's flag symbols do not represent the flags' *names* but rather the flags' *values*. Each flag can be set or cleared, and DEBUG displays the state of each flag by having a unique symbol for each state of each flag, for a total of 16 distinct symbols in all. The symbols' meanings are summarized in Table 7.4.

Table 7.4 DEBUG's Flag State Symbols

FLAG	NAME	SET SYMBOL	CLEAR SYMBOL
OF	Overflow flag	OV	NV
DF	Direction flag	DN	UP
IE	Interrupt enable flag	EI	DI
SF	Sign flag	NG	PL
ZF	Zero flag	ZR	NZ
AF	Auxiliary carry flag	AC	NA
PF	Parity flag	PE	PO
CF	Carry flag	CY	NC

The best I can say for this symbol set is that it's not obviously obscene. It is, however, nearly impossible to memorize. You'd best keep a reduced copy of this table (perhaps taped to the back of a business card) near your keyboard if you intend to watch the waving of the x86 CPU flags.

When you first run DEBUG, the flags are set to their default values, which are these:

```
NV UP EI PL NZ NA PO NC
```

You'll note that all these symbols are clear symbols except for EI, which must be set to allow interrupts to happen. Whether you are aware of it or not, interrupts are happening constantly within your PC. Each keystroke you type on the keyboard triggers an interrupt. Every 55 milliseconds, the system clock triggers an interrupt to allow the BIOS software to update the time and date values kept in memory as long as the PC has power. If you disabled interrupts for any period of time, your real-time clock would stop and your keyboard would freeze up. Needless to say, IE must be kept set nearly all the time.

Each time you execute an instruction with the Trace command, the flags display will be updated. If the instruction that was executed affected any of the flags, the appropriate symbol will be displayed over the previous symbol.

With Table 7.4 in hand, go back and examine the flags display for the four-instruction DEBUG trace shown a few pages back. The first display shows the default values for all the flags, since no instructions have been executed yet. No change appears for the second and third flags displays, because the **MOV** instruction affects none of the flags.

But look closely at the flags display after the **INC AX** instruction executes. Three of the flags have changed state: ZF has gone from NZ (clear) to ZR (set), indicating that the operand of **INC** went to zero as a result of the increment operation. AF has gone from NA to AC. (Let's just skip past that one; explaining what it means would be more confusing than helpful.) Parity flag PF has gone from PO to PE. This means that as a result of the increment operation, the number of bits present in the low byte of BX went from odd to even.

Finally, look at the last flags display, the one shown after the **DEC BX** instruction was executed. Again, ZF, AF, and PF changed. ZF went to NZ, indicating that the **DEC** instruction left a nonzero value in its operand. PF, moreover, went from PE to PO, indicating that the number of bits in the low byte of BX was odd after the **DEC BX** instruction.

One thing to keep in mind is that even when a flag doesn't change state from display to display, it was still *affected* by the previously executed instruction. Five out of nine flags affected by *every* **INC** and **DEC** instruction that the CPU executes. Not every **DEC** instruction decrements its operand down to zero, but every **DEC** instruction causes some value to be asserted in ZF. The same holds true for the other four affected flags: Even if the state of an affected flag doesn't *change* as a result of an instruction, the state is *asserted*, even if only reasserted to its existing value.

Thorough understanding of the flags comes with practice and dogged persistence. It's one of the more chaotic aspects of assembly language programming, but as we'll see when we get to conditional branches, flags are what make the CPU truly come alive to do our work for us.

Using Type Specifiers

Back on the sample reference appendix page (see page 212), notice the following example uses of the **NEG** instruction:

```
NEG BYTE [BX] ; Negates byte quantity at DS:BX
NEG WORD [DI] ; Negates word quantity at DS:BX
```

Why **BYTE [BX]**? Or **WORD [DI]**? Used in this way, **BYTE** and **WORD** are what we call *type specifiers*, and you literally can't use **NEG** (or numerous other machine instructions) on memory data without one or the other. They are not instructions in the same sense that **NEG** is an instruction. They exist in the broad class of things we call directives. *Directives* give instructions to the assembler. In this case, they tell the assembler how large the operand is when there is no other way for the assembler to know.

The problem is this: The **NEG** instruction negates its operand. The operand can be either a byte or a word; in real mode, **NEG** works equally well on both. But . . . how does **NEG** know whether to negate a byte or a word? The memory data operand [BX] only specifies an *address* in memory, using DS as the assumed segment register. The address DS:BX points to a byte—but it also points to a word, which is nothing more than two bytes in a row somewhere in memory. So, does **NEG** negate the byte located at address DS:BX? Or does it negate the *two* bytes (a word) that start at address DS:BX?

Unless you tell it somehow, **NEG** has no way to know.

Telling an instruction the size of its operand is what **BYTE** and **WORD** do. Several other instructions that work on single operands only (such as **INC**, **DEC**, and **NOT**) have the same problem and use type specifiers to resolve this ambiguity.

Types in Assembly Language

Unlike nearly all high-level languages such as Pascal and C++, the notion of *type* in assembly language is almost wholly a question of *size*. A word is a type, as is a byte, a double word, a quad word, and so on. The assembler is unconcerned with what an assembly language variable *means*. (Keeping track of such things is totally up to you.) The assembler only worries about how big it is. The assembler does not want to have to try to fit 10 pounds of kitty litter in a 5-pound bag, which is impossible, nor 5 pounds of kitty litter in a 10-pound bag, which can be confusing and under some circumstances possibly dangerous.

Register data always has a fixed and obvious type, since a register's size cannot be changed. BL is one byte and BX is two bytes.

The type of immediate data depends on the magnitude of the immediate value. If the immediate value is too large to fit in a single byte, that immediate value becomes word data and you can't load it into an 8-bit register half. An immediate value that can fit in a single byte may be loaded into either a byte-sized register half or a full word-sized register; its type is thus taken from the context of the instruction in which it exists and matches that of the register data operand into which it is to be loaded. But if you try to load immediate data into a destination that's too small for it, the assembler will give you an error. Here's a trivial example:

```
MOV BL,0FFFFH
```

When it encounters this, NASM will complain by saying, "Warning: Byte value exceeds bounds." BL can hold values from 0 to 0FFH. (0 to 255). The value 0FFFFH is out of bounds because it is much larger than 0FFH.

Memory data is something else again. We've spoken of memory data so far in terms of registers holding offsets without considering the use of named memory data. I discuss named memory data in the next chapter, but in brief terms, you can define named variables in your assembly language programs using such directives as **DB** and **DW**. It looks like this:

```
Counter    DB 0
MixTag     DW 32
```

Here, **Counter** is a variable allocated as a single byte in memory by the **DB** (**D**efine **B**yte) directive. Similarly, **MixTag** is a variable allocated as a word in memory by the **DW** (**D**efine **W**ord) directive.

By using **DB**, you give variable **Counter** a type and hence a size. You must match this type when you use the variable name **Counter** in an instruction to indicate memory data. The way to do this is to use the BYTE directive, as I mentioned a little earlier. This, for example, will be accepted by the assembler:

```
MOV BL,BYTE [Counter]
```

This instruction will take the current value located in memory at the address represented by the variable name **Counter** and will load that variable into register half BL. You might wonder: Why do I need to put the **BYTE** directive there? The assembler should know that **Counter** is 1 byte in size because it was defined using the directive **DB**.

In some assemblers, including Microsoft's MASM, it would. However, NASM's authors feel that it's important to be as explicit with assemblers as possible and leave little or nothing for the assembler to infer from context. So, although NASM uses the **DB** directive to allocate one byte of memory for the variable **Counter**, it does not remember that **Counter** takes up only one byte when you insert **Counter** as an operand in a machine instruction. You must build that specification into your source code, by using the **BYTE** directive. This will force you to think a little bit more about what you're doing at every point that you do it; that is, right where you use variable names as instruction operands. Doing so may help you avoid certain *really* stupid mistakes—like the ones I used to make all the time while I was working with MASM, most of which came out of trying to let the assembler do my thinking for me.

To me, this is a wonderful thing, and one of the main reasons I chose NASM as the focus of this book.

Now here's another case, one that NASM will assemble without a burp:

```
MOV BL,BYTE MixTag
```

This looks innocent enough until you remember that **MixTag** is actually 2 bytes (one word) in size, having been defined with the **DW** directive. You might think this is an error, because **MixTag** isn't the same size as BL. True enough—but the key is that there's no *ambiguity* here. The assembler knows what you want, even if what you want is peculiar. The type specifier **BYTE** forces the assembler to look upon **MixTag** as being 1 byte in size. **MixTag** is *not* byte-sized, however, so what actually happens is that the least significant (lowermost) byte of **MixTag** will be loaded into BL, with the most significant byte left high and dry.

Is this useful? It can be. Is it dangerous? You bet. It is up to you to decide whether overriding the type of memory data makes sense and is completely your responsibility to ensure that doing so doesn't sprinkle your code with bugs. *But nothing is left for the assembler to decide.* That's what type specifiers are for: to make it clear to the assembler *in every case* what it is supposed to do. Whether that in fact makes sense is up to you. Use your head—and know what you're doing. That's more important in assembly language than anywhere else in computer programming.

CHAPTER 8

Our Object All Sublime

Creating Programs that Work

They don't call it "assembly" for nothing. Facing the task of writing an assembly language program brings to mind images of Christmas morning: You've spilled 1,567 small metal parts out of a large box marked *Land Shark HyperBike* (Some Assembly Required) and now you have to somehow put them all together with nothing left over. (In the meantime, the kids seem more than happy playing in the box . . .)

I've actually explained just about all you absolutely *must* understand to create your first assembly language program. Still, there is a nontrivial leap from here to there; you are faced with many small parts with sharp edges that can fit together in an infinity of different ways, most wrong, some workable, but only a few that are ideal.

So here's the plan: In the following section I will present you with the completed and operable Land Shark HyperBike—which I will then tear apart before your eyes. This is the best way to learn to assemble: By pulling apart programs written by those who know what they're doing. Over the rest of this book we'll pull a few more programs apart, in the hope that by the time it's over you'll be able to move in the other direction all by yourself.

The Bones of an Assembly Language Program

The following listing is perhaps the simplest correct program that will do anything visible and still be comprehensible and expandable. This issue of comprehensibility is utterly central to quality assembly language programming. With no other computer language (not even APL or that old devil FORTH) is there anything even close to the risk of writing code that looks so much like something scraped off the wall of King Tut's tomb.

The program EAT.ASM displays one (short) line of text on your display screen:

```
Eat at Joe's!
```

For that you have to feed 28 lines of text file to the assembler. Many of those 28 lines are unnecessary in the strict sense, but serve instead as commentary to allow you to understand what the program is doing (or more important, *how* it's doing it) six months or a year from now.

One of the aims of assembly language coding is to use as few instructions as possible in getting the job done. This does *not* mean creating as short a source code file as possible. (The size of the source file has *nothing* to do with the size of the executable file assembled from it!) The more comments you put in your file, the better you'll remember how things work inside the program the next time you pick it up. I think you'll find it amazing how quickly the logic of a complicated assembly language file goes cold in your head. After no more than 48 hours of working on other projects, I've come back to assembler projects and had to struggle to get back to flank speed on development.

Comments are neither time nor space wasted. IBM used to say, One line of comments per line of code. That's good—and should be considered a *minimum* for assembly language work. A better course (that I will in fact follow in the more complicated examples later on) is to use one short line of commentary to the right of each line of code, along with a comment block at the start of each sequence of instructions that work together in accomplishing some discrete task.

Here's the program. Read it carefully:

```
; Source name     : EAT.ASM
; Executable name : EAT.COM
; Code model:      : Real mode flat model
```

```
; Version        : 1.0
; Created date   : 6/4/1999
; Last update    : 9/10/1999
; Author         : Jeff Duntemann
; Description     : A simple example of a DOS .COM file programmed using
;                   NASM-IDE 1.1 and NASM 0.98.


[BITS 16]          ; Set 16 bit code generation
[ORG 0100H]        ; Set code start address to 100h (COM file)

[SECTION .text]    ; Section containing code

START:

  mov  dx, eatmsg  ; Mem data ref without [] loads the ADDRESS!
  mov  ah,9        ; Function 9 displays text to standard output.
  int  21H         ; INT 21H makes the call into DOS.

  mov  ax, 04C00H  ; This DOS function exits the program
  int  21H         ; and returns control to DOS.

[SECTION .data]    ; Section containing initialized data

eatmsg  db "Eat at Joe's!", 13, 10, "$" ;Here's our message
```

The Simplicity of Flat Model

After all our discussion in previous chapters about segments, this program might seem, um, . . . *suspiciously* simple. And indeed it's simple, and it's simple almost entirely because it's written for the 16-bit real mode flat model. (I drew this model out in Figure 6.8.) The first thing you'll notice is that there are no references to segments or segment registers anywhere. The reason for this is that in real mode flat model, you are inside a single segment, and everything you do, you do within that single segment. If everything happens within one single segment, the segments (in a sense) "factor out" and you can imagine that they don't exist. Once we assemble EAT.ASM and create a runnable program from it, I'll show you what those segment registers are up to and how it is that you can almost ignore them in real mode flat model.

But first, let's talk about what all those lines are doing.

At the top is a summary comment block. This text is for your use only. When NASM processes a .ASM file, it strips out and discards all text between any semicolon and the end of the line the semicolon is in. Such lines are comments, and they serve only to explain what's going on in your program. They add nothing to the executable file, and they don't pass information to the assembler. I recommend placing a summary comment block like this at the top of every source code file you create. Fill it with information that will help someone else understand the file you've written or that will help you understand the file later on, after it's gone cold in your mind.

Beneath the comment block is a short sequence of commands directed to the assembler. These commands are placed in square brackets so that NASM knows that they are for its use, and are not to be interpreted as part of the program.

The first of these commands is this:

```
[BITS 16]          ; Set 16 bit code generation
```

The BITS command tells NASM that the program it's assembling is intended to be run in real mode, which is a 16-bit mode. Using [BITS 32] instead would have brought into play all the marvelous 32-bit protected mode goodies introduced with the 386 and later x86 CPUs. On the other hand, DOS can't run protected mode programs, so that wouldn't be especially useful.

The next command requires a little more explanation:

```
[ORG 0100h]          ; Set code start address to 100h (COM file)
```

"ORG" is an abbreviation of *origin*, and what it specifies is sometimes called the *origin* of the program, which is where code execution begins. Code execution begins at 0100H for this program. The 0100h value (the *h* and *H* are interchangeable) is loaded into the instruction pointer IP by DOS when the program is loaded and run. So, when DOS turns control over to your program (scary thought, that!), the first instruction to be executed is the one pointed to by IP—in this case, at 0100H.

Why 0100H? Look back at Figure 6.8. The real mode flat model (which is often called the .COM file model) has a 256-byte prefix at the beginning of its single segment. This is the Program Segment Prefix (PSP) and it has several uses that I won't be explaining here. The PSP is basically a data buffer and contains no code. The code cannot begin until after the PSP, so the 0100H value is there to tell DOS to skip those first 256 bytes.

The next command is this:

```
[SECTION .text]     ; Section containing code
```

NASM divides your programs into what it calls *sections*. These sections are less important in real mode flat model than in real mode segmented model, when sections map onto segments. (More on this later.) In flat model, you have only one segment. But the SECTION commands tell NASM where to look for particular types of things. In the .text section, NASM expects to find program code. A little further down the file you'll see another SECTION command, this one for the .data section. In the .data section, NASM expects to find the definitions for your initialized variables. A third section is possible, the .bss section, which contains uninitialized data. EAT.ASM does not use any uninitialized data, so this section does not exist in this program. I discuss uninitialized data later on, in connection with the stack.

Labels

The next item in the file is something called a label:

```
START:
```

A *label* is a sort of bookmark, holding a place in the program code and giving it a name that's easier to remember than a memory address. The START: label indicates where the program begins. Technically speaking, the START: label isn't necessary in EAT.ASM. You could eliminate the START: label and the program would still assemble and run. However, I think that every program should have a START: label as a matter of discipline. That's why EAT.ASM has one.

Labels are used to indicate where **JMP** instructions should jump to, and I explain that in detail later in this chapter and in later chapters. The only distinguishing characteristic of labels is that they're followed by colons. Some rules govern what constitutes a valid label:

- *Labels must begin with a letter or with an underscore, period, or question mark.* These last three have special meanings (especially the period), so I recommend sticking with letters until you're way further along in your study of assembly language and NASM.

- *Labels must be followed by a colon when they are defined.* This is basically what tells NASM that the identifier being defined is a label. NASM will punt if no colon is there and will not flag an error, but the colon nails it, and prevents a misspelled mnemonic from being mistaken for a label. So use the colon!

- *Labels are case sensitive.* So yikes:, Yikes:, and YIKES: are three completely different labels. This differs from practice in a lot of languages (Pascal particularly) so keep it in mind.

Later on, we'll see such labels used as the targets of jump instructions. For example, the following machine instruction transfers the flow of instruction execution to the location marked by the label **GoHome**:

```
JMP  GoHome
```

Notice that the colon is *not* used here. The colon is only placed where the label is *defined*, not where it is *referenced*. Think of it this way: Use the colon when you are *marking* a location, not when you are *going* there.

Variables for Initialized Data

The identifier **eatmsg** defines a *variable*. Specifically, **eatmsg** is a string variable (more on which follows) but still, as with all variables, it's one of a class of items we call *initialized data:* something that comes with a value, and not just a box that will accept a value at some future time. A variable is defined by associating an identifier with a *data definition directive.* Data definition directives look like this:

```
MyByte     DB 07H           ; 8 bits in size
MyWord     DW 0FFFFH        ; 16 bits in size
MyDouble   DD 0B8000000H    ; 32 bits in size
```

Think of the **DB** directive as "Define Byte." **DB** sets aside one byte of memory for data storage. Think of the **DW** directive as "Define Word." **DW** sets aside one word of memory for data storage. Think of the **DD** directive as "Define Double." **DD** sets aside a double word in memory for storage, typically for full 32-bit addresses.

I find it useful to put some recognizable value in a variable whenever I can, even if the value is to be replaced during the program's run. It helps to be able to spot a variable in a DEBUG dump of memory rather than to have to find it by dead reckoning—that is, by spotting the closest known location to the variable in question and counting bytes to determine where it is.

String Variables

String variables are an interesting special case. A *string* is just that: a sequence or string of characters, all in a row in memory. A string is defined in EAT.ASM:

```
eatmsg   DB "Eat at Joe's!", 13, 10, "$" ;Here's our message
```

Strings are a slight exception to the rule that a data definition directive sets aside a particular quantity of memory. The **DB** directive ordinarily sets aside one byte only. However, a string may be any length you like, as long as it remains on a single line of your source code file. Because there is no data directive that sets aside 16 bytes, or 42, strings are defined simply by associating a label with the place where the string *starts*. The **eatmsg** label and its **DB** directive specify one byte in memory as the string's starting point. The number of characters in the string is what tells the assembler how many bytes of storage to set aside for that string.

Either single quote (') or double quote (") characters may be used to delineate a string, and the choice is up to you, *unless* you're defining a string value that itself contains one or more quote characters. Notice in EAT.ASM the string variable **eatmsg** contains a single-quote character used as an apostrophe. Because the string contains a single-quote character, you *must* delineate it with double quotes. The reverse is also true: If you define a string that contains one or more double-quote characters, you must delineate it with single-quote characters:

```
Yukkh    DB    'He said, "How disgusting!" and threw up.',"$"
```

You may combine several separate substrings into a single string variable by separating the substrings with commas. Both **eatmsg** and **Yukkh** do this. Both add a dollar sign ($) in quotes to the end of the main string data. The dollar sign is used to mark the end of the string for the mechanism that displays the string to the screen. More on that mechanism and marking string lengths in a later section.

What, then, of the "13,10" in **eatmsg**? This is the carriage return and linefeed pair I discussed in an earlier chapter. Inherited from the ancient world of electromechanical Teletype machines, these two characters are recognized by DOS as meaning the end of a line of text that is output to the screen. If anything further is output to the screen, it will begin at the left margin of the next line below. You can concatenate such individual numbers within a string, but you must remember that they will not appear as numbers. A string is a string of *characters*. A number appended to a string will be interpreted by most operating system routines as an ASCII character. The correspondence between numbers and ASCII characters is shown in Appendix D.

Directives versus Instruction Mnemonics

Data definition directives look a little like machine instruction mnemonics, but they are emphatically *not* machine instructions. One very common mistake made by beginners is looking for the binary opcode represented by a directive such as **DB** or **DW**. There is no binary opcode for **DW**, **DB**, and the other directives. Machine instructions, as the name implies, are instructions to the CPU itself. Directives, by contrast, are instructions to the *assembler*.

Understanding directives is easier when you understand the nature of the assembler's job. (Look back to Chapter 4 for a detailed refresher if you've gotten fuzzy on what assemblers and linkers do.) The assembler scans your source code text file, and as it scans your source code file it builds an object code file on disk. It builds this object code file step by step, one byte at a time, starting at the beginning of the file and working its way through to the end. When it encounters a machine instruction mnemonic, it figures out what binary opcode is represented by that mnemonic and writes that binary opcode (which may be anywhere from one to six actual bytes) to the object code file.

When the assembler encounters a directive such as **DW**, it does not write any opcode to the object code file. DW is a kind of signpost to the assembler, reading "Set aside two bytes of memory right here, for the value that follows." The **DW** directive specifies an initial value for the variable, and so the assembler writes the bytes corresponding to that value in the two bytes it set aside. The assembler writes the address of the allocated space into a table, beside the label that names the variable. *Then* the assembler moves on, to the next directive (if there are further directives) or to whatever comes next in the source code file.

For example, when you write the following statement in your assembly language program:

```
MyVidOrg    DW    0B800H
```

what you are really doing is instructing the assembler to set aside two bytes of data (**D**efine **W**ord, remember) and place the value 0B800H in those two bytes. The assembler writes the identifier **MyVidOrg** and the variable's address into a table it builds of identifiers (both labels and variables) in the program for later use by other elements of the program, or the linker.

The Difference between a Variable's Address and Its Contents

I've left discussion of EAT.ASM's machine instructions for last—at least in part because they're easy to explain. All that EAT.ASM does, really, is hand a string to DOS and tell DOS to display it on the screen by sending it to something called *standard output*. It does this by passing the address of the string to DOS—*not* the character values contained in the string itself. This is a crucial distinction that trips up a lot of beginners. Here's the first instruction in EAT.ASM:

```
mov  dx, eatmsg    ; Mem data ref without [] loads the ADDRESS!
```

If you look at the program, you can see that while DX is 2 bytes in size, the string **eatmsg** is 15 bytes in size. At first glance, this **MOV** instruction would seem impossible—but that's because what's being moved is not the string itself, but the string's address, which (in the real mode flat model) is 16 bits—2 bytes—in size. The address will thus fit nicely in DX.

When you place a variable's identifier in a **MOV** instruction, you are accessing the variable's address, as explained previously. By contrast, if you want to work with the *value* stored in that variable, you must place the variable's identifier in square brackets. Suppose you had defined a variable in the .data section called **MyData** this way:

```
MyData    DW    0744H
```

The identifier **MyData** represents some address in memory, and at that address the assembler places the value 0744H. Now, if you want to copy the value contained in **MyData** to the AX register, you would use the following **MOV** instruction:

```
MOV AX,[MyData]
```

After this instruction, AX would contain 0744H.

There are many situations in which you need to move the *address* of a variable into a register rather than the *contents* of the variable. In fact, you may find yourself moving the addresses of variables around more than the contents of the variables, especially if you make a lot of calls to DOS and BIOS services.

If you've used higher-level languages such as Basic and Pascal, this distinction may seem inane. After all, who would mistake the contents of a variable for its location? Well, that's easy for you to say—in Basic and Pascal you rarely if ever even *think* about where a variable is. The language handles all that rigmarole for you. In assembly language, knowing where a variable is located is essential in order to do lots of important things.

Making DOS Calls

What EAT.ASM really does, as I mentioned previously, is call DOS and instruct DOS to display a string located at a particular place in memory. The string itself doesn't go anywhere; EAT.ASM tells DOS where the string is located, and then DOS reaches up into your .data section and does what it must with the string data.

Calling DOS is done with something called a *software interrupt*. I explain these in detail later in this chapter. But if you look at the code you can get a sense for what's going on:

```
mov  dx, eatmsg    ; Mem data ref without [] loads the ADDRESS!
mov  ah,9          ; Function 9 displays text to standard output.
int  21H           ; INT 21H makes the call into DOS.
```

Here, the first line loads the address of the string into register DX. The second line simply loads the constant value 9 into register AH. The third line makes the interrupt call, to interrupt 21H.

The DOS call has certain requirements that must be set up before the call is made. It must know what particular call you want to make, and each call has a number. This number must be placed in AH and, in this case, is call 09H (Display String). For this particular DOS call, DOS expects the address of the string to be displayed to be in register DX. If you satisfy those two conditions, you can make the DOS software interrupt call INT 21H—and there's your string on the screen!

Exiting the Program and Setting ERRORLEVEL

Finally, the job is done, Joe's has been properly advertised, and it's time to let DOS have the machine back. Another DOS service, 4CH (Terminate Process), handles the mechanics of courteously disentangling the machine from EAT.ASM's clutches. Terminate Process doesn't need the address of anything, but it will take whatever value it finds in the AL register and place it in the ERRORLEVEL DOS variable. DOS batch programs can test the value of ERRORLEVEL and branch on it.

EAT.ASM doesn't do anything worth testing in a batch program, but if ERRORLEVEL will be set anyway, it's a good idea to provide some reliable and harmless value for ERRORLEVEL to take. This is why 0 is loaded into AL prior to ending it all by the final **INT 21** instruction. If you were to test ERRORLEVEL after running EAT.EXE, you would find it set to 0 in every case.

That's really all there is to EAT.ASM. Now let's see what it takes to run it, and then let's look more closely at its innards in memory.

Assembling and Running EAT.ASM

To assemble and run EAT.ASM, we can load it into NASM-IDE, and then let NASM-IDE invoke NASM. That's how we're going to do it here. You should understand, however, that NASM-IDE is simply a "place to stand." NASM is what actually does the work of assembling the file.

Here's the sequence:

1. Run NASM-IDE.

2. Select the Open item from the File menu. (We would say this, in short-hand form, "Select File | Open.")

3. Highlight the name of file EAT.ASM, and click on the OK button. EAT.ASM will load and be displayed in a window. If EAT.ASM isn't in the same directory as NASM-IDE, you may have to navigate to the directory where EAT.ASM lives by clicking on directory names in the dialog box.

4. Select Assemble | Assemble. The Error window will appear in the lower half of the display, even if only to tell you, "No errors occurred."

5. Assuming no errors occurred, select Assemble | Run. The display will clear, and EAT's message will be displayed in the upper-left corner of the display. Beneath it you'll see DOS's message, "Press any key to continue . . ." Press any key, and the display will return to NASM-IDE, showing EAT.ASM.

Assembler and Interactive Development Environment

There it is: You've assembled and run an assembly language program. It's important at this point to ponder who's doing what on your system. If you read Chapter 5, you know that NASM-IDE is an interactive development environment (IDE) containing a source code editor and a few other tools. NASM-IDE is *not* the assembler. The assembler is called NASM, and NASM is a separate program that does not actually require NASM-IDE for its use. When you select Assemble | Assemble in NASM-IDE, the NASM-IDE program invokes the NASM assembler behind the scenes and passes the name of the program you're working on to NASM, which assembles it and writes the file EAT.COM to disk. Later, when you select Assemble | Run in NASM-IDE, the NASM-IDE program runs EAT.COM for you.

Technically, you don't need NASM-IDE. You can invoke the assembler yourself from the DOS command line, and you can of course run the generated EAT.COM file by naming it on the command line as well. NASM-IDE is there to save you time and let you make changes and reassemble your program quickly and with less keyboarding.

You should, however, understand what NASM-IDE is doing. One major thing it's doing for you is constructing a proper command line by which to invoke NASM. To treat EAT.ASM as a program written for real mode flat model and to generate EAT.COM from EAT.ASM, the following command line has to be used to invoke NASM:

```
C:\>NASM16 EAT.ASM -F BIN -O EAT.COM
```

It's certainly easier just selecting Assemble | Assemble, no? Still, over time you should study the various command-line options that NASM supports so that you can begin to do more advanced things than NASM-IDE is capable of doing. They're all described in detail in NASM's documentation, which is present on the CD ROM for this book.

This particular command line is fairly easy to explain:

1. NASM16 is the name of the version of NASM intended for use with real mode programs under DOS. On your disk it will be NASM16.EXE.

2. EAT.ASM is the name of the source code file you wish to assemble.

3. –F BIN indicates the output format. There are many different types of files that NASM is capable of producing. The one we want is the .COM file, which is generated as a simple binary image of the generated machine-code bytes and any initialized data. The "BIN" indicates "binary image." The other key thing about .COM files is the 0100H code origin, but that's handled in the source code, as I explained earlier.

4. –O EAT.COM is the name of the output file. You can call the generated code file anything you want. If you don't specify the name of the output file, NASM will just lop off the ".ASM" and call the file EAT. Unfortunately, the name "EAT" doesn't indicate to DOS that it's a runnable program, so DOS won't know what to do with it. That's why you have to specify the full output file name "EAT.COM" on the command line.

Later on in this book, we're going to invoke NASM from the command line to produce a type of file that NASM-IDE won't be able to tell NASM how to produce. Therefore, we'll have to do it ourselves.

What Happens When a .COM File Runs

It's often useful to know just what happens when you run a program of your own creation. DOS treats its two kinds of executable programs a little differently when it runs them. .COM files are the simpler of the two. (I speak of .EXE files a little later in this chapter.) .COM files are a simple image of the instructions and data assembled out of the source code file. When you execute a .COM program from the DOS command line, here's what happens:

1. The .COM file is loaded into memory at a location of DOS's choosing. It doesn't change the file when it loads the file; the file is loaded exactly as it was saved to disk by the assembler.

2. AX, BX, DX, BP, SI, and DI are set to 0.

3. The instruction pointer IP is set to 0100H.

4. The number of bytes loaded from disk and stored into memory is placed in the CX register.

5. The stack pointer is set to the highest address in the program's segment, minus one.

6. All four segment registers CS, SS, DS, and ES are set to the same value: the segment address of the single segment in which the .COM program must run. DOS chooses this value.

7. DOS transfers control to the instruction at CS:IP, and your program is off and running!

You can see this very plainly by loading EAT.COM with DEBUG. Here's a dump of the registers immediately after loading EAT.COM into memory:

```
-r
AX=0000 BX=0000 CX=001C DX=0000 SP=FFFE BP=0000 SI=0000 DI=0000
DS=1470 ES=1470 SS=1470 CS=1470 IP=0100  NV UP EI PL NZ NA PO NC
1470:0100 BA0C01    MOV    DX,010C
```

You'll sometimes hear the real mode flat model referred to as the Tiny model. This is a term that originated in the C programming community, which has separate names for several different arrangements of code and data, depending on whether there is a single segment for code and data or multiple segments.

The real mode flat model is simplicity itself—so simple, in fact, that it doesn't teach you much about segments. Maybe you don't need to know that much about segments to craft useful programs these days (especially in protected mode flat model), but I've found it very useful to know just how our CPUs evolved, and segments are a big part of that. So, that said, let's look at EAT.ASM crafted for the real mode segmented model.

One Program, Three Segments

The main problem with real mode flat model is that everything you do must fit into 64K of memory. This isn't much of a pinch for learning assembly language and just playing around writing small utilities, but once you try to create something ambitious—say, a word processor or database-driven e-mail client—you find that code and data begin to crowd one another in a big hurry. So, for all its trouble, real mode segmented model was the only way to make full use of real mode's megabyte of memory.

Today, of course, you'd either create a Windows application (which you would probably not attempt in assembly) or you'd work in protected mode flat model under an implementation of Unix for the Intel x86 CPUs. Nonetheless, if you understand segments, you have it in yourself to understand every other aspect of assembly work.

Let's do the Land Shark HyperBike trick again, this time with a version of EAT.ASM specifically written to use the real mode segmented model. Here's the bike—and then we'll take it apart just like last time:

```
; Source name      : EATSEG.ASM
; Executable name  : EATSEG.EXE
; Code model:      : Real mode segmented model
; Version          : 1.0
; Created date     : 9/10/1999
```

```
; Last update    : 9/10/1999
; Author         : Jeff Duntemann
; Description     : A simple example of a DOS .EXE file programmed for
;                   real mode segmented model, using NASM-IDE 1.1,
;                   NASM 0.98, and ALINK. This program demonstrates
;                   how segments are defined and initialized using NASM.


[BITS 16]              ; Set 16 bit code generation

      SEGMENT junk   ; Segment containing code

..start:               ; The two dots tell the linker to Start Here.
                       ; Note that this is a special symbol and MUST
                       ; be in lower case! "..start:"  "..START:"

; SEGMENT SETUP
;
;   In real mode segmented model, a program uses three segments, and it must
;   set up the addresses in the three corresponding segment registers. This
;   is what the ASSUME directive does in MASM; we ASSUME nothing in NASM!
;   Each of the three segments has a name (here, code, data, and stack) and
;   these names are identifiers indicating segment addresses. It is the
;   appropriate segment address that is moved into each segment register.
;   Note that you can't move an address directly into a segment register;
;   you must first move the address into a general purpose register. Also
;   note that we don't do anything with CS; the ..start: label tells the
;   linker where the code segment begins.

    mov   ax,data      ; Move segment address of data segment into AX
    mov   ds,ax        ; Copy address from AX into DS
    mov   ax,stack     ; Move segment address of stack segment into AX
    mov   ss,ax        ; Copy address from AX into SS

    mov   sp,stacktop  ; Point SP to the top of the stack

    mov   dx,eatmsg    ; Mem data ref without [] loads the ADDRESS!
    mov   ah,9         ; Function 9 displays text to standard output.
    int   21H          ; INT 21H makes the call into DOS.

    mov   ax, 04C00H   ; This DOS function exits the program
    int   21H          ;  and returns control to DOS.

      SEGMENT data   ; Segment containing initialized data

eatmsg   db "Eat at Joe's!", 13, 10, "$" ;Here's our message

      SEGMENT stack stack ;This means a segment of *type* "stack"
                          ; that is also *named* "stack"! Some
                          ; linkers demand that a stack segment
                          ; have the explicit type "stack"
```

```
        resb 64      ; Reserve 64 bytes for the program stack
stacktop:            ; It's significant that this label points to
                     ;  the *last* of the reserved 64 bytes, and
                     ;  not the first!
```

Three Segments

Assembly language programs written for real mode segmented model must contain at least three segments: One for code, one for data, and one for the stack. Larger programs may contain more than one code segment and more than one data segment, but real mode programs may contain only *one* stack segment at a time.

EATSEG.ASM has those three necessary segments. Each segment has a name: **stack**, **data**, and **code**, which indicate pretty clearly what the segment is for. The **code** segment, pretty obviously, contains the machine instructions that do the program's work. The **data** segment contains initialized variables.

The **stack** segment contains the program's stack. I haven't explained stacks just yet, and because you don't really need to understand stacks in order to understand how EATSEG.ASM works, I'm going to hold off just a little while longer. In short, a *stack* is simply an ordered place to stash things for the short term—and that will have to do until we cover the concept in depth in the next section.

Each of the three segments is declared using the **SEGMENT** directive, which is a command that tells NASM that a segment begins here. The **SEGMENT** directive must be followed by the segment's name. You can name the segments whatever you like, but custom suggests that when you have only three segments, they be called **stack**, **data**, and **code**. Why obscure the meaning of what you're writing?

The segment containing the stack has some special considerations attached to it, especially regarding the linking of several files together into one executable program. One of these considerations is that the stack have the type "stack" attached to it. This tells the linker (as I explain later) that this particular segment is special—it's a stack segment and not just a data segment. Hence the line:

```
SEGMENT stack stack
```

Nobody's stuttering here. The SEGMENT directive is creating a stack *named* "stack" that is of the type "stack." The first identifier is the name;

the second is the type. You could change the name of the segment to **My-Stack** or **GreasedPig** if you like, but it's important to let the type of the stack segment be precisely **stack**. More on this after we explain something else.

Don't ASSUME . . .

If you remember, in the real mode flat model, the operating system sets all four segment registers to the same value (one that it selects) when the program is loaded into memory and run. In the real mode segmented mode, the different segments are indeed different and distinct regions of memory and are not all the same place. When the program begins running, DOS doesn't set the segment registers to anything. Your program must do that on its own. (DOS does, of course, set CS to the start of the code segment before giving control to your program. The other segment registers it leaves alone.)

This is what the first part of EATSEG.ASM does: It takes the addresses represented by the segment names for the data and stack segments and loads them into DS and SS, the segment registers governing those segments:

```
mov  ax,data      ; Move segment address of data segment into AX
mov  ds,ax        ; Copy address from AX into DS
mov  ax,stack     ; Move segment address of stack segment into AX
mov  ss,ax        ; Copy address from AX into SS
```

Keep in mind that you can only load a segment register from a general-purpose register—you can't load it from anything else, either immediate data or memory data. This is why the segment addresses have to pass through AX to get into DS and SS. (Because we're not using ES to govern a segment defined at assembly time right there in our program, we don't need to load ES with anything right off the bat.)

This is a good place to point out a crucial difference between NASM (the assembler that we're using in this book) and Microsoft's extremely popular MASM, which is probably the most-used assembler in history: MASM attempts to associate segment names with segment types. *NASM does not.*

With one small exception done as a courtesy to the linker, NASM does not know which segment is the code segment, nor which segment is the data segment, nor which segment is the stack segment. You define a segment by name:

```
SEGMENT data      ; Segment containing initialized data
```

The name "data," however, tells *you* that it's the data segment. The assembler doesn't look for the string "data" and note somewhere that the segment named **data** is the data segment. This is why you could change the preceding line to this:

```
SEGMENT GreasedPig ; Segment containing initialized data
```

Nothing would change. **GreasedPig** is an odd name for a segment, but a completely legal one.

In MASM, Microsoft defines the **ASSUME** directive, which associates segment names with segment registers. This allows MASM to generate segment prefixes automatically when it creates the opcodes called out by a particular mnemonic in your source code. This is a tricky and subtle business, so to make this clearer, imagine a memory variable defined in a segment that is addressed via ES:

```
    SEGMENT JunkSegment
JunkChunk   DW   0FFA7H
```

At the beginning of the program, you have to make sure ES is loaded with the segment address of **JunkSegment**:

```
MOV AX, JunkSegment ; Load segment address of JunkSegment into ES via AX
MOV ES, AX
```

Ordinarily, using NASM, you have to specify when a piece of memory data is located relative to the ES register, because the default is DS:

```
MOV AX,[ES:JunkChunk] ; Move word variable JunkChunk from JunkSegment (ES) into AX
```

That's the NASM way. Using Microsoft's MASM, you can associate a segment name with ES using the **ASSUME** directive:

```
ASSUME ES:JunkSegment
```

Having associated ES and **JunkSegment** this way, you could now write the **MOV** instruction without explicitly including the ES: segment prefix:

```
MOV AX,[JunkChunk] ; Move word variable JunkChunk from JunkSegment (ES) into AX
```

Thanks to **ASSUME**, MASM knows that the variable **JunkChunk** is located in extra segment ES, so it inserts the ES: prefix behind the scenes as it generates the opcode for this mnemonic. Many of us (NASM's authors included) don't think this is a particularly good idea. It makes the source code less specific and hence less readable—a person not familiar with the program might assume (heh-heh) that **JunkChunk** is in the data segment associated with DS because there's no ES: prefix and DS is the default for memory variable references like that.

So, NASM has nothing like **ASSUME**. When you move away from the default addressing of memory variables relative to DS, you must include the segment register prefix inside the square brackets of all memory variable references!

Naming the Stack Segment

The exception I noted earlier is that NASM allows you to say which segment is the stack segment:

```
SEGMENT MyStack stack
```

Here, **MyStack** is the name of the segment (which can be any legal identifier) and **stack** is the type. This is not for NASM's benefit—it will not take any action of its own based on knowing that the segment named **MyStack** is in fact the stack segment. But some linkers need to know that there is a stack segment defined in the program. Stack segments are special as segments go, at least in part (kind of like Tigger) there can be only one—but there *must* be one! Some linkers check to see whether there is a segment in a program designated as the stack segment, and to keep such linkers quiet NASM allows you to give the **stack** type to a segment defined with **SEGMENT**.

This is a good idea and I recommend that you do it.

Choosing a Starting Point

There are no jumps, loops, or subroutines in EATSEG.ASM. If you've a smattering of assembly language smarts you may wonder if the **..start:** label at the beginning of the code segment is unnecessary except for readability purposes. After all, **start** is not referenced anywhere within the program.

On the other hand, code execution has to begin somewhere, and you need to tell the assembler (and especially the linker) where code execution must begin. This is the purpose of the **..start:** label.

The issue is this: DOS needs to know at what address to begin execution when it loads and runs the program. (DOS sets code segment register CS when it loads your program into memory prior to executing it.) You might think DOS could assume that execution would begin at the start of the code segment, but there may be more than one code segment, and under most circumstances the programmer does not specify the order of multiple code segments within a single program. (The linker has the power to rearrange multiple code segments for reasons that I can't explain in this book.) Better to have no doubt about it, and for that reason you the programmer should pick a starting point and tell the assembler what it is.

You may notice that leaving out **..start:** won't keep NASM from assembling a program, and while the linker will complain about the lack of a starting point, the linker will default to starting execution at the beginning of the code segment—which in our case is the *only* code segment, so there's no ambiguity there.

Nonetheless, it's bad practice to leave out the starting point label.

Assembling and Linking EATSEG.ASM

Although NASM can generate a .COM file (for a real mode flat model program) directly, it can't generate a .EXE file for a real mode segmented model program in the same way. Once you move away from a single segment in real mode flat model, NASM needs the help of a linker to generate the final .EXE file.

I've obtained permission to distribute an excellent free linker with this book's CD-ROM. The linker is ALINK, written by Anthony Williams. It's on the CD-ROM, and if you copied the executable file ALINK.EXE to your hard drive along with everything else, you can invoke it simply by naming it.

NASM-IDE was intended for writing programs in real mode flat model, so it relies exclusively on NASM and does not have any machinery for invoking a linker. That means that NASM-IDE won't be able to do the assemble and link tasks for us. It's time to face the fiendish command line.

If you're working from DOS you can simply assemble and link from the DOS command line. If you're working with NASM-IDE in a DOS box under Windows, it's probably easier to "shell out" to the DOS command line from inside NASM-IDE. This is done by selecting the menu item File | DOS Shell. You will see NASM-IDE vanish and be replaced by a blank screen with the DOS prompt. When you're done with the DOS shell, type EXIT followed by Enter to return to NASM-IDE.

Assembling EATSEG.ASM is done with the following command line:

```
C:\>NASM16 EATSEG.ASM -f obj -o EATSEG.OBJ
```

This command line will assemble EATSEG.ASM to the file EATSEG.OBJ, in the standard .OBJ linkable file format. Linking is even easier:

```
C:\>ALINK EATSEG.OBJ
```

Here, ALINK will convert EATSEG.OBJ into EATSEG.EXE. I explain more about linkers and what they do in the next chapter. Here, ALINK is acting more as a file format converter than anything else, since there's only one file to be linked. Later on, we'll see how ALINK can connect multiple .OBJ files into a single executable file.

After ALINK runs, you'll have the file EATSEG.EXE on your hard disk. That's the file that you can name at the DOS command line to run EAT-SEG.

Last In, First Out via the Stack

One problem with assembly language is that it's tough knowing where to put things. There are only so many registers to go around. Having variables in a data segment is helpful, but it isn't the whole story. People who come to assembly from higher-level languages such as Pascal and Basic find this particularly jarring, since they're used to being able to create new variables at any time as needed.

The x86 CPUs contain the machinery to create and manage a vital storage area called the *stack*. The name is appropriate, and for a usable metaphor I can go back to my high school days, when I was a dishwasher for Resurrection Hospital on Chicago's Northwest Side.

Five Hundred Plates an Hour

What I did most of the time was pull clean plates from a moving conveyor belt of little prongs that emerged endlessly from the steaming dragon's mouth of a 180° dishwashing machine. This was hot work, but it was a lot less slimy than stuffing the dirty plates into the other end of the machine.

When you pull 500 plates an hour out of a dishwashing machine, you had better have some place efficient to stash them. Obviously, you could simply stack them on a table, but stacked ceramic plates in any place habituated by rowdy teenage boys is asking for fragments. What the hospital had instead was an army of little wheeled stainless steel cabinets equipped with one or more spring-loaded circular plungers accessed from the top. When you had a handful of plates, you pushed them down into the plunger. The plunger's spring was adjusted such that the weight of the added plates pushed the whole stack of plates down just enough to make the new top plate flush with the top of the cabinet.

Each plunger held about 50 plates. We rolled one up next to the dragon's mouth, filled it with plates, and then rolled it back into the kitchen where the clean plates were used at the next meal shift to set patients' trays.

It's instructive to follow the path of the first plate out of the dishwashing machine on a given shift. That plate got into the plunger first and was subsequently shoved down into the bottom of the plunger by the remaining 49 plates that the cabinet could hold. After the cabinet was rolled into the kitchen, the kitchen girls pulled plates out of the cabinet one by one as they set trays. The *first* plate out of the cabinet was the *last* plate in. The *last* plate out of the cabinet had been the *first* plate to go in.

The x86 stack is like that. We call it a last in, first out, or *LIFO* stack.

An Upside-Down Segment

Two of the x86 registers team up to create and maintain the stack. Like everything else in 86-land, the stack must exist within a segment. The SS (Stack Segment) register holds the segment address of the segment chosen to be the stack segment, and the SP (Stack Pointer) register points to locations within the stack segment. As with all other segments in real mode, the stack segment may be as much as 65,536 bytes long, but it may be any length less than that as well. You'll find in practice that the stack rarely needs to be larger than a thousand bytes or so unless you're doing some really peculiar things.

The stack segment begins at SS:0, but the truly odd thing about it is that all the stack action happens at the *opposite* end of the stack segment. When a stack segment is set up, the SS register points to the base or beginning of the stack segment, and SP is set to point to the *end* of the stack segment. To store something in the stack segment (which we usually call "pushing something onto the stack"), we move SP "down the stack" (that is, closer to SS) and then copy the item to the memory location pointed to by SS:SP.

This takes some getting used to. Figure 8.1 provides the big picture of the stack segment and the two pointers that give it life. In real mode flat model, SS is set to the base of the stack segment by DOS when the program is loaded and begins running. (And all the other segment registers are set to the same address.) In real mode segmented model, you set SS from the address of the segment that you define within the program in two steps, first using NASM's **SEGMENT** directive:

```
SEGMENT stack stack
```

Then you need a couple of **MOV** instructions to get the address of segment **stack** into SS:

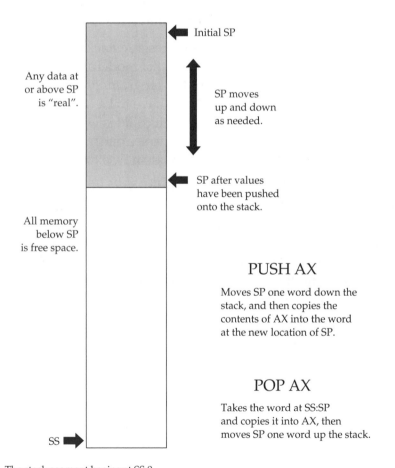

Initial SP

Any data at
or above SP
is "real".

SP moves
up and down
as needed.

SP after values
have been pushed
onto the stack.

All memory
below SP
is free space.

PUSH AX

Moves SP one word down the
stack, and then copies the
contents of AX into the word
at the new location of SP.

POP AX

Takes the word at SS:SP
and copies it into AX, then
moves SP one word up the stack.

SS

The stack segment begins at SS:0
and continues for up to 64K bytes.

Figure 8.1 The big picture of the real mode stack.

```
mov  ax,stack    ; Move segment address of stack segment into AX
mov  ss,ax       ; Copy address from AX into SS
```

Defining a stack segment just provides a starting point address for that segment. No room is actually reserved for the stack by the **SEGMENT** directive. That requires a new directive that we haven't discussed:

```
resb 64      ; Reserve 64 bytes for the program stack
```

RESB means "REServe Byte." And it means just that: It tells the assembler to set aside 64 bytes starting at the beginning of the stack segment and not to let anything else (such as memory variables) be defined in that reserved space. You can use **RESB** to reserve as much stack as you think you'll need; 64 bytes is enough for simple experimentation. If you're writing a more ambitious program, you may be better off looking at what it does and actually estimating a worst-case demand for stack space.

Note that you don't need to use **RESB** to reserve stack space if you're working in real mode flat model. The stack in that model exists at the very highest addresses of the single segment the program lives in. The space isn't reserved in the strictest sense, and you have to be careful not to let your code or data get so high in memory that it collides with your stack. This is called a *stack crash* and you're not likely to see one in your own programs until you get a lot further along in your assembly experience.

SP is set to the far (that is, the high, address-wise) end of the stack segment. (See Figure 8.1, where an arrow indicates the initial value of SP.) Again, if you're working in real mode flat model, DOS does it when your program is loaded—as you can see if you load EAT.COM with DEBUG and display the registers with the R command. SP will have a value something like 0FFFEH—in any case, something fairly high rather than close to 0000H.

And if you're working in real mode segmented model, you have to set SP yourself. This is done by first indicating the initial address to be contained in SP:

```
        resb 64    ; Reserve 64 bytes for the program stack
stacktop:          ; It's significant that this label points to
                   ;  the *last* of the reserved 64 bytes, and
                   ;  not the first!
```

Note that the label **stacktop:** is immediately *after* the **RESB 64** directive. The label **stacktop:** represents an address at the very end of the block of reserved memory locations set aside by **RESB**. Although the position of the two lines on the source code listing suggests that **stacktop:** points *beyond* the block of memory set aside by **RESB**, that's not the case. The **stacktop:** label resolves to the offset of the last byte in that block of 64 bytes.

You load the address represented by the **stacktop:** label into SP when the program begins, typically right after you set up the segment registers:

```
mov  sp,stacktop    ; Point SP to the top of the stack
```

After that's set up, you have valid values in both SS and SP, and you can begin using the stack.

Pushing Data

You can place data onto the stack in numerous ways, but the most straightforward way involves a trio of related machine instructions, **PUSH**, **PUSHF**, and **PUSHA**. The three are similar in how they work, and differ as to what they push onto the stack. **PUSHF** pushes the Flags register onto the stack. **PUSHA** pushes all eight of the 16-bit general-purpose registers. **PUSH** pushes a 16-bit register or memory value that is specified by you in your source code, like so:

```
PUSHF      ; Push the Flags register
PUSHA      ; Push AX, CX, DX, BX, SP, BP, SI, and DI, in that order, all at once
PUSHAD     ; Push EAX, ECX, EDX, EBX, ESP, ESP, EBP, ESI, and EDI, all at once
PUSH AX    ; Push the AX register
PUSH [BX]  ; Push the word stored in memory at DS:BX
PUSH DI    ; Push the DI register
PUSH ES    ; Push the ES register
```

Note that **PUSHF** takes no operands. You'll generate an assembler error if you try to hand it an operand; **PUSHF** pushes the flags and that's all it is capable of doing.

PUSH and **PUSHF** work this way: First SP is decremented by one word (two bytes) so that it points to an empty area of the stack segment that is two bytes long. Then whatever is to be pushed onto the stack is written to memory in the stack segment at the offset address in SP. Voila! The data is safe on the stack, and SP has crawled two bytes closer to SS. We call the word of memory pointed to by SP the *top of the stack.*

PUSHA works the same way, except that it pushes eight 16-bit registers at once, thus using 16 bytes of stack space at one swoop. One thing to remember is that **PUSHA** is a newer instruction that doesn't exist on the 8086 and 8088. It first appeared with the 286.

PUSHAD was added with the 386, and it pushes all eight 32-bit general-purpose registers onto the stack in one blow.

All memory between SP's initial position and its current position (the top of the stack) contains real data that was explicitly pushed on the stack and will presumably be fetched from the stack (we say *popped* from the stack) later on. In real mode segmented model, the stack exists in a separate segment, and memory between SS and SP is considered free and available and is used to store new data that is to be pushed onto the stack. This is not the case in real mode flat model, where the stack shares the same segment that everything else in the program is using.

What can and cannot be pushed onto the stack is complicated and depends on what CPU you're using. None of the x86 CPUs can push 8-bit registers onto the stack. You can't push AL or BH or any other of the 8-bit registers. Segment registers and 32-bit extended general-purpose registers can be pushed in real mode, assuming you have a 386 or later CPU. Similarly, immediate data can be pushed onto the stack, but only if you have a 286 or later CPU. Keeping track of all this used to be a problem, but you're unlikely to be running code on CPUs earlier than the 386 these days.

Your morbid curiosity may be wondering what happens when SP runs out of room in its downward crawl and collides with SS. Nothing good, certainly—it depends heavily on how your program is laid out—but I would lay money on your program crashing hard and possibly taking the system down with it. (If you're working in a DOS box under Windows NT you at least won't crash the operating system. All bets are off for Windows 9*x*!)

Stack crashes are serious business, at least in part because there is only one stack in action at a time in real mode. It's a little hard to explain (especially at this stage in our discussion), but this means that the stack you set up for your own program must be large enough to support as well the needs of DOS and any interrupt-driven code (typically in the BIOS) that may be active while your program is running. Even if you don't fully understand how someone else may be using your program's stack at the same time you are, give those other guys some extra room—and keep an eye on the proximity of SS and SP while you trace a program in DEBUG.

POP Goes the Opcode

In general, what gets pushed must get popped, or you can end up in any of several different kinds of trouble. Getting a word of data *off* the stack is done with another trio of instructions, **POP**, **POPF**, and **POPA**. As you might expect, **POP** is the general-purpose one-at-a-time popper, while **POPF** is dedicated to popping the flags off of the stack. **POPA** pops 16 bytes off the stack into the eight general-purpose 16-bit registers. **POPAD** is the flip side of **PUSHAD** and pops the top 32 bytes off the stack into the eight general-purpose 32-bit registers.

```
POPF     ; Pop the top of the stack into Flags
POPA     ; Pop the top 16 bytes from the stack into AX, CX, DX, BX, SP,
         ;  BP, SI, and DI
POPAD    ; Pop the top 32 bytes into EAX, ECX, EDX, EBX, ESP, ESP, EBP,
         ;  ESI, and EDI
POP SI   ; Pop the top of the stack into SI
POP CS   ; Pop the top of the stack into CS
POP [BX] ; Pop the top of the stack into memory at DS:BX
```

As with **PUSH**, **POP** only operates on word-sized operands. Don't try to pop data from the stack into an 8-bit register such as AH or CL.

POP works pretty much the way **PUSH** does, but in reverse: First the word of data at SS:SP is copied from the stack and placed in **POP**'s operand, whatever you specified that to be. Then, SP is incremented (rather than decremented) by two bytes, so that in effect it moves two bytes up the stack, away from SS.

It's significant that SP is decremented *before* placing a word on the stack at push time, but incremented *after* removing a word from the stack at pop time. Certain other CPUs work in the opposite manner, which is fine— just don't get confused. *Unless the stack is empty, SP points to real data, not empty space.*

Ordinarily, you don't have to remember that fact, as **PUSH** and **POP** handle it all for you and you don't have to manually keep track of what SP is pointing to. If you decide to manipulate the stack pointer directly, it helps to know the sequence of events behind **PUSH** and **POP**—and that's an advanced topic that I won't be going into in this book.

Figure 8.2 shows the stack's operation in a little more detail. The values of the four "X" registers at some hypothetical point in a program's execution are shown at the top of the figure. AX is pushed first on the stack.

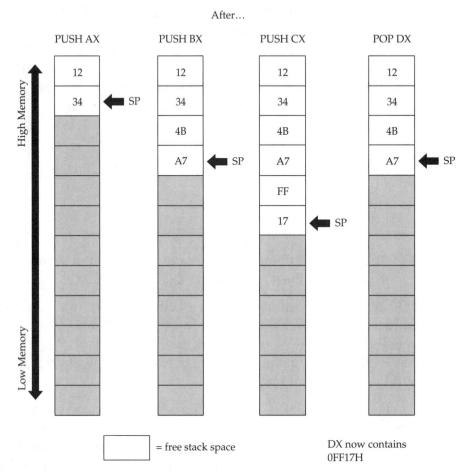

Given these initial register values:

AX = 01234H
BX = 04BA7H
CX = 0FF17H
DX = 034E0H

Figure 8.2 How the stack works.

Its least significant byte is at SS:SP, and its most significant byte is at SS:SP+1. (Remember that both bytes are pushed onto the stack at once, as a unit!)

Each time one of the registers is pushed onto the stack, SP is decremented two bytes down toward SS. The first three columns show AX, BX, and CX being pushed onto the stack, respectively. But note what happens in the fourth column, when the instruction **POP DX** is executed. The stack pointer is incremented by two bytes and moves away from SS. DX now contains a copy of the contents of CX. In effect, CX was pushed onto the stack, and then immediately popped off into DX.

That's a roundabout way to copy the value of CX into DX. **MOV DX,CX** is lots faster and more straightforward. However, *MOV will not operate on the Flags register*. If you want to load a copy of Flags into a register, you must first push the Flags register onto the stack with **PUSHF**, then pop the flags word off the stack into the register of your choice with **POP**. Getting the Flags register into BX is done like this:

```
PUSHF  ; Push the flags register onto the stack..
POP BX ; ..and pop it immediately into BX
```

Storage for the Short Term

The stack should be considered a place to stash things for the short term. Items stored on the stack have no names, and in general must be taken off the stack in the reverse order that they were put on. Last in, first out, remember. LIFO!

One excellent use of the stack allows the all-too-few registers to do multiple duty. If you need a register to temporarily hold some value to be operated on by the CPU and all the registers are in use, push one of the busy registers onto the stack. Its value will remain safe on the stack while you use the register for other things. When you're finished using the register, pop its old value off the stack—and you've gained the advantages of an additional register without really having one. (The cost, of course, is the time you spend moving that register's value onto and off of the stack. It's not something you want to do in the middle of an often-repeated loop!)

Using DOS Services through INT

I think of EAT.ASM as something of a Tom Sawyer program. It doesn't do much, and it does what it does in time-honored Tom Sawyer fashion—by getting somebody else to do all the work. All that EAT does is display a character string on your screen. The visible part of that string is the advertising slogan itself: **Eat at Joe's!** The other part is the pair of invisible characters we call *newline* or *EOL:* carriage return (0DH) followed by line feed (0AH). (For more on EOL markers and how they interact with text, see Chapter 4.) The EOL marker does nothing more than return the display cursor to the left margin of the next screen line, so that any subsequent text displayed will begin at the left margin and not nipping at the heels of **Eat at Joe's!**

Both parts of our advertising slogan are sent to the display at once, and via the same mechanism: through a *DOS service.*

As I explain in Chapter 4, DOS is both a god and a troll. It controls all the most important elements of the machine in godlike fashion: the disk drives, the printer, and (to some extent) the display. At the same time, DOS is like a troll living under a bridge to all those parts of your machine: You tell the troll what you want done, and the troll will go out and do it for you.

There is another troll guarding the bridges to other components of your machine called the BIOS, to which we'll return in a little while. DOS and BIOS both offer *services*, which are simple tasks that your programs would have to do themselves if the services were not provided. Quite apart from saving you the programmer a lot of work, having DOS and BIOS services helps guarantee that certain things will be done in identical fashion on all machines, which (especially in terms of disk storage) is a major reason software written for DOS runs on so many different machines: All the machine-dependent stuff is done the same way.

One of the services DOS provides is simple (far too simple, actually) access to your machine's display. For the purposes of EAT.ASM (which is just a lesson in getting your first assembly language program written and operating), simple services are enough.

So—how do we use DOS and BIOS services? The way is as easy to use as it is tricky to understand: through software interrupts.

An Interrupt That Doesn't Interrupt Anything

As one new to the x86 family of processors back in 1981, the notion of a *software interrupt* drove me nuts. I kept looking and looking for the interrupter and interruptee. Nothing was getting interrupted.

The name is unfortunate, even though I admit that there was some reason for calling software interrupts what they are. They are, in fact, courteous interrupts—if you can still call an interrupt an interrupt when it is so courteous that it does no interrupting at all.

The nature of software interrupts and DOS services is best explained by a real example illustrated twice in EAT.ASM. As I hinted previously, DOS keeps little sequences of machine instructions tucked away within itself. Each sequence does something useful—read something from a disk file, display something to the screen, send something to the printer. DOS uses them to do its own work, and it also makes them available (with its troll hat on) to you the programmer to access from your programs.

Well, there is the critical question: How do you find something tucked away inside of DOS? All code sequences, of course, have addresses, and Microsoft or IBM could publish a booklet of addresses indicating where all the code is hidden. There are numerous good reasons not to pass out the addresses of the code itself, however. DOS is evolving and (we should hope) being repaired on an ongoing basis. Repairing and improving code involves adding, changing, and removing machine instructions, which changes the size of those hidden code sequences—and also, in consequence, changes their location. Add a dozen instructions to one sequence, and all the other sequences up-memory from that one sequence will have to shove over, to make room. Once they shove over, they'll be at different addresses, so instantly the booklets are obsolete. Even *one byte* added to or removed from a code sequence in DOS could change *everything*. What if the first code sequence has a bug that must be fixed?

The solution is ingenious. At the very start of real mode memory, down at segment 0, offset 0, is a special table with 256 entries. Each entry is a complete address including segment and offset portions, for a total of 4 bytes per entry. The first 1,024 bytes of memory in *any* x86 machine are reserved for this table, and no code or data may be placed there.

Each of the addresses in the table is called an *interrupt vector*. The table as a whole is called the *interrupt vector table*. Each vector has a number, from 0 to 255. The vector occupying bytes 0 through 3 in the table is vector 0. The vector occupying bytes 4 through 7 is vector 1, and so on, as shown in Figure 8.3.

None of the addresses is burned into permanent memory the way BIOS routines are. When your machine starts up, DOS and BIOS fill many of the

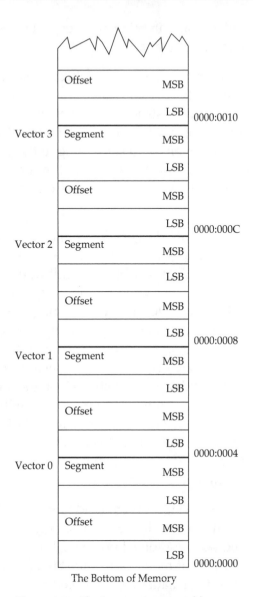

Figure 8.3 The interrupt vector table.

slots in the interrupt vector table with addresses of certain service routines within themselves. Each version of DOS knows the location of its inner-most parts, and when you upgrade to a new version of DOS, that new version will fill the appropriate slots in the vector table with upgraded and accurate addresses.

What *doesn't* change from DOS version to DOS version is the *number* of the interrupt that holds a particular address. In other words, since the PC first began, interrupt 21H has pointed the way into darkest DOS to DOS's *services dispatcher*, a sort of multiple-railway switch with spurs heading out to the many (over 50) individual DOS service routines. The address of the dispatcher has changed with every DOS version, but regardless of version, programs can find the address of the dispatcher in slot 21H of the interrupt vector table.

Furthermore, programs don't have to go snooping the table for the address themselves. The x86 CPUs include a machine instruction that makes use of the interrupt vector table. The **INT** (**INT**errupt) instruction is used by EAT.ASM to request the services of DOS in displaying two strings on the screen. At two places, EAT.ASM has an **INT 21H** instruction. When an **INT 21H** instruction is executed, the CPU goes down to the interrupt vector table, fetches the address from slot 21H, and then jumps execution to the address stored in slot 21H. Since the DOS services dispatcher lies at the address in slot 21H, the dispatcher gets control of the machine and does the work that it knows how to do.

The process is shown in Figure 8.4. When DOS loads itself at boot time, one of the many things it does to prepare the machine for use is put correct addresses in several of the vectors in the interrupt vector table. One of these addresses is the address of the dispatcher, which goes into slot 21H.

Later on, when you type the name of your program MYPROG on the DOS command line, DOS loads MYPROG.EXE into memory and gives it control of the machine. MYPROG.EXE does *not* know the address of the DOS dispatcher. MYPROG *does* know that the dispatcher's address will always be in slot 21H of the vector table, so it executes an **INT 21** instruction. The correct address lies in vector 21H, and MYPROG is content to remain ignorant and simply let the **INT 21** instruction and vector 21H take it where it needs to go.

Back on the Northwest Side of Chicago, where I grew up, there was a bus that ran along Milwaukee Avenue. All Chicago bus routes had numbers, and the Milwaukee Avenue route was number 56. It started somewhere in the tangled streets just north of Downtown, and ended up in a forest preserve just inside the city limits. The Forest Preserve District ran a swimming pool called Whelan Pool in that forest preserve. Kids all along Milwaukee Avenue could not necessarily have told you the address of

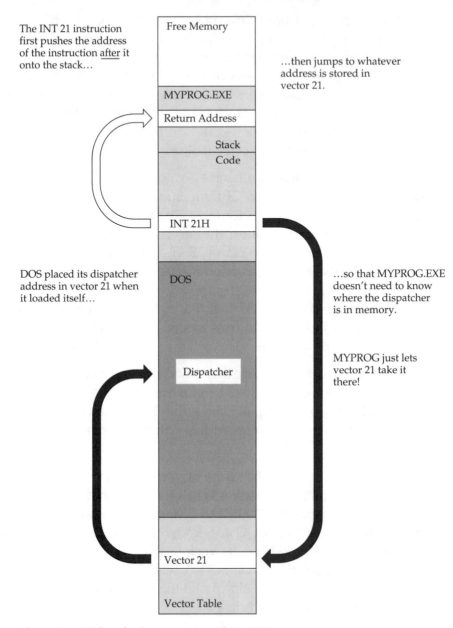

The INT 21 instruction first pushes the address of the instruction <u>after</u> it onto the stack…

…then jumps to whatever address is stored in vector 21.

DOS placed its dispatcher address in vector 21 when it loaded itself…

…so that MYPROG.EXE doesn't need to know where the dispatcher is in memory.

MYPROG just lets vector 21 take it there!

Free Memory

MYPROG.EXE

Return Address

Stack

Code

INT 21H

DOS

Dispatcher

Vector 21

Vector Table

Figure 8.4   Riding the interrupt vector into DOS.

Whelan Pool. But come summer, they'd tell you in a second how to get there: Just hop on bus number 56 and take it to the end of the line. It's like that with software interrupts. Find the number of the vector that reliably points to your destination, and ride that vector to the end of the line, without worrying about the winding route or the address of your destination.

Note that the **INT 21** instruction does something else: It pushes the address of the *next* instruction (that is, the instruction immediately following the **INT 21** instruction) on the stack before it follows vector 21H into the depths of DOS. Like Hansel and Gretel, the **INT 21** was pushing some breadcrumbs to the stack as a way of helping execution find its way back to MYPROG.EXE after the excursion down into DOS—but more on that later.

Now, the DOS dispatcher controls access to dozens of individual service routines. How does it know which one to execute? You have to tell the dispatcher which service you need, and you do so by placing the service's number in 8-bit register AH. The dispatcher may require other information as well and will expect you to provide that information in the correct place before executing **INT 21**.

Look at the following three lines of code from EAT.ASM:

```
mov  dx,eatmsg   ; Mem data ref without [] loads the ADDRESS!
mov  ah,09H      ; Function 9 displays text to standard output.
int  21H         ; INT 21H makes the call into DOS.
```

This sequence of instructions requests that DOS display a string on the screen. The first line sets up a vital piece of information: the offset address of the string to be displayed on the screen. Without that, DOS will not have any way to know what it is that we want to display. The dispatcher expects the offset address to be in DX and assumes that the segment address will be in DS.

In flat model, DS is initialized by DOS at execution time. In segmented model, the address of the data segment was loaded into DS earlier in the program by these two instructions:

```
mov  ax,data     ; Move segment address of data segment into AX
mov  ds,ax       ; Copy address from AX into DS
```

Once loaded, DS is not disturbed during the full run of the program, so the DOS dispatcher's assumption is valid even though DS is loaded at the start of program execution and *not* each time we want to display a string.

In moving 09H into register AH, we tell the dispatcher which service we want performed. Service 09H is DOS's Print String service. This is not the fastest nor in other ways the best way to display a string on the PC's screen, but it is most certainly the *easiest*.

DOS service 09H has a slightly odd requirement: That the end of the string be marked with a dollar sign ($). This is the reason for the dollar sign hung incongruously on the end of EAT.ASM's advertising slogan string. Given that DOS does not ask us to pass it a value indicating how long the string is, the end of the string has to be marked somehow, and the dollar sign is DOS's chosen way. It's a lousy way, unfortunately, because with the dollar sign acting as a marker, *there is no way to display a dollar sign*. If you intend to talk about money on the PC's screen, don't use DOS service 9! As I said, this is the easiest, but certainly not the best way to display text on the screen.

With the address of the string in DS:DX and service number 09H in AH, we take a trip to the dispatcher by executing **INT 21H**. The **INT** instruction is all it takes—*boom!*, and DOS has control, reading the string at DS:DX and sending it to the screen through mechanisms it keeps more or less to itself.

Getting Home Again

So much for getting into DOS. How do we get home again? The address in vector 21H took control into DOS, but how does DOS know where to go to pass execution back into EAT.EXE? Half of the cleverness of software interrupts is knowing how to get there, and the other half—just as clever—is knowing how to get back.

To get into DOS, a program looks in a completely reliable place for the address of where it wants to go: the address stored in vector 21H. This address takes execution deep into DOS, leaving the program sitting above DOS. To continue execution where it left off prior to the **INT 21** instruction, DOS has to look in a completely reliable place for the return address, and that completely reliable place is none other than the top of the stack.

I mentioned earlier (without much emphasis) that the **INT 21** instruction pushes an address to the top of the stack before it launches off into the unknown. This address is the address of the *next* instruction in line for execution: the instruction immediately following the **INT 21** instruction. This location is completely reliable because, just as there is only one interrupt vector table in the machine, there is only one stack in operation at any one time. This means that there is only one top of the stack—that is, SS:SP—and DOS can always send execution back to the program that called it by popping the address off the top of the stack and jumping to that address.

The process is shown in Figure 8.5, which is the continuation of Figure 8.4. Just as the **INT** instruction pushes a return address onto the stack and then jumps to the address stored in a particular vector, there is a

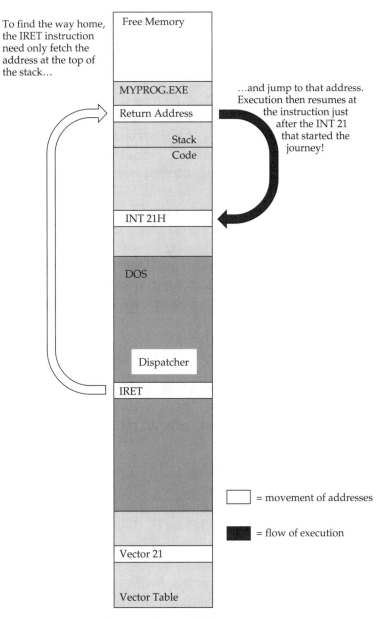

To find the way home, the IRET instruction need only fetch the address at the top of the stack…

Free Memory

MYPROG.EXE

Return Address

Stack

Code

…and jump to that address. Execution then resumes at the instruction just after the INT 21 that started the journey!

INT 21H

DOS

Dispatcher

IRET

□ = movement of addresses

■ = flow of execution

Vector 21

Vector Table

Figure 8.5 Returning home from an interrupt.

"combination" instruction that pops the return address off the stack and then jumps to the address. The instruction is **IRET** (for Interrupt **RET**urn), and it completes this complex but reliable system of jumping to an address when you really don't know the address. The trick, once again, is knowing where the address can reliably be found. (There's actually a little more to what the software interrupt mechanism pushes onto and pops from the stack, but it happens transparently enough that I don't want to complicate the explanation at this point—and you're unlikely to be writing your own software interrupt routines for a while.)

This should make it clear by now what happens when you execute an **INT 21** instruction. EAT.ASM uses DOS services to save it the trouble of writing its string data to the screen a byte at a time. The address into DOS is at a known location in the interrupt vector table, and the return address is at a known location on the stack. Whereas I've described the software interrupt system in terms of the DOS service dispatcher interrupt 21H, the system is precisely the same for all other software interrupts—and there are many. In the next chapter we use a few more and explore some of the many services available through the BIOS interrupts that control your video display and printer.

Software Interrupts versus Hardware Interrupts

Software interrupts evolved from an older mechanism that *did* involve some genuine interrupting: hardware interrupts. A *hardware interrupt* is your CPU's mechanism for paying attention to the world outside itself.

There is a fairly complex electrical system built into your PC that allows circuit boards to send signals to the CPU. An actual metal pin on the CPU chip is moved from one voltage level to another by a circuit board device like a disk drive controller or a serial port board. Through this pin, the CPU is tapped on the shoulder by the external device. The CPU recognizes this tap as a hardware interrupt. Like software interrupts, hardware interrupts are numbered, and for each interrupt number there is a slot reserved in the interrupt vector table. In this slot is the address of an *interrupt service routine* (ISR) that performs some action relevant to the device that tapped the CPU on the shoulder. For example, if the interrupt signal came from a serial port board, the CPU would then allow the serial port board to transfer a character byte from itself into the CPU.

Most properly, any routine that lies at the end of a vector address in the interrupt vector table is an ISR, but the term is usually reserved for hardware interrupt service routines.

The only difference between hardware and software interrupts is in the event that triggers the trip through the interrupt vector table. With a software interrupt the triggering event is part of the software; that is, an **INT** instruction. With a hardware interrupt, the triggering event is an electrical signal applied to the CPU chip itself without any **INT** instruction taking a hand in the process. The CPU itself pushes the return address on the stack when it recognizes the electrical pulse that triggers the interrupt; however, when the ISR is done, a **RET** instruction sends execution home, just as it does for a software interrupt.

Hardware ISRs can be (and usually are) written in assembly language. It's a difficult business, because the negotiations between the hardware and software must be done just *so*, or the machine may lock up or go berserk. This is no place for beginners, and I would advise you to develop some skill and obtain some considerable knowledge of your hardware setup before attempting to write a hardware ISR.

CHAPTER 9

Dividing and Conquering

Using Procedures and Macros to Battle Complexity

Programming in Martian

There is a computer language called APL (an acronym for *A Programming Language*, how clever) that has more than a little Martian in it. APL was the first computer language I learned (on a major IBM mainframe), and when I learned it, I learned a little more than just APL.

APL uses a very compact notation, with dozens of odd little symbols, each of which is capable of some astonishing power such as matrix inversion. You can do more in one line of APL than you can in one line of anything else I have learned since. The combination of the strange symbol set and the compact notation makes it very hard to read and remember what a line of code in APL actually does.

So it was in 1977. Having mastered (or so I thought) the whole library of symbols, I set out to write a text formatter program. The program would justify right and left, center headers, and do a few other things of a sort that we take for granted today but which were very exotic in the seventies.

The program grew over a period of a week to about 600 lines of squirmy little APL symbols. I got it to work, and it worked fine—as long as I didn't try to format a column that was more than 64 characters wide. Then everything came out scrambled.

Whoops. I printed the whole thing out and sat down to do some serious debugging. Then I realized with a feeling of sinking horror that, having finished the last part of the program, *I had no idea how the first part worked.*

The APL symbol set was only part of the problem. I soon came to realize that the most important mistake I had made was writing the whole thing as one 600-line monolithic block of code lines. There were no functional divisions, nothing to indicate what any 10-line portion of the code was trying to accomplish.

The Martians had won. I did the only thing possible: I scrapped it. And I settled for ragged margins in my text.

Boxes within Boxes

This sounds like Eastern mysticism, but it's just an observation from life: *Within any action is a host of smaller actions.* Look inside your common activities. When you brush your teeth you do the following:

- Pick up your toothpaste tube.
- Unscrew the cap.
- Place the cap on the sink counter.
- Pick up your toothbrush.
- Squeeze toothpaste onto the brush from the middle of the tube.
- Put your toothbrush into your mouth.
- Work it back and forth vigorously.

And so on. The original list went the entire page. When you brush your teeth, you perform every one of those actions. However, when you think about the sequence, you don't run through the whole list. You bring to mind the simple concept "brushing teeth."

Furthermore, when you think about what's behind the action we call "getting up in the morning," you might assemble a list of activities like this:

- Shut off the clock radio.
- Climb out of bed.

- Put on your robe.
- Let the dogs out.
- Make breakfast.
- Brush your teeth.
- Shave.
- Shower.
- Get dressed.

Brushing your teeth is on the list, but within the activity you call "brushing your teeth" is a whole list of smaller actions, as listed previously. The same can be said for most of the activities shown in the preceding list. How many individual actions, for example, does it take to put a reasonable breakfast together? And yet in one small, if sweeping, phrase, "getting up in the morning," you embrace that whole host of small and even smaller actions without having to laboriously trace through each one.

What I'm describing is the "Chinese boxes" method of fighting complexity. Getting up in the morning involves hundreds of little actions, so we divide the mass up into coherent chunks and set the chunks into little conceptual boxes. "Making breakfast" is in one box, "brushing teeth" is in another, and so on. Closer inspection of any box shows that its contents can also be divided into numerous boxes, and those smaller boxes into even smaller boxes.

This process doesn't (and can't) go on forever, but it should go on as long as it needs to in order to satisfy this criterion: *The contents of any one box should be understandable with only a little scrutiny.* No single box should contain anything so subtle or large and involved that it takes hours of hair-pulling to figure it out.

Procedures as Boxes for Code

The mistake I made in writing my APL text formatter is that I threw the whole collection of 600 lines of APL code into one huge box marked "text formatter."

While I was writing it, I should have been keeping my eyes open for sequences of code statements that worked together at some identifiable task. When I spotted such sequences, I should have set them off as *proce-*

dures. Each sequence would then have a name that would provide a memory tag for the sequence's function. If it took 10 statements to justify a line of text, those 10 statements should have been named **JustifyLine**, and so on.

Xerox's legendary APL programmer Jim Dunn later told me that I shouldn't ever write an APL procedure that wouldn't fit on a single 25-line terminal screen. "More than 25 lines and you're doing too much in one procedure. Split it up," he said. Whenever I worked in APL after that, I adhered to that rather sage rule of thumb. The Martians still struck from time to time, but when they did, it was no longer a total loss.

All computer languages have procedures of one sort or another, and assembly language is no exception. Your assembly language program may have numerous procedures. There's no limit to the *number* of procedures, as long as the total number of bytes of code contained by all the procedures together does not exceed 65,536 (one segment). Other complications arise at that point, but there are mechanisms in assembly language to deal sensibly with those complications.

But that's a lot of code. You needn't worry for a while, and certainly not while you're just learning assembly language. (I won't be treating the creation of multiple code segments in this book.) In the meantime, let's take a look at the "Eat at Joe's" program, expanded a little to include a couple of procedures:

```
; Source name      : EAT2.ASM
; Executable name  : EAT2.COM
; Code model       : Real Mode Flat Model
; Version          : 1.0
; Created date     : 7/31/1999
; Last update      : 9/11/1999
; Author           : Jeff Duntemann
; Description      : A simple example of a DOS .COM file programmed using
;                    NASM-IDE 1.1 and NASM 0.98 and incorporating procedures.


[BITS 16]          ; Set 16 bit code generation
[ORG 0x0100]       ; Set code start address to 100h (COM file)


[SECTION .text]    ; Section containing code

Start:
  mov DX,EatMsg1   ; Load offset of Eat1 string into DX
  call Writeln     ;  and display it
```

```
    mov DX,EatMsg2   ; Load offset of Ear2 string into DX
    call Writeln     ;  and display it

    mov ax, 04C00H   ; This function exits the program
    int 21H          ; and returns control to DOS.


;---------------------------
;      PROCEDURE SECTION
;---------------------------

Write:
    mov AH,09H       ; Select DOS service 9: Print String
    int 21H          ; Call DOS
    ret              ; Return to the caller


Writeln:
    call Write       ; Display the string proper through Write
    mov DX,CRLF      ; Load offset of newline string to DX
    call Write       ; Display the newline string through Write
    ret              ; Return to the caller

;---------------------------
;      DATA SECTION
;---------------------------


[SECTION .data]    ; Section containing initialized data

EatMsg1  DB   "Eat at Joe's . . . ",'$'
EatMsg2  DB   "...ten million flies can't ALL be wrong!",'$'
CRLF     DB   0DH,0AH,'$'
```

Calling and Returning

EAT2.ASM does about the same thing as EAT.ASM. It prints a second line as part of the advertising slogan, and that's all in the line of functional innovation. The way the two lines of the slogan are displayed, however, bears examination:

```
    mov DX,EatMsg1   ; Load offset of Eat1 string into DX
    call Writeln     ;  and display it
```

Here's a new machine instruction: **CALL**. The label **Writeln** refers to a procedure. As you might have gathered (especially if you've programmed in an older language such as Basic or FORTRAN), **CALL Writeln** simply tells the CPU to go off and execute a procedure named **Writeln**.

The means by which **CALL** operates may sound familiar: **CALL** first pushes the address of the *next* instruction after itself onto the stack. Then **CALL** transfers execution to the address represented by the name of the procedure. The instructions contained in the procedure execute. Finally, the procedure is terminated by **CALL**'s alter ego: **RET** (for **RET**urn). The **RET** instruction pops the address off the top of the stack and transfers execution to that address. Since the address pushed was the address of the first instruction *after* the **CALL** instruction, execution continues as though **CALL** had not changed the flow of instruction execution at all. See Figure 9.1.

This should remind you strongly of how software interrupts work. The main difference is that the caller *does* know the exact address of the routine it wishes to call. Apart from that, it's very close to being the same process. (Also note that **RET** and **IRET** are *not* interchangeable. **CALL** works with **RET** just as **INT** works with **IRET**. Don't get those return instructions confused!)

The structure of a procedure is simple and easy to understand. Look at the **Write** procedure from EAT2.ASM:

```
Write:
   mov AH,09H     ; Select DOS service 9: Print String
   int 21H        ; Call DOS
   ret            ; Return to the caller
```

The important points are these: A procedure must begin with a label, which is (as you should recall) an identifier followed by a colon. Also, somewhere within the procedure, and certainly as the last instruction in the procedure, there must be at least one **RET** instruction. There may be more than one **RET** instruction. Execution has to come back from a procedure by way of a **RET** instruction, but there can be more than one exit door from a procedure. Using more than one **RET** instruction requires the use of condition jump instructions, which I won't take up until the next chapter.

Calls within Calls

Within a procedure you can do anything that you can do within the main program. This includes calling other procedures from within a procedure. Even something as simple as EAT2.ASM does that. Look at the **Writeln** procedure:

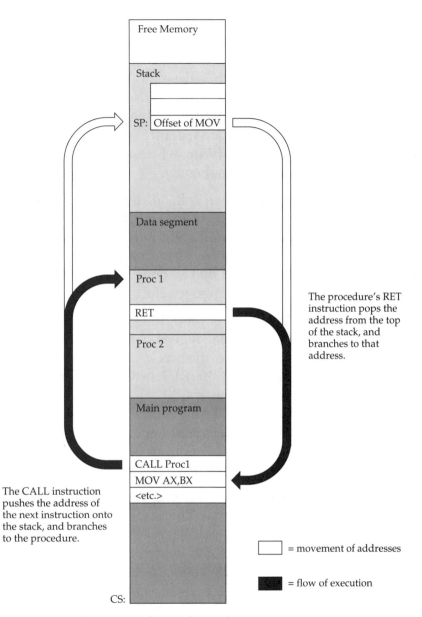

Figure 9.1 Calling a procedure and returning.

```
Writeln:
  call Write     ; Display the string proper through Write
  mov DX,CRLF    ; Load offset of newline string to DX
  call Write     ; Display the newline string through Write
  ret            ; Return to the caller
```

The **Writeln** procedure displays a string to your screen, and then returns the cursor to the left margin of the following screen line. This action is actually two distinct activities, and **Writeln** very economically uses a mechanism that already exists: the **Write** procedure. The first thing that **Writeln** does is call **Write** to display the string itself to the screen. Remember that the caller loaded the address of the string to be displayed into DX before calling **Writeln**. Nothing has disturbed DX, so **Writeln** can immediately call **Write**, which will fetch the address from DX and display the string to the screen.

Returning the cursor is done by displaying the newline sequence, which is stored in a string named **CRLF**. (If you recall, the carriage return and line feed character pair was built right into our message string in the EAT.ASM program that we dissected in Chapter 8.) **Writeln** again uses **Write** to display **CRLF**. Once that is done, the work is finished, and **Writeln** executes a **RET** instruction to return execution to the caller.

Calling procedures from within procedures requires you to pay attention to one thing: stack space. Remember that each procedure call pushes a return address onto the stack. This return address is not removed from the stack until the **RET** instruction for that procedure executes. If you execute another **CALL** instruction before returning from a procedure, the second **CALL** instruction pushes another return address onto the stack. If you keep calling procedures from within procedures, one return address will pile up on the stack for each **CALL** until you start returning from all those *nested* procedures.

If you run out of stack space, your program will crash and return to DOS, possibly taking DOS with it. This is why you should take care not to use more stack space than you have. Ironically, in small programs written in real mode flat model, this usually isn't a problem. Stack space isn't allocated in real mode flat model; instead the stack pointer points to the high end of the program's single segment, and the stack uses as much of the segment as it needs. For small programs with only a little data (such as the toy programs we're building and dissecting in this book), 95 percent of the space in the segment has nothing much to do and can be used by the stack if the stack needs it. (Which it doesn't—not in this kind of programming!)

Things are different when you move to real mode segmented model. In that model, you have to explicitly allocate a stack segment of some specific size, and that is all the space that the stack has to work with. So, ironically, in a program that can potentially make use of the full megabyte of real mode memory, it's much easier to foment a stack crash in segmented model than flat model. So, when you allocate space for the stack in real mode segmented model, it makes abundant sense to allocate considerably more stack space than you think you might ever conceivably need. EAT2.ASM at most uses 4 bytes of stack space, because it nests procedure calls two deep. (**Writeln** within itself calls **Write**.) In a program like this, stack allocation isn't an issue, even if you migrated it to the segmented model.

Nonetheless, I recommend allocating 512 bytes of stack to get you in the habit of not being stingy with stack space. Obviously, you won't always be able to keep a 128-to-1 ratio of need-to-have, but consider 512 bytes a *minimum* for stack space allocation in any reasonable program that uses the stack at all. (We allocated only 64 bytes of stack in EATSEG.ASM simply to show you what stack allocation was. The program does not, in fact, make any use of the stack at all.) If you need more, allocate it. Don't forget that there is only *one* stack in the system, and while your program is running, DOS and the BIOS and any active memory resident programs may well be using the same stack. If they fill it, you'll go down with the system—so leave room!

When to Make Something a Procedure

The single most important purpose of procedures is to manage complexity in your programs by replacing a sequence of machine instructions with a descriptive name. This might hardly seem to the point in the case of the **Write** procedure, which contains only two instructions apart from the structurally necessary **RET** instruction.

True. But—the **Writeln** procedure hides two separate calls to **Write** behind itself: one to display the string, and another to return the cursor to the left margin of the next line. The name **Writeln** is more readable and descriptive of what the underlying sequence of instructions does than the sequence of instructions itself. Extremely simple procedures such as **Write** don't themselves hide a great deal of complexity. They *do* give certain actions descriptive names, which is valuable in itself. They also provide basic building blocks for the creation of larger and more powerful procedures, as we'll see later on. And those larger procedures *will* hide considerable complexity, as you'll soon see.

In general, when looking for some action to turn into a procedure, see what actions tend to happen a lot in a program. Most programs spend a lot of time displaying things to the screen. Such procedures as **Write** and **Writeln** become general-purpose tools that may be used all over your programs. Furthermore, once you've written and tested them, they may be reused in future programs as well without adding to the burden of code that you must test for bugs.

Try to look ahead to your future programming tasks and create procedures of general usefulness. I show you more of those by way of examples as we continue, and tool building is a very good way to hone your assembly language skills.

On the other hand, a short sequence (5 to 10 instructions) that is only called once or perhaps twice within a middling program (that is, over hundreds of machine instructions) is a poor candidate for a procedure.

You may find it useful to define *large* procedures that are called only once when your program becomes big enough to require breaking it down into functional chunks. A thousand-line assembly language program might split well into a sequence of 9 or 10 largish procedures. Each is only called once from the main program, but this allows your main program to be very indicative of what the program is doing:

```
Start:   call Initialize
         call OpenFile
Input:   call GetRec
         call VerifyRec
         call WriteRec
         loop Input
         call CloseFile
         call CleanUp
         call ReturnToDOS
```

This is clean and readable and provides a necessary view from a height when you begin to approach a thousand-line assembly language program. Remember that the Martians are always hiding somewhere close by, anxious to turn your program into unreadable hieroglyphics.

There's no weapon against them with half the power of procedures.

Using BIOS Services

In the last chapter we looked closely at DOS services, which are accessed through the DOS services dispatcher. The DOS dispatcher lives at the other end of software interrupt 21H and offers a tremendous list of services at the disposal of your programs. There's another provider of services in your machine that lives even deeper than DOS: the ROM BIOS. *ROM* is an acronym for *read-only memory,* and it indicates memory chips whose contents are burned into their silicon and do not vanish when power is turned off. *BIOS* is an acronym for *Basic Input/Output System,* and it is just that: a collection of fundamental routines for dealing with your computer's input and output peripherals. These include disk drives, displays, printers, and the like. DOS uses BIOS services as part of some of the services that it provides.

Like DOS, BIOS services are accessed through software interrupts. Unlike DOS, which channels nearly all requests for its services through the single interrupt 21H, BIOS uses numerous interrupts (about 10) and groups similar categories of services beneath the control of different interrupts. For example, video display services are accessed through interrupt 10H, keyboard services come through interrupt 16H, printer services through interrupt 17H, and so on.

The overall method for using BIOS services, however, is very similar to that of DOS. You load a service number and sometimes other initial values into the registers and then execute an **INT <n>** instruction, where the **n** depends on the category of services you're requesting.

Nothing difficult about that at all. Let's start building some tools.

Positioning the Hardware Cursor

So far, in writing to the display, we've simply let the text fall where it may. In general this means one line of text following another, and when the screen fills, DOS *scrolls* the screen upward to make room on the bottom line for more text. This makes for dull programs, very similar to programming in the bad old days when everything was done on clunky mechanical printers called Teletypes. (Indeed, this kind of screen I/O is called "glass Teletype" I/O, due to its similarity to a printer scrolling paper up one line at a time.)

Let's leave the glass teletypes behind and take full control of the cursor. BIOS service 10H (often nicknamed VIDEO, in uppercase, for reasons that are obscure) offers a simple service to position the hardware cursor on the text screen. The service number is loaded into AH. This is a common thread through all BIOS services: The service number is placed into AH. A 0 must be placed in BH unless you intend to tinker with multiple text display pages. That's a story for another time (and not an especially useful feature in the twenty-first century), so while you're learning, assume BH should be set to 0 for cursor positioning.

The new position of the cursor must be loaded into the two halves of the DX register. Cursor positions are given as *X,Y* coordinate pairs. The *X* component of the cursor position is the number of character columns to the right of the left margin where we want the cursor to be. The *Y* component is the number of lines down from the top of the screen where we want the cursor to be. The *X* component is loaded into DL, and the *Y* component is loaded into DH. The routine itself is nothing more than this:

```
GotoXY:
   mov AH,02H   ; Select VIDEO service 2: Position cursor
   mov BH,0     ; Stay with display page 0
   int 10H      ; Call VIDEO
   ret          ; Return to the caller
```

Don't forget that the *X* and *Y* values must be loaded into DX *by the caller* (and that means you!). Using **GotoXY** is done this way:

```
   mov DX,[TextPos] ; TextPos contains X,Y position values
   call GotoXY      ; Position cursor
   mov DX,EatMsg1   ; Load offset of EatMsg1 string into DX
   call Write       ;  and display it
```

EAT3.ASM uses **GotoXY** to position the cursor, but it does something else as well: It clears the display. If you're going to be moving the cursor at will around the screen with **GotoXY**, it makes sense to start with a completely empty screen so that the remains of earlier programs and DOS commands don't clutter up the view.

There's another VIDEO service that can do the job. Service 6 is an interesting and powerful one: Not only does it clear the screen, it can scroll the screen as well, by any specified number of lines. Furthermore, it can clear or scroll the entire screen, or only a rectangular portion of the screen, leaving the rest of the screen undisturbed.

If the term *scrolling* is unfamiliar to you, just press Enter repeatedly at the DOS prompt and watch what happens when you reach the bottom line of the screen. The displayed text on the screen jumps up by one line, and an empty line appears at the bottom of the screen. The DOS prompt is then redisplayed in the empty line. Scrolling is the process of making the screen jump up by one or more lines and inserting one or more blank lines at the bottom as appropriate.

Using VIDEO Service 6

Understanding VIDEO service 6 involves a fair number of values that need to be passed to the service in registers. The one unchanging item is the service number itself, passed as 6 in (as with all BIOS services) register AH.

Service 6 acts upon a rectangular region of the display. This may be the full screen or it may be only part of the screen. You must pass the coordinates of the upper-left and lower-right corners of the region you want to work on in registers CX and DX. Because screen coordinates are always smaller than 255 (which is the largest value that can be expressed in 8 bits), the register halves of CX and DX are used independently to carry the X and Y values.

The upper-left corner's X coordinate is passed in CL, and the upper-left corner's Y coordinate is passed in CH. These are *zero-based* coordinates, meaning that they count from 0 rather than 1. Confusion is possible here because most high-level languages such as Borland Pascal number coordinates on the screen from 1. In other words, the upper-left corner of the screen in Borland Pascal is given by the coordinates 1,1. To the BIOS, however, that same corner of the screen is 0,0. The width and height values of a typical screen in Borland Pascal would be 80 x 25; the BIOS would say 79 x 24.

Similarly, the lower-right corner's X coordinate is passed in DL, and the lower-right corner's Y coordinate is passed in DH. (Again, counting from 0.)

Service 6 either scrolls or clears the region. It can scroll the screen upward by any arbitrary number of lines. This number is passed to service 6 in register AL. Clearing the region is a special case of scrolling it: When you specify that 0 lines be scrolled, the entire region is cleared instead.

The full screen is actually a special case of a rectangular region. By passing the coordinates of the upper-left and lower-right corners of the screen (0,0 and 79,24), the full screen is cleared.

Procedures with Multiple Entry Points

This is a lot of versatility for one service to handle, and it brings up a couple of questions. First of all, how versatile should a single procedure be? Should there be one procedure to clear the whole screen, another procedure to clear part of a screen, and a third procedure to scroll part of the screen?

The answer is that one procedure can do all three, and not duplicate any code at all. The method involves writing a single procedure that has four different *entry points*. Each entry point is a label, which may be called with a **CALL** instruction. When a given entry point's label is called, execution begins at the instruction specified by that label. There is only one **RET** instruction, so the procedure is in fact one procedure. It's like a house with three front doors but only one back door; having three front doors does not make it three separate houses.

Here's what such a creature might look like:

```
ClrScr:
    mov CX,0        ; Upper left corner of full screen
    mov DX,LRXY     ; Load lower-right XY coordinates into DX
ClrWin:
    mov AL,0        ; 0 specifies clear entire region
ScrlWin:
    mov BH,07H      ; Specify "normal" attribute for blanked line(s)
VIDEO6:
    mov AH,06H      ; Select VIDEO service 6: Initialize/Scroll
    int 10H         ; Call VIDEO
    ret             ; Return to the caller
```

There's nothing much to this. What we have here is a collection of **MOV** instructions which set up values in registers before calling VIDEO through interrupt 10H. Note that all of the entry points must be given as valid labels with colons.

The multiple entry points exist only to allow you to skip certain portions of the procedure that set up values that you don't want set. All the registers used by VIDEO service 6 must be set up *somewhere*. However, they can either be set within the procedure or in the caller's code just before the procedure is called. If the procedure sets them, they have to be set to some generally useful configuration (say, clearing the entire screen), whereas if the caller sets them, the registers can be set to serve the caller's needs and make service 6 perform any of its varied combinations.

So it is with procedure **ClrScr**. If you enter **ClrScr** through its main or top entry point, *all* of its internal code will be executed. CX and DX will be set to the upper-left and lower-right corner coordinates of the full screen, AL is set to 0 to clear the full screen rather than scroll it, and BH is loaded with the "normal" (that is, blank, for white text on a black background) text display attribute. Then service 6 is called.

If you wish to clear only a rectangular area of the screen (a *window*), you would use the **ClrWin** entry point. This entry point starts executing the code *after* CX and DX are set to the corners of the full screen. This means that the caller must load CX and DX with the upper-left and lower-right corners of the screen region to be cleared. Calling **ClrWin** *without* setting CX and DX at all will execute service 6 with whatever leftover garbage values happen to be in CX and DX. Something will happen, for certain. Whether it's something that you *want* to happen is far less certain.

Keeping in mind that for proper operation, all of service 6's required registers must be set, calling **ClrWin** would be done this way:

```
mov CX,0422H ; Set upper left corner to X=22H; Y=04H
mov DX,093AH ; Set lower right corner to X=3AH; Y=09H
call ClrWin  ; Call the window-clear procedure
```

The two **MOV** instructions are worth a closer look. Rather than use a separate instruction to load each half of DX and CX, the two halves are loaded together by loading a 16-bit immediate data value into the full 16-bit register. Thus, two **MOV** instructions can do the work that a first glance might think would take four **MOV** instructions. This is a good example of writing tight, efficient assembler code. The trick is to document it (as I've done in the preceding) to make sure you understand six weeks from now what the magic number 093AH really means!

The first instruction at the label **ClrWin** sets AL to 0. Setting AL to 0 indicates that the region is to be cleared, not scrolled. If, in fact, you *do* want to scroll the region, you need to skip the **MOV** instruction that loads 0 into AL. This is the purpose of the entry point labeled **ScrlWin**. It gets you into the procedure below the point at which you select clearing over scrolling. This means that you not only have to set the corners of the region to be scrolled, but also the number of lines to scroll as well:

```
mov CX,0422H ; Set upper left corner to  X=22H; Y=04H
mov DX,093AH ; Set lower right corner to X=3AH; Y=09H
mov AL,1     ; Set to scroll by one line
call ScrlWin ; Call the window-scroll procedure
```

As you can see, more and more of the work is being done by caller and less and less within the procedure.

Note that there is no entry point to scroll the full screen. To scroll the full screen, you need to load the coordinates of the corners of the full screen into CX and DX, and then call **ClrWin** as though you were clearing just a portion of the screen. If you do a lot of screen scrolling, you might define a separate routine for scrolling the full screen. As an interesting exercise, write such a routine and a program to test it.

As one more entry point, I included a label VIDEO6, which short-circuits all of the register setup apart from loading the service number itself into AH. This allows you to do something odd and infrequently done, such as scrolling the entire screen by three lines.

Memory Data or Immediate Data?

You may be wondering what the variable identifier **LRXY** is for and where it is defined. What it's for is simply to hold the current *X,Y* coordinates for the lower-right corner of the screen. Where it's defined is in the program's data segment, in the usual way variables are defined, as you'll see if you look ahead to the full listing of EAT3.ASM which follows.

The more interesting question is *why*. Most of the time I've been showing you values loaded into registers from immediate data, and this is often useful. The coordinates of the upper-left corner of the full screen, for example, are always going to be 0,0, and nothing will ever change that. The lower-right corner, however, is not necessarily always 79,24.

The original 1981 vintage IBM MDA and CGA graphics adapters are indeed capable of 80 by 25 text screens and no more. However, with an EGA, it is possible to have an 80 by either 25 or 43 text screen, and the VGA introduced in 1987 with the PS/2 line can display either 25- or 50-line screens, all 80 characters wide. The newer super VGA video boards are capable of even more different text modes, some of them with more than 80 characters in a visible line. If your program can determine what size screen is in force when it is invoked, it can modify its displays accordingly.

Avoid dropping immediate values into code (we call this *hard coding*) whenever you can. A better strategy, which I follow from now on, uses variables in the data segment initialized with currently correct values when the program begins running.

Use Comment Headers!

As time goes on, you'll find yourself creating dozens or even hundreds of procedures as a means of not reinventing the same old wheel. The libraries of available procedures that most high-level language vendors supply with their compilers just don't exist with assembly language. By and large, you create your own.

Keeping such a list of routines straight is no easy task when you've written them all yourself. You *must* document the essential facts about each individual procedure or you'll forget them, or remember them incorrectly and act on bad information. (The resultant bugs are often devilishly hard to find because you're *sure* you remember everything there is to know about that proc! After all, you *wrote* it!)

I recommend adding a comment header to every procedure you write, no matter how simple. Such a header should contain the following information:

- The name of the procedure
- The date it was last modified
- What it does
- What data items the caller must pass it to make it work correctly
- What data is returned by the procedure, if any, and where it is returned (for example, in register CX)
- What other procedures, if any, are called by the procedure
- Any "gotchas" that need to be kept in mind while writing code that uses the procedure

A typical workable procedure header is this:

```
;------------------------------------------------------------
;  WRITELN -- Displays information to the screen via DOS
;            service 9 and issues a newline
;  Last update 9/11/99
;
;  1 entry point:
;
;  Writeln:
;   Caller must pass:
;   DS: The segment of the string to be displayed
;   DX: The offset of the string to be displayed
;       String must be terminated by "$"
;   Action: Displays the string at DS:DX up to the "$" marker
;           marker, then issues a newline. Hardware cursor
;           will move to the left margin of the following
;           line. If the display is to the bottom screen
;           line, the screen will scroll.
;   Calls: Write
;------------------------------------------------------------
```

A comment header does not relieve you of the responsibility of commenting the individual lines of code within the procedure. It's a good idea to put a short comment to the right of every line that contains a machine instruction mnemonic, and also (in longer procedures) a comment block describing every major functional block within the procedure.

A program written to make use of procedures to control the screen follows. Examine EAT3.ASM, and notice the various commenting conventions. For a very short program such as this, such elaborate internal documentation might seem overkill. Once your programs get serious, however, you'll be very glad you expended the effort.

```
; Source name       : EAT3.ASM
; Executable name   : EAT3.COM
; Code model        : Real mode flat model
; Version           : 1.0
; Created date      : 7/31/1999
; Last update       : 9/11/1999
; Author            : Jeff Duntemann
; Description       : A DOS .COM file demonstrating the use of software
;                     interrupts to control the text mode display through
;                     calls into BIOS VIDEO interrupt 10H. Assemble with
;                     NASM 0.98.


[BITS 16]        ; Set 16 bit code generation
[ORG 0x0100]     ; Set code start address to 100h (.COM file)

[SECTION .text]  ; Section containing code

Start:
  call ClrScr    ; Clear the full display

  ; Make sure you understand the difference between
  ;   MOV DX,Identifier and MOV DX,[Identifier] !!!

mov word [TextPos],0914H  ; 0914H = X @ 20, Y @ 9

  mov DX,[TextPos] ; TextPos contains X,Y position values
  call GotoXY      ; Position cursor
  mov DX,EatMsg1   ; Load offset of EatMsg1 string into DX
  call Write       ;  and display it

  mov DX,[TextPos] ; Re-use text position variable
  mov DH,10        ; Put new Y value into DH but re-use X
  call GotoXY      ; Position cursor
  mov DX,EatMsg2   ; Load offset of EatMsg2 string into DX
  call Write       ;  and display it
```

```
    mov DX,1701H      ; Move cursor to bottom left corner of screen
    call GotoXY       ;  so that 'Press enter...' msg is out of the way.

    mov ax,4C00H      ; This function exits the program
    int 21H           ;  and returns control to DOS.


;---------------------------|
;      PROCEDURE SECTION     |
;---------------------------|


;-------------------------------------------------------------
;  GOTOXY  — Positions the hardware cursor to X,Y
;  Last update 7/31/99
;
;  1 entry point:
;
;  GotoXY:
;   Caller must pass:
;   DL: X value   These are both 0-based; i.e., they
;   DH: Y value     assume a screen 24 by 79, not 25 by 80
;   Action: Moves the hardware cursor to the X,Y position
;           loaded into DL and H.
;-------------------------------------------------------------
GotoXY:
    mov AH,02H  ; Select VIDEO service 2: Position cursor
    mov BH,0    ; Stay with display page 0
    int 10H     ; Call VIDEO
    ret         ; Return to the caller


;-------------------------------------------------------------
;  CLRSCR  — Clears or scrolls screens or windows
;  Last update 3/5/89
;
;  4 entry points:
;
;  ClrScr:
;   No values expected from caller
;   Action: Clears the entire screen to blanks with 07H as
;           the display attribute
;
;  ClrWin:
;   Caller must pass:
;   CH: Y coordinate, upper left corner of window
;   CL: X coordinate, upper left corner of window
;   DH: Y coordinate, lower right corner of window
;   DL: X coordinate, lower right corner of window
;   Action: Clears the window specified by the caller to
;           blanks with 07H as the display attribute
```

```
;
;   ScrlWin:
;    Caller must pass:
;    CH: Y coordinate, upper left corner of window
;    CL: X coordinate, upper left corner of window
;    DH: Y coordinate, lower right corner of window
;    DL: X coordinate, lower right corner of window
;    AL: number of lines to scroll window by (0 clears it)
;    Action: Scrolls the window specified by the caller by
;            the number of lines passed in AL. The blank
;            lines inserted at screen bottom are cleared
;            to blanks with 07H as the display attribute
;
;  VIDEO6:
;    Caller must pass:
;    CH: Y coordinate, upper left corner of window
;    CL: X coordinate, upper left corner of window
;    DH: Y coordinate, lower right corner of window
;    DL: X coordinate, lower right corner of window
;    AL: number of lines to scroll window by (0 clears it)
;    BH: display attribute for blanked lines (07H is "normal")
;    Action: Generic access to BIOS VIDEO service 6. Caller
;            must pass ALL register parameters as shown above
;--------------------------------------------------------------

ClrScr:
  mov CX,0      ; Upper left corner of full screen
  mov DX,LRXY   ; Load lower-right XY coordinates into DX
ClrWin:
  mov AL,0      ; 0 specifies clear entire region
ScrlWin:
  mov BH,07H    ; Specify "normal" attribute for blanked line(s)
VIDEO6:
  mov AH,06H    ; Select VIDEO service 6: Initialize/Scroll
  int 10H       ; Call VIDEO
  ret           ; Return to the caller


;--------------------------------------------------------------
;  WRITE — Displays information to the screen via DOS
;          service 9: Print String
;  Last update 7/31/99
;
;  1 entry point:
;
;  Write:
;    Caller must pass:
;    DS: The segment of the string to be displayed
;    DX: The offset of the string to be displayed
;        String must be terminated by "$"
;    Action: Displays the string at DS:DX up to the "$" marker
```

```
;--------------------------------------------------------------

Write:
  mov AH,09H    ; Select DOS service 9: Print String
  int 21H       ; Call DOS
  ret           ; Return to the caller



;--------------------------------------------------------------
;  WRITELN — Displays information to the screen via DOS
;           service 9 and issues a newline
;  Last update 7/31/99
;
;  1 entry point:
;
;  Writeln:
;   Caller must pass:
;   DS: The segment of the string to be displayed
;   DX: The offset of the string to be displayed
;       String must be terminated by "$"
;   Action: Displays the string at DS:DX up to the "$" marker
;           marker, then issues a newline. Hardware cursor
;           will move to the left margin of the following
;           line. If the display is to the bottom screen
;           line, the screen will scroll.
;   Calls: Write
;--------------------------------------------------------------

Writeln:
  call Write    ; Display the string proper through Write
  mov DX,CRLF   ; Load offset of newline string to DX
  call Write    ; Display the newline string through Write
  ret           ; Return to the caller



;----------------------------|
;      DATA SECTION          |
;----------------------------|


[SECTION .data]     ; Section containing initialized data

            ; Combined 0-based X,Y of 80 x 25 screen LR corner:
LRXY     DW    184FH ; 18H = 24D; 4FH = 79D

TextPos  DW    0  ; Memory variable to store text screen coordinates

EatMsg1  DB    "Eat at Joe's . . . ",'$'
EatMsg2  DB    "...ten million flies can't ALL be wrong!",'$'
CRLF     DB    0DH,0AH,'$'
Space    DB    " ",'$'
```

Building External Libraries of Procedures

You'll notice that the EAT3.ASM program given at the end of the previous section had most of its bulk devoted to procedures. This is as it should be, with the caution that the procedures it uses are the kind you're likely to use in any and all of your assembly language programs. Keeping cursor movement and screen-clearing routines in source code form in every single program you write is a waste of space and can clutter up the program in a way that makes it less easy to understand.

The answer is to break the utility procedures out into an external library that you can assemble only once, and then link into every program that uses its procedures without assembling the library every time you assemble the program. This is called *modular programming*, and it is an extremely effective tool for programming efficiently in any language, assembly language not excluded.

I describe this process briefly back in Chapter 4 and show it pictorially in Figures 4.4 and 4.5. A program might consist of three or four separate .ASM files, each of which is assembled separately to a separate .OBJ file. To produce the final executable .EXE file, the linker weaves all of the .OBJ files together, resolving all of the references from one to the other, finally creating an .EXE file.

Each .ASM file is considered a *module,* and each module contains one or more procedures and possibly some data definitions. When all the declarations are done correctly, all of the modules may freely call one another, and any procedure may refer to any data definition.

The trick, of course, is to get all the declarations right.

Public and External Declarations

If you reference a label in your program (by, say, including a **CALL** instruction to that label) without defining that label anywhere in the program, the assembler will gleefully give you an error message. (You've probably already experienced this if you've begun writing your own programs in assembly.) In modular programming, you're frequently going to be calling procedures that don't exist anywhere in the program that you're actually working on. How to get past the assembler's watchdogs?

The answer is to declare a procedure *external*. This works very much like it sounds: The assembler is told that a given label will have to be found outside the program somewhere, in another module. Once told that, that assembler is happy to give you a pass on an undefined label. You've promised the assembler that you'll provide it later, and the assembler accepts your promise and keeps going without flagging the undefined label.

The promise looks like this:

```
EXTERN ClrScr
```

Here, you've told the assembler that the label **ClrScr** represents a procedure and that it will be found somewhere external to the current module. That's all the assembler needs to know to withhold its error message.

And having done that, the assembler's part is finished. It leaves in place an empty socket in your program where the external procedure may later be plugged in. I sometimes think of it as an eyelet where the external procedure will later hook in.

Over in the other module where procedure **ClrScr** exists, it isn't enough just to define the procedure. An eyelet needs a hook. You have to warn the assembler that **ClrScr** will be referenced from outside the module. The assembler needs to forge the hook that will hook into the eyelet. You forge the hook by declaring the procedure *global*, meaning that other modules anywhere in the program may freely reference the procedure. Declaring a procedure global is simplicity itself:

```
GLOBAL ClrScr
```

That done, who actually connects the hook and the eyelet? The linker does that during the link operation. After all, why call it a linker if it doesn't link anything? At link time, the linker takes the two .OBJ files generated by the assembler, one from your program and the other from the module containing **ClrScr,** and combines them into a single .EXE executable file. (The number of .OBJ files isn't limited to two; you can have almost any number of separately assembled external modules.) When the .EXE file is loaded and run, the program can call **ClrScr** as cleanly and quickly as though both had been declared in the same source code file.

This process is summarized in Figure 9.2.

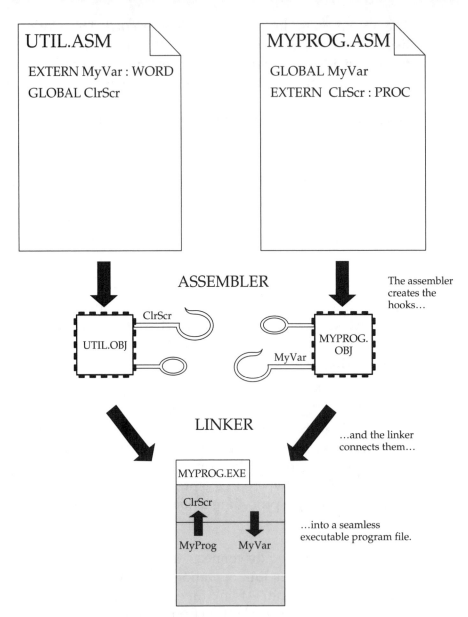

Figure 9.2 Connecting globals and externals.

What works for procedures works for data as well, and it can work in either direction. Your program can declare a variable as **GLOBAL**, and that variable may then be used by any module in which the same variable name is declared as external with the **EXTERN** directive. I show you how this works in the VIDLIB.ASM library presented a little later in this chapter. Finally, procedure libraries themselves may share data and procedures in any combination, as long as the declarations are handled correctly.

We sometimes say that a program or module containing procedures or variables declared as public *exports* those items. Also, we say that a program or module that uses procedures or variables that are external to it *imports* those items.

The Mechanics of Globals and Externals

I've described the source code mechanics of assembly language programs in detail in the last few chapters. External modules are similar to programs. There are two major differences, concerning things that external modules lack:

- *External modules do not contain a main program and hence have no start address.* That is, no label **..start:** exists to indicate to the linker that this is the point at which code execution is to begin. External modules are not intended to be run by themselves, so a start address is both unnecessary and (if one were added) a temptation to chaos.

- *External modules have no stack segment.* This is not an absolute requirement (there are few such requirements in assembler work), but for simple assembly language programming it's true enough. Your stack segment should be defined in your main program module. External modules should have none—they use the one defined by the programs that call them. Recall that in real mode segmented model, there is only one stack in operation at any given time, and that the one you define in your program is used by everything running on your machine—including the operating system—while your program has control.

External modules may have a data segment. If the external is to define a variable that is to be shared by the main program or by other externals, it obviously must have a data segment for that variable to reside in. But less obviously, if the external is to share a variable with another external or with the main program, it must *still* define a data segment, even if that data segment is empty except for the external declaration.

If a segment (whether a code segment or a data segment) is to export anything, that segment must be declared public. This is done with the

PUBLIC keyword, which instructs the linker to make access to the segment possible from outside the module that contains the segment:

```
SEGMENT data PUBLIC
SEGMENT code PUBLIC
```

This is easier to demonstrate than to explain. Take a look at the following external module, which is a library containing all of the simple display control procedures introduced in EAT3.ASM:

```
; Source name    : VIDLIB.ASM
; Compiled name  : VIDLIB.OBJ
; Code model:    : Real mode segmented model
; Version        : 1.0
; Created date   : 9/12/1999
; Last update    : 9/12/1999
; Author         : Jeff Duntemann
; Description    : A simple example of a separately assembled module
;                  containing utility procedures for controlling the
;                  PC display. Assembled using NASM 0.98. DOS programs
;                  can link to these routines by declaring them EXTERN
;                  and then linking the program .OBJ to VIDLIB.OBJ using
;                  a linker like ALINK.


[BITS 16]            ; Set 16 bit code generation


;----------------------------|
;   BEGIN DATA SEGMENT        |
;----------------------------|
        SEGMENT data PUBLIC

;Note that the following items are defined externally to this module, and
; for certain routines in this module to function these data items must
; be linked in from a properly assembled external module.

        EXTERN CRLF,LRXY

;Note also that there are no memory variables that reside in this data
; segment!
;The data segment must be here so that the EXTERN declarations may be
; made.

;----------------------------|
;   BEGIN CODE SEGMENT        |
;----------------------------|

        SEGMENT code PUBLIC ; This segment may be accessed externally

; Note that the following items are GLOBAL, and may be accessed by
;  external files that declare them EXTERN.
```

```
        GLOBAL GotoXY,ClrScr,ClrWin,ScrlWin,VIDEO6
        GLOBAL Write,Writeln



;-------------------------------------------------------------
; GOTOXY  -- Positions the hardware cursor to X,Y
; Last update 9/12/99
;
; 1 entry point:
;
; GotoXY:
;  Caller must pass:
;  DL: X value   These are both 0-based; i.e., they
;  DH: Y value     assume a screen 24 by 79, not 25 by 80
;  Action:  Moves the hardware cursor to the X,Y position
;              loaded into DL and H.
;-------------------------------------------------------------
GotoXY:
      mov AH,02H   ; Select VIDEO service 2: Position cursor
      mov BH,0     ; Stay with display page 0
      int 10H      ; Call VIDEO
      ret          ; Return to the caller


;-------------------------------------------------------------
; CLRSCR  -- Clears or scrolls screens or windows
; Last update 9/12/99
;
; 4 entry points:
;
; ClrScr:
;  No values expected from caller
;  Action:  Clears the entire screen to blanks with 07H as
;              the display attribute
;
; ClrWin:
;  Caller must pass:
;  CH: Y coordinate, upper left corner of window
;  CL: X coordinate, upper left corner of window
;  DH: Y coordinate, lower right corner of window
;  DL: X coordinate, lower right corner of window
;  Action:  Clears the window specified by the caller to
;              blanks with 07H as the display attribute
;
; ScrlWin:
;  Caller must pass:
;  CH: Y coordinate, upper left corner of window
;  CL: X coordinate, upper left corner of window
;  DH: Y coordinate, lower right corner of window
;  DL: X coordinate, lower right corner of window
;  AL: number of lines to scroll window by (0 clears it)
```

```
;   Action: Scrolls the window specified by the caller by
;           the number of lines passed in AL. The blank
;           lines inserted at screen bottom are cleared
;           to blanks with 07H as the display attribute
;
;  VIDEO6:
;   Caller must pass:
;   CH: Y coordinate, upper left corner of window
;   CL: X coordinate, upper left corner of window
;   DH: Y coordinate, lower right corner of window
;   DL: X coordinate, lower right corner of window
;   AL: number of lines to scroll window by (0 clears it)
;   BH: display attribute for blanked lines (07H is "normal")
;   Action:  Generic access to BIOS VIDEO service 6. Caller
;            must pass ALL register parameters as shown above
;-------------------------------------------------------------


ClrScr:
        mov CX,0           ; Upper left corner of full screen
        mov DX,word [LRXY] ; Load lower-right XY coordinates into DX
ClrWin: mov AL,0           ; 0 specifies clear entire region
ScrlWin: mov BH,07H        ; "Normal" attribute for blanked line(s)
VIDEO6: mov AH,06H         ; Select VIDEO service 6: Initialize/Scroll
        int 10H            ; Call VIDEO
        ret                ; Return to the caller




;-------------------------------------------------------------
;  WRITE  -- Displays information to the screen via DOS
;         service 9: Print String
;  Last update 9/12/99
;
;  1 entry point:
;
;  Write:
;   Caller must pass:
;   DS: The segment of the string to be displayed
;   DX: The offset of the string to be displayed
;       String must be terminated by "$"
;   Action: Displays the string at DS:DX up to the "$" marker
;-------------------------------------------------------------


Write:
        mov AH,09H   ; Select DOS service 9: Print String
        int 21H      ; Call DOS
        ret          ; Return to the caller




;-------------------------------------------------------------
;  WRITELN -- Displays information to the screen via DOS
```

```
;              service 9 and issues a newline
;  Last update 9/12/99
;
;  1 entry point:
;
;  Writeln:
;   Caller must pass:
;   DS: The segment of the string to be displayed
;   DX: The offset of the string to be displayed
;       String must be terminated by "$"
;   Action: Displays the string at DS:DX up to the "$" marker
;           marker, then issues a newline. Hardware cursor
;           will move to the left margin of the following
;           line. If the display is to the bottom screen
;           line, the screen will scroll.
;   Calls: Write
;-----------------------------------------------------------

Writeln:
      call Write   ; Display the string proper through Write
      mov DX,CRLF  ; Load address of newline string to DS:DX
      call Write   ; Display the newline string through Write
      ret          ; Return to the caller
```

VIDLIB.ASM has both a code segment and a data segment. Note well that both segments are declared with the **PUBLIC** keyword. A common mistake made by beginners is to declare the procedures and variables public, but not the segments that they reside in. Nonobvious it may be, but essential nonetheless: Make your module segments public if they contain any public declarations!

The code segment contains all the procedures declared as **GLOBAL**. VIDLIB, after all, exists to offer these procedures to programs and other libraries. The data segment, on the other hand, contains only the following statement:

```
EXTERN CRLF,LRXY
```

VIDLIB.ASM declares no variables of its own—that is, variables that are defined and exist within VIDLIB. Instead, it uses two variables that are declared and reside within the main program module EAT4.ASM. (EAT4.ASM is identical to EAT3.ASM, save that it has had its procedures removed and declared as external and two of its variables declared public. The program's function is exactly the same as that of EAT3.ASM.)

The preceding **EXTERN** statement indicates that two variables referenced within the module are to be imported from somewhere. *You don't have to specify from where.* The names of the variables have to be there, and that's all. Unlike many assemblers, NASM is case-sensitive for variable names and labels (though not for keywords and instruction mnemonics), so be careful of character case.

NASM declines the variable-typing syntax Microsoft uses with MASM and does not require that external variable identifiers be typed. That is, with NASM you don't have to say whether a variable is a byte, a word, a double word, and so on. NASM assumes that *the size of the item where it is declared governs its use in all places*—and the burden of enforcing that falls on you. If you declare an **EXTERN** to be a byte (say, with **DB**) and then try to link that **EXTERN** to a **GLOBAL** that is in fact a word, what actually happens may not be what you want.

Dividing a Segment across Module Boundaries

Note that the names of the code segment and data segment in the external module are the same as the names of the code segment and data segment in the main program module. The data segment is named **data** in both, and the code segment is named **code** in both. This is not an absolute requirement, but it simplifies things greatly and is a good way to set things up while you're just learning your way around in assembly language. Regardless of the number of external modules that link with your main program, *the program as a whole* contains only *one* code segment and *one* data segment. Until your data requirements and code size get *very* large, you won't need more than a single code and data segment. There are ways to use multiple code and data segments within a single assembly language program, but that's an advanced topic that I won't be addressing in this book.

As long as the code and data segments are declared with the **PUBLIC** directive in all the modules sharing the segments, the linker will consider all to be part of the same code and data segments.

Your Main Program Module

So here's our backhanded advertising program, as modified for use with an external display control module:

```
; Source name      : EAT4.ASM
; Executable name : EAT4.EXE
; Code model:       : Real mode segmented model
; Version           : 1.0
```

```
; Created date    : 9/12/1999
; Last update     : 9/12/1999
; Author          : Jeff Duntemann
; Description      : A simple example of a DOS .EXE file programmed for
;                    real mode segmented model, using NASM 0.98 and ALINK.
;                    This program demonstrates how separately-assembled
;                    modules sharing both code and data are linked into a
;                    single executable module.

[BITS 16]          ; Set 16 bit code generation


;----------------------------|
;   BEGIN CODE SEGMENT        |
;----------------------------|


; Note that the following items are external to EAT4.ASM, and must
;  be linked from the external file VIDLIB.OBJ. Assemble VIDLIB.ASM
;  first to VIDLIB.OBJ before attempting the link.

        EXTERN GotoXY,Write,Writeln,ClrScr

        SEGMENT code PUBLIC

; SEGMENT SETUP
;
;  In real mode segmented model, a program uses three segments, and it must
;  set up the addresses in the three corresponding segment registers. This
;  is what the ASSUME directive does in MASM; we ASSUME nothing in NASM!
;  Each of the three segments has a name (here, code, data, and stack) and
;  these names are identifiers indicating segment addresses. It is the
;  appropriate segment address that is moved into each segment register.
;  Note that you can't move an address directly into a segment register;
;  you must first move the address into a general purpose register. Also
;  note that we don't do anything with CS; the ..start: label tells the
;  linker where the code segment begins.

..start:               ; This is where program execution begins:
     mov ax,data       ; Move segment address of data segment into AX
     mov ds,ax         ; Copy address from AX into DS
     mov ax,stack      ; Move segment address of stack segment into AX
     mov ss,ax         ; Copy address from AX into SS

     mov sp,stacktop   ; Point SP to the top of the stack

     call ClrScr       ; Clear the full display

     mov word [TextPos], 0914H  ; 0914H = X @ 20, Y @ 9

     mov DX,[TextPos]  ; TextPos contains X,Y position values
     call GotoXY       ; Position cursor
     mov DX,Eat1       ; Load offset of Eat1 string into DX
```

```
        call Write        ;  and display it

        mov DX,[TextPos] ; Re-use text position variable
        mov DH,10         ; Put new Y value into DH
        call GotoXY        ; Position cursor
        mov DX,Eat2       ; Load offset of Ear2 string into DX
        call Writeln       ;  and display it

        mov AH,4CH        ; Terminate process DOS service
        mov AL,0          ; Pass this value back to ERRORLEVEL
        int 21H           ; Control returns to DOS


;----------------------------|
;   BEGIN DATA SEGMENT        |
;----------------------------|
        SEGMENT data PUBLIC
        GLOBAL LRXY,CRLF

LRXY    DW   184FH ; 18H = 24D; 4FH = 79D; 0-based XY of LR screen corner

TextPos DW   0
Eat1    DB   "Eat at Joe's . . . ",'$'
Eat2    DB   "...ten million flies can't ALL be wrong!",'$'
CRLF    DB   0DH,0AH,'$'


;----------------------------|
;   END DATA SEGMENT          |
;----------------------------|



;----------------------------|
;   BEGIN STACK SEGMENT       |
;----------------------------|

        SEGMENT stack stack ;This means a segment of *type* "stack"
                            ; that is also *named* "stack"! Some
                            ; linkers demand that a stack segment
                            ; have the explicit type "stack"

        resb 64             ; Reserve 64 bytes for the program stack
stacktop:                   ; It's significant that this label points to
                            ;  the *last* of the reserved 64 bytes, and
                            ;  not the first!


;----------------------------|
;   END STACK SEGMENT         |
;----------------------------|
```

EAT4.ASM differs in only a few ways from EAT3.ASM. First of all, the
data and code segment declarations now include the **PUBLIC** directive:

```
SEGMENT data PUBLIC
SEGMENT code PUBLIC
```

This is easy to forget but you must keep it in mind: The segments containing imported or exported items *as well as the imported or exported items themselves* must be declared as public.

Take note of the declaration of two of the variables in the data segment as global:

```
GLOBAL LRXY,CRLF
```

This allows external modules to use these two variables. The other variables declared in the main program, **Eat1**, **Eat2**, and **TextPos**, are not declared as public and are inaccessible from external modules. We would say that those three variables are *private* to the main program module EAT4.ASM.

EAT4.ASM contains no procedure declarations of its own. All the procedures it uses are imported from VIDLIB.ASM, and all are therefore declared as external in the code segment, using this statement:

```
EXTERN GotoXY,Write,Writeln,ClrScr
```

Something to keep in mind is that while VIDLIB.ASM exports seven procedures (seven labels, actually, since four are entry points to the **ClrScr** procedure), EAT4.ASM only imports the four immediately previous. The **ClrWin**, **ScrlWin**, and **VIDEO6** entry points to procedure **ClrScr** are declared as global in VIDLIB.ASM, but they are not declared as external in EAT4.ASM. EAT4.ASM only uses the four it imports. The other three are available, but the EAT4.ASM does not call them and therefore does not bother declaring them as external. If you were to expand EAT4.ASM to use one of the three other entry points to **ClrScr**, you would have to add the entry point to the **EXTERN** list.

Once all the external and global declarations are in place, your machine instructions may reference procedures and variables across module boundaries as though they were all within the same large program. No special qualifiers have to be added to the instructions. **CALL ClrScr** is written the same way, whether **ClrScr** is declared in the main program module or in an external module such as VIDLIB.ASM.

Linking Multiple Modules

The linker hasn't had to do much linking so far. Once you have multiple modules, however, the linker begins to earn its keep. To link multiple modules, you must specify the name of the .OBJ file for each module on the linker command line.

Up until now, the linker command line contained only the name of the main program module:

```
ALINK EAT3
```

Now you must add the names of all external modules to the linker command line:

```
ALINK EAT4 VIDLIB
```

Pretty obviously, if you forget to name an external module on the linker command line, the linker will not be able to resolve the external references involving the missing .OBJ file, and you will get linker error messages like this one, one for each unresolved external reference:

```
Undefined symbol 'CLRSCR' in module EAT4.ASM
```

Batch Files for Building Modular Programs

NASM-IDE was created for use with real mode flat model programs, which cannot, strictly speaking, be modular in nature and assembled with a linker from separately assembled modules. So, if you're going to be doing a lot of work in real mode segmented model, you might consider creating batch files containing the commands you need to issue to the assembler and the linker. This will save you a lot of typing: Instead of typing two full commands on the DOS command line every time you want to build a program, you type only the name of the batch file, and DOS executes any commands in the batch file just as though you had typed them by hand.

Here's a batch file I created (called BUILD4.BAT) to build EAT4.EXE:

```
NASM16 EAT4.ASM -f obj -o EAT4.OBJ
NASM16 VIDLIB.ASM -f obj -o VIDLIB.OBJ
ALINK EAT4.OBJ VIDLIB.OBJ
```

It's nothing more than a simple text file containing the three commands you would need to type separately: two for the assembler and a third to link the two assembled files together into the finished .EXE program. To run this batch program, just type "BUILD4" at the DOS prompt. You'll be able to follow the progress of the three program runs, including any error messages or warnings.

External Module Summary

Here are some points to keep in mind when you're faced with splitting a single program up into a main program and one or more external modules. The assumption here is that the final program will consist of only one code segment and only one data segment. Larger arrangements of segments are possible (especially with multiple code segments) but require additional considerations I won't be covering in this book.

- Declare the code segments PUBLIC in all modules, and give them all the same name.
- Declare the data segments PUBLIC in all modules, and give them all the same name.
- Declare all exported procedures, entry points, and variables as GLOBAL. Put the exported declaration statement inside the segment where the exported items are declared.
- Declare all imported procedures, entry points, and variables as EXTERN. Put the imported declaration statement inside the segment where the imported items are to be used. Data is used in the data segment, code in the code segment.
- Finally, don't forget to add the names of all external modules to the linker command line in the link step. For example, ALINK MYPROG MODULE1 MODULE2 MODULE3.

If this still seems fuzzy to you, follow VIDLIB.ASM and EAT4.ASM as a model. Certainly it would be worth beefing up VIDLIB.ASM by adding more screen control procedures.

Creating and Using Macros

There is more than one way to split an assembly language program into more manageable chunks. Procedures are the most obvious way, and certainly the easiest to understand. The mechanism for calling and returning from procedures is built right into the CPU and is independent of any given assembler product.

Today's major assemblers provide another complexity-management tool that works a little differently: *macros*. Macros are a different breed of cat entirely. Whereas procedures are implemented by the use of **CALL** and **RET** instructions built right into the instruction set, macros are a trick of the assembler and do not depend on any particular instruction or group of instructions.

Most simply put, a macro is a label that stands for some sequence of text lines. This sequence of text lines can be (but is not necessarily) a sequence of instructions. When the assembler encounters the macro label in a source code file, it replaces the macro label with the text lines that the macro label represents. This is called *expanding* the macro, because the name of the macro (occupying one text line) is replaced by several lines of text, which are then assembled just as though they had appeared in the source code file all along. (Of course, a macro doesn't have to be several lines of text. It can be only one—but then there's a lot less advantage to using them!)

Macros bear some resemblance to include files in high-level languages such as Pascal. In Turbo Pascal, an include command might look like this:

```
{$I ENGINE.DEF}
```

When this include command is encountered, the compiler goes out to disk and finds the file named ENGINE.DEF. It then opens the file and starts feeding the text contained in that file into the source code file at the point where the include command was placed. The compiler then processes those lines as though they had always been in the source code file.

You might think of a macro as an include file that's built right into the source code file. It's a sequence of text lines that is defined once, given a name, and then may be dropped into the source code again and again by simply using the name.

This process is shown in Figure 9.3. The source code as stored on disk has a definition of the macro, bracketed between **%macro** and **%end-macro** directives. Later in the file, the name of the macro appears several times. When the assembler processes this file, it copies the macro definition into a buffer somewhere in memory. As it assembles the text read from disk, the assembler drops the statements contained in the macro into the text wherever the macro name appears. The disk file is not affected; the expansion of the macros occurs *only* in memory.

Macros versus Procedures: Pro and Con

There are advantages to macros over procedures. One of them is speed. It takes time to execute the **CALL** and **RET** instructions that control entry to and exit from a procedure. In a macro, neither instruction is

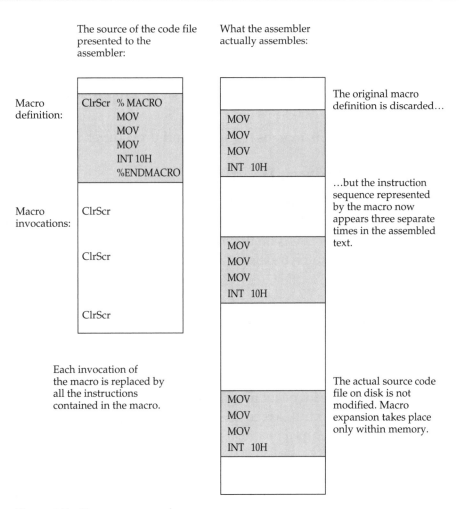

The source of the code file presented to the assembler:

What the assembler actually assembles:

Macro definition:

ClrScr % MACRO
　　　MOV
　　　MOV
　　　MOV
　　　INT 10H
　　　%ENDMACRO

The original macro definition is discarded...

MOV
MOV
MOV
INT 10H

Macro invocations:

ClrScr

ClrScr

ClrScr

...but the instruction sequence represented by the macro now appears three separate times in the assembled text.

MOV
MOV
MOV
INT 10H

Each invocation of the macro is replaced by all the instructions contained in the macro.

MOV
MOV
MOV
INT 10H

The actual source code file on disk is not modified. Macro expansion takes place only within memory.

Figure 9.3　How macros work.

used. Only the instructions that perform the actual work of the macro are executed, so the macro's work is performed as quickly as possible.

There is a cost to this speed, and the cost is in extra memory used, especially if the macro is called a great many times. Notice in Figure 9.3 that three invocations of the macro generate a total of 12 instructions in memory. If the macro had been set up as a procedure, it would have required the four instructions in the body of the procedure, plus one **RET** instruction and three **CALL** instructions to do the same work. This would give you a total of eight instructions for the procedure and 12 for the macro. And if the macro were called five or seven times or more, the difference would grow. *Every time a macro is called, all of its instructions are duplicated in the program another time.*

In short programs, this may not be a problem, and in situations where the code must be as fast as possible—as in graphics drivers—macros have a lot going for them.

By and large, think macros for speed and procedures for compactness.

The Mechanics of Macro Definition

A macro definition looks a little like a procedure definition, framed between a pair of directives: **%macro** and **%endmacro**. Note that the **%endmacro** directive is on the line *after* the last line of the macro. Don't make the mistake of treating **%endmacro** like a label that marks the macro's last line.

One important shortcoming of macros vis-à-vis procedures is that macros can have only *one* entry point. A macro, after all, is a line of code that is inserted into your program in the midst of the flow of execution; execution has to go through the whole thing. The **ClrScr** procedure described in the last section cannot be converted into a macro without splitting it up into four separate invocations of VIDEO interrupt 10H. If the **ClrScr** function (clearing the full screen to blanks for the normal video attribute) alone were written as a macro, it would look like this:

```
%macro ClrScr
    mov CX,0        ; Upper left corner of full screen
    mov DX,LRXY     ; Load lower-right XY coordinates into DX
    mov AL,0        ; 0 specifies clear entire region
    mov BH,07H      ; Specify "normal" attribute for blanked line(s)
    mov AH,06H      ; Select VIDEO service 6: Initialize/Scroll
    int 10H         ; Call VIDEO
%endmacro
```

You can see that **ClrScr** has shed its **RET** instruction and its additional entry points, but apart from that, it's exactly the same sequence of instructions. Functionally it works the same way, except that *every* time you clear your screen, **ClrScr**'s six instructions are dropped into the source code.

Macros are called simply by naming them. Don't use the **CALL** instruction! Just place the macro name on a line:

```
ClrScr
```

The assembler will handle the rest.

Defining Macros with Parameters

So far, macros may seem useful but perhaps not especially compelling. What makes macros really sing is their ability to mimic high-level language subroutines and take arguments through parameters. For example, if you were to define a macro named **GotoXY** that would position the hardware cursor, you could pass it the *X* and *Y* values as arguments, separated by a comma:

```
GotoXY 17,3          ; Move the cursor to the Name field
```

You'd have to pinch yourself to be sure you weren't working in Basic, no?

Macro parameters are, again, artifacts of the assembler. They are not pushed on the stack or set into **COMMON** or anything like that. The parameters are simply placeholders for the actual values (called *arguments*) that you pass to the macro through its parameters.

I've converted the **GotoXY** procedure to a macro to show you how this works. Here's the macro:

```
%macro   GotoXY 2     ; NewX,NewY
         mov DH,%2    ; The NewY parameter loads into DH
         mov DL,%1    ; The NewX parameter loads into DL
         mov AH,02H   ; Select VIDEO service 2: Position cursor
         mov BH,0     ; Stay with display page 0
         int 10H      ; Call VIDEO
%endmacro
```

So where are the parameters? This is another area where NASM differs radically from MASM. MASM allows you to use symbolic names—such as the words *NewX* and *NewY*—to stand for parameters. NASM relies on a simpler system that declares the number of parameters, and then refers to the parameters by number rather than symbolic name.

In the definition of macro **GotoXY**, the number 2 after the name of the macro indicates that the assembler is to look for two parameters. This number must be present—as 0—even when you have a macro with no parameters. Later down in the macro, the two parameters are referenced by number. "%1" indicates the first parameter used after the name "GotoXY," and "%2" indicates the second parameter:

```
GotoXY 11,14
Name   %1 %2
```

I call the two parameters **NewX** and **NewY**—but they don't exist anywhere in the code! They're strictly creatures of the imagination to help me remember what the macro is doing. This is one place (perhaps the only one) where I think I prefer MASM's way of doing things to NASM's.

Macro parameters are a kind of label, and they may be referenced anywhere *within* the macro—but only within the macro. Here, the parameters are referenced as operands to a couple of **MOV** instructions. The arguments passed to the macro in **%1** (**NewX**) and **%2** (**NewY**) are thus loaded into DL and DH.

The actual values passed into the parameters are referred to as *arguments*. Don't confuse the actual values with the parameters. If you understand Pascal, it's *exactly* like the difference between formal parameters and actual parameters. A macro's parameters correspond to Pascal's formal parameters, whereas a macro's arguments correspond to Pascal's actual parameters. The macro's parameters are the labels following the name of the macro in the line in which it is *defined*. The arguments are the values specified on the line where the macro is *invoked*.

The Mechanics of Macro Parameters

A macro may have as many parameters as will fit on one line. This is a rather arbitrary restriction, leaving you no recourse but to use short parameter names if you need lots of parameters for a single macro.

When a macro is invoked, arguments are separated by commas. The arguments are dropped into the macro's parameters in order, from left to right. If you pass only two arguments to a macro with three parameters, you're likely to get an error message from the assembler, depending on how you've referenced the unfilled parameter. The assembler is building opcodes depending on the types of operands passed as arguments; if you don't pass an argument for a given parameter, any instructions that reference that parameter won't be constructable by the assembler, hence the errors.

If you pass *more* arguments to a macro than there are parameters to receive the arguments, the extraneous arguments will be ignored.

Local Labels within Macros

I haven't really gone into labels and branches yet, but there's an important problem with labels used inside macros. Labels in assembly language programs must be unique, and yet a macro is essentially duplicated in the source code as many times as it is invoked. This means there will be error messages flagging duplicate labels . . . unless a macro's labels are treated as local. *Local* items have no meaning outside the immediate framework within which they are defined. Labels local to a macro are not known outside the macro definition.

All labels defined within a macro are considered local to the macro and are handled specially by the assembler. Here's an example from the file MYLIB.MAC; don't worry if you don't fully understand all of the instructions it uses:

```
%macro  UpCase 2               ; Target,Length
        mov CX,%2              ; CX is acting as length counter for loop
        mov BX,%1              ; String will be at DS:BX
%%Tester: cmp BYTE [BX],'a'    ; Is string character below 'a'?
        jb %%Bump             ; If so, leave character alone
        cmp BYTE [BX],'z'     ; Is string character above 'z'?
        ja %%Bump             ; If so, leave character alone
        and BYTE [BX],11011111b ; Char is lc alpha, so force bit 5 to 0
%%Bump:  inc BX               ; Bump BX to point to next char in string
        loop %%Tester         ; And go back and do it again!
%endmacro
```

A label in a macro is made local by beginning it with two percent signs: "%%." When marking a location in the macro, the local label should be followed by a colon. When used as an operand to a jump or call instruction (such as **JB** and **LOOP** in the preceding), the local label is *not* followed by a colon. The important thing is to understand that unless the labels **Tester** and **Bump** were made local to the macro by adding the prefix "%%," there would be multiple instances of a label in the program and the assembler would generate a duplicate label error on the second and every subsequent invocation of the macro.

Because labels must in fact be unique within your program, NASM takes a formal label such as **%%Tester** and generates an actual label from it that will be unique in your program by using the prefix "..@" plus a four-digit number and the name of the label. Each time your macro is invoked, NASM will change the number, and thus generate unique synonyms for each local label within the macro. The label **%%Tester**, for example, might become **..@1771.Tester** and the number would be different each time the macro is invoked. This happens behind the scenes and you'll rarely be aware that it's going on unless you read the code dump listing files generated by NASM.

Macro Libraries

Just as procedures may be gathered in libraries external to your program, so may macros be gathered into macro libraries. A *macro library* is really nothing but a text file that contains the source code for the macros in the library. Unlike procedures gathered into a module, macro libraries are not separately assembled and must be passed through the assembler each time the program is assembled. This is a problem with macros in general, not only with macros that are gathered into libraries. Programs that manage complexity by dividing code up into macros will assemble more slowly than programs that have been divided up into separately assembled modules.

Macro libraries are used by including them into your program's source code file. The means to do this is the **%include** directive. The **%include** directive precedes the name of the macro library:

```
%include "MYLIB.MAC"
```

Technically this statement may be anywhere in your source code file, but you must keep in mind that all macros must be fully defined before they are invoked. For this reason, it's a good idea to use the **%include** directive near the top of your source code file, before any possible invocation of one of the library macros could occur.

If the macro file you want to include in a program is not in the same directory as NASM itself, you may need to provide a more complete DOS path specification as part of the **%include** directive:

```
%include "BOOK\MYLIB.MAC"
```

Otherwise, NASM may not be able to locate the macro file and will hand you a relatively unhelpful error message:

```
D:\NASM\BOOK\EAT5.ASM:18: unable to open include file 'MYLIB.MAC'
```

The following is a macro library containing macro versions of all the procedures we discussed in the previous section, plus a few more:

```
; Source name    : MYLIB.MAC
; File type      : NASM macro library
; Code model:    : Real mode segmented OR flat model
; Version        : 2.0
; Created date   : 9/12/1999
; Last update    : 9/18/1999
; Author         : Jeff Duntemann
; Description    : A simple example of a multi-line macro file
;                  for NASM containing utility procedures for
```

```
;                     controlling the PC display. Assembled using
;                     NASM 0.98. Include this file in your programs
;                     with the directive:
;                        %include "MYLIB.MAC"



;-----------------------------------------------------------------
;  CLEAR  -- Clears the entire visible screen buffer
;  Last update 9/16/99
;
;   Caller must pass:
;   In VidAddress: The address of the video refresh buffer
;   In ClearAtom:  The character/attribute pair to fill the
;                  buffer with. The high byte contains the
;                  attribute and the low byte the character.
;   In BufLength:  The number of *characters* in the visible
;                  display buffer, *not* the number of bytes!
;                  This is typically 2000 for a 25-line screen
;                  or 4000 for a 50-line screen.
;   Action:        Clears the screen by machine-gunning the
;                  character/attribute pair in AX into the
;                  display buffer beginning at VidAddress.
;-----------------------------------------------------------------
%macro   Clear 3 ;VidAddress,ClearAtom,BufLength
         les DI,[%1]    ;VidAddress
         mov AX,%2      ;ClearAtom
         mov CX,%3      ;BufLength
         rep stosw
         GotoXY 0,0
%endmacro



;-----------------------------------------------------------------
;  RULER  -- Displays a "1234567890"-style ruler on-screen
;  Last update 9/16/99
;
;   Caller must pass:
;   In VidAddress: The address of the start of the video buffer
;   In Length:     The length of the ruler to be displayed
;   In ScreenW:    The width of the current screen (usually 80)
;   In ScreenY:    The line of the screen where the ruler is
;                  to be displayed (0-24)
;   In ScreenX:    The row of the screen where the ruler should
;                  start (0-79)
;   Action:        Displays an ASCII ruler at ScreenX,ScreenY.
;-----------------------------------------------------------------
%macro   Ruler 5       ;VidAddress,Length,ScreenW,ScreenX,ScreenY
         les   DI,[%1] ; Load video address to ES:DI
         mov   AL,%5   ; Move Y position to AL
         mov   AH,%3   ; Move screen width to AH
         imul  AH      ; Do 8-bit multiply AL*AH to AX
```

```
        add  DI,AX       ; Add Y offset into vidbuff to DI
        add  DI,%4       ; Add X offset into vidbuf to DI
        shl  DI,1        ; Multiply by two for final address
        mov  CX,%2       ; CX monitors the ruler length
        mov  AH,07       ; Attribute 7 is "normal" text
        mov  AL,'1'      ; Start with digit "1"

%%DoChar: stosw          ; Note that there's no REP prefix!
        add  AL,'1'      ; Bump the character value in AL up by 1
        aaa              ; Adjust AX to make this a BCD addition
        add  AL,'0'      ; Basically, put binary 3 in AL's high nybble
        mov  AH,07       ; Make sure our attribute is still 7
        loop %%DoChar    ; Go back & do another char until BL goes to 0
%endmacro


;-------------------------------------------------------------
;   UPCASE -- Converts lowercase to uppercase characters
;             in a string.
;   Last update 9/18/99
;
;       Caller must pass:
;       In Target: The offset (relative to DS) of the string
;       In Length: The length of the string in characters
;       Action:    Scans the string at DS:BX and replaces chars
;                  in the range 'a'..'z' to 'A'..'Z'.
;-------------------------------------------------------------
%macro  UpCase 2                 ; Target,Length
        mov CX,%2                ; CX is acting as length counter for
                                 ; loop
        mov BX,%1                ; String will be at DS:BX
%%Tester: cmp BYTE [BX],'a'  ; Is string character below 'a'?
        jb %%Bump                ; If so, leave character alone
        cmp BYTE [BX],'z'        ; Is string character above 'z'?
        ja %%Bump                ; If so, leave character alone
        and BYTE [BX],11011111b ; Char is lc alpha, so force bit 5 to 0
%%Bump:  inc BX                  ; Bump BX to point to next char in
                                 ; string
        loop %%Tester            ; And go back and do it again!
%endmacro


;-------------------------------------------------------------
;   GOTOXY  -- Positions the hardware cursor to X,Y
;   Last update 9/18/99
;
;       Caller must pass:
;       In NewX: The new X value
;       In NewY: The new Y value
;          These are both 0-based; i.e., they assume a screen
```

```
;       whose dimensions are 24 by 79, not 25 by 80.
;    Action:  Moves the hardware cursor to the X,Y position
;             passed as NewX and NewY.
;-----------------------------------------------------------------
%macro   GotoXY 2      ;NewX,NewY
         mov DH,%2     ;NewY
         mov DL,%1     ;NewX
         mov AH,02H    ; Select VIDEO service 2: Position cursor
         mov BH,0      ; Stay with display page 0
         int 10H       ; Call VIDEO
%endmacro



;-----------------------------------------------------------------
;  NEWLINE -- Sends a newline sequence to DOS Standard Output
;             via DOS service 40H
;  Last update 9/16/99
;
;    Caller need not pass any parameters.
;    Action:  Sends a newline sequence DOS Standard Output
;-----------------------------------------------------------------
%macro   Newline 0
         Write CRLF,2
%endmacro



;-----------------------------------------------------------------
;  POKECHAR  -- Inserts a single character into a string
;  Last update 9/16/99
;
;    Caller must pass:
;    In Target:  The name of the string to be poked at
;    In TheChar: The character to be poked into the string
;    In ToPos:   The 0-based position in the string to poke to
;    Action:     Pokes character passed in TheChar into string
;                passed in Target to position passed in ToPos.
;                The first character in the string is 0, etc.
;-----------------------------------------------------------------
%macro   PokeChar 3         ;Target,TheChar,ToPos
         mov BX,%1          ; Load the address of target string into BX
         mov BYTE [BX+%3],%2 ; Move char into the string
%endmacro



;-----------------------------------------------------------------
;  WRITE  -- Displays information to the screen via DOS
;            service 40: Print String to Standard Output
;  Last update 9/16/99
;
;    Caller must pass:
;    In ShowIt:    The name of the string to be displayed
```

```
;    In ShowLength: The length of the string to be displayed
;    Action:  Displays the string to DOS Standard Output
;-------------------------------------------------------------
%macro   Write 2     ;ShowIt,ShowLength
         mov BX,1   ; Selects DOS file handle 1: Standard Output
         mov CX,%2  ; ShowLength: Length of string passed in CX
         mov DX,%1  ; Showit: Offset address of string passed in DX
         mov AH,40H ; Select DOS service 40: Print String
         int 21H    ; Call DOS
%endmacro


;-------------------------------------------------------------
;  WRITELN -- Displays information to the screen via DOS
;             service 40H: Display to Standard Output, then
;             issues a newline
;  Last update 9/16/99
;
;     Caller must pass:
;     In ShowIt:     The name of the string to be displayed
;     In ShowLength: The length of the string to be displayed
;     Action:        Displays the string in ShowIt, then issues a
;                    newline. Hardware cursor will move to the
;                    left margin of the following line. If the
;                    display is to the bottom screen line, the
;                    screen will scroll.
;     Calls: Write
;-------------------------------------------------------------
%macro   Writeln 2   ;ShowIt,ShowLength
         Write %1,%2 ; Display the string proper through Write
         Write CRLF,2 ; Display the newline string through Write
%endmacro
```

And, finally, yet another version of EAT.ASM, this time rearranged to make use of the macros in MYLIB.MAC. The macro library is included by way of the **%include** directive immediately after the **[SECTION .text]** command near the top of the file. Note that although EAT5 uses real mode flat model, there is nothing model-specific about the macros in MYLIB.MAC. I've created a version of EAT5 for real mode segmented model called EAT5SEG.ASM, which uses the exact same macros and runs precisely the same way. (EAT5SEG.ASM is on the CD-ROM, but not printed here in the book text.)

```
; Source name      : EAT5.ASM
; Executable name  : EAT5.COM
; Code model:      : Real mode flat model
; Version          : 1.0
; Created date     : 9/15/1999
```

```
; Last update      : 9/18/1999
; Author           : Jeff Duntemann
; Description       : A simple example of a DOS .COM file programmed for
;                     real mode flat model, using NASM 0.98 and ALINK.
;                     This program demonstrates how multi-line macros are
;                     used with NASM.

[BITS 16]               ; Set 16 bit code generation
[ORG 0100H]             ; Set code start address to 100h (COM file)


[SECTION .text]         ; Section containing code

%include "MYLIB.MAC" ; Load in screen control macro library

START:                  ; This is where program execution begins:

        Clear VidOrigin,07B0H,4000 ; Replace B0 with 20 for space clear

        GotoXY 14H,09H              ; Position cursor
        Write Eat1,Eat1Length      ; and display first text line

        GotoXY 14H,0AH             ; Position cursor
        Writeln Eat2,Eat2Length    ; and display second text line

        mov AH,4CH    ; Terminate process DOS service
        mov AL,0      ; Pass this value back to ERRORLEVEL
        int 21H       ; Control returns to DOS


[SECTION .data]     ; Section containing initialized data

LRXY        DW  184FH ; 18H = 24D; 4FH = 79D; 0-based XY of LR screen corner

VidOrigin  DD  0B8000000H  ; Change to 0B0000000H if you have a mono CRT!
Eat1        DB  "Eat at Joe's..."
Eat1Length EQU $-Eat1
Eat2        DB  "...ten million flies can't ALL be wrong!"
Eat2Length EQU $-Eat2
CRLF        DB  0DH,0AH
```

EAT5 goes back to real mode flat model and should be assembled and
run from within NASM-IDE. The ALINK linker is not required.

You'll spot something odd in EAT5.ASM: Instead of using **ClrScr** to
clear the screen as I have been for the last several incarnations of EAT,
I've replaced **ClrScr** with a new macro called **Clear**. **Clear** (defined in
VIDLIB.MAC) uses some technology I haven't explained yet, but will
return to in Chapter 11. The lesson is that there are numerous ways to

skin a screen, and we've moved here from having the BIOS do it for us to doing it all on our own. Take it on faith for now, until I come back to it. More to the point for the current discussion is the use of the **GotoXY** and **Write** and **Writeln** macros.

Additionally, if you look closely at the main program procedure in EAT5.ASM, something odd may occur to you: It's starting to look like something other than an assembly language program. This is true, and it's certainly possible to create so many macros that your programs will begin to look like some odd high-level language. I actually used such a language in my first job as a programmer, and so complete was the transformation that I didn't actually realize I was using assembly macros until someone pointed it out.

The danger there is that unless you name your macros carefully and document them both in their macro library files and on the lines where they are invoked, your programs will not be any more comprehensible for their presence. Dividing complexity into numerous compartments is only half the job—labeling the compartments is just as (or more) important!

CHAPTER 10

Bits, Flags, Branches, and Tables

Easing into Mainstream Assembly Programming

Y ou don't take off until all your flight checks are made.

That's the reason that we haven't done a lot of instruction arranging in this book up until here, now that we are in the last quarter of the book. I've found that machine instructions aren't the most important part of assembly language programming. What's most important is understanding your machine and your tools and how everything fits together. Higher-level languages such as Pascal and Modula-2 hide much of those essential details from you. In assembly language you must see to them yourself. For some reason, authors of previous beginner books on assembly language haven't caught on to this fact.

This fact (in fact) was the major motivation for my writing this book.

If you've digested everything I've said so far, however, you're ready to get in and understand the remainder of the x86 instruction set. I won't teach it all in this book, but the phrase *ready to understand* is germane. You can now find yourself a reference and learn what instructions I don't cover on your own. The skills you need to build programming expertise are now yours, and if this book has accomplished that much, I'd say it's accomplished a lot.

So, let the fun begin.

Bits Is Bits (and Bytes Is Bits)

Assembly language is big on bits.

Bits, after all, are what bytes are made of, and one essential assembly language skill is building bytes and taking them apart again. A technique called bit mapping is widely used in assembly language. *Bit mapping* assigns special meanings to individual bits within a byte to save space and squeeze the last little bit of utility out of a given amount of memory.

There is a family of instructions in the x86 instruction set that allows you to manipulate the bits within the bytes by applying Boolean logical operations to the bytes on a bit-by-bit basis. These are the *bitwise logical instructions*: **AND**, **OR**, **XOR**, and **NOT**. Another family of instructions allows you to slide bits back and forth within a single byte or word. These are the most-used shift/rotate instructions: **ROL**, **ROR**, **RCL**, **RCR**, **SHL**, and **SHR**. (There are a few others that I will not be discussing in this book.)

Bit Numbering

Dealing with bits requires that we have a way of specifying which bits we're dealing with. By convention, bits in assembly language are numbered, starting from 0, at the *least-significant bit* in the byte, word, or other item we're using as a bit map. The least-significant bit is the one with the least value in the binary number system. (Return to Chapter 2 and reread the material on base 2 if that seems fuzzy to you.) It's also the bit on the far right, if you write the value down as a binary number.

It works best as a visual metaphor. See Figure 10.1.

When you count bits, start with the bit on the right, and number them from 0.

"It's the Logical Thing to Do, Jim . . ."

Boolean logic sounds arcane and forbidding, but remarkably, it reflects the realities of ordinary thought and action. The Boolean operator AND, for instance, pops up in many of the decisions you make every day of your life. For example, to write a check that doesn't bounce, you must have money in your checking account AND checks in your checkbook. Neither alone will do the job. ("How can I be overdrawn?" goes the classic question, "I still have checks in my checkbook!") You can't

Bits are numbered from right to left, starting from 0:

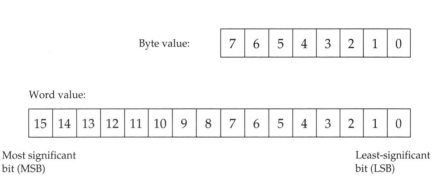

Byte value:

| 7 | 6 | 5 | 4 | 3 | 2 | 1 | 0 |

Word value:

| 15 | 14 | 13 | 12 | 11 | 10 | 9 | 8 | 7 | 6 | 5 | 4 | 3 | 2 | 1 | 0 |

Most significant bit (MSB)

Least-significant bit (LSB)

Figure 10.1 Bit numbering.

write a check you don't have, and a check without money behind it will bounce. People who live out of their checkbooks (and they always end up ahead of me in the checkout line at Safeway) must use the AND operator frequently.

When mathematicians speak of Boolean logic, they manipulate abstract values called True and False. The AND operator works like this. Condition1 AND Condition2 will be considered True if *both* Condition1 and Condition2 are True. If either condition is False, the result will be False.

There are in fact four different combinations of the two input values, so logical operations between two values are usually summarized in a form called a *truth table*. The truth table for the AND operator is shown in Table 10.1.

There's nothing mysterious about the truth table. It's just a summary of all possibilities of the AND operator as applied to two input conditions. The important thing to remember is that *only* when both input values are True will the result also be True.

Table 10.1 The AND Truth Table for Formal Logic

CONDITION1	OPERATOR	CONDITION2		RESULT
False	AND	False	=	False
False	AND	True	=	False
True	AND	False	=	False
True	AND	True	=	True

That's the way mathematicians see AND. In assembly language terms, the **AND** instruction looks at two bits and yields a third bit based on the values of the first two bits. By convention, we consider a 1 bit to be True and a 0 bit to be False. The *logic* is identical; we're just using different symbols to represent True and False. Keeping that in mind, we can rewrite AND's truth table to make it more meaningful for assembly language work. See Table 10.2.

The AND Instruction

The **AND** instruction embodies this concept in the x86 instruction set. The **AND** instruction performs the AND logical operation on two like-sized operands and replaces its *first* operand with the result of the operation. (By first, I mean the operand closest to the mnemonic.) In other words, consider this instruction:

```
AND AL,BL
```

What will happen here is that the CPU will perform a gang of eight bit-wise AND operations on the eight bits in AL and BL. Bit 0 of AL is ANDed with bit 0 of BL, bit 1 of AL is ANDed with bit 1 of BL, and so on. Each AND operation generates a result bit, and that bit is placed in the first operand (here, AL) *after all eight* AND operations occur. This is a common thread among machine instructions that perform some operation on two operands and produce a result: The result replaces the first operand, not the second!

Masking Out Bits

A major use of the **AND** instruction is to isolate one or more bits out of a byte value or a word value. *Isolate* here simply means to set all *unwanted* bits to a reliable 0 value. As an example, suppose we are interested in testing bits 4 and 5 of a value to see what those bits are. To do

Table 10.2 The AND Truth Table for Assembly Language

BIT 1	OPERATOR	BIT 2		RESULT BIT
0	AND	0	=	0
0	AND	1	=	0
1	AND	0	=	0
1	AND	1	=	1

that, we have to be able to ignore the other bits (bits 0 through 3 and 6 through 7), and the only way to safely ignore bits is to set them to 0.

AND is the way to go. We set up a *bit mask* in which the bit numbers that we want to inspect and test are set to 1, and the bits we wish to ignore are set to 0. To mask out all bits but bits 4 and 5, we must set up a mask in which bits 4 and 5 are set to 1, with all other bits at 0. This mask in binary is 00110000B, or 30H. (To verify it, count the bits from the right-hand end of the binary number, starting with 0.) This bit mask is then ANDed against the value in question. Figure 10.2 shows this operation in action, with the 30H bit mask just described and an initial value of 9DH.

The three binary values involved are shown laid out vertically, with the LSB (that is, the right-hand end) of each value at the top. You should be able to trace each AND operation and verify it by looking at Table 10.2.

The end result is that all but bits 4 and 5 are *guaranteed* to be 0 and can thus be safely ignored. Bits 4 and 5 could be either 0 or 1. (That's why

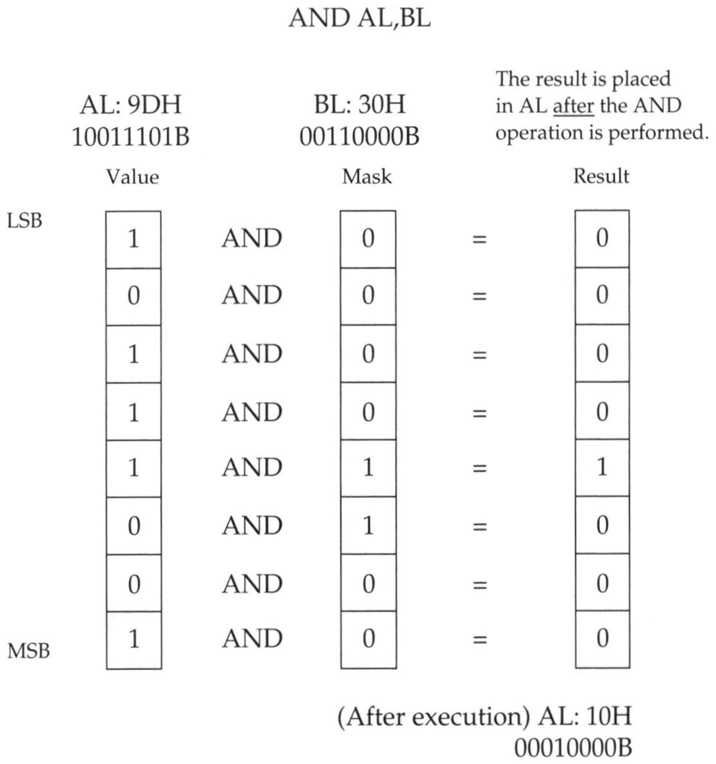

AND AL,BL

	AL: 9DH 10011101B		BL: 30H 00110000B	The result is placed in AL <u>after</u> the AND operation is performed.
	Value		Mask		Result

LSB	1	AND	0	=	0
	0	AND	0	=	0
	1	AND	0	=	0
	1	AND	0	=	0
	1	AND	1	=	1
	0	AND	1	=	0
	0	AND	0	=	0
MSB	1	AND	0	=	0

(After execution) AL: 10H
00010000B

Figure 10.2 The anatomy of an **AND** instruction.

we need to test them; we don't *know* what they are.) With the initial value of 9DH, bit 4 turns out to be a 1, and bit 5 turns out to be a 0. If the initial value were something else, bits 4 and 5 could both be 0, both be 1, or some combination of the two.

Don't forget: The result of the AND operation replaces the first operand after the operation is complete.

For an example of the **AND** instruction in operation isolating bits in a word, look ahead to the **Byte2Str** procedure, which follows later in this chapter.

The OR Instruction

Closely related to the AND logical operation is OR, which, like the AND logical operation, has an embodiment with the same name in the x86 instruction set. Structurally, the **OR** instruction works identically to **AND**. Only its truth table is different: While **AND** requires that both its operands be 1 for the result to be 1, **OR** is satisfied that at least *one* operand has a 1 value. The truth table for **OR** is shown in Table 10.3.

Because it's unsuitable for isolating bits, **OR** is used much more rarely than **AND.**

The XOR Instruction

In a class by itself is the exclusive OR operation, embodied in the **XOR** instruction. **XOR**, again, does in broad terms what **AND** and **OR** do: It performs a logical operation on two operands, and the result replaces the first operand. The logical operation, however, is *exclusive or,* meaning that the result is 1 only if the two operands are *different* (that is, 1 and 0 or 0 and 1). The truth table for **XOR** (Table 10.4) should make this slippery notion a little clearer.

Table 10.3 The OR Truth Table for Assembly Language

BIT 1	OPERATOR	BIT 2		RESULT BIT
0	OR	0	=	0
0	OR	1	=	1
1	OR	0	=	1
1	OR	1	=	1

Table 10.4 The XOR Truth Table for Assembly Language

BIT 1	OPERATOR	BIT 2		RESULT BIT
0	XOR	0	=	0
0	XOR	1	=	1
1	XOR	0	=	1
1	XOR	1	=	0

Look Table 10.4 over carefully! In the first and last cases, where the two operands are the *same*, the result is 0. In the middle two cases, where the two operands are *different*, the result is 1.

Some interesting things can be done with **XOR**, but most of them are a little arcane for a beginners' book. I will show you one handy **XOR** trick, however: **XOR**ing any value against *itself* yields 0. In the old days, this was faster than loading a 0 into a register from immediate data. Although that's no longer the case, it's an interesting trick to know. How it works should be obvious from reading the truth table, but to drive it home I've laid it out in Figure 10.3.

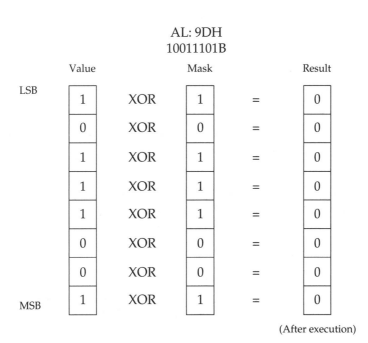

Figure 10.3 Using XOR to zero a register.

Follow each of the individual XOR operations across the figure to its result value. Because each bit in AL is XORed against itself, in every case the XOR operations happen between two operands that are identical. Sometimes both are 1, sometimes both are 0, but in every case the two are the same. With the XOR operation, when the two operands are the same, the result is always 0. Voila! Zero in a register.

The NOT Instruction

Easiest to understand of all the bitwise logical instructions is **NOT**. The truth table for **NOT** is simpler than the others we've looked at because **NOT** only takes one operand. And what it does is simple as well: **NOT** takes the state of each bit in its single operand and changes it to its opposite state. What was 1 becomes 0 and what was 0 becomes 1. I show it in Table 10.5.

Segment Registers Don't Respond to Logic!

One limitation of the segment registers CS, DS, SS, ES, FS, and GS is that they cannot be used with any of the bitwise logical instructions. If you try, the assembler will hand you an "Illegal use of segment register" error. If you need to perform a logical operation on a segment register, you must first copy the segment register's value into one of the registers AX, BX, CX, DX, BP, SI, and DI; perform the logical operation on the new register; and then copy the result back into the segment register.

Banging bits in segment registers is a dicey business if what's in the segment register is truly a segment address. Sometimes it would be handy to use segment registers as spare, general-purpose registers, but this can only be done in real mode. In real work in today's world, you're likely to be working in protected mode, where segment registers can only be used as segment registers. So, it's really not losing any genuine chip features, but gaining 4 gigabytes of memory instead. That's a bargain I can live with.

Table 10.5   The NOT Truth Table for Assembly Language

BIT	OPERATOR	RESULT BIT
0	NOT	1
1	NOT	0

Shifting Bits

The other way of manipulating bits within a byte is a little more straight-forward: You *shift* them to one side or the other. There are a few wrinkles to the process, but the simplest shift instructions are pretty obvious: **SHL** **SH**ifts its operand **L**eft, whereas **SHR SH**ifts its operand **R**ight.

All of the shift instructions (including the slightly more complex ones I describe a little later) have the same general form, illustrated here by the **SHL** instruction:

```
SHL <register/memory>,<count>
```

The first operand is the target of the shift operation, that is, the value that you're going to be shifting. It can be register data or memory data, but not immediate data. The second operand specifies the number of bits by which to shift.

Shift by What?

This **<count>** operand is a little peculiar. On the 8086 and 8088, it can be one of two things: the immediate digit 1, or else the register CL. (*Not* CX!) If you specify the count as 1, then the shift will be by one bit. If you wish to shift by more than one bit at a time, you must load the shift count into register CL. Counting things is CX's (and hence CL's) hidden agenda; it counts shifts, loops, string elements, and a few other things that we look at later in this book. That's why it's sometimes called the *count register* and can be remembered by the C in *count*.

Although you can load a number as large as 255 into CL, it really only makes sense to use count values up to 32. If you shift any bit in a dou-ble word by 32, you shift it completely out of the double word—not to mention out of any byte or word!

Starting with the 286, the **<count>** operand may be any immediate value from 1 to 255. If you're quite sure your code will never have to run on an 8086 or 8088, using an immediate operand instead of loading CL can save you an instruction and a little time.

How Bit Shifting Works

Understanding the shift instructions requires that you think of the num-bers being shifted as *binary* numbers, and not hexadecimal or decimal numbers. (If you're fuzzy on binary notation, again, take another slip through Chapter 1.) A simple example would start with register AX containing a value of 0B76FH. Expressed as a binary number (and hence as a bit pattern), 0B76FH is as follows:

```
1011011101101111
```

Keep in mind that each digit in a binary number is one bit. If you execute an **SHL AX,1** instruction, what you'd find in AX after the shift is the following:

```
0110111011011110
```

A 0 has been inserted at the right-hand end of the number, and the whole shebang has been bumped toward the left by one digit. Notice that a 1 bit has been bumped off the left end of the number into cosmic nothingness.

Bumping Bits into the Carry Flag

Well, not exactly cosmic nothingness . . . The last bit shifted out is bumped into a temporary bucket for bits called the *Carry flag*, often abbreviated as CF. The Carry flag is one of those odd bits lumped together as the Flags register, which I described in Chapter 6. You can test the state of the Carry flag with a branching instruction, as I explain later in this chapter.

Keep in mind when using shift instructions, however, that a *lot* of different instructions use the Carry flag as well as the shift instructions. If you bump a bit into the Carry flag with the intent of testing that bit to see what it is, test it *before* you execute another instruction that affects the Carry flag. This includes all the arithmetic instructions, all the bitwise logical instructions, a few miscellaneous instructions—and, of course, all the other shift instructions.

If you shift a bit into the Carry flag and then immediately execute another shift instruction, the first bit *will* be bumped off the end of the world and into cosmic nothingness.

Byte2Str: Converting Numbers to Displayable Strings

As we've seen, DOS has a fairly convenient method for displaying text to your screen. The problem is that it only displays *text*—if you want to display a numeric value from a register as a pair of digits, DOS won't help. You first have to convert the numeric value into its string representation, and then display the string representation through DOS.

Converting hexadecimal numbers to hexadecimal digits isn't difficult, and the routine to do the job demonstrates several of the new concepts we're exploring in this chapter. Read the code for procedure **Byte2Str** carefully:

```
;-------------------------------------------------------------
; Byte2Str -- Converts a byte passed in AL to a string at
;             DS:SI
; Last update 9/18/99
;
; 1 entry point:
;
; Byte2Str:
;   Caller must pass:
;   AL : Byte to be converted
;   DS : Segment of destination string
;   SI : Offset of destination string
;
;   This routine converts 8-bit values to 2-digit hexadecimal
;   string representations at DS:SI. The "H" specifier is
;   *not* included. Four separate output examples:
;   02  B7  FF  6C
;-------------------------------------------------------------

Byte2Str:
    mov DI,AX           ; Duplicate byte in DI
    and DI,000FH        ; Mask out high 12 bits of DI
    mov BX,Digits       ; Load offset of Digits into DI
    mov AH,BYTE [BX+DI] ; Load digit from table into AH
    mov [SI+1],AH       ;  and store digit into string
    xor AH,AH           ; Zero out AH
    mov DI,AX           ; And move byte into DI
    ; WARNING: The following instruction requires 286 or better!
    shr DI,4            ; Shift high nybble of byte to low
    mov AH,BYTE [BX+DI] ; Load digit from table into AH
    mov [SI],AH         ;  and store digit into string
    ret                 ; We're done—go home!
```

Note that this is a procedure, and not a macro. (It could be turned into a macro, however. Why not give it a shot?)

To call **Byte2Str**, you must pass the value to be converted to a string in AL and the address of the string into which the string representation is to be stored as DS:SI. Typically, DS will already contain the segment address of your data segment, so you most likely will only need to pass the offset of the start of the string in SI.

In addition to the code shown here, **Byte2Str** requires the presence of a second string in the data segment. This string, whose name must be **Digits**, contains all 16 of the digits used to express hexadecimal numbers. The definition of **Digits** looks like this:

```
Digits DB '0123456789ABCDEF'
```

The important thing to note about **Digits** is that each digit occupies a position in the string whose offset from the start of the string is the value it represents. In other words, "0" is at the start of the string, zero bytes offset from the string's beginning. The character "7" lies seven bytes from the start of the string, and so on. **Digits** is what we call a *lookup table* and it represents (as I explain in the following sections) an extremely useful mechanism in assembly language.

Splitting a Byte into Two Nybbles

Displaying the value stored in a byte requires two hexadecimal digits. The bottom four bits in a byte are represented by one digit (the least-significant, or rightmost, digit) and the top four bits in the byte are represented by another digit (the most significant, or leftmost, digit). Converting the two digits must be done one at a time, which means that we have to separate the single byte into two 4-bit quantities, which are often called *nybbles*.

To split a byte in two, we need to *mask out* the unwanted half. This is done with an **AND** instruction. Note in **Byte2Str** that the first instruction, **MOV DI,AX**, copies the value to be converted (which is in AL) into DI. You don't need to move AH into DI here, but there is no instruction to move an 8-bit register half such as AL into a 16-bit register such as DI. AH comes along for the ride, but we really don't need it. The second instruction masks out the high 12 bits of DI using **AND**. This eliminates whatever might have earlier been in free rider AH, as well as the high 4 bits of AL. What's left in DI is all we want: the lower 4 bits of what was originally passed to the routine in AL.

Using a Lookup Table

The low nybble of the value to be converted is now in DI. The address of **Digits** is loaded into BX. Then the appropriate digit character is copied from **Digits** into AH. The whole trick of using a lookup table lies in the way the character in the table is addressed:

```
MOV AH,BYTE [BX+DI]
```

DS:BX points to the start of **Digits**, so [BX] would address the *first* character in **Digits**. To get at the desired digit, we must *index* into the lookup table by adding the offset into the table to BX. There is an x86 addressing mode intended precisely for use with lookup tables, called *base indexed addressing*. That sounds more arcane than it is; what it means is that instead of specifying a memory location at [BX], we add an index contained in register DI to BX and address a memory location at [BX+DI].

If you recall, we masked out all of DI but the four lowest bits of the byte we are converting. These bits will contain some value from 0 through 0FH. **Digits** contains the hexadecimal digit characters from 0 to F. By using DI as the index, the value in DI will select its corresponding digit character in **Digits**. We are using the value in DI to look up its equivalent hexadecimal digit character in the lookup table **Digits**. See Figure 10.4.

So far, we've read a character from the lookup table into AH. Now, we use yet another addressing mode to move the character from AX back into the second character of the destination string, whose address was passed to **Byte2Str** in DS:SI. This addressing mode is called *indirect displacement* addressing, though I question the wisdom of memorizing that term. The mode is nothing more than indirect addressing (that is, addressing the contents of memory at [SI]) with the addition of a literal displacement:

```
MOV [SI+1],AH
```

This looks a lot like base indexed addressing (which is why the jargon may not be all that useful) with the sole exception that what is added to SI is not a *register* but a *literal constant*.

Once this **MOV** is done, the first of the two nybbles passed to **Byte2Str** in AL has been converted to its character equivalent and stored in the destination string variable at DS:SI.

Now we have to do it again, this time for the high nybble.

Shifting the High Nybble into the Low Nybble

The high nybble of the value to be converted has been waiting patiently all this time in AL. We didn't mask out the high nybble until we moved AX into DI and did our masking on DI instead of AX. So, AL is still just as it was when **Byte2Str** began.

The first thing to do is clear AH to 0. **Byte2Str** uses the **XOR AH,AH** trick I described in the last section. Then we copy AX into DI with **MOV**.

MOV AH,BYTE PTR [BX+DI]

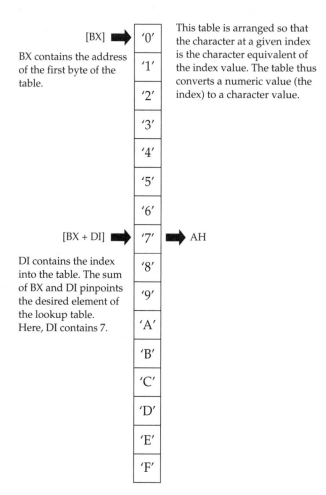

Figure 10.4 Using a lookup table.

All that remains to be done is to somehow move the high nybble of the low byte of DI into the position occupied by the low nybble. The fastest way to do this is simply to shift DI to the right by four bits. This is what the four **SHR DI,4** instructions in **Byte2Str** do. The low nybble is simply shifted off the edge of DI, into the Carry flag, and then out into nothingness. After the shift, what was the high nybble is now the low nybble, and once again, DI can be used as an index into the **Digits** lookup table to **MOV** the appropriate digit into AH.

One minor caution: The instruction **SHR DI,4** does not exist on the 8086 and 8088 CPUs. Prior to the 286, you could not provide any immediate operand to the shift instructions except for 1. Now, any immediate value that may be expressed in 8 bits may be used as the shift count operand. If your code *must* be able to run on *any* x86 CPU, you have to replace **SHR DI,4** with four **SHR DI,1** instructions. It's a good idea to flag any use of instructions that do not exist on early CPUs in your source code. While it's true that there are damned few 8088s and 8086s left out there, there are a few, and the reaction of old chips to undefined instructions is always a crapshoot and may produce some crazy bugs.

Finally, there is the matter of storing the digit into the target string at DS:SI. Notice that *this* time, there is no +1 in the **MOV** instruction:

```
MOV [SI],AH
```

Why not? The high nybble is the digit on the left, so it must be moved into the first byte in the target string. Earlier, we moved the low nybble into the byte on the right. String indexing begins at the left and works toward the right, so if the left digit is at index 0 of the string, the right digit must be at index 0+1.

Byte2Str does a fair amount of data fiddling in only a few lines. Read it over a few times while following the preceding discussion through its course until the whole thing makes sense to you.

Converting Words to Their String Form

Having converted a byte-sized value to a string, it's a snap to convert 16-bit words to their string forms. In fact, it's not much more difficult than calling **Byte2Str** . . . twice:

```
;-------------------------------------------------------------
;  Word2Str -- Converts a word passed in AX to a string at
;         DS:SI
;  Last update 9/18/99
;
;  1 entry point:
;
;  Word2Str:
;    Caller must pass:
;    AX : Word to be converted
;    DS : Segment of destination string
;    SI : Offset of destination string
;-------------------------------------------------------------
```

```
Word2Str:
    mov CX,AX       ; Save a copy of convertee in CX
    xchg AH,AL      ; Swap high and low AX bytes to do high first
    call Byte2Str   ; Convert AL to string at DS:SI
    add SI,2        ; Bump SI to point to second 2 characters
    mov AX,CX       ; Reload convertee into AX
    call Byte2Str   ; Convert AL to string at DS:SI
    ret             ; And we're done!
```

The logic here is fairly simple—if you understand how **Byte2Str** works. Moving AX into CX simply saves an unmodified copy of the word to be converted in CX. Something to watch out for here: If **Byte2Str** were to use CX for something, this saved copy would be mangled, and you might be caught wondering why things weren't working correctly. This is a common enough bug for the following reason: You create **Byte2Str**, and then create **Word2Str** to call **Byte2Str**. The first version of **Byte2Str** does not make use of CX, so it's safe to use CX as a storage bucket.

However—later on you beef up **Byte2Str** somehow, and in the process add some instructions that use CX. You plum forgot that **Word2Str** stored a value in CX *while Word2Str was calling Byte2Str*. It's pointless arguing whether the bug is that **Byte2Str** uses CX, or that **Word2Str** assumes that no one else is using CX. To make things work again, you would have to stash the value somewhere other than in CX. Pushing it onto the stack is your best bet if you run out of registers. (You might hit on the idea of stashing it in an unused segment register such as ES—but I warn against it! Later on, if you try to use these utility routines in a program that makes use of ES, you'll be in a position to mess over your memory addressing royally, and once you move to protected mode you can't play with the segment registers at all. Let segment registers hold segments. Use the stack instead.)

Virtually everything that **Word2Str** does involves getting the converted digits into the proper positions in the target string. A word requires four hexadecimal digits altogether. In a string representation, the high byte occupies the left two digits, and the low byte occupies the right two digits. Since strings are indexed from the left to the right, it makes a certain sense to convert the left end of the string first.

This is the reason for the **XCHG** instruction. It swaps the high and low bytes of AX, so that the *first* time **Byte2Str** is called, the high byte is actually in AL instead of AH. (Remember that **Byte2Str** converts the value passed in AL.) **Byte2Str** does the conversion and stores the two converted digits in the first two bytes of the string at DS:SI.

For the second call to **Byte2Str**, AH and AL are not exchanged. Therefore, the low byte will be the one converted. Notice the following instruction:

```
ADD SI,2
```

This is not heavy-duty math, but it's a good example of how to add a literal constant to a register in assembly language. The idea is to pass the address of the *second* two bytes of the string to **Byte2Str** as though they were actually the start of the string. This means that when **Byte2Str** converts the low byte of AX, it stores the two equivalent digits into the second two bytes of the string.

For example, if the high byte was 0C7H, the digits C and 7 would be stored in the first two bytes of the string, counting from the left. Then, if the low byte were 042H, the digits 4 and 2 would be stored at the third and fourth bytes of the string, respectively. The whole string would look like this when the conversion was complete:

```
C742
```

As I've said numerous times before: Understand memory addressing and you've got the greater part of assembly language in your hip pocket. Most of the trick of **Byte2Str** and **Word2Str** lies in the different ways they address memory. If you study them, study the machinery behind the lookup table and target string addressing. The logic and shift instructions are pretty obvious and easy to figure out by comparison.

Flags, Tests, and Branches

Those assembler-knowledgeable folk who have stuck with me this long may be wondering why I haven't covered conditional jumps until this late in the book. I mean, we've explained procedures already and haven't even gotten to jumps yet.

Indeed. That's the whole point. I explained procedures before jumps because when people learn those two concepts the other way around, they have a tendency to use jumps for *everything*, even when procedures are called for. Unlike some high-level languages such as Pascal and Modula-2, there is no way around jumps—what Pascal and Modula people so derisively call "GOTOs"—in assembly language. Sadly, some people then assume that jumps are It, and don't bother imposing any structure at all on their assembly language programs. By teaching procedures first, I feel that I've at least made possible a more balanced approach on the part of the learner.

Besides, I felt it wise to teach how to *manage* complexity before teaching the number one means of *creating* complexity.

Unconditional Jumps

A *jump* is just that: an abrupt change in the flow of instruction execution. Ordinarily, instructions are executed one after the other, in order, moving from low memory toward high memory. *Jump instructions* alter the address of the next instruction to be executed. Execute a jump instruction, and *zap!* All of a sudden you're somewhere else in the code segment. A jump instruction can move execution forward in memory or backward. It can bend execution back into a loop. (And it can tie your program logic in knots . . .)

There are two kinds of jumps: conditional and unconditional. An *unconditional* jump is a jump that *always* happens. It takes this form:

```
JMP <label>
```

When this instruction executes, the sequence of execution moves to the instruction located at the label specified by **<label>**. It's just that simple.

The unconditional **JMP** instruction is of limited use by itself. It almost always works in conjunction with the conditional jump instructions that test the state of the various x86 flags. You'll see how this works in just a little while, once we've gone through conditional jumps too.

Conditional Jumps

A *conditional* jump instruction is one of those fabled tests I introduced in Chapter 1. When executed, a conditional jump tests something, usually one of the flags in the Flags register. If the flag being tested happens to be in a particular state, execution may jump to a label somewhere else in the code segment, or it may simply fall through to the next instruction in sequence.

This two-way nature is important. A conditional jump instruction either jumps, or it falls through. Jump, or no jump. It can't jump to one of two places, or three. Whether it jumps or not depends on the current value of one single bit within the CPU.

For example, there is a flag that is set to 1 by certain instructions when the result of that instruction is zero: the Zero flag ZF. The **DEC** (**DEC**rement) instruction is a good example. **DEC** subtracts one from its operand. If by that subtraction the operand becomes zero, ZF is set to 1. One of the conditional jump instructions, **JZ** (Jump if **Z**ero) tests ZF. If ZF is found set to 1, a jump occurs, and execution transfers to a label. If ZF is found to be 0, execution falls through to the next instruction in line.

Here's a simple (and nonoptimal) example, using instructions you should already understand:

```
            mov byte [Counter],17 ; We're going to do this 17 times
WorkLoop: call DoWork          ; Process the data
            dec byte [Counter]   ; Subtract 1 from the counter
            jz  AllDone          ; If the counter is zero, we're done!
            jmp WorkLoop         ; Otherwise, go back and execute the loop again
```

The label **AllDone** isn't shown in the example because it's somewhere else in the program, maybe a long way off. The important thing is that the **JZ** instruction is a two-way switch. If ZF is equal to 1, execution moves to the location marked by the label **AllDone**. If ZF is equal to 0, execution falls through to the next instruction in sequence. Here, that would be the unconditional jump instruction **JMP WorkLoop**.

This simple loop is one way to perform a call to a procedure some set number of times. A count value is stored in a variable named **Counter**. The procedure is called. After control returns from the procedure, **Counter** is decremented by one. If that drops the counter to 0, the procedure has been called the full number of times, and the loop sends execution elsewhere. If the counter still has some count in it, execution loops back to the procedure call and begins the loop again.

Note the use of an unconditional jump instruction to close the loop.

Beware Endless Loops!

This is a good place to warn you of a common sort of bug that produces the dreaded *endless loop*, which locks up your machine and forces you to reboot to get out. Suppose the preceding code snippet was instead done the following way:

```
WorkLoop: mov byte [Counter],17 ; We're going to do this 17 times
            call DoWork          ; Process the data
            dec byte [Counter]   ; Subtract 1 from the counter
            jz  AllDone          ; If the counter is zero, we're done!
            jmp WorkLoop         ; Otherwise, go back and execute the loop again
```

This becomes a pretty obvious endless loop. (However, you'll be appalled at how often such an obvious bug will dance in your face for hours without being recognized as such . . .) The key point is that the instruction that loads the initial value to the counter is *inside* the loop! Every time the loop happens, the counter is counted down by one . . . and then immediately reloaded with the original count value. The count value thus never gets smaller than the original value minus one, and the loop (which is waiting for the counter to become zero) never ends.

You're unlikely to do something like this deliberately, of course. But it's *very* easy to type a label at the wrong place or (easier still!) to type the name of the wrong label, a label that might be at or before the point where a counter is loaded with its initial value.

Assembly language programming requires concentration and endless attention to detail. If you pay attention to what you're doing, you'll make fewer "stupid" errors like the preceding one.

But I can promise you that you'll still make a few.

Jumping on the Absence of a Condition

There are a fair number of conditional jump instructions, of which I'll discuss only the most common in this book. Their number is increased by the fact that almost every conditional jump instruction has an alter ego: a jump when the specified condition is *not* set to 1.

The **JZ** instruction provides a good example. **JZ** jumps to a new location in the code segment if the Zero flag (ZF) is set to 1. **JZ**'s alter ego is **JNZ** (**J**ump if **N**ot **Z**ero). **JNZ** jumps to a label if ZF is 0 and falls through if ZF is 1.

This may be confusing at first, because **JNZ** jumps when ZF is equal to 0. Keep in mind that the name of the instruction applies to the *condition* being tested and not necessarily the binary bit value of the flag. In the previous code example, **JZ** jumped when the **DEC** instruction decremented a counter to zero. The condition being tested is something connected with an earlier instruction, *not* simply the state of ZF.

Think of it this way: A condition raises a flag. "Raising a flag" means setting the flag to 1. When one of numerous instructions forces an operand to a value of zero (which is the condition), the Zero flag is raised. The logic of the instruction refers to the condition, *not* to the flag.

As an example, let's improve the little loop shown on page 333. I should caution you that its first implementation, while correct and workable in the strictest sense, is awkward and not the best way to code that kind of thing. It can be improved in several ways. Here's one:

```
         mov byte [Counter],17  ; We're going to do this 17 times
WorkLoop: call DoWork           ; Process the data
```

```
        dec byte [Counter]      ; Subtract 1 from the counter
        jnz WorkLoop            ; If the counter is zero, we're done!
        < more code >
```

The **JZ** instruction has been replaced with a **JNZ** instruction. That makes much more sense, since to close the loop we have to jump, and we only close the loop while the counter is greater than 0. The jump back to label **WorkLoop** will happen only while the counter is greater than 0.

Once the counter decrements to 0, the loop is considered finished. **JNZ** falls through, and the code that follows the loop (which I don't show here) executes. The next instruction could be a **JMP** to label **AllDone**, as shown earlier, or it could be the next bit of work that the assembly language program has to do. The point is that if you can position the program's next task immediately after the **JNZ** instruction, you don't need to use the **JMP** instruction *at all*. Instruction execution will just flow naturally into the next task that needs performing. The program will have a more natural and less-tangled top-to-bottom flow and will be easier to read and understand.

Flags

Back in Chapter 6, I explained the Flags register and briefly described the purposes of all the flags it contains. Most flags are not terribly useful, especially when you're first starting out as a programmer. The Carry flag (CF) and the Zero flag (ZF) will be 90 percent of your involvement in flags as a beginner, with the Direction flag (DF), Sign flag (SF), and Overflow flag (OF) together making up an additional 9.998 percent. It might be a good idea to reread that part of Chapter 6 now, just in case your grasp of flag etiquette has gotten a little rusty.

As explained earlier, **JZ** jumps when ZF is 1, whereas **JNZ** jumps when ZF is 0. Most instructions that perform some operation on an operand (such as **AND**, **OR**, **XOR**, **INC**, **DEC**, and all arithmetic instructions) set ZF according to the results of the operation. On the other hand, instructions that simply move data around (such as **MOV**, **XCHG**, **PUSH**, and **POP**) do not affect ZF or any of the other flags. (Obviously, **POPF** affects the flags by popping the top-of-stack value into them.) One irritating exception is the **NOT** instruction, which performs a logical operation on its operand but does *not* set any flags—even when it causes its operand to become 0. Before you write code that depends on flags, *check your instruction reference* to make sure that you have the flag etiquette down correctly.

Comparisons with CMP

One major use of flags is in controlling loops. Another is in comparisons between two values. Your programs will often need to know whether a value in a register or memory is equal to some other value. Further, you may want to know if a value is greater than a value or less than a value if it is not equal to that value. There is a jump instruction to satisfy every need, but something has to set the flags for the benefit of the jump instruction. The **CMP** (CoMPare) instruction is what sets the flags for comparison tasks.

CMP's use is straightforward and intuitive. The second operand is compared with the first, and several flags are set accordingly:

```
cmp <op1>,<op2>    ; Sets OF, SF, ZF, AF, PF, and CF
```

The sense of the comparison can be remembered if you simply recast the comparison in arithmetic terms:

```
Result = <op1> - <op2>
```

CMP is very much a subtraction operation where the result of the subtraction is thrown away, and only the flags are affected. The second operand is subtracted from the first. Based on the results of the subtraction, the other flags are set to appropriate values.

After a **CMP** instruction, you can jump based on several arithmetic conditions. People who have a fair grounding in math, and FORTRAN or Pascal programmers will recognize the conditions: *Equal, Not equal, Greater than, Less than, Greater than or equal to,* and *Less than or equal to.* The sense of these operators follows from their names and is exactly like the sense of the equivalent operators in most high-level languages.

A Jungle of Jump Instructions

There is a bewildering array of jump instruction mnemonics, but those dealing with arithmetic relationships sort out well into just six categories, one category for each of the six preceding conditions. Complication arises out of the fact that there are *two* mnemonics for each machine instruction, for example, **JLE** (Jump if **L**ess than or **E**qual) and **JNG** (Jump if **N**ot **G**reater than). These two mnemonics are *synonyms* in that the assembler generates the identical binary opcode when it encounters either mnemonic. The synonyms are a convenience to you the programmer in that they provide two alternate ways to think about a given jump instruction. In the preceding example, *Jump if Less than or Equal to* is logically identical to *Jump if Not Greater than*. (Think about it!) If the importance of the preceding compare was to see if one value is less than or equal to another, you'd use the **JLE** mnemonic. On the other hand, if you were testing to be sure one quantity was not greater than another, you'd use **JNG**. The choice is yours.

Another complication is that there is a separate set of instructions for signed and unsigned comparisons. I haven't spoken much about assembly language math in this book, and thus haven't said much about the difference between signed and unsigned quantities. A *signed* quantity is one in which the high bit of the quantity is considered a built-in flag indicating whether the quantity is negative. If that bit is 1, the quantity is considered negative. If that bit is 0, the quantity is considered positive.

Signed arithmetic in assembly language is complex and subtle, and not as useful as you might immediately think. I won't be covering it in detail in this book, though most all assembly language books treat it to some extent. All you need know to get a high-level understanding of signed arithmetic is that in signed arithmetic, negative quantities are legal. Unsigned arithmetic, on the other hand, does not recognize negative numbers.

Greater Than versus Above

To tell the signed jumps apart from the unsigned jumps, the mnemonics use two different expressions for the relationships between two values:

- *Signed values* are thought of as being *greater than* or *less than*. For example, to test whether one signed operand is greater than another, you would use the **JG** (Jump if Greater) mnemonic after a **CMP** instruction.

- *Unsigned values* are thought of as being *above* or *below*. For example, to tell whether one unsigned operand is greater than (above) another, you would use the **JA** (Jump if Above) mnemonic after a **CMP** instruction.

Table 10.6 summarizes the arithmetic jump mnemonics and their synonyms. Any mnemonics containing the words *above* or *below* are for unsigned values, while any mnemonics containing the words *greater* or *less* are for signed values. Compare the mnemonics with their synonyms and see how the two represent opposite viewpoints from which to look at identical instructions.

Table 10.6 Arithmetic Jump Mnemonics and Their Synonyms

MNEMONICS		SYNONYMS	
JA	Jump If Above	JNBE	Jump If Not Below or Equal
JAE	Jump If Above or Equal	JNB	Jump If Not Below
JB	Jump If Below	JNAE	Jump If Not Above or Equal
JBE	Jump If Below or Equal	JNA	Jump If Not Above
JE	Jump If Equal	JZ	Jump If Result is Zero
JNE	Jump If Not Equal	JNZ	Jump If Result is Not Zero
JG	Jump If Greater	JNLE	Jump If Not Less Than or Equal
JGE	Jump If Greater or Equal	JNL	Jump If Not Less
JL	Jump If Less	JNGE	Jump If Not Greater or Equal
JLE	Jump If Less or Equal	JNG	Jump If Not Greater

Table 10.6 simply serves to expand the mnemonics into a more comprehensible form and associate a mnemonic with its synonym. Table 10.7, on the other hand, sorts the mnemonics out by logical condition and according to their use with signed and unsigned values. Also listed in Table 10.7 are the flags whose values are considered in each jump instruction. Notice

Table 10.7 Arithmetic Tests Useful After a **CMP** Instruction

CONDITION	PASCAL OPERATOR	UNSIGNED VALUES	JUMPS WHEN	SIGNED VALUES	JUMPS WHEN
Equal	=	JE	ZF=1	JE	ZF=1
Not Equal	<>	JNE	ZF=0	JNE	ZF=0
Greater than	>	JA	CF=0 and	JG	ZF=0 or
Not Less than or equal to		JNBE	ZF=0	JNLE	SF=OF
Less than	<	JB	CF=1	JL	SF<>OF
Not Greater than or equal to		JNAE		JNGE	
Greater than or equal to	>=	JAE	CF=0	JGE	SF=OF
Not Less than		JNB		JNL	
Less than or equal to	<=	JBE	CF=1 or ZF=1	JLE	ZF=1 and SF<>OF
Not Greater than		JNA		JNG	

that some of the jump instructions require one of two possible flag values in order to take the jump, while others require *both* of two flag values.

Several of the signed jumps compare two of the flags against one another. **JG**, for example, will jump when either ZF is 0, or when the Sign flag (SF) is equal to the Overflow flag (OF). I won't spend any further time explaining the nature of the Sign flag or Overflow flag. As long as you have the sense of each instruction under your belt, understanding exactly how the instructions test the flags can wait until you've gained some programming experience.

Some people have trouble understanding how it is that **JE** and **JZ** mnemonics are synonyms, as are **JNE** and **JNZ**. Think again of the way a comparison is done within the CPU: The second operand is subtracted from the first, and if the result is 0 (indicating that the two operands were in fact equal), the Zero flag is set to 1. That's why **JE** and **JZ** are synonyms: Both are simply testing the state of the Zero flag.

Detecting the Installed Display Adapter

A useful example of **CMP** and the conditional jump instructions in action involves detecting the installed display adapter. At the beginning of the 1990s, there were five different mainstream IBM display adapters in reasonably common use in PCs, from the first generation introduced with the original PC in 1981 to the VGA and MCGA introduced with the PS/2 series in 1987. Going into the twenty-first century, nearly all of those adapters except for the VGA are mostly extinct.

So, the code I'm about to show you is mostly a technical exercise, but if you work with older machines (and one reason to work in assembly is to create software that works quickly enough on older machines), it may be useful for sorting out what any given machine can do from a text video standpoint.

It isn't quite enough to know which board is installed in a given machine. The way a certain board operates can change severely depending on whether a monochrome or color monitor is attached to the board. The most obvious difference (and the one of most interest to the programmer) is that memory address of the video display buffer is one address for the color monitor and a different address for the monochrome monitor. This schizophrenic quality of the EGA, VGA, and MCGA is so pronounced that it makes sense to consider the EGA/color monitor combination an entirely separate display adapter from the EGA/monochrome monitor combination, and ditto for the VGA. (The MCGA is one of those adapters approaching extinction asymptotically.)

In my method, I use a separate numeric code to represent each legal adapter/monitor combination. There are nine possibilities in all, summarized in Table 10.8.

The codes are not consecutive; note that there is no code 3, 6, or 9. I didn't make these codes up arbitrarily. They are, in fact, the display adapter/monitor combination codes returned by one of the VGA BIOS services.

The procedure **DispID** given in the following listing determines which display adapter is installed in the machine upon which **DispID** is running. **DispID** then returns one of the codes listed in Table 10.8. I recommend that your programs define a byte-sized variable in their data segments where this code can be stored throughout the programs' duration. If you detect the adapter with **DispID** immediately on program startup, your program can inspect the code any time it needs to make a decision as to which video features to use.

Given what I've told you about **CMP** and conditional jump instructions so far, see if you can follow the logic in **DispID** before we go through it blow by blow:

Table 10.8   Legal PC Display Adapter/Monitor Combinations

CODE	ADAPTER/MONITOR	SEGMENT OF DISPLAY BUFFER
00	None	None
01H	MDA/monochrome	0B000H
02H	CGA/color	0B800H
04H	EGA/color	0B800H
05H	EGA/monochrome	0B000H
07H	VGA/monochrome	0B000H
08H	VGA/color	0B800H
0AH	MCGA/color (digital)	0B800H
0BH	MCGA/monochrome	0B000H
0CH	MCGA/color (analog)	0B800H

```
;--------------------------------------------------------------
;  DispID — Identifies the installed display adapter
;  Last update 9/18/99
;
;  1 entry point:
;
;  DispID:
;   Caller passes no parameters
;   Routine returns a code value in AX.
;   The codes are these:
;   0 : Adapter is unknown; recommend aborting
;   1 : MDA (Monochrome Display Adapter)
;   2 : CGA (Color Graphics Adapter)
;
;--------------------------------------------------------------

DispID:
     mov AH,1AH     ; Select PS/2 Identify Adapter Service
     xor AL,AL      ; Select Get Combination Code Subservice (AL=0)
     int 10H        ; Call VIDEO
     cmp AL,1AH     ; If AL comes back with 1AH, we have a PS/2
     jne TryEGA     ; If not, jump down to test for the EGA
     mov AL,BL      ; Put Combination Code into AL
     ret            ;  and go home!
TryEGA: mov AH,12H  ; Select EGA Alternate Function
     mov BX,10H     ; Select Get Configuration Information subservice
     int 10H        ; Call VIDEO
     cmp BX,10H     ; If BX comes back unchanged, EGA is *not* there
     je  OldBords   ; Go see whether it's an MDA or CGA
     cmp BH,0       ; If BH = 0, it's an EGA/color combo
     je  EGAColor   ;  otherwise it's EGA/mono
     mov AL,5       ; Store code 5 for EGA mono
     ret            ;  and go home!
EGAColor:
     mov AL,4       ; Store code 4 for EGA color
     ret            ;  and go home!
OldBords:
     int 11H        ; Call Equipment Configuration interrupt
     and AL,30H     ; Mask out all but bits 4 & 5
     cmp AL,30H     ; If bits 4 & 5 are both =1, it's an MDA
     jne CGA        ;  otherwise it's a CGA
     mov AL,1       ; Store code 1 for MDA
     ret            ;  and go home!
CGA: mov AL,2       ; Store code 2 for CGA
     ret            ;  and go home!
```

DispID is the most complex piece of code shown so far in this book. The overall strategy is not obvious and warrants some attention.

IBM's standard display boards appeared in three generations. The first generation consisted of the original Color Graphics Adapter (CGA) and

Monochrome Display Adapter (MDA). The second generation consisted solely of the Enhanced Graphics Adapter (EGA). Finally, the third generation came in with the PS/2 in April of 1987 and provided the Video Graphics Array (VGA) and Multi-Color Graphics Array (MCGA). Although "super" successors of the VGA appeared regularly going into the 1990s, their superness was strictly on the graphics side. The evolution of the PC text display pretty much ceased with the VGA and MCGA.

The simplest way to find out what display board is installed in a machine is to ask the machine by querying BIOS services. There are BIOS services specific to each generation of display board, and by some quirk of fate all such services are well behaved, by which I mean that querying a service that doesn't exist (because an older generation of video board is installed) will not crash the system. (IBM's BIOS standard is extremely downward compatible in that newer generations all contain everything the older generations do.) Furthermore, if a BIOS service specific to a generation of boards is found *not* to exist, that tells us that the installed board is not a member of that generation or a newer generation.

Assuming that the target machine could have any of the standard IBM display boards in it, it makes sense to test for the presence of the newest boards first. Then, through a process of elimination, we move to the older and older boards.

The first test that **DispID** makes, then, is for the VGA or MCGA generation, that is, the PS/2 boards. The PS/2 machines contain in their ROM BIOS a service (VIDEO Service 1AH) designed specifically to identify the installed display adapter. **DispID** calls VIDEO service 1AH, having cleared AL to 0 via **XOR**. As it happens, if a PS/2 BIOS is present on the bus, the 1AH service number is returned in register AL. On return from the **INT 10H** call, we test AL for 1AH using **CMP**. If 1AH is *not* found in AL, we know up front that there is no PS/2 BIOS in the system, and therefore no VGA or MCGA.

After the **CMP** instruction is the **JNE TryEGA** conditional branch. If the **CMP** instruction finds that AL is *not* equal to 1AH, then control jumps down to the code that tests for the next older generation of video boards: the EGA. If AL *is* equal to 1AH, then the PS/2 BIOS is present and has placed the display adapter code in BL. **DispID** then copies BL into AL (which is where **DispID** returns the display code) and executes a **RET** instruction to pass control back to the caller.

Testing for the EGA is done a little differently, but the same general idea holds: We call an EGA-specific VIDEO service not present in the oldest generation of boards. The key test, again, is whether a certain register comes back unchanged. There is a twist, however: If BX comes back with the *same* value it held when the VIDEO call was made (here, 10H), then an EGA BIOS does *not* exist in the machine. (Isn't the PC wonderful?) Here, after the **CMP BX,10H** instruction, we do a **JE OldBords** and not a **JNE** as we did when testing for the PS/2 generation. If BX comes back in an altered state, we assume an EGA is present and that BX contains information on the display configuration.

If an EGA BIOS is found, a value in BH tells us whether the EGA is connected to a monochrome or color monitor. (Remember, there is a different code for each.) The value in BH is not the code itself, as it was with the PS/2 BIOS, so we have to do a little more testing to get the right code into AL. If BH contains 0, then the attached monitor is color. Any other value in BH indicates a monochrome system. The following sequence of instructions from **DispID** takes care of loading the proper EGA-specific code into AL:

```
      cmp BH,0      ; If BH = 0, it's an EGA/color combo
      je  EGAColor  ;  otherwise it's EGA/mono
      mov AL,5      ; Store code 5 for EGA mono
      ret           ;  and go home!
EGAColor:
      mov AL,4      ; Store code 4 for EGA color
      ret           ;  and go home!
```

You'll find yourself writing sequences like this a lot, when a single test decides between one of two courses of action. One course here is to load the value 5 into AL, and the other course is to load 4 into AL. Notice that after the appropriate **MOV** instruction is executed, a **RET** takes care of passing execution back to the caller. If **DispID** were not a procedure, but simply a sequence coded into the main line of instructions, you would need an unconditional jump (**JMP**) after each **MOV** to continue on with instruction execution somewhere else in the program. Using **RET** is much neater—which is yet another reason to wrap up small tasks such as display adapter identification in a procedure wrapper.

Finally, if neither PS/2 nor EGA are present, **DispID** realizes that, by default, one of the original generation of display boards is on the bus.

Telling MDA from CGA is not done with a BIOS call at all, because the first generation BIOS did not know which display board was present. (That was a feature instituted with the EGA in 1984.) Instead, there is a separate software interrupt, 11H, that returns machine configuration information.

Testing Bits with TEST

Service 11H returns a word's worth of bits in AX. Singly or in twos or threes, the bits tell a tale about specific hardware options on the installed PC. These hardware options are summarized in Figure 10.5.

The bits we need to examine are bits 4 and 5. If both are set to 1, then we know we have a Monochrome Display Adapter. If the two bits are set to any other combination, the adapter must be a Color Graphics Adapter; all other alternatives have by this time been eliminated.

Testing for two 1 bits in a byte is an interesting exercise—which is one reason I've retained this code in the book, even though it's not as compellingly useful as it was 10 years ago. The x86 instruction set recognizes that bit testing is done a lot in assembly language, and it provides what amounts to a **CMP** instruction for bits: **TEST**.

The Phantoms of the Opcodes

TEST performs an AND logical operation between two operands, and then sets the flags as **AND** would, *without* altering the destination operation, as **AND** would. Here's the **TEST** instruction syntax:

```
TEST <operand>,<bit mask>
```

The bit mask operand should contain a 1 bit in each position where a 1 bit is to be sought in the operand, and 0 bits in all the other bits.

What **TEST** does is AND the operand against the bit mask and set the flags as **AND** would. The operand doesn't change. For example, if you want to determine if bit 3 of AX is set to 1, you would use this instruction:

```
TEST AX,3      ; 3 in binary is 00001000B
```

AX doesn't change as a result of the operation, but the AND truth table is asserted between AX and the binary pattern 00001000. If bit 3 in AX is a 1 bit, then the Zero flag is cleared to 0. If bit 3 in AX is a 0 bit, then the Zero flag is set to 1. Why? If you AND 1 (in the bit mask) with 0 (in AX),

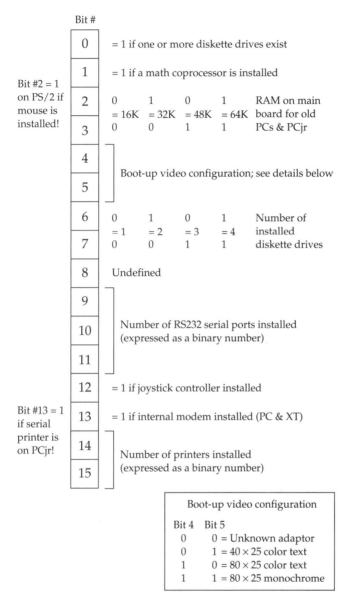

Bit #

Bit #					
0	= 1 if one or more diskette drives exist				
1	= 1 if a math coprocessor is installed				
2	0	1	0	1	RAM on main
	= 16K	= 32K	= 48K	= 64K	board for old
3	0	0	1	1	PCs & PCjr

Bit #2 = 1 on PS/2 if mouse is installed!

4	
	Boot-up video configuration; see details below
5	

6	0	1	0	1	Number of
	= 1	= 2	= 3	= 4	installed
7	0	0	1	1	diskette drives

8	Undefined

9	
10	Number of RS232 serial ports installed (expressed as a binary number)
11	

12	= 1 if joystick controller installed
13	= 1 if internal modem installed (PC & XT)

Bit #13 = 1 if serial printer is on PCjr!

14	
	Number of printers installed (expressed as a binary number)
15	

Boot-up video configuration

Bit 4	Bit 5	
0	0	= Unknown adaptor
0	1	= 40 × 25 color text
1	0	= 80 × 25 color text
1	1	= 80 × 25 monochrome

Figure 10.5 Interrupt 11H configuration information.

you get 0. (Look it up in Table 10.2, the AND truth table.) And if all eight bitwise AND operations come up 0, the result is 0, and the Zero flag is raised to 1, indicating that the result is 0.

Key to understanding **TEST** is thinking of **TEST** as a sort of Phantom of the Opcode, where the Opcode is **AND**. **TEST** pretends it is **AND**, but doesn't follow through with the results of the operation. It simply sets the flags *as though* an AND operation had occurred.

CMP is another Phantom of the Opcode and bears the same relation to **SUB** as **TEST** bears to **AND**. **CMP** subtracts its second operand from its first, but doesn't follow through and store the result in the first operand. It just sets the flags *as though* a subtraction had occurred.

TEST Pointers

Here's something important to keep in mind: *TEST is only useful for finding 1 bits.* If you need to identify 0 bits, you must first flip each bit to its opposite state with the logical **NOT** instruction, as I explained earlier. **NOT** changes all 1 bits to 0 bits, and all 0 bits to 1 bits. Once all 0 bits are flipped to 1 bits, you can test for a 1 bit where you need to find a 0 bit. (Sometimes it helps to map it out on paper to keep it all straight in your head.)

Also, **TEST** will *not* reliably test for two or more 1 bits in the operand *at one time*. **TEST** doesn't check for the presence of a bit pattern; *it checks for the presence of a single 1 bit*. In other words, if you need to check to make sure that *both* bits 4 and 5 are set to 1, **TEST** won't hack it.

And unfortunately, that's what we have to do in **DispID**.

What we're looking for in the last part of **DispID** is the monochrome code in bits 4 and 5, which is the value 30H; that is, both bits 4 and 5 set to 1. Don't make the mistake (as I did once, in ages long past) of assuming that we can use **TEST** to spot the two 1 bits in bits 4 and 5:

```
test AL,30H   ; If bits 4 & 5 are both =1, it's an MDA
jnz CGA       ;    otherwise it's a CGA
```

This doesn't work! The Zero flag will be set *only* if both bits are zero. If either bit is 1, ZF will become 0, and the branch will be taken. However, we *only* want to take the branch if *both* bits are 1.

Here's where your right brain can sometimes save both sides of your butt. **TEST** only spots a single 1 bit at a time. We need to detect a condition where two 1 bits are present. So let's get inspired and first flip the state of all bits in the Equipment Identification Byte with **NOT**, and then look at the byte with **TEST**. After using **NOT**, what we need to find are two 0 bits, not two 1 bits. And if the two bits in question (4 and 5) are now both zero, the whole byte is zero, and the Zero flag will be set and ready to test via **JNZ**:

```
not AL       ; Invert all bits in the equipment ID byte
test AL,30H  ; See if either of bits 4 or 5 are 1-bits
jnz CGA      ; If both = 0, they originally were both 1's,
             ; and the adapter is a monochrome
```

Tricky, tricky. But as you get accustomed to the instruction set and its quirks, you'll hit upon lots of nonobvious solutions to difficult problems of that kind.

So, get that right brain working: How would you test for a specific pattern that was a *mix* of 0 bits and 1 bits?

Assembly Odds 'n Ends

Practice is the word.

You can do a lot with what you've learned so far, and certainly, you've learned enough to be able to figure out the rest with the help of an assembly language reference and perhaps a more advanced book on the subject. For the remainder of this chapter we're going to do some practicing, flexing some assembly language muscles and picking up a few more instructions in the process.

Yet Another Lookup Table

The lookup table named **Digits** (used by **Byte2Str** and **Word2Str** in the previous section) is so obvious that it didn't need much in the line of comments or explanations. **Digits** simply converted the table's index into the ASCII character equivalent to the value of the index. **Digits** is only 16 bytes long, and its contents pretty much indicate what it's for:

```
Digits  DB '0123456789ABCDEF'
```

Most of the time, your lookup tables will be a little less obvious. A lookup table does *not* have to be one single **DB** variable definition. You can define it pretty much as you need to, either with all table elements defined on a single line (as with **Digits**) or with each table element on its own line.

Consider the following lookup table:

```
OriginTbl DW    0B000H  ; Code 0: No adapter identified
          DW    0B000H  ; Code 1: MDA
          DW    0B800H  ; Code 2: CGA
          DW    0B000H  ; Undefined
```

```
DW    0B800H  ; Code 4: EGA/color
DW    0B000H  ; Code 5: EGA/mono
DW    0B000H  ; Undefined
DW    0B000H  ; Code 7: VGA/mono
DW    0B800H  ; Code 8: VGA/color
DW    0B000H  ; Undefined
DW    0B800H  ; Code 0AH: MCGA/color (digital)
DW    0B000H  ; Code 0BH: MCGA/mono
DW    0B800H  ; Code 0CH: MCGA/color (analog)
```

Here's a table in which each table element has its own **DW** definition statement on its own line. This table treats a problem connected with the numerous different kinds of display adapters installable in a PC. There are two different addresses where the video refresh buffer begins. On boards connected to color or color/gray scale monitors, the address is B800:0000, whereas on monochrome monitors, the address is B000:0000. (Refer back to Figure 6.11 and the accompanying text if you've forgotten what the video refresh buffer is.)

If you intend to address video memory directly (and doing so is much faster than working through DOS as we have been), then you have to know at which address the video refresh buffer lies. Knowing which display adapter is installed is the hardest part—and the **DispID** procedure described in the previous section answers that question. Each of the nine codes returned by **DispID** has a video refresh buffer address associated with it. But which goes with which? You could use a long and interwoven series of **CMP** and **JE** tests, but that's the hard road and is grossly wasteful of memory and machine cycles. A lookup table is simpler, faster in execution, and much easier to read and understand.

The following routine uses the **OriginTbl** lookup table shown previously to return the segment portion of the video refresh buffer address in AX. **OriginTbl** must be present in the data segment, and the display adapter code must be passed to **VidOrg** in AL:

```
;-----------------------------------------------------------
;  VidOrg -- Returns origin segment of video buffer
;  Last update 9/20/99
;
;  1 entry point:
;
;  VidOrg:
;   Caller must pass:
;   AL : Code specifying display adapter type
;   VidOrg returns the buffer origin segment in AX
;-----------------------------------------------------------
```

```
VidOrg:
    xor AH,AH          ; Zero AH
    mov DI,AX          ; Copy AX (with code in AL) into DI
    shl DI,1           ; Multiply code by 2 to act as word index
    mov BX,OriginTbl   ; Load address of origin table into BX
    mov AX,[BX+DI]     ; Index into table using code as index
    ret                ; Done; go home!
```

This works a lot like the **Digits** lookup table mechanism in **Byte2Str**. There's an important difference, however: Each entry in the **OriginTbl** lookup table is *two* bytes in size, whereas each entry in **Digits** was *one* byte in size.

Using Shift Instructions to Multiply by Powers of Two

To use the **Digits** lookup table, we simply used the value to be converted as the index into the table. Because each element in the table was one byte in size, this worked. When table elements are more than one byte long, you have to multiply the index by the number of bytes in each table element, or the lookup won't find the correct table element.

OriginTbl is a good working example. Suppose you get a code 2 back from **DispID**, indicating that you have a CGA in the system. Adding the 2 code to the starting address of the table (as we did with **Digits**) takes us to the start of the second element in the table. Read across to the comment at the right of that second element and see which code it applies to: code 1, the MDA! Not cool . . .

If you scan down to find the table element associated with the CGA, you'll find that it starts at an offset of four from the start of the table. To index into the table correctly, you have to add 4, not 2, to the offset address of the start of the table. This is where multiplication comes in.

There is a general-purpose multiply instruction in the x86 CPU, but **MUL** is outrageously slow as machine instructions go. There's a better way— in some cases. When you need to multiply a value by some power of 2 (that is, 2, 4, 8, 16, 32, and so on), you can do it by using the shift left instruction, **SHL**. Shifting a value to the left by one bit multiplies the overall value by 2. Shifting a value to the left by two bits multiplies the value by 4. Shifting a value to the left by three bits multiplies the value by 8, and so on.

Magic? Not at all. Work it out on paper by expressing a number as a bit pattern (that is, in binary form), shifting the bit pattern one bit to the right, and then converting the binary form back to decimal or hex. Like so:

```
00110101        Binary equivalent of 35H, 53 decimal
<--- by one bit yields
01101010        Binary equivalent of 6AH, 106 decimal
```

Sharp readers may have guessed that shifting to the right *divides* by powers of two—and that's also correct. Shifting right by one bit divides by 2; shifting right by two bits divides by 4, and so on.

The advantage to multiplying with shift instructions is that it's *fast*. Even on the oldest and slowest x86 CPUs, shifting a byte-sized value in a register to the left by one bit *takes only two machine cycles*—2 . . . as opposed to 77 (on those same older machines) with **MUL**. And **MUL** can do no better than 13 cycles even on the newest Pentium-class processors.

As we say, no contest.

Once the index is multiplied by two with **SHL**, the index is added to the starting address of the table, just as with **Digits**. A word-sized **MOV** then copies the correct segment address from the table into AX, for return to the caller.

This illustrates how you can realize enormous speed advantages by structuring your tables properly. Even if it means leaving a little wasted space at the end of each element, do your best to make the length of your table elements equal to some power of two. That means making each element 1, 2, 4, 8, 16, 32, or some larger power of two in size, but not 3, 7, 12, 20, or 25 bytes in size.

Tables within Tables

Tables are about the handiest means at your disposal for grouping data together and organizing them. Sometimes tables can be as simple as those I've just shown you, which are simply sequences of single values.

In most cases, you'll need something a little more sophisticated. Sometimes you'll need a table of tables, and (surprise!) the x86 instruction set contains some built-in machinery to handle such nested tables quickly and easily.

Let's continue on with the issue of video support. In the previous section we looked at a table containing the display buffer addresses for each of the display adapters identified by **DispID**. This is good, but not enough: Each adapter has a name, a display buffer address, and a screen size dictated by the size of the current character font. These items comprise a table of information about a display adapter, and if you wanted to put together a summary of all that information about all legal display adapters, you'd have to create such a table of tables.

Below is such a two-level table:

```
;-------------------------------------------------------------
; DISPLAY ADAPTER INFORMATION LOOKUP TABLE
;
; This is the lookup table containing information on all legal
; display adapters. The first field in each element is a 26-
; character string containing a brief description of the
; adapter. The next field is the segment of the video refresh
; buffer. The last three fields are the number of screen lines
; an adapter displays when the 8-pixel, 14-pixel, and 16-pixel
; fonts are loaded, respectively. Note that not all adapters
; support all fonts, but a screen line count is given for all
; three fonts for all adapter types. Illegal combinations will
; not be accessed.
;-------------------------------------------------------------
VidInfoTbl DB   'No adapter identified     '  ; Code 0
           DW   0B000H
           DB   25,25,25
           DB   'Monochrome Display Adapter '  ; Code 1
           DW   0B000H
           DB   25,25,25
           DB   'Color Graphics Adapter    '  ; Code 2
           DW   0B800H
           DB   25,25,25
           DB   'Code 3: Undefined         '  ; Code 3
           DW   0B000H
           DB   25,25,25
           DB   'EGA with color monitor    '  ; Code 4
           DW   0B800H
           DB   43,25,25
           DB   'EGA with mono monitor     '  ; Code 5
           DW   0B000H
           DB   43,25,25
           DB   'Code 6: Undefined         '  ; Code 6
           DW   0B000H
           DB   25,25,25
           DB   'VGA with mono monitor     '  ; Code 7
           DW   0B000H
           DB   50,27,25
           DB   'VGA with color monitor    '  ; Code 8
           DW   0B800H
           DB   50,27,25
```

```
DB    'Code 9: Undefined          '  ; Code 9
DW    0B000H
DB    25,25,25
DB    'MCGA with digital color    '  ; Code 0AH
DW    0B800H
DB    25,25,25
DB    'MCGA with monochrome       '  ; Code 0BH
DW    0B000H
DB    25,25,25
DB    'MCGA with analog color     '  ; Code 0CH
DW    0B800H
DB    25,25,25
```

The table consists of 12 subtables, one for each possible code returned by **DispID** as well as a subtable for several undefined codes. Why a subtable for undefined codes? We're going to follow the same general strategy of indexing into the table based on the value of the code. In other words, to get the information for code 4, we have to look at the fifth table (counting from zero) which requires that tables 0 through 4 already exist. Code 3 is undefined, yet something must hold its place in the table for our indexing scheme to work.

Each subtable occupies three lines, for clarity's sake. Here's a typical subtable:

```
DB    'EGA with color monitor   '  ; Code 4
DW    0B800H
DB    43,25,25
```

The first line is a 27-character quoted string containing the name of the display adapter. The second line is a word-sized address, the segment address of the visible display buffer corresponding to that name. The third line contains three numeric values. These are screen sizes, in lines, relating to the font sizes currently in force. The first value is the number of lines on the screen with the 8-pixel font in force. The second value is the number of lines on the screen with the 14-pixel font in force. The third value is the number of lines on the screen with the 16-pixel font in force. The items stored in the subtables give you just about everything you'd really need to know about a given display adapter to do useful work with it. The character string is set to precisely 27 characters in length so that with the addition of the display buffer segment address and the three screen size values, the length of the whole table entry comes out to exactly 32 bytes.

When your assembly language programs begin executing, they should inspect such a table and extract the values pertinent to the currently installed display adapter. These extracted values should be ordinary variables in the data segment, easily accessible without further table searching. These variables should be defined together, as a block, with comments explaining how they are related:

```
;----------------------------------------------------------------
; DISPLAY INFORMATION VARIABLES
;
; The following block of variables all relate to the video
; system and are initialized by the VidCheck procedure:
;----------------------------------------------------------------
DispType    DB    0        ; Code for display adapter type
VidSegment  DW    0B000H   ; Segment of installed display buffer
VidOrigin   DW    0        ; Offset for FAR pointer to refresh buffer
VisibleX    DB    80       ; Number of columns on screen
VisibleY    DB    25       ; Number of lines on screen
VidBufSize  DW    4000     ; Default to 25 X 80 X 2 (char & attribute)
FontSize    DB    8        ; Either 8, 14, or 16; default to 8
BordName    DW    0        ; NEAR pointer to name string of installed board
; 18H = 24D; 4FH = 79D; Combined 0-based X,Y of 80 x 25 screen LR corner:
LRXY        DW    184FH
```

As the comments indicate, a single routine named **VidCheck** reads values from the two-level lookup table **VidInfoTbl** and loads those values into the variables shown in the preceding listing.

VidCheck is an interesting creature and demonstrates the way of dealing with two-level tables. Read it over carefully—again, this is as complex a piece of code as you're going to see in this book:

```
;----------------------------------------------------------------
;  VidCheck -- Identifies display board & display parameters
;  Last update 9/18/99
;
;  1 entry point:
;
;  VidCheck:
;    Caller need pass no parameters.
;    VidCheck identifies the installed display board by
;    calling DispID. It then calculates numerous display
;    information values, which it then stores in the block
;    of display information variables in the data segment.
;----------------------------------------------------------------

VidCheck:
        ; First task is to figure out which board is on the bus:
        call DispID          ; Ask BIOS for adapter code; returns in AL
        mov [DispType],AL    ; Store display adapter code in DispType

        ; Next we determine the font size currently in force:
```

```
        cmp AL,0AH              ; See if board is an MCGA
        jl TryOld               ; If less than code 0AH, it's not an MCGA
        mov [FontSize],BYTE 16  ; MCGA supports *only* 16 pixel text font
        jmp GetName             ; Jump ahead to look up adapter name string
TryOld: cmp [DispType],BYTE 01  ; Is the display adapter code 1, for MDA?
        jne TryCGA              ; If not, go test for CGA code 2
        mov [FontSize],BYTE 14  ; MDA uses *only* 14-pixel text font
        jmp GetName             ; Jump ahead to look up adapter name string
TryCGA: cmp [DispType],BYTE 02  ; Is the display adapter code 2, for CGA?
        jne TryVGA              ; If not, go test for EGA/VGA font size
        mov [FontSize],BYTE 08  ; CGA uses *only* 8-pixel text font
        jmp GetName             ; Jump ahead to look up adapter name string
TryVGA: mov AH,11H              ; Select VIDEO Get Font Information subservice
        mov AL,30H              ;  requires AH = 11H and AL = 30H
        mov BH,0                ; 0 = Get info about current font
        int 10H                 ; Call VIDEO
        mov [FontSize],CL       ; Font size in pixels is returned in CL

        ; Next we get the name string for the board from the info table:
GetName:
        mov AL,[DispType]       ; Load display adapter code into AL
        xor AH,AH               ; Zero AH so we don't copy trash into DI
        mov DI,AX               ; Copy AX (with code in AL) into DI
        mov CL,5                ; We must shift the code 5 bits to mult. by 32
        shl DI,CL               ; Multiply code by 32 to act as table index
        mov BX,VidInfoTbl       ; Load address of origin table into BX
        mov [BordName],BX       ; Save pointer to video info. table in BordName
        add [BordName],DI       ; Add offset into table to right element

        ; Next we get the refresh buffer segment from the table:
        mov AX,[BX+DI+27]       ; Index into table past name string to segment
        mov [VidSegment],AX     ; Store segment from table to VidSegment variable

        ; Here we calculate the number of lines on-screen from font size:
        xor AH,AH               ; Make sure AH has no trash in it
        mov AL,[FontSize]       ; Load the font size in pixels into AL
        cmp AL,8                ; Is it the 8-pixel font?
        jne Try14               ; If not, try the 14-pixel font
        mov AL,1                ; The 8-pixel font is table offset 1
        jmp ReadLns             ; Jump ahead to read screen lines from table
Try14:  cmp AL,14               ; Is it the 14-pixel font?
        jne Do16                ; If not, it has to be the 16-pixel font
        mov AL,2                ; The 14-pixel font is table offset 2
        jmp ReadLns             ; Jump ahead to read screen lines from table
Do16:   mov AL,3                ; The 16-pixel font is table offset 3
ReadLns:
        add DI,AX               ; Add font size offset to table element offset
        mov AL,[BX+DI+28]       ; Load the screen lines value from the table
        mov [VisibleY],AL       ; and store it in the VisibleY variable
        mov AH,[VisibleX]       ; Load the screen columns value to AH
```

```
xchg AH,AL            ; Exchange AH & AL for 0-basing
dec AL                ; Subtract one from column count for 0-basing
dec AH                ; Subtract one from line count for zero-basing
mov [LRXY],AX         ; And store 0-based X,Y word into LRXY variable

; Finally, we calculate the size of the refresh buffer in bytes:
mov AL,[VisibleY]     ; We multiply screen lines time screen columns
mul BYTE [VisibleX]   ; times 2 (for attributes) to get buffer size
shl AX,1              ; Multiply lines * columns by 2
mov [VidBufSize],AX   ; Store refresh buffer size in VidBufSize

ret                   ; Return to caller
```

The first thing **VidCheck** does is call **DispID** to determine which display adapter is installed. Build on your own tools—there's no need to duplicate logic if you can avoid it. The adapter ID code is stored in the variable **DispType**.

It's possible to use the table to look up the number of lines on the screen from the current text font size, but to do that you have to determine the font size. Determining the font size is a good exercise in the use of the **CMP** instruction and conditional jumps. Certain adapters support only one font size. The MCGA has only the 16-pixel font. The CGA has only the 8-pixel font. The MDA has only the 14-pixel font. A series of compares and jumps selects a font size based on the display adapter ID code. The trickiness comes in with the EGA and VGA, which are versatile operatives capable of using more than one size of font. Fortunately, BIOS has a service that reports the size in pixels of the text font currently being used, and this service is used to query the font size. Whatever it turns out to be, the font size is stored in the **FontSize** variable in the data segment.

Base-Indexed-Displacement Memory Addressing

So far, we haven't dealt with the **VidInfoTbl** table at all. This changes when we want to look up the string containing the English-language description of the installed display adapter. There are three general steps to be taken in reading *any* two-level lookup table:

1. Derive the offset of the subtable from the beginning of the larger table.

2. Derive the offset of the desired information within the subtable.

3. Read the information from the subtable.

Each of the subtables is exactly 32 bytes in size. To move from the start of the **VidInfoTbl** to a desired subtable, we multiply the index of the subtable by 32, just as we did in the previous section, in reading one single value from **OriginTbl**. The index, here, is the display adapter ID code. We multiply the index by 32 by loading it into register DI, and then shifting DI to the left by 5 bits. (Shifting left by 5 bits multiplies the shifted quantity by 32.) We use the form:

```
mov CL,5
shl DI,CL
```

because it is shorter and faster to shift by CL than to shift by using five SHL DI,1 opcodes in sequence. This sequence is universal in that any x86 processor can execute it. For the 286 and newer CPUs, you can simply shift left by 5 as an immediate operand:

```
shl DI,5
```

Once you graduate to protected mode programming, you can begin using such newer opcodes with complete safety, because protected mode works only on the newer CPUs.

Because the display adapter description is the first item in every subtable, no offset into the subtable is necessary. (The offset, if you must think of an offset, is 0.) The shifted quantity in DI is added to the address of the larger table, and the sum becomes the 16-bit address to the display adapter description string. This address is saved in the **BordName** variable.

At this point within **VidCheck,** we have the address of the **VidInfoTbl** table itself in BX and the offset of the desired subtable in DI. Now we want to fetch the segment address of the display buffer from the middle of the subtable. The segment address is at some fixed offset from the start of the subtable. I say "fixed" because it never changes and will be the same regardless of which subtable is selected by the adapter ID code. In the case of the segment address, the offset is 27, since the segment address is 27 bytes from the start of the subtable.

Expressed as a sum, the segment address is at the following offset from the start of **VidInfoTbl:** DI + 27. Since BX contains the offset of **VidInfoTbl** from the start of the data segment, we can pin down the segment address in the data segment with this sum: BX + DI + 27.

Is there a way to address memory using this three-part sum?

There is, indeed, and it is the most complex of the numerous x86 addressing modes: *Base-indexed-displacement addressing*, a term you probably can't memorize and shouldn't try. Specifically to serve two-level lookup tables like this one, the CPU understands **MOV** statements such as the following:

```
mov AX, [BX+DI+27]
```

Here, the *base* is the address of the larger table in BX; the *index* is the offset of the subtable within the larger table, stored in DI; and the *displacement* is the fixed distance between the start of the subtable and the data we wish to address.

You can't just use any registers in building a memory address using based-indexed-displacement addressing. The base register may be *only* BP or BX. (Think of general-purpose register BX's hidden agenda as that of *base register*; the *B* is your memory hook.) The index register may be *only* SI or DI. These registers' names, *Source Index* and *Destination Index*, should provide you with their own memory hooks.

Finally, the displacement may not be a register at all, but may be only a literal value such as 27 or 14 or 3.

Finding the Number of Lines in the Screen

Reading the screen line count from the subtable is the trickiest part of the whole process. In one sense, the list of three different line count values is a table within a table within a table, but x86 addressing only goes down two levels. What we must do is point BX and DI plus a displacement to the first of the three values, and then add a second index to DI that selects one of the three line counts.

This second index is placed into AL, which is eventually (as part of AX) added to DI. The line count is read from the table with the following instruction:

```
mov AL, [BX+DI+28]
```

with the second index already built into DI.

The rest of **VidCheck** fills a few other video-related variables such as LRXY, which bundles the *X,Y* position of the lower-right corner of the screen into a single 16-bit quantity. The size of the video buffer in bytes is calculated as the *X* size of the screen times the *Y* size of the screen times 2, and stored in **VidBufSize**.

Equates and the Current Location Counter

To make **VidCheck** show its stuff, I've written a short program called INFO.ASM that reports certain facts about the installed display controller. As a program, INFO.ASM doesn't present any assembly language mechanisms we haven't used before, except in one respect: string lengths.

To display a string, you have to tell DOS just how long the string is, in characters. Counting characters is difficult, and if you get it wrong, you'll either display too much string or not enough.

The solution is simple: The assembler can do the counting. Here's the notation:

```
VidIDStr  DB  ' The installed video board is: '
LVidIDStr EQU $-VidIDStr
```

The first statement is nothing more than a simple string constant definition that we've been using all along. The second statement is a new kind of statement, an *equate*, which looks a lot like a data definition but is not.

A data definition sets aside and initializes an area of memory to some value. An equate, by contrast, generates a value similar to a simple constant in such languages as Pascal. An equate allocates no memory, but instead generates a value that is stored in the assembler's symbol table. This value may then be used anywhere a literal constant of that type may be used.

Here, we're using an equate to generate a value giving us the length of the string defined immediately before the equate. The expression **$-VidIDStr** resolves to the difference between two addresses: One is the address of the first byte of the string variable **VidIDStr,** and the other is the *current location counter*, the assembler's way of keeping track of the code and data it's generating. (The current location counter bears *no relation whatsoever* to IP, the instruction pointer!) When the assembler is generating information (either code or data) inside a segment, it begins with a counter set to zero for the start of the segment. As it works its way through the segment, generating code or allocating data, it increments this value by one for each byte of generated code or allocated data.

The expression **$-VidIDStr** is evaluated immediately after the string **VidIDStr** is allocated. This means the assembler's current location counter is pointing to the first byte *after* **VidIDStr**. Because the variable name **VidIDStr** itself resolves to the address of **VidIDStr**, and **$** resolves to the location counter immediately after **VidIDStr** is allocated, the expression **$-VidIDStr** evaluates to the length of **VidIDStr**. Even if you add or delete characters to the contents of **VidIDStr**, the length count will always come out correct, because the calculation always subtracts the address of the beginning of the string from the address just past the end of the string.

This mechanism is used to pass a reliable string length to DOS when using DOS call 40H in the **Write** macro. The **Write** macro illustrates an advance in another way:

```
%macro   Write 2 ;ShowIt,ShowLength
      mov BX,1   ; Selects DOS file handle 1: Standard Output
      mov CX,%2  ; ShowLength: Length of string passed in CX
      mov DX,%1  ; Showit: Offset address of string passed in DX
      mov AH,40H ; Select DOS service 40: Print String
      int 21H    ; Call DOS
%endmacro
```

This is a mechanism different from the one we used in the earliest iterations of the EAT program. If you recall, when using DOS service 09H, you had to mark the end of a string passed to DOS with a dollar sign symbol. This was a crude holdover from CP/M, and more modern DOS programs all use DOS service 40H. This allows you to display strings containing dollar signs—not a feature without value in some applications, such as financial programming.

Here's how you use DOS interrupt 21H service 40H: You must pass the offset address of the string in DX, the length of the string in CX, and a *file handle* in BX. I won't explain file handles in detail in this book, but any good DOS reference will be adequate in picking up the details. By passing the handle of a disk-based text file to DOS service 40H, you can write text to a disk-based text file instead of to the screen.

As given, **Write** uses standard file handle 1, which is *standard output*. Standard output is by default directed to the screen display, but you can use various DOS commands to redirect standard output to other destinations, such as the printer or a disk file.

Finally, here is the whole of the INFO.ASM program:

```
; Source name    : INFO.ASM
; Executable name : INFO.COM
; Code model:     : Real mode flat model
; Version         : 2.0
; Created date    : 9/18/1999
; Last update     : 9/19/1999
; Author          : Jeff Duntemann
; Description     : A utility to query and display information about
;                   the installed PC video adapter, programmed for
;                   real mode flat model, using NASM 0.98 and ALINK.
;                   This program demonstrates how lookup tables and
;                   numerous instructions are used.

[BITS 16]                    ; Set 16 bit code generation
[ORG 0100H]                  ; Set code start address to 100h (COM file)


[SECTION .text]              ; Section containing code

%include "BOOK\MYLIB.MAC"    ; Load in screen control macro library

START:                       ; This is where program execution begins:
      call VidCheck          ; Initialize all video information variables

      Clear VidSegment,ClearAtom,VidBufSize ; Clear the screen

      ; Here we display the name of the program and its author:
      Writeln IDString,LIDString    ; Display the program name
      Writeln AuthorStr,LAuthorStr  ; display the author name
      Newline

      ; Here we display the name of the installed video board:
      Write VidIDStr,LVidIDStr      ; Display the intro string
      mov BX,1            ; Select DOS file handle 1: Standard Output
      mov CX,27           ; The name strings are 27 bytes long
      mov DX,[BordName];  The string address is stored in BordName
      mov AH,40H          ; Service 40H: Write string to file
      int 21H             ; Call DOS to display to Standard Output
      Newline

      ; Here we display the segment address of the refresh buffer:
      Write OrgIDStr,LOrgIDStr ; Display the intro string
      mov AX,[VidSegment]      ; AX gets the value to convert to a string
      mov SI,DigitStr          ; String equivalent is written to DigitStr
      call Word2Str            ; Do the actual string conversion
      PokeChar DigitStr,'H',4  ; Append 'H' on the end of the string
      Writeln DigitStr,5       ; and display the string equivalent

      ; Here we display the size of the current text font:
      Write FontSzStr,LFontSzStr ; Display the intro string
      mov AL,[FontSize]          ; AL gets the value to convert to a string
      mov SI,DigitStr            ; String equivalent is written to DigitStr
```

```
        call Byte2Str          ; Do the actual string conversion
        PokeChar DigitStr,'H',2  ; Append 'H' on the end of the string
        Writeln DigitStr,3       ; and display the string equivalent

        ; Here we display the number of lines on the screen:
        Write ScrnLnStr,LScrnLnStr
        mov AL,[VisibleY]      ; AL gets the value to convert to a string
        mov SI,DigitStr        ; String equivalent is written to DigitStr
        call Byte2Str          ; Do the actual string conversion
        PokeChar DigitStr,'H',2 ; Append 'H' on the end of the string
        Writeln DigitStr,3      ; and display the string equivalent

        ;Finally, we display the size of the video refresh buffer:
        Write BufSizStr,LBufSizStr ; Display the intro string
        mov AX,[VidBufSize]      ; AX gets the value to convert to a string
        mov SI,DigitStr          ; String equivalent is written to DigitStr
        call Word2Str            ; Do the actual string conversion
        PokeChar DigitStr,'H',4  ; Append 'H' on the end of the string
        Writeln DigitStr,5       ; and display the string equivalent
        Newline

        mov AH,4CH              ; Terminate process DOS service
        mov AL,0               ; Pass this value back to ERRORLEVEL
        int 21H                ; Control returns to DOS


;--------------------------------------------------------------
;  Byte2Str -- Converts a byte passed in AL to a string at
;         DS:SI
;  Last update 9/18/99
;
;  1 entry point:
;
;  Byte2Str:
;   Caller must pass:
;   AL : Byte to be converted
;   DS : Segment of destination string
;   SI : Offset of destination string
;
;  This routine converts 8-bit values to 2-digit hexadecimal
;   string representations at DS:SI.
;--------------------------------------------------------------

Byte2Str:
        mov DI,AX              ; Duplicate byte in DI
        and DI,000FH          ; Mask out high 12 bits of DI
        mov BX,Digits         ; Load offset of Digits into DI
        mov AH,BYTE [BX+DI]   ; Load digit from table into AH
        mov [SI+1],AH         ;  and store digit into string
        xor AH,AH             ; Zero out AH
        mov DI,AX             ; And move byte into DI
```

```
;     shr DI,4           ; This can do the four shifts on 286 and later
      shr DI,1           ; Shift high nybble of byte to
      shr DI,1           ;  low nybble
      shr DI,1
      shr DI,1
      mov AH,BYTE [BX+DI] ; Load digit from table into AH
      mov [SI],AH        ;  and store digit into string
      ret                ; We're done—go home!


;----------------------------------------------------------------
;  Word2Str -- Converts a word passed in AX to a string at
;         DS:SI
;  Last update 9/19/99
;
;  1 entry point:
;
;  Word2Str:
;   Caller must pass:
;   AX : Word value (16 bits) to be converted
;   DS : Segment of destination string
;   SI : Offset of destination string
;----------------------------------------------------------------

Word2Str:
      mov CX,AX      ; Save a copy of convertee in CX
      xchg AH,AL     ; Swap high and low AX bytes to do high first
      call Byte2Str  ; Convert AL to string at DS:SI
      add SI,2       ; Bump SI to point to second 2 characters
      mov AX,CX      ; Reload convertee into AX
      call Byte2Str  ; Convert AL to string at DS:SI
      ret            ; And we're done!


;----------------------------------------------------------------
;  VidCheck -- Identifies display board & display parameters
;  Last update 9/18/99
;
;  1 entry point:
;
;  VidCheck:
;   Caller need pass no parameters.
;   VidCheck identifies the installed display board by
;   calling DispID. It then calculates numerous display
;   information values, which it then stores in the block
;   of display information variables in the data segment.
;----------------------------------------------------------------

VidCheck:
      ; First task is to figure out which board is on the bus:
      call DispID       ; Ask BIOS for adapter code; returns in AL
```

```
        mov [DispType],AL ; Store display adapter code in DispType

        ; Next we determine the font size currently in force:
        cmp AL,0AH              ; See if board is an MCGA
        jl  TryOld              ; If less than code 0AH, it's not an MCGA
        mov [FontSize],BYTE 16  ; MCGA supports *only* 16 pixel text font
        jmp GetName             ; Jump ahead to look up adapter name string
TryOld: cmp [DispType],BYTE 01  ; Is the display adapter code 1, for MDA?
        jne TryCGA              ; If not, go test for CGA code 2
        mov [FontSize],BYTE 14  ; MDA uses *only* 14-pixel text font
        jmp GetName             ; Jump ahead to look up adapter name string
TryCGA: cmp [DispType],BYTE 02  ; Is the display adapter code 2, for CGA?
        jne TryVGA              ; If not, go test for EGA/VGA font size
        mov [FontSize],BYTE 08  ; CGA uses *only* 8-pixel text font
        jmp GetName             ; Jump ahead to look up adapter name string
TryVGA: mov AH,11H              ; Select VIDEO Get Font Information subservice
        mov AL,30H              ;  requires AH = 11H and AL = 30H
        mov BH,0                ; 0 = Get info about current font
        int 10H                 ; Call VIDEO
        mov [FontSize],CL       ; Font size in pixels is returned in CL

        ; Next we get the name string for the board from the info table:
GetName:
        mov AL,[DispType]       ; Load display adapter code into AL
        xor AH,AH               ; Zero AH so we don't copy trash into DI
        mov DI,AX               ; Copy AX (with code in AL) into DI
        mov CL,5                ; We must shift the code 5 bits to mult. by 32
        shl DI,CL               ; Multiply code by 32 to act as table index
        mov BX,VidInfoTbl       ; Load address of origin table into BX
        mov [BordName],BX       ; Save pointer to video info. table in BordName
        add [BordName],DI       ; Add offset into table to right element

        ; Next we get the refresh buffer segment from the table:
        mov AX,[BX+DI+27]       ; Index into table past name string to segment
        mov [VidSegment],AX     ; Store segment from table to VidSegment variable

        ; Here we calculate the number of lines on-screen from font size:
        xor AH,AH               ; Make sure AH has no trash in it
        mov AL,[FontSize]       ; Load the font size in pixels into AL
        cmp AL,8                ; Is it the 8-pixel font?
        jne Try14               ; If not, try the 14-pixel font
        mov AL,1                ; The 8-pixel font is table offset 1
        jmp ReadLns             ; Jump ahead to read screen lines from table
Try14:  cmp AL,14               ; Is it the 14-pixel font?
        jne Do16                ; If not, it has to be the 16-pixel font
        mov AL,2                ; The 14-pixel font is table offset 2
        jmp ReadLns             ; Jump ahead to read screen lines from table
Do16:   mov AL,3                ; The 16-pixel font is table offset 3
ReadLns:
        add DI,AX               ; Add font size offset to table element offset
        mov AL,[BX+DI+28]       ; Load the screen lines value from the table
```

```
            mov [VisibleY],AL       ; and store it in the VisibleY variable
            mov AH,[VisibleX]       ; Load the screen columns value to AH
            xchg AH,AL              ; Exchange AH & AL for 0-basing
            dec AL                  ; Subtract one from column count for 0-basing
            dec AH                  ; Subtract one from line count for zero-basing
            mov [LRXY],AX           ; And store 0-based X,Y word into LRXY variable

            ; Finally, we calculate the size of the refresh buffer in bytes:
            mov AL,[VisibleY]       ; We multiply screen lines time screen columns
            mul BYTE [VisibleX]     ; times 2 (for attributes) to get buffer size
            shl AX,1                ; Multiply lines * columns by 2
            mov [VidBufSize],AX     ; Store refresh buffer size in VidBufSize

            ret                     ; Return to caller


;----------------------------------------------------------------
;  DispID — Identifies the installed display adapter
;  Last update 9/18/99
;
;  1 entry point:
;
;  DispID:
;   Caller passes no parameters
;   Routine returns a code value in AX.
;   The codes are these:
;   0 : Adapter is unknown; recommend aborting
;   1 : MDA (Monochrome Display Adapter)
;   2 : CGA (Color Graphics Adapter)
;
;----------------------------------------------------------------

DispID:
            mov AH,1AH    ; Select PS/2 Identify Adapter Service
            xor AL,AL     ; Select Get Combination Code Subservice (AL=0)
            int 10H       ; Call VIDEO
            cmp AL,1AH    ; If AL comes back with 1AH, we have a PS/2
            jne TryEGA    ; If not, jump down to test for the EGA
            mov AL,BL     ; Put Combination Code into AL
            ret           ;  and go home!
TryEGA:     mov AH,12H    ; Select EGA Alternate Function
            mov BX,10H    ; Select Get Configuration Information subservice
            int 10H       ; Call VIDEO
            cmp BX,10H    ; If BX comes back unchanged, EGA is *not* there
            je  OldBords  ; Go see whether it's an MDA or CGA
            cmp BH,0      ; If BH = 0, it's an EGA/color combo
            je  EGAColor  ;  otherwise it's EGA/mono
            mov AL,5      ; Store code 5 for EGA mono
            ret           ;  and go home!
EGAColor:
            mov AL,4      ; Store code 4 for EGA color
```

```
        ret             ;  and go home!
OldBords:
        int 11H         ; Call Equipment Configuration interrupt
        and AL,30H      ; Mask out all but bits 4 & 5
        cmp AL,30H      ; If bits 4 & 5 are both =1, it's an MDA
        jne CGA         ;  otherwise it's a CGA
        mov AL,1        ; Store code 1 for MDA
        ret             ;  and go home!
CGA:    mov AL,2        ; Store code 2 for CGA
        ret             ;  and go home!


[SECTION .data]

;----------------------------------------------------------------
; DISPLAY INFORMATION VARIABLES
;
; The following block of variables all relate to the video
; system and are initialized by the VidCheck procedure:
;----------------------------------------------------------------
DispType    DB   0      ; Code for display adapter type
VidSegment  DW   0B000H ; Segment of installed display buffer
VidOrigin   DW   0      ; Offset for FAR pointer to refresh buffer
VisibleX    DB   80     ; Number of columns on screen
VisibleY    DB   25     ; Number of lines on screen
VidBufSize  DW   4000   ; Default to 25 X 80 X 2 (char & attribute)
FontSize    DB   8      ; Either 8, 14, or 16; default to 8
BordName    DW   0      ; NEAR pointer to name string of installed board
; 18H = 24D; 4FH = 79D; Combined 0-based X,Y of 80 x 25 screen LR corner:
LRXY        DW   184FH


;----------------------------------------------------------------
; DISPLAY ADAPTER INFORMATION LOOKUP TABLE
;
; This is the lookup table containing information on all legal
; display adapters. The first field in each element is a 26-
; character string containing a brief description of the
; adapter. The next field is the segment of the video refresh
; buffer. The last three fields are the number of screen lines
; an adapter displays when the 8-pixel, 14-pixel, and 16-pixel
; fonts are loaded, respectively. Note that not all adapters
; support all fonts, but a screen line count is given for all
; three fonts for all adapter types. Illegal combinations will
; not be accessed.
;----------------------------------------------------------------
VidInfoTbl DB    'No adapter identified     '  ; Code 0
           DW    0B000H
           DB    25,25,25
           DB    'Monochrome Display Adapter '  ; Code 1
           DW    0B000H
           DB    25,25,25
```

```
            DB    'Color Graphics Adapter   '  ; Code 2
            DW    0B800H
            DB    25,25,25
            DB    'Code 3: Undefined        '  ; Code 3
            DW    0B000H
            DB    25,25,25
            DB    'EGA with color monitor   '  ; Code 4
            DW    0B800H
            DB    43,25,25
            DB    'EGA with mono monitor    '  ; Code 5
            DW    0B000H
            DB    43,25,25
            DB    'Code 6: Undefined        '  ; Code 6
            DW    0B000H
            DB    25,25,25
            DB    'VGA with mono monitor    '  ; Code 7
            DW    0B000H
            DB    50,27,25
            DB    'VGA with color monitor   '  ; Code 8
            DW    0B800H
            DB    50,27,25
            DB    'Code 9: Undefined        '  ; Code 9
            DW    0B000H
            DB    25,25,25
            DB    'MCGA with digital color  '  ; Code 0AH
            DW    0B800H
            DB    25,25,25
            DB    'MCGA with monochrome     '  ; Code 0BH
            DW    0B000H
            DB    25,25,25
            DB    'MCGA with analog color   '  ; Code 0CH
            DW    0B800H
            DB    25,25,25

Digits      DB    '0123456789ABCDEF' ; Lookup table for numeric/string conv.


;--------------------------------------------------------------
; These two variables are screen-clear "atoms" useable by the
; Clear macro. The high byte is the display attribute, while
; the low byte is the character with which Clear fills the
; video refresh buffer to clear the screen.
;--------------------------------------------------------------
HToneAtom DW    07B0H     ; Clears screen to halftone pattern
ClearAtom DW    0720H     ; Clears screen to blanks


;--------------------------------------------------------------
; This is where all predefined string variables are stored.
;--------------------------------------------------------------
CRLF        DB    0DH,0AH   ; Newline string
IDString    DB    '>>>INFO V2.0'
LIDString   EQU   $-IDString
```

```
AuthorStr   DB    '  by Jeff Duntemann K7JPD'
LAuthorStr  EQU   $-AuthorStr
VidIDStr    DB    '  The installed video board is: '
LVidIDStr   EQU   $-VidIDStr
OrgIDStr    DB    '  The segment of the video refresh buffer is: '
LOrgIDStr   EQU   $-OrgIDStr
FontSzStr   DB    '  The size of the current text font is: '
LFontSzStr  EQU   $-FontSzStr
ScrnLnStr   DB    '  The number of lines currently on the screen is: '
LScrnLnStr  EQU   $-ScrnLnStr
BufSizStr   DB    '  The size of the refresh buffer in bytes is: '
LBufSizStr  EQU   $-BufSizStr
DigitStr    DB    '    '
LDigitStr   EQU   $-DigitStr
```

CHAPTER 11

Stringing Them Up

Those Amazing String Instructions

Most people, having learned a little assembly language, grumble about the seemingly huge number of instructions it takes to do anything useful. By and large, this is a legitimate gripe—and the major reason people write programs in higher-level languages such as Pascal and Basic. The x86 instruction set, on the other hand, is full of surprises, and the surprise most likely to make apprentice assembly programmers gasp is the instruction group we call the *string instructions*.

They alone of all the instructions in the x86 instruction set have the power to deal with long sequences of bytes or words at one time. (In assembly language, any contiguous sequence of bytes or words in memory may be considered a string—not simply sequences of human-readable characters.) More amazingly, they deal with these large sequences of bytes or words in an extraordinarily compact way: by executing an instruction loop entirely *inside* the CPU! A string instruction is, in effect, a complete instruction loop baked into a single instruction.

The string instructions are subtle and complicated, and I won't be able to treat them exhaustively in this book. Much of what they do qualifies as an advanced topic. Still, you can get a good start on understanding the string instructions by using them to build some simple tools to add to your video toolkit.

Besides, for my money, the string instructions are easily the single most fascinating aspect of assembly language work.

The Notion of an Assembly Language String

Words fail us sometimes by picking up meanings as readily as a magnet picks up iron filings. The word *string* is a major offender here. It means roughly the same thing in all computer programming, but there is a multitude of small variations on that single theme. If you learned about strings in Turbo Pascal, you'll find that what you know isn't totally applicable when you program in C, or Basic, or assembly.

So here's the Big View: A *string* is any contiguous group of bytes, of any arbitrary size up to the size of a segment. The main concept of a string is that its component bytes are right there in a row, with no interruptions.

That's pretty fundamental. Most higher-level languages build on the string concept in several ways. Turbo Pascal treats strings as a separate data type, limited to 255 characters in length, with a single byte at the start of the string to indicate how many bytes are in the string. In C, a string may be longer than 255 bytes, and it has no length byte in front of it. Instead, a C string is said to end when a byte with a binary value of 0 is encountered. In Basic, strings are stored in something called *string space*, which has a lot of built-in code machinery associated with it.

When you begin working in assembly, you have to give up all that high-level language stuff. Assembly strings are just contiguous regions of memory. They start at some specified address, go for some number of bytes, and stop. There is no length byte to tell how many bytes are in the string and no standard boundary characters such as binary 0 to indicate where a string starts or ends.

You can certainly write assembly language routines that allocate Turbo Pascal–style strings or C-style strings and manipulate them. To avoid confusion, however, you must think of the data operated on by your routines to be Pascal or C strings rather than assembly strings.

Turning Your "String Sense" Inside-Out

Assembly strings have no boundary values or length indicators. They can contain any value at all, including binary 0. In fact, you really have to stop thinking of strings in terms of specific regions in memory. You should instead think of strings in much the same way you think of segments: in terms of the register values that define them.

It's slightly inside-out compared to how you think of strings in such languages as Pascal, but it works: *You've got a string when you set up a pair of registers to point to one* (or a single register, if you're working in real mode or protected mode flat model). And once you point to a string, the length of that string is defined by the value you place in register CX.

This is key: Assembly strings are wholly defined by values you place in registers. There is a set of assumptions about strings and registers baked into the silicon of the CPU. When you execute one of the string instructions (as I describe a little later), the CPU uses those assumptions to determine which area of memory it reads from or writes to.

Source Strings and Destination Strings

There are two kinds of strings in assembly work. *Source strings* are strings that you read from. *Destination strings* are strings that you write to. The difference between the two is *only* a matter of registers; source strings and destination strings can overlap. In fact, the very same region of memory can be *both* a source string and a destination string, all at the same time.

Here are the assumptions the CPU makes about strings when it executes a string instruction:

- A source string is pointed to by DS:SI.
- A destination string is pointed to by ES:DI.
- The length of both kinds of strings is the value you place in CX.
- Data coming from a source string or going to a destination string must pass through register AX.

Note that the use of segment registers mostly applies to real mode segmented model. In real mode flat model, as you should know by now, all the segment registers contain the same value, and are therefore basically factored out of consideration for many things, string work included. (The same is true of protected mode flat model, as you'll learn in later chapters.) The CPU can recognize both a source string and a destination string simultaneously, because DS:SI and ES:DI can hold values independent of one another. However, because there is only one CX register, the length of source and destination strings must be identical when they are used simultaneously, as in copying a source string to a destination string.

One way to remember the difference between source strings and destination strings is by their offset registers. *SI* means "source index," and *DI* means "destination index."

REP STOSW, the Software Machine Gun

The best way to cement all that string background information in your mind is to see a string instruction at work. In this section I lay out a very useful video display tool that makes use of the simplest string instruction, **STOSW**. (Think: **STO**re **S**tring by **W**ord.) The discussion involves something called a *prefix*, which I haven't gone into yet. Bear with me for now. We'll discuss prefixes in a little while.

Machine-Gunning the Video Display Buffer

The **ClrScr** procedure we discussed earlier relied on BIOS to handle the actual clearing of the screen. BIOS is very much a black box, and we're not expected to know how it works. The trouble with BIOS is that it only knows how to clear the screen to blanks. Some programs (such as the most recent releases of Borland/Turbo Pascal) give themselves a stylish, sculpted look by clearing the screen to one of the PC's halftone characters, which are character codes 176 to 178. BIOS can't do this. If you want the halftone look, you'll have to do it yourself. It doesn't involve anything more complex than replicating a single word value (two bytes) into every position in your video refresh buffer.

Such things should always be done in tight loops. The obvious way is to put the video refresh buffer segment into the extra segment register ES, the refresh buffer offset into DI, the number of words in your refresh buffer into CX, the word value to clear the buffer to into AX, and then code up a tight loop this way:

```
Clear:  mov ES:[DI],AX  ; Copy AX to ES:DI
        inc DI          ; Bump DI to next *word* in buffer,
        inc DI          ;   which means incrementing by 1 twice
        dec CX          ; Decrement CX by one position
        jnz Clear       ; And loop again until CX is 0
```

This will work. It's even tolerably fast, especially on newer CPUs. But *all* of the preceding code is equivalent to this one single instruction:

```
rep stosw
```

Really. *Really.*

There are two parts to this instruction, actually. As I said, **REP** is a new type of critter, called a *prefix*. We'll get back to it. Right now, let's look at **STOSW**. The mnemonic means **STO**re **S**tring by **W**ord. Like all the string instructions, **STOSW** makes certain assumptions about some CPU registers. It works only on the destination string, so DS and SI are not involved. However, these assumptions must be respected and dealt with:

1. ES must be loaded with the segment address of the destination string (that is, the string into which data will be stored). This is automatically the case in flat model and does not have to be set up by you.

2. DI must be loaded with the offset address of the destination string. (Think: DI, the destination index.)

3. CX (think: the Count register) must be loaded with the number of times the copy of AX is to be stored into the string. Note that this does *not* mean the size of the string in bytes!

4. AX must be loaded with the word value to be stored into the string.

Executing the STOSW Instruction

Once you set up these four registers, you can safely execute a **STOSW** instruction. When you do, this is what happens:

1. The word value in AX is copied to the word at ES:DI.

2. DI is incremented by 2, such that ES:DI now points to the next word in memory following the one just written to.

Note that we're *not* machine-gunning here. *One* copy of AX gets copied to *one* word in memory. The DI register is adjusted so that it'll be ready for the *next* time **STOSW** is executed.

One very important point to remember is that CX is *not* decremented by **STOSW**. CX is decremented automatically *only* if you put the **REP** prefix in front of **STOSW**. Lacking the **REP** prefix, you have to do the decrementing yourself, either explicitly through **DEC** or through the **LOOP** instruction, as I explain a little later in this chapter.

So, you can't make **STOSW** run automatically without **REP**. However, you can, if you like, execute other instructions before executing another **STOSW**. As long as you don't disturb ES, DI, or CX, you can do whatever you wish. Then when you execute **STOSW** again, another copy of AX will go out to the location pointed to by ES:DI, and DI will be adjusted yet again. (You have to remember to decrement CX somehow.) Note that you can change AX if you like, but the changed value will be copied into memory. (You may want to do that—there's no law saying you have to fill a string with only one single value.)

However, this is like the difference between a semiautomatic weapon (which fires one round every time you press and release the trigger) and a fully automatic weapon, which fires rounds continually as long as you hold the trigger down. To make **STOSW** fully automatic, just hang the **REP** prefix ahead of it. What **REP** does is beautifully simple: It sets up the tightest of all tight loops completely *inside* the CPU and fires copies of AX into memory repeatedly (hence its name), incrementing DI by 2 each time and decrementing CX by 1, until CX is decremented down to 0. Then it stops, and when the smoke clears, you'll see that your whole destination string, however large, has been filled with copies of AX.

Man, now *that's* programming!

The following macro sets up and triggers **REP STOSW** to clear the video refresh buffer. **Clear** was designed to be used with the block of video information variables initialized by the **VidCheck** procedure I described in Chapter 10. It needs to be passed a far pointer (which is nothing more than a full 32-bit address consisting of a segment and an offset laid end to end) to the video refresh buffer, the word value to be blasted into the buffer, and the size of the buffer in bytes.

```
;----------------------------------------------------------------
;  CLEAR  -- Clears the entire visible screen buffer
;  Last update 9/20/99
;
;   Caller must pass:
;   In VidAddress: The address of the video refresh buffer
;   In ClearAtom:  The character/attribute pair to fill the
;                  buffer with. The high byte contains the
;                  attribute and the low byte the character.
;   In BufLength:  The number of *characters* in the visible
;                  display buffer, *not* the number of bytes!
;                  This is typically 2000 for a 25-line screen
;                  or 4000 for a 50-line screen.
;   Action:        Clears the screen by machine-gunning the
;                  character/attribute pair in AX into the
;                  display buffer beginning at VidAddress.
;----------------------------------------------------------------
%macro Clear 3  ;VidAddress,ClearAtom,BufLength
     les DI,[%1]   ; Load ES and DI from FAR pointer
     mov AX,%2     ; Load AX with word to blast into memory
     mov CX,%3     ; Load CX with length of buffer in bytes
     shr CX,1      ; Divide size of buffer by 2 for word count
     cld           ; Set direction flag so we blast up-memory
```

```
        rep stosw       ; Blast away!
        GotoXY 0,0      ; Move hardware cursor to UL corner of screen
    %endmacro
```

Don't let the notion of a far pointer throw you. It's jargon you're going to hear again and again, and this was a good point at which to introduce it. A pointer is an address, quite simply. A *near pointer* is an offset address only, used in conjunction with some value in some segment register that presumably doesn't change. All pointers to objects inside a real mode flat model program are by definition near pointers.

A *far pointer* is a pointer that consists of both a segment value and an off-set value, both of which may be changed at any time, working together. The video refresh buffer is not usually part of your data segment, so if you're going to work with it, you're probably going to have to access it with a far pointer, as we're doing here. Any time you need to reference something that exists outside the 64K boundaries of a real mode flat model program (such as your system's text video buffer), you're going to have to work with a far pointer.

Note that most of **Clear** is setup work. The **LES** instruction loads both ES and DI with the address of the destination string. The screen atom (display character plus attribute value) is loaded into AX.

The handling of CX deserves a little explanation. The value in **BufLength** is the size *in bytes* of the video refresh buffer. Remember, however, that CX is assumed to contain the number of times that AX is to be machine-gunned into memory. AX is a word, and a word is 2 bytes long. So, each time **STOSW** fires, 2 bytes of the video refresh buffer will be written to. Therefore, in order to tell CX how many times to fire the gun, we have to divide the size of the refresh buffer (which is given in bytes) by 2, in order to express the size of the refresh buffer in words.

As I explained in Chapter 10, dividing a value in a register by 2 is easy. All you have to do is shift the value of the register to the right by one bit. This what the **SHR CX,1** instruction does: divides CX by 2.

STOSW and the Direction Flag DF

Note the **CLD** instruction in the **Clear** macro. I've avoided mentioning it until now to avoid confusing you. Most of the time you'll be using **STOSW**, you'll want to run it "uphill" in memory; that is, from a lower memory address to a higher memory address. In **Clear**, you put the address of the start of the video refresh buffer into ES and DI, and then blast character/attribute pairs into memory at successively higher memory addresses. Each time **STOSW** fires a word into memory, DI is incremented twice to point to the *next higher* word in memory.

This is the logical way to work it, but it doesn't have to be done that way. **STOSW** can just as easily begin at a high address and move downward in memory. On each store into memory, DI can be *decremented* by 2 instead.

Which way **STOSW** fires—uphill toward successively higher addresses, or downhill toward successively lower addresses—is governed by one of the flags in the Flags register. This is the *Direction flag* DF. DF's sole job in life is to control the direction of certain instructions that, like **STOSW**, can move in one of two directions in memory. Most of these (like **STOSW**) are string instructions.

The sense of DF is this: When DF is *set* (that is, when DF has the value 1), **STOSW** and its fellow string instructions work downhill, from higher to lower addresses. When DF is *cleared* (that is, when it has the value 0), **STOSW** and its siblings work uphill from lower to higher addresses. This in turn is simply the direction in which the DI register is adjusted: When DF is set, DI is decremented. When DF is cleared, DI is incremented.

The Direction flag defaults to 0 (uphill) when the CPU is reset. It is generally changed in one of two ways: with the **CLD** instruction, or with the **STD** instruction. **CLD** clears DF, and **STD** sets DF. (You should keep in mind when debugging that the **POPF** instruction can also change DF, by popping an entire new set of flags from the stack into the Flags register.) It's always a good idea to place the appropriate one of **CLD** or **STD** right before a string instruction to make sure that your machine gun fires in the right direction!

People sometimes get confused and think that DF also governs whether CX is incremented or decremented by the string instructions. Not so! Nothing in a string instruction ever increments CX! You place a count in CX and it counts down, period. DF has nothing to say about it.

The **Clear** macro is part of the MYLIB.MAC macro library on the CD-ROM for this book. As you build new macro tools, you might place them in MYLIB.MAC as well.

The Semiautomatic Weapon: STOSW without REP

I chose to show you **REP STOSW** first because it's dramatic in the extreme. But even more, it's actually simpler to use **REP** than not to use **REP**. **REP** simplifies string processing from the programmer's perspective, because it brings the instruction loop *inside* the CPU. You can use the **STOSW** instruction without **REP**, but it's a little more work. The work involves setting up the instruction loop outside the CPU and making sure it's correct.

Why bother? Simply this: With **REP STOSW**, you can only store the *same* value into the destination string. Whatever you put into AX before executing **REP STOSW** is the value that gets fired into memory CX times. **STOSW** can be used to store *different* values into the destination string by firing it semiautomatically and changing the value in AX between each squeeze of the trigger.

Also, by firing each character individually, you can change the value in DI periodically to break up the data transfer into separated regions of memory instead of one contiguous area as you must with **REP STOSW**. This may be hard to picture until you see it in action. The SHOWCHAR program listing I present a little later will give you a for instance that will make it instantly clear what I mean.

You lose a little time in handling the loop yourself, outside the CPU. This is because there is a certain amount of time spent in fetching the loop's instruction bytes from memory. Still, if you keep your loop as tight as you can, you don't lose an objectionable amount of speed, especially on the newer processors like the Pentium.

Who Decrements CX?

Early in my experience with assembly language, I recall being massively confused about where and when the CX register was decremented when using string instructions. It's a key issue, especially when you *don't* use the **REP** prefix.

When you use **REP STOSW** (or **REP** with any of the string instructions), CX is decremented automatically, by 1, for each memory access the instruction makes. And once CX gets itself decremented down to 0, **REP STOSW** detects that CX is now 0 and stops firing into memory. Control then passes down to the next instruction in line. But take away **REP**, and the automatic decrementing of CX stops. So, also, does the automatic detection of when CX has been counted down to 0.

Obviously, something has to decrement CX, since CX governs how many times the string instruction accesses memory. If **STOSW** doesn't do it—you guessed it—you have to do it somewhere else, with another instruction.

The obvious way to decrement CX is to use **DEC CX.** And the obvious way to determine if CX has been decremented to 0 is to follow the **DEC CX** instruction with a **JNZ** (Jump if Not Zero) instruction. **JNZ** tests the Zero flag ZF and jumps back to the **STOSW** instruction until ZF becomes true. And ZF becomes true when a **DEC** instruction causes its operand (here, CX) to become 0.

The LOOP Instructions

With all that in mind, consider the following assembly language instruction loop. Note that I've split it into three parts by inserting blank lines:

```
DoChar: stosw          ; Note that there's no REP prefix!

        add  AL,'1'  ; Bump the character value in AL up by 1
        aaa            ; Adjust AX to make this a BCD addition
        add  AL,'0'  ; Basically, put binary 3 in AL's high nybble
        mov  AH,07   ; Make sure our attribute is still 7

        dec  CX      ; Decrement the count by 1..
        jnz  DoChar  ; ..and loop again if CX > 0
```

Ignore the block of instructions in the middle for the time being. What it does is what I suggested could be done a little earlier: change AX inbetween each store of AX into memory. I'll explain in detail shortly. Look instead (for now) to see how the loop runs. **STOSW** fires, AX is modified, and then CX is decremented. The **JNZ** instruction tests to see if the **DEC** instruction has forced CX to zero. If so, the Zero flag ZF is set, and the loop will terminate. But until ZF is set, the jump is made to the label **DoChar**, where **STOSW** fires yet again.

There is a simpler way, using an instruction I haven't discussed until now: **LOOP**. The **LOOP** instruction combines the decrementing of CX with a test and jump based on ZF. It looks like this:

```
DoChar:  stosw          ; Note that there's no REP prefix!

         add   AL,'1'   ; Bump the character value in AL up by 1
         aaa            ; Adjust AX to make this a BCD addition
         add   AL,'0'   ; Basically, put binary 3 in AL's high nybble
         mov   AH,07    ; Make sure our attribute is still 7

         loop  DoChar   ; Go back & do another char until CX goes to 0
```

The **LOOP** instruction first decrements CX by 1. It then checks the Zero flag to see if the decrement operation forced CX to zero. If so, it falls through to the next instruction. If not (that is, if ZF remains 0, indicating that CX was still greater than 0), **LOOP** branches to the label specified as its operand.

So, the loop keeps looping the **LOOP** until CX counts down to 0. At that point, the loop is finished, and execution falls through and continues with the next instruction following the loop.

Displaying a Ruler on the Screen

As a useful demonstration of when it makes sense to use **STOSW** without **REP** (but with **LOOP**) let me offer you another item for your video toolkit.

The **Ruler** macro which follows displays a repeating sequence of ascending digits from 1 at some selectable location on your screen. In other words, you can display a string of digits like this at the top of a window:

```
12345678901234567890123456789012345678901234567890
```

This might allow you to determine where in the horizontal dimension of the window a line begins or some character falls. The macro allows you to specify how long the ruler is, in digits, and where on the screen it will be displayed.

A call to **Ruler** would look like this:

```
Ruler VidOrigin,20,80,15,5
```

This invocation (assuming you had defined **VidOrigin** to be the address of the start of the video refresh buffer in your machine) places a 20-character long ruler at position 15,5. The "80" argument indicates to **Ruler** that your screen is 80 characters wide. If you had a wider or narrower text screen, you would have to change the "80" to reflect the true width of your screen in text mode.

Don't just read the code inside **Ruler**! Load it up into a copy of EAT5.ASM, and display some rulers on the screen. You don't learn half as much by just reading assembly code as you do by loading and using it!

```
;-----------------------------------------------------------
;   RULER  -- Displays a "1234567890"-style ruler on-screen
;   Last update 9/16/99
;
;   Caller must pass:
;   In VidAddress: The address of the start of the video buffer
;   In Length:     The length of the ruler to be displayed
;   In ScreenW:    The width of the current screen (usually 80)
;   In ScreenY:    The line of the screen where the ruler is
;                  to be displayed (0-24)
;   In ScreenX:    The row of the screen where the ruler should
;                  start (0-79)
;   Action:        Displays an ASCII ruler at ScreenX,ScreenY.
;-----------------------------------------------------------
%macro   Ruler  5 ;VidAddress,Length,ScreenW,ScreenX,ScreenY
         les    DI,[%1] ; Load video address to ES:DI
         mov    AL,%5   ; Move Y position to AL
         mov    AH,%3   ; Move screen width to AH
         imul   AH      ; Do 8-bit multiply AL*AH to AX
         add    DI,AX   ; Add Y offset into vidbuff to DI
         add    DI,%4   ; Add X offset into vidbuf to DI
         shl    DI,1    ; Multiply by two for final address
         mov    CX,%2   ; CX monitors the ruler length
         mov    AH,07   ; Attribute 7 is "normal" text
         mov    AL,'1'  ; Start with digit "1"

%%DoChar: stosw        ; Note that there's no REP prefix!
          add   AL,'1' ; Bump the character value in AL up by 1
          aaa          ; Adjust AX to make this a BCD addition
          add   AL,'0' ; Basically, put binary 3 in AL's high nybble
          mov   AH,07  ; Make sure our attribute is still 7
          loop  %%DoChar ; Go back & do another char until BL goes to 0
%endmacro
```

Over and above the **LOOP** instruction, there's a fair amount of new assembly technology at work here that could stand explaining. Let's detour from the string instructions for a bit and take a closer look.

Simple Multiplies with IMUL

Ruler can put its ruler anywhere on the screen at all, to a position passed as **ScreenX** and **ScreenY**. It's not using **GotoXY**, either. It's actually calculating a position in the video refresh buffer where the ruler characters must be placed—and then using **STOSW** to place them there.

Locations in the text video refresh buffer are always expressed as offsets from a single segment address that is either B000H or B800H. The algorithm for determining the offset in bytes for any given *X* and *Y* values looks like this:

```
Offset = ((Y * width in characters of a screen line) + X) * 2
```

Pretty obviously, you have to move *Y* lines down in the screen buffer, and then move *X* bytes over from the left margin of the screen to reach your *X,Y* position.

The trickiest part of implementing the algorithm lies in multiplying the *Y* value by the screen width. There is an instruction to do the job, **IMUL**, but it's a little quirky and (as assembly instructions go) not very fast.

It is, however, fast enough for what we're doing here, which is just positioning the ruler somewhere on the screen. The positioning only needs to be done once, not many times within a tight loop. So, even if **IMUL** is slow as instructions go (and it's much faster than it used to be on ancient machines like the 8086 and 8088), when you only need to use it to set up something else, it's certainly fast enough.

IMUL *always* operates in conjunction with the AX register. In every case, the destination for the product value is AX, or else AX and DX for products larger than 32,767.

On the simpler CPUs operating in real mode, there are basically two variations on **IMUL**, and the difference turns on the size of the operands. If you are multiplying two 8-bit quantities, you can put one in AL and the other in some 8-bit register or memory location. The product will be placed in AX. If you are multiplying two 16-bit quantities, one can be placed in AX and one in a 16-bit register or memory location. The product from multiplying two 16-bit quantities is too large to fit in a single 16-bit register, so the low-order 16 bits are placed in AX, and the high-order 16 bits are placed in DX. You have no control over the destination; it's either AX or AX:DX. Also, one of the operands *must* be in AL (for 8-bit multiples) or AX (for 16-bit multiples). You have no control over that; it's impossible to multiply (for example) CX x BX, or DX x DS:[BX].

One very common bug you may commit when using **IMUL** is simply forgetting that when given 16-bit operands, **IMUL** changes the value in DX. The easiest way to avoid this problem is to use **IMUL** in its 8-bit mode whenever possible, which is when *both* multiplier and multiplicand are less than 256. If either operand is 16 bits in size, DX will be altered.

Here are some examples of some legal forms of **IMUL**:

```
imul  byte [bx] ; multiplies AL x byte at DS:[BX]
imul  bh        ; multiplies AL x BH

imul  word [bx] ; multiplies AX x word at DS:[BX]
imul  bx        ; multiplies AX x BX
```

In the first two lines, the destination for the product is AX. In the second two lines, the destination for the product is DX:AX

IMUL sets two flags in those cases where the product is larger than the two operands. The flags involved are the Carry flag CF and the Overflow flag OF. For example, if you're multiplying two 8-bit operands and the product is larger than 8 bits, both CF and OF will be set. Otherwise, the two flags will be cleared.

Now, why the final multiplication by 2? Keep in mind that every character position in the screen buffer is represented by 2 bytes: One character byte and one attribute byte. So, moving X characters from the left margin actually moves X x 2 bytes into the screen buffer. You might think of an 80-character line on the screen as being 80 characters long, but it's actually 160 characters long in the screen buffer, to account for the invisible attribute bytes.

This multiplication by 2 is done by using the **SHL** instruction to shift DI to the left by one bit. As I explained in Chapter 10, this is exactly the same as multiplying DI by 2.

The Limitations of Macro Arguments

There's another problem you will eventually run into if you're like most people. Given the macro header for **Ruler**:

```
%macro Ruler 5 ;VidAddress,Length,ScreenW,ScreenX,ScreenY
```

you might be tempted to write something like this:

```
mov  al,%5
imul %3
```

No go! The assembler will call you on it, complaining of an *illegal immediate*. What went wrong? You can freely use constructions like these:

```
mov  al,%5
add  di,%4
cmp  al,%2
```

All of these use arguments from the macro header. So what's that assembler complaining about? The problem here is that on the simpler CPUs, the **IMUL** instruction cannot work with immediate operands. (Starting with the 386, a separate form of **IMUL** can take an immediate operand.) And this isn't just a problem with **IMUL**; *all* instructions that cannot work with immediate operands will reject a macro argument under these circumstances.

And "these circumstances" involve the way that the macro is invoked. In an early test version of the Ruler macro that used the **IMUL %3** instruction shown previously, I tried to use the following line, which invokes the macro to display a ruler:

```
Ruler VidOrigin,20,80,50,10 ; Draw ruler
```

It didn't work! Except for the video origin address argument, all of these arguments are numeric literals. A numeric literal, when used in an assembly language instruction, is called *immediate data*. When the macro is expanded, the argument you pass to the macro is substituted into the actual instruction that uses a macro argument, just as you passed it to the macro.

In other words, if you pass the value 10 in the %5 argument (ScreenY), the instruction **MOV AL,%5** becomes **MOV AL,10** once the macro is expanded by the assembler. Now, **MOV AL,10** is a completely legal instruction. But if you pass the literal value 80 in the %3 argument (ScreenW), you cannot use **IMUL %3**, because after expansion this becomes **IMUL 80**, which is not a legal instruction on anything older than the 386.

The problem is *not* that you're using macro arguments with **IMUL**. The problem is that you're passing a numeric literal in a macro argument to an instruction that (in the form we're using it) cannot accept immediate data.

The version of **Ruler** given in MYLIB.MAC loads the %3 (ScreenW) argument into AH using a **MOV** instruction. This means that you can use numeric literals when invoking **Ruler**. Using literals saves memory by making memory variables unnecessary, and if you'd prefer to define a meaningful name for the screen width rather than hard coding the value 80 in the source (which is unwise), you can define a symbol called **ScreenWidth** as an *equate*. I explained equates at the end of Chapter 10. The SHOWCHAR.ASM routine defines a **ScreenWidth** value as an equate.

Adding ASCII Digits

Once the correct offset into the buffer for the ruler's beginning is calculated in DI (and once we set up initial values for CX and AX), we're ready to start making rulers.

Immediately before the **STOSW** instruction, we load the ASCII digit '1' into AL. Note that the instruction **MOV AL,'1'** does *not* move the numeric value 01 into AL! The '1' is an ASCII character, and the character '1' (the "one" digit) has a numeric value of 31H, or 49 decimal.

This becomes a problem immediately after we store the digit '1' into video memory with **STOSW**. After digit '1,' we need to display digit '2,' and to do that we need to change the value stored in AL from '1' to '2.'

Ordinarily, you can't just add '1' to '1' and get '2'; 31H + 31H will give you 62H, which (when seen as an ASCII character) is lowercase letter *b*, *not* '2'! However, in this case the x86 instruction set comes to the rescue, in the form of a somewhat peculiar instruction called **AAA**, **A**djust **A**L after BCD **A**ddition.

What **AAA** does is allow us, in fact, to add ASCII character digits rather than numeric values. **AAA** is one of a group of instructions called the BCD instructions, so called because they support arithmetic with Binary Coded Decimal (BCD) values. BCD is just another way of expressing a numeric value, somewhere between a pure binary value like 01 and an ASCII digit like '1.' A BCD value is a 4-bit value, occupying the low nybble of a byte. It expresses values between 0 and 9 *only*. (That's what the "decimal" part of "Binary Coded Decimal" indicates.) It's possible to express values greater than 9 (from 9 to 15, actually) in 4 bits, but those additional values are not valid BCD values. See Figure 11.1.

The value 31H is a valid BCD value, because the low nybble contains 1. BCD is a 4-bit numbering system, and the high nybble (which in the case of 31H contains a 3) is ignored. In fact, all of the ASCII digits from '0' through '9' may be considered legal BCD values, because in each case the characters' low 4 bits contain a valid BCD value. The 3 stored in the high four bits of each digit is ignored.

So, if there were a way to perform BCD addition on the 86-family CPUs, adding '1' and '1' would indeed give us '2' because '1' and '2' can be manipulated as legal BCD values.

AAA (and several other instructions I don't have room to discuss here) gives us that ability to perform BCD math. The actual technique may

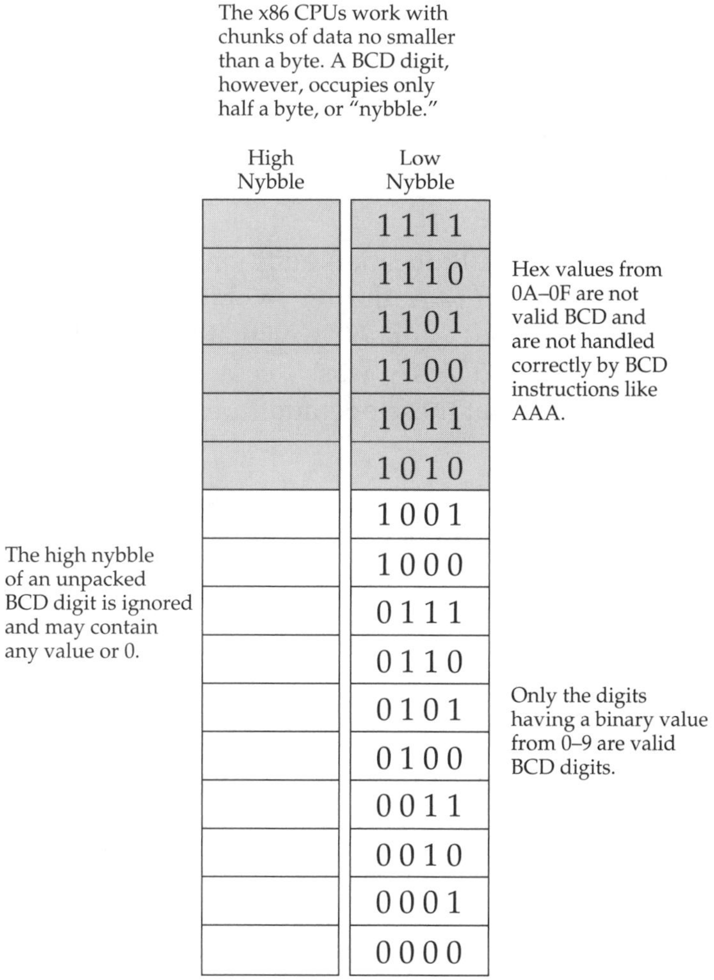

The x86 CPUs work with
chunks of data no smaller
than a byte. A BCD digit,
however, occupies only
half a byte, or "nybble."

High Nybble	Low Nybble	
	1 1 1 1	
	1 1 1 0	Hex values from 0A–0F are not valid BCD and are not handled correctly by BCD instructions like AAA.
	1 1 0 1	
	1 1 0 0	
	1 0 1 1	
	1 0 1 0	
	1 0 0 1	
	1 0 0 0	
	0 1 1 1	
	0 1 1 0	
	0 1 0 1	Only the digits having a binary value from 0–9 are valid BCD digits.
	0 1 0 0	
	0 0 1 1	
	0 0 1 0	
	0 0 0 1	
	0 0 0 0	

The high nybble
of an unpacked
BCD digit is ignored
and may contain
any value or 0.

Figure 11.1 Unpacked BCD digits.

seem a little odd, but it does work. **AAA** is in fact a sort of a fudge factor, in that you execute **AAA** after performing an addition using the normal addition instruction **ADD**. **AAA** takes the results of the **ADD** instruction and forces them to come out right in terms of BCD math.

AAA basically does these two things:

- It forces the value in the low 4 bits of AL (which could be any value from 0 to F) to a value between 0 and 9 if they were greater than 9. This is done by adding 6 to AL and then forcing the high nybble of AL to 0. Obviously, if the low nybble of AL contains a valid BCD digit, the digit in the low nybble is left alone.

- If the value in AL had to be adjusted, it indicates that there was a carry in the addition, and thus AH is incremented. Also, the Carry flag CF is set to 1, as is the Auxiliary carry flag AF. Again, if the low nybble of AL contained a valid BCD digit when AAA was executed, AH is not incremented, and the two Carry flags are cleared (forced to 0) rather than set.

AAA thus facilitates base 10 (decimal) addition on the low nybble of AL. After AL is adjusted by **AAA**, the low nybble contains a valid BCD digit and the high nybble is 0. (But note well that this will be true *only* if the addition that preceded **AAA** was executed on two valid BCD operands! And ensuring that those operands are valid is *your* responsibility, not the CPU's!)

This allows us to add ASCII digits such as '1' and '2' using the **ADD** instruction. **Ruler** does this immediately after the **STOSW** instruction:

```
add  AL,'1'    ; Bump the character value in AL up by 1
aaa            ; Adjust AX to make this a BCD addition
```

If prior to the addition the contents of AL's low nybble were 9, adding '1' would make the value 0AH, which is not legal BCD. **AAA** would then adjust AL by adding 6 to AL and clearing the high nybble. Adding 6 to 0A would give 10, so once the high nybble is cleared the new value in AL would be 00. Also, AH would have been incremented by 1.

In **Ruler** we're not adding multiple columns but instead are simply rolling over a count in a single column and displaying the number in that column to the screen. Therefore, we just ignore the incremented value in AH and use AL alone.

Adjusting AAA's Adjustments

There is one problem: AAA clears the high nybble to 0. This means that adding '1' and '1' doesn't *quite* equal '2,' the displayable digit. Instead, AL becomes 02, which in ASCII is the dark "smiley face" character. To make AL a displayable ASCII digit again, we have to add 30H to AL. This is easy to do: Just add '0' to AL, which has a numeric value of 30H. So, adding '0' takes 02H back up to 32H, which is the numeric equivalent of the ASCII digit character '2.' This is the reason for the **ADD AL,'0'** instruction that immediately follows **AAA**.

There's a lot more to BCD math than what I've explained here. When you want to perform multiple-column BCD math, you have to take carries into account, which involves a new flag called the *Auxiliary carry flag* AF. There are also the **AAD**, **AAM**, and **AAS** instructions for adjusting AL after BCD divides, multiplications, and subtractions, respectively. The same general idea applies: All the BCD adjustment instructions force the standard binary arithmetic instructions to come out right for BCD operands.

And yet another problem: **AAA** increments AH whenever it finds a value in the low nybble of AL greater than 9. In **Ruler**, AH contains the text attribute we're using to display our ruler, and if AH is incremented, the attribute will change and we'll end up displaying parts of the ruler in different colors. This is why we have to do one last adjustment to **AAA**'s adjustments: We reassert our desired text attribute in AH each time we change the ASCII digit in AL.

An interesting thing to do is comment out the **ADD AL,'0'** instruction in the **Ruler** macro and then run the RULER.ASM test program. Another interesting thing to do (especially if you work on a color screen, as you almost certainly do) is to comment out the **MOV AH,07** instruction in **Ruler** and then run RULER.ASM. Details count, big time!

Ruler's Lessons

The **Ruler** macro is a good example of using **STOSW** *without* the **REP** prefix. We have to change the value in AX every time we store AX to memory, and thus can't use **REP STOSW**. Note that nothing is done to ES:DI or CX while changing the digit to be displayed, and thus the values stored in those registers are held over for the next execution of **STOSW**. **Ruler** is a good example of how **LOOP** works with **STOSW** to adjust CX downward and return control to the top of the loop. **LOOP**, in a sense, does outside the CPU what **REP** does inside the CPU: adjust CX and close the loop. Try to keep that straight in your head when using any of the string instructions!

Storing Data to Discontinuous Strings

Sometimes you have to break the rules. Until now I've been explaining the string instructions under the assumption that the destination string is always one continuous sequence of bytes in memory. This isn't necessarily the case. In addition to changing the value in AX between executions of **STOSW**, you can change the *destination address* as well. The end result is that you can store data to several different areas of memory within a single very tight loop.

Displaying an ASCII Table in a Big Hurry

I've created a small demo program to show you what I mean. It's not as useful a tool as the **Ruler** macro, but it makes its point and is easy to understand. The SHOWCHAR.ASM program clears the screen and shows a table containing all 256 ASCII characters, neatly displayed in four lines of 64 characters each. The table includes the "undisplayable" ASCII characters corresponding to the control characters whose values are less than 32. They are displayable from SHOWCHAR because the program writes them directly into video memory. Neither DOS nor BIOS are aware of the display of the control characters, so they have no opportunity to interpret or filter out those characters with special meanings.

SHOWCHAR.ASM introduces a number of new concepts and instructions, all related to program loops. (String instructions such as **STOSW** and program loops are intimately related.) Read over the main body of the SHOWCHAR.ASM program carefully. We go over it idea by idea through the next several pages.

```
; Source name      : SHOWCHAR.ASM
; Executable name  : SHOWCHAR.COM
; Code model:       : Real mode flat model
; Version          : 1.0
; Created date      : 9/18/1999
; Last update       : 9/18/1999
; Author            : Jeff Duntemann
; Description      : A simple example of a DOS .COM file programmed for
;                    real mode flat model, using NASM 0.98 and ALINK.
;                    This program demonstrates how multi-line macros are
;                    used with NASM.

[BITS 16]             ; Set 16 bit code generation
[ORG 0100H]           ; Set code start address to 100h (COM file)

[SECTION .text]       ; Section containing code

%include "MYLIB.MAC"  ; Load in screen control macro library

START:                ; This is where program execution begins:

    Clear VidOrigin,0720H,4000    ; Clear full video buffer to spaces
    ; Show a 64-character rule above the table display:
```

```
            Ruler VidOrigin,LineLen,ScrnWidth,0,LinesDown-1
            les  DI,[VidOrigin]          ; Put vid seg in ES & offset in DI
            add  DI,ScrnWidth*LinesDown*2 ; Start table display down a ways
            mov  CX,256      ; There are 256 chars in the ASCII set
            mov  AX,0700H    ; Start with char 0, attribute 7

DoLine:     mov  BL,LineLen  ; Each line will consist of 64 characters
DoChar:     stosw            ; Note that there's no REP prefix!
            jcxz AllDone     ; When the full set is printed, quit
            inc  AL          ; Bump the character value in AL up by 1
            dec  BL          ; Decrement the line counter by one
            loopnz DoChar    ; Go back & do another char until BL goes to 0
            add  DI,(ScrnWidth - LineLen)*2 ; Move DI to start of next line
            jmp  DoLine      ; Start display of the next line

AllDone:    GotoXY 0,12      ; Move hardware cursor down below char. table
            mov  AH,4CH      ; Terminate process DOS service
            mov  AL,0        ; Pass this value back to ERRORLEVEL
            int  21H         ; Control returns to DOS

[SECTION .data]             ; Section containing initialized data

LRXY     DW  184FH ; 18H = 24D; 4FH = 79D; 0-based XY of LR screen corner

VidOrigin DD  0B8000000H  ; Change to 0B0000000H if you have a mono CRT!
CRLF      DB  0DH,0AH

ScrnWidth EQU 80            ; Width of the screen in characters
LineLen   EQU 64            ; Length of one line of the ASCII table
LinesDown EQU 4             ; Number of lines down to start ASCII table
```

The Nature of Equates

You might remember (and it wouldn't hurt to go back and take another look) how we calculated the offset from the beginning of the video refresh buffer to the memory location corresponding to an arbitrary X,Y position on the screen. We used the **ADD** instruction, along with the **SHL** instruction to multiply by 2.

There is another way to perform calculations of that general sort in assembly work: by letting the assembler itself do them, while the program is being assembled. Take a look at the following line, lifted from SHOWCHAR.ASM:

```
add  DI,ScrnWidth*LinesDown*2 ; Start table display down a ways
```

This is new indeed. What can we make of this? What sort of an operand is **ScrnWidth*LinesDown*2**? The answer is that it's a simple integer operand, no different from the value 12, 169, or 15,324.

The key is to go back to SHOWCHAR and find out what **ScrnWidth** and **LinesDown** are. You might have thought that these were variables in memory, defined with the **DW** operator. Instead, they're something I touched on only briefly at the end of Chapter 10: *equates*. Equates are defined with the **EQU** operator, and if you find yourself confused over the differences between **EQU** and **DW**, don't despair. It's an easy enough thing to do.

One road to understanding harkens back to the Pascal language. What is the difference between a variable and a simple constant? A variable is located at one and only one particular place in memory. A simple constant, on the other hand, is a value dropped into the program anywhere it is used and exists at no particular place in memory. Simple constants are used mostly in expressions calculated by the compiler during compilation.

It's the same thing here. The **DW** and **DB** operators define and set aside areas of memory for storage of data. A **DW** exists somewhere at some address and only exists in one place. The **EQU**, by contrast, is a symbol you define mostly for the assembler's use. It sets aside no memory and has no particular address. Consider this line from SHOWCHAR:

```
LinesDown EQU   4    ; Number of lines down to start ASCII table
```

The value defined as **LinesDown** exists at no single place in the SHOW-CHAR program. It allocates no storage. It's actually a notation in the assembler's symbol table, telling the assembler to substitute the value 4 for the symbol **LinesDown**, anywhere it encounters the symbol **Lines-Down**. The same is true of the equates for **ScrnWidth** and **LineLen**.

When the assembler encounters equates in a program, it performs a simple textual substitution of the values assigned to the symbol defined in the equate. The symbol is dumped, and the value is dropped in. *Then* assembly continues, using the substituted values rather than the symbols. In a very real sense, the assembler is pausing to alter the source code when it processes an equate, then picks up its assembly task again. This is exactly what happens when the assembler processes a macro, by the way.

An example may help. Imagine that the assembler is assembling SHOW-CHAR.ASM when it encounters the following line from SHOWCHAR:

```
add  DI,ScrnWidth*LinesDown*2 ; Start table display down a ways
```

It looks up **ScrnWidth** and **LinesDown** in its symbol table and discovers that they are equates. It then calls time-out from assembling and processes the two equates by substituting their values into the line of source code for their text symbols. The line of source code changes to the following:

```
add  DI,80*4*2       ; Start table display down a ways
```

Assembly-Time Calculations

But in assembling the preceding line, the assembler has to pull another trick out of its hat. It has to be able to deal with the expression 80*4*2. We've not seen this before in our discussions, but the assembler happily parses the expression and performs the math exactly as you would imagine: It cooks 80*4*2 down to the single integer value 640. It then performs another substitution on the line in question, which finally cooks down to this:

```
add  DI,640          ; Start table display down a ways
```

At last, the line becomes an utterly ordinary line of assembly language code, which is turned to object code in a trice.

So, the assembler can in fact do a little math on its own, quite apart from the arithmetic instructions supported by the CPU. This is called assembly-time math, and it has some very important limitations:

- Assembly-time calculations may *only* be done on values that are fixed and unambiguous at assembly time. This most pointedly excludes the contents of variables. Equates are fine. **DBs**, **DWs**, and **DDs** are *not*. Variables are empty containers at assembly time; just buckets into which values will be thrown later on at runtime. You can't perform a calculation with the contents of an empty bucket!

- Assembly-time calculations are performed *once*, at assembly time, and cannot be recalculated at runtime for a different set of values. This should be obvious, but it's easy enough to misconstrue the nature of assembly-time math while you're a beginner.

Let me point out an important consequence of the use of assembly-time math in SHOWCHAR. In SHOWCHAR, the ASCII table is displayed four lines down from the top of the screen, at the left margin. Now, what do we need to do to allow the ASCII table to be moved around the screen at runtime?

Oh, not much: Just rewrite the whole thing.

I'm not trying to be funny. That's the price you pay for the convenience of assembly-time calculation. We baked the screen position of the ASCII table into the program at the source code level. If we wanted to parameterize the position of the ASCII table, we'd have to take a whole different approach and do what we did with RULER.ASM: use the **IMUL** instruction to perform the multiplication that calculates the offset into the screen buffer, at runtime.

We can change the **LinesDown** equate in SHOWCHAR.ASM to have a value of 6 or 10—but we then have to reassemble SHOWCHAR for the change to take. The calculation is done only once, at assembly time. Thereafter, as long as we use the resulting .EXE file, the ASCII table will be the number of lines down the screen that we defined in the **Lines-Down** equate.

Assembly-time calculations may not seem very useful now, in the light of these restrictions. However, they serve a purpose that may not be immediately obvious: They make it a little easier for us to read the sense in our own source code. We could have just skipped the equates and the assembly-time math, done the math in our heads and written the line of code like this:

```
add  DI,640          ; Start table display down a ways
```

How obvious is it to you that adding 640 to DI starts the display of the table down the screen by 4 lines? Using equates and assembly-time math builds the screen-positioning algorithm into the source code, right there where it's used.

Equates and assembly-time math cost you *nothing* in terms of runtime speed or memory usage. They *do* slow down the assembly process a little, but the person who uses your programs never knows that—and it's the user that you want to wow with your assembly language brilliance. And anything that makes your own source code easier to read and modify is well worth the minuscule extra time it takes to assemble.

Nested Instruction Loops

Once all the registers are set up correctly according to the assumptions made by **STOSW**, the real work of SHOWCHAR is performed by two instruction loops, one inside the other. The inner loop displays a line consisting of 64 characters. The outer loop breaks up the display into four such lines. The inner loop is by far the more interesting of the two. Here it is:

```
DoChar: stosw        ; Note that there's no REP prefix!
        jcxz  AllDone ; When the full set is printed, quit
```

```
inc  AL       ; Bump the character value in AL up by 1
dec  BL       ; Decrement the line counter by one
loopnz DoChar ; Go back & do another char until BL goes to 0
```

The work here (putting a character/attribute pair into the video buffer) is again done by **STOSW**. Once again, **STOSW** is working solo, without **REP**. Without **REP** to pull the loop inside the CPU, you have to set the loop up yourself.

Keep in mind what happens each time **STOSW** fires. The character in AX is copied to ES:DI and DI is incremented by 2. At the other end of the loop, the **LOOPNZ** instruction decrements CX by 1 and closes the loop.

During register setup, we loaded CX with the number of characters we wanted to display—in this case, 256. Each time **STOSW** fires, it places another character on the screen, and there is one fewer character left to display. CX acts as the master counter, keeping track of when we finally display the last remaining character. When CX goes to zero, we've displayed the full ASCII character set and the job is done.

Jumping When CX Goes to 0

Hence the instruction **JCXZ**. This is a special branching instruction created specifically to help with loops like this. Back in Chapter 10, I explained how it's possible to branch using one of the many variations of the **JMP** instruction, based on the state of one of the machine flags. Earlier in this chapter, I explained the **LOOP** instruction, which is a special-purpose sort of a **JMP** instruction, one combined with an implied **DEC CX** instruction. **JCXZ** is yet another variety of **JMP** instruction, but one that doesn't watch any of the flags or decrement any registers. Instead, **JCXZ** watches the CX register. When it sees that CX has just gone to zero, it jumps to the specified label. If CX is still nonzero, execution falls through to the next instruction in line.

In the case of the inner loop shown previously, **JCXZ** branches to the "close up shop" code when it sees that CX has finally gone to 0. This is how the SHOWCHAR program terminates.

Most of the other **JMP** instructions have partners that branch when the governing flag is *not* true. That is, **JC** (Jump on Carry) branches when the Carry flag equals 1. Its partner, **JNC** (Jump on Not Carry), jumps if the Carry flag is *not* 1. However, **JCXZ** is a loner. There is *no* **JCXNZ** instruction, so don't go looking for one in the instruction reference!

Closing the Inner Loop

Assuming that CX has not yet been decremented down to 0 by the **STOSW** instruction (a condition watched for by **JCXZ**), the loop continues. AL is incremented. This is how the next ASCII character in line is selected. The value in AX is sent to the location at ES:DI by **STOSW**, and the character code proper is stored in AL. If you increment the value in AL, you change the displayed character to the next one in line. For example, if AL contains the value for the character *A* (65), incrementing AL changes the *A* character to a B (66). On the next pass through the loop, **STOSW** will fire a *B* at the screen instead of an *A*.

Why not just increment AX? The AH half of AX contains the attribute byte, and we do *not* want to change that. By explicitly incrementing AL instead of AX, we ensure that AH will never be altered.

After the character code in AL is incremented, BL is decremented. Now, BL is not directly related to the string instructions. Nothing in any of the assumptions made by the string instructions involves BL. We're using BL for something else entirely here. BL is acting as a counter that governs the length of the lines of characters shown on the screen. BL was loaded earlier with the value represented by **LineLen**; here, 64. On each pass through the loop, the **DEC BL** instruction decrements the value of BL by 1. Then the **LOOPNZ** instruction gets its moment in the sun.

LOOPNZ is a little bit different from our friend **LOOP** that we examined earlier. It's just different enough to get you into trouble if you don't truly understand how it works. Both **LOOP** and **LOOPNZ** decrement the CX register by 1. **LOOP** watches the state of the CX register and closes the loop until CX goes to 0. **LOOPNZ** watches *both* the state of the CX register *and* the state of the Zero flag ZF. (**LOOP** ignores ZF.) **LOOPNZ** will only close the loop if CX <> 0 *and* ZF = 0. In other words, **LOOPNZ** closes the loop only if CX still has something left in it, *and* if the Zero flag ZF is not set.

So, what exactly is **LOOPNZ** watching for here? Remember that immediately prior to the **LOOPNZ** instruction, we're decrementing BL by 1 through a **DEC BL** instruction. The **DEC** instruction always affects ZF. If **DEC**'s operand goes to zero as a result of the **DEC** instruction, ZF goes to 1 (is set). Otherwise, ZF stays at 0 (remains cleared). So, in effect, **LOOPNZ** is watching the state of the BL register. Until BL is decremented to 0 (setting ZF), **LOOPNZ** closes the loop. After BL goes to zero, the inner loop is finished and execution falls through **LOOPNZ** to the next instruction.

What about CX? Well, **LOOPNZ** is watching CX—but so is **JCXZ**. **JCXZ** is actually the switch that governs when the whole loop—both inner and outer portions—has done its work and must stop. So, while **LOOPNZ** does watch CX, somebody else is doing that task, and that somebody else will take action on CX before **LOOPNZ** can. **LOOPNZ**'s job is thus to decrement CX, but to watch BL. It governs the inner of the two loops.

Closing the Outer Loop

But does that mean **JCXZ** closes the outer loop? No. **JCXZ** tells us when *both* loops are finished. Closing the outer loop is done a little differently from closing the inner loop. Take another look at the two nested loops:

```
DoLine: mov  BL,LineLen ; Each line will consist of 64 characters
DoChar: stosw           ; Note that there's no REP prefix!
        jcxz  AllDone    ; When the full set is printed, quit
        inc  AL          ; Bump the character value in AL up by 1
        dec  BL          ; Decrement the line counter by one
        loopnz DoChar    ; Go back & do another char until BL goes to 0
        add  DI,(ScrnWidth - LineLen)*2 ; Move DI to start of next line
        jmp  DoLine      ; Start display of the next line
```

The inner loop is considered complete when we've displayed one full line of the ASCII table to the screen. BL governs the length of a line, and when BL goes to zero (which the **LOOPNZ** instruction detects), a line is finished. **LOOPNZ** then falls through to the **ADD** instruction that modifies DI.

We modify DI to jump from the end of a completed line to the start of the next line at the left margin. This means we have to "wrap" by some number of characters from the end of the ASCII table line to the end of the visible screen. The number of bytes this requires is given by the assembly-time expression **(ScrnWidth-LineLen)*2**. This is basically the difference between the length of one ASCII table line and width of the visible screen. Multiplying by 2 is done because each character position is actually represented by both a character and an attribute byte in the video refresh buffer. The result of the expression is the number of bytes we must move into the video refresh buffer to come to the start of the next line at the left screen margin.

But after that wrap is accomplished by modifying DI, the outer loop's work is done, and we close the loop. This time, we do it *unconditionally*, by way of a simple **JMP** instruction. The target of the **JMP** instruction is the **DoLine** label. No ifs, no arguments. At the top of the outer loop (represented by the **DoLine** label), we load the length of a line back into the now-empty BL register and drop back into the inner loop. The inner loop starts firing characters at the screen again, and will continue to do so until **JCXZ** detects that CX has gone to 0.

At that point, both the inner and outer loops are finished, and the full ASCII table has been displayed. SHOWCHAR's work is done, and it terminates.

SHOWCHAR.ASM Recap

Let's look back at what we've just been through. SHOWCHAR.ASM contains two nested loops. The inner loop shoots characters at the screen via **STOSW**. The outer loop shoots *lines* of characters at the screen, by repeating the inner loop some number of times. (Here, four.)

The inner loop is governed by the value in the BL register, which is initially set up to take the length of a line of characters. (Here, 64.) The outer loop is not explicitly governed by the number of lines to be displayed. That is, you don't load the number 4 into a register and decrement it. Instead, the outer loop continues until the value in CX goes to 0, indicating that the whole job is done.

The inner and outer loops both modify the registers that **STOSW** works with. The inner loop modifies AL after each character is fired at the screen. This makes it possible to display a different character each time **STOSW** fires. The outer loop modifies DI (the destination index register) each time a *line* of characters is complete. This allows us to break the destination string up into four separate, noncontinuous lines.

The Other String Instructions

STOSW is only one of the several string instructions in the x86 instruction set. I would have liked to cover the others here, but space won't allow in this edition at least. In particular, the **MOVSW** instruction is useful, because it allows you to copy entire regions of memory from one place to another, screamingly fast, and with only a single instruction:

```
REP MOVSW
```

You probably understand enough about string instruction etiquette now to pick up **MOVSW** yourself from an assembly language reference. All of the same register conventions apply, only with **MOVS** you're working with both the source and destination strings at the same time.

I felt it important to discuss not only the string instructions, but their supporting cast of characters: **LOOP**, **LOOPNZ**, and **JCXZ**. Individual instructions are important, but not nearly as important as the full context within which they work. Now that you've seen how **STOSW** is used in non-**REP** loops, you should be able to apply the same knowledge to the other string instructions as well.

Further Research: Building Your Assembly Language Video Toolkit

Video is important—it's the fundamental way your programs communicate with their users. *Fast* video is essential, and BIOS-based video generally fails in that regard—especially on older and slower machines. The **Clear** and **Ruler** macros are good examples of just how fast video routines can be made with solid knowledge of assembly language.

You have the fundamentals of a really good and extremely fast toolkit of video routines for your assembly language programs. To get some serious practice in assembly language design and implementation, it's up to you to fill that toolkit out.

Here's a list of some of the new routines you should design and perfect for your video toolkit:

WriteFast. A routine to move a string of characters from your data segment to the visible display buffer. You can do this easily using instructions we've discussed so far. A suggestion: Use the **LOOP** instruction for an easy time of it, or research the **MOVSW** instruction for a trickier—but much faster—routine.

WritelnFast. Like **WriteFast**, but moves the hardware cursor to the beginning of the following line after the write. If the write is to the bottom line on the screen, scroll the screen using INT 10 BIOS calls, or for more speed, **MOVSW**.

WriteDown. A routine to move a string of characters from the data segment to the visible display buffer, only *vertically*. This is useful for displaying boxes for menus and other screen forms, using the

PC's line-drawing characters. SHOWCHAR.ASM gives you a hint as to how to approach this one.

DrawBox. Using **WriteFast** and **WriteDown**, create a routine that draws a box on the screen using the PC's suite of predefined text box draw characters. Allow the programmer to specify whether it is made of single-line or double-line line-drawing characters.

GetString. A delimited field-entry routine. Delineate a field somehow, by highlighting the background or framing a portion of a line with vertical bar characters, and allow the user to move the cursor and enter characters within the bounds of the field. When the user presses Enter, return the entered characters to a buffer somewhere in the data segment. This is ambitious and might require 70 or 80 instructions, but it's likely to be a lot of fun and will be extremely useful if you write a full-screen text application that puts particular things at particular places on the screen.

Getting your video tools in order will allow you to move on to other, more involved subjects such as file I/O and interface to the serial and parallel ports. "Real" assembly-language programs require all these things, and you should strive to create them as small, easily read and understood toolkit-style procedures and macros. Create them so that they call one another rather than duplicating function—assembly language is difficult enough without creating routines that do the same old things over and over again.

CHAPTER 12

The Programmer's View of Linux

Tools and Skills to Help You Write Assembly Code under a True 32-Bit OS

Where to Now?

Where indeed? If you've followed me this far, you've been exposed to nearly every concept commonly used in assembly language work. As a working environment we've been using MS-DOS, which made a lot of things easier—made most of it possible, in fact. DOS is simple, forgiving, and present in nearly all Windows machines either as a lurker-beneath-the-windows (for Windows 9x) or a very high quality emulation (Windows NT). Either way, it was likely that you had access to DOS if you had a PC anywhere in your life.

The trouble is, DOS is the past. At best, it's a training ground for understanding the environments where all the real action is now taking place. And that's basically one of two places these days: Windows and Unix. Most other environments have withered severely and exist primarily as "legacy support"—that is, for people who can't afford the money or effort required to move from where they are to Windows or Unix.

On the x86 family of processors (which is what we've been discussing), the undisputed king of Unix implementations is Linux. And where we're going is Linux. It's a true 32-bit protected mode operating system, and it offers the chance to create real 32-bit flat model programs in assembly without a prohibitive amount of head banging. So, what remains of this book will serve to get you started on learning assembly coding for Linux.

Why Not Windows?

The first edition of this book was published in 1992. In the last few years, I've received many letters from readers of the first edition, requesting a second edition that explained how to write Microsoft Windows programs in assembly code. I looked into it. I paled. And I shook my head. Don't go there—you may never come back.

The problem is this: A Windows application isn't so much a stand-alone program as a custom-built extension of Windows itself. A DOS assembly program begins at the top, runs down from there, may do some looping back, but eventually it ends. It may touch the operating system from time to time by making system calls, but the nature of those calls is simple: You set up some parameters in registers or on the stack, and you make an INT 21H call into DOS. When DOS does what it must, it returns control to your program. That's about all there is to it.

The relationship between Windows and its applications is much closer and far more complex. When a Windows program is running and the user presses a mouse button, Windows intercepts the mouse signal and (in effect) taps your program on the shoulder and whispers: "The user just clicked the right mouse button. What are you going to do about it?" A tremendously complex system of events and responses, of messages passed and messages intercepted, runs through Windows and all of its applications like the threads of water flowing over a rocky streambed. From a distance, it's gorgeous. Up close, it borders on chaotic. And in assembly language, you're up as close as it gets.

Just understanding how Windows and Windows applications work at the assembly level could take you months of study. Coding a sizeable app could take a year. Balance against this the fact that a lot of the work in dealing with Windows is always done in precisely the same ways, and you have a tailor-made excuse for drop-in software components and boilerplate code. This is what you get with programming environments like Visual C++, Visual Basic, and Delphi, which basically hand you a generic Windows program with all the infrastructure in place—windows, scroll bars, mouse support, the works—but nothing in the line of specifics.

Nonetheless, getting that massive a head start pretty much eliminates any advantage you might have in working in assembly.

But what about speed and size? Nothing beats assembly at speed and size, right? Well, nothing beats *good* assembly at the speed and size game. However . . . you need to keep in mind that when a Windows application is running, much or even most of the time code execution is actually somewhere down in Windows, executing DLLs or other Windows machinery that you have no control over. The parts that you actually write will not likely be what dominate the user's perception of the application's speed.

Besides, today's C and Pascal compilers have gotten mighty *damned* good at generating near-optimal machine code for a specified sequence of high-level language statements. Ace assembly hacks can do better, but it's a little discouraging to ponder just how close to your heels the wolves are snapping.

In truth, coding in assembly for Windows is good for one thing and one thing only: to gain a bit-level, way-down-deep under-the-skin understanding of how Windows works. This can be a very good and valuable thing, and if you want to pursue it, I salute you. I also suspect that once you gain that hard-won understanding of Windows internals, you'll run screaming to the most efficient Windows RAD (Rapid Application Development) environment you can find. (For me, that was Delphi.)

Only one book to my knowledge has ever been written about coding in assembly for Windows: *Windows Assembly Language and Systems Programming*, by Barry Kauler (R & D Books, 1997). And for all that it's 400 pages long, it's only a start. Most of what you need to know will have to be found elsewhere, in Microsoft's massive technical documentation.

Good luck. Heh-heh. You'll need it.

And Why Linux?

The decision to cover Linux was not automatic. There were actually two other contenders—or maybe a contender and a half. The half-of-a-contender was DOS protected mode, using a 32-bit DOS extender and the DOS Protected Mode Interface, or DPMI. This would have been reasonably simple, and I almost went that way. I turned back because DOS and DPMI just aren't used anymore by anything that isn't legacy. Why make brand-new antiques? No, strike that—the metaphor is inapt; antiques are by definition valuable. Why make brand-new kitsch?

Besides, DPMI, for all that it works, is really a crutch under a small and very unpowerful OS. For all the effort you will eventually put into learning assembly technology, you deserve to work with more horsepower than that.

The true alternate contender was something called a *Windows console application*. These are special programs written to be run under Windows NT, in a *console*—basically, a true 32-bit text-mode window rather than a 16-bit text-mode DOS emulation window. NT console applications are genuine 32-bit programs and are relatively simple to write. They can even do cool Windows-ish things such as display graphical message boxes without a prohibitive amount of fuss. One problem: You must run them under Windows NT, which isn't cheap and currently isn't all that common. On DOS and Windows 9*x* systems, Windows console applications won't run at all.

Ultimately, I chose Linux because it was every bit as powerful as Windows NT (especially in the realm we're discussing in this book) as well as free. Furthermore, there is an immense amount of free code out there on the Internet written for use with Linux. You can install a Linux partition on the same hard disk as a Windows partition, so you don't have to give up your "real work" in Windows to play around with Linux coding.

Finally, Linux (as the reigning x86 king of the Unix world) is one of the last places where x86 text-mode programming is still done in a big way. Windows console applications are little-used exceptions to the GUI rule in the Microsoft world. In Linux, text mode is still mainstream.

That's where we're going. Let's see what it'll take to get there.

Prerequisites—Yukkh!

Yes, I know, patience isn't one of your virtues. It's not one of mine either. But before you write your first line of assembly code under Linux, there are a number of things that you had better do, or you'll end of up thrashing a lot and wasting a lot of time. That's the only way some people learn, but it's hard on the hair and sucks up valuable hours out of your life that you will never have again. (This seems not to matter much when you're 18—but when you're 47, as I am at this writing, it matters a *lot*.) The list is short, but plan to spend some time on it:

1. Learn Linux.
2. Learn EMACS.
3. Learn C programming.

These three things—surprise!—are way too much for me to attempt to explain in this book. I recommend you buy or borrow a full book (or more) on each of them, work through tutorials, and do your best to become a journeyman practitioner in all three areas. Allow me to explain why.

Linux Is Not DOS!

The single most important thing to remember if you're coming to Linux for the first time is that although Linux bears some functional resemblance to a grown-up DOS, it's radically different in a great many ways. Some of these ways are so fundamental that people who use Linux (and other versions of Unix) on a total lifestyle basis no longer think of them as notable—and, thus, even beginner books will not fully prepare you for the sense of alienness that you'll encounter in your first few days in front of the beast.

The best example I can give you is this: In the first few days that I began working with Linux, I wrote a short C program that generated a date display. The program was trivial, and it compiled without difficulty. But when I named the compiled binary program in order to run it, bash (a user shell and roughly equivalent to DOS's COMMAND.COM) told me the file wasn't there! This drove me nuts for some time. The executable file I had generated was right there in the current directory, as I could verify with the ls command. However, when I typed the name of the file followed by Enter, bash pleaded ignorance of its existence. What I hadn't learned yet is that to run a Unix (and hence a Linux) executable, you have to enter the full path name, put the directory in which the executable file exists on the path, or prepend the explicit current directory specifier "./". Absent one of those location specifiers, bash doesn't search the current directory for a named executable file!

Yes, to me this is stupid—but I came up through DOS. People who started out with Linux or some other flavor of Unix don't think of this as remarkable at all, and there are some technical reasons why it may be better to do things this way. But the lesson here is that you need to be very attentive as you learn Linux, and try very hard not to make assumptions based on your DOS or Windows experience.

If you've never touched a Unix system before, trust me, it's a lot to swallow in a hurry. See if there's a local community college course you can take on it, or corral a couple of your Unix friends, buy them beer and pizza, and encourage them to talk while you take furious notes. At minimum, buy several books on Linux and read them through, following along at your keyboard and typing the commands as they're presented. At the simple user level, Linux *is* Unix, so any good beginner book on Unix will be useful, and there are currently a multitude of new Linux-specific beginner books on the stands. (Books that are specific to a particular *distribution* of Linux—Red Hat, Debian, or Caldera, for example— are now beginning to appear and these may be even more helpful. Haunt the local Borders regularly and keep your eyes open. If you install Red Hat Linux, I recommend *Learning Red Hat Linux* by Bill McCarty, from O'Reilly.)

In going forward, I am going to assume that you know how to log in and out, navigate around within Unix directories, and all that elementary user-level stuff. If I use a term or cite a Unix command that you're not familiar with, look it up in one of those other books that you ought to have close at hand.

The distribution I used in preparing this book in the late summer and fall of 1999 was Red Hat 6. It's by far the Linux distribution in widest use, and if you adopt it, you will have plenty of company, which in the computer business is always a plus.

EMACS: More than an Editor

I didn't bother looking for a Linux programming editor/environment to put on this book's CD-ROM, because if you have Linux you've already got one—or several. In fact, if you've been using Linux as a programmer for more than half an hour, you've probably already glommed onto an editor and would be unwilling to switch to anything I would likely be able to hand you. Although there are dozens or (perhaps) hundreds of text editors available for Unix, most Unix people use one of either vi or EMACS. And in the Linux world, as best I can tell, EMACS is the editor of choice.

EMACS is *way* more than just an editor. It's much closer to the integrated text-mode environments used in the last days of DOS for such products as Borland C++ and Borland Pascal. It understands C syntax, C++ syntax, and assembly syntax—though, alas, not the assembly syntax we'll be using. (More on this sad little disconnect later.) EMACS can build an executable from inside the editor and do an awful lot of other things I've never had occasion to fool with. Whole books have been written on EMACS (O'Reilly has one) and it would be worthwhile to grab such a book and digest it. If you intend to stick with Linux and do any significant programming for it, EMACS is indispensable. Learn as much of it as you can.

It's a C World

I'm a notorious Pascal bigot, and it pains me to say this, but Linux (as a genuine implementation of Unix) is inescapably a C world. Most of Linux is written in C, and what little isn't in C is in assembly. Virtually all the programming examples you'll see for Linux that don't involve interpreted languages such as Perl or Tcl will be in C. Most significantly (as I explain in greater detail later), the runtime library your assembly programs will use to communicate with the operating system is written in C and requires that you use the C protocols for function calling, rather than the more sensible Pascal ones.

So, before you attempt your first assembly program, buy a book and get down and hack some C. You don't need to do a lot of it, but make sure you understand all the basic C concepts, especially as they apply to function calls. I'll try to fill in the lower-level gaps in this book, but I can't teach the language itself nor all the baggage that comes with it. You may find it distasteful (as I did and do) or you may love it, but what you must understand is that *you can't escape it*, even if your main interest in Linux is assembly language.

There are some excellent Pascal implementations for Linux, most of them free, so if you don't stick with assembly you have some alternatives to C. My choice is FreePascal 32. Go to the following Web site for more details and for the software itself: http://gd.tuwien.ac.at/languages/pascal/fpc/www/.

NASM for Linux

Another (minor) reason that I chose NASM as the focus assembler for this book is that a very good implementation—still free—exists for Linux. I've included NASM for Linux, version 0.98, on the CD-ROM for this book. That's the version with which I wrote all the code examples published here. However, there's no saying how long this book will remain in use, and if it's for more than a year or so (and the first edition lasted over seven years), you might check the NASM Web site to see if a newer release is available at www.web-sites.co.uk/nasm/.

This is its home page in early 2000. If it moves in subsequent years, you may have to hunt with a Web search engine. My hunch is that it will always exist *somewhere*. Free software never dies, though it sometimes gets a little dusty.

You can download NASM in either source code form or in assembled binary form, as an RPM (Red Hat Package Manager) archive. Installing the RPM file might seem to be easier, but there's a catch: You must choose one of two different RPM archives, depending on whether you're using libc5 or libc6. If you know your Linux system well, you probably know which version of the C library it uses; on the other hand, if you're relatively new to Linux, you might not. That's why I have not included the RPM version on the CD-ROM but NASM's full source code in C, which you rebuild in the process of installing it.

Installing NASM's Source Code

Don't faint, newcomers. It's not that hard, and rebuilding tools is a fact of Linux life. Installing the source code and rebuilding it from scratch avoids the libc version problem, as gcc (the Linux C compiler) knows what C library it has, and it uses it to build the NASM assembler binary correctly. That's why you'll find the file nasm-0.98.tar on the CD-ROM for this book. A *tar file* is an archive file, like a .ZIP file in the DOS world, only without compression. It's simply a way to combine multiple files into one file for easy transport over a network.

Your Linux system probably has a directory /usr/local/src on it. That's a good place to start. (If it doesn't, consider creating a directory with that pathname.) Copy the nasm-0.98.tar file from the CD-ROM into /usr/local/src, and then use tar to extract all the files from it. The tar utility is one of my least-favorite Unix utilities, because it has a whole different mindset for dealing with command-line parameters, and if you type something it doesn't understand or like, it will just sit there mute until you Ctrl-C out of it.

So, use this command line, and make sure you get it *precisely* as shown here:

```
tar xvf nasm-0.98.tar
```

Rebuilding NASM

Once you get tar to extract all the files from the archive, you'll notice that tar has created a new directory on your hard drive. Use cd to move to this directory:

```
cd nasm-0.98
```

There will be a fair number of files in this directory. The next step configures NASM's make files for rebuilding. You execute this step with the following command:

```
./configure
```

The configure step looks at your system, sees what C compilers you have installed, and tests those it finds for suitability. It looks to see what C library your system is using, checks a few other things, and finally creates the make files it will need to recreate the NASM binaries. Once configure has completed its job, you need to execute one very simple command:

```
./make
```

This will do a lot, though it won't take a great deal of time, especially if you have a reasonably fast machine and a fast hard drive. (Mine is a 400-MHz Pentium II and the whole build took about 15 seconds.) A great many obscure messages will flow by on your screen. Many of them will be warnings, but you don't need to be concerned about those—the compiler is simply complaining about things in the NASM source code that aren't simon-pure by its own reckoning. A warning is not an indication that the compiler can't understand something or generate correct code.

Once NASM is installed, it makes sense to add to your search path the path to the bin directory where NASM is installed. This command will do it:

```
PATH=$PATH:/usr/local/bin
```

Obviously, if you installed NASM somewhere else (and the preceding path is simply where the NASM make process installs it by default), enter the full path after the colon. At this point, NASM is there, installed as a brand-new binary, and ready to go to work.

But there's a lot to talk about first. NASM, like a lot of things in the Linux world, does not work alone, nor in a vacuum.

What's GNU?

Way back in the late 1970s, a wild-eyed Unix hacker named Richard Stallman wanted his own copy of Unix. He didn't want to pay for it, however, so he did the obvious thing: He began writing his own version. (If it's not obvious to you, well, you don't understand Unix culture.) However, he was unsatisfied with all the programming tools currently available and objected to their priciness as well. So, as a prerequisite to writing his own version of Unix, Stallman set out to write his own compiler, assembler, and debugger. (He had already written his own editor, the legendary EMACS.)

Stallman had named his version of Unix *GNU*, a recursive acronym meaning GNU's Not Unix. This was a good chuckle, and one way of getting past AT&T's trademark lawyers, who were fussy in those days about who used the word *Unix* and how. As time went on, the GNU tools (the C compiler and its other Swiss army knife go-alongs) took on a life of their own, and as it happened, Stallman never actually finished GNU itself. Other free versions of Unix appeared, and there was some soap opera for a few years regarding who actually owned what parts of which. This so disgusted Stallman that he created the Free Software Foundation as the home base for GNU tools development and created a radical sort of software license called the GNU Public License (GPL), which is sometimes informally called "copyleft." Stallman released the GNU tools under the GPL, which not only required that the software be free (including all source code), but prevented people from making minor mods to the software and claiming the derivative work as their own. Changes and improvements had to be given back to the GNU community.

This seemed to be major nuttiness at the time, but over the years since then it has taken on a peculiar logic and life of its own. The GPL has allowed software released under the GPL to evolve tremendously quickly, because large numbers of people were using it and improving it and giving back the improvements without charge or restriction. Out of this bubbling open source pot eventually arose Linux, the premier GPL operating system. Linux was built with and is maintained with the

GNU tool set. If you're going to program under Linux, regardless of what language you're using, you will eventually use one or more of the GNU tools.

The Swiss Army Compiler

The copy of EMACS that you will find on modern distributions of Linux doesn't have a whole lot of Richard Stallman left in it—it's been rewritten umpteen times by many other people over the past 20-odd years. Where the Stallman legacy persists most strongly is in the GNU compilers. There are a number of them, but the one that you must understand as thoroughly as possible is the GNU C Compiler, gcc. (Lowercase letters are something of an obsession in the Unix world, a fetish not well understood by a lot of people, myself included.)

Why use a C compiler for working in assembly? Two reasons:

- Most of Linux and all of the standard C library for Linux are written in C for gcc. The C library is the only reasonable way to communicate with Linux from an assembly program. Gcc has a great deal of intimate knowledge of the standard C library that you'll need to learn if you choose not to use it. Love Linux, love gcc. There's no way around it.

- More interestingly, gcc does much more than simply compile C code. It's a sort of Swiss army knife development tool. In fact, I might better characterize what it does as *building* software rather than simply *compiling* it. In addition to compiling C code to object code, gcc governs both the assembly step and the link step.

Assembly step? Yes, indeedy. There is a GNU assembler, gas. And a GNU linker, ld. What gcc does is control them like puppets on strings. If you use gcc (especially at the beginner level), you don't have to do much messing around with gas and ld.

Let's talk more about this.

Building Code the GNU Way

Assembly language work is a departure from C work, and gcc is first and foremost a C compiler. So, we need to look first at the process of building C code. On the surface, building a C program for Linux using the GNU tools is pretty simple. Behind the scenes, however, it's a seriously hairy business. While it looks like gcc does all the work, what gcc really does is act as master controller for several GNU tools, supervising a code assembly line that you don't need to see unless you specifically want to.

Theoretically, this is all you need to do to generate an executable binary file from C source code:

```
gcc eatc.c -o eatc
```

Here, gcc takes the file eatc.c (which is a C source code file) and crunches it to produce the file eatc. (The –o option tells gcc what to name the executable output file.) Note well that in the Linux world, executable files typically do *not* have file extensions, as they do under DOS and Windows. What might be eatc.com or eatc.exe under DOS is simply eatc under Linux.

However, there's more going on here than meets the eye. Take a look at Figure 12.1 as we go through it. In the figure, shaded arrows indicate movement of information. Blank arrows indicate program control.

The programmer invokes gcc from the shell command line. gcc takes control of the system and immediately invokes a utility called the C preprocessor, cpp. The preprocessor takes the original C source code file and handles certain items like #includes and #defines. It can be thought of as a sort of macro expansion pass on the source code file, if "macro expansion pass" means anything to you. If not, don't fret it—it's a C thing and not germane to assembly work.

When cpp is finished with its work, gcc takes over in earnest. From the preprocessed source code file, gcc generates an assembly language source code file with a .s file extension. This is literally the assembly code equivalent of the C statements in the original .c file, in human-readable form. If you develop any skill in reading AT&T assembly syntax and mnemonics, you can learn a *lot* from inspecting the .s files produced by gcc.

When gcc has completed generating the assembly language equivalent of the C source code file, it invokes the GNU assembler, gas, to assemble the .s file into object code. This object code is written out in a file with a .o extension.

The final step involves the GNU linker, ld. The .o file contains binary code, but it's *only* the binary code generated from statements in the original .c file. The .o file does *not* contain the code from the standard C

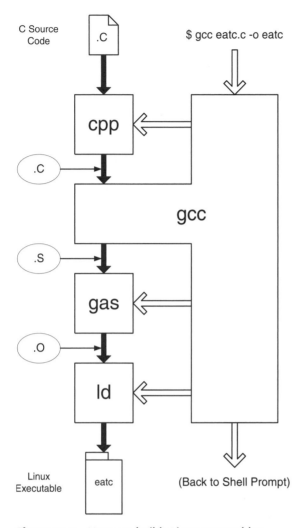

Figure 12.1 How gcc builds Linux executables.

libraries that are so important in C programming. Those libraries have already been compiled and simply need to be linked into your application. The linker ld does this work at gcc's direction. The good part is that gcc knows precisely which of the standard C libraries need to be linked to your application to make it work, and it always includes the right libraries in their right versions. So, although gcc doesn't actually do the linking, *it knows what needs to be linked*—and that is valuable knowledge indeed, as you will learn if you ever try to invoke ld manually.

At the end of the line, ld spits out the fully linked and executable program file. At that point, the build is done, and gcc returns control to the Linux shell. Note that all of this is typically done with one simple command to gcc!

How We Use gcc in Assembly Work

The process I just described, and drew out for you in Figure 12.1, is how a C program is built under Linux using the GNU tools. I went into some detail here because we're going to use part—though only part—of this process to make our assembly programming easier. It's true that we don't need to convert C source code to assembly code—and in fact, we don't need gas to convert gas assembly source code to object code. *But we need gcc's expertise at linking.* Linking a Linux program is much more complex than linking a simple DOS program. So we're going to tap in to the GNU code-building process at the link stage, so that gcc can coordinate the link step for us.

When we assemble a Linux program using NASM, NASM generates a .o file containing binary object code. Invoking NASM under Linux is typically done this way:

```
nasm -f elf eatlinux.asm
```

This command will direct NASM to assemble the file eatlinux.asm and generate a file called eatlinux.o. The "–f elf" part of it tells NASM to generate object code in the ELF format (the acronym means Executable and Linking Format, so saying "ELF format" is redundant even though everyone does it) rather than one of the numerous other object code formats that NASM is capable of producing. The eatlinux.o file is not by itself executable. It needs to be linked. So, we call gcc and instruct it to link the program for us:

```
gcc eatlinux.o -o eatlinux
```

What of this tells gcc to link and not compile? The only input file called out in the command is a .o file containing object code. This fact alone tells gcc that all that needs to be done is to link the file with the C library to produce the final executable. The "–o eatlinux" tells gcc that the name of the final executable file is to be "eatlinux." (Remember that Linux does not use file extensions on executable program files.)

Including the –o specifier is important. If you don't tell gcc precisely what to name the final executable file, it will name that file "a.out." Yes, "a.out," every time—irrespective of what your object file or source files are called.

Why Not gas?

You might be wondering why, if there's a perfectly good assembler installed automatically with every copy of Linux, I'm bothering to show you how to install and use another one. First of all, there is no gas look-alike for DOS as best I know, so you can't take your first steps in gas assembly while working with DOS. But more important, gas uses a peculiar syntax that is utterly unlike that of all the other familiar assemblers used in the x86 world (MASM and TASM as well as NASM) and a whole set of instruction mnemonics unique to itself. I find them ugly, nonintuitive, and hard to read. This is the AT&T syntax, so called because it was created by AT&T as a portable assembly notation to make Unix easier to port from one underlying CPU to another. It's ugly because it was designed to be generic, and it can be recast for any reasonable CPU you could come up with. (Don't forget that Unix significantly predates the x86, and gas's predecessor is older than the x86.)

If it were this simple, I wouldn't mention gas at all, since you don't need to use it to write Linux code in NASM. However, one of the major ways you'll end up learning many of the standard C library calls is by using them in short C programs and then inspecting the assembly output gcc generates. (I have more to say about this later on.) What gcc generates first when it compiles a C program is a file (with a .s extension) of assembly language source code using the AT&T syntax and mnemonics. It may not be necessary to learn the AT&T syntax thoroughly enough to write it, but it will be very helpful if you can pick it up well enough to read it. I'll show you an example later on, and when I do I'll summarize the important differences between AT&T and the NASM syntax and mnemonics, which are more properly called the Intel syntax and mnemonics.

The make Utility and Dependencies

If you've done any programming in C at all, you're almost certainly familiar with the idea of the make utility. The make mechanism grew up in the C world, and although it's been adopted by many other programming languages and environments, it's never been adopted quite as thoroughly (or as nakedly) as in the C world.

What the make mechanism does is build executable program files from their component parts. Like gcc, the make utility is a puppet master that executes other programs according to a master plan, which is a simple text file called a make file. The *make file* (which by default is named "makefile") is a little like a computer program in that it specifies how something is to be done. But unlike a computer program, it doesn't specify the precise sequence of operations to be taken. What it does is specify what pieces of a program are required to build other pieces of the program, and in doing so ultimately defines what it takes to build the final executable file. It does this by specifying certain rules called *dependencies*.

Dependencies

Throughout this book we've been looking at teeny little programs with a hundred lines of code or less. In the real world, useful programs can take thousands, tens of thousands, or even millions of lines of source code. (The current release of Linux represents about 10 million lines of source code, depending on how you define what's a "part" of Linux. At last realizing that program bugs increase at least linearly with the size of a program's source code suite, Microsoft has stopped bragging about how many lines of code it took to create Windows NT. In truth, I'm not sure I want to know.) Managing such an immense quantity of source code is *the* central problem in software engineering. Making programs modular is the oldest and most-used method of dealing with program complexity. Cutting up a large program into smaller chunks and working on the chunks separately helps a great deal. In ambitious programs, some of the chunks are further cut into even smaller chunks, and sometimes the various chunks are written in more than one programming language. Of course, that creates the additional challenge of knowing how the chunks are created and how they all fit together. For that you really need a blueprint.

A make file is such a blueprint.

In a modular program, each chunk of code is created somehow, generally by using a compiler or an assembler and a linker. Compilers, assemblers, and linkers take one or more files and create new files from them. An assembler, as you've learned, takes a .asm file full of assembly language source code and uses it to create a linkable object code file or (in some cases) an executable program file. You can't create the object code file without having and working with the source code file. The object code file *depends* on the source code file for its very existence.

Similarly, a linker connects multiple object code files into a single executable file. The executable file depends on the existence of the object code files for its existence. The contents of a make file specify which files are necessary to create which other files, and what steps are necessary to accomplish that creation. The make utility looks at the rules (called *dependencies*) in the make file and invokes whatever compilers, assemblers, and other utilities it sees are necessary to build the final executable or library file.

There are numerous flavors of make utilities, and not all make files are comprehensible to all make utilities everywhere. The Unix make utility is pretty standard, however, and the one that comes with Linux is the one we'll be discussing here.

Let's take an example that actually makes a simple Linux assembly program. Typically, in creating a make file, you begin by determining which file or files are necessary to create the executable program file. The executable file is created in the link step, so the first dependency you have to define is which files the linker requires to create the executable file. As I explained earlier in this chapter, under Linux the link step is handled for us by the GNU C compiler, gcc. (Turn back to Figure 12.1 and the associated discussion if it's still fuzzy as to why a C compiler is required to link an assembly program.) The dependency itself can be pretty simply stated:

```
eatlinux: eatlinux.o
```

All this says is that to generate the executable file eatlinux, we first need to have the file eatlinux.o. The line is actually a dependency line written as it should be for inclusion in a make file. In any but the smallest programs (such as this one) the linker will have to link more than one .o file. So this is probably the simplest possible sort of dependency: One executable file depends on one object code file. If there are additional files that must be linked to generate the executable file, these are placed in a list, separated by spaces:

```
linkbase: linkbase.o linkparse.o linkfile.o
```

This line tells us that the executable file linkbase depends on *three* object code files, and all three of these files must exist before we can generate the executable file that we want.

Lines like these tell us what files are required, but not what must be done with them. That's an essential part of the blueprint, and it's handled in a line that follows the dependency line. The two lines work together. Here's both lines for our simple example:

```
eatlinux: eatlinux.o
    gcc eatlinux.o -o eatlinux
```

The second line is indented by custom. The two lines together should be pretty easy to understand: The first line tells us what file or files are required to do the job. The second line tells us how the job is to be done: in this case, by using gcc to link eatlinux.o into the executable file eatlinux.

Nice and neat: We specify which files are necessary and what has to be done with them. The make mechanism, however, has one more very important aspect: knowing whether the job as a whole actually has to be done at all.

When a File Is Up to Date

It may seem idiotic to have to come out and say so, but once a file has been compiled or linked, it's been done, and it doesn't have to be done again . . . *until we modify one of the required source or object code files*. The make utility knows this. It can tell when a compile or a link task needs to be done at all, and if the job doesn't have to be done, make will refuse to do it.

How does make know if the job needs doing? Consider this dependency:

```
eatlinux: eatlinux.o
```

Make looks at this and understands that the executable file eatlinux depends on the object code file eatlinux.o, and that you can't generate eatlinux without having eatlinux.o. It also knows when both files were last changed, and if the executable file eatlinux is *newer* than eatlinux.o, it deduces that any changes made to eatlinux.o are already reflected in eatlinux. (It can be absolutely sure of this because the only way to generate eatlinux is by processing eatlinux.o.)

The make utility pays close attention to Linux timestamps. Whenever you edit a source code file, or generate an object code file or an executable file, Linux updates that file's timestamp to the moment that the changes were finally completed. And even though you may have created the original file six months ago, by convention we say that a file is *newer* than another if the time value in its timestamp is more recent than that of another file, even one that was created only 10 minutes ago.

(In case you're unfamiliar with the notion of a *timestamp*, it's simply a value that an operating system keeps in a file system directory for every file in the directory. A file's timestamp is updated to the current clock time whenever the file is changed.)

When a file is newer than all of the files that it depends upon (according to the dependencies called out in the make file), that file is said to be *up to date*. Nothing will be accomplished by generating it again, because all information contained in the component files is reflected in the dependent file.

Chains of Dependencies

So far, this may seem like a lot of fuss to no great purpose. But the real value in the make mechanism begins to appear when a single make file contains *chains* of dependencies. Even in the simplest make files, there will be dependencies that depend on other dependencies. Our completely trivial example program requires two dependency statements in its make file.

Consider that the following dependency statement specifies how to generate an executable file from an object code (.o) file:

```
eatlinux: eatlinux.o
    gcc eatlinux.o -o eatlinux
```

The gist here is that to make eatlinux, you start with eatlinux.o and process it according to the recipe in the second line. Okay, . . . so where does eatlinux.o come from? That requires a second dependency statement:

```
eatlinux.o: eatlinux.asm
    nasm -f elf eatlinux.asm
```

Here we explain that to generate eatlinux.o, we need eatlinux .asm . . . and to generate it we follow the recipe in the second line. The full makefile would contain nothing more than these two dependencies:

```
eatlinux: eatlinux.o
    gcc eatlinux.o -o eatlinux
eatlinux.o: eatlinux.asm
    nasm -f elf eatlinux.asm
```

These two dependency statements define the two steps that we must take to generate an executable program file from our very simple assembly language source code file eatlinux.asm. However, it's not obvious from the two dependencies I show here that all the fuss is worthwhile. Assembling eatlinux.asm pretty much requires that we link eatlinux.o to create eatlinux. The two steps go together in virtually all cases.

But consider a real-world programming project, in which there are hundreds of separate source code files. Only some of those files might be "on the rack" and undergoing change on any given day. However, to build and test the final program, all of the files are required. But . . . are all the compilation steps and assembly steps required? Not at all.

An executable program is knit together by the linker from one or more—often *many* more—object code files. If all but (let's say) two of the object code files are up to date, there's no reason to compile the other 147 source code files. You just compile the two source code files that have been changed, and then link all 149 object code files into the executable.

The challenge, of course, is correctly remembering *which* two files have changed—and being sure that *all* changes that have been recently made to *any* of the 149 source code files are reflected in the final executable file. That's a lot of remembering, or referring to notes. And it gets worse when more than one person is working on the project, as will be the case in nearly all commercial software development projects. The make utility makes remembering any of this unnecessary. Make figures it out and does only what must be done, no more, no less.

The make utility looks at the make file, and it looks at the timestamps of all the source code and object code files called out in the make file. If the executable file is newer than all of the object code files, nothing needs to be done. However, if any of the object code files are newer than the executable file, the executable file must be relinked. And if one or more of the source code files are newer than either the executable file or their respective object code files, some compiling must be done before any linking is done.

What make does is start with the executable file and look for chains of dependency moving away from that. The executable file depends on one or more object files, which depend on one or more source code files, and make walks the path up the various chains, taking note of what's newer than what and what must be done to put it all right. Make then executes the compiler, assembler, and linker selectively to be sure that the executable file is ultimately newer than all of the files that it depends on. Make ensures that all work that needs to be done gets done. Furthermore, make avoids spending unnecessary time compiling and assembling files that are already up to date and do not need to be compiled or assembled. Given that a full build (by which I mean the recompilation and relinking of every single file in the project) can take several hours on an ambitious program, make saves an enormous amount of idle time when all you need to do is test changes made to one small part of the program.

There is actually a lot more to the Unix make facility than this, but what I've described are the fundamental principles. You have the power to make compiling conditional, inclusion of files conditional, and much more. You won't need to fuss with such things on your first forays into assembly language (or C programming, for that matter), but it's good to know that the power is there as your programming skills improve and you take on more ambitious projects.

Using make from within EMACS

The EMACS source code editor has the power to invoke the make facility without forcing you to leave the editor. This means that you can change a source code file in the editor and then compile it without dropping back out to the Linux shell. EMACS has a command called Compile, which is an item in its Tools menu. When you select Tools | Compile, EMACS will place the following command in the command line at the bottom of its window and wait for you to do something:

```
compile command: make -k
```

You can add additional text to this command line, you can backspace over it and delete parts of it (like the –k option), or you can press Enter and execute the command as EMACS wrote it. In most cases (especially while you're just getting started) all you need to do is press Enter.

Here's what happens: EMACS invokes the make utility. Unless you typed another name for the make file, make assumes that the make file will be called "makefile." The –k option instructs make to stop building any file in which an error occurs and to leave the previous copy of the target file undisturbed. If this doesn't make sense to you right now, don't worry—it's a good idea to use –k until you're *really* sure you don't need to. EMACS places it on the command line automatically, and you have to explicitly backspace over it to make it go away.

When it invokes make, EMACS opens a new text buffer and pipes all text output from the make process into that buffer. It will typically split your EMACS window so that the make buffer window is below the buffer you were in when you selected Tools | Compile. This allows you to see the progress of the make operation (including any error or warning messages) without leaving EMACS.

Of course, if make determines that the executable file is up to date, it will do nothing beyond displaying a message to that effect:

```
make: 'eatlinux' is up to date.
```

If you're using EMACS in an X Window window (which is what will happen automatically if you have X Window running when you invoke EMACS), you can switch from window to window by clicking with the mouse on the window you want to work in. This way you can click your way right back to the window in which you're editing source code.

One advantage to having make pipe its output into an EMACS buffer is that you can save the buffer to a text file for later reference. To do this, just keep the cursor in the make window, select the Files | Save Buffer As command, and then give the new buffer file a name.

Understanding AT&T Instruction Mnemonics

I've alluded a time or two in this book to the fact that there is more than one set of mnemonics for the x86 instructions set. There is only one set of machine instructions, but the machine instructions are pure binary bit patterns that were never intended for human consumption. A mnemonic is just that: a way for human beings to remember what the binary bit pattern 1000100111000011 means to the CPU. Instead of writing 16 ones and zeros in a row (or even the slightly more graspable hexadecimal equivalent $89 $C3), we say **MOV BX,AX**.

Keep in mind that mnemonics are just that—memory joggers for humans—and are creatures unknown to the CPU itself. Assemblers translate mnemonics to machine instructions. Although we can agree among ourselves that **MOV BX,AX** will translate to 1000100111000011, there's nothing magical about the string **MOV BX,AX**. We could as well have agreed on "COPY AX TO BX" or "STICK GPREGA INTO GPREGB." We use **MOV BX,AX** because that was what Intel suggested we do, and since it designed and manufactures the CPU chips, we feel that it has no small privilege in such matters.

There is another set of mnemonics for the x86 processors, and, as luck would have it, those mnemonics predominate in the Linux world. They didn't come about out of cussedness or contrariness, but because the people who originally created Unix also wished to create a family of nearly portable assemblers to help implement Unix on new platforms. I say "nearly portable" because a truly portable assembler is impossible. (Supposedly, the C language originated as an attempt to create a genuinely portable assembler notation—which, of course, is the definition of a higher-level language.) What they did do was create a set of global conventions that all assemblers within the Unix family would adhere to, and thus make creating a CPU-specific assembler faster and less trouble. These conventions actually predate the creation of the x86 processors themselves.

When gcc compiles a C source code file to machine code, what it really does is translate the C source code to assembly language source code, using what most people call the *AT&T mnemonics*. (Unix was created at AT&T in the sixties, and the assembler conventions for Unix assemblers were defined there as well.) Look back to Figure 12.1. The gcc compiler takes as input a .c source code file, and outputs a .s assembly source file, which is then handed to the GNU assembler gas for assembly. This is the way the GNU tools work on all platforms. In a sense, assembly language is an intermediate language used mostly for the C compiler's benefit. In most cases, programmers never see it and don't have to fool with it.

In most cases. However, if you're going to deal with the GNU debugger gdb at a machine-code level (rather than at the C source code level), the AT&T mnemonics will be in your face at every single step of the way, heh-heh. In my view the usefulness of gdb is greatly reduced by its strict dependence on the AT&T instruction mnemonics. I keep looking for somebody to create a DEBUG-style debugger for Linux that uses Intel's own mnemonics, but so far I've come up empty.

Therefore, it would make sense to become at least passingly familiar with the AT&T mnemonic set. There are some general rules that, once digested, make it much easier. Here's the list in short form:

- *AT&T mnemonics and register names are invariably in lowercase.* This is in keeping with the Unix convention of case sensitivity, and at complete variance with the Intel convention of uppercase for assembly language source. I've mixed uppercase and lowercase in the text and examples to get you used to seeing assembly source both ways, but you have to remember that while Intel (and hence NASM) suggests uppercase but will accept lowercase, AT&T *requires* lowercase.

- *Register names are always preceded by the percent symbol, %.* That is, what Intel would write as AX or EBX, AT&T would write as %ax and %ebx. This helps the assembler recognize register names.

- *Every AT&T machine instruction mnemonic that has operands has a single-character suffix indicating how large its operands are.* The suffix letters are *b, w,* and *l,* indicating byte (8 bits), word (16 bits), or long (32 bits). What Intel would write as MOV BX,AX, AT&T would write as movw %ax,%bx. (The changed order of %ax and %bx is *not* an error. See the next rule!)

- *In the AT&T syntax, source and destination operands are placed in the opposite order from Intel syntax.* That is, what Intel would write as MOV BX,AX, AT&T would write as movw %ax,%bx. In other words, in AT&T syntax, the source operand comes first, followed by the destination. This actually makes a little more sense than Intel conventions, but confusion and errors are inevitable.

- *In the AT&T syntax, immediate operands are always preceded by the dollar sign, $.* What Intel would write as PUSH DWORD 32, AT&T would write as pushl $32. This helps the assembler recognize immediate operands.

- *AT&T documentation refers to "sections" where we would say "segments."* A *segment override* is thus a *section override* in AT&T parlance. This doesn't come into play much because segments are not a big issue in 32-bit flat model programming. Still, be aware of it.

- *Not all Intel instruction mnemonics have AT&T equivalents.* JCXZ, JECXZ, LOOP, LOOPZ, LOOPE, LOOPNZ, and LOOPNE do not exist in the AT&T mnemonic set, and gcc never generates code that uses them. This won't be a problem for us, as we're using NASM, but you won't see these instructions in gdb displays.

- *In the AT&T syntax, displacements in memory references are signed quantities placed outside parentheses containing the base, index, and scale values*. I'll treat this one separately a little later, as you'll see it a lot in .s files and you should be able to understand it.

There are a handful of other issues that would be involved in programs more complex than we'll take up in this book. These mostly involve near versus far calls and jumps and their associated return instructions.

Examining gas Source Files Created by gcc

The best way to get a sense for the AT&T assembly syntax is to look at an actual AT&T-style .s file produced by gcc. Doing this actually has two benefits: First of all, it will help you become familiar with the AT&T mnemonics and formatting conventions. In addition, you may find it useful, when struggling to figure out how to call a C library function from assembly, to create a short C program that calls the function of interest and then examines the .s file that gcc produces when it compiles your C program. The dateis.c program which follows was part of my early research, and I used it to get a sense for how **ctime()** was called at the assembly level. Obviously, for this trick to work you must have at least a journeyman understanding of the AT&T mnemonics. (I discuss **ctime()** and other time-related C library calls in detail in the next chapter.)

You don't automatically get a .s file every time you compile a C program. The .s file is created, but once gas assembles the .s file to a binary object code file (typically a .o file), it deletes the .s file. If you want to examine a .s file created by gcc, you must compile with the –S option. (Note that this is an uppercase *S*. Case matters big time in the Unix world!) The command would look like this:

```
gcc dateis.c -S
```

Note that the output of this command is *the assembly source file only*. If you specify the –S option, gcc understands that you want to generate assembly source rather than an executable program file, so all it will generate is the .s file. To compile a C program to an executable program file, you must compile it again *without* the –S option.

Here's dateis.c. It does nothing more than print out the date and time as returned by the standard C library function **ctime()**:

```
#include <time.h>
#include <stdio.h>
```

```
int main()
  {
    time_t timeval;

    (void)time(&timeval);
    printf("The date is: %s", ctime(&timeval));
    exit(0);
  }
```

It's not much of a program, but it does illustrate the use of three C library function calls, **time()**, **ctime()**, and **printf()**. When gcc compiles the preceding program (dateis.c), it produces the file dateis.s, which follows. I have manually added the equivalent Intel mnemonics as comments to the right of the AT&T mnemonics, so you can see what equals what in the two systems. (Alas, neither gcc nor any other utility I have ever seen will do this for you!)

```
        .file       "dateis.c"
        .version    "01.01"
gcc2_compiled.:
.section  .rodata
.LC0:
        .string     "The date is: %s"
.text
        .align 4
.globl main
        .type       main,@function
main:
        pushl %ebp          # push ebp
        movl %esp,%ebp      # mov ebp,esp
        subl $4,%esp        # sub esp,4
        leal -4(%ebp),%eax  # lea eax,ebp-4
        pushl %eax          # push eax
        call time           # call time
        addl $4,%esp        # add esp,4
        leal -4(%ebp),%eax  # lea eax,ebp-4
        pushl %eax          # push eax
        call ctime          # call ctime
        addl $4,%esp        # add esp,4
        movl %eax,%eax      # mov eax,eax
        pushl %eax          # push eax
        pushl $.LC0         # push dword .LC0
        call printf         # call printf
        addl $8,%esp        # add esp,8
        pushl $0            # push dword 0
        call exit           # call exit
        addl $4,%esp        # add esp,4
        .p2align 4,,7
.L1:
        leave               # leave
```

```
    ret              # ret
.Lfe1:
    .size     main,.Lfe1-main
    .ident    "GCC: (GNU) egcs-2.91.66 19990314/Linux (egcs-1.1.2 release)"
```

One thing to keep in mind when reading this is that dateis.s is assembly language code produced mechanically by a compiler, and *not* by a human programmer! Some things about the code (such as why the label .L1 is present but never referenced) are less than ideal and can only be explained as artifacts of gcc's compilation machinery. In a more complex program there may be some customary use of a label .L1 that doesn't exist in a program this simple.

Some quick things to note here while reading the preceding listing:

- When an instruction does not take operands (call, leave, ret), it does not have an operand-size suffix. Calls and returns look pretty much alike in both Intel and AT&T syntax.

- When referenced, the name of a message string is prefixed by a dollar sign ($) the same way that numeric literals are. In NASM, a named string variable is considered a variable and not a literal. This is just another AT&T peccadillo to be aware of.

- Note that the comment delimiter in the AT&T scheme is the pound sign (#) rather than the semicolon used in nearly all Intel-style assemblers, including NASM.

AT&T Memory Reference Syntax

As you'll remember from earlier chapters, referencing a memory location (as distinct from referencing its address) is done by enclosing the location of the address in square brackets, like so:

```
mov ax, dword [ebp]
```

Here, we're taking whatever 32-bit quantity is located at the address contained in EBP and loading it into register AX. The x86 processors allow a number of different ways of specifying the address. To a core address called a *base* we can add another register called an *index*, and to that a constant value called a *displacement*. We used this sort of addressing to locate a string within a table of strings back in Chapter 11. Such addressing modes can look like this:

```
mov eax, dword [ebx-4]    ; Base minus displacement
mov al, byte [bx+di+28]   ; Base plus index plus displacement
```

I haven't really covered this, but you can add an additional factor to the index called a *scale*, which is a power of two by which you multiply the index:

```
mov al, byte [bx+di*4]
```

The scale can't be any arbitrary value, but must be one of 2, 4, or 8. (The value 1 is legal but doesn't accomplish anything useful.) This mode, called *scaled indexed addressing*, is only available in 32-bit flat model and will not work in 16-bit modes at all—which is why I haven't mentioned it in this book before now.

All of the examples I've shown you so far use the Intel syntax. The AT&T syntax for memory addressing is considerably different. In place of square brackets, AT&T uses parentheses to enclose the components of a memory address:

```
movb (%ebx),%al     # mov byte al,[ebx] in Intel syntax
```

Here, we're moving the byte quantity at [ebx] to AL. (Don't forget that the order of operands is reversed from what Intel syntax does!) Inside the parentheses you place the base, the index, and the scale, when present. (The base must always be there.) The displacement, when one exists, must go in front of and outside the parentheses:

```
movl -4(%ebx),%eax        # mov dword eax,[ebx-4] in Intel syntax
movb 28(%ebx,%edi),%eax   # mov byte eax,[ebx+edi+28] in Intel syntax
```

Note that in AT&T syntax, you don't do the math inside the parentheses. The base, index, and scale are separated by commas, and plus signs and asterisks are not allowed. The schema for interpreting an AT&T memory reference is as follows:

```
±disp(base,index,scale)
```

The ± symbol indicates that the displacement is *signed*; that is, it may be either positive or negative, to indicate whether the displacement value is added to or subtracted from the rest of the address. Typically, you only see the sign as explicitly negative; without the minus symbol, the assumption is that the displacement is positive. The displacement value is optional. You may omit it entirely if there's no displacement in the memory reference. Similarly, you may omit the scale if there is no scale value present in the effective address.

What you will see most of the time, however, is a very simple type of memory reference:

```
-16(%ebp)
```

The displacements will vary, of course, but what this almost always means is that an instruction is referencing a data item somewhere on the stack. C code allocates its variables on the stack, in a stack frame, and then references those variables by constant offsets from the value in EBP. EBP acts as a "thumb in the stack," and items on the stack may be referenced in terms of offsets (either positive or negative) away from EBP. The preceding reference would tell a machine instruction to work with an item at the address in EBP minus 16 bytes.

I have a lot more to say about stack frames in the next chapter.

Using the GNU Debugger

The first thing you have to understand about the GNU debugger gdb is that it was designed to work as a high-level debugger on C programs. That is, gdb allows programmers to single-step a C program by stepping from one C statement to another, setting breakpoints on C statements, and so on. It isn't nearly as good as DOS DEBUG at poking around assembly code programs, or any programs at the binary level irrespective of their source language. I've been looking for some sort of DEBUG clone for Linux, but as yet haven't found it. If you're going to use a debugger to work on your assembly code, gdb will have to do. (And if you find a DEBUG clone for Linux, please let me know! There will be a third edition of this book someday.)

In terms of their basic concepts, DEBUG and gdb are very much alike. Both load a program into memory and allow you to examine its innards, as well as examine memory and registers. How they look to you sitting in your chair, however, is radically different. And some of that difference has to do with the nature of Linux assembly programs versus DOS assembly programs.

Your Code, My Code, and Our Code

When you write a DOS assembly language program, as I explained in the earlier parts of this book, you write *all* of it. All the code that runs is only the code that you write, or that you explicitly and optionally link into it. When you run that program, DOS hands control of the machine to the program, right at the first machine instruction you wrote at the start of your program. It continues to run your code until you return control back to DOS with a call to service 04CH of INT 21H.

This is simple and easy to understand, which is one important reason I started you off with DOS programming rather than Linux programming. Linux is different. *Lots* different. And once you begin using a debugger to go inside the binary space of a program you've written, you have to understand that difference thoroughly.

To communicate with the Linux kernel, an assembly language program should use the C library as its communications layer. It's possible to make direct kernel calls, but it's not a good idea, as the details of making those calls may change from version to version of Linux. We're going to play it straight in this book and make all input and output calls through the standard C library.

This means we have to link the C library into an assembly language program. Doing so allows us to call C library functions such as **printf()**, **ctime()**, and so on. However, linking in those function calls comes with a certain amount of baggage, and the baggage consists of startup and shutdown code.

In truth, when you create a Linux assembly language program as I explain in this and the next chapter, you're creating a sort of a hybrid. The structure of this hybrid is shown in Figure 12.2.

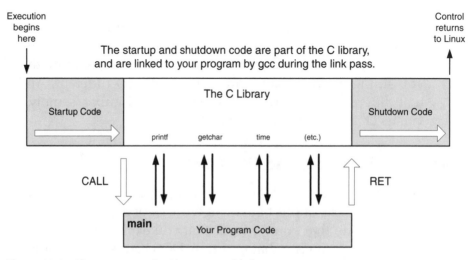

Figure 12.2 The structure of a Linux assembly language program.

Linking your assembly language program to the C library adds in all the code shown in the top bar. In addition to the code containing library calls such as **printf()**, there is a block of code that runs before your program begins, and another block that runs after your program ends. In a sense, your program is only a subroutine called by a boilerplate empty program in the C library. Your program is called as though it were a subroutine (with the **CALL** instruction) and it returns control to the C library code using a **RET** instruction.

Technically, your program *is* a subroutine, and it helps to think of it as one. That's how I've drawn it in Figure 12.2. When Linux begins executing your program, it actually starts, not at the top of the code *you* wrote, but at the beginning of the startup code. When the startup code has done what it must, it executes a **CALL** instruction that takes execution down into your assembly code. When the assembly language program you wrote returns control to its caller via **RET**, the shutdown code begins executing, and it's the shutdown code that actually returns control to Linux.

In between, you can make as many calls into the C runtime library code as you like. When you link your program with gcc, the code containing the C library routines that you call is linked into the program. Note well that the startup and shutdown code, as well as all the code for the library calls, are all physically present in the executable file that you generate with gcc. You're not making calls into a DLL somewhere. Whatever calls are made into the Linux kernel are made by the C library code.

The problem caused by the presence of the startup code in your executable file is that when you begin single-stepping the program, you're single-stepping through C library code. That can be enlightening, and I encourage you to do it a few times while you're first getting your Linux legs. However, after a while you'll be pounding on the keyboard trying to get through it so that you can figure out why *your* code isn't working correctly. You need a way to skip past the startup code. And skipping code means you need some signposts in the executable file so that you have someplace to skip to. For this you need symbols in your executable file.

Spotting Symbols in an Executable File

To use gdb, you need to be able to access symbols defined within your program, that is, labels for variables and locations in the code. They allow you to jump from one place in the program forward to another without single-stepping through the intervening code. Such symbols are usually included in the executable file by default but can be stripped out to make the executable file smaller.

To determine whether symbols are present in one of your executable files, execute the nm utility on that file:

```
nm hilinux
```

No one's ever explained to me what *nm* stands for; my hunch is it's a scrunched form of "name." (When it was created, people communicated with Unix on electromechanical Teletype machines, which were ponderously slow and difficult to type on. There was a *big* payback in using short names for things.) What you'll see when you run nm will either be a list of symbols, or else this message:

```
hilinux: no symbols
```

The list, when you get one, will be quite long—and most of the symbols on the list will be unfamiliar to you. That's because they're symbols of elements of the C library that have been linked into your program. Your symbols, the ones defined in your assembly language program, will be there somewhere—alas, they're not all clustered conveniently together. Look for **main**—assuming you defined a label **main** in your program (and you must or you will have trouble linking it with the C library), it will be there, probably near the end of the list. Here's a typical nm listing for a very simple program that I present in the next chapter:

```
0804943c ? _DYNAMIC
08049420 ? _GLOBAL_OFFSET_TABLE_
080483fc R _IO_stdin_used
08049414 ? __CTOR_END__
08049410 ? __CTOR_LIST__
0804941c ? __DTOR_END__
08049418 ? __DTOR_LIST__
0804940c ? __EH_FRAME_BEGIN__
0804940c ? __FRAME_END__
080494dc A __bss_start
08049400 D __data_start
         U __deregister_frame_info@@GLIBC_2.0
080483b0 t __do_global_ctors_aux
08048320 t __do_global_dtors_aux
         U __gmon_start__
         U __libc_start_main@@GLIBC_2.0
         U __register_frame_info@@GLIBC_2.0
080494dc A _edata
080494f4 A _end
080483dc A _etext
080483dc ? _fini
```

```
          U _fp_hw
08048274 ? _init
080482f0 T _start
08049408 d completed.3
08049400 W data_start
08048368 t fini_dummy
0804940c d force_to_data
0804940c d force_to_data
08048370 t frame_dummy
08048314 t gcc2_compiled.
08048320 t gcc2_compiled.
080483b0 t gcc2_compiled.
080483dc t gcc2_compiled.
08048390 t init_dummy
080483d4 t init_dummy
080483a0 T main
080494dc b object.8
08049404 d p.2
```

The program this listing was generated from, boiler.asm, has only one symbol in it: **main**. The capital *T* to the left of the symbol **main** indicates that the symbol resides in the [text] section of your program, and the fact that it's capitalized indicates that **main** is global. Local symbols (which means all symbols you do not explicitly mark as global) are indicated by small letters here. Because nm is virtually undocumented, I don't know what all the various tags mean, but *t* or *T* indicates items residing in the [text] section, and *d* or *D* indicates items residing in the [data] section.

What are all the rest of these symbols? Mostly, they're code labels and data items from the C library, which gcc links into your program. Most of the time you won't have to fool with them, especially when you're just getting started.

Stripping Symbols out of an Executable File

When you're done debugging a program, you can strip the symbols out of the program to reduce the size of the program on disk. For small programs the reduction can be substantial; the eatlinux.asm program I show you in the next chapter went from 12 to 3K bytes after I stripped the symbols out of it.

Stripping the symbols out of a program is trivial. You use the strip command, followed by the name of the executable:

```
strip eatlinux
```

And that's it! Like most Unix utilities, strip is a taciturn creature and won't say anything unless something goes wrong. No comment, no problems.

Loading a Program for Debugging

Loading a program for debugging via gdb is easy: On the Linux shell command line, you follow the command gdb with the name of the executable file you wish to debug:

```
gdb eatlinux
```

This command runs gdb and loads the file to be debugged into memory, much as you did with DEBUG under DOS. Once loaded, you'll see gdb's command prompt:

```
(gdb)
```

Alas, that's where the resemblance ends. You'll get a command prompt from gdb, but you can't begin single-stepping the program or inspecting registers yet.

The problem is this: Linux, like all versions of Unix, is a multiuser, multitasking operating system, orders of magnitude more complex than DOS. Other programs are running and continue running while you're in there with your assembly program and gdb, single-stepping. This means that special measures must be taken by Linux to allow your program to share the machine with all other running programs, and those measures cannot be taken until you explicitly run the program. Most critical to your efforts as a programmer is the fact that Linux doesn't calculate initial register values for a program until it has spawned a process in which to run it. A *process* is a sort of operational frame within which a program is run. I think of a process as a frying pan into which you pour your executable code from its "can" on disk in order to do something with it. In a very real sense, a debuggable program (that is to say, something you can look at with a debugger and glean useful information from) doesn't really exist until the program has been run. You can't cook your Spam while it's still in the can, brother.

Now, the command to run a program from within gdb is "run"; however, there's a catch. If you issue the run command (which is roughly equivalent to DEBUG's G command), the program will run, and run until completion, then stop running. It won't pause anywhere for you to start single-stepping or inspecting registers or memory.

Before you run the program from within gdb, you must set at least one breakpoint.

Setting Breakpoints in gdb

Setting breakpoints in gdb isn't difficult. It does require that debugging symbols be present in your executable file, as I mentioned a little earlier in this chapter. You can set a breakpoint on any symbol listed by the nm utility as being in the [text] section of your program by the *t* or *T* symbol to the left of the symbol's name. While you're just getting started, many or most of these symbols will be of locations within the startup or shutdown code, or within the C library. On the other hand, you should be able to recognize your own symbols.

The symbol you're most likely to want to set a breakpoint on is **main**, which in nearly all cases will be the beginning of your program. (The C library assumes—and hence requires—that the main program it is linked to be called "main.") Setting a breakpoint on **main** is easy enough to do:

```
(gdb) break main
```

Gdb will respond by confirming the breakpoint, giving it an identification number, and telling you its machine address:

```
Breakpoint 1 at 0x80483d6
```

Additional breakpoints will be called out as Breakpoint 2, Breakpoint 3, and so forth. Once you've set at least one breakpoint, you can execute the run command. When you do, you'll see a message like this, specific to your system, of course:

```
Starting program: /usr/local/nasmbook/showargs

Breakpoint 1, 0x80483d6 in main ()
(gdb)
```

What this means is that program execution is paused at the breakpoint called out in the message. The big hex number is the 32-bit address where execution was paused. If you have set other breakpoints, you can skip to them, in sequence, by executing the continue command to move from breakpoint to breakpoint. Another way to do this (if you know how many breakpoints away from your destination you are) is to give a numeric parameter to the continue command:

```
continue 2
```

This will skip past the next two breakpoints and is equivalent to executing the continue command twice. Leaving out the number entirely is equivalent to "continue 1."

If you decide you no longer need a breakpoint and it's getting in your way, you can remove the breakpoint with the delete command. You must provide delete with the identification number of the breakpoint to be removed:

```
delete 1
```

On the other hand, you can disable a breakpoint without removing it completely. A disabled breakpoint remains in gdb's breakpoint table, but execution will not pause there. To disable a breakpoint, use the disable command followed by the breakpoint's identification number:

```
disable 1
```

Turning a disabled breakpoint back on is done with the enable command, followed by the breakpoint's identification number:

```
enable 1
```

Keeping track of what's enabled and what's disabled can be a challenge. To help out, you can request at any time a summary description of all existing breakpoints by using the info breakpoints command:

```
(gdb) info breakpoints
Num Type           Disp Enb Address    What
1   breakpoint     keep y   0x080483d6 <main+6>
2   breakpoint     keep y   0x080483de <showit>
(gdb)
```

Here, the breakpoint's identification number is at the left margin, with the type of the item (here, "breakpoint") to the right, followed by the breakpoint's disposition and enable status. An enabled breakpoint will show the letter y under the Enb header. A disabled breakpoint will show an n.

A breakpoint's disposition status is an advanced topic that I won't take up in detail. Basically, the disposition status specifies what happens to the breakpoint when the breakpoint is hit during program execution. "Keep" is the default and indicates that nothing happens; the breakpoint remains in existence and enabled. Other disposition status values can direct gdb to delete or disable the breakpoint when it is hit.

The address of a breakpoint is the memory address in hex of the instruction on which the breakpoint has been set. The What header is more useful when you're debugging C code. For assembly work, it indicates the location of the breakpoint relative to a symbol—usually the symbol on which you set the breakpoint.

Sharp readers may be wondering why the "What" value for Breakpoint 1 in the preceding listing is given as <main+6>. Why not just <main>? There's a small and very technical oddity here that stems from the special nature of the label **main**. For gcc to successfully link your assembly programs to the C library, the starting point of your programs must be labeled **main**, and the label **main** must be declared as **global**. The main program part of all C programs *must* be called **main**, and what you're doing in a sense is writing a C program in which the main program is written in assembly. (All the rest of it, in the libraries, is written in C.)

So, this special label **main** is hard-coded into the GNU tools in a number of ways. One of these ways involves breakpoints set by gdb. If you want to begin single-stepping your program, but you don't want to single-step through the startup code first, a breakpoint at **main** is a natural thing to want. (Single-stepping through the startup code is possible, and can be educational, but it involves some special techniques that I'm not going to take it up here.)

However, . . . at the very beginning of your assembly language main program are some required instructions, sometimes called *prolog code*, that create a stack frame for your program. I explain this in detail in the next chapter; consider it a "forward reference" for now. That prolog is required, and all the programs you'll see me present in the next chapter will have this identical sequence at their beginnings:

```
main:
    push ebp        ; Set up stack frame for debugger
    mov ebp,esp
    push ebx        ; Program must preserve ebp, ebx, esi, & edi
    push esi
    push edi
    ;;; Everything before this is boilerplate; use it for all ordinary apps!
```

Following the **main** label are exactly five instructions. These instructions are crucial for your program to be able to access the stack and avoid trashing important register values, and the GNU debugger gdb makes the assumption that in nearly all cases you'll want to begin single-stepping *after* these instructions have executed. (Its reasoning: Your program won't work correctly until they've executed, so why waste the time stepping through them?) So, when you request a breakpoint on the main program with this command:

```
break main
```

gdb will actually set a breakpoint six instructions *after* the label **main**. This guarantees that the stack frame has been set up, allowing you to access variables on the stack. These variables include any command line parameters passed to your program at startup, so it is an important consideration.

If you really and truly do want to set a breakpoint precisely at the **main** label, you need to execute this command:

```
break *main
```

There's not a whole lot of advantage in it, unless you want to watch stack frame setup actually happen. (There's nothing wrong with that, of course. But once you've seen it happen a time or two there's not much sense in watching it every time you debug!)

Providing Command-Line Arguments

It's often useful to be able to provide command-line arguments when debugging a program. Doing it is easy: Just follow the run command with whatever arguments you would type on the command line for the program, exactly as you would type them:

```
(gdb) run fee fie foe fum
```

Here, four command-line arguments will be passed to the program being run under gdb. One nice touch is that these same arguments will be retained by gdb and used every time you begin program execution with the run command. That is, you don't have to retype them every time you use run to start program execution again. (Obviously, they are lost when you exit gdb.)

If you want to provide a different set of command-line arguments while debugging the same program, you can use the set args command to enter a new set:

```
(gdb) set args foo bar bas bat
```

And if you've forgotten precisely which arguments are being stored by gdb for your next program run, you can display them with show args:

```
(gdb) show args
Argument list to give program being debugged when it is started is:
    foo bar bas bat
```

Given the extreme brevity of most gdb (and all Unix) prompts and messages, show args takes the award for about the gabbiest command you'll encounter.

Examining Registers

Whatever DEBUG can show you, gdb can show you as well. I don't think the gdb display formats are as intuitive and easy to grasp as DEBUG's, but with some practice they're perfectly usable.

You can display the contents of CPU registers with the info reg command. The command and its display look like this:

```
(gdb) info reg
      eax: 0x40101db8  1074798008
      ecx:  0x80483d0   134513616
      edx: 0x40100234  1074790964
      ebx: 0x401031b4  1074803124
      esp: 0xbffffbac -1073742932
      ebp: 0xbffffbb8 -1073742920
      esi: 0xbffffc04 -1073742844
      edi:        0x1           1
      eip:  0x80483d6   134513622
   eflags:       0x246 IOPL: 0; flags: PF ZF IF
 orig_eax: 0xffffffff          -1
       cs:        0x23          35
       ss:        0x2b          43
       ds:        0x2b          43
       es:        0x2b          43
       fs:         0x0           0
       gs:         0x0           0
(gdb)
```

This is straightforward. Every value except for eflags is given both in hex (the left-hand value) and decimal. The way that the Flags register is displayed is one place where I think gdb has it way better than DEBUG: Every flag that is *set* appears in the list, after "flags:". Flags that are cleared are not displayed at all. "IOPL" means "I/O Privilege Level" and is an indicator of what permissions your program has been given to perform I/O. In most cases this will be 0, meaning no permission at all! (This is one reason why it's useful to let the C library handle I/O, since the C library then gets to deal with the complexities of requesting I/O permissions.)

Once you've moved beyond the assembly language basics I'm teaching in this book, you may wish to examine the floating-point processor registers, and for this you need a slightly different command:

```
(gdb) info all-reg
      eax: 0x40101db8  1074798008
      ecx:  0x80483d0   134513616
      edx: 0x40100234  1074790964
      ebx: 0x401031b4  1074803124
      esp: 0xbffffbac -1073742932
      ebp: 0xbffffbb8 -1073742920
      esi: 0xbffffc04 -1073742844
      edi:        0x1          1
      eip: 0x80483d6   134513622
   eflags:      0x246 IOPL: 0; flags: PF ZF IF
 orig_eax: 0xffffffff          -1
       cs:       0x23          35
       ss:       0x2b          43
       ds:       0x2b          43
       es:       0x2b          43
       fs:        0x0           0
       gs:        0x0           0
      st0: 0x00000000000000000000 Empty Zero   0
      st1: 0x00000000000000000000 Empty Zero   0
      st2: 0x00000000000000000000 Empty Zero   0
      st3: 0x4004a400000000000000 Empty Normal 41
      st4: 0x4007ce00000000000000 Empty Normal 412
      st5: 0x00000000000000000000 Empty Zero   0
      st6: 0x4002c000000000000000 Empty Normal 12
      st7: 0x40018000000000000000 Empty Normal 4
    fctrl:   0x037f 64 bit; NEAR; mask INVAL DENOR DIVZ OVERF UNDER LOS;
    fstat: 0x0000 flags 0000; top 0;
     ftag: 0xffff
      fip: 0x0809ffaa
      fcs: 0x035d0023
   fopoff: 0xbfffead8
   fopsel:     0x002b
   fopsel:     0x002b
(gdb)
```

I can't take up the floating-point processor (FPU) in this book, but once you begin to program it you'll need to understand most of what info all-reg displays.

Examining Program Variables and Individual Registers

Whereas you can use the info regs command to see a dump of all the registers at once, you can also examine both registers and program variables individually. There are two distinct mechanisms for displaying individual items in gdb, and when you're working with assembly language in NASM, you're going to have to use both of them.

The first is the easiest to understand. The print command will display the value stored in any of the general-purpose registers. The only trick is to prefix the name of the register with a dollar sign:

```
(gdb) print $edx
```

What gdb displays in response will take just a little explaining:

```
$1 = 1074790964
```

(Obviously, you may see some other value than the one shown here.) Unless you apply a format code (more on which follows), the default display of register values will be in decimal. The "$1 =" indicates that the display has been logged in the value history. The *value history* is a memory-based table in which gdb keeps values displayed using the print command. Each time you display something using print, gdb tucks the displayed value away in the value history and gives it an identification number, starting with 1. You can then redisplay the value by executing the print command on the value history identification number:

```
(gdb) print $$1
```

Note that there is an additional "$" symbol here.

One important caution is that gdb *cannot* display values for 8-bit or 16-bit registers. In other words, you cannot display AX all by itself, or AH or AL. The symbols $ax, $ah, and $al (and their opposite numbers in the other registers) are not defined in gdb's symbol table.

The print command is the best way to display values of program variables other than ASCII strings or other arrays. You can specify how the variable will be displayed (and this applies to registers as well) with a format code. The *format code* allows you to display registers or variables in decimal, octal, binary, or hex, or as ASCII characters. The code is placed after a slash, before the name of the register or variable to be displayed:

```
(gdb) print /x seconds
$5 = 0x2a
```

Here, an integer program variable named **seconds** is displayed in hexadecimal. You could as well display it as an ASCII character:

```
(gdb) print /c seconds
$6 = 42 '*'
```

It's the same value (decimal 42, hex 2A) but displayed as its ASCII equivalent, which is the asterisk character (*). You can display a register or a variable in binary by using the t format code. This is useful when you're interpreting a register value as a bitmap or as a set of flags:

```
(gdb) print /t $ebx
$7 = 1000000001001000010100010000
```

Note that when using the t format code, leading zeros in the display are suppressed, so you will not always get 32 ones or zeros. (There are only 28 in the preceding value. The four highest-order bits in the value are 0 and have been suppressed.) A summary of all the format codes available to the print command is given in Table 12.1.

Here, however, is a problem: The print command has no way to display anything that won't fit in a character or integer value, so strings can't be displayed that way. Instead, you must display null-terminated string variables with the x command (think "examine"), which is intended for use in examining memory. Program variables exist in memory, and hence can be displayed with the x command. Here's a typical use of the x command to display a string variable:

```
(gdb) x /s &eatmsg
```

As with the print command, the format codes are placed first, preceded by a slash symbol (/). The name of the variable follows, preceded by an ampersand (&). C programmers will recognize the use of the ampersand here: It's the "address of" operator in C. In C, the expression **&eatmsg** would return the address of the variable **eatmsg**. That's just what we're

Table 12.1 Format Codes for gdb's Print and x Commands

CODE	CMD	DEFINITION
c	Both	Assume the data is a single byte, and display it as an ASCII character
d	Both	Assume data is an integer, and display it in signed decimal
i	x	Display the memory value as a machine instruction mnemonic
o	Both	Assume data is an integer, and display it in octal
s	x	Assume data is a null-terminated string, and display it as a string
t	Both	Display data in binary (think: base 2)
u	Both	Assume the data is an integer, and display it in unsigned decimal
x	Both	Assume the data is an integer, and display it in hexadecimal

doing here: We're handing the x command the address of the variable **eatmsg**, so that it can display memory starting at that address.

Note that values displayed by the x command are not retained in the value history!

The format code s indicates that the x command should treat memory as a null-terminated string. Starting with the address indicated by **&eatmsg**, x will then display memory as a null-terminated string. Table 12.1 shows the various format codes available for use with the x command. Note that two of the format codes, s and I, are available *only* with the x command. Print does not support them.

You can use the address-of operator with the print command to determine the memory address of a program variable. To display the address of a variable named **seconds**, you would issue this command:

```
(gdb) print &seconds
$8 = (<data variable, no debug info> *) 0x80496d5
```

This will also work for code labels, to determine the address at which a label exists.

The x command can dump memory for a specified number of bytes beginning at a specified address. The two additional tricks (over and above the format code) are the repeat count and the unit size. The *repeat count* is a number placed immediately after the slash in the x command, and it specifies the number of units to dump. The *format command* comes next and indicates which way the data must be displayed. Finally, the unit size specifies how large each displayed unit is. For a traditional memory count, this is best done as a byte, for which the code is b. The address may be specified as a literal address in hex, or as the address in a register, or as the address of a specific variable name or program label. Here's an example of a memory dump of 64 bytes, each formatted in hex:

```
(gdb) x /64xb 0x8049500
0x8049500:    0x55   0x89   0xe5   0xc9   0xc3   0x90   0x90   0x90
0x8049508:    0x90   0x90   0x90   0x90   0x90   0x90   0x90   0x90
0x8049510:    0x55   0x89   0xe5   0x60   0x68   0x00   0x00   0x00
0x8049518:    0x00   0xe8   0xfe   0xfe   0xff   0xff   0x83   0xc4
0x8049520:    0x04   0xa3   0xe0   0x97   0x04   0x08   0x68   0xe0
0x8049528:    0x97   0x04   0x08   0xe8   0x1c   0xff   0xff   0xff
0x8049530:    0x83   0xc4   0x04   0x50   0x68   0x2c   0x96   0x04
0x8049538:    0x08   0xe8   0xfe   0xfe   0xff   0xff   0x83   0xc4
(gdb)
```

The "/64xb" tells you first how many units, then how to format it (in hex), and finally the size of the displayed units (bytes). Table 12.2 lists all the available unit size codes.

Half an hour experimenting with the various codes will give you a good feeling for how you can display memory and items in memory using gdb. The memory dump display isn't as nice as DEBUG's side-by-side hex-and-ASCII display, but once you've worked with it for a while you can get a good feel for what's out there lurking in memory.

Changing Register and Program Variable Values

Changing values within machine registers and simple variables (that is, variables that are not strings or arrays) can be done with the print command. Just as print can show you what's in a register or a variable, it can place new values in them as well. The notation looks a lot like an assignment statement in C:

```
(gdb) print $edx=42
$9 = 42
```

Here, the EDX register will be given the new value 42. Print will echo the new value and assign it a number in the value history. This can be done with simple program variables as well. For example, given a 32-bit integer variable named **seconds**, you can store a new value into **seconds** this way:

```
(gdb) print seconds=57
$9 = 57
```

There's another way to do the same thing. The set var command will change the value of a variable without echoing the value back to you, and without adding another record to the value history:

Table 12.2 Unit Size Codes for gdb's x Command

CODE	INDICATED SIZE
b	Byte (8 bits)
h	Half word (16 bits or 2 bytes)
w	Word (32 bits or 4 bytes)
g	Giant word (64 bits or 8 bytes)

```
(gdb) set var seconds=17
```

That's all it takes—and that's all you'll see. The effect of the set var command on the program variable is the same as though you had used print.

Patching memory at arbitrary addresses is something you may need to do from time to time. Another variation of the set command will get you there. You need to provide the name of a valid simple data type so that gdb knows what size and range to allow for the intended data. The notation for storing an integer value into memory at an arbitrary address looks like this:

```
(gdb) set {int}0x80964d5 = 68
```

C programmers may understand this as a sort of type cast into a raw memory location that has no notion of type, size, or range. You're using the type identifier **int** as a template so that gdb can correctly store the new value at that address. The preceding statement will use 4 bytes starting at the specified address, because an integer is 4 bytes in size. The following set command stores the same value a little differently:

```
(gdb) set {char}0x80964d5 = 68
```

Here, we're using the **char** (character) type as our template. The **char** type occupies only 1 byte, so in this case, the very same value of 68 (ASCII character "D") is stored in only 1 byte at the specified address, rather than at 4 consecutive bytes.

Single-Stepping Your Programs

As I explained earlier in this book with respect to DOS DEBUG, perhaps the most important job of a debugger is to let you execute an assembly language program one instruction at a time, so that you can determine *exactly* when it begins to malfunction. What occurs inside a debugger to make this possible is interesting, but way beyond the scope of this book. For our purposes here, it's enough to understand how to make it happen, and how to interpret what you see as you go.

I've explained how to set breakpoints, and it's important to understand what's going on when the program you're testing is paused at a breakpoint: The program is still *running*—in other words, it is an active Linux process—but through its own brand of magic, gdb has seized control of the machine back from your program for the time being. While the program is paused at a breakpoint, you can examine its register and variable values, examine any location in memory that you have permission to examine, change register and program variable values, and patch any memory location that you have permission to change. Finally, you can pick up execution again, in one of two ways:

- You can continue program execution at full speed, so that your program will run without pause until the point of execution encounters another breakpoint, or until it ends normally—or abnormally.

- You can continue execution one step at a time, using gdb's single-stepping commands.

Both are useful techniques. The continue command takes your program out of pause mode, and simply lets it run as though it were running outside the debugger. (It actually runs a little bit more slowly, because gdb is still there, watching for breakpoints as your program goes.) Once you pick up execution again with continue, the program will run until it encounters any breakpoint, at which time it will pause once again.

You can also pick up execution with the until command, which allows you to specify a particular breakpoint at which to pause. You must follow the word *until* with the identification number of the breakpoint at which you want to pause:

```
(gdb) until 2
```

Note well that if execution for some reason never passes breakpoint 2 (if your code branches around that breakpoint, for example), your program could well execute to completion (or to some problem that halts it) without pausing again.

The continue and until commands are useful ways to move from breakpoint to breakpoint within a program. But the really cool way to move around inside your code is one instruction at a time, watching things happen as you go. This is what single-stepping is all about, and with gdb it's remarkably easy.

Single-stepping is simple in principle: You type a gdb command that executes a single machine instruction. You type the command again, and you execute the instruction after that. In between instruction executions, you can look at registers, memory locations, and other things that might provide telltales to your program's operation.

There are two commands that single-step at the machine-instruction level: stepi and nexti. The *i* at the end of each command indicates that these step by machine instruction, and not by C source code statements. The two related commands, step and next, work with C and Modula 2 code only. (Never forget that the overwhelming majority of gdb's users are debugging C code at the C source code level, and not assembly code at all.)

The nexti and stepi instructions have shorthand forms: ni and si.

The difference between stepi and nexti may seem odd at first: Stepi executes the next machine instruction in the execution path, irrespective of which instruction it is, whereas nexti executes the next machine instruction in the execution path *unless* that instruction is a CALL instruction. If nexti executes a CALL instruction, it executes the *whole* of the subroutine invoked by that CALL instruction *without* pausing.

Users of Borland's programming languages are probably familiar with two debugging commands built into Borland's interactive environments: Step Over and Trace Into. Trace Into corresponds to gdb's stepi command, and Step Over corresponds to gdb's nexti command.

The idea is this: While you're stepping along through a program, you may wish to avoid climbing down into subroutines and stepping through them instruction by instruction—unless you're debugging the subroutine. This is especially true of subroutines that are in fact calls into the standard C library. If you're hitting a bug, it's unlikely to be in the C library. (Suspect your own code in virtually every case. Those library routines are *extremely* robust!) So, assuming you can trust the C library functions your program is calling, you probably don't want to waste time going through them an instruction at a time. The same may be true of subroutines in your own personal code library. You may have written them and proven them out long ago, so rather than go through them an instruction at a time, you'd prefer to execute the whole subroutine at once.

If this is the case, you should single-step with nexti. When nexti encounters a CALL instruction, it executes CALL and all the instructions within the subroutine invoked by that CALL instruction as though the whole subroutine were a single instruction. Boom! The subroutine has run, and you go on to the next instruction in the code execution sequence.

Stepi, on the other hand, treats all machine instructions identically: It follows the CALL instruction down into its subroutine and executes each of the subroutine's instructions in turn, coming back when the subroutine executes a RET instruction.

It really is that simple. The trick, as usual, is knowing what's happening based on what you see on your screen. Without some preparation, nexti and stepi are pretty closed-mouthed and unhelpful. Stop at a breakpoint and execute nexti, and this is what you'll see:

```
(gdb) nexti
0x80483d9 in main ()
```

The hex number is the 32-bit value of the program counter at that instruction. And that's all it tells you. You can, however, instruct gdb to be a little more verbose. This is done with the display command, using the following syntax:

```
(gdb) display /i $pc
1: x/i $eip 0x80483d6 <main+6>    movl 0x8(%ebp),%ecx
```

More like it! Here we have three major pieces of information: the machine address of the next instruction to be executed, its offset in instructions from the nearest label, and the machine instruction mnemonic, in AT&T format. The /i portion of the display command instructs gdb to display what it finds in memory as machine instructions, using gdb's built-in disassembler. The $pc is a built-in symbol that specifies what address to use in this display: the address currently stored in the program counter register, EIP.

The "1:" at the left margin is the identification number of this *display format*. It's possible to have several display formats active at the same time, so that you can automatically display one or more register or other items every time execution pauses. For example, if you're watching what happens to ECX, you might issue this display command as well:

```
(gdb) display /x $ecx
2: /x $ecx = 0x1
```

Now we have a second active display format, showing us the value of register ECX in hex format. Now, every time you issue the nexti command, you'll see something like this:

```
2: /x $ecx = 0x1
1: x/i $eip 0x80483d9 <main+9>    movl 0xc(%ebp),%ebx
```

This way, you can watch the effects that executing instructions have on registers or program variables as the program progresses.

Note that as you create new display formats, they stack up with the oldest at the bottom. If you want to delete a display format so that it doesn't display, you can issue the delete display command, passing it the identification number of the display format:

```
(gdb) delete display 2
```

Display format 2 will be deleted. Note that gdb does not reuse display identification numbers within a single session. If you create yet another display format after deleting format 2, the new display format will get the number 3 rather than reusing the number 2.

To summarize: Here's the process you'll take to single-step an assembly program with gdb, outlined in step-by-step (how else?) fashion:

1. Run gdb with the name of the executable file as your sole command-line argument:

   ```
   gdb eattime
   ```

2. Set a breakpoint at the label where you wish to start single-stepping. In many cases that will be **main,** but not always . . . Once your programs get more complex than the ones I show in this book, you'll usually be able to zero in on one malfunctioning portion of your program quickly without having to step through the whole thing from the beginning:

   ```
   (gdb) break main
   ```

3. Issue the display command to create a display format that shows the memory location at the program counter as a machine instruction:

   ```
   (gdb) display /i $pc
   ```

   (Don't forget: $pc is a special predefined symbol that means "program counter" and contains the current value of EIP.) The display format created by the display command will show you the machine instruction that will be executed next, in AT&T mnemonics. You can create additional display formats to watch the values of registers or program variables and memory locations.

4. Run the program so that it will execute until it pauses at the breakpoint you set:

   ```
   (gdb) run
   ```

5. To begin single-stepping, execute the nexti or stepi commands, as needed, to execute that displayed machine instruction:

   ```
   nexti
   ```

6. Assuming you've first issued the display command shown in step 3, after nexti or stepi executes the instruction you saw in response to the

display command, gdb will display the instruction that is in turn up next for execution. You can immediately use nexti or stepi to execute another instruction or use the print or x commands to look at registers, program variables, or memory.

That's really all there is to single-stepping. In my early explorations with gdb under Linux I found that single-stepping my way through a program was a superb way to become bilingual with respect to the AT&T assembly mnemonics. I printed out a copy of the original NASM source code file that I had written, using Intel mnemonics, and kept that beside me while I followed the action of the program on the screen. Very quickly I found that I could read and understand the AT&T mnemonics without any trouble at all.

There is a great deal more to gdb than I have room to cover in this chapter. I encourage you to look up the full gdb documentation on the Web and read through it, and perhaps print it to paper and put it in a binder. I hate to put specific URLs in a book that may be in print for many years (considering that the half-life of most URLs seems to be months if not mere weeks), so the best way to proceed is to search for the string "gdb documentation" using a Web search engine such as Alta Vista. The documentation set for the GNU tools has been posted on a great many Web sites around the world, and you should be able to find copies very quickly.

Your Work Strategy

There are smart ways to work and dumb ways to work. The dumb ways often get the same things done, but for twice the expended time. (Maybe more. How much is your time worth?) It pays to have an organized approach to any kind of programming work, and in this section I'm going to suggest a way of setting up your working environment so that you will waste as little time as possible.

Put Only One Project in One Directory

Traditional practice in the Unix world has long been "one makefile, one directory." What this means is that you should create a separate directory for every project whose end result is a single executable program file. Don't just create one directory for assembly language work and then fill it with umpty-several different projects. This invites confusion, and it makes certain things (such as using the make facility) trickier and more error-prone.

If you confine each project to its own directory, you can keep the default make file named "makefile" and not worry about typing the name of the make file into EMACS each time you want to rebuild the project. (And with only one make file in the directory, you won't have to worry about accidentally invoking make on the wrong make file. I've done this. If you block on it, you'll soon be doubting your sanity.)

This also allows you to have standard names for test files, log files, and so on, that will be identical irrespective of which project you happen to be working on at any given time. If all the files were glommed together in one huge directory, you'd have to remember a whole set of unique names, one set for each project. Why bother? Directories cost little in disk space and do an enormous amount to manage complexity.

Consider EMACS Home

All of the various steps required for programming can be done right from inside EMACS. You can edit source code files and make files. You can assemble files and link them to generate executable files. You can run the executable program files to test them. You can invoke the GNU debugger. You can execute nearly any Unix command that can be issued from inside a Unix shell such as bash. Why waste time ducking in and out of EMACS as though it were nothing more than a text editor?

More than one book has been written about EMACS. I recommend the book *Learning GNU EMACS* by Debra Cameron, Bill Rosenblatt, and Eric S. Raymond (O'Reilly, 1996). My one gripe is that it doesn't cover the X Window version of EMACS specifically, but all the key commands are the same. I don't want to duplicate a lot of that book's excellent material here, and EMACS is relatively intuitive on the editing side.

The important big-picture thing to understand about EMACS is that it is buffer-based, and those buffers either may be related to disk files, or may simply contain other text that is not from a disk file. When you open a file, EMACS opens a buffer and loads text from the opened file into that buffer. You can also open a buffer as a scratch buffer, type something in it, cut or copy portions of that buffer into another buffer, and then just kill the scratch buffer (delete it) without saving it to disk. (There is a separate EMACS menu item for killing buffers.)

When EMACS runs the make facility, it pipes output from make and from the tools that make invokes into a new buffer. That buffer is the same as any other EMACS buffer, and if you want, you can give the buffer a name and save it to a disk file as a record of the make session. It does the same when you invoke the GNU debugger from inside EMACS: gdb's output is piped into a buffer, which you can save to disk if you choose for later reference.

Most usefully, you can invoke a Unix shell (I use bash) from inside EMACS, and EMACS will pipe its output into a new buffer, which like any buffer can be saved to disk. Especially while you're learning, there's very little that you'll need to do that can't be done either from the EMACS menus or from a shell opened from within EMACS.

Opening a Shell from inside EMACS

This last is worth explaining, because it is less obvious than most of the editing commands. There is currently no EMACS menu item that opens a shell in a window. (There *should* be!) To open a shell, the command is "Esc x shell." You press the Esc key followed by the lowercase *x* key (don't press both at once!) and, in its command line at the bottom of its window, EMACS will display the unhelpful string "M-x." This is its way of expressing the sequence Esc x on a PC. (The *M* stands for "Meta," which was the name of a control key on some ancient and mercifully forgotten minicomputer dumb terminal.) On other computers or terminals that may lack an Esc key, there may be other ways of initiating the command. EMACS was written to be portable. After the string "M-x" you must type "shell" and then press Enter.

EMACS will open a new buffer in a window and will begin piping shell output from the default shell into that window. At the top of the window will be your familiar shell prompt, waiting for you to type shell commands just as you did before you invoked EMACS. You can invoke the executables you build with make by naming them (usually prepended by "./") just as you would from the shell.

Note that you can exit the shell by typing "exit," but the window and buffer that EMACS opened for the shell will not go away by themselves. You have to kill the buffer as a separate operation, using the Files | Kill Current Buffer menu item.

I mentioned it earlier, but keep in mind that you can launch the GNU Debugger by selecting the EMACS menu item Tools | Debugger.

CHAPTER 13

Coding for Linux

Applying What You've Learned to a True Protected Mode Operating System

I can see the "fan" mail now: "How can you claim your book is about Linux assembly language when you don't present any Linux code until *the very last chapter?*" (I get notes like this every time the book I wrote isn't exactly the book that a reader has hoped to find.) The answer here, of course, is that this book isn't about Linux assembly language. It's about assembly language for Intel's x86 family of processors. Most people still start fooling around with x86 assembly under DOS, so that's where I started. Many who started with assembly under DOS would like to move on to something more powerful and more pertinent to real computing today, and more and more people see that destination as Linux.

So, whereas I began this book against a DOS backdrop, I'm finishing it against a Linux backdrop. The book, however, is about neither DOS nor Linux. Nearly everything that I've taught you so far applies to Linux as truly as DOS: addressing modes, machine instructions, and one- and two-level data tables, to name just a few. In truth, some things don't apply: real mode segmented model and DOS calls, primarily. The rest is as good under Linux as it is under DOS.

That being the case, you now have most of what you need to write assembly language programs for x86 processors under Linux. This chapter fills in the essentials of how Linux work differs from DOS work at the code level. If in fact there is a third edition of this book someday (and I hope there will be), I am considering rewriting it almost completely so that DOS at last vanishes into the mists of history, and we begin with Linux and stay with Linux throughout. You may be surprised at how little of what I've taught you will have to change. Stay tuned.

Genuflecting to the C Culture

I made it plain in the previous chapter that Linux was a C world from top to bottom. Some people think that by this I mean most of the programs written for Linux are written in C, that the people who created Linux were C people, and so on. True enough—but not enough truth. C was created for Unix, and Unix was created in C. The two evolved together and left indelible marks on one another. Even if Linux or some other species of Unix were reimplemented in Pascal (a very good idea, in my view), the C flavor would still be there, and would *have* to be there, or what we would have would not be Unix at all.

The Primacy of Libraries

Not all of this C culture is pertinent to assembly language work, but a good part of it is. The part that most affects assembly work, ironically, is the primacy of the standard C libraries. Linux and the standard C libraries are inseparable. The libraries are the way that applications and utilities communicate with the Linux kernel. They stand in place of the DOS INT 21H interface I explained in early chapters.

There are basically three reasons for this:

- *Portability.* This is less important than it used to be, and for those of us who feel that the CPU wars were won by Intel long ago, it may not be important at all. But it's a fact that the standard C libraries were created to make the porting of Unix to other processors easier.

- *Complexity management.* Linux is an order of magnitude (at least) more complex than DOS. It can do more, and can do it (thanks to some of that complexity) with far greater robustness and flexibility. Much of that complexity can be hidden from typical end-user utilities and applications, and the C library is the most important means by which that hiding is done.

- *Kernel evolution.* Linux—like Unix itself—is a work in progress. One reason Unix has had such staying power is that it has been able to evolve to meet the needs of modern users on modern machines, irrespective of its origins on creaking ancient minicomputers with less processor power than a Wal-Mart video game. One reason that this has been possible is that the kernel is not much burdened by layers of "legacy obligations" like those that have made the DOS/Windows 9x chimera such an unholy and crash-prone muddle. The main reason it remains thus unburdened is that the kernel is off limits and not accessed directly by utility and application code. Any legacy burden is borne by the standard C library. The kernel is free to move in the directions that it must, and the standard C libraries are rewritten as necessary so that the same face is presented to utilities and applications.

The INT 80H Kernel Function Interface

This last item brings up a subject I'm asked about a lot: the Linux INT 80H kernel function call interface. Just as there is a software interrupt–based function call interface to DOS, there is a way to call the Linux kernel through software interrupts. Instead of INT 21H it uses INT 80H, but the basic idea is almost identical: You set up parameters in registers and then call INT 80H. There are over 200 kernel primitives that may be called this way. If you keep to these primitives, you don't need the C library.

The INT 80H interface seems to pull at the imaginations of people who have an aversion to C. Many of these are Europeans, on whose continent Pascal still thrives; and being a Pascal guy myself, I can well understand it. That being said, I advise against it, and I won't explain the INT 80H mechanism further in this book. Some information can be found at the Web site of Konstantin Boldyshev at http://lightning.voshod.com/asm. This is a marvelous (and humbling) site, and worth digesting for the context even if you never intend to try some of the tricks he describes.

The INT 80H interface is what the C library uses to communicate with the kernel, and the authors of Linux make it clear that they reserve the right to change the parameters and semantics (that is, what the calls do) of kernel primitives as necessary without notice or apology. If you make use of kernel primitives through INT 80H, your Linux programs will become version-specific. This is not a good thing and will not endear you to users of your software.

If you intend to do any kind of programming at all under Linux, you will have to cut a personal karmic truce with the C language. If you intend to work in assembly, you will have to move beyond an uneasy truce (hey, is there ever an *easy* truce?) to active and willing collaboration. It can be done. I do it all the time.

Get used to it.

C Calling Conventions

One of the most peculiar things I learned early about Linux programs (peculiar to me, at least) is that the main portion of a Linux program is a subroutine call—called from the startup code linked in at the link stage. That is, when Linux executes a program, it loads that program into memory and runs it—but before your code runs, some standard library code runs, and then executes a CALL instruction to the **main:** label in the program. (Yes, ye purists and gurus, there is some other grimbling involved). This is the reason that the main program portion of a C program is called the main *function*. It really is a function, the standard C library code calls it, and it returns control to the standard C library code by executing a RET instruction. I diagrammed this in Figure 12.2 in the previous chapter, and it might be useful to take another look at the figure if this still isn't clear to you.

The way the main program obtains control is therefore the first example you'll see of a set of rules we call the *C calling conventions*. The C library is nothing if not consistent, and that is its greatest virtue. All C library functions implemented on x86 processors follow these rules. Bake them into your synapses early, and you'll lose a lot less hair than I did trying to figure them out by beating your head against them.

Perforce:

- A procedure (which is the more generic term for what C calls a function) must preserve the values of the EBX, ESP, EBP, ESI, and EDI 32-bit registers. That is, although it may use those registers, when it returns control to its caller, the values those registers have must be the same values they had before the function was called. The contents of all other general-purpose registers may be altered at will. (Because Linux is a protected mode operating system, this pointedly does *not* include the segment registers, which are off limits and should not be altered for any reason.)

- A procedure's return value is returned in EAX if it is a value 32 bits in size or smaller. Sixty-four-bit integer values are returned in EDX and EAX, with the low 32 bits in EAX and the high 32 bits in EDX. Floating-point return values are returned at the top of the floating-point stack. (I won't be covering floating-point numerics work in this book.) Strings, structures, and other items larger than 32 bits in size are returned by reference; that is, the procedure returns a pointer to them in EAX.

- Parameters passed to procedures are pushed onto the stack in *reverse* order. That is, given the C function **MyFunc(foo, bar, bas)**, **bas** is pushed onto the stack first, **bar** second, and **foo** last. More on this later.

- Procedures do *not* remove parameters from the stack. The caller must do that after the procedure returns, either by popping the procedures off or (more commonly, since it is usually faster) by adding an offset to the stack pointer ESP. (Again, I'll explain what this means in detail later on, when we actually do it.)

Understanding these rules thoroughly will allow you to make calls to the multitude of functions in the standard C library, as well as other extremely useful libraries such as ncurses, all of which are written in C (either currently or originally) and follow the conventions as I've described them. Much of what I have to teach you about Linux assembly language work involves how to call library functions. Most of the rest of it is no different from DOS—and that you already know!

A Framework to Build On

We've been through some pretty substantial programs at the end of our DOS sojourn, so rather than start again with the most primitive "eat at Joe's" one-liner, I'll present a sort of boilerplate assembly program that provides some useful mechanisms that nearly all programs will find handy. The beginning and end are set up for you; when you want to create a new assembly language program for Linux, you just load the boilerplate program and fill in the middle with your own code.

So let's get started. Here it is. Read it over carefully:

```
; Source name    : BOILER.ASM
; Executable name : BOILER -- though this isn't intended to be run!
; Version         : 1.0
; Created date    : 10/1/1999
; Last update     : 10/18/1999
; Author          : Jeff Duntemann
; Description     : A "skeleton" program in assembly for Linux, using NASM 0.98
;
; Build using these commands:
;   nasm -f elf boiler.asm
;   gcc boiler.o -o boiler
;
; HOWEVER, the program as given here is "boilerplate" and has nothing "useful"
;   to do. The idea is to give you a head start on new projects, by providing
;   the things that every (or nearly every) simple Linux assembly program must
;   have.


[SECTION .text]          ; Section containing code

global main              ; Required so linker can find entry point

main:
        push ebp         ; Set up stack frame
        mov ebp,esp      ; ebp is our "thumb" in the stack
        push ebx         ; Program must preserve ebp, ebx, esi, & edi
        push esi
        push edi
        ;;; Everything before this is boilerplate; use it for all ordinary apps!
        ;;; This is where you put your own code!

        ;;; Everything after this is boilerplate; use it for all ordinary apps!
        pop edi          ; Restore saved registers
        pop esi
        pop ebx
        mov esp,ebp      ; Destroy stack frame before returning
        pop ebp
        ret              ; Return control to Linux


[SECTION .data]          ; Section containing initialized data


[SECTION .bss]           ; Section containing uninitialized data
```

Saving and Restoring Registers

One of the odder provisions of the C calling conventions that I described earlier is that a program may not arbitrarily change all general-purpose registers. To me this is dumb; if the operating system doesn't want an application to change certain registers, it should save those register values before handing control to the application. However, we must deal with what is, as they say, and the best way to do that is to just save the registers that must be saved before we begin, and restore them again before we pack it up and go home.

The registers that cannot be changed by a Linux application are EBX, ESP, EBP, ESI, and EDI. You'll notice that BOILER.ASM saves these registers onto the stack when the program begins, and then restores them from the stack before control returns to Linux.

One very important but extremely nonobvious conclusion you must draw from this requirement to save EBX, ESP, EBP, ESI, and EDI is that *the other general-purpose registers may be trashed*. Yes, trashed—and not only by you. When you call procedures written by other people—primarily in the standard C libraries and in utility libraries such as ncurses—those procedures may alter the values in EAX, ECX, and EDX. (The stack pointer ESP is a special case and needs special care of a sort not applicable to other registers.) What this means for you is that you *cannot* assume that (for example) a counter value you're tracking in ECX will be left untouched when you call a C library function such as **printf**. If you're using ECX to count passes through a loop that calls a library function—or any function that you yourself didn't write—you must save your value of ECX on the stack before you call the library function and restore it after the library function returns. The same applies to EAX and EDX. (EAX is often used to return values from library functions, so it's not a good idea to use it to store counters and addresses and such when you're making library function calls.) If you need to keep their values intact across a call to a library function, you must save them to the stack before the library function is called.

On the other hand, the sacred nature of EBX, EBP, ESI, and EDI means that these registers *will* keep their values when you make C library calls. What is binding on you is binding on the C library as well. Library functions that must use these registers save and restore them without any attention from you.

Setting Up a Stack Frame

The stack is extremely important in assembly language work, and this is doubly true in Linux work, because Linux is a C world, and in C (as in most high-level languages including Pascal) the stack has a central role. The reason for this is simple: Compilers are machines that write assembly language code, and they are not human and clever like you. (Although I've met some people who appear less intelligent than some of your better compilers . . .) This means a compiler has to use what might seem brute force methods to create its code, and most of those methods depend heavily on the use of the stack.

Compiler code generation is doctoral thesis stuff and I won't have much more to say about it in this book. One compiler mechanism that bears on Linux assembly work is that of the *stack frame*. Compilers depend on stack frames to create local variables in functions (in Pascal we call them procedures), and while stack frames are less useful in assembly work, you must understand them, because they provide an easy way to access command-line arguments and environment variables.

A stack frame is a location on the stack marked as belonging to a particular function. It is basically the region between the addresses contained in two registers: base pointer EBP, and stack pointer ESP. This draws better than it explains; see Figure 13.1.

A stack frame is created by pushing the caller's copy of EBP on the stack to save it, and then copying the caller's stack pointer ESP into register EBP. The first two instructions in any assembly program that honors the C calling conventions must be these:

```
push ebp
mov ebp,esp
```

After this, you must either leave EBP alone, or else if you must use it in a serious pinch make sure you can restore it before the change violates any C library assumptions. (I recommend leaving it alone!) EBP is considered the anchor of your new stack frame, which is the main reason it shouldn't be changed. There are things stored on the stack above (that is, at higher addresses than) your stack frame that often need to be referenced in your code, and EBP is the only safe way to reference them. (These things aren't shown in Figure 13.1, but I return to them later in this chapter.)

Less obvious is the fact that EBP is also the hidey-hole in which you stash the caller's stack pointer value, ESP. This is yet another reason not to

The Stack

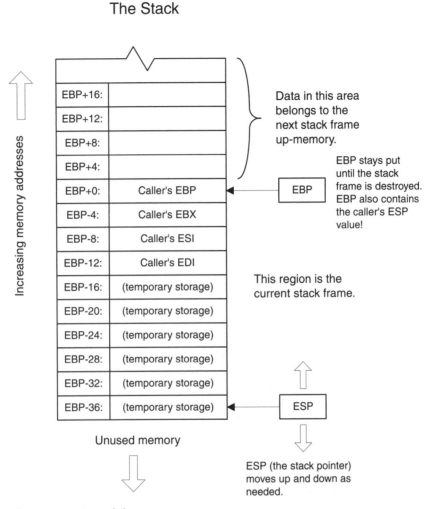

Figure 13.1 A stack frame.

change EBP once you create your stack frame. Returning control at the end of your program with a random value in ESP is the shortest path to trouble I could name.

Once EBP is safely anchored as one end of your stack frame, the stack pointer ESP is free to move up and down the stack as required. The first things you need to put on the stack, however, are the caller's values for EBX, ESI, and EDI, as shown in Figure 13.1. The order in which these three are saved isn't crucial, but the order I show in Figure 13.1 is customary. They will be popped back off the stack when the stack frame is destroyed at the end of your program, handing back to the caller (which in our case is the startup/shutdown code from the C library) the same values those registers had when the startup code called your program as the function **main**.

But once EBX, ESI, and EDI are there, you can push and pop whatever you need to for temporary storage. Calling C library functions requires a fair amount of pushing and popping, as we see shortly.

Destroying a Stack Frame

Before your program ends its execution by returning control to the startup/shutdown code (refer back to Figure 12.2 if this relationship isn't clear), its stack frame must be destroyed. This sounds to many people like something wrong is happening, but not so: The stack frame must be destroyed, or your program will crash. "Put away" might be a better term than "destroyed" . . . but let it pass. What we must do is leave the stack and the sacred registers in the same state they had when your program received control from the startup code.

Your stack must be clean before you destroy the stack frame and return control. This simply means that any temporary values that you may have pushed onto the stack during the program's run must be gone. All that is left on the stack should be the caller's EBP, EBX, ESI, and EDI values. Basically, if EDI was the last of the caller's values that you saved on the stack, ESP (the stack pointer) had better be pointing to that saved EDI value, or there will be trouble.

Once your stack is clean, to destroy the stack frame you must first pop the caller's register values back into their registers, making sure your pops are in the correct order. Handing back the caller's EBX value in EDI will still crash your program! With that done, we undo the logic we followed in creating the stack frame: We restore the caller's ESP by moving the value from EBP into ESP, and finally pop the caller's EBP value off the stack:

```
mov esp,ebp
pop ebp
```

That's it! The stack frame is gone, and the stack and sacred registers are now in the same state they were in when the startup code handed control to our program. It's now safe to execute the RET instruction that sends control to the shutdown code from the C library.

The file BOILER.ASM I showed earlier (it's on the CD-ROM for this book) is a boilerplate Linux assembly language program. It has a comment header, the three sections [.text], [.data], and [.bss], and all the code necessary to create and then destroy a stack frame. In between, you place the code for your own programs. All of the programs we create in the rest of this chapter will be built on this common framework.

The Perks of Protected Mode

I've said plenty of times that x86 protected mode is a wonderful thing, but I've never actually come out and said what it gives you. It's a long list, and I can't cover it all in detail, but in truth, while you're just starting out, most of it will be under the covers inside the operating system and not something you can build into your own programs.

In short, from the perspective of beginning assembly programmers, it comes down to more instructions, more versatile registers, a more stable and predictable environment, and *no segments!* (Can you tell which part I like best?)

You Know You Have a 386 or Better

An excellent and underappreciated thing about protected mode is simply this: You know you're running on a 386 or more advanced Intel processor. There's much less to be concerned about in terms of whether you can use certain instructions as there are when you're running DOS. Nearly every new processor family that Intel has released has added some instructions to the x86 instruction set, but the really *big* gulf is between the 386 and those CPUs that came before it. Thirty-two-bit protected mode is not present in the 8088, 8086, or 286, so whatever limitations are attached to those processors you can just forget.

No Segments!

I explained the nature of 32-bit flat model in earlier chapters and won't recap too thoroughly here. Segments still exist in 32-bit protected mode, but as each segment can be as large as 4 GB, all the segments are basically in the same memory space, and thus factor out. (This is why we call it "flat.") The 32-bit offset address can be considered the *sole* address for an item, and it may be contained in a single 32-bit register.

This means that we need no longer be concerned about such things as segment overrides, or recalling whether a data item is addressed relative to DS or ES. This banishes a good deal of complexity from programs, and you'll find that flat model coding is remarkably simple compared to the segment wrestling DOS programmers suffered through starting in 1981.

More Versatile Registers and Addressing

One of the more aggravating limitations of ancient Intel CPUs such as the 8086 and 8088 is that the general-purpose registers weren't exactly general. Addressing memory, for example, was limited to EBX and EBP in most cases, which meant a lot of fancy footwork when several separate items had to be addressed at the same time.

This restriction has pretty much gone away. You can address memory with any of the general-purpose registers. You can even address memory directly with ESP, something that its predecessor SP could not do. (You shouldn't *change* the value in ESP without considerable care, but ESP can now take part in addressing modes from which the stack pointer was excluded in 16-bit land.)

There's now a general-purpose memory-addressing scheme in which all the GP registers can participate equally, and I've sketched it out in Figure 13.2.

When I first saw this, wounds still bleeding from 16-bit 8088-class segmented memory addressing, it looked too good to be true. But it is! Here are the rules:

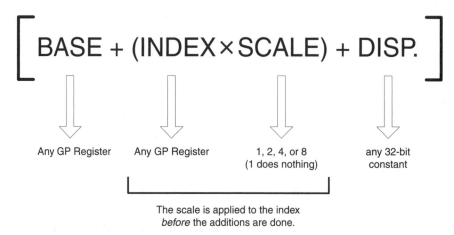

$$\left[\ \text{BASE} + (\text{INDEX} \times \text{SCALE}) + \text{DISP.}\ \right]$$

Any GP Register   Any GP Register   1, 2, 4, or 8 (1 does nothing)   any 32-bit constant

The scale is applied to the index *before* the additions are done.

Figure 13.2   Protected mode memory addressing.

- The base and index registers may be any of the 32-bit general-purpose registers, including ESP.

- The displacement may be any 32-bit constant. Obviously, 0, while legal, isn't useful.

- The scale must be one of the values 1, 2, 4, or 8. That's it! The value 1 is legal but doesn't do anything useful, so it's never used.

- The index register is multiplied by the scale before the additions are done. In other words, it's not (base + index) x scale. Only the index register is multiplied by the scale.

- All of the elements are optional and may be used in almost any combination.

This last point is worth enlarging upon. There are several different ways you can address memory, by gathering the components in the figure in different combinations. Examples are shown in Table 13.1.

Note here that the displacement term in an address can be *any* constant value from 0 to 0xffffffff. (Hey, all those little *f*s look funny to me, too, but we're in Unixland now, where Capital Letters Are For Engraving In Stone, sheesh.) So, although 0x4044d72a may seem like a different beast than the number 17, they're both legal 32-bit quantities. The numbers are probably used for different things: 0x4044d72a is most likely a full 32-bit address, whereas 17 is probably an offset into a table. However, both are legal and may be considered valid displacement components in a protected mode memory address.

There's a slightly dark flip side to this new and expanded register picture:

Table 13.1 Protected Mode Memory-Addressing Schemes

SCHEME	EXAMPLE	DESCRIPTION
[BASE]	[edx]	Base only
[DISP.]	[0x4044d72a]	Displacement (constant address) only
[BASE + DISP.]	[ecx + 17]	Base plus displacement
[INDEX × SCALE]	[ebx * 4]	Index times scale
[INDEX × SCALE + DISP.]	[eax * 8 + 65]	Index times scale plus displacement
[BASE + INDEX × SCALE]	[esp + edi * 2]	Base plus index times scale
[BASE + INDEX × SCALE + DISP.]	[esi + ebp * 4 + 9]	Base plus index times scale plus displacement

Using the 16-bit general-purpose registers AX, BX, CX, DX, SP, BP, SI, and DI will slow you down. Now that 32-bit registers rule, making use of the 16-bit registers is considered a special case that adds to the size of the opcodes that the assembler generates, and slows your code down. Now, note well that by "use" I mean explicitly reference in your source code. The AX register, for example, is still there inside the silicon of the CPU (as part of the larger EAX register) and placing data there won't slow you down. You just can't place data in AX by using "AX" as an operand in an opcode and not slow down. This syntax generates a slow opcode:

```
mov ax,542
```

You can do the same thing this way, and the opcode NASM generates will execute much more quickly:

```
mov eax,542
```

It's time to kiss those old 16-bit register names good-bye.

More Instructions

Most beginners probably think that the "new" instructions available with the 386 and later processors are the best part of working in 32-bit protected mode, but that's a pretty naïve view. I think of those new instructions as the *least* of the advantages of protected mode. There are two major reasons for this opinion:

- The majority of the new instructions are way-down-deep items of use almost exclusively by those who write system software, that is, device drivers and especially operating systems. These new instructions are in fact the machinery by which protected mode is configured and managed. In most cases the operating system won't let you use them—not that they're especially useful in writing simple applications and utilities.

- The really useful new instructions aren't new at all, but are simply more powerful ways of using the old familiar instructions such as PUSH, SHL, and SHR, coupled with the more versatile memory addressing I just finished explaining. Even these are relatively few.

All that being said, there are some useful new instructions that were introduced with the 386, and I'll take a little time to highlight the most useful of them. One thing I won't be covering here are the instructions introduced with the 486 and Pentium family. Why? To use them, you have to be sure you're using a 486, a Pentium, or whatever CPU in which the instructions were first implemented, or later—and that's generally more trouble than it's worth, especially when you're first starting out. (My favorite of those gotchas is this: The Pentium introduced an instruction called CPUID, which tells you what CPU you're using . . . but you have to be sure you have at least a Pentium under the sheet metal before you dare use it!)

More Versatile Pushes and Pops

First of all, you can now push immediate values onto the stack with the PUSH instruction. This is *most* useful when calling C library functions that expect certain values to be placed on the stack before the call, as we'll see later in this chapter. Here's an example:

```
push 0x4044d72a
```

The immediate operand can be any value that fits in 32 bits.

The 386 introduced the ability to push and pop all 32-bit GP registers at once. The PUSHAD instruction pushes EAX, ECX, EDX, EBX, ESP, EBP, ESI, and EDI onto the stack. The POPAD instruction pops values off the stack into these same registers. (Sixteen-bit equivalents to PUSHAD and POPAD were introduced with the 286, but are not particularly useful in a 32-bit memory model like the one Linux uses.) It's possible to use PUSHAD and POPAD to save and restore the registers coming into and going out of the main programs you write under Linux. However, in creating BOILER.ASM, I stuck with the more limited C calling conventions, which only saves EBX, EBP, ESI, and EDI—and ESP inside EBP. Note that the value pushed onto the stack for ESP is *not* popped back into ESP by POPAD, but is simply discarded.

The related instructions PUSHFD and POPFD push and pop the EFLAGS register to and from the stack. They are the 32-bit equivalents of PUSHF and POPF, which were available on the 8086/8088. Pushing EFLAGS onto the stack with PUSHFD and then popping the pushed value off the stack into a 32-bit register is one way to get a copy of the EFLAGS register that can be examined at your leisure.

More Versatile Shifts and Rotates

As I said earlier, the best of the new instructions are simply enhancements to instructions you encountered on the 8086/8088. Among the best of these are enhancements to the shift and rotate instructions. There are six such instructions: SHL, SHR, ROL, ROR, RCL, and RCR. (The instructions SAL and SAR are just duplicate names for SHL and SHR.) I dealt with the shift instructions in Chapter 10, as they exist on the 8088 and 8086. For those ancient CPUs, you can express the number of bits by which to shift in one of only two ways:

```
shl AX,1  ; Shift left by 1
shl AX,CL ; Shift left by number in CL
```

(Note that this discussion applies to any of the shift/rotate instructions, and not just SHL.) To shift an operand by 1 bit, you could specify the literal value 1. To shift by any greater number of bits greater than 1, you had to first load a count value into the CL register, and then use CL as the second operand. Well, that was the 16-bit world. In 32-bit protected mode you can drop the use of CL and use an immediate value for *any* legal shift values, 1 or whatever up to 31. It becomes legal to use instructions that look like this:

```
shl eax,17
```

Note that the shift count is limited to 31. If you shift a 32-bit operand by 32 or more bits in either direction, you're left with nothing but zeros in the operand, because all significant bits will be shifted completely out of the operand into nothingness. So, for the shift instructions, at least, shifting by more than 31 bits is meaningless.

It's less obviously true for the rotate instructions, but here, too, there's no advantage to rotating a value by more than 31 bits. The rotate instructions, if you recall, rotate bits off one end of the operand and then feed them back into the opposite end of the operand, to begin the trip again. If you mentally follow a single bit through the rotation process, you'll realize that after 32 rotations, any given bit is where it was when you started rotating the value. What's true of one bit is true of them all, so 31 rotations is as much as will be useful on a 32-bit value. This is why, in protected mode programming (and on the 286 as well), the shift-by count is truncated to 5 bits: The largest value expressible in 5 bits is . . . 32!

Looking for 0 Bits with BT

Back in Chapter 10 I introduced the **TEST** instruction, which allows you to determine whether any given bit in a byte or word is set to 1. As I explained, **TEST** has its limits: It's not cut out for determining when a bit is set to 0.

The 386 and newer processors have an instruction that allows you to test for either 0 bits or 1 bits. BT (Bit Test) performs a very simple task: It copies the specified bit from the first operand into the Carry flag CF. In other words, if the selected bit was a 1 bit, the Carry flag becomes set. If the selected bit was a 0 bit, the Carry flag is cleared. You can then use any of the conditional jump instructions that examine and act on the state of CF.

BT is easy to use. It takes two operands: The first one is the value containing the bit in question. The second operand is the ordinal number of the bit you want to test, starting from 0:

```
bt <value containing bit>,<bit number>
```

Once you execute a **BT** instruction, you should immediately test the value in the Carry flag and branch based on its value. Here's an example:

```
bt eax,4    ; Test bit 4 of AX
jnc quit    ; We're all done if bit 4 = 0
```

Note that we're branching if CF is *not* set; that's what JNC (Jump if Not Carry) does.

I hate to discuss code efficiency too much in a beginners' book, but there is a caution here: The BT instruction is pretty slow as instructions go—and bit-banging is often something you do a great many times inside tight loops, where instruction speed can be crucial. Using it here and there is fine, but if you're inside a loop, consider whether there might be a better way to test bits. Creaky old TEST is much faster . . . but TEST only tests for 1 bits. Depending on your application, you may be able to test for 0 bits more quickly another way, perhaps shifting a value into the Carry flag with SHL or SHR, using NOT to invert a value . . . There are no hard and fast rules, and everything depends on the dynamics of what you're doing. (That's why I'm not teaching optimization in this book!)

Crash Protection

This sounds wonderful, but you have to understand: The protection in "protected mode" is for the operating system. Programs that you write will crash right and left, trust me. However, no matter what idiotic things your program might do, either accidentally or on purpose, its chances of bringing down Linux in flames are close to nil. In all the time I've been using Linux, I have never crashed the operating system. Not even once. It is far and away the most robust OS I've ever touched, and that includes Windows NT, which I use every day and have for five years.

On the other hand, this benefit cuts both ways. Linux is a multitasking operating system, and many programs can be executing at the same time. The features of protected mode also serve to protect the other programs from your program—and your programs from the other programs. Bullying is prohibited.

You will encounter the protection mechanism sooner or later, most likely when you try to address a portion of memory for which your program does not have permission. You must keep in mind that although a 32-bit memory address can theoretically run from 0 to 0xffffffff, *your program does not have permission to access all of those addresses.* And by *access* I mean write *or* read! You can't just start from address 0 and inspect every memory location your computer has. Snooping is prohibited too—except for your own little corner of Linux's world.

The message that comes up under Red Hat 6 for protection errors is this:

```
Segmentation fault (core dumped)
```

Not very helpful in and of itself, huh? This is why gdb is so crucial—and why I spent so much of Chapter 12 on it. If you're single-stepping through gdb, you will (in most cases) know precisely which instruction causes the problem, because the fault will be thrown as soon as you single-step that instruction. If that instruction references memory, you can probably assume that it references a region of memory for which you don't have permission. You may also discover that a protection fault occurs during a C library call, but what that means is that you passed a bad value of some sort to the C library. This is less common, and you simply have to take a much closer look at what you're passing to the library code.

What does the "core dumped" part of the message mean? When a segmentation fault occurs, Linux creates a kind of postmortem file containing a description of the machine's state when the fault happened, including a snapshot of your program's binary code. This file's name defaults to "core" and it could be useful in debugging *except* that NASM does not currently embed the same information in its .o files that gcc embeds in its .o files generated from C programs. The core file is therefore *much* more difficult to interpret for NASM programs than for C programs. The NASM team indicates that this is on its to-do list for the assembler, and with some luck we'll see that feature added soon. All the more reason to watch the NASM Web site for new releases!

Characters Out

Enough warm-up—it's time to start writing programs! Actually, we've already been through a complete and assemble-able program called BOILER.ASM. However, if you assemble BOILER.ASM and run it, you won't see anything. It takes no real action and doesn't display any output. Making an "Eat at Joe's" program out of it requires that we make a C library function call to display text on the screen. This isn't particularly difficult, and it's good practice in learning the conventions for making C library calls from assembly. I explained the C calling conventions in some detail in an earlier section of this chapter, and now we'll actually put them to work. Consider the following assembly program, which is built on the BOILER.ASM foundation I showed you earlier:

```
; Source name      : EATLINUX.ASM
; Executable name  : EATLINUX
; Version          : 1.0
; Created date     : 11/12/1999
; Last update      : 11/22/1999
; Author           : Jeff Duntemann
; Description      : A simple program in assembly for Linux, using NASM 0.98,
;   demonstrating the use of the puts C library routine to display text.
;
; Build using these commands:
;   nasm -f elf eatlinux.asm
;   gcc eatlinux.o -o eatlinux
;

[SECTION .text]          ; Section containing code

extern puts
global main              ; Required so linker can find entry point

main:
    push ebp             ; Set up stack frame for debugger
    mov ebp,esp
    push ebx             ; Program must preserve ebp, ebx, esi, & edi
    push esi
    push edi
    ;;; Everything before this is boilerplate; use it for all ordinary apps!

    push dword eatmsg    ; Push a 32-bit pointer to the message on the stack
    call puts            ; Call the clib function for displaying strings
    add esp, 4           ; Clean stack by adjusting esp back 4 bytes

    ;;; Everything after this is boilerplate; use it for all ordinary apps!
    pop edi              ; Restore saved registers
```

```
        pop esi
        pop ebx
        mov esp,ebp          ; Destroy stack frame before returning
        pop ebp
        ret                  ; Return control to Linux


[SECTION .data]              ; Section containing initialized data

eatmsg: db "Eat at Joe's!",10,0

[SECTION .bss]               ; Section containing uninitialized data
```

The C library has a number of routines for displaying text to the screen. The simplest of all of them to understand is **puts,** which, as its name implies, puts a string to standard output. (I explain what *standard output* is very shortly.) Here's the code required to call **puts** from within an assembly program:

```
push dword eatmsg  ; Push a 32-bit pointer to the message on the stack
call puts           ; Call the clib function for displaying strings
add esp,4           ; Call cleans stack by adjusting esp back 4 bytes
```

This is a wonderful example, in miniature, of the process you'll use to call most any C library routine. All library routines take their parameters on the stack, which means you have to push either numeric values that fit in 32 bits, or else pointers to strings or other larger data objects. In this case, we push a 32-bit pointer to a text string on the stack. The string itself is defined in the [.data] section of the program, and by now it should be pretty familiar:

```
eatmsg: db "Eat at Joe's!",10,0
```

Note well that in the PUSH instruction we specify **eatmsg** and not **[eatmsg]**. What we need to push is the *address* of **eatmsg**, and not the data that **eatmsg** contains. As you should recall from earlier chapters, when you reference the name of a data item you're actually referencing its address. To reference its *contents* you must surround it by brackets. Here, we leave out the brackets and thus push the string's address on the stack instead.

The text to be displayed is followed by two numbers: a 10 and a 0. The 10 is the numeric code for what Unix people call *newline*, which is the character that, when sent to the screen or to a text file, moves the current position to the left margin of the next line. In the x86 Unix world, newline is equivalent to ASCII linefeed, Ctrl-A, which has a numeric value of 10. On other hardware systems, newline might be something else entirely, but as long as you're working on Linux for the x86 processors, the 10 will be interpreted by the system as newline.

In Unix jargon the 0 is called a *null*, and it is used almost everywhere in the standard C library to indicate the end of a string. The **puts** library function displays the text at the location passed to it in the pointer pushed on the stack, from the first character up to the first null that it encounters. The null is important. If you don't append a null to the end of the string, **puts** will keep stuffing bytes from memory to the screen until it encounters a null somewhere up-memory of the original string—which could mean that hundreds of random garbage characters will appear on your screen.

The Three Standard Files

This is a good place to explain that **puts** and the other character-output library functions don't send text explicitly to your screen display. They send it to a special Unix mechanism called *standard output*, which is a destination to which you can send text. Standard output defaults to the screen display. Unless you *redirect* standard output to some other place (such as a disk-based text file), characters written to standard output will appear on your screen.

Standard output is one of three standard text streams that Linux will open and make available to a running Linux application, no matter how small. A *stream* is a logical file intended for use with text information. These are the three standard streams:

- *Standard output (stdout) which defaults to the screen display.* It can be redirected to a text file or some other text-oriented device such as a printer.

- *Standard error (stderr) which also defaults to the screen display.* The availability of this standard file allows programs to write their error messages to something other than the screen display, for debugging or logging purposes. This "something other" is typically a text file, which then provides a persistent record of what errors occurred during the program's execution.

- *Standard input (stdin) which (in contrast to stdout and stderr) is a source of text.* It defaults to the system keyboard, but it can be redirected to a text file, which can allow you to drive a program with "canned" inputs stored in a separate file.

If your program sends text to standard output (which is what happens by default), you can redirect its output to a text file when executing the program on the Unix command line:

```
# ./eatlinux > eattext.txt
```

Here, instead of appearing on your screen, the text displayed by the EATLINUX program is sent to the text file eattext.txt instead.

I don't have the room in this book to discuss how to programmatically redirect the standard streams to other sources or destinations, but any good book on Unix or Linux C programming will explain it in detail. Like most everything else, it's nothing more complex than a function call.

Formatted Text with printf

The **puts** library routine may seem pretty useful, but compared to a few of its more sophisticated siblings, it's kid stuff. With **puts** you can only send a simple text string to a stream, without any sort of formatting. Worse, **puts** always includes a newline at the end of its display, whether you include one in your displayed string or not. (Notice when you run the executable program EATLINUX that there is a blank line after its output. That's the second newline, inserted by the **puts** routine.) This prevents you from using multiple calls to **puts** to output several text strings all on a single line.

About the best you can say for **puts** is that it has the virtue of simplicity. For nearly all of your character output needs, you're way better off using a much more powerful library routine: **printf**. The **printf** routine allows you to do a number of truly useful things, all with one function call:

- Output text without a newline
- Convert numeric data to text in numerous formats by passing formatting codes along with the data
- Output text to a stream that includes multiple strings stored separately

If you've worked with C for more than half an hour, **printf** will be perfectly obvious to you, but for people coming from other languages (such as Pascal, which has no direct equivalent), it may take a little explaining.

The **printf** routine will gladly display a simple string like "Eat at Joe's!"— but you can merge other text strings and converted numeric data with that base string as it travels toward standard output, and show it all seamlessly together. This is done by dropping *formatting codes* into the base string, and then passing a data item to **printf** for each of those formatting codes, along with the base string. A formatting code begins with a percent sign and includes information relating to the type and size of the data item being merged with the base string, as well as how that information should be presented.

Let's look at a very simple example to start out. Here's a base string containing one formatting code:

```
"The answer is %d, and don't you forget it!"
```

The %d formatting code simply tells **printf** to convert a signed integer value to text, and substitute that text for the formatting code in the base string. Of course, you must now pass an integer value to **printf** (and I show you how that's done shortly), but when you do, **printf** will convert the integer to text and merge it with the base string as it sends text to the stream. If the decimal value passed is 42, on your screen you'll see this:

```
The answer is 42, and don't you forget it!
```

A formatting code actually has a fair amount of structure, and the **printf** mechanism as a whole has more wrinkles than I have room here to describe. Any good C reference will explain the whole thing in detail— one more reason why it's useful to know C before you attempt Linux assembly work. Table 13.2 lists the most common and useful ones.

The most significant enhancement you can make to the formatting codes is to place an integer value between the % symbol and the code letter:

```
%5d
```

Table 13.2 Common **printf** Formatting Codes

CODE	BASE	DESCRIPTION
%c	n/a	Displays a character as a character
%d	10	Converts an integer and displays it in decimal
%s	n/a	Displays a string as a string
%x	16	Converts an integer and displays it in hex
%%	n/a	Displays a percent sign

This code tells **printf** to display the value right-justified within a field 5 characters wide. If you don't put a field width value there, **printf** will simply give the value as much room as its digits require.

Passing Arguments to printf

The real challenge in working with **printf**, assuming you understand how it works logically, is knowing how to pass it all the arguments that it needs to pull off any particular display. Like the **Writeln** function in Pascal, **printf** has no set number of arguments. It can take as few arguments as one base string, or as many arguments as you need, including additional strings, character values, and numeric values of various sorts.

All arguments to C library functions are passed on the stack. This is done either directly, by pushing the argument value itself on the stack, or indirectly, by pushing a 32-bit pointer to the argument onto the stack. For 32-bit or 64-bit data values, you push the values themselves onto the stack. (The big instruction set win with protected mode is that you can push immediate values onto the stack, something that was impossible prior to the introduction of the 386.) For larger data items such as strings and arrays, you push a pointer to the items onto the stack.

When there are multiple arguments passed to **printf**, they all have to be pushed onto the stack, and in a very particular and nonintuitive order: from right to left as they would appear if you were to call **printf()** from C. The base string is considered the leftmost argument and is always pushed onto the stack last. A simple example will help here:

```
printf('%d + %d = %d ... for large values of %d.',2,2,5,2);
```

This is a C statement that calls **printf()**. The base string is enclosed in quotes and is the first argument. After the string are several numeric arguments. There must be one numeric value for each of the %d formatting codes embedded in the base string. The order that these items must go onto the stack is from the right reading toward the left: 2,5,2,2, and finally the base string. In assembly, you'd do it this way:

```
push dword 2
push dword 5
push dword 2
push dword 2
push dword mathmsg
call printf
add esp,20
```

The identifier **mathmsg** is the base string, and its address is pushed last of all the arguments. Remember that you don't push the string itself onto the stack. You push the string's *address,* and the C library code will follow the address and fetch the string's data using its own machinery.

The **ADD** instruction at the end of the sequence represents what you'll hear described as "cleaning up the stack." Each time you push something onto the stack with a **PUSH** instruction, the stack pointer ESP moves toward low memory by a number of bytes equal to the size of whatever was pushed. In our case here, all arguments are exactly 4 bytes in size. Five such arguments thus represent 20 bytes of change in ESP for the sake of making the call. After the call is done, ESP must be moved back to where it was before you started pushing arguments on the stack. By adding 20 to the value in ESP, the stack pointer moves back up by 20 bytes and will then be where it was before you began to set up the **printf** call.

If you forget to clean up the stack, or if you clean it up by the wrong number of bytes, your program will almost certainly throw a segmentation fault. Details—dare I call it neatness?—count!

Here's another example, in which three separate strings are merged at standard output by the call to **printf**:

```
        push dword dugongs      ; Rightmost arg is pushed first
        push dword mammals      ; Next arg to the left
        push dword setbase      ; Base string is pushed last
        call printf             ; Make the printf call
        add esp,12              ; Stack cleanup: 3 args x 4 bytes = 12

        [SECTION .data]         ; Section containing initialized data

  setbase db 'Does the set of %s contain the set of %s?',10,0
  mammals db 'mammals',0
  dugongs db 'dugongs',0
```

I haven't shown everything here for the sake of brevity—how often do you need to see the comment headers?—but by now you should be catching the sense of making calls to **printf**. The three crucial things to remember are these:

- Arguments are pushed onto the stack from right to left, starting with the function call as it would be written in C. The base string is pushed last. If you're doing anything even a little complex with **printf**, it helps to write the call out first in C form, and then translate it from there into assembly.

- After the call to **printf**, you must add to ESP a value equal to the total size of all arguments pushed onto the stack. Don't forget that for strings you're pushing the address of the string and *not* the data contained in the string! For most arguments this will be 4 bytes.

- The **printf** function call trashes everything but the sacred registers. Don't expect to keep values in other registers intact through a call to **printf**! (If you try to keep a counter value in ECX while executing a loop that calls **printf**, the call to **printf** will destroy the value in your counter. You must save ECX on the stack before each call to a library function, and restore it after the library call returns—or use a sacred register such as ESI, EDI, or EBX.)

If you can't get a **printf** call to work in assembly, write up a simple one-liner C program containing the call, and see if it works there. If it does, you're probably getting the order or number of the arguments wrong. Never forget that there must be one argument for each formatting code!

Characters In

Reading characters from the Linux keyboard is as easy as sending characters to the screen display. In fact, the C library calls for reading data from the keyboard (which is the default data source assigned to standard input) are almost the inverse of those that display data to standard output. This was deliberate, even though there are times when the symmetry gets in the way, as I'll explain.

String Input with fgets

If you poke around in a C library reference (and you should—there are a multitude of interesting routines there that you can call from assembly programs), you may discover the **gets** routine. You may have wondered (if I didn't choose to tell you here) why I didn't cover it. The **gets** routine is simplicity itself: You pass it the name of a string array in which to place characters, and then the user types characters at the keyboard, which are placed in the array. When the user presses Enter, **gets** appends a null at the end of the entered text and returns. What's not to love?

Well, how big is the array? And how dumb is your user?

Here's the catch: There's no way to tell **gets** when to stop accepting characters. If the user types in more characters than you've allocated room to accept them in an array, **gets** will gleefully keep accepting characters, and overwrite whatever data is sitting next to your array in memory. If that something is something important, your program will crash hard.

That's why, if you try to use **gets**, gcc will warn you that **gets** is dangerous. It's old, and much better machinery has been created in times since. The designated successor to **gets** is **fgets**, which has some safety equipment built-in—and some complications, too.

The complications stem from the fact that you must pass a file handle to **fgets**. In general, standard C library routines whose names begin with *f* act on files. (I explain how to work with disk files later in this chapter.) You can use **fgets** to read text from a disk file—but remember, in Unix terms, your keyboard is connected to a file, the file called standard input. If we can connect **fgets** to standard input, we can read text from the keyboard, which is what the old and hazardous **gets** does automatically.

The bonus in using **fgets** is that it allows us to specify a maximum number of characters for the routine to accept from the keyboard. Anything else the user types will be truncated and discarded. If this maximum value is no larger than the string buffer you define to hold characters entered by the user, there's no chance that using **fgets** will crash your program.

Connecting **fgets** to the standard input file is easy. The C library predefines three standard file handles, and these handles are linked into your program automatically. The three are **stdin** (standard input), **stdout** (standard output), and **stderr** (standard error). For accepting input from the keyboard through **fgets**, we want to use **stdin**. It's there; you simply have to declare it as **extern**.

So here's how to use the **fgets** routine:

1. Make sure you have declared **extern fgets** and **extern stdin** along with your other external declarations at the top of the .text section.

2. Declare a buffer variable large enough to hold the string data you want the user to enter. Use the RESB directive in the [.bss] section of your program.

3. To call **fgets**, first push the file handle. You must push *the handle itself*, not the handle's address! So use the form **push dword [stdin]**.

4. Next, push the value indicating the maximum number of characters you want **fgets** to accept. Make sure it is no larger than the buffer vari-

able you declare in [.bss]! The stack must contain the actual value—don't just push the *address* of a variable holding the value. Pushing an immediate value or the contents of a memory variable will work.

5. Next, push the address of the buffer variable where **fgets** is to store the characters entered by the user.

6. Finally, call **fgets** itself.

7. (And as with all library function calls, don't forget to clean up the stack!)

In terms of actual code, it should look something like this:

```
push dword [stdin]  ; Push predefined file handle for standard input
push dword 72       ; Accept no more than 72 characters from keyboard
push dword instring ; Push address of buffer for entered characters
call fgets          ; Call fgets
add esp,12          ; 3 args X 4 bytes = 12 for stack cleanup
```

Here, the identifier **instring** is a memory variable defined like this:

```
[SECTION .bss]      ; Section containing uninitialized data
instring resb 96    ; Reserve 96 bytes for string entry buffer
```

Recall that the RESB directive just sets aside space for your variable; that space is not preloaded with any particular value, with spaces, or nulls, or anything. Until the user enters data through **fgets**, the string storage you allocate using RESB is uninitialized and could contain any garbage values at all.

From the user side of the screen, **fgets** simply accepts characters until the user presses Enter. It doesn't automatically return after the user types the maximum permitted number of characters. (That would prevent the user from backing over input and correcting it.) However, anything the user types beyond the number of permitted characters is discarded.

The CHARSIN.ASM file shown later in this chapter contains the preceding code.

Using scanf for Entry of Numeric Values

In a peculiar sort of way, the C library function **scanf** is **printf** running backward: Instead of outputting formatted data in a character stream, **scanf** takes a stream of character data from the keyboard and converts it to numeric data stored in a numeric variable. **Scanf** works very well, and it understands a great many formats that I won't be able to explain in this book, especially for the entry of floating-point numbers. (Floating-point values are a special problem in assembly work, and I won't be taking them up in this edition of this book.)

For most simple programs you may write while you're getting your bearings in Linux assembly, you'll be entering simple integers, and **scanf** is very good at that. You pass **scanf** the name of a numeric variable in which to store the entered value and a formatting code indicating what form that value will take on data entry. The **scanf** function will take the characters typed by the user and convert them to the integer value that the characters represent. That is, **scanf** will take the two ASCII characters "4" and "2" entered successively and convert them to the integer value 42 after the user presses Enter.

What about a prompt string, instructing the user what to type? Well, many newcomers get the idea that you can combine the prompt with the format code in a single string handed to **scanf**—but that won't work. It seems like it should—hey, after all, you can combine formatting codes with the base string to be displayed using **printf**. And in **scanf**, you can theoretically use a base string containing formatting codes . . . but the user would then have to type the prompt as well as the numeric data!

So, in actual use, the only string used by **scanf** is a string containing the formatting codes. If you want a prompt, you must display the prompt before calling **scanf**, using **printf**. To keep the prompt and the data entry on the same line, make sure you *don't* have a newline called out at the end of your prompt string!

The **scanf** function automatically takes character input from standard input. You don't have to pass it the file handle **stdin**, as with **fgets**. (There is a C library routine **fscanf** to which you *do* have to pass a file handle, but for integer data entry, there's no hazard in using **scanf**.)

Here's how to use the **scanf** routine:

1. Make sure you have declared **extern scanf** along with your other external declarations at the top of the [.text] section.
2. Declare a memory variable of the proper type to hold the numeric data read and converted by **scanf.** My examples here will be for integer data, so you would create such a variable with either the DD directive or the RESD directive. Obviously, if you're going to keep several separate values, you'll need to declare one variable per value entered.

3. To call **scanf** for entry of a single value, first push the address of the memory variable that will hold the value. (See the following discussion about entry of multiple values in one call.)

4. Next, push the address of the format string that specifies what format that data will arrive in. For integer values, this is typically the string "%d."

5. Call **scanf**.

6. Clean up the stack.

The code for a typical call would look like this:

```
push dword intval    ; Push the address of the integer buffer
push dword iformat   ; Push the address of the integer format string
call scanf           ; Call scanf to enter numeric data
add esp,8            ; Clean up the stack
```

It's possible to present **scanf** with a string containing multiple formatting codes, so that the user could enter multiple numeric values with only one call to **scanf**. I've tried this, and it makes for a very peculiar user interface. The feature is better used if you're writing a program to read a text file containing rows of integer values expressed as text, and convert them to actual integer variables in memory. For simply obtaining numeric values from the user through the keyboard, it's best to accept only one value per call to **scanf**.

The following program shows how you would set up prompts alongside a data entry field for accepting both string data and numeric data from the user through the keyboard. After accepting the data, the program displays what was entered, using **printf**.

```
; Source name      : CHARSIN.ASM
; Executable name  : CHARSIN
; Version          : 1.0
; Created date     : 11/21/1999
; Last update      : 11/30/1999
; Author           : Jeff Duntemann
; Description      : A data input demo for Linux, using NASM 0.98
;
; Build using these commands:
;   nasm -f elf charsin.asm
;   gcc charsin.o -o charsin
;

[SECTION .text]          ; Section containing code

extern stdin             ; Standard file variable for input
```

```
        extern fgets
        extern printf
        extern scanf
        global main            ; Required so linker can find entry point

main:
        push ebp               ; Set up stack frame for debugger
        mov ebp,esp
        push ebx               ; Program must preserve ebp, ebx, esi, & edi
        push esi
        push edi
        ;;; Everything before this is boilerplate; use it for all ordinary apps!

        ;; First, an example of safely limited string input using fgets. Unlike
        ;; gets, which does not allow limiting the number of chars entered, fgets
        ;; lets you specify a maximum number. However, you must also specify a
        ;; file (hence the 'f' in 'fgets') so we must push the stdin handle.

        push dword sprompt     ; Push address of the string input prompt string
        call printf            ; Display it
        add esp,4              ; Clean up stack for 1 arg

        push dword [stdin]     ; Push predefined file handle for standard input
        push dword 72          ; Accept no more than 72 characters from keybd.
        push dword instring    ; Push address of buffer for entered characters
        call fgets             ; Call fgets
        add esp,12             ; 3 args X 4 bytes = 12 for stack cleanup

        push dword instring    ; Push address of entered string data buffer
        push dword sshow       ; Push address of the string display prompt
        call printf            ; Call printf
        add esp,8              ; Clean up the stack

        ;; Next, we'll use scanf to enter numeric data. This is easier, because
        ;; unlike strings, integers can only be so big and hence are self-
        ;; limiting.

        push dword iprompt     ; Push address of the integer input prompt
        call printf            ; Display it
        add esp,4              ; Clean up the stack

        push dword intval      ; Push the address of the integer buffer
        push dword iformat     ; Push the address of the integer format string
        call scanf             ; Call scanf to enter numeric data
        add esp,8              ; Clean up the stack

        push dword [intval]    ; Push integer value to display
        push dword ishow       ; Push base string
        call printf            ; Call printf to convert & display the integer
        add esp,8              ; Clean up the stack
```

```
;;; Everything after this is boilerplate; use it for all ordinary apps!
pop edi              ; Restore saved registers
pop esi
pop ebx
mov esp,ebp          ; Destroy stack frame before returning
pop ebp
ret                  ; Return control to Linux


[SECTION .data]          ; Section containing initialized data

sprompt db 'Enter string data, followed by Enter: ',0
iprompt db 'Enter an integer value, followed by Enter:    ',0
iformat db '%d',0
sshow   db 'The string you entered was: %s',10,0
ishow   db 'The integer value you entered was: %5d',10,0


[SECTION .bss]           ; Section containing uninitialized data

intval    resd  1        ; Reserve one uninitialized double word
instring  resb 128       ; Reserve 128 bytes for string entry buffer
```

Be a Time Lord

The standard C libraries contain a pretty substantial group of functions that manipulate dates and times. Although these functions were originally designed to handle date values generated by the real-time clock in ancient AT&T minicomputer hardware, they have by now become a standard interface to any operating system's real-time clock support. People who program in C under DOS or for Windows use the very same group of functions, and they work more or less the same way irrespective of what platform you're working with.

By understanding how to call these functions as assembly language procedures, you'll be able to read the current date, express time and date values in numerous formats, apply timestamps to files, and do many other useful things.

Let's take a look at how it works.

The C Library's Time Machine

Somewhere deep inside the standard C library, there is a block of code that, when invoked, looks at the real-time clock in the computer, reads the current date and time, and translates that into a standard, 32-bit unsigned integer value. This value is the number of seconds that have passed in the "Unix Epoch," which began on January 1, 1970, 00:00:00 universal time. Every second that passes adds one to this value. When you read the current time or date via the C library, what you'll retrieve is the current value of this number.

The number is called **time_t**. The **time_t** value is currently in the high 900,000,000s, and will flip to 10 digits (1 billion seconds since January 1, 1970) on September 9, 2001, at 7:46:40 A.M. UTC. This isn't a Y2K-style hazard in the immediate future, since even a signed 32-bit integer can express a quantity over 2 billion, and an unsigned 32-bit integer can express over 4 billion. Furthermore, a properly implemented C library doesn't assume that this is a 32-bit quantity at all. So, when the whole thing flips in the year 2069, we'll already be using at least 64-bit values for everything and the whole problem will be put off for another 292 billion years or so. If we haven't fixed it once and for all by then, we'll deserve to go down in the Cosmic Crunch that cosmologists are predicting.

A **time_t** value is just an arbitrary seconds count and doesn't tell you much on its own, though it can be useful for calculating elapsed times in seconds. A second standard data type implemented by the standard C library is much more useful. A **tm** structure (which is often called a *struct*, and which is what Pascal people would call a *record*) is a grouping of nine 32-bit values that express the current time and date in separately useful chunks, as summarized in Table 13.3. Note that although a struct (or record) is nominally a grouping of unlike values, in the current x86 Linux implementation, a **tm** value is more like an array or a data table, because all nine elements are the same size, which is 32 bits, or 4 bytes. I've described it that way in Table 13.3, by including a value that is the offset from the beginning of the structure for each element in the structure. This allows you to use a pointer to the beginning of the structure and an offset from the beginning to close in on any given element of the structure.

There are C library functions that convert **time_t** values to **tm** values and back. I cover a few of them in this book, but they're all pretty straightforward, and once you've thoroughly internalized the C calling conventions, you should be able to work out an assembly calling mechanism for any of them.

Fetching time_t Values from the System Clock

Any single second of time (at least those seconds after January 1, 1970) can be represented as a 32-bit unsigned integer in the Unix system.

Table 13.3 The Values Contained in the **tm** Structure

OFFSET IN BYTES	C LIBRARY NAME	DEFINITION
0	tm_sec	Seconds after the minute, from 0
4	tm_min	Minutes after the hour, from 0
8	tm_hour	Hour of the day, from 0
12	tm_mday	Day of the month, from 1
16	tm_mon	Month of the year, from 0
20	tm_year	Year since 1900, from 0
24	tm_wday	Days since Sunday, from 0
28	tm_yday	Day of the year, from 0
32	tm_isdst	Daylight Savings Time flag

Fetching the value for the current time is done by calling the **time** function:

```
push dword 0        ; Push a 32-bit null pointer to stack, since
                    ; we don't need a buffer. Time value is
                    ; returned in eax.
call time           ; Returns calendar time in eax
add esp, byte 4     ; Clean up stack after call
mov [oldtime],eax   ; Save time value in memory variable
```

The **time** function can potentially return the time value in two places: In EAX, or in a buffer that you allocate somewhere. To have **time** place the value in a buffer, you pass it a pointer to that buffer on the stack. If you don't want to store the time value in a buffer, you must still hand it a null pointer on the stack. That's why we push a 0 value in the preceding code; 0 is the value of a null pointer.

No other arguments need to be passed to **time.** On return, you'll have the current time value (what Unixoids call **time_t**) in EAX. That's all there is to it.

Converting a time_t Value to a Formatted String

At this writing, **time_t** is up to about 950,000,000. (Scary to think that that many seconds have passed since the middle of my senior year in high school—which is precisely the time I first learned about computers!) By itself, **time_t** doesn't tell you a great deal. The C library contains a function that will return a pointer to a formatted string representation of a given **time_t**. This is the **ctime** function. It returns a pointer to a string buried somewhere in the runtime library. This string has the following format:

```
Thu Dec 2 13:59:20 1999
```

The first field is a three-character code for the day of the week, followed by a three-character code for the month and a two-space field for the day of the month. The time follows, in 24-hour format, and the year brings up the rear. For good measure (though it is sometimes a nuisance), the string is terminated by a newline.

Here's how you use **ctime**:

```
push dword oldtime ; Push *address* of calendar time value
call ctime         ; Returns pointer to ASCII time string in eax
add esp, byte 4    ; Clean up stack after call
```

This looks pretty conventional, but there is something here that you must notice, as it's a little unconventional: You pass **ctime** the *address* of a **time_t** value, not the value itself! You're used to passing 32-bit integer values by pushing the values themselves onto the stack, say, for display by **printf**. Not so here. A **time_t** value is currently, under Linux, represented as a 4-byte integer, but there is no promise that it will always be thus. So, to keep its options open (and to ensure that Unix can be used for thousands or even millions of years to come, egad), the C library requires a pointer to the current time. Maybe in a thousand years it'll be a quad word . . . who's to say?

So you push a pointer to the **time_t** value that you want to represent as a string, and then call **ctime**. What **ctime** returns is a pointer to the string, which it keeps somewhere inside the library. You can use that pointer to display the string on the screen via **printf** or to write it to a text file.

Generating Separate Local Time Values

The C library also gives you a function to break out the various components of the date and time into separate values, so you can use them separately or in various combinations. This function is **localtime**, and given a **time_t** value, it will break out the date and time into the fields of a **tm** structure described in Table 13.3. Here's the code to call it:

```
push dword oldtime   ; Push address of calendar time value
call localtime       ; Returns pointer to static time structure in eax
add esp, byte 4      ; Clean up stack after call
```

Here, oldtime is a **time_t** value. Given this value, **localtime** returns in EAX—much in the fashion of **ctime**—a pointer to a **tm** structure within the runtime library somewhere. By using this pointer as a base address, you can access the fields in the structure by using a constant displacement from the base (here, shown as stored in EAX):

```
mov edx, dword [eax+20] ; Year value is 20 bytes offset into tm
push edx                ; Push value onto the stack
push dword yrmsg        ; Push address of the base string
call printf             ; Display string and year value with printf
add esp, byte 8         ; Clean up the stack
```

By using the displacements shown in Table 13.3, you can access all the other components of the time and the date in the **tm** structure, stored as 32-bit integer values.

Uninitialized Storage and [.bss]

To newcomers, the difference between the [.data] and [.bss] sections of the program may be obscure. Both are used for holding variables . . . so, what's the deal? Is it (like many other things in computing) just more, . . . um, . . . bss?

Not really. Again, the difference is more a matter of convention than anything else. The [.data] section was intended to contain *initialized* data; that is, variables that you provide with initial values. Most of the time, these will be base strings for data display containing prompts and other string data that doesn't change during the course of a program's execution. Sometimes you'll store count values there that define the number of lines in an output report, and so on. These values are much like values defined as CONSTANT in Pascal. They're defined at compile time and are not supposed to change.

In assembly, of course, you can change them if you want. But for variables that begin without values (that is, are *uninitialized*) which are given values over the course of a program's execution (which is the way most high-level language programmers think of variables), you should probably allocate them in the [.bss] section.

There are two groups of data-definition pseudoinstructions that I've used informally all along. They are what I call the defines and the reserves. The *define* pseudoinstructions give a name, a size, and a value to a data item. The *reserves* only give a name and a size. Here are some examples:

```
rowcount dd 6
fileop   db 'w',0
timemsg  db "Hey, what time is it? It's %s",10,0

timediff resd 1  ; Reserve 1 integer (4 bytes) for time difference
timestr  resb 40 ; Reserve 40 bytes for time string
tmcopy   resd 9  ; Reserve 9 integer fields for time struct tm
```

The first group are the defines. The ones you'll use most often are DD (define double) and DB (define byte). The DB pseudoinstruction is unique in that it allows you to define character arrays very easily, and it is generally used for string constants. For more advanced work, NASM provides you with DW (define word) for 16-bit quantities, DQ (define quad word) for 64-byte quantities, and DT (define ten-byte) for 80-bit quantities. These larger types are used for floating-point arithmetic, which I won't be covering in this book.

The second group are reserves. They all begin with "RES," followed by the code that indicates the size of the item to be reserved. NASM defines RESB, RESW, RESD, RESQ, and REST for bytes, words, doubles, quads, and 10-bytes. The reserves allow you to allocate arrays of any type, by specifying an integer constant after the pseudoinstruction. RESB 40 allocates 40 bytes, and RESD 9 allocates 9 doubles (32-bit quantities) all in a contiguous array.

Making a Copy of clib's tm Struct with MOVSD

It's sometimes handy to be able to keep a separate copy of a **tm** structure, especially if you're working with several date/time values at once. So, after you use **localtime** to fill the C library's hidden **tm** structure with date/time values, you can copy that structure to a structure allocated in the [.bss] section of your program.

Doing such a copy is a straightforward use of the REP **MOVSD** (Repeat Move String Double) instruction. **MOVSD** is an almost magical thing: Once you set up pointers to the data area you want to copy, and the place you want to copy it to, you store the size of the area in ECX and let REP **MOVSD** do the rest. In one operation it will copy an entire buffer from one place in memory to another.

To use REP **MOVSD**, you place the address of the source data—that is, the data to be copied—into ESI. You move the address of the destination location—where the data is to be placed—in EDI. The number of items to be moved is placed in ECX. You make sure the Direction flag is cleared (for more on this, see Chapter 11) and then execute REP **MOVSD**:

```
mov esi, eax          ; Copy address of static tm from eax to esi
mov edi, dword tmcopy ; Put the address of the local tm copy in edi
mov ecx,9             ; A tm struct is 9 dwords in size under Linux
cld                   ; Clear df to 0 so we move up-memory
rep movsd             ; Copy static tm struct to local copy in .bss
```

Here, we're moving the C library's **tm** structure to a buffer allocated in the [.bss] section of the program. The **tm** structure is 9 double words—36 bytes—in size. So, we have to reserve that much space and give it a name:

```
tmcopy    resd 9      ; Reserve 9 integer fields for time struct tm
```

The preceding code assumes that the address of the C library's already-filled **tm** structure is in EAX, and that a **tm** structure **tmcopy** has been allocated. Once executed, it will copy all of the **tm** data from its hidey-hole inside the C runtime library to your freshly allocated buffer.

The REP prefix puts **MOVSD** in automatic-rifle mode, as I explained in Chapter 11. That is, **MOVSD** will keep moving data from the address in ESI to the address in EDI, counting ECX down by one with each move, until ECX goes to zero. Then it stops.

One oft-made mistake is forgetting that the count in ECX is the count of data items to be moved, *not* the number of bytes to be moved! By virtue of the *D* on the end of its mnemonic, **MOVSD** moves double words, and the value you place in ECX must be *the number of 4-byte items* to be moved. So, in moving 9 double words, **MOVSD** actually transports 36 bytes from one location to another—but you're counting doubles here, not bytes.

The following program knits all of these snippets together into a demo of the major Unix time features. There are many more time functions to be studied in the C library, and with what you now know about C function calls, you should be able to work any of them out.

```
; Source name     : TIMETEST.ASM
; Executable name : TIMETEST
; Version         : 1.0
; Created date    : 12/2/1999
; Last update     : 12/3/1999
```

```
; Author         : Jeff Duntemann
; Description     : A demo of time-related functions for Linux, using NASM 0.98
;
; Build using these commands:
;   nasm -f elf timetest.asm
;   gcc timetest.o -o timetest
;

[SECTION .text]              ; Section containing code

extern ctime
extern getchar
extern printf
extern localtime
extern time

global main                  ; Required so linker can find entry point

main:
    push ebp                 ; Set up stack frame for debugger
    mov ebp,esp
    push ebx                 ; Program must preserve ebp, ebx, esi, & edi
    push esi
    push edi
    ;;; Everything before this is boilerplate; use it for all ordinary apps!

;;; Generate a time_t calendar time value with clib's time function============
    push dword 0             ; Push a 32-bit null pointer to stack, since
                             ;   we don't need a buffer. Time value is
                             ;   returned in eax.
    call time                ; Returns calendar time in eax
    add esp, byte 4          ; Clean up stack after call
    mov [oldtime],eax        ; Save time value in memory variable

;;; Generate a string summary of local time with clib's ctime function=========
    push dword oldtime       ; Push address of calendar time value
    call ctime               ; Returns pointer to ASCII time string in eax
    add esp, byte 4          ; Clean up stack after call

    push eax                 ; Push pointer to ASCII time string on stack
    push dword timemsg       ; Push pointer to base message text string
    call printf              ; Merge and display the two strings
    add esp, byte 8          ; Clean up stack after call

;;; Generate local time values into clib's static tm struct====================
    push dword oldtime       ; Push address of calendar time value
    call localtime           ; Returns pointer to static time structure in eax
    add esp, byte 4          ; Clean up stack after call

;;; Make a local copy of clib's static tm struct===============================
```

```
        mov esi, eax            ; Copy address of static tm from eax to esi
        mov edi, dword tmcopy   ; Put the address of the local tm copy in edi
        mov ecx,9               ; A tm struct is 9 dwords in size under Linux
        cld                     ; Clear df to 0 so we move up-memory
        rep movsd               ; Copy static tm struct to local copy in .bss

;;; Display one of the fields in the tm structure===============================
        mov edx, dword [tmcopy+20] ; Year value is 20 bytes offset into tm
        push edx                ; Push value onto the stack
        push dword yrmsg        ; Push address of the base string
        call printf             ; Display string and year value with printf
        add esp, byte 8         ; Clean up the stack

;;; Wait a few seconds for user to press Enter so we have a time difference====

        call getchar

;;; Calculating seconds passed since program began running with difftime=======
        push dword 0            ; Push null ptr; we'll take value in eax
        call time               ; Get current time value; return in eax
        add esp, byte 4         ; Clean up the stack
        mov [newtime],eax       ; Save new time value

        sub eax,[oldtime]       ; Calculate time difference value
        mov [timediff],eax      ; Save time difference value

        push dword [timediff]   ; Push difference in seconds onto the stack
        push dword elapsed      ; Push addr. of elapsed time message string
        call printf             ; Display elapsed time
        add esp, byte 8         ; Clean up the stack

;;; Everything after this is boilerplate; use it for all ordinary apps!
        pop edi                 ; Restore saved registers
        pop esi
        pop ebx
        mov esp,ebp             ; Destroy stack frame before returning
        pop ebp
        ret                     ; Return control to Linux


[SECTION .data]                 ; Section containing initialized data

timemsg db "Hey, what time is it? It's %s",10,0
yrmsg   db "The year is 19%d.",10,0
elapsed db "A total of %d seconds has elapsed since program began running.",10,0

[SECTION .bss]                  ; Section containing uninitialized data

oldtime  resd 1                 ; Reserve 3 integers (doubles) for time values
```

```
newtime   resd 1
timediff  resd 1
timestr   resb 40         ; Reserve 40 bytes for time string
tmcopy    resd 9          ; Reserve 9 integer fields for time struct tm
```

Generating Random Numbers

As our next jump on this quick tour of Unix library calls from assembly, let's get seriously random. (Or modestly pseudorandom, at least.) The standard C library has a pair of functions that allow programs to generate pseudorandom numbers. The *pseudo* is significant here. Research indicates that there is no provable way to generate a truly *random* random number strictly from software. In fact, the whole notion of what *random* really means is a spooky one and keeps a lot of mathematicians off the streets these days. Theoretically you'd need to obtain triggers from some sort of quantum phenomenon (radioactivity is the one most often mentioned) to achieve true randomness. But lacking a nuclear-powered random-number generator, we'll have to fall back on pseudoness and learn to live with it.

A simplified definition of *pseudorandom* would run something like this: A *pseudorandom*-number generator yields a sequence of numbers of no recognizable pattern, but the sequence can be repeated by passing the same *seed value* to the generator. A *seed value* is simply a whole number that acts as an input value to an arcane algorithm that creates the sequence of pseudorandom numbers. Pass the same seed to the generator, and you get the same sequence. However, within the sequence, the distribution of numbers within the generator's range is reasonably scattered and random.

The standard C library contains two functions relating to pseudorandom numbers:

- The **srand** function passes a new seed value to the random-number generator. This value must be a 32-bit integer. If no seed value is passed, the value defaults to 1.

- The **rand** function returns a 31-bit pseudorandom number. The high bit is always 0 and thus the value is always positive if treated as a 32-bit signed integer.

Once you understand how they work, using them is close to trivial.

Seeding the Generator with srand

Getting the seed value into the generator is actually more involved than making the call that pulls the next pseudorandom number in the current sequence. And it's not that the call to **srand** is that difficult: You push the seed value onto the stack, and then call **srand**:

```
push eax    ; Here, the seed value is in eax
call srand  ; Seed the pseudorandom number generator
add esp,4   ; Clean up the stack
```

That's all you have to do! The **srand** function does not return a value. But . . . what do you use as a seed value?

That's the rub.

If it's important that your programs not work with the same exact sequence of pseudorandom numbers every time they run, you clearly don't want to use an ordinary integer hard-coded into the program. You'd ideally want to get a different seed value each time you run the program. The best way to do that (though there are others) is to seed **srand** with the seconds count since January 1, 1970, as returned by the **time** function, which I explained in the previous section. This value (called **time_t**) is an unsigned integer that is currently (February 2000) in the high 900 millions and will flip to 1 billion in 2001. It changes every second, so with every passing second you have a new seed value at your disposal, one that by definition will *never* repeat.

Almost everyone does this, and the only caution is that you must make certain that you don't call **srand** to reseed the sequence more often than once per second. In most cases, for programs that are run, do their work, and terminate in a few minutes or hours, you only need to call **srand** once, when the program begins executing. If you are writing a program that will remain running for days or weeks or longer without terminating (such as a server), it might be a good idea to reseed your random-number generator once per day.

Here's a short code sequence that calls **time** to retrieve the time value, and then hands the time value to **srand**:

```
push dword 0 ; Push a 32-bit null pointer to stack, since
             ; we don't need a buffer.
call time    ; Returns time_t value (32-bit integer) in eax
add esp,4    ; Clean up stack
push eax     ; Push time value in eax onto stack
```

```
    call srand    ; Time value is the seed value for random gen.
    add esp,4     ; Clean up stack
```

The initial push of a zero simply indicates to **time** that you're not passing in a variable to accept the time value. The null pointer (which is what a zero value is in this context) has to be there on the stack to keep the **time** function happy, however. The value you want to keep is returned in EAX.

Generating Pseudorandom Numbers

Once you've seeded the generator, getting numbers in the pseudorandom sequence is easy: You pull the next number in the sequence with each call to **rand**. And the **rand** function is as easy to use as anything in the C library: It takes no arguments (so you don't need to push anything onto the stack or clean up the stack afterward) and the pseudorandom number is returned in EAX.

The following program demonstrates how **srand** and **rand** work. It also shows off a couple of interesting assembly tricks, and I spend the rest of this section discussing them.

```
; Source name      : RANDTEST.ASM
; Executable name  : RANDTEST
; Version          : 1.0
; Created date     : 12/1/1999
; Last update      : 12/2/1999
; Author           : Jeff Duntemann
; Description       : A demo of Unix rand & srand using NASM 0.98
;
; Build using these commands:
;   nasm -f elf randtest.asm
;   gcc randtest.o -o randtest
;

extern printf
extern puts
extern rand
extern scanf
extern srand
extern time

[SECTION .text]           ; Section containing code

global main               ; Required so linker can find entry point

main:
    push ebp              ; Set up stack frame for debugger
```

```
        mov ebp,esp
        push ebx                ; Program must preserve ebp, ebx, esi, & edi
        push esi
        push edi
        ;;; Everything before this is boilerplate; use it for all ordinary apps!

        ;; Start by seeding the random number generator with a time value:
Seedit: push dword 0     ; Push a 32-bit null pointer to stack, since
                         ; we don't need a buffer.
        call time               ; Returns time_t value (32-bit integer) in eax
        add esp,4               ; Clean up stack
        push eax                ; Push time value in eax onto stack
        call srand              ; Time value is the seed value for random gen.
        add esp,4               ; Clean up stack

        ;; All of the following code blocks are identical except for the size of
        ;; the random value being generated.

        ;; Create and display an array of 31-bit random values:
        mov edi, dword pull31 ; Copy address of random # subroutine into edi
        call puller             ; Pull as many numbers as called for in [pulls]
        push dword 32           ; Size of numbers being pulled, in bits
        push dword [pulls]      ; Number of random numbers generated
        push dword display      ; Address of base display string
        call printf             ; Display the label
        add esp,12              ; Clean up stack from printf call
        call shownums           ; Display the rows of random numbers

        ;; Create and display an array of 16-bit random values:
        mov edi, dword pull16 ; Copy address of random # subroutine into edi
        call puller             ; Pull as many numbers as called for in [pulls]
        push dword 16           ; Size of numbers being pulled, in bits
        push dword [pulls]      ; Number of random numbers generated
        push dword display      ; Address of base display string
        call printf             ; Display the label
        add esp,12              ; Clean up stack from printf call
        call shownums           ; Display the rows of random numbers

        ;; Create and display an array of 8-bit random values:
        mov edi, dword pull8  ; Copy address of random # subroutine into edi
        call puller             ; Pull as many numbers as called for in [pulls]
        push dword 8            ; Size of numbers being pulled, in bits
        push dword [pulls]      ; Number of random numbers generated
        push dword display      ; Address of base display string
        call printf             ; Display the label
        add esp,12              ; Clean up stack from printf call
        call shownums           ; Display the rows of random numbers

        ;; Create and display an array of 7-bit random values:
        mov edi, dword pull7  ; Copy address of random # subroutine into edi
        call puller             ; Pull as many numbers as called for in [pulls]
```

```
        push dword 7            ; Size of numbers being pulled, in bits
        push dword [pulls]      ; Number of random numbers generated
        push dword display      ; Address of base display string
        call printf             ; Display the label
        add esp,12              ; Clean up stack from printf call
        call shownums           ; Display the rows of random numbers

        ;; Create and display an array of 4-bit random values:
        mov edi, dword pull4    ; Copy address of random # subroutine into edi
        call puller             ; Pull as many numbers as called for in [pulls]
        push dword 4            ; Size of numbers being pulled, in bits
        push dword [pulls]      ; Number of random numbers generated
        push dword display      ; Address of base display string
        call printf             ; Display the label
        add esp,12              ; Clean up stack from printf call
        call shownums           ; Display the rows of random numbers

        ;; Clear a buffer to nulls
Bufclr: mov ecx, BUFSIZE+5 ; Fill whole buffer plus 5 for safety
.loop:  dec ecx             ; BUFSIZE is 1-based so decrement first!
        mov byte [randchar+ecx],0 ; Mov null into the buffer
        cmp ecx,0               ; Are we done yet?
        jnz .loop               ; If not, go back and stuff another null

        ;; Create a string of random alphanumeric characters
Pulchr: mov ebx, BUFSIZE ; BUFSIZE tells us how many chars to pull
.loop: dec ebx              ; BUFSIZE is 1-based, so decrement first!
        mov edi, dword pull6    ; For random in the range 0-63
        call puller             ; Go get a random number from 0-63
        mov cl,[chartbl+eax]    ; Use random # in eax as offset into table
                                ;  and copy character from table into cl
        mov [randchar+ebx],cl   ; Copy char from cl to character buffer
        cmp ebx,0               ; Are we done having fun yet?
        jne .loop               ; If not, go back and pull another

        ;; Display the string
        mov eax,1               ; Output a newline
        call newline            ;  using the newline subroutine
        push dword randchar     ; Push the address of the char buffer
        call puts               ; Call puts to display it
        add esp,4               ; Clean up the stack
        mov eax,1               ; Output a newline
        call newline            ;  using the newline subroutine

        ;;; Everything after this is boilerplate; use it for all ordinary apps!
        pop edi                 ; Restore saved registers
        pop esi
        pop ebx
        mov esp,ebp             ; Destroy stack frame before returning
        pop ebp
        ret                     ; Return control to Linux
```

```
;;; SUBROUTINES===============================================================


;---------------------------------------------------------------
; Random number generator subroutines -- Last update 12/1/1999
;
; This routine provides 5 entry points, and returns 5 different "sizes" of
; pseudorandom numbers based on the value returned by rand. Note first of
; all that rand pulls a 31-bit value. The high 16 bits are the most "random"
; so to return numbers in a smaller range, you fetch a 31-bit value and then
; right shift it zero-fill all but the number of bits you want. An 8-bit
; random value will range from 0-255, a 7-bit value from 0-127, and so on.
; Respects ebp, esi, edi, ebx, and esp. Returns random value in eax.
;---------------------------------------------------------------
pull31: mov ecx,0  ; For 31 bit random, we don't shift
        jmp pull
pull16: mov ecx,15 ; For 16 bit random, shift by 15 bits
        jmp pull
pull8:  mov ecx,23 ; For 8 bit random, shift by 23 bits
        jmp pull
pull7:  mov ecx,24 ; For 7 bit random, shift by 24 bits
        jmp pull
pull6:  mov ecx,25 ; For 6 bit random, shift by 25 bits
        jmp pull
pull4:  mov ecx,27 ; For 4 bit random, shift by 27 bits
pull:   push ecx   ; rand trashes ecx; save shift value on stack
        call rand  ; Call rand for random value; returned in eax
        pop ecx    ; Pop stashed shift value back into ecx
        shr eax,cl ; Shift the random value by the chosen factor
                   ;  keeping in mind that part we want is in cl
        ret        ; Go home with random number in eax


;---------------------------------------------------------------
; Newline outputter -- Last update 12/1/1999
;
; This routine allows you to output a number of newlines to stdout, given by
; the value passed in eax. Legal values are 1-10. All sacred registers are
; respected. Passing a 0 value in eax will result in no newlines being issued.
;---------------------------------------------------------------
newline:
    mov ecx,10        ; We need a skip value, which is 10 minus the
    sub ecx,eax       ;  number of newlines the caller wants.
    add ecx, dword nl ; This skip value is added to the address of
    push dword ecx    ;  the newline buffer nl before calling printf.
    call printf       ; Display the selected number of newlines
    add esp,4         ; Clean up the stack
    ret               ; Go home
nl db 10,10,10,10,10,10,10,10,10,10,0


    ;; This subroutine displays numbers six at a time
    ;; Not intended to be general-purpose...
```

```
shownums:
    mov esi, dword [pulls]    ; Put pull count into esi
.dorow: mov edi,6             ; Put row element counter into edi
.pushr: dec edi               ; Decrement row element counter
    dec esi                   ; Decrement pulls counter
    push dword [stash+esi*4]  ; Push number from array onto stack
    cmp edi,0                 ; Have we filled the row yet?
    jne .pushr                ; If not, go push another one
    push dword showarray      ; Push address of base display string
    call printf               ; Display the random numbers
    add esp,28                ; Clean up the stack
    cmp esi,0                 ; See if pull count has gone to <> 0
    jnz .dorow                ; If not, we go back and do another row!
    ret                       ; Done, so go home!


    ;; This subroutine pulls random values and stuffs them into an
    ;; integer array. Not intended to be general purpose. Note that
    ;; the address of the random number generator entry point must
    ;; be loaded into edi before this is called, or you'll seg fault!
puller:
    mov esi, dword [pulls]    ; Put pull count into esi
.grab: dec esi                ; Decrement counter in esi
    call edi                  ; Pull the value; it's returned in eax
    mov [stash+esi*4],eax     ; Store random value in the array
    cmp esi,0                 ; See if we've pulled 4 yet
    jne .grab                 ; Do another if esi <> 0
    ret                       ; Otherwise, go home!


[SECTION .data]              ; Section containing initialized data


pulls    dd 36               ; How many numbers do we pull?
display  db 10,'Here is an array of %d %d-bit random numbers:',10,0
showarray db '%10d %10d %10d %10d %10d %10d',10,0
chartbl  db '0123456789ABCDEFGHIJKLMNOPQRSTUVWXYZabcdefghijklmnopqrstuvwxyz-@'


[SECTION .bss]               ; Section containing uninitialized data


BUFSIZE equ 70
randval resd 1               ; Reserve an integer variable
stash  resd 72               ; Reserve an array of 72 integers for randoms
randchar resb BUFSIZE+5      ; Buffer for storing randomly chosen characters
```

Some Bits Are More Random than Others

Under Linux, the **rand** function returns a 31-bit unsigned value in a 32-bit integer. (The sign bit of the integer—the highest of all 32 bits—is always cleared.) The Unix documentation for **rand** and **srand** indicates that the low-order bits of a value generated by **rand** are less random than the high-order bits. This means that if you're going to use only some of the bits of the value generated by **rand**, you should use the highest-order bits you can.

I honestly don't know why this should be so, nor how bad the problem is. I'm not a math guy, and I will take the word of the people who wrote the **rand** documentation. But it bears on the issue of how to limit the range of the random numbers that you generate.

The issue is pretty obvious: Suppose you want to pull a number of random alphanumeric ASCII characters? You don't need numbers that range from 0 to 2 billion. There are only 127 ASCII characters, and in fact only 62 are letters and numbers. (The rest are punctuation marks, whitespace, control characters, or nonprinting characters such as the smiley faces.) What you want to do is pull random numbers between 0 and 61.

Pulling numbers that range from 0 to 2 billion until you find one less than 62 will take a long time. Clearly, you need a different approach. The one I took treats the 31-bit value returned by **rand** as a collection of random bits. I extracted a subset of those bits just large enough to meet my needs. Six bits can express values from 0 to 63, so I took the highest-order 6 bits from the original 31-bit value and used those to specify random characters.

It's easy: I simply shifted the 31-bit value to the right until all bits but the highest-order 6 bits had been shifted off the right end of the value into oblivion. The same trick works with any (reasonable) number of bits. All you have to do is select by how many bits to shift. I created a subroutine with multiple entry points, each entry point selecting a number of bits to select from the random value:

```
pull31: mov ecx,0  ; For 31 bit random, we don't shift
        jmp pull
pull16: mov ecx,15 ; For 16 bit random, shift by 15 bits
        jmp pull
pull8:  mov ecx,23 ; For 8 bit random, shift by 23 bits
        jmp pull
pull7:  mov ecx,24 ; For 7 bit random, shift by 24 bits
        jmp pull
pull6:  mov ecx,25 ; For 6 bit random, shift by 25 bits
        jmp pull
pull4:  mov ecx,27 ; For 4 bit random, shift by 27 bits
pull:   push ecx   ; rand trashes ecx; save shift value on stack
        call rand  ; Call rand for random value; returned in eax
```

```
pop ecx    ; Pop stashed shift value back into ecx
shr eax,cl ; Shift the random value by the chosen factor
           ;  keeping in mind that part we want is in cl
ret        ; Go home with random number in eax
```

To pull a 16-bit random number, call **pull16**. To pull an 8-bit random number, call **pull8**, and so on. I did discover that the smaller numbers are not as random as the larger numbers, and the numbers returned by **pull4** are probably not random enough to be useful. (I left the **pull4** code in so you could see for yourself by running RANDTEST.)

The logic here should be easy to follow: You select a shift value, put it in ECX, push ECX on the stack, call **rand**, pop ECX from the stack, and then shift the random number (which **rand** returns in EAX) by the value in CL—which, of course, is the lowest 8 bits of ECX.

Why does ECX go onto the stack? ECX is not one of the sacred registers in the C calling conventions, and virtually all C library routines use ECX and trash its value. If you want to keep a value in ECX across a call to a library function, you have to save your value somewhere before the call, and restore it after the call is complete. The stack is the best place to do this.

I used the **pull6** routine to pull random 6-bit numbers to select characters from a character table, thus creating a string of random alphanumeric characters. I padded the table to 64 elements with two additional characters (- and @) so that I wouldn't have to test each pulled number to see if it was less than 62. If you need to limit random values to some range that is not a power of 2, choose the next largest power of 2—but try to design your program so that you don't have to choose randoms in a range like 0 to 65. Much has been written on random numbers in the algorithm books, so if the concept fascinates you, I direct you there for further study.

Calls to Addresses in Registers

I use a technique in RANDTEST.ASM that sometimes gets forgotten by assembly newcomers: You can execute a **CALL** instruction to a subroutine address held in a register. You don't always have to use **CALL** with an immediate label. In other words, the following two **CALL** instructions are both completely legal and equivalent:

```
mov ebx, dword pull8
call pull8
call ebx
```

Why do this? You'll find your own reasons over time, but in general it allows you to treat subroutine calls as parameters. In RANDTEST.ASM, I factored out a lot of code into a subroutine called **puller**, and then called **puller** several times for different sizes of random number. I passed **puller** the address of the correct random-number subroutine to call by loading the address of that subroutine into EDI:

```
;; Create and display an array of 8-bit random values:
mov edi, dword pull8 ; Copy address of random # subroutine into edi
call puller           ; Pull as many numbers as called for in [pulls]
```

Down in the **puller** subroutine, the code calls the requested random-number subroutine this way:

```
puller:
    mov esi, dword [pulls] ; Put pull count into esi
.grab: dec esi            ; Decrement counter in esi
    call edi              ; Pull the value; it's returned in eax
    mov [stash+esi*4],eax ; Store random value in the array
    cmp esi,0            ; See if we've pulled enough yet
    jne .grab            ; Do another if esi <> 0
    ret                  ; Otherwise, go home!
```

See the CALL EDI instruction? In this situation (where EDI was previously loaded with the address of subroutine **pull8**), what is called is **pull8**—even though the label **"pull8"** is nowhere present in subroutine **puller**. The same code in **puller** can be used to fill a buffer with all the different sizes of random numbers, by calling the subroutine address passed to it in EDI.

This technique was available in the 8086/8088, but was not often used because in the older processors it was *very* slow. Since the 486, it's been only slightly slower than calling an immediate label. Calling an address in a register gives you a lot of power to generalize code—just make sure you document what you're up to, since the label which you're calling is not contained in the **CALL** instruction.

Local Labels

I haven't presented any particularly long or complex programs in this book, so having problems with code labels conflicting with one another hasn't really been an issue. But as you begin to write "real" code for Linux, you'll eventually be writing programs hundreds or even (with some practice and persistence) thousands of lines long. You will soon find that duplicate code labels will be a problem. How will you always remember that you already used the label **loop** on line 187 of a 1,432-line program?

You won't. And sooner or later, you'll try and use the label **loop** again. NASM will call you on it with an error.

This is a common enough problem (especially with obviously useful labels such as **loop**) that NASM's authors created a feature to deal with it: *local labels*. Local labels are founded on the fact that nearly all labels in assembly work (outside of names of subroutines and major sections) are "local" in nature, by which I mean that they are only referenced by **JMP** instructions that are *very* close to them—perhaps only two or three instructions away. Such labels are usually parts of tight loops and are not referenced from far away in the code.

Here's an example:

```
        ;; Clear a buffer to nulls
Bufclr: mov ecx, BUFSIZE+5   ; Fill whole buffer plus 5 for safety
.loop:  dec ecx              ; BUFSIZE is 1-based so decrement first!
    mov byte [randchar+ecx],0 ; Mov null into the buffer
    cmp ecx,0                ; Are we done yet?
    jnz .loop                ; If not, go back and stuff another null


        ;; Create a string of random alphanumeric characters
Pulchr: mov ebx, BUFSIZE     ; BUFSIZE tells us how many chars to pull
.loop:  dec ebx              ; BUFSIZE is 1-based, so decrement first!
    mov edi, dword pull6     ; For random in the range 0-63
    call puller              ; Go get a random number from 0-63
    mov cl,[chartbl+eax]     ; Use random # in eax as offset into table
                             ; and copy character from table into cl
    mov [randchar+ebx],cl    ; Copy char from cl to character buffer
    cmp ebx,0                ; Are we done having fun yet?
    jne .loop                ; If not, go back and pull another
```

You'll see that throughout this code snippet the label **.loop** has a period in front of it. This period marks it as a local label—and there are two **.loop** labels here, each a separate and distinguishable label. Local labels are local to the first *nonlocal* label (that is, the first label not prefixed by a period; we call these *global*) that precedes them in the code. In the preceding code snippet, the first label **.loop** is local to the global label **Buf-clr**. It is not visible further up the source code past **Bufclr**, and once you get above **Bufclr**, there may be another local label called **.loop**, without any conflict with the two **.loop** local labels.

Going down the source code from the global label **Bufclr**, the local label **.loop** is referenceable until the *next* global label, **Pulchr**, is encountered.

You'll see that after **Pulchr**, there is another **.loop**, which does not conflict with the **.loop** that "belongs" to **Bufclr**. As long as a global label exists between the two of them, NASM has no trouble distinguishing them.

Some notes on local labels:

- In a library of subroutines, local labels are *at least* local to the subroutine in which they are defined. Each subroutine begins with a label (the name of the subroutine, which is a label), so a local label defined within a subroutine will at most be visible until the beginning of the next subroutine. You may, of course, have global labels within subroutines, which will confine visibility of local labels even further.

- It's perfectly legal and often helpful to define global labels that are never referenced, simply to provide a context for local labels. If you're writing a utility program that executes in straight-through fashion without a lot of jumping or long-distance looping back, you may go a long way without needing to insert a global label. I like to use global labels to set off major functional parts of a program, whether those labels are ever called or not. This allows me to use local labels freely within those major functional modules. As a personal stylistic convention, I mark such nonreferenced global labels by using a capital letter for the first letter in the label. All labels meant to be referenced begin with lowercase letters. As a side benefit, these labels can be used as breakpoints when debugging with gdb.

- Local labels, unfortunately, are not accessible as breakpoints within gdb. I'm not entirely sure why this is so, but gdb will refuse to set a breakpoint on a local label.

- A rule of thumb that I use: Global labels and all references to them should occur within a single screen's worth of code. In other words, you should be able to see both a local label and everything that refers to it without scrolling your program editor. This is just a guide to help you keep sense in your programs, but I've found it very useful in my own work.

- If you're writing dense code with a lot of intermixed global and local labels, be careful that you don't try to **JMP** to a local label on the other side of a global label. This is one reason *not* to have 15 local labels called **.loop** within one part of a program—you can easily get them confused, and in trying to jump to one five instructions up, you may unknowingly be jumping to one seven instructions down. NASM won't warn you if there is a local label with the same name on your side of a global label and you try to jump to a local label on the other side of the global label. Bugs like this can be insanely difficult to find sometimes. Like any tool, local labels have to be used carefully to be of greatest benefit.

Placing Constant Data in a Subroutine

By now you're used to thinking of code as living in the [.text] section, and data as living in the [.data] section. In almost all cases this is a good way to organize things, but there's no absolute demand that you separate code and data in this way. It's possible to define data within a subroutine using NASM's pseudoinstructions including DB, DW, and DD. I've created a useful subroutine that shows how this is done and is a good example of when to do it.

The subroutine allows you to issue some number of newline characters to standard output, specified by a value passed to the subroutine in EAX:

```
newline:
      mov ecx,10        ; We need a skip value, which is 10 minus the
      sub ecx,eax       ;  number of newlines the caller wants.
      add ecx, dword nl ; This skip value is added to the address of
      push dword ecx    ;  the newline buffer nl before calling printf.
      call printf       ; Display the selected number of newlines
      add esp,4         ; Clean up the stack
      ret               ; Go home
  nl  db 10,10,10,10,10,10,10,10,10,10,0
```

The buffer **nl** contains 10 newline characters, followed by a null. It is thus a null-terminated string of newline characters, and you can pass all of it—or any chunk starting in the middle and going to the end—to **printf**. If you pass **printf** the address of the beginning of the string, **printf** will output all 10 newlines, and your display will scroll by 10 lines. If you pass **printf** the address of the third newline, **printf** will output only 8 newlines, having skipped the first 2. If you only want **printf** to output a single newline, you pass **printf** the address of the very last newline, so that the only things that **printf** actually sends to standard output will be the final newline and the null character.

All the trickery is in calculating the address to pass to **printf**. The algorithm: To output x newline(s), we need to skip past $10 - x$ newline(s). This is why we load 10 into ECX and subtract EAX from it. The resulting value in EAX becomes the offset that, when added to the address represented by **nl**, gives you the address of the place in the string where **printf** should begin outputting.

Having the data right in the subroutine means that it's easy to cut and paste the subroutine from one program into another without leaving the essential table of newline characters behind. And because the only code that ever uses the newline table is the subroutine itself, there's no benefit to placing the newline table in the more centrally visible [.data] section.

Accessing Command-Line Arguments

One of the most useful things to be able to do when writing simple utilities is to pass them parameters—C people call them *arguments*—on the command line. If you're working in C or Pascal, these are set up as predefined arrays or functions and are a snap to use. In assembly, there's no such convenience. (Surprise!) You have to know where and how they're stored, which is (alas) nontrivial.

On the other hand, getting at command-line arguments is a wonderful exercise both in the use of pointers and also of accessing the stack *up-memory* from EBP, where a number of interesting things live. EBP is your marker driven into the stack, and it anchors your access to both your own items (stored down-memory from EBP) and those owned by the runtime library, which are up-memory.

Because we're talking about a pointer to a pointer to a table of pointers to the actual argument strings, the best way to begin is to draw a picture of the lay of the land. Figure 13.3 shows the pointer relationships and stack structures we have to understand to identify and read the command-line arguments.

As I explained earlier in this chapter, when Linux passes control to your program, the C library's startup code gets control first, and it sets up a number of things for you, before the code that you wrote ever begins executing. One of the things the startup code does is set up your program's access to the command-line arguments. It does this by building a table of pointers to the arguments and placing a pointer to that table of pointers on the stack, up-memory from EBP.

The startup code places other things on the stack as well. Immediately above EBP is the return address for your portion of the code. When

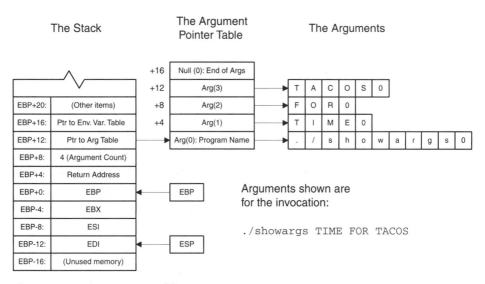

Figure 13.3 Linux command-line arguments.

your code is done, it executes a RET instruction, which takes execution back into the runtime library code's shutdown sequence. This RET instruction uses the return address just above EBP to take execution to the shutdown sequence. The shutdown sequence has its own return address, which eventually takes it back into Linux. You don't need to access the return address for anything; and certainly don't change it!

Immediately above the return address, at offset 8 from EBP (as the literature would say, at EBP+8) is an integer count of the number of arguments. There will always be at least one, because the name of the program is the first command-line argument. (After all, you typed the name on the command line, no?)

Immediately above the argument count, at EBP+12, is a pointer to the argument table. Immediately above that, at EBP+16, is a pointer to the table of environment variable pairs. Reading environment variable pairs is done pretty much the same way as reading command-line arguments, so if you understand one, you won't have much trouble with the other.

Addressing the Stack Relative to EBP

Our crooked trail to the command-line arguments begins at the address stored in EBP. EBP is your anchor point in the stack. It allows you to access the stack using more than just the **PUSH** and **POP** instructions. The stack is just memory, after all, and can be addressed through registers just as any area of memory can (assuming you have permissions in that area, one always has to say when speaking of Unix . . .).

Such addressing is done via offsets from the address stored in EBP. Here's a simple example:

```
mov ecx,[ebp+8]    ; Load argument count into ecx
mov ebx,[ebp+12]   ; Load pointer to argument table into ebx
```

The first instruction copies the argument count from the stack into ECX. If you refer to Figure 13.3, you'll see that the argument count is stored on the stack 8 bytes up-memory from EBP. So, by adding the displacement 8 to the address in EBP, you go right to it. Similarly, the second instruction copies the pointer to the argument table from its spot on the stack, 12 bytes up-memory from EBP, into EBX.

Once you have these two items in registers, you're most of the way there. With the pointer to the argument table in EBX (as the preceding code snippet shows), you now have a pointer to the first element in the argument table, which is always a pointer to the program name as you typed it on the command line. (You're following all this on Figure 13.3, aren't you?)

Scaled Addressing

One of the marvelous new features introduced on the x86 architecture with the 386 is *scaled addressing*. I described this earlier in this chapter, but it's worth recapping as I explain how to use it to access the rest of the arguments through the table of argument pointers.

We now have a pointer to the beginning of the argument pointer table, stored in EBX. Obtaining the other pointers in the table requires that we somehow index into that table. Scaled addressing is the best way to do it. With scaled addressing, we can multiply a register value by 2, 4, or 8, and add it to the base register to generate the final address.

Consider the argument pointer I marked as Arg(1) in Figure 13.3. It's a pointer, and like all pointers in protected mode flat model, it's 32 bits—4 bytes—in size. With another 4-byte pointer beneath it, Arg(1) is 4 bytes from the beginning of the pointer table.

So, let's do some pointer math. We start with the address of pointer Arg(0), lying at the very beginning of the table. We need to add 4 to it to reach Arg(1). Here's the algorithm:

```
<BASE POINTER> + (<ARGUMENT INDEX> X 4)
```

The base pointer we already have in EBX. The argument index for Arg(0) is 0, for Arg(1) is 1, and so on. The address for Arg(1) would thus be the base pointer plus 1 times 4—which points at the pointer to Arg(1). The address for Arg(3) would be the base pointer plus 3 times 4, or 12 bytes from the start of the table. As you can see in Figure 13.3, that's exactly where Arg(3) is. The way this encodes in NASM syntax is this:

```
push dword [ebx+esi*4]      ; Push address of an arg on the stack
```

We're pushing the pointer onto the stack here, but scaled addressing can of course be used anywhere you can use a memory address in assembly work. The important part of the notation is [EBX + ESI * 4]. This is the implementation of our addressing algorithm, and it's baked right into the silicon of the CPU!

I've written a short program that displays all the command-line arguments, and in doing so demonstrates how to use scaled addressing to get the address of any given argument. Read it carefully:

```
; Source name     : SHOWARGS.ASM
; Executable name  : SHOWARGS
; Version          : 1.0
; Created date     : 10/1/1999
; Last update      : 12/3/1999
; Author           : Jeff Duntemann
; Description      : A demo that shows how to access command line arguments
;                    stored on the stack by addressing them relative to ebp.
;
; Build using these commands:
;   nasm -f elf showargs.asm
;   gcc showargs.o -o showargs
;
; To test, execute with some command-line arguments:
;   ./showargs foo bar bas bat

[SECTION .text]        ; Section containing code

global main            ; Required so linker can find entry point
extern printf          ; Notify linker that we're calling printf

main:
push ebp               ; Set up stack frame for debugger
   mov ebp,esp
   push ebx            ; Program must preserve ebp, ebx, esi, & edi
   push esi
   push edi
   ;;; Everything before this is boilerplate; use it for all ordinary apps!
```

```
    mov edi,[ebp+8]    ; Load argument count into edi
    mov ebx,[ebp+12]   ; Load pointer to argument table into ebx
    xor esi,esi        ; Clear esi to 0
.showit:
    push dword [ebx+esi*4] ; Push address of an arg on the stack
    push esi           ; Push arg number on the stack
    push dword argmsg  ; Push address of display string on the stack
    call printf        ; Display the arg number and arg
    add esp, byte 12   ; Clean up stack after printf call
    inc esi            ; Bump arg number to next arg
    dec edi            ; Decrement arg counter by 1
    jnz .showit        ; If arg count is 0, we're done

    ;;; Everything after this is boilerplate; use it for all ordinary apps!
    pop edi            ; Restore saved registers
    pop esi
    pop ebx
    mov esp,ebp        ; Destroy stack frame before returning
    pop ebp
    ret                ; Return control to Linux


[SECTION .data]        ; Section containing initialized data

argmsg    db "Argument %d: %s",10,0

[SECTION .bss]         ; Section containing uninitialized data
```

The logic I followed is this: We begin by copying the argument count into EDI and the pointer to the start of the argument pointer table into EBX. We clear ESI to 0 by **XOR**ing it against itself. With that accomplished, we go into a loop that pushes the argument pointer, the argument number, and a base string onto the stack and calls **printf** to display them. After printing each argument, we increment the argument number in ESI and decrement the argument count in EDI. When EDI goes to 0, we've displayed all the arguments, and we're done.

One final note on this program, which I've said before but must emphasize: If you're calling a C library function in a loop, you must either use the sacred registers to hold your counters that govern the loop, or you must push them onto the stack before making a library call. The library trashes the nonsacred registers such as EAX, ECX, and EDX. If you had tried to store the argument count in ECX, the count would have been destroyed the first time you called **printf**. The sacred nature of EBX, ESI, and EDI makes them ideal for this use. (EBP is reserved for use in addressing data on the stack, so don't try to use it for anything like counters unless you *very* carefully save its value on the stack!)

There is a pointer to a table of environment variables on the stack at EBP+16. It's set up pretty much the same way, so you could very easily create a program to print out all the environment strings in that table. The major difference is this: There is no count of the number of environment variables stored anywhere. The end of the table of pointers to environment variables is marked by a null pointer; that is, a pointer whose value is 0. You have to fetch each pointer and test it against 0 before attempting to display data at the pointer address.

For tomorrow's assignment, modify SHOWARGS.ASM to display the environment variables as well. (I've written such a program, but it isn't printed here in the chapter. Find it on the CD-ROM to check your work: SHOWENV.ASM.)

Simple File I/O

The last example program I present in this book is nominally about working with disk-based text files. However, it pulls together a lot of assembly tricks and features I've explained in previous sections and adds a few more. It's the largest and most complex program in this book, and if you can read it and follow the flow of the logic, you've gotten everything from this book that I set out to teach you. It's more like a "real" program than anything else in this book, in that it works with command-line arguments, writes output to a disk file, and does other useful things that any utility you'll set out to build will likely use.

The program TEXTFILE.ASM creates and fills a text file with text. You can specify the number of lines to be filled in the file, as well as text for the lines. If you don't specify text for the file, the program will generate a line of randomly chosen characters and use that instead. Invoking the program would thus be done like this:

```
#./textfile 150 Time for tacos!
```

This invocation would create a new file (the name of which is fixed in the program as "testeroo.txt") and write the text "Time for tacos!" to the file 150 times before closing the file. If the file TESTEROO.TXT already exists, it will be overwritten from the beginning. If you don't type anything after the line count number, the program will fill the file with random alphanumeric characters. If you don't type an integer as the first argument, TEXTFILE will display an error message. If you only type the program name and press Enter, TEXTFILE will display several lines explaining what it is and how to use it.

That's about all there is to say about the program TEXTFILE. The whole program is printed at the end of this chapter. I pull out short sequences for discussion as we go.

Converting Strings into Numbers with sscanf

When you type a number on the command line when invoking a program, you can access that number as one of the command-line arguments, through the mechanisms I described a little earlier in this chapter. However, there's a catch: The number is present *as text*, and you can't just take the textual string "751" and load it into a register or an integer variable. To make use of numeric arguments as numbers, you must convert their textual expression into numeric form.

The C library has several functions to handle this challenge. Some of them, such as **strtod**, are pretty specific and limited, and convert text to only one numeric type. One of them, however, has the ability to convert almost any textual expression of a legal numeric value into an appropriate numeric form. This is **sscanf**, and it's the one we'll look at in TEXTFILE.ASM.

The **sscanf** function takes three parameters, which you must push on the stack in the following order:

1. First push a pointer to a numeric variable to contain the numeric value generated by **sscanf**. We're generating a 32-bit integer here, which is also called a double. So, in TEXTFILE.ASM, we pass the address of the memory variable **linecount**, which is a 32-bit integer.

2. Next push the address of a formatting code string that tells **sscanf** what numeric format you want the input text to be converted to. Here the code string is "%d," which as you may recall from our **printf** discussion is the code for doubles (32-bit integers).

3. Finally, push the address of the text string to be converted to the numeric value that it represents. In TEXTFILE.ASM, we push the address of arg(1), which is the first command-line argument you type on the command line when you invoke the program.

Once these three parameters are pushed onto the stack, call **sscanf**. It returns the converted value in the numeric variable whose address you passed as the first parameter. It also returns a code in EAX to indicate whether the conversion was successful. If the return value in EAX is 0, then an error occurred, and you shouldn't assume you have anything useful in your numeric variable. If the conversion went through successfully, you'll see the number 1 in EAX.

This is the simplest way to use **sscanf**. It can convert whole arrays of numbers at once, but this is a more specialized use that you're unlikely to need when you're just starting out. The string passed to **sscanf** as the third parameter can contain multiple formatting codes, and then the string whose address you pass it as the third parameter should have text describing numeric values for each code in the format string.

The whole process looks like this:

```
mov ebx,[ebp+12]        ; Put pointer to argument table into ebx
push dword linecount    ; Push address of line count integer for sscanf
push dword intformat    ; Push address of integer formatting code
push dword [ebx+4]      ; Push pointer to arg(1)
call sscanf             ; Call sscanf to convert arg(1) to an integer
add esp,12              ; Clean up the stack
cmp eax,1               ; Return value of 1 says we got a number
je chkdata              ; If we got a number, go on; else abort
```

Assuming the user entered at least one argument on the command line (and the program has already verified this), a pointer to that first argument is located at an offset of 4 from the beginning of the command-line argument pointer table. (The very first element in the table, which we call arg(0), points to the name of the program as the user typed it on the command line.) That's why we push the contents of location [EBX+4] onto the stack; we had already loaded EBX with the address of the argument pointer table. What's located at [EBX+4] is the pointer to arg(1), the first command-line argument. Refer to Figure 13.3 if this is still fuzzy.

Creating and Opening Files

By this time you should be pretty comfortable with the general mechanism for making C library calls from assembly. And whether you realize it or not, you're already pretty comfortable with some of the machinery for manipulating text files. You've already used **printf** to display formatted text to the screen by way of standard output. The very same mechanism is used to write formatted text to disk-based text files—you're basically substituting a real disk file for standard output. So, understanding text file I/O shouldn't be much of a conceptual leap.

But unlike standard output, which is predefined for you by the C library and always available, you have to create or open a disk-based text file in order to use it. The **fopen** function is what does the job.

There are three general ways to open a file: for reading, for writing, and for appending. When you open a file for reading, you can read text from it via such functions as **fgets**, but you can't write to the file. When you open a file for writing, whatever may have been in the file before is thrown away, and new material is written at the beginning of the file. When you open a file for appending, you may write to the file, but new material is written *after* any existing material, and whatever was originally in the file is retained.

Ordinarily, when you open a file for writing you can't read from it, but there are special modes that allow both reading from and writing to a file. For text files especially (which are what we're speaking of here) that introduces some complications, so for the most part, text files are opened for either reading or for writing, but not both at once.

In the Unix file system, if you open a file for either writing or appending and the file does not already exist, the file is created. If you don't know if a file exists and you need to find out, attempt to open it for *reading* and not for writing, or you'll get the file whether it exists or not!

To use **fopen**, you must push the following parameters onto the stack before the call:

1. First onto the stack is a pointer to a code indicating which mode the file should be opened for. The various available modes are listed in Table 13.4. The ones you'll typically use for text files are "r," "w," and "a." These should be defined as short character strings, followed by a null:

```
writecode   db 'w',0
opencode    db 'r',0
```

2. Next onto the stack is the address of the character string containing the name of the file to be opened.

With those two items on the stack, you make the call to **fopen**. If the file was successfully opened, **fopen** returns a file handle in EAX. If the open was unsuccessful, EAX will contain 0. Here's how opening a file for reading looks in code:

```
push dword opencode ; Push pointer to open-for-read code "r"
push ebx            ; Pointer to name of help file is passed in ebx
```

Table 13.4 File Access Codes for Use with **fopen**

CODE SENSE	DESCRIPTION
"r"	Opens an existing text file for reading
"w"	Creates a new text file, or opens and truncates an existing file
"a"	Creates a new text file, or opens an existing file so that new text is added at the end
"r+"	Opens an existing text file for either writing or reading
"w+"	Creates a new text file, or opens and truncates an existing file for both read and write access
"a+"	Creates a new text file, or opens an existing file for reading or for writing so that new text may be added at the end

```
    call fopen          ; Attempt to open the file for reading
    cmp eax,0           ; fopen returns null if attempted open failed
    <jump as needed>
```

The process to create a file and then write to it is identical, except that you must push the "w" code onto the stack instead of the "r" code.

Reading Text from Files with fgets

When **fopen** successfully creates or opens a file for you, it returns a file handle in EAX. Keep that file handle safe somewhere—I recommend either copying it to a memory variable allocated for that purpose or putting it in one of the sacred registers. If you store it in EAX, ECX, or EDX and then make a call to almost any C library function, the file handle in the register will be trashed and you'll lose it.

Once a file is opened for reading, you can read text lines from it sequentially with the **fgets** function. Each time you call **fgets** on an opened text file, it will read one line of the file, which is defined as all the characters up to the next newline character, which in the Unix world always indicates the end of a text line.

Now, in any given file there's no way of knowing how many characters there will be until the next newline, so it would be dangerous to just turn **fgets** loose to bring back characters until it encounters a newline. If you attempt to open the wrong kind of file (a binary code file is one possibility, or a compressed data file), you might bring in thousands of bytes before encountering the binary 10H value that the file system considers a newline. Whatever buffer you had allocated to hold the incoming text would overflow and **fgets** would perhaps destroy adjacent data or crash your program.

For that reason, you must also pass a limit value to **fgets**. When it begins reading a line, **fgets** keeps track of how many characters it has brought in from the file, and when it gets to one short of the limit value, it stops reading characters. It then adds a newline to the buffer for the final character and returns.

Set up calls to **fgets** this way:

1. First, push the file handle onto the stack.

2. Next, push the character count limit value. This must be the actual integer value, and not a pointer to the value!

3. Finally, push the address of the character buffer into which **fgets** should store the characters that it reads from the file.

With all that done, call **fgets**. If **fgets** returns a 0 in EAX, then you've either reached the end of the file, or else a file error happened during the read. Either way, there's no more data forthcoming from the file. But without a 0 coming back in EAX, you can assume that valid text is present in the buffer at the address you passed to **fgets** on the stack.

I used **fgets** to create a simple disk-based help system for TEXTFILE. ASM. When the user enters no command-line arguments at all, TEXTFILE reads a short text file from disk and displays it to standard output. This is a common and courteous thing to do with command-line programs, and I recommend that all utilities you build for everyday use work this way.

The code for the help system is relatively simple and demonstrates both **fopen** and **fgets**:

```
diskhelp:
    push dword opencode ; Push pointer to open-for-read code "r"
    push ebx            ; Pointer to name of help file is passed in ebx
    call fopen          ; Attempt to open the file for reading
    cmp eax,0           ; fopen returns null if attempted open failed
    jne .disk           ; Read help info from disk, else from memory
    call memhelp
    ret
.disk: mov ebx,eax      ; Save handle of opened file in ebx
.rdln: push ebx         ; Push file handle on the stack
```

```
        push dword HELPLEN    ; Limit line length of text read
        push dword helpline   ; Push address of help text line buffer
        call fgets            ; Read a line of text from the file
        add esp,12            ; Clean up the stack
        cmp eax,0             ; A returned null indicates error or EOF
        je .done              ; If we get 0 in eax, close up & return
        push dword helpline   ; Push address of help line on the stack
        call printf           ; Call printf to display help line
        add esp,4             ; Clean up the stack
        jmp .rdln

.done:  push ebx              ; Push the handle of the file to be closed
        call fclose           ; Closes the file whose handle is on the stack
        add esp,4             ; Clean up the stack
        ret                   ; Go home
```

When subroutine **diskhelp** is called, the caller passes a pointer to the
name of the help file to be read in EBX. The file is first opened. If the
attempt to open the help file fails, a very short "fail safe" help message
is displayed from strings stored in the [.data] section of the program.
(This is the call to **memhelp**, which is another short subroutine in TEXT-
FILE.ASM.) Never leave the user staring at a mute cursor, wondering
what's going on!

Once the help file is opened, we start looping through a sequence that
reads text lines from the opened file with **fgets**, and then writes those
lines to standard output with **printf**. The maximum length of the lines
to be read is defined by the equate HELPLEN. (As a convention, things
in a program defined as macros or equates are named in uppercase letters.) Pushing an equate value on the stack is no different from pushing
an immediate value, and that's how the instruction is encoded. But
instead of being specified (perhaps differently) at several places all over
your source code, the maximum length of your help file lines is defined
in only one place and may be changed by changing that one equate
only. Equates are good. Use them whenever you can.

Each time a line is read from the file, the address of the line is pushed
onto the stack and displayed with **printf**. When no more lines are available to be read in the help file, **fgets** returns a 0 in EAX, and the program
branches to the function call that closes the file.

Note the **fclose** function, which is quite simple: You push the file handle of the open file onto the stack, and call **fclose**. That's all it takes to
close a file!

Writing Text to Files with **fprintf**

Earlier in this chapter, I explained how to write formatted text to the display by way of standard output, using the **printf** function. The C library provides a function that writes the very same formatted text to *any* opened text file. The **fprintf** function does exactly what **printf** does, but it takes one additional parameter on the stack: the file handle of an opened text file. The same text stream that **printf** would send to standard output is sent by **fprintf** to that opened file.

So I won't bother reexplaining how to format text for **printf** using formatting codes and base strings. It's done the same way, with the same codes. Instead, I'll simply summarize how to set up a call to **fprintf**:

1. First push any values or pointers to values (as appropriate) onto the stack. There's no difference here from the way it's done for a call to **printf**.

2. Next push the base string containing the formatting codes. Again, just as for **printf**.

3. Finally (and here's where **fprintf** differs from **printf**), push the file handle of the file to which the text should be written.

Then call **fprintf**. Your text will be written to the open file. Note that to use **fprintf**, the destination file must have been opened *for either writing or appending*. If you attempt to use **fprintf** on a file opened for reading, you will generate an error and **fprintf** will return without writing any data.

An error code is returned in EAX. However, unlike the other functions we've discussed, the error code is a negative number, *not* 0! So, although you should compare the returned value against 0, you actually need to jump on a value *less* than 0—rather than 0 itself. Typically, to jump on an **fprintf** error condition, you would use **JL** (Jump if Less), which will jump on a value less than 0.

Here's the **fprintf** call from TEXTFILE.ASM:

```
mov edi,[linecount]    ; The number of lines to be filled is in edi

push esi               ; esi is the pointer to the line of text
push dword 1           ; The first line number
push dword writebase   ; Push address of the base string
push ebx               ; Push the file handle of the open file
```

```
writeline:
    cmp dword edi,0        ; Has the line count gone to 0?
    je donewrite           ; If so, go down & clean up stack
    call fprintf           ; Write the text line to the file
    dec edi                ; Decrement the count of lines to be written
    add dword [esp+8],1    ; Update the line number on the stack
    jmp writeline          ; Loop back and do it again
donewrite:
    add esp,16             ; Clean up stack after call to fprintf
```

The call to **fprintf** is a pretty minor part of this. But there's still something very interesting to see here: The code doesn't clean up the stack immediately after the call to **fprintf**. In every other case of a call to a C library function, I have adjusted the stack to remove parameters immediately after the function call. What's different here?

This part of the code from TEXTFILE.ASM writes a single text line to the output file repeatedly, for a number of times specified in the memory variable **linecount**. Instead of wasting time pushing and removing the parameters for every write to the file, I waited until all the calls to **fprintf** were finished, and only then (at the label **donewrite**) cleaned up the stack.

But that leaves the question of changing the line number value for each write. TEXTFILE writes an initial line number before each line of text written to the file, and that number changes for each line. But instead of pushing a new line number value for each call to **fprintf** (which would require removing and repushing everything else, too), reach right into the stack and update the value that has been pushed on the stack, after each call to **fprintf**:

```
add dword [esp+8],1  ; Update the line number on the stack
```

I counted the number of bytes in each of the parameters passed to **fprintf**, and worked out where the pushed line number value was on the stack. In this case (and it may change depending on how many values you pass to **fprintf**) it was 8 bytes higher on the stack than the position of the stack pointer ESP.

There's nothing dicey about changing parameters that have already been pushed onto the stack, especially if it can save you a whole bunch of pushing and popping. *Just make sure you know where the things are that you want to change!* Needless to say, attempting to update a counter but changing an address instead can lead to a quick crash. This is assembly, guys. Your cushy chair is gone.

Gathering Your Subroutines into Libraries

Just as with DOS, you can build your own libraries of subroutines that you develop and use them in all your programs. Here's how to go about it in general terms:

- No entry-point definition or register saving has to happen. Just create a new source code file and paste the subroutine source code into the file, which must have a .ASM file extension.

- List all of the callable entry points to all subroutines, as well as any other identifiers that may be used by other programs and libraries, as **global**.

- If the subroutines call any C library routines, or routines in other libraries you own or have created, or use variables or other identifiers defined outside the library, declare all such external identifiers as **extern**.

- When adding library routines to a program, update the make file for that program so that the final executable has a dependency on the library.

This last point is the only one that requires additional discussion. The following make file builds the TEXTFILE.ASM demo program, which links in a library called LINLIB.ASM. Note that there is a whole new line specifying how the object file LINLIB.O is assembled, and also that the final binary file TEXTFILE depends on both TEXTFILE.O and LINLIB.O.

Because the TEXTFILE executable depends on both TEXTFILE.O and LINLIB.O, any time you make changes to either TEXTFILE.ASM or LINLIB.ASM, the make utility will completely relink the executable file via gcc. However, unless you change both .ASM files, only the .ASM file that is changed will be assembled. The magic of make is that it does nothing that doesn't need to be done.

```
textfile: textfile.o linlib.o
        gcc textfile.o linlib.o -o textfile
textfile.o: textfile.asm
        nasm -f elf textfile.asm
linlib.o: linlib.asm
        nasm -f elf linlib.asm
```

The file LINLIB.ASM is on the CD-ROM for this book. The subroutines it contains have been gathered from other programs in this chapter, so it would be repetitive to reprint them all here.

Finally, the TEXTFILE.ASM program follows, in its entirety. Make sure you can read all of it—there's nothing here I haven't covered somewhere in the book. And if you want a challenge, here's one for your next project: Expand TEXTFILE to read in a text file, and write it out again with line numbers in front of each line of text. This sort of utility is called a *text filter*, and it's one of the most common sorts of Unix programs there is.

```
; Source name     : TEXTFILE.ASM
; Executable name : TEXTFILE
; Version         : 1.0
; Created date    : 11/21/1999
; Last update     : 12/4/1999
; Author          : Jeff Duntemann
; Description     : A text file I/O demo for Linux, using NASM 0.98
;
; Build using these commands:
;   nasm -f elf textfile.asm
;   nasm -f elf linlib.asm
;   gcc textfile.o linlib.o -o textfile
;
; Note that this program requires several subroutines in an external
; library named LINLIB.ASM.

[SECTION .text]          ; Section containing code

;; These externals are all from the standard C library:
extern fopen
extern fclose
extern fgets
extern fprintf
extern printf
extern sscanf
extern time

;; These externals are from the associated library LINLIB.ASM:
extern seedit            ; Seeds the random number generator
extern pull6             ; Generates a 6-bit random number from 0-63
extern newline           ; Outputs a specified number of newline chars

global main              ; Required so linker can find entry point

main:
      push ebp           ; Set up stack frame for debugger
      mov ebp,esp
      push ebx           ; Program must preserve ebp, ebx, esi, & edi
      push esi
      push edi
      ;;; Everything before this is boilerplate; use it for all ordinary apps!
```

```
        call seedit          ; Seed the random number generator

        ;; First test is to see if there are command line arguments at all.
        ;; If there are none, we show the help info as several lines. Don't
        ;; forget that the first arg is always the program name, so there's
        ;; always at least 1 command-line argument!
        mov eax,[ebp+8]      ; Load argument count from stack into eax
        cmp eax,1            ; If count is 1, there are no args
        ja chkarg2           ; Continue if arg count is > 1
        mov ebx, dword diskhelpnm ; Put address of help file name in ebx
        call diskhelp        ; If only 1 arg, show help info...
        jmp gohome           ; ...and exit the program

        ;; Next we check for a numeric command line argument 1:
chkarg2:
        mov ebx,[ebp+12]     ; Put pointer to argument table into ebx
        push dword linecount ; Push address of line count integer for sscanf
        push dword intformat ; Push address of integer formatting code
        push dword [ebx+4]   ; Push pointer to arg(1)
        call sscanf          ; Call sscanf to convert arg(1) to an integer
        add esp,12           ; Clean up the stack
        cmp eax,1            ; Return value of 1 says we got a number
        je chkdata           ; If we got a number, go on; else abort
        mov eax, dword err1  ; Load eax with address of error message #1
        call showerr         ; Show the error message
        jmp gohome           ; Exit the program

        ;; Here we're looking to see if there are more arguments. If there
        ;; are, we concatenate them into a single string no more than BUFSIZE
        ;; chars in size. (Yes, I *know* this does what strncat does...)
chkdata:
        cmp dword [ebp+8],3  ; Is there a second argument?
        jae getlns           ; If so, we have text to fill a file with
        call randline        ; If not, generate a line of random text
                             ; Note that randline returns ptr to line in esi
        jmp genfile          ; Go on to create the file

        ;; Here we copy as much command line text as we have, up to BUFSIZE
        ;; chars, into the line buffer buff. We skip the first two args
        ;; (which at this point we know exist) but we know we have at least
        ;; one text arg in arg(2). Going into this section, we know that
        ;; ebx contains the pointer to the arg table. All other bets are off.
getlns: mov edx,2            ; We know we have at least arg(2), start there
        mov edi,dword buff   ; Destination pointer is start of char buffer
        xor eax,eax          ; Clear eax to 0 for the character counter
        cld                  ; Clear direction flag for up-memory movsb

grab: mov esi,[ebx+edx*4] ; Copy pointer to next arg into esi
.copy: cmp byte [esi],0 ; Have we found the end of the arg?
```

```
        je .next            ; If so, bounce to the next arg
        movsb               ; Copy char from [esi] to [edi]; inc edi & esi
        inc eax             ; Increment total character count
        cmp eax,BUFSIZE     ; See if we've filled the buffer to max count
        je addnul           ; If so, go add a null to buff & we're done
        jmp .copy

.next:  mov byte [edi],' ' ; Copy space to buff to separate args
        inc edi             ; Increment destination pointer for space
        inc eax             ; Add one to character count too
        cmp eax,BUFSIZE     ; See if we've now filled buff
        je addnul           ; If so, go down to add a null and we're done
        inc edx             ; Otherwise, increment the argument count
        cmp edx, dword [ebp+8] ; Compare against argument count
        jae addnul          ; If edx = arg count, we're done
        jmp grab            ; And go back and copy it

addnul: mov byte [edi],0 ; Tuck a null on the end of buff
        mov esi, dword buff  ; File write code expects ptr to text in esi

        ;; Now we create a file to fill with the text we have:
genfile:
        push dword writecode ; Push pointer to file write/create code ('w')
        push dword newfilename ; Push pointer to new file name
        call fopen          ; Create/open file
        add esp,8           ; Clean up the stack
        mov ebx,eax         ; eax contains the file handle; save in ebx

        ;; File is open. Now let's fill it with text:
        mov edi,[linecount] ; The number of lines to be filled is in edi

        push esi            ; esi is the pointer to the line of text
        push dword 1        ; The first line number
        push dword writebase ; Push address of the base string
        push ebx            ; Push the file handle of the open file

writeline:
        cmp dword edi,0     ; Has the line count gone to 0?
        je donewrite        ; If so, go down & clean up stack
        call fprintf        ; Write the text line to the file
        dec edi             ; Decrement the count of lines to be written
        add dword [esp+8],1 ; Update the line number on the stack
        jmp writeline       ; Loop back and do it again
donewrite:
        add esp,16          ; Clean up stack after call to fprintf

        ;; We're done writing text; now let's close the file:
closeit:
        push ebx            ; Push the handle of the file to be closed
        call fclose         ; Closes the file whose handle is on the stack
```

```
        add esp,4

    ;;; Everything after this is boilerplate; use it for all ordinary apps!
gohome: pop edi          ; Restore saved registers
    pop esi
    pop ebx
    mov esp,ebp          ; Destroy stack frame before returning
    pop ebp
    ret                  ; Return control to to the C shutdown code


;;;
SUBROUTINES=======================================================================


;-------------------------------------------------------------
; Disk-based mini-help subroutine -- Last update 12/5/1999
;
; This routine reads text from a text file, the name of which is passed by
; way of a pointer to the name string in ebx. The routine opens the text file,
; reads the text from it, and displays it to standard output. If the file
; cannot be opened, a very short memory-based message is displayed instead.
;-------------------------------------------------------------
diskhelp:
    push dword opencode  ; Push pointer to open-for-read code "r"
    push ebx             ; Pointer to name of help file is passed in ebx
    call fopen           ; Attempt to open the file for reading
    add esp,8            ; Clean up the stack
    cmp eax,0            ; fopen returns null if attempted open failed
    jne .disk            ; Read help info from disk, else from memory
    call memhelp
    ret
.disk: mov ebx,eax       ; Save handle of opened file in ebx
.rdln: push ebx          ; Push file handle on the stack
    push dword HELPLEN   ; Limit line length of text read
    push dword helpline  ; Push address of help text line buffer
    call fgets           ; Read a line of text from the file
    add esp,12           ; Clean up the stack
    cmp eax,0            ; A returned null indicates error or EOF
    jle .done            ; If we get 0 in eax, close up & return
    push dword helpline  ; Push address of help line on the stack
    call printf          ; Call printf to display help line
    add esp,4            ; Clean up the stack
    jmp .rdln

.done: push ebx          ; Push the handle of the file to be closed
    call fclose          ; Closes the file whose handle is on the stack
    add esp,4            ; Clean up the stack
    ret                  ; Go home

memhelp:
    mov eax,1
```

```
      call newline
      mov ebx, dword helpmsg ; Load address of help text into eax
.chkln: cmp dword [ebx],0 ; Does help msg pointer point to a null?
      jne .show              ; If not, show the help lines
      mov eax,1              ; Load eax with number of newslines to output
      call newline           ; Output the newlines
      ret                    ; If yes, go home
.show: push ebx              ; Push address of help line on the stack
      call printf            ; Display the line
      add esp,4              ; Clean up the stack
      add ebx,HELPSIZE       ; Increment address by length of help line
      jmp .chkln             ; Loop back and check to see if we done yet



showerr:
      push eax               ; On entry, eax contains address of error message
      call printf            ; Show the error message
      add esp,4              ; Clean up the stack
      ret                    ; Go home; no returned values



randline:
      mov ebx, BUFSIZE       ; BUFSIZE tells us how many chars to pull
      mov byte [buff+BUFSIZE+1],0 ; Put a null at the end of the buffer first
.loop: dec ebx               ; BUFSIZE is 1-based, so decrement
      call pull6             ; Go get a random number from 0-63
      mov cl,[chartbl+eax]   ; Use random # in eax as offset into table
                             ;  and copy character from table into cl
      mov [buff+ebx],cl      ; Copy char from cl to character buffer
      cmp ebx,0              ; Are we done having fun yet?
      jne .loop              ; If not, go back and pull another
      mov esi, dword buff    ; Copy address of the buffer into esi
      ret                    ;  and go home


[SECTION .data]             ; Section containing initialized data


intformat   dd '%d',0
writebase   db 'Line #%d: %s',10,0
newfilename db 'testeroo.txt',0
diskhelpnm  db 'helptextfile.txt',0
writecode   db 'w',0
opencode    db 'r',0
chartbl     db '0123456789ABCDEFGHIJKLMNOPQRSTUVWXYZabcdefghijklmnopqrstuvwxyz-@'
err1        db 'ERROR: The first command line argument must be an integer!',10,0
helpmsg     db 'TEXTTEST: Generates a test file. Arg(1) should be the # of ',10,0
HELPSIZE EQU $-helpmsg
            db 'lines to write to the file. All other args are concatenated',10,0
            db 'into a single line and written to the file. If no text args',10,0
            db 'are entered, random text is written to the file. This msg ',10,0
            db 'appears only if the file HELPTEXTFILE.TXT cannot be opened. ',10,0
```

```
helpend  dd 0

[SECTION .bss]              ; Section containing uninitialized data

linecount resd 1           ; Reserve integer to hold line count
HELPLEN   EQU 72           ; Define length of a line of help text data
helpline  resb HELPLEN     ; Reserve space for disk-based help text line
BUFSIZE   EQU 64           ; Define length of text line buffer buff
buff      resb BUFSIZE+5   ; Reserve space for a line of text
```

Not the End, But Only the Beginning

You never really *learn* assembly language.

You can improve your skills over time, by reading good books on the subject, by reading good code that others have written, and most of all, by writing lots and lots of code yourself. But at no point will you be able to stand up and say, I *know* it.

You shouldn't feel bad about this. In fact, I take some encouragement from occasionally hearing that Michael Abrash, author of *Zen of Assembly Language*, *Zen of Code Optimization*, and his giant compendium *Michael Abrash's Graphics Programming Black Book*, has learned something new about assembly language. Michael has been writing high-performance assembly code for almost 20 years and has evolved into one of the two or three best assembly language programmers in the Western hemisphere.

If Michael is still learning, is there hope for the rest of us?

Wrong question. *Silly* question. If Michael is still learning, it means that *all* of us are students and will always be students. It means that the journey is the goal, and as long as we continue to probe and hack and fiddle and try things we never tried before, that over time we will advance the state of the art and create programs that would have made the pioneers in our field catch their breath in 1977.

For the point is not to conquer the subject, but to live with it, and grow with your knowledge of it. The journey *is* the goal, and with this book I've tried hard to help those people who have been frozen with fear at the thought of starting the journey, staring at the complexity of it all and wondering where the first brick in that Yellow Brick Road might be.

It's *here*, with nothing more than the conviction that you can do it.

I got out of school in recession year 1974 with a B.A. in English, summa cum laude, and not much in reliable prospects outside of driving a cab. I finessed my way into a job with Xerox Corporation, repairing copy machines. Books were fun, but paperwork makes money—so I picked up a tool bag and had a fine old time for several years, before finessing my way into a computer programming position.

But I'll never forget that first awful moment when I looked over the shoulder of an accomplished technician at a model 660 copier with its panels off, to see what looked like a bottomless pit of little cams and gears and drums and sprocket chains turning and flipping and knocking switch actuators back and forth. Mesmerized by the complexity, I forgot to notice that a sheet of paper had been fed through the machine and turned into a copy of the original document. I was terrified of never learning what all the little cams did and missed the comforting simplicity of the Big Picture—that a copy machine makes copies.

That's Square One—discover the Big Picture. Ignore the cams and gears for a bit. You can do it. Find out what's important in holding the Big Picture together (ask someone if it's not obvious) and study that before getting down to the cams and gears. Locate the processes that happen. Divide the Big Picture into subpictures. See how things flow. Only then should you focus on something as small and as lost in the mess as an individual cam or switch.

That's how you conquer complexity, and that's how I've presented assembly language in this book. Some might say I've shorted the instruction set, but covering the instruction set was never the real goal here.

The real goal was to conquer your fear of the complexity of the subject, with some metaphors and some pictures and some funny stories to bleed the tension away.

Did it work? You tell me. I'd really like to know.

Where to Now?

If you've followed me so far, you've probably lost your fear of assembly language, picked up some skills and a good part of the instruction set, and are ready to move on. What's next? Ideally, you need an intermediate book on assembly language. The bad news is, assembly language has had a bad couple of years in the book industry, and most of the useful books I've found are now out of print. Tom Swan's masterful *Mastering Turbo Assembler* (Howard W. Sams & Co., 1995) is the most significant exception, and is still in print as of early 2000.

Worse, every single one of them focuses on DOS. There has never been an x86 assembly language book focusing on Linux, as best I know. This isn't to say there will never be one, but I don't see one on the immediate horizon.

On the other hand, the Internet has made it much easier to find out-of-print books. There are two sites that you simply *must* bookmark, and visit regularly, if you want to find books that are no longer available from the publisher or through Amazon.com. Both of these sites are brokers of used books, and what they do is direct you to an independent used bookstore somewhere that contributed listings of books to their master Web database. Here they are:

- *Alibris* has better shipping but a more limited database. You deal directly with Alibris itself rather than the separate used book dealers. It's at www.alibris.com.
- *Bibliofind* is less direct, but its listings are larger and I've found a number of things listed here that Alibris does not list. You send your order to Bibliofind via the Web, and Bibliofind forwards it to the bookstore that listed the book you want. You then conclude the order by sending payment to the bookstore rather than Bibliofind. It's at www.bibliofind.com.

I've used both firms very successfully and I endorse them both without hesitation.

Mastering Turbo Assembler

Tom Swan

Howard W. Sams & Co., 1995

ISBN 0-672-30526-7

Tom's intermediate-level assembly volume is a natural next step if you're working with the Borland tools. I have never seen a better intermediate-level text. It has gone through a couple of editions and is reasonably abundant on the used market. The downside, of course, is that it was published some years back and focuses on DOS real mode segmented model. The TASM assembly code is easily converted to NASM, and the principles Tom teaches apply well to Linux assembly as well, even though Tom does not mention Linux or NASM.

Mastering Turbo Debugger

Tom Swan

Howard W. Sams & Co, 1990

ISBN 0-672-48454-4

For my money, this is the only good book on debugging ever published, and for what I consider an advanced topic, it's remarkably approachable. Again, it focuses on DOS and the Borland tools, but Tom's higher-level strategies for finding and nuking bugs in your code are absolutely essential reading, no matter *what* assembler you're using, now or at any time in the future. It's been out of print for some time, but you can find it regularly on the used book market.

PC Magazine Programmer's Technical Reference: The Processor and Coprocessor

Robert L. Hummel

Ziff-Davis Press, 1992

ISBN 1-562-76016-5

This is not a tutorial but a reference on Intel's x86 processors through the 486, and it's by far the best one ever written or likely to be written for some time. It has the best discussion of that mysterious protected mode that I've ever seen, and its description of the individual assembly instructions is wonderfully crafted. I'm tempted to have my own copy taken apart and rebound as hardcover—if I don't, it's going to fall to pieces any day now! Alas, out of print but you should grab it if you find it.

Michael Abrash's Graphics Programming Black Book

Michael Abrash

Coriolis Group Books, 1997

ISBN 1-576-10174-6

This is a *huge* book (1,300+ pages) covering code optimization, largely for graphics applications (where it matters the most) but explained in a way that can be applied to almost anything. Some of it involves C programming, but much of it is pure, expert-level assembly—and on the CD-ROM is the original text of Michael's 1989 classic *Zen of Assembly Language*, which was barely off press when its publisher went under. The book was thus lost in the crush of a big business reorganization, and it never recovered. You'll need to get some practice and some context before all of this book will be completely comprehensible, but it's beautifully written and whether you can read it now, grab it if you see it so it'll be there on your shelf when you're ready for it. (Alas, it went out of print in early 2000, just as I am completing the book you're now reading.)

Stepping off Square One

Okay—with a couple of new books in hand and good night's sleep behind you, strike out on your own a little. Set yourself a goal, and try to achieve it: something *tough*, say, an assembly language utility that locates all files anywhere on a hard disk drive with a given ambiguous file name. That's ambitious for a newcomer and will take some research and study and (perhaps) a few false starts. But you can do it, and once you do it you'll be a real journeyman assembly language programmer.

Becoming a master takes work, and time. Michael Abrash's massive *Graphics Programming Black Book* (recently out of print but still in some stores) is a compilation of the secret knowledge of a programming master. It's not easy reading, but it will give you a good idea where your mind has to be to consider yourself an expert assembly language programmer.

Keep programming. Michael can show you things that would have taken you years to discover on your own, but they won't stick in your mind unless you *use* them. Set yourself a real challenge, something that has to be both correct and *fast*: Rotate graphics objects in 3-D, transfer data through a serial port at 19,200 bits per second, things like that.

You can do it.

Coming to believe the truth in that statement is the essence of stepping away from Square One—and the rest of the road, like all roads, is taken one step at a time.

Partial 8086/8088 Instruction Set Reference

Instruction	Reference Page	Text Page	
JMP	558	190	
LEA	559	Only in Appendix A	
LOOP	560	276	
LOOPNZ/LOOPNE	561	389	
LOOPZ/LOOPE	562	422	
MOV	563	75	
NEG	564	212	
NOP	565	Only in Appendix A	
NOT	566	213	
OR	567	67	
POP	568	214	
POPA	569	253	286+
POPAD		253	386+
POPF	570	253	
POPFD	571	465	386+
PUSH	572	115	
PUSHA	573	251	286+
PUSHAD	574	251	386+
PUSHF	575	85	
PUSHFD	576	465	386+
RET	577	263	
ROL	578	316	
ROR	580	316	
SBB	582	11	
SHL	583	316	
SHR	585	316	
STC	587	Only in Appendix A	
STD	588	376	
STOS	589	596	
SUB	590	140	
XCHG	592	198	
XOR	593	86	

Notes on the Instruction Set Reference

Instruction Operands

When an instruction takes two operands, the destination operand is the one on the *left*, and the source operand is the one on the *right*. In general, when a result is produced by an instruction, the result replaces the destination operand. For example, in this instruction:

```
ADD BX,SI
```

the BX register is added to the SI register, and the sum is then placed in the BX register, overwriting whatever was in BX before the addition.

Flag Results

Each instruction contains a flag summary that looks like this (the asterisks will vary from instruction to instruction):

```
O D I T S Z A P C   OF: Overflow flag  TF: Trap flag AF: Aux carry
F F F F F F F F F   DF: Direction flag SF: Sign flag PF: Parity flag
*       * * * * *   IF: Interrupt flag ZF: Zero flag CF: Carry flag
```

The nine flags are all represented here. An asterisk indicates that the instruction on that page affects that flag. If a flag is affected at all (that is, if it has an asterisk beneath it), it will be affected according to these rules:

OF Set if the result is too large to fit in the destination operand.

IF Set by the STI instruction; cleared by CLI.

TF For debuggers; not used in normal programming and may be ignored.

SF Set when the sign of the result forces the destination operand to become negative.

ZF Set if the result of an operation is zero. If the result is nonzero, ZF is cleared.

AF Auxiliary carry used for 4-bit BCD math. Set when an operation causes a carry out of a 4-bit BCD quantity.

PF Set if the number of 1 bits in the low byte of the result is even; cleared if the number of 1 bits in the low byte of the result is odd. Used in data communications applications but little else.

CF Set if the result of an add or shift operation carries out a bit beyond the destination operand; otherwise cleared. May be manually set by STC and manually cleared by CLC when CF must be in a known state before an operation begins.

Some instructions force certain flags to become undefined. When this is the case, it is noted under "Notes." *Undefined* means *don't count on it being in any particular state.*

AAA Adjust AL after BCD Addition

Flags affected:

```
O D I T S Z A P C   OF: Overflow flag  TF: Trap flag AF: Aux carry
F F F F F F F F F   DF: Direction flag SF: Sign flag PF: Parity flag
          *   *     IF: Interrupt flag ZF: Zero flag CF: Carry flag
```

Legal forms:

```
AAA
```

Examples:

```
AAA
```

Notes:

AAA makes an addition come out right in AL when what you're adding are BCD values rather than ordinary binary values. Note well that AAA does *not* perform the arithmetic itself, but is a postprocessor after ADD or ADC. The AL register is an *implied* operand and may not be explicitly stated—so make sure that the preceding ADD or ADC instruction leaves its results in AL!

A BCD digit is a byte with the high 4 bits set to 0, and the low 4 bits containing a digit from 0 to 9. AAA will yield garbage results if the preceding ADD or ADC acted upon one or both operands with values greater than 09.

After the addition of two legal BCD values, AAA will adjust a non-BCD result (that is, a result greater than 09 in AL) to a value between 0 and 9. This is called a *decimal carry*, since it is the carry of a BCD digit and not simply the carry of a binary bit.

For example, if ADD added 08 and 04 (both legal BCD values) to produce 0C in AL, AAA will take the 0C and adjust it to 02. The decimal carry goes to AH, *not* to the upper 4 bits of AL, which are *always* cleared to 0 by AAA.

If the preceding ADD or ADC resulted in a decimal carry (as in the preceding example), *both* CF and AF are set to 1 and AH is incremented by 1. Otherwise, AH is not incremented and CF and AF are cleared to 0.

This instruction is subtle. See the detailed discussion in Chapter 11.

```
r8 = AL AH BL BH CL CH DL DH      r16 = AX BX CX DX BP SP SI DI
sr = CS DS SS ES FS GS            r32 = EAX EBX ECX EDX EBP ESP ESI EDI
m8 = 8-bit memory data            m16 = 16-bit memory data
m32 = 32-bit memory data          i8 = 8-bit immediate data
i16 = 16-bit immediate data       i32 = 32-bit immediate data
d8 = 8-bit signed displacement    d16 = 16-bit signed displacement
d32 = 32-bit unsigned displacement
```

ADC Arithmetic Addition with Carry

Flags affected:

```
O D I T S Z A P C   OF: Overflow flag  TF: Trap flag AF: Aux carry
F F F F F F F F F   DF: Direction flag SF: Sign flag PF: Parity flag
*       * * * *     IF: Interrupt flag ZF: Zero flag CF: Carry flag
```

Legal forms:

```
ADC r8,r8
ADC m8,r8
ADC r8,m8
ADC r16,r16
ADC m16,r16
ADC r16,m16
ADC r32,r32     386+
ADC m32,r32     386+
ADC r32,m32     386+
ADC r8,i8
ADC m8,i8
ADC r16,i16
ADC m16,i16
ADC r32,i32     386+
ADC m32,i32     386+
ADC r16,i8
ADC m16,i8
ADC r32,i8      386+
ADC m32,i8      386+
ADC AL,i8
ADC AX,i16
ADC EAX,i32     386+
```

Examples:

```
ADC BX,DI
ADC EAX,5
ADC AX,0FFFFH              ;Uses single-byte opcode
ADC AL,42H                ;Uses single-byte opcode
ADC BP,17H
ADC WORD [BX+SI+Inset],5
ADC WORD ES:[BX],0B800H
```

Notes:

ADC adds the source operand and the Carry flag to the destination operand, and after the operation, the result replaces the destination operand. The add operation is an arithmetic add, and the carry allows multiple-precision additions across several registers or memory locations. (To add without taking the Carry flag into account, use the ADD instruction.) All affected flags are set according to the operation. Most importantly, if the result does not fit into the destination operand, the Carry flag is set to 1.

```
r8  = AL AH BL BH CL CH DL DH        r16 = AX BX CX DX BP SP SI DI
sr  = CS DS SS ES FS GS              r32 = EAX EBX ECX EDX EBP ESP ESI EDI
m8  = 8-bit memory data              m16 = 16-bit memory data
m32 = 32-bit memory data             i8  = 8-bit immediate data
i16 = 16-bit immediate data          i32 = 32-bit immediate data
d8  = 8-bit signed displacement      d16 = 16-bit signed displacement
d32 = 32-bit unsigned displacement
```

ADD Arithmetic Addition

Flags affected:

```
O D I T S Z A P C   OF: Overflow flag  TF: Trap flag AF: Aux carry
F F F F F F F F F    DF: Direction flag SF: Sign flag PF: Parity flag
*       * * * *      IF: Interrupt flag ZF: Zero flag CF: Carry flag
```

Legal forms:

```
ADD r8,r8
ADD m8,r8
ADD r8,m8
ADD r16,r16
ADD m16,r16
ADD r16,m16
ADD r32,r32     386+
ADD m32,r32     386+
ADD r32,m32     386+
ADD r8,i8
ADD m8,i8
ADD r16,i16
ADD m16,i16
ADD r32,i32     386+
ADD m32,i32     386+
ADD r16,i8
ADD m16,i8
ADD r32,i8      386+
ADD m32,i8      386+
ADD AL,i8
ADD AX,i16
ADD EAX,i32     386+
```

Examples:

```
ADD BX,DI
ADD AX,0FFFFH              ;Uses single-byte opcode
ADD AL,42H                 ;Uses single-byte opcode
ADD EAX,5
ADD BP,17H
AND DWORD [EDI],EAX
ADD WORD [BX+SI+Inset],5
ADD WORD ES:[BX],0B800H
```

Notes:

ADD adds the source operand to the destination operand, and after the operation, the result replaces the destination operand. The add operation is an arithmetic add, and does *not* take the Carry flag into account. (To add using the Carry flag, use the ADC Add with

Carry instruction.) All affected flags are set according to the operation. Most importantly, if the result does not fit into the destination operand, the Carry flag is set to 1.

```
r8  = AL AH BL BH CL CH DL DH      r16 = AX BX CX DX BP SP SI DI
sr  = CS DS SS ES FS GS            r32 = EAX EBX ECX EDX EBP ESP ESI EDI
m8  = 8-bit memory data            m16 = 16-bit memory data
m32 = 32-bit memory data           i8  = 8-bit immediate data
i16 = 16-bit immediate data        i32 = 32-bit immediate data
d8  = 8-bit signed displacement    d16 = 16-bit signed displacement
d32 = 32-bit unsigned displacement
```

AND Logical AND

Flags affected:

```
O D I T S Z A P C   OF: Overflow flag  TF: Trap flag AF: Aux carry
F F F F F F F F F   DF: Direction flag SF: Sign flag PF: Parity flag
*       * * * *     IF: Interrupt flag ZF: Zero flag CF: Carry flag
```

Legal forms:

```
AND r8,r8
AND m8,r8
AND r8,m8
AND r16,r16
AND m16,r16
AND r16,m16
AND r32,r32     386+
AND m32,r32     386+
AND r32,m32     386+
AND r8,i8
AND m8,i8
AND r16,i16
AND m16,i16
AND r32,i32     386+
AND m32,i32     386+
AND AL,i8
AND AX,i16
AND EAX,i32     386+
```

Examples:

```
AND BX,DI
AND EAX,5
AND AX,0FFFFH          ;Uses single-byte opcode
AND AL,42H             ;Uses single-byte opcode
AND DWORD [EDI],EAX
AND WORD ES:[BX],0B800H
AND WORD [BP+SI],DX
```

Notes:

AND performs the AND logical operation on its two operands. Once the operation is complete, the result replaces the destination operand. AND is performed on a bit-by-bit basis, such that bit 0 of the source is ANDed with bit 0 of the destination, bit 1 of the source is ANDed with bit 1 of the destination, and so on. The AND operation yields a 1 if *both* of the operands are 1; and a 0 only if *either* operand is 0. Note that the operation makes the Auxiliary carry flag undefined. CF and OF are cleared to 0, and the other affected flags are set according to the operation's results.

```
r8 = AL AH BL BH CL CH DL DH        r16 = AX BX CX DX BP SP SI DI
sr = CS DS SS ES FS GS              r32 = EAX EBX ECX EDX EBP ESP ESI EDI
m8 = 8-bit memory data              m16 = 16-bit memory data
m32 = 32-bit memory data            i8 = 8-bit immediate data
i16 = 16-bit immediate data         i32 = 32-bit immediate data
d8 = 8-bit signed displacement      d16 = 16-bit signed displacement
d32 = 32-bit unsigned displacement
```

BT   Bit Test (386+)

Flags affected:

```
O D I T S Z A P C   OF: Overflow flag  TF: Trap flag AF: Aux carry
F F F F F F F F F    DF: Direction flag SF: Sign flag PF: Parity flag
            *        IF: Interrupt flag ZF: Zero flag CF: Carry flag
```

Legal forms:

```
BT r16,r16     386+
BT m16,r16     386+
BT r32,r32     386+
BT m32,r32     386+
BT r16,i8      386+
BT m16,i8      386+
BT r32,i8      386+
BT m32,i8      386+
```

Examples:

```
BT AX,CX
BT [BX+DI],DX
BT AX,64
BT EAX,EDX
BT ECX,17
```

Notes:

BT copies a single specified bit from the left operand to the Carry flag, where it can be tested or fed back into a quantity using one of the shift/rotate instructions. Which bit is copied is specified by the right operand. Neither operand is altered by BT.

When the right operand is an 8-bit immediate value, the value specifies the number of the bit to be copied. In BT AX,5, bit 5 of AX is copied into CF. When the immediate value exceeds the size of the left operand, the value is expressed modulo the size of the left operand. That is, because there are not 66 bits in EAX, BT EAX,66 pulls out as many 32s from the immediate value as can be taken, and what remains is the bit number. (Here, 2.) When the right operand is *not* an immediate value, the right operand not only specifies the bit to be tested but also an offset from the memory reference in the left operand. This is complicated. See a detailed discussion in a full assembly language reference.

```
r8 = AL AH BL BH CL CH DL DH    r16 = AX BX CX DX BP SP SI DI
sr = CS DS SS ES FS GS          r32 = EAX EBX ECX EDX EBP ESP ESI EDI
m8 = 8-bit memory data          m16 = 16-bit memory data
m32 = 32-bit memory data        i8 = 8-bit immediate data
i16 = 16-bit immediate data     i32 = 32-bit immediate data
d8 = 8-bit signed displacement  d16 = 16-bit signed displacement
d32 = 32-bit unsigned displacement
```

CALL   Call Procedure

Flags affected:

```
O D I T S Z A P C   OF: Overflow flag  TF: Trap flag AF: Aux carry
F F F F F F F F F   DF: Direction flag SF: Sign flag PF: Parity flag
    <none>          IF: Interrupt flag ZF: Zero flag CF: Carry flag
```

Legal forms:

```
CALL <near label>
CALL <far label>
CALL r16
CALL m16
CALL r32      386+
CALL m32      386+
```

Examples:

```
CALL InsideMySegment     ;InsideMySegment is a Near label
CALL OutsideMySegment    ;OutsideMySegment is a Far label
CALL BX
CALL EDX
CALL WORD [BX+DI+17]     ;Calls Near address at [BX+DI+17]
CALL DWORD [BX+DI+17]    ;Calls full 32-bit address at [BX+DI+17]
```

Notes:

CALL transfers control to a procedure address. Before transferring control, CALL pushes the address of the instruction immediately after itself onto the stack. This allows a RET instruction (see also) to pop the return address into either CS:IP or IP only (depending on whether it is a Near or Far call) and thus return control to the instruction immediately after the CALL instruction.

In addition to the obvious CALL to a defined label, CALL can transfer control to a Near address within a 16-bit general-purpose register, and also to an address located in memory. These are shown in the Legal Forms column as m16 and m32. m32 is simply a full 32-bit address stored at a location in memory that may be addressed through any legal x86 memory-addressing mode. CALL m16 and CALL m32 are useful for creating jump tables of procedure addresses.

There are many more variants of the CALL instruction with provisions for working with the protection mechanisms of operating systems. These are not covered here, and for more information you should see an advanced text or a full assembly language reference.

```
r8 = AL AH BL BH CL CH DL DH     r16 = AX BX CX DX BP SP SI DI
sr = CS DS SS ES FS GS           r32 = EAX EBX ECX EDX EBP ESP ESI EDI
m8 = 8-bit memory data           m16 = 16-bit memory data
m32 = 32-bit memory data         i8 = 8-bit immediate data
i16 = 16-bit immediate data      i32 = 32-bit immediate data
d8 = 8-bit signed displacement   d16 = 16-bit signed displacement
d32 = 32-bit unsigned displacement
```

CLC Clear Carry Flag (CF)

Flags affected:

```
O D I T S Z A P C   OF: Overflow flag  TF: Trap flag AF: Aux carry
F F F F F F F F F   DF: Direction flag SF: Sign flag PF: Parity flag
              *     IF: Interrupt flag ZF: Zero flag CF: Carry flag
```

Legal forms:

```
CLC <none>
```

Examples:

```
CLC
```

Notes:

CLC simply sets the Carry flag (CF) to the cleared (0) state. Use CLC in situations where the Carry flag *must* be in a known cleared state before work begins, as when you are rotating a series of words or bytes using the rotate instructions RCL and RCR. It can also be used to put CF into a known state before returning from a procedure, to indicate that the procedure had succeeded or failed, as desired.

```
r8  = AL AH BL BH CL CH DL DH      r16 = AX BX CX DX BP SP SI DI
sr  = CS DS SS ES FS GS            r32 = EAX EBX ECX EDX EBP ESP ESI EDI
m8  = 8-bit memory data            m16 = 16-bit memory data
m32 = 32-bit memory data           i8  = 8-bit immediate data
i16 = 16-bit immediate data        i32 = 32-bit immediate data
d8  = 8-bit signed displacement    16  = 16-bit signed displacement
d32 = 32-bit unsigned displacement
```

CLD Clear Direction Flag (DF)

Flags affected:

```
O D I T S Z A P C   OF: Overflow flag  TF: Trap flag AF: Aux carry
F F F F F F F F F   DF: Direction flag SF: Sign flag PF: Parity flag
    *               IF: Interrupt flag ZF: Zero flag CF: Carry flag
```

Legal forms:

```
CLD <none>
```

Examples:

```
CLD
```

Notes:

CLD simply sets the Direction flag (DF) to the cleared (0) state. This affects the adjustment performed by repeated string instructions such as STOS, SCAS, and MOVS. Typically, when DF = 0, the destination pointer is increased, and decreased when DF = 1. DF is set to one with the STD instruction.

```
r8 = AL AH BL BH CL CH DL DH        r16 = AX BX CX DX BP SP SI DI
sr = CS DS SS ES FS GS              r32 = EAX EBX ECX EDX EBP ESP ESI EDI
m8 = 8-bit memory data             m16 = 16-bit memory data
m32 = 32-bit memory data           i8 = 8-bit immediate data
i16 = 16-bit immediate data        i32 = 32-bit immediate data
d8 = 8-bit signed displacement     d16 = 16-bit signed displacement
d32 = 32-bit unsigned displacement
```

CMP Arithmetic Comparison

Flags affected:

```
O D I T S Z A P C   OF: Overflow flag  TF: Trap flag AF: Aux carry
F F F F F F F F F   DF: Direction flag SF: Sign flag PF: Parity flag
*       * * * *     IF: Interrupt flag ZF: Zero flag CF: Carry flag
```

Legal forms:

```
CMP r8,r8
CMP m8,r8
CMP r8,m8
CMP r16,r16
CMP m16,r16
CMP r16,m16
CMP r32,r32     386+
CMP m32,r32     386+
CMP r32,m32     386+
CMP r8,i8
CMP m8,i8
CMP r16,i16
CMP m16,i16
CMP r32,i32     386+
CMP m32,i32     386+
CMP r16,i8
CMP m16,i8
CMP r32,i8      386+
CMP m32,i8      386+
CMP AL,i8
CMP AX,i16
CMP EAX,i32     386+
```

Examples:

```
CMP BX,DI
CMP EAX,5
CMP AX,0FFFFH               ;Uses single-byte opcode
CMP AL,42H                  ;Uses single-byte opcode
CMP BP,17H
CMP WORD [BX+SI+Inset],5
CMP WORD ES:[BX],0B800H
```

Notes:

CMP compares its two operations, and sets the flags to indicate the results of the comparison. *The destination operand is not affected.* The operation itself is identical to subtraction of the source from the destination without borrow (SUB), save that the result does not replace the destination. Typically, CMP is followed by one of the conditional jump instructions; that is, JE to jump if the operands were equal; JNE if they were unequal; and so forth.

```
r8 = AL AH BL BH CL CH DL DH        r16 = AX BX CX DX BP SP SI DI
sr = CS DS SS ES FS GS              r32 = EAX EBX ECX EDX EBP ESP ESI EDI
m8 = 8-bit memory data              m16 = 16-bit memory data
m32 = 32-bit memory data            i8 = 8-bit immediate data
i16 = 16-bit immediate data         i32 = 32-bit immediate data
d8 = 8-bit signed displacement      d16 = 16-bit signed displacement
d32 = 32-bit unsigned displacement
```

DEC Decrement Operand

Flags affected:

```
O D I T S Z A P C   OF: Overflow flag  TF: Trap flag AF: Aux carry
F F F F F F F F F   DF: Direction flag SF: Sign flag PF: Parity flag
*         * * * *   IF: Interrupt flag ZF: Zero flag CF: Carry flag
```

Legal forms:

```
DEC m8
DEC m16
DEC m32
DEC r8
DEC r16
DEC r32
```

Examples:

```
DEC AL
DEC CX
DEC EBX
DEC BYTE [BP]   ; Decrements the BYTE at [BP]
DEC WORD [BX]   ; Decrements the WORD at [BX]
DEC DWORD [EDX] ; Decrements the DWORD at [EDX]
```

Notes:

Remember that segment registers *cannot* be decremented with DEC. All register-half opcodes are 2 bytes in length, but all 16-bit register opcodes are 1 byte in length. If you can decrement an entire register of which only the lower half contains data, use the 16-bit opcode and save a byte.

As with all instructions that act on memory, memory data forms *must* be used with a data size specifier such as BYTE, WORD, and DWORD! NASM doesn't assume anything!

```
r8 = AL AH BL BH CL CH DL DH      r16 = AX BX CX DX BP SP SI DI
sr = CS DS SS ES FS GS            r32 = EAX EBX ECX EDX EBP ESP ESI EDI
m8 = 8-bit memory data            m16 = 16-bit memory data
m32 = 32-bit memory data          i8 = 8-bit immediate data
i16 = 16-bit immediate data       i32 = 32-bit immediate data
d8 = 8-bit signed displacement    d16 = 16-bit signed displacement
d32 = 32-bit unsigned displacement
```

IMUL Signed Integer Multiplication

Flags affected:

```
O D I T S Z A P C   OF: Overflow flag  TF: Trap flag AF: Aux carry
F F F F F F F F F   DF: Direction flag SF: Sign flag PF: Parity flag
*               *   IF: Interrupt flag ZF: Zero flag CF: Carry flag
```

Legal forms:

```
IMUL r8
IMUL m8
IMUL r16
IMUL m16
IMUL r32              386+
IMUL i32              386+
IMUL r16,i8           286+
IMUL r16,i16          286+
IMUL r32,i8           386+
IMUL r32,i16          386+
IMUL r16,r16          386+
IMUL r16,m16          386+
IMUL r32,r32          386+
IMUL r32,m32          386+
IMUL r16,r16,i8       286+
IMUL r16,m16,i8       286+
IMUL r16,r16,i16      286+
IMUL r16,m16,i16      286+
IMUL r32,r32,i8       386+
IMUL r32,m32,i8       386+
IMUL r32,r32,i32      386+
IMUL r32,m32,i32      386+
```

Examples:

```
IMUL CH            ; AL * CH --> AX
IMUL BX            ; AX * BX --> DX:AX
IMUL ECX           ; EAX * ECX --> EDX:EAX
IMUL WORD [BX+DI]  ; AX * DS:[BX+DI] --> DX:AX
IMUL EAX,ECX       ; EAX * ECX --> EAX
IMUL ECX,EAX,15    ; EAX * 15 --> ECX
```

Notes:

In its oldest, single-operand form (usable on all processors), IMUL multiplies its operand by AL, AX, or EAX, and the result is placed in AX, in DX:AX, or in EDX:EAX. If IMUL is given an 8-bit operand (either an 8-bit register or an 8-bit memory operand), the results will be placed in AX. This means that AH will be affected, even if the results will fit entirely in AL.

Similarly, if IMUL is given a 16-bit operand, the results will be placed in DX:AX, *even if the entire result will fit in AX!* It's easy to forget that IMUL affects DX on 16-bit multiples, and EDX in 32-bit multiples. Keep that in mind!

In *both* the two- and three-operand forms, the product replaces the contents of the *first* operand. In the two-operand form, the two operands are multiplied together, and the product replaces the first operand. In this it is like most other arithmetic and logical instructions. In the three-operand form, the second and third operand are multiplied, and the product replaces the first operand.

Note that with the two- and three-operand forms, there is the possibility that the product will not entirely fit in the destination register. When using those forms, the CF and OF flags will *both* be 0 (cleared) only if the product fits entirely in the destination. It's best to use the original forms in cases where you aren't sure of the range the product might take.

```
r8  = AL AH BL BH CL CH DL DH        r16 = AX BX CX DX BP SP SI DI
sr  = CS DS SS ES FS GS              r32 = EAX EBX ECX EDX EBP ESP ESI EDI
m8  = 8-bit memory data              m16 = 16-bit memory data
m32 = 32-bit memory data             i8  = 8-bit immediate data
i16 = 16-bit immediate data          i32 = 32-bit immediate data
d8  = 8-bit signed displacement      d16 = 16-bit signed displacement
d32 = 32-bit unsigned displacement
```

INC   Increment Operand

Flags affected:

```
O D I T S Z A P C   OF: Overflow flag  TF: Trap flag AF: Aux carry
F F F F F F F F F   DF: Direction flag SF: Sign flag PF: Parity flag
*         * * * *    IF: Interrupt flag ZF: Zero flag CF: Carry flag
```

Legal forms:

```
INC r8
INC m8
INC r16
INC m16
INC r32    386+
INC m32    386+
```

Examples:

```
INC AL
INC BX
INC EDX
INC BYTE [BP]    ; Increments the BYTE at [BP]
INC WORD [BX]    ; Increments the WORD at [BX]
INC DWORD [ESI]  ; Increments the DWORD at [ESI]
```

Notes:

Remember that segment registers *cannot* be incremented with INC. All register-half (r8) opcodes are 2 bytes in length, but all 16-bit register (r16) opcodes are 1 byte in length. If you can increment an entire register of which only the lower half contains data, use the 16-bit opcode and save a byte.

As with all instructions that act on memory, memory data forms *must* be used with a data size specifier such as BYTE, WORD, and DWORD! NASM doesn't assume anything!

```
r8 = AL AH BL BH CL CH DL DH        r16 = AX BX CX DX BP SP SI DI
sr = CS DS SS ES FS GS              r32 = EAX EBX ECX EDX EBP ESP ESI EDI
m8 = 8-bit memory data              m16 = 16-bit memory data
m32 = 32-bit memory data            i8 = 8-bit immediate data
i16 = 16-bit immediate data         i32 = 32-bit immediate data
d8 = 8-bit signed displacement      d16 = 16-bit signed displacement
d32 = 32-bit unsigned displacement
```

INT Software Interrupt

Flags affected:

```
O D I T S Z A P C   OF: Overflow flag  TF: Trap flag AF: Aux carry
F F F F F F F F F   DF: Direction flag SF: Sign flag PF: Parity flag
    * *             IF: Interrupt flag ZF: Zero flag CF: Carry flag
```

Legal forms:

```
INT3          NASM-specific shorthand for INT 3
INT i8
```

Examples:

```
INT3      ; NASM requires this to generate an INT 3 instruction
INT 10H
```

Notes:

INT triggers a software interrupt to one of 256 vectors in the first 1,024 bytes of memory. The operand specifies which vector, from 0 to 255. When an interrupt is called, the Flags register is pushed on the stack along with the return address. The IF flag is cleared, which prevents further interrupts (either hardware or software) from being recognized until IF is set again. TF is also cleared.

A special form of the instruction allows calling Interrupt 3 with a single-byte instruction. Debuggers use Interrupt 3 to set breakpoints in code by replacing an instruction with the single-byte opcode for calling Interrupt 3. NASM does not recognize this, and if you want to use INT 3 for some reason (and that instruction form isn't of much use unless you're writing a debugger), you must use a special mnemonic form INT3 rather than INT 3. This is advanced stuff; be careful.

Virtually all your applications of INT will use the other form, which takes an 8-bit immediate numeric value.

Always return from a software interrupt service routine with the IRET instruction. IRET restores the flags that were pushed onto the stack by INT, and in doing so clears IF, allowing further interrupts.

```
r8 = AL AH BL BH CL CH DL DH      r16 = AX BX CX DX BP SP SI DI
sr = CS DS SS ES FS GS            r32 = EAX EBX ECX EDX EBP ESP ESI EDI
m8 = 8-bit memory data            m16 = 16-bit memory data
m32 = 32-bit memory data          i8 = 8-bit immediate data
i16 = 16-bit immediate data       i32 = 32-bit immediate data
d8 = 8-bit signed displacement    d16 = 16-bit signed displacement
d32 = 32-bit unsigned displacement
```

IRET Return from Interrupt

Flags affected:

```
O D I T S Z A P C   OF: Overflow flag  TF: Trap flag AF: Aux carry
F F F F F F F F F   DF: Direction flag SF: Sign flag PF: Parity flag
* * * * * * * * *   IF: Interrupt flag ZF: Zero flag CF: Carry flag
```

Legal forms:

```
IRET
```

Examples:

```
IRET
```

Notes:

IRET *must* be used to exit from interrupt service routines called through INT or through interrupt hardware such as serial ports and the like. IRET pops the return address from the top of the stack into CS and IP, and then pops the next word from the stack into the Flags register. *All flags are affected.*

If the interrupt was triggered by hardware, there may be additional steps to be taken to prepare the hardware for another interrupt before IRET is executed. Consult your hardware documentation.

When using NASM, the actual opcode generated for IRET depends on the setting of the BITS setting, and governs whether a 16-bit return or 32-bit return is generated.

```
r8 = AL AH BL BH CL CH DL DH        r16 = AX BX CX DX BP SP SI DI
sr = CS DS SS ES FS GS              r32 = EAX EBX ECX EDX EBP ESP ESI EDI
m8 = 8-bit memory data              m16 = 16-bit memory data
m32 = 32-bit memory data            i8 = 8-bit immediate data
i16 = 16-bit immediate data         i32 = 32-bit immediate data
d8 = 8-bit signed displacement      d16 = 16-bit signed displacement
d32 = 32-bit unsigned displacement
```

J? Jump on Condition

Flags affected:

```
O D I T S Z A P C    OF: Overflow flag  TF: Trap flag AF: Aux carry
F F F F F F F F F    DF: Direction flag SF: Sign flag PF: Parity flag
      <none>         IF: Interrupt flag ZF: Zero flag CF: Carry flag
```

Legal forms: Descriptions   Jump if flags are

JA/JNBE d	(Jump If Above/Jump If Not Below or Equal)	CF=0 AND ZF=0
JAE/JNB d	(Jump If Above or Equal/Jump If Not Below)	CF=0
JB/JNAE d	(Jump If Below/Jump If Not Above or Equal)	CF=1
JBE/JNA d	(Jump If Below or Equal/Jump If Not Above)	CF=1 OR ZF=1
JE/JZ d	(Jump If Equal/Jump If Zero)	ZF=1
JNE/JNZ d	(Jump If Not Equal/Jump If Not Zero)	ZF=0
JG/JNLE d	(Jump If Greater/Jump If Not Less or Equal)	ZF=0 OR SF=OF
JGE/JNL d	(Jump If Greater or Equal/Jump If Not Less)	SF=OF
JL/JNGE d	(Jump If Less/Jump If Not Greater or Equal)	SFOF
JLE/JNG d	(Jump If Less or Equal/Jump If Not Greater)	ZF=1 OR SFOF
JC d	(Jump If Carry flag set)	CF=1
JNC d	(Jump If Carry flag Not set)	CF=0
JO d	(Jump If Overflow flag set)	OF=1
JNO d	(Jump If Overflow flag Not set)	OF=0
JP/JPE d	(Jump If PF set/Jump if Parity Even)	PF=1
JNP/JPO d	(Jump If PF Not set/Jump if Parity Odd)	PF=0
JS d	(Jump If Sign flag set)	SF=1
JNS d	(Jump If Sign flag Not set)	SF=0

```
d without NEAR = 8-bit signed displacement; use NEAR before d to specify
segment-wide displacement.
```

Examples:

```
JB HalfSplit       ;Jumps if CF=1
JLE TooLow         ;Jumps if either ZF=1 or SFOF
JG NEAR WayOut     ;Jumps if greater to 16-bit displacement
                   ; in real mode or 32-bit displacement in
                   ; 32-bit protected mode.
```

Notes:

By default all these instructions make a short jump (127 bytes forward or 128 bytes back) if some condition is true, or fall through if the condition is not true. The conditions all involve flags, and the flag conditions in question are given to the right of the mnemonic and its description.

The mnemonics incorporating "above" or "below" are for use after unsigned comparisons, whereas the mnemonics incorporating "less" or "greater" are for use after signed comparisons. "Equal" and "Zero" may be used after unsigned or signed comparisons.

NASM allows use of the segmentwide form by inserting the NEAR keyword after the instruction mnemonic. In real mode this allows the use of a 16-bit signed displacement, and in 32-bit protected mode this allows the use of a 32-bit signed displacement. Use of NEAR is only supported with 386 and newer CPUs.

```
r8  = AL AH BL BH CL CH DL DH        r16 = AX BX CX DX BP SP SI DI
sr  = CS DS SS ES FS GS              r32 = EAX EBX ECX EDX EBP ESP ESI EDI
m8  = 8-bit memory data              m16 = 16-bit memory data
m32 = 32-bit memory data             i8  = 8-bit immediate data
i16 = 16-bit immediate data          i32 = 32-bit immediate data
d8  = 8-bit signed displacement      d16 = 16-bit signed displacement
d32 = 32-bit unsigned displacement
```

JCXZ Jump If CX = 0

Flags affected:

```
O D I T S Z A P C   OF: Overflow flag  TF: Trap flag AF: Aux carry
F F F F F F F F F   DF: Direction flag SF: Sign flag PF: Parity flag
     <none>         IF: Interrupt flag ZF: Zero flag CF: Carry flag
```

Legal forms:

```
JCXZ <short displacement>
```

Examples:

```
JCXZ AllDone    ;Label AllDone must be within 127 bytes!
```

Notes:

Many instructions use CX as a count register, and JCXZ allows you to test and jump to see if CX has become 0. The jump may only be a short jump (that is, no more than 127 bytes forward or 128 bytes back) and will be taken if CX = 0 at the time the instruction is executed. If CX is any other value than 0, execution falls through to the next instruction. *See also* the *Jump on Condition* instructions.

JCXZ is most often used to bypass the CX = 0 condition when using the LOOP instruction. Because LOOP decrements CX before testing for CX = 0, if you enter a loop governed by LOOP with CX = 0, you will end up iterating the loop 65,536 times, hence JCXZ.

```
r8  = AL AH BL BH CL CH DL DH      r16 = AX BX CX DX BP SP SI DI
sr  = CS DS SS ES FS GS            r32 = EAX EBX ECX EDX EBP ESP ESI EDI
m8  = 8-bit memory data            m16 = 16-bit memory data
m32 = 32-bit memory data           i8  = 8-bit immediate data
i16 = 16-bit immediate data        i32 = 32-bit immediate data
d8  = 8-bit signed displacement    d16 = 16-bit signed displacement
d32 = 32-bit unsigned displacement
```

JECXZ   Jump If ECX = 0

Flags affected:

```
O D I T S Z A P C   OF: Overflow flag  TF: Trap flag AF: Aux carry
F F F F F F F F F   DF: Direction flag SF: Sign flag PF: Parity flag
      <none>        IF: Interrupt flag ZF: Zero flag CF: Carry flag
```

Legal forms:

```
JECXZ <short displacement>     386+
```

Examples:

```
JECXZ AllDone  ;Label AllDone must be within 127 bytes!
```

Notes:

This instruction operates identically to JCXZ, except that the register tested is ECX, and not CX.

JECXZ is most often used to bypass the ECX = 0 condition when using the LOOP instruction. Because LOOP decrements ECX before testing for ECX = 0, if you enter a loop governed by LOOP with ECX = 0, you will end up iterating the loop 2,147,483,648 times, hence JECXZ.

```
r8 = AL AH BL BH CL CH DL DH      r16 = AX BX CX DX BP SP SI DI
sr = CS DS SS ES FS GS            r32 = EAX EBX ECX EDX EBP ESP ESI EDI
m8 = 8-bit memory data            m16 = 16-bit memory data
m32 = 32-bit memory data          i8 = 8-bit immediate data
i16 = 16-bit immediate data       i32 = 32-bit immediate data
d8 = 8-bit signed displacement    d16 = 16-bit signed displacement
d32 = 32-bit unsigned displacement
```

JMP Unconditional Jump

Flags affected:

```
O D I T S Z A P C   OF: Overflow flag  TF: Trap flag AF: Aux carry
F F F F F F F F F   DF: Direction flag SF: Sign flag PF: Parity flag
     <none>         IF: Interrupt flag ZF: Zero flag CF: Carry flag
```

Legal forms:

```
JMP <short displacement>
JMP <near label>
JMP <far label>
JMP r16
JMP r32         386+
JMP m16
JMP m32
```

Examples:

```
JMP RightCloseBy          ;Plus or minus 128 bytes
JMP InsideMySegment       ;To 16-bit offset from CS
JMP OutsideMySegment      ;To immediate 32-bit address
JMP DX                    ;To 16-bit offset stored in DX register
JMP EAX                   ;To 32-bit offset stored in EAX register
JMP WORD [BX+DI+17]       ;To Near address stored at [BX+DI+17]
JMP DWORD [BX+DI+17]      ;To full 32-bit address stored at [BX+DI+17]
```

Notes:

JMP transfers control unconditionally to the destination given as the single operand. In addition to defined labels, JMP can transfer control to a 16-bit signed offset from IP (or 32-bit signed offset from EIP) stored in a general-purpose register, or to an address (either Near or Far) stored in memory and accessed through any legal addressing mode. These m16 and m32 forms are useful for creating jump tables in memory, where a jump table is an array of addresses. For example, JMP [BX+DI+17] would transfer control to the 16-bit offset into the code segment found at the based-indexed-displacement address [BX+DI+17].

No flags are affected, and, unlike CALL, no return address is pushed onto the stack.

```
r8 = AL AH BL BH CL CH DL DH      r16 = AX BX CX DX BP SP SI DI
sr = CS DS SS ES FS GS            r32 = EAX EBX ECX EDX EBP ESP ESI EDI
m8 = 8-bit memory data            m16 = 16-bit memory data
m32 = 32-bit memory data          i8 = 8-bit immediate data
i16 = 16-bit immediate data       i32 = 32-bit immediate data
d8 = 8-bit signed displacement    16 = 16-bit signed displacement
d32 = 32-bit unsigned displacement
```

LEA Load Effective Address

Flags affected:

```
O  D  I  T  S  Z  A  P  C    OF: Overflow flag   TF: Trap flag AF: Aux carry
F  F  F  F  F  F  F  F  F    DF: Direction flag  SF: Sign flag PF: Parity flag
      <none>                 IF: Interrupt flag  ZF: Zero flag CF: Carry flag
```

Legal forms:

```
LEA r16,m<any size>
LEA r32,m<any size>
```

Examples:

```
LEA EBX,[EAX+EDX*4+128]      ;Loads calculated address into EBX
LEA BP,MyWordVar             ;Loads offset of MyWordVar to BP
```

Notes:

LEA derives the offset of the source operand from the start of its segment and loads that offset into the destination operand. The destination operand must be a register and *cannot* be memory. The source operand must be a memory operand, but it can be any size. The address stored in the destination operand is the address of the first byte of the source in memory, and the size of the source in memory is unimportant.

This is a good, clean way to place the address of a variable into a register prior to a procedure or interrupt call.

LEA can also be used to perform register math, since the address specified in the second operand is *calculated* but not *accessed*. The address can thus be an address for which your program does not have permission to access. Any math that can be expressed as a valid address calculation may be done with LEA.

This is one of the few places where NASM does not require a size specifier before an operand that gives a memory address, again, because LEA calculates the address but moves no data to or from that address.

```
r8 = AL AH BL BH CL CH DL DH      r16 = AX BX CX DX BP SP SI DI
sr = CS DS SS ES FS GS            r32 = EAX EBX ECX EDX EBP ESP ESI EDI
m8 = 8-bit memory data            m16 = 16-bit memory data
m32 = 32-bit memory data          i8 = 8-bit immediate data
i16 = 16-bit immediate data       i32 = 32-bit immediate data
d8 = 8-bit signed displacement    d16 = 16-bit signed displacement
d32 = 32-bit unsigned displacement
```

LOOP Loop until CX/ECX = 0

Flags affected:

```
O D I T S Z A P C    OF: Overflow flag  TF: Trap flag AF: Aux carry
F F F F F F F F F    DF: Direction flag SF: Sign flag PF: Parity flag
      <none>         IF: Interrupt flag ZF: Zero flag CF: Carry flag
```

Legal forms:

```
LOOP d8
```

Examples:

```
LOOP PokeValue
```

Notes:

LOOP is a combination decrement counter, test, and jump instruction. It uses the CX register in 16-bit modes, and ECX in 32-bit modes. The operation of LOOP is logistically identical in both modes, and I use 16-bit coding as an example here.

LOOP simplifies code by acting as a DEC CX instruction, a CMP CX,0 instruction, and JZ instruction, all at once. A repeat count must be initially loaded into CX. When the LOOP instruction is executed, it first decrements CX. Then it tests to see if CX = 0. If CX is *not* 0, LOOP transfers control to the displacement specified as its operand:

```
        MOV CX,17
DoIt:   CALL CrunchIt
        CALL StuffIt
        LOOP DoIt
```

Here, the two procedure CALLs will be made 17 times. The first 16 times through, CX will still be nonzero and LOOP will transfer control to DoIt. On the 17th pass, however, LOOP will decrement CX to 0, and then fall through to the next instruction in sequence when it tests CX.

LOOP does not alter any flags, even when CX is decremented to 0. *Warning:* Watch your initial conditions! If CX is initially 0, LOOP will decrement it to 65,535 (0FFFFH) and then perform the loop 65,535 times. Worse, if you're working in 32-bit protected mode and enter a loop with ECX = 0, the loop will be performed over 2 *billion* times, which might be long enough to look like a system lockup.

```
r8  = AL AH BL BH CL CH DL DH     r16 = AX BX CX DX BP SP SI DI
sr  = CS DS SS ES FS GS           r32 = EAX EBX ECX EDX EBP ESP ESI EDI
m8  = 8-bit memory data           m16 = 16-bit memory data
m32 = 32-bit memory data          i8  = 8-bit immediate data
i16 = 16-bit immediate data       i32 = 32-bit immediate data
d8  = 8-bit signed displacement   d16 = 16-bit signed displacement
d32 = 32-bit unsigned displacement
```

LOOPNZ/LOOPNE Loop While CX/ECX > 0 and ZF = 0

Flags affected:

```
O D I T S Z A P C    OF: Overflow flag   TF: Trap flag  AF: Aux carry
F F F F F F F F F    DF: Direction flag  SF: Sign flag  PF: Parity flag
      <none>         IF: Interrupt flag  ZF: Zero flag  CF: Carry flag
```

Legal forms:

```
LOOPNZ d8
LOOPNE d8
```

Examples:

```
LOOPNZ StartProcess
LOOPNE GoSomewhere
```

Notes:

LOOPNZ and LOOPNE are synonyms and generate identical opcodes. Like LOOP, they use either CX or ECX depending on the BITS setting and hence the mode. LOOPNZ/LOOPNE decrements CX and jumps to the location specified in the target operand if CX is not 0 and the Zero flag ZF is 0. Otherwise, execution falls through to the next instruction.

What this means is that the loop is pretty much controlled by ZF. If ZF remains 0, the loop is looped until CX is decremented to 0. But as soon as ZF is set to 1, the loop terminates. Think of it as "Loop While Not Zero Flag."

Keep in mind that LOOPNZ does not itself affect ZF. Some instruction within the loop (typically one of the string instructions) must do something to affect ZF to terminate the loop before CX/ECX counts down to 0.

```
r8  = AL AH BL BH CL CH DL DH      r16 = AX BX CX DX BP SP SI DI
sr  = CS DS SS ES FS GS            r32 = EAX EBX ECX EDX EBP ESP ESI EDI
m8  = 8-bit memory data            m16 = 16-bit memory data
m32 = 32-bit memory data           i8  = 8-bit immediate data
i16 = 16-bit immediate data        i32 = 32-bit immediate data
d8  = 8-bit signed displacement    d16 = 16-bit signed displacement
d32 = 32-bit unsigned displacement
```

LOOPZ/LOOPE Loop While CX/ECX > 0 and ZF = 1

Flags affected:

```
O  D  I  T  S  Z  A  P  C    OF: Overflow flag  TF: Trap flag AF: Aux carry
F  F  F  F  F  F  F  F  F    DF: Direction flag SF: Sign flag PF: Parity flag
        <none>               IF: Interrupt flag ZF: Zero flag CF: Carry flag
```

Legal forms:

```
LOOPZ d8
LOOPE d8
```

Examples:

```
LOOPZ SenseOneShots
LOOPE CRCGenerate
```

Notes:

LOOPZ and LOOPE are synonyms and generate identical opcodes. Like LOOP, they use either CX or ECX depending on the BITS setting and hence the mode. LOOPZ/LOOPE decrements CX and jumps to the location specified in the target operand if CX is not 0 and the Zero flag ZF is 1. Otherwise, execution falls through to the next instruction.

What this means is that the loop is pretty much controlled by ZF. If ZF remains 1, the loop is looped until CX is decremented to 0. But as soon as ZF is cleared to 0, the loop terminates. Think of it as "Loop While Zero Flag."

Keep in mind that LOOPZ does not itself affect ZF. Some instruction within the loop (typically one of the string instructions) must do something to affect ZF to terminate the loop before CX/ECX counts down to 0.

```
r8  = AL AH BL BH CL CH DL DH      r16 = AX BX CX DX BP SP SI DI
sr  = CS DS SS ES FS GS            r32 = EAX EBX ECX EDX EBP ESP ESI EDI
m8  = 8-bit memory data            m16 = 16-bit memory data
m32 = 32-bit memory data           i8  = 8-bit immediate data
i16 = 16-bit immediate data        i32 = 32-bit immediate data
d8  = 8-bit signed displacement    d16 = 16-bit signed displacement
d32 = 32-bit unsigned displacement
```

MOV   Move (Copy) Right Operand into Left Operand

Flags affected:

```
O D I T S Z A P C   OF: Overflow flag  TF: Trap flag AF: Aux carry
F F F F F F F F F   DF: Direction flag SF: Sign flag PF: Parity flag
      <none>        IF: Interrupt flag ZF: Zero flag CF: Carry flag
```

Legal forms:

```
MOV r8,r8
MOV m8,r8
MOV r8,m8
MOV r8,i8
MOV m8,i8
MOV r16,r16
MOV m16,r16
MOV r16,m16
MOV m16,i16
MOV r16,i16
MOV r32,r32    386+
MOV m32,r32    386+
MOV r32,m32    386+
MOV r32,i32    386+
MOV m32,i32    386+
MOV sr,r16
MOV sr,m16
MOV r16,sr
MOV m16,sr
```

Examples:

```
MOV AL,BH
MOV EBX,EDI
MOV BP,ES
MOV ES,AX
MOV AX,0B800H
MOV ES:[BX],0FFFFH
MOV CX,[SI+Inset]
```

Notes:

This is perhaps the most used of all instructions. The flags are not affected.

```
r8 = AL AH BL BH CL CH DL DH     r16 = AX BX CX DX BP SP SI DI
sr = CS DS SS ES FS GS           r32 = EAX EBX ECX EDX EBP ESP ESI EDI
m8 = 8-bit memory data           m16 = 16-bit memory data
m32 = 32-bit memory data         i8 = 8-bit immediate data
i16 = 16-bit immediate data      i32 = 32-bit immediate data
d8 = 8-bit signed displacement   d16 = 16-bit signed displacement
d32 = 32-bit unsigned displacement
```

NEG Negate (Two's Complement; i.e., Multiply by -1)

Flags affected:

```
O D I T S Z A P C   OF: Overflow flag  TF: Trap flag AF: Aux carry
F F F F F F F F F   DF: Direction flag SF: Sign flag PF: Parity flag
*       * * * * *   IF: Interrupt flag ZF: Zero flag CF: Carry flag
```

Legal forms:

```
NEG r8
NEG m8
NEG r16
NEG m16
NEG r32      386+
NEG m32      386+
```

Examples:

```
NEG AL
NEG DX
NEG ECX
NEG BYTE [BX]   ; Negates BYTE quantity at [BX]
NEG WORD [DI]   ; Negates WORD quantity at [BX]
NEG DWORD [EAX] ; Negates DWORD quantity at [EAX]
```

Notes:

This is the assembly language equivalent of multiplying a value by −1. Keep in mind that negation is *not* the same as simply inverting each bit in the operand. (Another instruction, NOT, does that.) The process is also known as generating the *two's complement* of a value. The two's complement of a value added to that value yields zero. −1 = $FF; −2 = $FE; −3 = $FD; and so forth.

If the operand is 0, CF is cleared and ZF is set; otherwise, CF is set and ZF is cleared. If the operand contains the maximum negative value (−128 for 8-bit or −32,768 for 16-bit), the operand does not change, but OF and CF are set. SF is set if the result is negative, or else SF is cleared. PF is set if the low-order 8 bits of the result contain an even number of set (1) bits; otherwise, PF is cleared.

Note: You *must* use a size specifier (BYTE, WORD, DWORD) with memory data!

```
r8 = AL AH BL BH CL CH DL DH      r16 = AX BX CX DX BP SP SI DI
sr = CS DS SS ES FS GS            r32 = EAX EBX ECX EDX EBP ESP ESI EDI
m8 = 8-bit memory data            m16 = 16-bit memory data
m32 = 32-bit memory data          i8 = 8-bit immediate data
i16 = 16-bit immediate data       i32 = 32-bit immediate data
d8 = 8-bit signed displacement    d16 = 16-bit signed displacement
d32 = 32-bit unsigned displacement
```

NOP No Operation

Flags affected:

```
O D I T S Z A P C   OF: Overflow flag  TF: Trap flag AF: Aux carry
F F F F F F F F F   DF: Direction flag SF: Sign flag PF: Parity flag
        <none>      IF: Interrupt flag ZF: Zero flag CF: Carry flag
```

Legal forms:

```
NOP <none>
```

Examples:

```
NOP
```

Notes:

This, the easiest-to-understand of all 86-family machine instructions, simply does nothing. Its job is to take up space in sequences of instructions. When fetched by the CPU, NOP is executed as XCHG AX,AX. So, some work is actually done, but it's not *useful* work, and no data is altered anywhere. The flags are not affected. NOP is used for "NOPping out" machine instructions during debugging, leaving space for future procedure or interrupt calls, or padding timing loops.

```
r8  = AL AH BL BH CL CH DL DH      r16 = AX BX CX DX BP SP SI DI
sr  = CS DS SS ES FS GS            r32 = EAX EBX ECX EDX EBP ESP ESI EDI
m8  = 8-bit memory data            m16 = 16-bit memory data
m32 = 32-bit memory data           i8  = 8-bit immediate data
i16 = 16-bit immediate data        i32 = 32-bit immediate data
d8  = 8-bit signed displacement    d16 = 16-bit signed displacement
d32 = 32-bit unsigned displacement
```

NOT Logical NOT (One's Complement)

Flags affected:

```
O D I T S Z A P C    OF: Overflow flag  TF: Trap flag AF: Aux carry
F F F F F F F F F    DF: Direction flag SF: Sign flag PF: Parity flag
     <none>          IF: Interrupt flag ZF: Zero flag CF: Carry flag
```

Legal forms:

```
NOT r8
NOT m8
NOT r16
NOT m16
NOT r32       386+
NOT m32       386+
```

Examples:

```
NOT CL
NOT DX
NOT EBX
NOT WORD [SI+5]
```

Notes:

NOT inverts each individual bit within the operand separately. That is, every bit that was 1 becomes 0, and every bit that was 0 becomes 1. This is the "logical NOT" or "one's complement" operation. *See* the *NEG* instruction for the negation, or two's complement, operation.

After execution of NOT, the value FFH would become 0; the value AAH would become 55H.

Note: You *must* use a size specifier (BYTE, WORD, DWORD) with memory data!

```
r8 = AL AH BL BH CL CH DL DH      r16 = AX BX CX DX BP SP SI DI
sr = CS DS SS ES FS GS            r32 = EAX EBX ECX EDX EBP ESP ESI EDI
m8 = 8-bit memory data            m16 = 16-bit memory data
m32 = 32-bit memory data          i8 = 8-bit immediate data
i16 = 16-bit immediate data       i32 = 32-bit immediate data
d8 = 8-bit signed displacement    d16 = 16-bit signed displacement
d32 = 32-bit unsigned displacement
```

OR   Logical OR

Flags affected:

```
O D I T S Z A P C   OF: Overflow flag  TF: Trap flag AF: Aux carry
F F F F F F F F F    DF: Direction flag SF: Sign flag PF: Parity flag
*       * * * *      IF: Interrupt flag ZF: Zero flag CF: Carry flag
```

Legal forms:

```
OR r8,r8
OR m8,r8
OR r8,m8
OR r16,r16
OR m16,r16
OR r16,m16
OR r32,r32      386+
OR m32,r32      386+
OR r32,m32      386+
OR r8,i8
OR m8,i8
OR r16,i16
OR m16,i16
OR r32,i32      386+
OR m32,i32      386+
OR AL,i8
OR AX,i16
OR EAX,i32      386+
```

Examples:

```
OR EBX,EDI
OR AX,0FFFFH            ;Uses single-byte opcode
OR AL,42H              ;Uses single-byte opcode
OR WORD [ES:BX],0B800H
OR WORD [BP+SI],DX
```

Notes:

OR performs the OR logical operation between its two operands. Once the operation is complete, the result replaces the destination operand. OR is performed on a bit-by-bit basis, such that bit 0 of the source is ORed with bit 0 of the destination, bit 1 of the source is ORed with bit 1 of the destination, and so on. The OR operation yields a 1 if one of the operands is 1; and a 0 only if both operands are 0. Note that the operation makes the Auxiliary carry flag undefined. CF and OF are cleared to 0, and the other affected flags are set according to the operation's results.

Note: You *must* use a size specifier (BYTE, WORD, DWORD) with memory data!

```
r8 = AL AH BL BH CL CH DL DH      r16 = AX BX CX DX BP SP SI DI
sr = CS DS SS ES FS GS            r32 = EAX EBX ECX EDX EBP ESP ESI EDI
m8 = 8-bit memory data            m16 = 16-bit memory data
m32 = 32-bit memory data          i8 = 8-bit immediate data
i16 = 16-bit immediate data       i32 = 32-bit immediate data
d8 = 8-bit signed displacement    d16 = 16-bit signed displacement
d32 = 32-bit unsigned displacement
```

POP Pop Top of Stack into Operand

Flags affected:

```
O D I T S Z A P C   OF: Overflow flag  TF: Trap flag AF: Aux carry
F F F F F F F F F   DF: Direction flag SF: Sign flag PF: Parity flag
      <none>        IF: Interrupt flag ZF: Zero flag CF: Carry flag
```

Legal forms:

```
POP r16
POP m16
POP r32
POP m32
POP sr
```

Examples:

```
POP WORD [BX]
POP EAX
POP DX
POP DWORD [EAX+ECX]
POP ES
```

Notes:

It is impossible to pop an 8-bit item from the stack. Also remember that the *top of the stack* is defined (in 16-bit modes) as the word at address SS:SP, and there's no way to override that using prefixes. In 32-bit modes, the top of the stack is the DWORD at [ESP]. There is a separate pair of instructions, PUSHF and POPF, for pushing and popping the Flags register.

All register forms have single-byte opcodes. NASM recognizes them and generates them automatically, even though there are larger forms in the CPU instruction decoding logic.

```
r8 = AL AH BL BH CL CH DL DH      r16 = AX BX CX DX BP SP SI DI
sr = CS DS SS ES FS GS            r32 = EAX EBX ECX EDX EBP ESP ESI EDI
m8 = 8-bit memory data            m16 = 16-bit memory data
m32 = 32-bit memory data          i8 = 8-bit immediate data
i16 = 16-bit immediate data       i32 = 32-bit immediate data
d8 = 8-bit signed displacement    d16 = 16-bit signed displacement
d32 = 32-bit unsigned displacement
```

POPA Pop All 16-Bit Registers (286+)

Flags affected:

```
O D I T S Z A P C   OF: Overflow flag  TF: Trap flag AF: Aux carry
F F F F F F F F F   DF: Direction flag SF: Sign flag PF: Parity flag
      <none>        IF: Interrupt flag ZF: Zero flag CF: Carry flag
```

Legal forms:

```
POPA
```

Examples:

```
POPA
```

Notes:

PUSHA pushes all 16-bit general-purpose registers onto the stack. This instruction is present on the 286 and later CPUs and is not available in the 8086/8088.

The 16-bit general-purpose registers are popped in this order:

DI, SI, BP, SP, BX, DX, CX, AX

There's one wrinkle here: The SP value popped off the stack is *not* popped back into SP! (That would be insane, since we're using SP to manage the stack as we pop values off of it.) The value in SP's position on the stack is simply discarded when instruction execution reaches it.

POPA is usually used in conjunction with PUSHA, but nothing guarantees this. If you pop garbage values off the stack into the general registers, well, interesting things (in the sense of the old Chinese curse) can and probably will happen.

```
r8 = AL AH BL BH CL CH DL DH      r16 = AX BX CX DX BP SP SI DI
sr = CS DS SS ES FS GS            r32 = EAX EBX ECX EDX EBP ESP ESI EDI
m8 = 8-bit memory data            m16 = 16-bit memory data
m32 = 32-bit memory data          i8 = 8-bit immediate data
i16 = 16-bit immediate data       i32 = 32-bit immediate data
d8 = 8-bit signed displacement    d16 = 16-bit signed displacement
d32 = 32-bit unsigned displacement
```

POPF Pop Top of Stack into Flags

Flags affected:

```
O D I T S Z A P C   OF: Overflow flag  TF: Trap flag AF: Aux carry
F F F F F F F F F   DF: Direction flag SF: Sign flag PF: Parity flag
* * * * * * * * *   IF: Interrupt flag ZF: Zero flag CF: Carry flag
```

Legal forms:

```
POPF <none>
```

Examples:

```
POPF
```

Notes:

POPF pops the 16-bit word at the top of the stack into the Flags register. *The top of the stack* is defined as the word at SS:SP, and there is no way to override that with prefixes.

SP is incremented by two *after* the word comes off the stack. Remember that SP always points to either an empty stack or else real data. There is a separate pair of instructions, PUSH and POP, for pushing and popping other register data and memory data.

PUSHF and POPF are most used in writing 16-bit interrupt service routines, where you must be able to save and restore the environment, that is, all machine registers, to avoid disrupting machine operations while servicing the interrupt.

```
r8 = AL AH BL BH CL CH DL DH      r16 = AX BX CX DX BP SP SI DI
sr = CS DS SS ES FS GS            r32 = EAX EBX ECX EDX EBP ESP ESI EDI
m8 = 8-bit memory data            m16 = 16-bit memory data
m32 = 32-bit memory data          i8 = 8-bit immediate data
i16 = 16-bit immediate data       i32 = 32-bit immediate data
d8 = 8-bit signed displacement    d16 = 16-bit signed displacement
d32 = 32-bit unsigned displacement
```

POPFD Pop Top of Stack into EFlags (386+)

Flags affected:

```
O  D  I  T  S  Z  A  P  C    OF: Overflow flag  TF: Trap flag AF: Aux carry
F  F  F  F  F  F  F  F  F    DF: Direction flag SF: Sign flag PF: Parity flag
*  *  *  *  *  *  *  *  *    IF: Interrupt flag ZF: Zero flag CF: Carry flag
```

Legal forms:

```
POPFD <none>
```

Examples:

```
POPFD
```

Notes:

POPFD pops the double word (4 bytes) at the top of the stack into the EFlags register. In 32-bit protected mode, the *top of the stack* is defined as the DWORD at [ESP], and there is no way to override the SS segment with prefixes.

ESP is incremented by 4 *after* the word comes off the stack. Remember that ESP always points to either an empty stack or else real data. There is a separate pair of instructions, PUSH and POP, for pushing and popping other register data and memory data, in both 16-bit and 32-bit sizes.

PUSHFD and POPFD are most used in writing 32-bit interrupt service routines, where you must be able to save and restore the environment, that is, all machine registers, to avoid disrupting machine operations while servicing the interrupt.

```
r8  = AL AH BL BH CL CH DL DH      r16 = AX BX CX DX BP SP SI DI
sr  = CS DS SS ES FS GS            r32 = EAX EBX ECX EDX EBP ESP ESI EDI
m8  = 8-bit memory data            m16 = 16-bit memory data
m32 = 32-bit memory data           i8  = 8-bit immediate data
i16 = 16-bit immediate data        i32 = 32-bit immediate data
d8  = 8-bit signed displacement    d16 = 16-bit signed displacement
d32 = 32-bit unsigned displacement
```

PUSH Push Operand onto Top of Stack

Flags affected:

```
O D I T S Z A P C    OF: Overflow flag  TF: Trap flag AF: Aux carry
F F F F F F F F F    DF: Direction flag SF: Sign flag PF: Parity flag
    <none>           IF: Interrupt flag ZF: Zero flag CF: Carry flag
```

Legal forms:

```
PUSH r16
PUSH m16
PUSH r32        386+
PUSH m32        386+
PUSH sr
PUSH i8         286+
PUSH i16        286+
PUSH i32        386+
```

Examples:

```
PUSH WORD [BX]
PUSH EAX
PUSH DI
PUSH ES
PUSH DWORD 5
PUSH WORD 1000H
```

Notes:

It is impossible to push an 8-bit item onto the stack. Also remember that the *top of the stack* is defined (in 16-bit modes) as the word at address SS:SP, and there's no way to override that using prefixes. In 32-bit modes the top of the stack is the DWORD at [ESP]. There is a separate pair of instructions, PUSHF and POPF, for pushing and popping the Flags register.

Also remember that SP/ESP is decremented *before* the push takes place; SP points to either an empty stack or else real data.

```
r8 = AL AH BL BH CL CH DL DH     r16 = AX BX CX DX BP SP SI DI
sr = CS DS SS ES FS GS           r32 = EAX EBX ECX EDX EBP ESP ESI EDI
m8 = 8-bit memory data           m16 = 16-bit memory data
m32 = 32-bit memory data         i8 = 8-bit immediate data
i16 = 16-bit immediate data      i32 = 32-bit immediate data
d8 = 8-bit signed displacement   d16 = 16-bit signed displacement
d32 = 32-bit unsigned displacement
```

PUSHA Push All 16-Bit GP Registers (286+)

Flags affected:

```
O D I T S Z A P C    OF: Overflow flag  TF: Trap flag AF: Aux carry
F F F F F F F F F    DF: Direction flag SF: Sign flag PF: Parity flag
    <none>           IF: Interrupt flag ZF: Zero flag CF: Carry flag
```

Legal forms:

```
PUSHA               286+
```

Examples:

```
PUSHA
```

Notes:

PUSHA pushes all 16-bit general-purpose registers onto the stack. This instruction is present on the 286 and later CPUs and is not available in the 8086/8088.

The registers are pushed in this order:

AX, CX, DX, BX, SP, BP, SI, DI

However, note that the value of SP pushed is the value SP had *before* the first register was pushed onto the stack. In the course of executing PUSHA, the stack pointer is decremented by 16 bytes (8 registers x 2 bytes each).

The Flags register is not pushed onto the stack by PUSHA; *see PUSHF*.

```
r8  = AL AH BL BH CL CH DL DH        r16 = AX BX CX DX BP SP SI DI
sr  = CS DS SS ES FS GS              r32 = EAX EBX ECX EDX EBP ESP ESI EDI
m8  = 8-bit memory data              m16 = 16-bit memory data
m32 = 32-bit memory data             i8  = 8-bit immediate data
i16 = 16-bit immediate data          i32 = 32-bit immediate data
d8  = 8-bit signed displacement      d16 = 16-bit signed displacement
d32 = 32-bit unsigned displacement
```

PUSHAD Push All 32-Bit GP Registers (386+)

Flags affected:

```
O  D  I  T  S  Z  A  P  C    OF: Overflow flag  TF: Trap flag AF: Aux carry
F  F  F  F  F  F  F  F  F    DF: Direction flag SF: Sign flag PF: Parity flag
       <none>                IF: Interrupt flag ZF: Zero flag CF: Carry flag
```

Legal forms:

```
PUSHAD          386+
```

Examples:

```
PUSHAD
```

Notes:

PUSHA pushes all 32-bit general-purpose registers onto the stack. This instruction is present on the 386 and later CPUs and is not available in the 8086, 8088, or 286.

The registers are pushed in this order:

EAX, ECX, EDX, EBX, ESP, EBP, ESI, EDI

However, note that the value of ESP pushed is the value SP had *before* the first register was pushed onto the stack. In the course of executing PUSHAD, the stack pointer is decremented by 32 bytes (8 registers x 4 bytes each).

The EFlags register is not pushed onto the stack by PUSHAD; *see PUSHFD*.

```
r8  = AL AH BL BH CL CH DL DH      r16 = AX BX CX DX BP SP SI DI
sr  = CS DS SS ES FS GS            r32 = EAX EBX ECX EDX EBP ESP ESI EDI
m8  = 8-bit memory data            m16 = 16-bit memory data
m32 = 32-bit memory data           i8  = 8-bit immediate data
i16 = 16-bit immediate data        i32 = 32-bit immediate data
d8  = 8-bit signed displacement    d16 = 16-bit signed displacement
d32 = 32-bit unsigned displacement
```

PUSHF Push 16-Bit Flags onto Stack

Flags affected:

```
O D I T S Z A P C   OF: Overflow flag  TF: Trap flag AF: Aux carry
F F F F F F F F F   DF: Direction flag SF: Sign flag PF: Parity flag
      <none>         IF: Interrupt flag ZF: Zero flag CF: Carry flag
```

Legal forms:

```
PUSHF <none>
```

Examples:

```
PUSHF
```

Notes:

PUSHF simply pushes the current contents of the Flags register onto the top of the stack. *The top of the stack* is defined as the word at SS:SP, and there is no way to override that with prefixes.

SP is decremented *before* the word goes onto the stack. Remember that SP always points to either an empty stack or else real data. There is a separate pair of instructions, PUSH and POP, for pushing and popping other register data and memory data.

The Flags register is not affected when you *push* the flags, but only when you pop them back with POPF.

PUSHF and POPF are most used in writing interrupt service routines, where you must be able to save and restore the environment, that is, all machine registers, to avoid disrupting machine operations while servicing the interrupt.

```
r8 = AL AH BL BH CL CH DL DH      r16 = AX BX CX DX BP SP SI DI
sr = CS DS SS ES FS GS            r32 = EAX EBX ECX EDX EBP ESP ESI EDI
m8 = 8-bit memory data            m16 = 16-bit memory data
m32 = 32-bit memory data          i8 = 8-bit immediate data
i16 = 16-bit immediate data       i32 = 32-bit immediate data
d8 = 8-bit signed displacement    d16 = 16-bit signed displacement
d32 = 32-bit unsigned displacement
```

PUSHFD Push 32-Bit EFlags onto Stack (386+)

Flags affected:

```
O D I T S Z A P C   OF: Overflow flag  TF: Trap flag AF: Aux carry
F F F F F F F F F   DF: Direction flag SF: Sign flag PF: Parity flag
      <none>        IF: Interrupt flag ZF: Zero flag CF: Carry flag
```

Legal forms:

```
PUSHFD <none>      386+
```

Examples:

```
PUSHFD
```

Notes:

PUSHFD simply pushes the current contents of the 32-bit EFlags register onto the top of the stack. The *top of the stack* in 32-bit modes is defined as the word at [SS:ESP], and there is no way to override that with prefixes.

ESP is decremented *before* the EFlags double word goes onto the stack. Remember that ESP always points to either an empty stack or else real data. There is a separate pair of instructions, PUSH and POP, for pushing and popping other register data and memory data, and (in the 286 and later processors) immediate data.

The EFlags register is not affected when you *push* the flags, but only when you pop them back with POPFD.

PUSHFD and POPFD are most used in writing interrupt service routines, where you must be able to save and restore the environment, that is, all machine registers, to avoid disrupting machine operations while servicing the interrupt.

```
r8 = AL AH BL BH CL CH DL DH     r16 = AX BX CX DX BP SP SI DI
sr = CS DS SS ES FS GS           r32 = EAX EBX ECX EDX EBP ESP ESI EDI
m8 = 8-bit memory data           m16 = 16-bit memory data
m32 = 32-bit memory data         i8 = 8-bit immediate data
i16 = 16-bit immediate data      i32 = 32-bit immediate data
d8 = 8-bit signed displacement   d16 = 16-bit signed displacement
d32 = 32-bit unsigned displacement
```

RET Return from Procedure

Flags affected:

```
O  D  I  T  S  Z  A  P  C    OF: Overflow flag  TF: Trap flag  AF: Aux carry
F  F  F  F  F  F  F  F  F    DF: Direction flag SF: Sign flag  PF: Parity flag
       <none>               IF: Interrupt flag ZF: Zero flag  CF: Carry flag
```

Legal forms:

```
RET
RETN
RETF
RET i8
RETN i8
RET i16
RETF i16
```

Examples:

```
RET
RET 12H
RETN
RETF 117H
```

Notes:

There are two kinds of returns: Near and Far, where Near is within the current code segment and Far is to some other code segment. Ordinarily, the RET form is used, and the assembler resolves it to a Near or Far return opcode to match the procedure definition's use of the NEAR or FAR specifier. Specifying RETF or RETN may be done when necessary.

RET may take an operand indicating how many bytes of stack space are to be released on returning from the procedure. This figure is subtracted from the stack pointer to erase data items that had been pushed onto the stack for the procedure's use immediately prior to the procedure call.

The RETF and RETN forms are *not* available in Microsoft's MASM prior to V5.0!

```
r8  = AL AH BL BH CL CH DL DH       r16 = AX BX CX DX BP SP SI DI
sr  = CS DS SS ES FS GS             r32 = EAX EBX ECX EDX EBP ESP ESI EDI
m8  = 8-bit memory data             m16 = 16-bit memory data
m32 = 32-bit memory data            i8  = 8-bit immediate data
i16 = 16-bit immediate data         i32 = 32-bit immediate data
d8  = 8-bit signed displacement     d16 = 16-bit signed displacement
d32 = 32-bit unsigned displacement
```

ROL Rotate Left

Flags affected:

```
O D I T S Z A P C   OF: Overflow flag   TF: Trap flag AF: Aux carry
F F F F F F F F F    DF: Direction flag  SF: Sign flag PF: Parity flag
*               *    IF: Interrupt flag  ZF: Zero flag CF: Carry flag
```

Legal forms:

```
ROL r8,1
ROL m8,1
ROL r16,1
ROL m16,1
ROL r32,1    386+
ROL m32,1    386+
ROL r8,CL
ROL m8,CL
ROL r16,CL
ROL m16,CL
ROL r32,CL   386+
ROL m32,CL   386+
ROL r8,i8    286+
ROL m8,i8    286+
ROL r16,i8   286+
ROL m16,i8   286+
ROL r32,i8   386+
ROL m32,i8   386+
```

Examples:

```
ROL AL,1
ROL WORD [BX+SI],CL
ROL BP,1
ROL DWORD [EBX+ESI],9
ROL BP,CL
```

Notes:

ROL rotates the bits within the destination operand to the left, where left is toward the most significant bit (MSB). A rotate is a shift (*see SHL* and *SHR*) that wraps around; the leftmost bit of the operand is shifted into the rightmost bit, and all intermediate bits are shifted one bit to the left. Except for the direction the shift operation takes, ROL is identical to ROR.

The number of bit positions shifted may be specified either as an 8-bit immediate value, or by the value in CL—*not* CX or ECX. (The 8086 and 8088 are limited to the immediate value 1.) Note that while CL may accept a value up to 255, it is meaningless to shift by any value larger than 16, *even though the shifts are actually performed on the 8086 and 8088*. (The 286 and later limit the number of shift operations performed to the native word size except when running in Virtual 86 mode.)

The leftmost bit is copied into the Carry flag on each shift operation. OF is modified *only* by the shift-by-one forms of ROL; after shift-by-CL forms, OF becomes undefined.

```
r8  = AL AH BL BH CL CH DL DH      r16 = AX BX CX DX BP SP SI DI
sr  = CS DS SS ES FS GS            r32 = EAX EBX ECX EDX EBP ESP ESI EDI
m8  = 8-bit memory data            m16 = 16-bit memory data
m32 = 32-bit memory data           i8  = 8-bit immediate data
i16 = 16-bit immediate data        i32 = 32-bit immediate data
d8  = 8-bit signed displacement    d16 = 16-bit signed displacement
d32 = 32-bit unsigned displacement
```

ROR Rotate Right

Flags affected:

```
O  D  I  T  S  Z  A  P  C    OF: Overflow flag   TF: Trap flag AF: Aux carry
F  F  F  F  F  F  F  F  F    DF: Direction flag SF: Sign flag PF: Parity flag
*                    *       IF: Interrupt flag ZF: Zero flag CF: Carry flag
```

Legal forms:

```
ROR r8,1
ROR m8,1
ROR r16,1
ROR m16,1
ROR r32,1     386+
ROR m32,1     386+
ROR r8,CL
ROR m8,CL
ROR r16,CL
ROR m16,CL
ROR r32,CL    386+
ROR m32,CL    386+
ROR r8,i8     286+
ROR m8,i8     286+
ROR r16,i8    286+
ROR m16,i8    286+
ROR r32,i8    386+
ROR m32,i8    386+
```

Examples:

```
ROR AL,1
ROR WORD [BX+SI],CL
ROR BP,1
ROR DWORD [EBX+ESI],9
ROR BP,CL
```

Notes:

ROR rotates the bits within the destination operand to the right, where right is toward the least significant bit (LSB). A rotate is a shift (*see SHL* and *SHR*) that wraps around; the rightmost bit of the operand is shifted into the leftmost bit, and all intermediate bits are shifted one bit to the right. Except for the direction the shift operation takes, ROR is identical to ROL.

The number of bit positions shifted may be specified either as an 8-bit immediate value, or by the value in CL—*not* CX or ECX. (The 8086 and 8088 are limited to the immediate value 1.) Note that while CL may accept a value up to 255, it is meaningless to shift by any value larger than 16—or 32 in 32-bit mode—*even though the shifts are actually performed on the 8086 and 8088.* (The 286 and later limit the number of shift operations performed to the native word size except when running in Virtual 86 mode.)

The rightmost bit is copied into the Carry flag on each shift operation. OF is modified *only* by the shift-by-one forms of ROR; after shift-by-CL forms, OF becomes undefined.

```
r8 = AL AH BL BH CL CH DL DH      r16 = AX BX CX DX BP SP SI DI
sr = CS DS SS ES FS GS            r32 = EAX EBX ECX EDX EBP ESP ESI EDI
m8 = 8-bit memory data            m16 = 16-bit memory data
m32 = 32-bit memory data          i8 = 8-bit immediate data
i16 = 16-bit immediate data       i32 = 32-bit immediate data
d8 = 8-bit signed displacement    d16 = 16-bit signed displacement
d32 = 32-bit unsigned displacement
```

SBB Arithmetic Subtraction with Borrow

Flags affected:

```
O D I T S Z A P C   OF: Overflow flag   TF: Trap flag  AF: Aux carry
F F F F F F F F F   DF: Direction flag  SF: Sign flag  PF: Parity flag
*       * * * *     IF: Interrupt flag  ZF: Zero flag  CF: Carry flag
```

Legal forms:

```
SBB r8,r8
SBB m8,r8
SBB r8,m8
SBB r16,r16
SBB m16,r16
SBB r16,m16
SBB r32,r32    386+
SBB m32,r32    386+
SBB r32,m32    386+
SBB r8,i8
SBB m8,i8
SBB r16,i16
SBB m16,i16
SBB r32,i32    386+
SBB m32,i32    386+
SBB r16,i8
SBB m16,i8
SBB r32,i8     386+
SBB m32,i8     386+
SBB AL,i8
SBB AX,i16
SBB EAX,i32    386+
```

Examples:

```
SBB BX,DI
SBB AX,0FFFFH        ;Uses single-byte opcode
SBB AL,42H           ;Uses single-byte opcode
SBB BP,17H
SBB WORD [BX+SI+Inset],5
SBB WORD [ES:BX],0B800H
```

Notes:

SBB performs a subtraction with borrow, where the source is subtracted from the destination, and then the Carry flag is subtracted from the result. The result then replaces the destination. If the result is negative, the Carry flag is set. To subtract without taking the Carry flag into account (i.e., without borrowing), use the SUB instruction.

```
r8 = AL AH BL BH CL CH DL DH      r16 = AX BX CX DX BP SP SI DI
sr = CS DS SS ES FS GS            r32 = EAX EBX ECX EDX EBP ESP ESI EDI
m8 = 8-bit memory data            m16 = 16-bit memory data
m32 = 32-bit memory data          i8 = 8-bit immediate data
i16 = 16-bit immediate data       i32 = 32-bit immediate data
d8 = 8-bit signed displacement    d16 = 16-bit signed displacement
d32 = 32-bit unsigned displacement
```

SHL Shift Left

Flags affected:

```
O D I T S Z A P C   OF: Overflow flag  TF: Trap flag AF: Aux carry
F F F F F F F F F   DF: Direction flag SF: Sign flag PF: Parity flag
*       * * * * *   IF: Interrupt flag ZF: Zero flag CF: Carry flag
```

Legal forms:

```
SHL r8,1
SHL m8,1
SHL r16,1
SHL m16,1
SHL r32,1     386+
SHL m32,1     386+
SHL r8,CL
SHL m8,CL
SHL r16,CL
SHL m16,CL
SHL r32,CL    386+
SHL m32,CL    386+
SHL r8,i8     286+
SHL m8,i8     286+
SHL r16,i8    286+
SHL m16,i8    286+
SHL r32,i8    386+
SHL m32,i8    386+
```

Examples:

```
SHL AL,1
SHL WORD [BX+SI],CL
SHL BP,1
SHL EAX,9
SHL BP,CL
```

Notes:

SHL shifts the bits within the destination operand to the left, where left is toward the most significant bit (MSB). The number of bit positions shifted may be specified either as an 8-bit immediate value, or by the value in CL—*not* CX or ECX. (The 8086 and 8088 are limited to the immediate value 1.) Note that while CL may accept a value up to 255, it is meaningless to shift by any value larger than 16—or 32 in 32-bit mode—*even though the shifts are actually performed on the 8086 and 8088.* (The 286 and later limit the number of shift operations performed to the native word size except when running in Virtual 86 mode.) The leftmost bit of the operand is shifted into the Carry flag; the rightmost bit is cleared to 0. The Auxiliary carry flag (AF) becomes undefined after this instruction. OF is modified *only* by the shift-by-one forms of SHL; after shift-by-CL forms, OF becomes undefined.

SHL is a synonym for SAL (Shift Arithmetic Left). Except for the direction the shift operation takes, SHL is identical to SHR.

```
r8  = AL AH BL BH CL CH DL DH     r16 = AX BX CX DX BP SP SI DI
sr  = CS DS SS ES FS GS           r32 = EAX EBX ECX EDX EBP ESP ESI EDI
m8  = 8-bit memory data           m16 = 16-bit memory data
m32 = 32-bit memory data          i8  = 8-bit immediate data
i16 = 16-bit immediate data       i32 = 32-bit immediate data
d8  = 8-bit signed displacement   d16 = 16-bit signed displacement
d32 = 32-bit unsigned displacement
```

SHR Shift Right

Flags affected:

```
O D I T S Z A P C   OF: Overflow flag  TF: Trap flag AF: Aux carry
F F F F F F F F F   DF: Direction flag SF: Sign flag PF: Parity flag
*       * * * *     IF: Interrupt flag ZF: Zero flag CF: Carry flag
```

Legal forms:

```
SHR r8,1
SHR m8,1
SHR r16,1
SHR m16,1
SHR r32,1    386+
SHR m32,1    386+
SHR r8,CL
SHR m8,CL
SHR r16,CL
SHR m16,CL
SHR r32,CL   386+
SHR m32,CL   386+
SHR r8,i8    286+
SHR m8,i8    286+
SHR r16,i8   286+
SHR m16,i8   286+
SHR r32,i8   386+
SHR m32,i8   386+
```

Examples:

```
SHR AL,1
SHR WORD [BX+SI],CL
SHR BP,1
SHR EAX,9
SHR BP,CL
```

Notes:

SHR shifts the bits within the destination operand to the right, where right is toward the least-significant bit (LSB). The number of bit positions shifted may be specified either as an 8-bit immediate value, or by the value in CL—*not* CX or ECX. (The 8086 and 8088 are limited to the immediate value 1.) Note that while CL may accept a value up to 255, it is meaningless to shift by any value larger than 16—or 32 in 32-bit mode—*even though the shifts are actually performed on the 8086 and 8088.* (The 286 and later limit the number of shift operations performed to the native word size except when running in Virtual 86 mode.) The rightmost bit of the operand is shifted into the Carry flag; the leftmost bit is cleared to 0. The Auxiliary carry flag (AF) becomes undefined after this instruction. OF is modified *only* by the shift-by-one forms of SHL; after shift-by-CL forms, OF becomes undefined.

SHR is a synonym for SAR (Shift Arithmetic Right). Except for the direction the shift operation takes, SHR is identical to SHL.

```
r8  = AL AH BL BH CL CH DL DH        r16 = AX BX CX DX BP SP SI DI
sr  = CS DS SS ES FS GS              r32 = EAX EBX ECX EDX EBP ESP ESI EDI
m8  = 8-bit memory data              m16 = 16-bit memory data
m32 = 32-bit memory data             i8  = 8-bit immediate data
i16 = 16-bit immediate data          i32 = 32-bit immediate data
d8  = 8-bit signed displacement      d16 = 16-bit signed displacement
d32 = 32-bit unsigned displacement
```

STC   Set Carry Flag (CF)

Flags affected:

```
O D I T S Z A P C   OF: Overflow flag  TF: Trap flag AF: Aux carry
F F F F F F F F F   DF: Direction flag SF: Sign flag PF: Parity flag
              *  IF: Interrupt flag ZF: Zero flag CF: Carry flag
```

Legal forms:

```
STC <none>
```

Examples:

```
STC
```

Notes:

STC asserts the Carry flag (CF) to a known set state (1). Use it prior to some task that needs a bit in the Carry flag. It can also be used to put CF into a known state before returning from a procedure, to indicate that the procedure had succeeded or failed, as desired.

```
r8 = AL AH BL BH CL CH DL DH      r16 = AX BX CX DX BP SP SI DI
sr = CS DS SS ES FS GS            r32 = EAX EBX ECX EDX EBP ESP ESI EDI
m8 = 8-bit memory data            m16 = 16-bit memory data
m32 = 32-bit memory data          i8 = 8-bit immediate data
i16 = 16-bit immediate data       i32 = 32-bit immediate data
d8 = 8-bit signed displacement    d16 = 16-bit signed displacement
d32 = 32-bit unsigned displacement
```

STD Set Direction Flag (DF)

Flags affected:

```
O D I T S Z A P C    OF: Overflow flag   TF: Trap flag AF: Aux carry
F F F F F F F F F    DF: Direction flag  SF: Sign flag PF: Parity flag
    *                IF: Interrupt flag  ZF: Zero flag CF: Carry flag
```

Legal forms:

```
STD <none>
```

Examples:

```
STD
```

Notes:

STD simply asserts the Direction flag (DF) to the set (1) state. This affects the adjustment performed by repeated string instructions such as STOS, SCAS, and MOVS. Typically, when DF = 0, the destination pointer is increased, and decreased when DF = 1. DF is set to 0 with the CLD instruction.

```
r8 = AL AH BL BH CL CH DL DH      r16 = AX BX CX DX BP SP SI DI
sr = CS DS SS ES FS GS            r32 = EAX EBX ECX EDX EBP ESP ESI EDI
m8 = 8-bit memory data            m16 = 16-bit memory data
m32 = 32-bit memory data          i8 = 8-bit immediate data
i16 = 16-bit immediate data       i32 = 32-bit immediate data
d8 = 8-bit signed displacement    d16 = 16-bit signed displacement
d32 = 32-bit unsigned displacement
```

STOS Store String

Flags affected:

```
O  D  I  T  S  Z  A  P  C    OF: Overflow flag   TF: Trap flag AF: Aux carry
F  F  F  F  F  F  F  F  F     DF: Direction flag  SF: Sign flag  PF: Parity flag
      <none>                 IF: Interrupt flag  ZF: Zero flag  CF: Carry flag
```

Legal forms:

```
STOS ES:m8
STOS ES:m16
STOSB
STOSW
STOSD             386+
```

Examples:

```
STOS ES:WordVar    ;Stores AX to [ES:DI]
STOS ES:ByteVar    ;Stores AL to [ES:DI]
STOSB              ;Stores AL to [ES:DI]
STOSW              ;Stores AX to [ES:DI]
STOSD              ;Stores EAX to [EDI]
REP STOSW          ;Stores AX to [ES:DI] and up, for CX repeats
```

Notes:

Stores either AL (for 8-bit store operations), AX (for 16-bit operations), or EAX (for 32-bit operations) to the location at [ES:DI] or (for 32-bit operations) [EDI]. ES must be the segment of the destination and cannot be overridden. (For 32-bit protected mode flat model, all segments are congruent and thus ES does not need to be specified explicitly.) Similarly, DI or EDI must always be the destination offset.

By placing an operation repeat count (not a byte, word, or dword count!) in CX/ECX and preceding the mnemonic with the REP prefix, STOS can do an automatic "machine-gun" store of AL/AX/EAX into successive memory locations beginning at the initial [ES:DI] or [EDI]. After each store, DI/EDI is adjusted (see next paragraph) by either by 1 (for 8-bit store operations), 2 (for 16-bit store operations), or 4 (for 32-bit store operations), and CX is decremented by 1. Don't forget that CX/ECX counts *operations* (the number of times a data item is stored to memory) and not bytes!

Adjusting means incrementing if the Direction flag is cleared (by CLD) or decrementing if the Direction flag has been set.

```
r8  = AL AH BL BH CL CH DL DH      r16 = AX BX CX DX BP SP SI DI
sr  = CS DS SS ES FS GS            r32 = EAX EBX ECX EDX EBP ESP ESI EDI
m8  = 8-bit memory data            m16 = 16-bit memory data
m32 = 32-bit memory data           i8  = 8-bit immediate data
i16 = 16-bit immediate data        i32 = 32-bit immediate data
d8  = 8-bit signed displacement    d16 = 16-bit signed displacement
d32 = 32-bit unsigned displacement
```

SUB　Arithmetic Subtraction

Flags affected:

```
O D I T S Z A P C   OF: Overflow flag  TF: Trap flag AF: Aux carry
F F F F F F F F F   DF: Direction flag SF: Sign flag PF: Parity flag
*       * * * *     IF: Interrupt flag ZF: Zero flag CF: Carry flag
```

Legal forms:

```
SUB r8,r8
SUB m8,r8
SUB r8,m8
SUB r16,r16
SUB m16,r16
SUB r16,m16
SUB r32,r32      386+
SUB m32,r32      386+
SUB r32,m32      386+
SUB r8,i8
SUB m8,i8
SUB r16,i16
SUB m16,i16
SUB r32,i32      386+
SUB m32,i32      386+
SUB r16,i8
SUB m16,i8
SUB r32,i8       386+
SUB m32,i8       386+
SUB AL,i8
SUB AX,i16
SUB EAX,i32      386+
```

Examples:

```
SUB BX,DI
SUB AX,0FFFFH            ;Uses single-byte opcode
SUB AL,42H              ;Uses single-byte opcode
SUB BP,17H
SUB ECX,DWORD [ESI+5]
SUB EAX,17
SUB WORD [BX+SI+Inset],5
SUB WORD [ES:BX],0B800H
```

Notes:

SUB performs a subtraction without borrow, where the source is subtracted from the destination, and the result replaces the destination. If the result is negative, the Carry flag is set. Multiple-precision subtraction can be performed by following SUB with SBB (Subtract with Borrow) which takes the Carry flag into account as a borrow.

```
r8 = AL AH BL BH CL CH DL DH        r16 = AX BX CX DX BP SP SI DI
sr = CS DS SS ES FS GS              r32 = EAX EBX ECX EDX EBP ESP ESI EDI
m8 = 8-bit memory data              m16 = 16-bit memory data
m32 = 32-bit memory data            i8 = 8-bit immediate data
i16 = 16-bit immediate data         i32 = 32-bit immediate data
d8 = 8-bit signed displacement      d16 = 16-bit signed displacement
d32 = 32-bit unsigned displacement
```

XCHG Exchange Operands

Flags affected:

```
O D I T S Z A P C   OF: Overflow flag  TF: Trap flag AF: Aux carry
F F F F F F F F F   DF: Direction flag SF: Sign flag PF: Parity flag
      <none>        IF: Interrupt flag ZF: Zero flag CF: Carry flag
```

Legal forms:

```
XCHG r8,r8
XCHG r8,m8
XCHG r16,r16
XCHG r16,m16
XCHG r32,r32     386+
XCHG r32,m32     386+
```

Examples:

```
XCHG AL,DH
XCHG BH,BYTE [SI]
XCHG SP,BP
XCHG DX,WORD [DI]
XCHG ESI,EDI
XCHG ECX,DWORD [EBP+38]
XCHG AX,BX   ; Uses single-byte opcode
```

Notes:

XCHG exchanges the contents of its two operands. This is why there is no form of XCHG for identical operands; that is, XCHG AX,AX is not a legal form since exchanging a register with itself makes no logical sense.

Exchanging an operand with AX may be accomplished with a single-byte opcode, saving fetch time and code space. All good assemblers recognize these cases and optimize for them, but if you are hand-assembling INLINE statements for some high-level language, keep the single-byte special cases in mind.

```
r8 = AL AH BL BH CL CH DL DH        r16 = AX BX CX DX BP SP SI DI
sr = CS DS SS ES FS GS              r32 = EAX EBX ECX EDX EBP ESP ESI EDI
m8 = 8-bit memory data             m16 = 16-bit memory data
m32 = 32-bit memory data           i8 = 8-bit immediate data
i16 = 16-bit immediate data        i32 = 32-bit immediate data
d8 = 8-bit signed displacement     d16 = 16-bit signed displacement
d32 = 32-bit unsigned displacement
```

XOR Exclusive Or

Flags affected:

```
O D I T S Z A P C   OF: Overflow flag  TF: Trap flag AF: Aux carry
F F F F F F F F F   DF: Direction flag SF: Sign flag PF: Parity flag
*       * * * * *   IF: Interrupt flag ZF: Zero flag CF: Carry flag
```

Legal forms:

```
XOR r8,r8
XOR m8,r8
XOR r8,m8
XOR r16,r16
XOR m16,r16
XOR r16,m16
XOR r32,r32      386+
XOR m32,r32      386+
XOR r32,m32      386+
XOR r8,i8
XOR m8,i8
XOR r16,i16
XOR m16,i16
XOR r32,i32      386+
XOR m32,i32      386+
XOR AL,i8
XOR AX,i16
XOR EAX,i32      386+
```

Examples:

```
XOR BX,DI
XOR AX,0FFFFH             ;Uses single-byte opcode
XOR AL,42H               ;Uses single-byte opcode
XOR EBX,DWORD [EDI]
XOR WORD [ES:BX],0B800H
XOR WORD [BP+SI],DX
```

Notes:

XOR performs the exclusive OR logical operation between its two operands. Once the operation is complete, the result replaces the destination operand. XOR is performed on a bit-by-bit basis, such that bit 0 of the source is XORed with bit 0 of the destination, bit 1 of the source is XORed with bit 1 of the destination, and so on. The XOR operation yields a 1 if the operands are different, and a 0 if the operands are the same. Note that the operation makes the Auxiliary carry flag undefined. CF and OF are cleared to 0, and the other affected flags are set according to the operation's results.

```
r8 = AL AH BL BH CL CH DL DH      r16 = AX BX CX DX BP SP SI DI
sr = CS DS SS ES FS GS            r32 = EAX EBX ECX EDX EBP ESP ESI EDI
m8 = 8-bit memory data            m16 = 16-bit memory data
m32 = 32-bit memory data          i8 = 8-bit immediate data
i16 = 16-bit immediate data       i32 = 32-bit immediate data
d8 = 8-bit signed displacement    d16 = 16-bit signed displacement
d32 = 32-bit unsigned displacement
```

Segment Register Assumptions for Real Mode Segmented Model

One reason the segmented modes are so awful is that there is a whole layer of assumptions to be remembered about which segments are used in which ways with which instructions, and what may be overridden with override prefixes. Here's a quick summary you can refer to if it ever gets all turned around in your head. Keep in mind that this applies *only* to real mode segmented model. In 32-bit protected mode (as in Linux), all the segments point to the same memory space, and thus you don't need to "mess with" segments and overrides.

Where allowed, segment assumptions may be overridden with the segment override prefixes. These are DS:, SS:, CS:, and ES:. Under NASM, they must be placed *inside* the memory reference brackets. (MASM and TASM place them outside the brackets.) Here's an example of such an override in action:

```
mov [ES:BX],AX
```

The assumptions are these:

1. When the offset is specified in BX, SI, or DI, the assumed segment register is DS.

2. When the offset is specified in SP, the assumed segment register is SS. *This may not be overridden!*

3. When the offset is specified in BP, the assumed segment register is SS.

4. For string instruction LODS, the assumed segment is DS and the assumed offset is SI. *This may not be overridden!*

5. For string instructions STOS and SCAS, the assumed segment is ES and the assumed offset is DI. *This may not be overridden!*

6. For string instruction MOVS, the source must be pointed to by DS:SI and the destination must be pointed to by ES:DI. *This may not be overridden!*

Web URLs for Assembly Programmers

M any assembly language books have gone out of print, but a great deal of assembly language information can be found on the Web. I include a number of sites that were current in early 2000 in the following list. Web addresses change or go bad on an aggravatingly regular basis, so if you can't find one of these sites, assume first that it's been moved, and only after some unsuccessful effort with the search engines, assume that the site is gone forever. (And for some things such as NASM, you can almost assume that it's been moved. Software as potent as NASM doesn't just disappear!)

- The NASM home page: www.web-sites.co.uk/nasm/
- The ALINK home page: http://alink.home.dhs.org/
- The NASM-IDE home page: www.inglenook.co.uk/nasmide/
- Linux assembly language page: http://lightning.voshod.com/asm/
- Jan's Linux assembly page: http://bewoner.dma.be/JanW/eng.html
- The 80x86 Assembly Pages: www.fys.ruu.nl/~faber/Amain.html

These are the best pages I've seen, and they've all been around for a while. You'll find links pages on some of them that may direct you to newer Web sites that don't exist as I write this. The Web is a living organism, and you never surf the same wave twice. Keep both eyes open, so you don't miss anything!

Segment Register Assumptions

Where allowed, segment assumptions can be overridden with the segment override prefixes. These are DS: SS: CS: ES:. For example:

```
mov ES:[BX],AX
```

The assumptions are these:

1. When the offset is specified in BX, SI, or DI, the assumed segment register is DS.

2. When the offset is specified in SP, the assumed segment register is SS. CANNOT BE OVERRIDDEN.

3. When the offset is specified in BP, the assumed segment register is SS.

4. For string instruction LODS, the assumed segment is DS and the assumed offset is SI. CANNOT BE OVERRIDDEN.

5. For string instruction STOS and SCAS, the assumed segment is ES and the assumed offset is DI. CANNOT BE OVERRIDDEN.

6. For string instruction MOVS, the source must be pointed to be DS:SI and the destination must be pointed to by ES:DI. CANNOT BE OVERRIDDEN.

What's on the CD-ROM?

The CD-ROM included with *Assembly Language Step-by-Step, Second Edition* includes the following items:

- The x86 NASM assembler for DOS
- The x86 NASM assembler for Linux
- Anthony Williams's ALINK free linker for DOS
- Robert Anderton's NASM-IDE programming environment for DOS
- All the example programs presented in the book, in source code form
- The author's JLIST10 LaserJet source code print utility